W9-AHN-709

WINTER PARK PUBLIC LIBRARY
460 E. NEW ENGLAND AVENUE
WINTER PARK, FL 32789

The Correspondence of Walter Benjamin

Paris, 1927. *Photo credit: Suhrkamp Verlag, Frankfurt.*

The Correspondence of Walter Benjamin 1910–1940

Edited and Annotated by
Gershom Scholem and Theodor W. Adorno

Translated by
Manfred R. Jacobson and Evelyn M. Jacobson

The University of Chicago Press
Chicago and London

838
Benjamin

Walter Benjamin was born in Berlin in 1892. He studied philosophy and theology in Berlin and Switzerland, and lived in various places in Europe including several years in Paris. He was a regular contributor to magazines and literary sections of newspapers. His numerous works include *The Origin of German Tragedy,* "The Task of the Translator," and "The Work of Art in the Age of Mechanical Reproduction." In 1940, while fleeing the Gestapo at the Franco-Spanish border, he took his own life.

The University of Chicago Press, Chicago 60637
The University of Chicago Press, Ltd., London
© 1994 by The University of Chicago
All rights reserved. Published 1994
Printed in the United States of America
03 02 01 00 99 98 97 96 95 94 1 2 3 4 5
ISBN: 0-226-04237-5 (cloth)

Originally published in Germany in 1978 as a two-volume edition under the titles *Briefe 1, 1910–1928* and *Briefe 2, 1929–1940,* © Suhrkamp Verlag, Frankfurt am Main 1966.

Library of Congress Cataloging-in-Publication Data

Benjamin, Walter, 1892–1940.
[Correspondence. English]
The correspondence of Walter Benjamin, 1910–1940 / edited and annotated by Gershom Scholem and Theodor W. Adorno ; translated by Manfred R. Jacobson and Evelyn M. Jacobson.
p. cm.
"Originally published in Germany in 1978 as a two-volume edition under the titles Briefe 1, 1910–1928 and Briefe 2, 1929–1940, copyright Suhrkamp Verlag, Frankfurt am Main 1966"—T.p. verso.
Includes index.
1. Benjamin, Walter, 1892–1940—Correspondence. 2. Authors, German—20th century—Correspondence. I. Scholem, Gershom Gerhard, 1897– . II. Adorno, Theodor W., 1903–1969. III. Title.
PT2603.E455Z48 1994
838′.91209—dc20
[B] 93-41005
CIP

The paper used in this publication meets the minimum requirements of the American National Standard for Information Sciences—Permanence of Paper for Printed Library Materials, ANSI Z39.48-1984.

Contents

Note on Sources

Most of the letters that appear here, along with their annotation, were translated by Manfred R. Jacobson and Evelyn M. Jacobson from the two-volume German edition, *Walter Benjamin: Briefe,* edited by Gershom Scholem and Theodor W. Adorno. That edition, copyrighted in 1966, was published only in 1978. Bracketed notes marked "Trans." were added by these translators.

Thirty-three letters, dating from 1932 on, were translated by Gary Smith and are reprinted here from *The Correspondence of Walter Benjamin and Gershom Scholem, 1932–1940* (New York: Schocken Books, 1989). The letters are as follows (the first number denoting the letter number in the present edition, the numbers in parentheses denoting the page numbers of the Schocken edition): 212 (13–15), 214 (25–26), 215 (27–30), 216 (33–35), 218 (40–42), 220 (50–53), 221 (57–60), 225 (68–70), 227 (82–83), 230 (94–97), 233 (109–12), 236 (119–21), 237 (122–25), 238 (128–30), 240 (134–36), 241 (138–40), 244 (143–45), 249 (148–50), 257 (158–61), 264 (164–66), 268 (169–72), 278 (178–79), 286 (193–94), 287 (197–99), 289 (202–3), 292 (208–9), 296 (216–17), 299 (220–26), 300 (230–31), 308 (240–43), 309 (244), 311 (251–54), 326 (262–64). These letters are marked by an asterisk in the present edition. Gershom Scholem's notes to these letters have been edited only to eliminate repetition or cross-references. Bracketed notes are marked "Smith."

"Benjamin the Letter Writer," by Theodor Adorno (p. xvii), was translated by Howard Stern and is reprinted here with the publisher's permission from *On Walter Benjamin: Critical Essays and Recollections,* edited by Gary Smith (Cambridge: MIT Press, 1988), pp. 329–37.

Publisher's Note. This English-language edition follows exactly (with the exception of the Translators' Note and the Note on Sources), the original publication of the Suhrkamp Verlag's 1978 edition, including the notes and the prefaces of the editors. Under the terms of their contract, we were not permitted to revise the notes or to include any additional comments, prefaces, afterwords, etc., considering that a second scholarly edition had yet to be published in German.

Translators' Note

Titles of French and German works that are commonly known or easily accessible under English titles are referred to by the English titles, with the original German or French in parentheses the first time they appear in the letters. Lesser-known or untranslated works of Benjamin (often with working titles) are given in the original language with an English translation in parentheses the first time they appear. Other French and German works that are known primarily or only in the original are referred to in those languages.

Foreword

Gershom Scholem

Walter Benjamin's natural and extraordinary talent for letter writing was one of the most captivating facets of his nature. When I suggested to Theodor Adorno that we jointly publish a collection of Benjamin's letters, I was able to do so because a significant number of letters constituting a representative core for such a collection was already available. A selection of his letters could be assembled around this core, which consisted of the extensive correspondence spanning twenty-five years that Benjamin conducted with me, as well as his letters to the members of the Institute for Social Research during his years as an émigré, especially those to Max Horkheimer and Adorno. We knew of other correspondence that had been preserved and would be accessible to us: letters to Florens Christian Rang, Hofmannsthal, and the later letters to Werner Kraft. Once we had elected to do the project, we could also expect to find still more material that would have survived the storms and catastrophes of the past decades. We were not disappointed. Benjamin was a much too impressive and significant phenomenon to almost all who knew him more intimately for them not to have preserved all or some of his letters to them. The natural charm and the splendor of his power of expression, which manifests itself even in spontaneous communication, were additional factors that inevitably made these letters precious to those who received them. Thus, in spite of everything, it turned out that we had a surprising wealth of material at our disposal. This volume offers the reader an extensive sampling from this material. We were fortunate in being able to present an almost uninterrupted sequence of letters spanning thirty years, from Benjamin's eighteenth birthday to shortly before his suicide while in flight from the murderers. These very diverse letters are addressed to friends of his youth and to men and women with whom he later maintained literary and personal relationships. They constitute valuable documentation of his personal and intellectual biography, and we hope they will at the same time allow the image of his person, which has made such an unforgettable impression on us, to emerge in clear contours for the reader as well. These letters begin with the Youth Movement of the years immediately preceding the First World War. Notwithstanding all his exuberance and youthful vagueness, Benjamin assumed a sharply defined stance in this movement in his particularly visible role as the main contributor to *Der Anfang,* the journal published by Gustav Wyneken; as the main spokesman of the

Young People's Discussion Hall in Berlin; and as president of the Free Students at the University of Berlin. The letters then take us through his years of total withdrawal, or even reclusion, to the years when he was active as an author and journalist. They attend his confrontations with the great intellectual movements and phenomena of these years and forcibly attest to the transformations of his genius, from the metaphysician who dreamed of becoming an exegete of the great Hebrew texts, to the Marxist he wanted to be in his later years.[1] The purpose of this collection is to make evident the life story and physiognomy of one of the deepest thinkers and most articulate individuals to emerge from the German-speaking Jewish community in the generation before its destruction.

Of course much of the correspondence has been lost, including Benjamin's letters to his parents; to his siblings, George and Dora; from the period of the Youth Movement, the letters to Kurt Tuchler, Franz Sachs, Gustav Wyneken, Fritz Heinle, and Georg Barbizon; from the First World War to the twenties and thirties, the letters to Wolf Heinle, Erich Gutkind, Ernst Bloch, and Siegfried Kracauer. We did not have access to the letters saved by Brecht. Among the letters to women who were close to him, those to Grete Cohn-Radt, his first fiancée, and to Dora Benjamin, his wife, who died in 1964, have all been lost. Only right before the collection went to press did we learn that his friend Asja Lacis, to whom *One-Way Street* is dedicated, was living in Riga. For many years Benjamin felt particularly close to Jula Cohn, the sister of his boyhood friend Alfred Cohn. Of the letters to her, the only ones that have been preserved date from the period after her marriage to Fritz Radt (1925). Among letters to French correspondents, those to André Breton, for example, have been lost or cannot be located, and very few of those written to French acquaintances have been preserved or made available to us. Between 1915 and 1921, Benjamin conducted an occasionally lively correspondence with Werner Kraft, in which he primarily voiced at length his opinions on literary questions. Indeed, as he told me at the time, he sometimes thought of using these letters as the basis for a sequel to the *Briefe zur neuern Literatur*. They have been lost due to particularly unhappy circumstances, and only Benjamin's letters to Kraft after the resumption of their relationship in the thirties have been preserved.

Here I would like to say a word about his letters to me, which consti-

1. Adorno wrote more exhaustively about WB in "Charakteristik Walter Benjamins," in *Prismen* (Berlin and Frankfurt am Main, 1955) [translated by Samuel Weber and Shierry Weber, "A Portrait of Walter Benjamin," in *Prisms* (Cambridge: MIT Press, 1967), pp. 227–41], and in the foreword to the *Gesammelte Schriften* [hereafter *Schriften*—Trans.]; Scholem in "Walter Benjamin," *Neue Rundschau* (1965), 1–21.

tute something like a mainstay for many years of the selection now before us. I became acquainted with Walter Benjamin three months after his final break with Wyneken, and my passionate ties to Judaism and the cause of Zionism, no less than our shared intense interest in philosophical and literary matters, paved my way to him. I was very young at the time. I was studying mathematics and Hebrew with equal intensity and deluged him with information, questions, and thoughts concerning my Jewish studies, but also my youthful encounter with mathematics and philosophy. From the beginning of our correspondence, substantive and personal interests were joined, and this combination defines the approximately three hundred letters I have from him. Since we usually did not live in the same place and, especially after I went to Palestine in 1923, we had to rely almost exclusively on written communication, letters constituted the medium of our later relationship in a quite exemplary way. After 1923, there were only two occasions on which personal conversation was able to take the place of correspondence. Therefore, while in his relationships with other people most of the interaction occurred through the medium of productive conversation and spontaneous speech, his letters to me had to take the place of everything denied us in the way of personal contact. The result was that much of what amounted to personal reports and self-reflections, which would otherwise have been lost, was preserved, while much, of course, could not be expressed in this medium, precisely because of our physical separation. I am also convinced that he spoke to others about me with the same critical candor and ironic edge with which he expressed himself about others in his letters to me. We always knew where we stood with each other.

Of the approximately six hundred letters that were available to us, we have selected more than three hundred that, we believe, combine to form a whole. The tone, even the intonation, of these letters varies according to the person to whom they are addressed. It is precisely this that reflects the fecundity of Benjamin's personality, refracted in a medium appropriate to him. In large part, the letters are long, in keeping with his need for reflection and for communication with his friends. Since the short letters are often only of a technical nature, they could be excluded without loss. Other letters were excluded because their subject matter was less important or because they repeated what is adequately treated in letters included in the collection. There is much I had to omit, especially many of the letters to me, for reasons of space if nothing else. Omissions made within the letters selected for inclusion are always indicated by ellipsis dots in brackets [. . .]. They concern purely technical and financial matters, his relationships with his parents, and personal comments about people still living that we did not think we had the authority to make public. We did leave in objective criticism of individuals, even when it was of an ironic nature; beyond that, discretion seemed to be in order.

In the footnotes, we have limited ourselves to what was absolutely necessary. In a letter to Ernst Schoen on September 19, 1919, Benjamin criticizes the use of footnotes in collections of letters by comparing them to leeches. This had to be interpreted as a warning directed to us as editors to proceed with caution. We did not bother to include footnotes to explain literary matters that are common knowledge. In many cases when an explanation would not have been amiss, we were no longer able to determine the precise circumstances to which Benjamin alludes. This is primarily true of the letters before 1915, before I knew Benjamin better. For the next fifteen years I could resort to my own fairly detailed memory and, for the time after that, to both Adorno's and my memory, as well as to other written documents (such as my diaries from 1915 to 1919). Over the years, Benjamin's wife, who lived in London during and after the Second World War until her death, also provided me with a lot of information. I must also thank Herbert Belmore (Rome), Franz Sachs (Johannesburg), and Jula Radt-Cohn (Naarden, Holland) for valuable information concerning specific details of the letters written during his youth. Unfortunately Ernst Schoen, whose friendship with Benjamin goes all the way back to those early years, died before we had gathered the material for this collection and before we were able to ask him about details only he was in a position to clarify.

We have uniformly placed the date in the top right-hand corner of each letter. Benjamin himself usually placed it at the bottom left-hand, next to his signature. We have normalized the use of the comma after the salutation. The punctuation of the letters themselves posed a difficult problem. For years, mainly between 1914 and 1924, as a matter of principle Benjamin did not adhere to established usage, and proceeded entirely according to his own inclinations, in particular resisting the use of the comma in personal letters. He used relatively conventional punctuation only in more or less formal letters. After 1921 he began, at first very hesitantly but then increasingly, to conform to orthographic conventions even in this respect. Therefore, in the letters before 1921, I have corrected the punctuation only rarely, when it seemed totally necessary because of syntactical considerations; later we made it conform more to established usage.

Letters written *to* Benjamin have been as good as completely lost until now, with the exception of the letters written to him by Horkheimer and Adorno in his very last years. They were typed and preserved in carbon copies. Of the hundreds of letters I wrote to him, I now have copies of only five. We decided to include three of my letters and two of Adorno's in this collection, and to incorporate them at their proper chronological place, because they seemed to be of special significance for the theoretical questions we were debating. They also have much to contribute to an understanding of his letters and beyond that, to an understanding of his very person. Finally, they transmit an image of the give-and-take of living speech in this correspondence. I have also included two of my own poems, to which Benjamin referred in several letters, at the proper chronological place in the text: one poem on Paul Klee's painting *Angelus Novus,* the name Benjamin wanted to use for a journal he was planning to publish; the other a didactic poem on Kafka's *Trial.*

We divided editorial duties as follows, and accordingly bear separate responsibility for the final shape of the letters and the notes: I edited all the letters prior to 1921 and, after 1921, the letters written to me, Max Rychner, Martin Buber, Alfred Cohn, Jula Radt, Werner Kraft, Fritz Lieb, Kitty Marx-Steinschneider, and Hannah Arendt. Adorno was responsible for the letters written to himself and his wife, to Florens Christian Rang, Hofmannsthal, Brecht and the members of his circle, Karl Thieme, Adrienne Monnier, and Horkheimer. Rolf Tiedemann made a significant contribution to the footnotes of the letters edited by Adorno. Each of us has read and commented on the part edited by the other.

Finally, I would like to extend our most heartfelt gratitude to everybody who has assisted in making this book a reality by contributing letters, above all to Mr. Herbert Belmore (Rome), Mrs. Hansi Schoen (Countess Johanna Rogendorf, London), Mrs. Jula Radt-Cohn (Naarden), Mrs. Grete Cohn-Radt (Paris), Dr. Werner Kraft (Jerusalem), Dr. Kitty Steinschneider (Jerusalem), Prof. Fritz Lieb (Basel), and Mrs. Susanne Thieme (Lörrach), as well as the heirs and executors of the estates of Brecht, Hofmannsthal, and Rang. Our warmest thanks are due the Suhrkamp Verlag, which was receptive to our suggestions and wishes, and Walter Boehlich, an editor at Suhrkamp, who was of tremendous help to us in many ways. The work of collecting the material, the preparation of the manuscript, and its printing took over four years. Quite a few letters were made available to us only during the printing, and some even after we had finished reading galley proofs. Thus this collection, which is meant to be a living monument to our deceased friend, now appears twenty-five years after his death.

Benjamin the Letter Writer

Theodor W. Adorno

Walter Benjamin the person was from the very beginning so completely the medium of his work—his felicity was so much one of the mind—that anything one might call "immediacy of life" was refracted. Not that he was ascetic, or even gave such an impression by his appearance; but there was something almost incorporeal about him. Master of his ego as few others have been, he seemed alienated from his own *physis*. That is perhaps one root of his philosophical intentions: to render accessible by rational means that range of experience that announces itself in schizophrenia. Just as Benjamin's thinking constitutes the antithesis of the existential concept of the person, he seems empirically, despite extreme individuation, hardly to have been a person at all, but rather an arena of movement in which a certain content forced its way, through him, into language. It would be idle to reflect on the psychological origin of this trait; to do so would be to postulate precisely the standard image of a living being that Benjamin's speculation exploded, and to which general consensus clings all the more obdurately the less of a life life becomes. A remark about his own handwriting (Benjamin was a good graphologist), namely that its object was above all to pretend that nothing had happened, attests at any rate his attitude toward this dimension of himself; but otherwise he never bothered much about his psychology.

It is doubtful whether anyone else ever succeeded in making his own neurosis—if indeed it was a neurosis—so productive. The psychoanalytic concept of neurosis implies the fettering of productive forces, the misdirection of energies. Nothing of the sort in Benjamin's case. His productivity in spite of self-alienation can be explained only by the fact that the *difficile* subjective mode of his reactions was the precipitate of an objective historical reality, which enabled him to transform himself into an organ of objectivity. What he may have lacked in immediacy, or what must soon have become second nature to him to conceal, is forfeit in a world subject to the abstract law of relations between people. Only at the price of the severest pain, or else untruthfully, as tolerated nature, may it show itself. Benjamin had acknowledged the consequences long before he was consciously aware of such matters. In himself and his relations with others he insisted unreservedly upon the primacy of the mind; which, in lieu of immediacy, became for him immediate. His private demeanor at times approached the ritualistic. The influence of Stefan George and his school, with whom Benjamin had nothing in common philosophically even as a youth, amounts to this: from George he learned the patterns of ritual. In the letters this ritual element extends to the graphic image, indeed even to the selection of writing paper, about which he was uncommonly particular; during the period of emigration his friend Alfred Cohn continued a longstanding practice of presenting him with a specific grade of paper. Benjamin's ritual behavior was most pronounced in his youth, and only toward the end of his life did it begin to relax; as if the apprehension of catastrophe, of what was worse than death, had awakened the long-buried spontaneity of expression that he had banished through mimesis to the hour of death.

Benjamin was a great letter writer, and obviously he wrote letters with a passion. Despite two wars, the Hitler Reich, and emigration, very many of them have been preserved; it was difficult to make a selection. The letter became one of his literary forms; as such, it does transmit the primary impulses, but interposes something between them and the addressee: the process of shaping the written material as if in conformance with the law of objectification—in spite of the particular occasion and also by virtue of it—as though the impulse were otherwise not legitimate. Thinkers of major significance and power will often produce insights that address their objects with utmost fidelity and yet at the same time are insights into the thinkers themselves. This was the case with Benjamin; a model would be the well-known remark about the old Goethe as chancery clerk of his own interior. Such second nature has nothing affected or posed about it, though Benjamin would have taken the reproach with equanimity. The letter form suited him because it predisposes to mediated, objectified immediacy. Letter writing simulates life in the medium of the frozen word. In a letter one can disavow isolation and nonetheless remain distant, apart, isolated.

One anecdote that does not directly involve correspondence at all may shed some light on Benjamin's distinctive features as a letter writer. The conversation once came round to differences between the written and the spoken word; for instance, the fact that in lively conversation, for the sake of humaneness, one speaks somewhat less formally and uses the comfortable perfect tense where German grammar would strictly require the simple past. Benjamin, who had a very delicate ear for linguistic nuances, was unreceptive to this idea and challenged it with some intensity, as if a sore spot had been touched. His letters are figures of a speaking voice that writes when it speaks.

For the renunciation that bears them, however, these letters have been richly rewarded; and the reward justifies their being made accessible to a wide readership. It is true that Benjamin experienced the present moment in the "prismatic splendor" of reflection;[1] but he was granted power over the past. The letter form is an anachronism and was already becoming one in Benjamin's lifetime; his own letters are not thereby impugned. Characteristically, he wrote them by hand whenever possible, long after the typewriter had prevailed. The pleasure he took in the physical act of writing—he loved to prepare excerpts and fair copies—was as great as his aversion to mechanical expedients; in this respect the essay "The Work of Art in the Age of Mechanical Reproduction," like many another stage of his intellectual biography, was an act of identification with the aggressor. Letter writing registers a claim of the individual, but is nowadays quite as ineffectual in advancing that claim as the world is set against honoring it. When Benjamin remarked that it was no longer possible to caricature anyone, he was dealing with a closely related issue; likewise in the essay "The Storyteller." In a total constitution of society that demotes every individual to a function, no one is now entitled to give an account of himself in a letter as though he were still the uncomprehended individual, which is what the letter claims; the "I" in a letter has something about it of the merely apparent.

Subjectively, though, in the age of disintegrating experience people are no longer disposed to write letters.[2] For the time being it seems that technology is undercutting their premise. Since letters are no longer necessary, in view of the speedier means of communication and the dwindling of space-time distances, their very substance is dissolving. Benjamin brought to them an uninhibited talent for antiquities; he celebrated the wedding of a vanishing institution to its utopian restoration. What enticed him to write letters was thus connected with his habitual mode of experience; for he regarded historical forms—and the letter is one such form—as nature that required deciphering, that issued a binding commandment. His posture as a letter writer inclines to that of the allegorist: letters were for Benjamin natural-history illustrations of what survives the ruin of time. His own letters, by virtue of not at all resembling the ephemeral utterances of life, develop their objective force: that of formulation and nuance indeed worthy of a human being. Here the eye, grieving for the losses about to overtake it, still lingers over things with a patient intensity that itself needs to be restored as a possibility. "I am not interested in people; I am interested only in things"—this private remark of Benjamin's

1. The reference is to Goethe's *Faust,* Act 2, scene 1, line 4727—Stern.

2. The word for "experience" is *Erfahrung;* Benjamin's formulation of the distinction between *Erfahrung* and *Erlebnis* is developed, for example, in the essay "On Some Motifs in Baudelaire," *Illuminations*—Stern.

broaches the secret of his letters. The energy of negation that emanates from it is identical with his productive energy.

The early letters are all to friends from the Free German Youth Movement, a radical group headed by Gustav Wyneken that came closest to realizing its program in the Free School Community at Wickersdorf. Benjamin was also an influential contributor to that circle's periodical publication *Der Anfang,* which attracted much attention in 1913–14. It is difficult to imagine him, with his thoroughly idiosyncratic reactions, involved in such a movement, or in fact in any movement. That he plunged in so unreservedly, that he took so very seriously the controversies of the "discussion halls" and all who participated in them—by now the issues are incomprehensible to an outsider—was surely the result of psychic compensation. Benjamin was by nature inclined to express the general through an extreme of the particular, through what was proper to himself; and he suffered so acutely on that account that he searched for collectivities—to be sure, fitfully and in vain—even in his maturity. Furthermore (and on the other hand!) he shared the general tendency of young intellectuals to overestimate the people they first associate with. As a matter of course he credited his friends with the same intentness upon achieving the utmost that animated his own intellectual existence from its first to its final day; such confidence befits the pure will. It cannot have been the most trifling of his painful experiences to discover that most people do not have the power of elevation that his own example led him to assume in others; and what is more, they do not even aspire to that utmost of which he considered them capable, because it is the potential of humanity.

To be sure, Benjamin's experience of young people, with whom he fervently identified, and also his experience of himself as a youth were already in the mode of reflection. Being young became for him an attitude of consciousness. He was supremely indifferent to the contradiction here: one negates naïveté by adopting it as a standpoint, let alone contemplating a "Metaphysics of Youth." Later, Benjamin's melancholy observation that he "revered youth" aptly named the trait that left its distinguishing mark on the early letters. Between his own proclivities and the circle he joined there was a gulf that he seems to have attempted to bridge by indulging his need to dominate; even afterward, while working on the baroque book, he once remarked that images such as that of the king had attracted him very strongly from the beginning. Flashes of imperiousness dart through the often nebulous early letters like lightning bolts in search of tinder; the gesture anticipates what intellectual energy will later accomplish. Benjamin must have typified the behavior that young people, say university students, are so quick to censure in the most gifted among them as arrogant. And such arrogance is not to be denied. It marks the difference between what persons of the highest intellectual rank know to be their potential and what they already are; a difference for which they adjust by means of behavior that necessarily gives the surface appearance of presumption. Later, the mature Benjamin exhibited as little arrogance as desire to dominate. His politeness was consummate and extremely gracious; it is documented also in the letters. In this quality he resembled Brecht, and without it the friendship between them could hardly have lasted very long.

With a sense of abashment at his beginnings, such as commonly overtakes those of high aspiration—an abashment quite the equal of the earlier self-assessment—Benjamin closed accounts on the period of his participation in the Youth Movement when he came to full self-awareness. He stayed in touch with only a handful of friends, like Alfred Cohn. And of course with Ernst Schoen; that was a lifelong friendship. Schoen's indescribably distinguished bearing and sensitivity must have touched him to the quick, and certainly Schoen was among the first acquaintances to match him in caliber. If Benjamin enjoyed a few years of more or less secure income between the collapse of his academic plans and the outbreak of fascism, he owed them in no small measure to the solidarity of Ernst Schoen, who as program director of Radio Frankfurt commissioned his regular and frequent contributions. Schoen was one of those profoundly self-assured individuals who loved to yield the limelight—without a trace of resentment and to the point of self-effacement; all the more reason to remember him when speaking of Benjamin's personal history.

Aside from the marriage to Dora Kellner, the friendship with Scholem was of decisive importance during the period of Benjamin's emancipation; Scholem was his intellectual peer, and the friendship probably the closest he ever contracted. Benjamin's talent for friendship resembled his talent for letter writing in many features, even in such eccentric ones as the mystery-mongering with which he kept his friends apart whenever possible; although, within a necessarily limited circle, they did as a rule eventually make each other's acquaintance. Out of aversion to clichés of the human sciences, Benjamin rejected the idea that there had been any development in his work; but the difference between his first letters to Scholem and all the previous ones, as well as the trajectory of the *oeuvre* itself, demonstrates how much he did in fact develop. Here, suddenly, he is free of all contrived superiority; which is replaced by the infinitely delicate irony that made him so extraordinarily charming also in private life, despite his strangely objectified and untouchable personality. That irony resides in part in the incongruousness of a touchy and fastidious Benjamin toying with folksiness, say with the Berlin idiom or with typically Jewish expressions.

The letters from the early twenties on have not dated as much as those written before World War I. Benjamin unfolds himself in loving reportage and narrative, in precise epigrammatic formulations, and occasionally also—*not* altogether too often!—in theoretical argument. To the last of these he felt compelled whenever his extensive travels prevented personal discussion with the correspondent. His literary relations are widely ramified. Benjamin was anything but a misunderstood writer who would not be rediscovered until today. His quality remained hidden only from the envious; through journalistic media like the *Frankfurter Zeitung* and the *Literarische Welt* it became generally visible. Not until the eve of fascism was he rebuffed; and even in the first years of Hitler's dictatorship he was still able to publish pseudonymously here and there in Germany. The letters convey a progressive picture not only of him, but also of the spiritual climate of the age. The breadth of his professional and personal contacts was not restricted by politics of any sort. These contacts ranged from Florens Christian Rang and Hofmannsthal to Brecht; the intricate texture of theological and social motifs becomes perspicuous in the correspondence. Time and again he adapted himself to the recipient without thereby diminishing his individuality; reserve and a sense of etiquette, the constituents of any Benjamin letter, then enter the service of a certain diplomacy. There is something touching about that diplomacy when one remembers how little the sometimes artfully considered sentences actually facilitated his life; how incommensurate he remained with existing conditions and how unassimilable, in spite of temporary successes.

I should like to mention the dignity and, until it became a question of sheer survival, the patient self-possession with which Benjamin endured the period of emigration, although the first years imposed upon him the most pitiful material circumstances, and although he never for a moment deceived himself about the danger of sojourning in France. For the sake of his magnum opus, the *Paris Arcades* project, he accepted the danger. In maintaining such an attitude at that time, he benefited greatly from his impersonality and disregard of private concerns: since he understood himself as the instrument of his thought, and refused to set up his life as an end in itself—in spite, or rather because, of the unfathomable wealth of substance and experience that he incorporated—he never bemoaned his fate as a private misfortune. Insight into the objective conditions of that fate gave him the strength to raise himself above it; the very strength that allowed him in 1940, doubtless with thoughts of death, to formulate the theses "On the Concept of History."

Only by sacrificing life did Benjamin become the spirit that lived by this idea: there must be a human estate that demands no sacrifices.

The Correspondence of

Walter Benjamin

Svendborg, summer 1938. *Photo credit: Suhrkamp Verlag, Frankfurt.*

The Letters

1. To Herbert Belmore

[Vaduz]
July 15, 1910[1]

Dear Herbert,

Why don't I write you once? Why not? That's easy. I haven't yet received a single line from you in response to my many postcards. Nevertheless, out of the boundless goodness of my heart and since I want to consecrate the first day of the new year of my life with a good deed, I intend to find it in my heart to write a timely, precise, long, and real letter. And to begin, I hereby give notice that I want an answer to this letter, sent general delivery to: St. Moritz (Dorf). For on Sunday I intend to leave Vaduz, where I have spent many a beautiful day, walking in the cool valley and climbing to the mountain peak. Now my feet, and perhaps the smoky train, will transplant me from here to Ragaz, whence a few hours' journey will bring me to St. Moritz. It is still uncertain whether from there I might travel to Italy or return soon to Germany.—So much for the actual facts. As far as my spirit is concerned, today it received bounteous nourishment to celebrate my eighteenth birthday. I would like to tell you about it in more detail, but this kind of subject matter will not tolerate the constraints of the strict cadences in which I write. And thus the technical limitations of my creative writing compel me to conclude this letter against my will.

1. Written on WB's eighteenth birthday. Herbert Belmore was a fellow student at the Kaiser Friedrich Gymnasium in Berlin.

2. To Herbert Belmore

St. Moritz
July 27, [*sic*—Trans.] 1910

Dear Herbert,

I'm approaching the end of my "Romance." Partly out of a surfeit of material (which I can't master), partly out of a lack of time (which I don't have), partly because I have to write you a great deal about something else (which I won't do). So I have to go on writing the "Romance" anyway. But first an editorial and a geographical observation.

1. I hope that you have also received my other letters and cards (because—believe me!—you only ever mention the first ones I wrote). They were all sent to your home address.

2. Liechtenstein is not in Austria, but is a small sovereign principality and has only Austrian postage stamps (postage 5 pfennigs). But that is no longer relevant, because I am now in Switzerland. My address is care of the Petersburg Hotel, St. Moritz. I'll be here until about Thursday the 29th. (Postage for a postcard, 10 pf.; for a letter, 20 pf. You will have to inquire at the post office what the postage is for two-page letters.)

Well:

On the morning of July 17 in the year of our Lord 1910, a two-horse carriage rolled out of the village of Vaduz onto the country road that lay basking in the sunshine. The larks exulted in the air, the sky was blue, and the mountain peaks sparkled in the sunlight. The attentive female reader will have already surmised who was sitting in the carriage—none other than our renowned Walter. A yellow panama hat picturesquely concealed part of his tanned face, out of which two steel-blue, unflinching eyes flashed underneath dark brows. The attentive female reader, who has already read two to three dozen romances, will know that the same Walter reached his destination (in this case Balzers, near the Swiss border) after a one- to two-hour journey; that he pushed his slouch hat—pardon me, his panama—farther down on his face; that he furrowed his brow and entered the lonely inn on the country road (in this case, the Post Hotel). She will know that he allowed himself only a short rest and soon emerged in order to reach the hostile city (in this case, Bad Ragaz) before evening fell. But what she will not know is that he had to walk for two hours in the heat of the sun into the most horrible foehn before he could take refreshment at an inn on the country road. In short, toward evening he was in Ragaz. Here our hero had an impression of Ragaz as a beautifully situated, terribly desolate tourist spa, which he had visited only because he wanted to see the Tamina Gorge, just an hour away. He did this on the following day and, after his return home, told his astonished comrades about the magnificent impression it had made on him. Our hero has been in St. Moritz since yesterday evening. That he had the most horrible toothache during his trip on the magnificent Albula railway need not be mentioned to those who are well acquainted with him and the general cussedness of things. In St. Moritz, he has not yet spoken with Böninger, who, however, is still here.[1] This morning during the open-air concert, he observed the life of the spa, which generally yields some aperçus. Because of a shortage of space, however, there is no room for them here. He continues to create aphorisms from time to time, a pastime suitable to and recommended for spiritually ruinous toothaches. This afternoon he will pay a visit to the Segantini Museum. And because this style would no longer be appropriate to the subject, he will close this portion of the "Romance" with a happy heart and in the hope of soon receiving an "antiromance" from

Herbert Bl.[2]

1. Theodor Böninger, a classmate of WB and Belmore, died in 1914 during the war. He was the son of a high public official.

2. Written as a signature.

3. To Herbert Belmore

St. Moritz
July 22, 1910

Dear Herbert,

In order to write you, I will put down Mauthner's *Die Sprache,* a book I received as a birthday gift after asking for it. And indeed I put it down with a happy heart. Less because I want to write you than because I no longer have to read it. The book is extremely heavy going, and I think I will forego it for the time being. I also received Gurlitt's *Die Schule,* Burkhard's *Das Theater,*[1] Spitteler's two-volume (new) edition of *Der olympische Frühling,* two volumes of Storm. And *Das zweite Buch der Ernte.* Pompous! Incomparable! The foreword, printed as usual on the dust jacket, begins, "Two years of total absorption in compiling and sifting have brought to fruition this, the second and last book of the *Ernte.*" Käthe Vesper-Waentig has provided a few more rose-shaped doodles: otherwise the old ones are still there. Two poems by Will-Vesper [*sic*] are again included, good ones, incidentally. Otherwise it contains some odd things: for this second collection (it is not actually a sequel beginning with the modern era, but again starts around 3000 B.C.), Will Vesper has discovered Eichendorff and Hölderlin, among others—by chance, at the same time as I have. Anything by Goethe that was not included in the first volume is in the second. Based on this, two things become clear: first, that Goethe is a poet of genius; second, that he does not belong in an anthology but that you are better off obtaining his collected works. In the interval between the publication of the first and second *Ernte* volumes (as you may know), the poems of Angelus Silesius (a medieval poet) have appeared, published by Diederichs. By a remarkable coincidence, the very same poet has suddenly been discovered by Will Vesper during his "two years of total absorption in compiling and sifting." By the way, Angelus's pieces, at least those included in the *Ernte,* are wonderful, but they are not lyric poetry. It is pathetic that Will Vesper needed another two years to discover a few poems by Nietzsche and Hoffmannstal [*sic*], which have already appeared in all the other anthologies. Furthermore, in contrast to the first volume, not everything printed in this one is flawless. Otherwise there is surely much that is good in this second volume—I have not yet read very much of it but rather have skimmed it. This time, what is very good—much better than in the first volume—are the medieval poems.

That's it for a St. Moritz literary letter. Now comes a St. Moritz nature letter. Under the circumstances I'm at a loss to write anything at all. At first quite a few things here seemed to me to be a bit too civilized, but once you take a few steps back, everything is wonderful. When I see the mountains from this perspective, I sometimes ask myself why all this culture exists at all. Yet we forget to take into account the extent to which it is precisely culture (and even superculture) that enables us to enjoy nature.

Yesterday W. from Berlin permitted himself a rendevous [*sic*]. We (i.e. our family) went on an outing with Teddy,[2] and met your parents, your sister, and a stranger who was with them. Your parents silenced my complaints. To my horror, I learned that all my letters to you were forwarded here to your parents—it's no wonder I haven't heard from you. Yesterday your father gave me yet another card I had written you from Vaduz. This has surely been one of the most remarkable exchanges of correspondence in existence. Because of the postage due, it also turned out to be rather expensive for your parents.

I have learned that you are supervising the cleaning up of your house. My heartfelt sympathy to you and those who are doing the cleaning.

Yours, Walter Benjamin

1. All are volumes in the collection *Die Gesellschaft*.
2. Böninger.

4. To Herbert Belmore

Weggis
July 18, 1911

Lucky you! Twice lucky!

Namely: 1) you were already in Sils-Maria when I was granted the honor of receiving my grade (IIB) in the auditorium (!) of the Kaiser Friedrich School. Twice lucky, for you benefit from my being too lazy to get down my picture postcards and will consequently receive a longer written communication (letter) from me. This is to inform you: first and foremost, that I am also in Switzerland, and today for the last time in Weggis (in the Hotel [Albana], which is so generously providing me with stationery). But tomorrow, as far as it is possible for any mortal traveler to make this kind of prediction, I will be in Wengen (Bernese Oberland).

I will refrain from giving you descriptions of the local countryside, because they would merely provoke a flaccid smile from the pale lips of the blasé traveler who dwells in the Engadine. Therefore, to the purely pragmatic (excerpt from a travel diary yet to be written):

Lake Lucerne looks like a lopsided cross (writes Bädecker [*sic*]). Steamboats provide for the tourists and traffic on the lake's surface (says Karlchen).[1] This style is tedious (you say). Sorry! . . .

Well::: By early morning I was in Lucerne. It is the most magnificent lakeside resort I have ever seen (and I saw it for three-quarters of an hr.), and I am convinced that at a certain age, in certain places (should you be interested, on the spa's promenade), you can't walk more than 100 paces without getting engaged. In this region, the Alps are still conspicuously restrained.—I was already in Weggis for lunch. (How else is a person to orient himself on trips but by the five (holy) meals, since time is not divided up as it is by the daily grind of work.) In Weggis the Alps are already more concrete. Mount Rigi is high and has **. Here, as almost everywhere, we did not go to the top. Here, as almost everywhere, a mountain railway goes to the top. (I believe that no country on earth is as accessible to the lame and the fragile as mountainous Switzerland.)—Today I walked the most beautiful stretch of the famous Axen Road, which runs along Lake Lucerne.[2] The road continues above the Gotthard railway and in places has been blasted out of the cliffs. Amazing views. You walk along the extremely high mountain face; on the opposite side you see wooded mountains, snow-topped mountains, and glaciers; in the midst of these, the lake displays a continuous, very clearly defined transition from dark green to blue- or light green, depending on the position of the sun. In Flüelen (at the end of the lake), there is a restaurant where they don't serve liquor. My daily routine begins at nine o'clock. I usually spend the morning on a shady terrace or in the hotel park, day-dreaming with a Latin primer in my hand (notice the well-worn "poetic contrast"!), or, in a state of extreme excitement, holding *The Culture of the Renaissance in Italy* [*Die Kultur der Renaissance in Italien*] (by Burkhardt [*sic*]). Unfortunately, I have only the first volume with me since I didn't hope to finish even this one. But now I have almost finished it. Thrilling and often unbelievable. (Pietro Aretino received an annual pension from Karl V and Franz I so that he would spare them in his satirical poems.) Cf. Bruhn.[3] I am also slowly nearing the end of *Anna Karenina* and just as slowly, but surely, Tolstoy is becoming more interesting to me than his heroine. In addition, I have a lot of other nice things with me, among others *Kaspar Hauser*.[4]

In conclusion, I will leave you with the following good, probably superfluous, advice. After many years of experience, I have recently become *aware* of how much more peculiar and, above all, how completely different nature appears after sundown (from 8:45 to 9:15). Beautiful and strange. Well, if you have not yet observed this, then do so. I await your response in Wengen, general delivery.

Yours, Walter Benjamin

1. This is probably a reference to the then popular humorist Karlchen (Ettlinger).
2. [In German, the Vierwaldstätter See.—Trans.] Drawn as a rebus: the number 4, trees, a townsman.
3. The publisher of a Berlin newspaper, about whose conduct similar rumors were in circulation.
4. Wassermann's novel.

5. To Herbert Belmore

Wengen
July 19, 1911

Isis . . . Pythia . . . Demeter,

Behold, my unfettered soul openly betook itself to you, from Weggis to the Engadine. Yet it discovered no charming Swiss cottage. Rather, in the midst of the eternal glacier, an altar rose up (it is true that I did not see anything on its base), but beneath it was written "Isis Moralitas." And my soul donned its armor and dispensed incense . . . and proceeded thence, swung itself upon the Jungfrau, and the Jungfrau spoke on its behalf:

Sublime maternal Demeter! first let me offer my greetings and all the esteem due you: for out of your infinite loftiness you stoop to promote men's fashion.

But hear, oh maternal Demeter! Your song of morality makes its way to me only in a confused and insipid manner, and even though it comes from a great distance, it nonetheless still comes out of the depths. (And in Sils, where a human being thought and wrote "beyond good and evil," you, the goddess, raise the brazen trumpet of morality.)

(And I may not say more to you, for the Jungfrau speaks on my behalf.)

The Jungfrau solves the Oracle of Pythia:

Pythia speaks ambiguously, and when she is of the opinion that matter weighs nothing and the spirit too much, it is a sign that she is not master of the latest philosophical terminology, because she is of the opinion that matter *still* weighs too much and there is all too little spirit. But when Pythia is of the opinion that the One is strawberry colored, this is explicable, for she is blindfolded, and color is hard to define in any case. This One, however, is usable, specifically as the blueprint of *neue Secession* as produced by commercial artists.

So this is the One, and I have already received it because the colored illustration was enclosed in your letter.

The other, however, is really not usable, and it is only praiseworthy and natural that Pythia should say nothing about it.

And I have already received it as well and it is the other postcard. Thus I will thank God and Pythia if I receive nothing else.

Nevertheless, I have a soft heart, and the Jungfrau's icy tone confuses it and it descends and speaks in a human voice among beasts. For I call the music that the Berlin Opera Repertory imports and imparts as witness to the fact that the beast resides primarily in human beings. Of course, I did not hear this music in the billiard hall, but I was playing billiards there and risked my first shots in the absence of an audience.

I thank you for the excerpts; I have not yet read everything. The criticism in Schaffner's essay interested me greatly. I had no time to go to the public library to immerse myself in this labyrinth. I am intentionally ignoring one point in your commemorative volume:[1] I have received too many good wishes on this point and am somewhat depressed.

I am unable to draft any kind of romantic descriptions of Wengen, and do not know how to produce homemade postcards. That is to say, I've only been here for two hours. Through the beautiful, pouring rain, you catch sight of the Jungfrau.

And now my thirst for vengeance has been slaked and I close with a heartfelt:

Thank you very much!
Yours, Walter

1. Apparently a birthday letter Belmore wrote WB.

6. To Herbert Belmore

Wengen
July 24, 1911

Dear Herbert!

You owe the continuing bulletins about my spiritual condition to neither your soulful and edifying tracts, nor to your malicious contributions to my file of newspaper clippings, nor to the dried Alpine flowers picked on the edge of the pernicious abyss. Rather, you owe them solely to my horrible isolation. Seriously: a lively social life has unfortunately become a necessity for me (as I take this opportunity to note), and I am so lonely here that I fear I will become interesting and, in the course of time, acquire soulful eyes. A condition that even a get-together arranged by the maître d'hôtel could not remedy because I did not attend it. On the other hand, since I am now pretty much the only "young man" at the hotel (perhaps with the exception of my brother[1]), today, in a conversation that took place at some remove from me, I had to listen to scathing words about the blasé attitude of contemporary youth. That is to say, the get-together was generally poorly attended.

By the way, there is even a female here with whom it would be possible to carry on a conversation. Yet we dine at small tables! And thus I struggle with books, whenever I am not outside or at my desk writing in my diary. That is, I struggle primarily with one book, with a demon and a paragon (with a piece of a book, as Horazio-Schlegel would say), with a dragon of a book on which, however, I have been standing for the last ten minutes, just as St. George did in days of yore. I've finished it! I've finished *Anna Karenina* by Count Leo Tolstoy! The second volume: 499 pages. And in reading this book I have experienced genuine rage at the blue, fat-bellied monster in Reclam format that I daily led either to the meadow or into the woods, and that returned to its stall (i.e. my vest pocket) seemingly even fatter instead of thinner. The said monster of a book is nourished on Russian politics. On the new economic system, on self-government, on the Serbian question, on the family unit, and on several dozen other questions, among which the religious question must be particularly stressed. And the reader puts up with all of this for 1,000 pages, in the silent, unfortunately unfounded, assumption that somehow it is part of Anna Karenina's fate. But when after 1,000 pages the heroine is dead and yet another 100 pages are devoted to new discussions about political and social matters (you know: Russian discussions, à la Steinfeld[2]); when in these same 100 pages a subplot is concluded that had gradually and in Homeric breadth crept out of the main plot without ever again joining it; then even the most conscientious reader is gripped by a desire to skip 1–20 pages. But I manfully resisted. And at the end I must say: no matter how defective the novel's structure; no matter how much of it is superfluous in terms of a novel; no matter how much of what appears in the several discussions and digressions is fruitless—the portrait of Russian culture and the Russian soul that seems to be unintentionally, but completely organically, distilled from all of this is extremely powerful. Nowhere but, in great part, in the modern Russians is there another portrait of the soul with such vast areas of squalor, or at least of misery and apathy (portrayed psychologically). In any case, very rarely. The novel is set among the Russian nobility. Ultimately, however, the social position, as well as the soul, of both the nobleman and the peasant is made clear and the main contours of the spiritual features of the rest of the population can be surmised. Maybe more about this when we can talk. It is complicated and difficult to put into words.

Did I already write you about *The Culture of the Renaissance?* I have finished reading the first volume; I don't have the second with me. I lack the historical knowledge to enjoy it fully. What I miss in Burkhard [*sic*] is an enumeration of the reasons for a movement, reasons he continuously presents as "necessary." The book is extraordinarily objective. Almost too objective for a layman who occasionally would like something more in the way of generalizing and summarizing retrospectives. Where such retrospective judgments do appear, they are very clear; and the mass of detail in the book still yields a vivid picture (*especially* for the person who has a great deal of historical knowledge).

Aside from that (!), I have even improved my mind. (Now I see you bowing your head while quivering with awe.) I read a novella by Zschokke. *Ein Buckliger*. The critic's standard tools and thermometer prove useless in evaluating this work, and he must reach into the personal realm. So, just imagine a novella by the gentle, affable Korschel,[3] and you will get the picture.

And finally, I am enjoying the nether regions of domestic and foreign newspapers. The upper regions are indeed meant to look threatening! At such a distance from Morocco, I immerse myself in "Natural Philosophy," "The Prison in the Dunes" (*Tageblatt*), and "The Limits of Psychoanalysis" (*Frankfurter Allgemeine*). Important pieces, and today, in one of the latest issues of the *Neue Zürcher Zeitung,* an article by Spitteler on poetry and literature came into my hands. The notion that the preoccupation of the literarily inclined with poetry is an obstacle to its vigorous development has been frequently alluded to in the "laughing truths." An intense bitterness also comes through in this article. There will apparently be a second installment which may have something more original by way of examples.

I look over what I have written with horror. I can already hear a speech entitled "The Stay-at-Home," presented at one of our literary evenings,[4] but veiled by a friendly smile. I also expect some indication in your next communication as to "how a sojourn in the open air may be made pleasant and productive, for the benefit of one's body and the strengthening of one's limbs."

So nothing more remains for me to do than to draft a large-scale description of adventurous journeys and mountain climbs. (Provided that I don't send reports about devastating thunderstorms that could be exposed as fake by weather reports.)

Granted! The weather is beautiful. Thus, in beautiful weather, a steep (!!) climb down into the Lauterbrunn Valley. From there to Grütschalp, in some places a climb with a ninety-degree slope (which can be accomplished by means of the mountain railway), on a glowing hot morning.

From Grütschalp to Myrrhen, a real Engadine road. This suddenly became obvious to me after I had been walking for quite a while. And with that I believe I have discovered a main characteristic of the Engadine landscape. Namely, the interplay of grandiose elements that complement and harmoniously temper each other. For you will surely concede that you can speak about something's being purely grandiose and overwhelming in only a very few instances; and that an austere kind of charm predominates much more often. And, as I said, in my opinion it is based on contrasts: primarily the contrast between light-green and white; the opposition of barren rocky areas to bright masses of snow (in comparison with which the glaciers seem charming); the grass of the meadows, the deep blue sky, and the gray rocks again produce an interplay that I would call "austere charm." The lakes, of course, should not be forgotten.

Some of these elements made the road from Grütschalp to Myrrhen so beautiful. The glaciers lie before you, and below them the dark pine forest and, in front of it, the road and bright meadows . . . on one side the valley, behind it rocky mountains, and in front of everything the meadow rising up on the other side, out of which darker rocky areas loom intermittently (overgrown with solitary dark conifers), and the deep blue sky. This, moreover, during the midday heat. Do you remember the passage about "the so-called midday heat" in *Gerold und Hansli?*[5] The hotter it is, the more colors there are between heaven and earth . . . or something to that effect. Finally, in the vicinity of Myrrhen, when I came ever closer to the glacier and all I could see was its whiteness, for quite a while I felt (unconsciously) as if I were out walking on a beautiful winter morning.

Nothing is more alien to the luxuriating nature lover than pedantic chronology. And so he will now portray the charms of a hike that, according to central European time, probably took place eighty hours before the hike that was just briefly mentioned. It was my hike on the Jungfrau, for which your warnings and advice came too late.

The Wengernalp railway, which we used to get to Scheidegg, must be very beautiful: and its scenic charms are especially splendid when you do not sit facing the rear—which was naturally what I had to do. For once, on the stretch from Scheidegg to the Eiger glacier, we cut ourselves loose from the railway, "the Jungfrau railway," which looks unexpectedly harmless at its starting point. From a restaurant, you climb down to the Eiger glacier which is now immediately in front of you. A very large mass, and you are hemmed in by snow on three sides. An ice cave (we passed up a visit to it), guides, people with sleds.

Then the Jungfrau railway. (Due to the late hour, my description will be condensed and will dispense with anything lyrical since you have already analyzed the region with a journalist's unerring eye.) I rode with my sister[6] only as far as the Eiger wall since, because of my heart, my parents did not want me to subject myself to too drastic a change in altitude. I find that one nice feature about the tunnel is that you are aware that it leads to the Jungfrau. With this, however, my enjoyment of the trip comes to an end. I spent a melancholy half hour on the face of the Eiger, alone with a station master, a Zeiss telescope, and my sister. A description of mood (main factor: the cold) will be oral. A pleasant return journey from the Eiger glacier to Wengen. Through a wayside telescope, you could occasionally see somebody climbing the Jungfrau; you frequently hear the thunder of avalanches and see what appear to be small amounts of snow dust on the massif. The road across from the massif travels parallel to it for two hours. (To my horror, I realize that I have also forgotten to weave a description of an exciting mountain climb into my account: forgive me!)

Forgive me yet again for the fact that neither alpine flowers nor scraps of newspaper are enclosed with this letter. I have neither the money nor the imagination to pick the former from the abyss (pooh! how trite!); I am too cowardly to cut up the newspapers the hotel gets (oh! how disgusting!).

In the spirit of friendship, I warn you against spreading nonsense in word and image through all of Europe! Fearing a speedy response, countersigned:

Walter

Excuse my handwriting: my writing materials are of poor quality.

1. Georg Benjamin.
2. Alfred Steinfeld, WB's fellow student.
3. Another fellow student.
4. WB, Belmore, Steinfeld, Franz Sachs, and Willi Wolfradt (who later became an art critic) were all fellow students. From 1908, when WB returned from Hanbinda and reenrolled in the Kaiser Friedrich Gymnasium, until the beginning of the First World War, they had a weekly literary evening, when plays by Shakespeare, Hebbel, Ibsen, Strindberg, Wedekind, et al. were read, with each of the participants assuming different roles. They also read their own criticism to each other, written after visits to the theater. This criticism was "often publishable, but never published" (letter from Franz Sachs, Johannesburg).
5. A story by Carl Spitteler.
6. Dora Benjamin (1899–1946).

7. To Herbert Belmore

[Freiburg]
[May 14, 1912]

In the year
MVII ten C88th
one year before the great French Revolution.

My dear friend,

What great variety the world displays! Tonight I had to think of you yet again, my dear friend, since the moon with full cheeks shone into my room. You, my goddess! Luna, the beloved of quiet nights. Silver clouds travel across the dark sky like round silver dollars.——My dear friend, forgive the torrent of emotions which, like a roaring cataract, has taken control of my pen. But tell me whose breast is able to remain silent at the sight of eternally sublime nature! Nature, thou magic word: oh, I know well that this word also awakens a divine image in your imagination. Friedrich Mathisson [*sic*] is conjured up in your imagination. O my dear friend! I will be silent, because I am far too deeply moved. Even I.[1]

Dear Herr Bert,[2]

Forgive this inarticulate chorale of soulful feelings to which I was enticed by your winged missive, glowing with friendship, that I received in the late afternoon mail. I intend to get a grip on myself. It is very beautiful here. How are you? O my dear friend——enough! restrain the waves of my emotions.——The laughter of spring resounds from the houses. The sky is blue and only dark at night, when the sun does not radiate its lovely light. The Free Students are also here and, in absolute terms, the city must be called a university town. Yet only in small part is it situated in a world that is imaginable; for the most part it lies in a world that is unimaginable. This can be proven primarily by the peculiar consistency of Freiburg time. It is not enough that it is not central European. Nowhere, of course, is time a concrete substance. It is strangely fleeting in nature. But the proximity of the local philosophical faculty[3] absolutely forces it to assume its true being—i.e. always to exist in the past and the future, but never in the present. If you designate the quantity of time available at each moment as x, you get the equation

$$x = 16 - 327 + 311.$$

In the same way, the *fille de Sophie* (i.e. daughter of wisdom [French]) exerts her demoralizing influence on men. They regain—like true lovers—consciousness only in the evening—and their individuality also corresponds to a lover's insofar as they live much more through the beloved (phrenology, art, literature, school reform, pistol shooting), rather than somehow being substantial personalities in their own right. So they sit in cafés late in the evening, and you come to realize that there are many valuable things but proportionately few valuable people.

Dear Herbert:

Science is a cow
It goes: moo
I sit in the lecture hall and listen too!

(It is a fact that in Freiburg I am able to think independently about scholarly matters only about one-tenth as often as in Berlin.)

And now forgive this crazy letter. If you want to know about practical matters, have my parents show you my twenty-page letter. You can't expect me to repeat my factual descriptions. You will also know that, in every respect, a first semester is a time of beginning and of chaos (cum grano salis . . . with some sun)—and that in such a state nothing is more difficult than to write rational letters.

On the other hand, things like that must come easy to you.

Best regards.
Yours, Walter

1. Written in a different handwriting.
2. A play on Herbert.
3. WB studied philosophy with Heinrich Rickert.

8. To Herbert Belmore

[Freiburg]
[June 21, 1912]

Dear Herbert,

I have had a moral Achilles heel from time immemorial—and out of pure necessity, in order not to become more fatally afflicted, I will cover it with a 5-pf. postcard—to be sure, not to tell you something about Freiburg, much less about Italy, for your amusement. In addition to that, I am unfortunately aware that every line I write and, even more, every letter I do not write, arouses in you the most tremendous expectations from me, a hero of school reform and a sacrificial offering to learning—the Anhalt railroad station groans under the weight of the man returning home—and Kant's sentences flow from his mouth "like lemonade from the gullet of a raven." (This to show that I have not developed poetically either! I have not written one line of poetry since I've been here: nothing, ουδεν, nichts, nihil, rien!) Instead, I can only tell you the expectations with which I will arrive in Berlin: to be fed into a highly therapeutic "work machine," to be pressed between books, and to groan aloud in delight at rational conversation.

To put it metaphorically: it is impossible to harvest while one is plowing. Or in other words: the Freiburg air.———

I hope you have realized that, in response to your letter, I am engaged only in the idle and senseless business of making myself interesting instead of being interesting as a reporter. From this you will draw the conclusion that, in the future, you must send a greater number of descriptive letters from Berlin to me—without any attempts at extortion, internal or external. Because, my God! everything has already been squeezed out of me.

A trip to Italy is slowly taking shape. An essay I wrote, "Die Schulreform, eine Kulturbewegung" [School reform: a cultural movement],[1] will soon appear in a school reform pamphlet directed at the students. While here, I have read two longish novels: *The Picture of Dorian Gray*—it is perfect and a dangerous book—and *Gösta Berling*—problematical in terms of its structure, but filled with beautiful individual passages.

Many regards. Please write!
Yours, Walter

1. It appeared under the pseudonym "Eckart, phil." in the pamphlet *Student und Schulreform*, published by the . . . Free Students (Freiburg, 1912).

9. To Herbert Belmore

Stolpmünde
Park Hotel
August 12, 1912

The day before yesterday, your latest letter to Freiburg reached me. The letter contains much that is interesting, and between the lines showed me that a thank-you letter I sent from Freiburg did not find you way up north. Or was it your evil intention to ignore my letters?

This coherent introduction will have already brought the idea home to you that my GNI (generally normal intellect) is again surfacing from the deluge of the first semester. There are still snakes of nonsense in its hair, but a coy smile of more mature experience at the corners of its mouth.

As an indication of this:

There is quite a to-do here about Wölfflin's *Klassische Kunst* and Ninon's letters. For me, Wölfflin's book is one of the most useful I have ever read about concrete art. I rate the following on the same level: Dilthey's "Hölderlin,"[1] isolated Shakespeare commentaries, but otherwise nothing I have ever read about the fine arts (*in concreto*).

Thus I rescue myself from oceans of inactivity in the harbor of work and am hospitably welcomed by my good conscience, which did not tire of waiting for me for three months.

Whom shall I introduce to my conscience. A clever and clever . . . charming young lady (tutor?). I became acquainted with her in the Skerries of the *côte d'esprit*. In spite of her youth, she is generally thought to be about three hundred years old—hence, a degree of youthful health, which metaphysicists designate with the word *immortality* (*athanasia sempiterna*). The letters Ninon writes to me (in recognition of my merits, she addresses me as *cher Marquis*) say everything clever and irrational that can be said about such a—basically so reasonable—matter as gallantry, while avoiding some really ungallant [(accidental properties)] of love. A trinity of depth, sobriety, and beauty, so that we dub Ninon a wise woman.

I am also most enthusiastically reading the extremely exhaustive history of the genesis of a drama, *Andrea Sezno*. Dear Herbert, even though I read every day, the end is still not in sight, since the wonderfully well-preserved manuscripts [*sic!*] of the apparently still little-known author repeat the first scene of the third act in ever new variations. Nonetheless, such a detailed invasion of an author's workshop hones one's often much too indulgent critical judgment.—N.B. I might have almost forgotten to point out the bibliophilist value of this history, of which there is only one copy in print.

You naturally don't believe any of this. With a diabolic smile you whisper "Stolpmünde" and the intrinsic mendacity of the above assertions is proven.

I can only confess to so much: that Stolpmünde certainly framed my honest attempts at rehabilitation with sandy mornings, and projects the images of my activity onto a background of coffee-drenched afternoons.

Stolpmünde can still perhaps exert a serious influence on me. Here for the first time I have been confronted with Zionism and Zionist activity as a possibility and hence perhaps as a duty.[2]

When I'm back in Berlin, I'll explain how, in spite of that—of course—I would remain completely dedicated to the Wickersdorf movement.[3]

You will soon hear if Freiburg begins to fade into the past.

Yours, Walter

(I'm coming to Berlin next week.)[4]

1. In *Poetry and Experience* [*Das Erlebnis und die Dichtung*] (1905).

2. In conversations with Kurt Tuchler from Stolp (born 1894), who at that time was a senior. Tuchler writes: "In the summer vacation, Franz Sachs brought Walter Benjamin along to Stolpmünde. During the entire vacation, I was with Walter Benjamin on a daily,

one might even say hourly, basis, and we had an inexhaustible topic of conversation. I tried to introduce him to my view of Zionism. For his part, he tried to draw me into his way of thinking. We continued our exchange of ideas through correspondence and with great intensity. This correspondence was lost during the Nazi period" (letter of February 26, 1963, from Tel Aviv). A series of letters written by WB to Ludwig Strauß, however, specifically concerning the question of Zionism, has been preserved. The letters dated September 11, October 10, and November 21, 1912, and January 7, 1913, are devoted to the debate on Zionism. WB also expressed his opinion on the *Kunstwart* debate of 1912. He finally rejected political Zionism.

3. The movement centering on Wyneken and radical school reform.
4. Where WB stayed until April 1913.

10. To Herbert Belmore

Freiburg
April 29, 1913

Dear Herbert,

I know: I ought to write you. But what? I feel so irresponsible! Outside my window, the church square with a tall poplar (the yellow sun in its green foliage) and in front of that an old fountain and the sun-drenched walls of the houses—I can stare at this for fifteen minutes at a time. Then—as you might expect—I lie down on the sofa for a while and pick up a volume of Goethe. As soon as I come upon a phrase like "the breadth of the divinity," I have already lost control again. You know: In *Groß ist die Diana der Epheser*—perhaps the most beautiful title of any German poem. Have Franz [Sachs] tell you what I wrote him about my room. Keller[1] expressed it very nicely: "Here you're always a visitor." This sunny spaciousness with respectable saints on the walls. I sit in a small armchair and know of no better place for philosophy.

The kind of people I associate with! You'll also hear about that from Sachs. There's Keller, with the beginning of a new important novel and with a beautiful girlfriend whom I often see. There's Heinle,[2] a good fellow. "Drinks, eats a lot, and writes poems." They are supposed to be very beautiful—I will soon get to hear some. An eternal dreamer and German. Not well dressed.

Englert—he dresses even worse. Also has a girlfriend. His childishness is of immense proportions. He worships Keller as a god and values me as a demon.

Finally there's Manning. A Berliner. Note that all the people with whom I associate here are Christians, and tell me what this means. I can't figure it out at all myself. Manning and I talk mostly about girls and women. I am surprised that I have a lot to say to him on this topic (just as I had to Keller in the first semester) without having any actual experiences. In return, he supplies me with accounts thereof, and this way I move forward.

All of this naturally forces me to work a lot, for otherwise I could not endure this atmosphere.

This evening I'll be at the University Club. Our group will be there, plus one or two guests, and some female students. Keller rules despotically and reads aloud to us incessantly. I will also make an effort to get a lively discussion going. Tomorrow Ewer's *Wundermädchen von Berlin* will premiere here, and the day after tomorrow I will go climbing with Heinle.

In the evening, we have long conversations in the very dark, warm air. If you want to know anything else, just ask. Because unless I were willing to write fifty pages, I can't give you more than aphorisms like this. Yet, so you will see that I am doing everything I can in throwing you these scraps of experience, I am enclosing a kind of "poem" that you can just as well take for madness.

Sincerely, Walter

Alienated country subdivided into many provinces.
There blind feelings go begging,
They stagger, as if in lofty rooms.
Planet of the I!
Symbollike
Motility, how you wordlessly plunge into emptiness,
and where you fall, space is created out of eons,
gaping figurativeness will wash round me,
Sapping thoughts, all zones have
Surrendered their "nonetheless" and "hardly."
Decaying, rationality emits odors of finality—
and its colorfully streaked maledictions,
wings beating, at the inner core have become
rigid and furtively steal away.
Blindness has a divine back
and carries the hymnic man across wooden bridges.

Please write. Regards[3]

1. Philipp Keller, with whom WB associated in Freiburg. The author of a novel, *Gemischte Gefühle* (Leipzig, 1915), which WB praised even later. See *Schriften* 3:173.

2. Friedrich C. Heinle, with whom WB was then cultivating a more intimate relationship.

3. One word is illegible.

11. To Carla Seligson

Freiburg i.B.
April 30, 1913

Dear Miss Seligson,

As you have seen, contrary to my promise, you haven't heard a peep out of me since my return from Schreiberhau.[1] I can't tell you how sorry I am about this, but it was unavoidable. The few beautiful spring days in the valley (with deep snow on the peak) made me feel that I had to avoid human contact whenever possible. I was totally lost in meditation and charged with intellectual explosives, which anyone could have unwittingly set off. You may ask yourself whether this is the usual effect that a beautiful landscape has on me? No—but in Schreiberhau I induced it in the following way: for half the day I walked, the other half I read. My reading: Kant, *Prolegomena to a Metaphysics of Morals* [*Grundlegung zur Metaphysik der Sitten*]. Kierkegaard, *Either/Or*. Gottfried Keller, *Das Sinngedicht*. But no normal person can endure a colossal and exclusive association with these writings for an entire week. Whenever a few pages of Kant had tired me out, I fled to Kierkegaard. You probably know that he demands heroism of us on the grounds of Christian ethics (or Jewish ethics, if you will) as mercilessly as Nietzsche does on other grounds, and that he engages in psychological analyses that are as devastating as Nietzsche's. *Either/Or* is the ultimatum: aestheticism or morality? In short, this book confronted me with question after question that I had always divined but never articulated to myself, and excited (even) me more than any other book. And after that it is not easy to stretch your mind on Keller's difficult style, which demands that each sentence be read slowly.

Kierkegaard and a friend's letter also prompted me to go to Freiburg, but, as I said, after the nature of my stay in Schreiberhau I was completely incapable of conversation.

Now, in the course of this magnificent summer, I have achieved serenity: and when I look at the church square outside my window, an old fountain, a single very tall poplar in the sun, behind it houses that look like they belong in Goethe's Weimar (very small)—I can hardly imagine the horror had I stayed in Berlin, as I might have done (if Mrs. St. had chosen me).

Here I have few friends, but good ones, very different from my Berlin friends and mostly older than I. Having become used to things, I find it very pleasant here. Totally apart from the Free Students, who are incapable of work—we have a university club where we (both male and female students) get together on Tuesday evening. We read things to each other and converse. Each of us can bring guests along, but that rarely happens; usually it's the same group of about seven to nine students.

As I said, nothing can be done with the Free Students. I already told Dr. Wyneken in Berlin that I would lead the Division for School Reform only if a well-organized free student union were already in place. There is no indication of that here. There are no announcements to be seen on the bulletin board, no organized groups, no lectures. Now, at a remove from Berlin, I have also become generally clearer in my mind about the Free Students. I want to tell you what I think about this sometime when I am back in Berlin.

Now on to something that will please you. Before my departure, I visited Mrs. Lesser. Our conversation was perhaps not the same as it was the first time we talked, for the same reason that I did not write you—but it may also have been due to where we were. Nonetheless, I was once again very pleased. She asked about you and told me that she was quite taken with you and, "if I had as much time for people, which I in fact do not," she would ask you to visit her. But she did express the hope that we would still occasionally get together—which is indeed possible—on the winter days when she is receiving.

In a few days, the first issue of *Der Anfang* will probably appear. I would be very happy if you were to write me, perhaps even about *Der Anfang* once it has appeared.

In a few weeks I hope to be able to send you something I wrote. This winter I finished writing a *Dialog über die Religiosität der Gegenwart* [Dialogue on contemporary religiosity],[2] which is now being typed. More about this when the occasion arises.

My best regards and please remember me to your mother

Yours, Walter Benjamin

P.S. Please excuse my handwriting if it is bad (as I believe it is).

1. This is where WB spent Easter vacation with his brother and mother in the larger circle of the Josephy family.

2. Preserved among his papers.

12. To Herbert Belmore

[Freiburg]
[May 2, 1913]

Dear Herbert,

A stroke of fortune has befallen me, who might have endured (and serenely endured) Pentecost in Freiburg by reading philosophy while listening to the rain. I will most likely leave here on the 9th and stay in Paris until the 22d. In the company of Kurt Tuchler and a certain Mr. [Siegfried] Lehmann,[1] who is now Tuchler's fraternity brother and was my playmate twelve years ago. Once more, as so often, I do not take childish delight in making a decision, but do so cautiously and with strict self-control, as if I were at a border crossing. This will be explained in a later letter. I am writing to find out if you know of any literature on Paris or have any other tips about the city. The three of us will share the expense of buying Karl Scheffler's *Paris*. But beyond that. Does *Der gefühlvolle Bädecker* [*sic*][2] have a chapter on Paris? If it is good, please write me the essentials—I can't get it here. What *good* art guides to Paris are there. Good essays. Books about Parisian culture and impressionism. About Parisiennes? Please write *quickly*.—My parents do not need to hear about this card right away. I will write them about my plans, but not just yet since I am still waiting for a letter from home. On the other hand, I want to be the first one to tell them about my decision.

Yesterday I was on the Kandel with the nineteen-year-old poet—young Heinle. We get on well. In the antology [*sic*] *Mistral*, which will soon be published by A. R. Meyer, there is one poem each by him[3] and by Quentin.[4]

With a sense of well-being, I send you my regards.

Yours, Walter

1. Lehmann later founded the Jewish People's Home in Berlin and the Ben-Schemen Children's Village in Palestine.
2. Kurt Münzer, *Der gefühlvolle Baedecker* (Berlin, 1911).
3. "Tannenwald im Schnee," 22.
4. Franz Quentin, the literary pseudonym occasionally used by Ludwig Strauß.

13. To Herbert Belmore

Freiburg
May 5, 1913

Dear Herbert,

I admit that the introduction to the *Critique of Judgment* [*Kritik der Urteilskraft*] is on my agenda for this morning. Yet I will put it off for a moment—in order to *thank* you for your letter, but also to tell you that I do not feel entirely comfortable with the intense mystical aura with which all of you in Berlin are surrounding me. I am a simple child of humanity. Now I would like to answer you with a few theses of my own, so that yours will not overwhelm me. First and foremost, however, I refer you to my last twenty-four-page letter to Franz. It contains not only diary entries but also an enclosure that is somewhat similar to what I am about to write here. Since that time, moreover, a conversation has taken place that told me more than I knew and you surmise: I am not saving myself—I am not lifting off from, but rather I am *conquering* on this soil.

Now to the theses.

1. I am and feel myself in a state of ὕβρις, the most impious certainty about gods and men.

2. I came to alien peoples who do not honor me and see that my being continues even without being honored.

3. I see my being prove itself; finally it expands and takes on earthly form, instead of steeply climbing. This happened through sensual resistance.

4. I see that it is not my conscience, but rather my nature, which limits me. My conscience is my nature. I cannot go against it: thus it is no longer a conscience. In school I never copied: that was not conscience, but rather intelligence, nearsightedness (nature).

5. Once this nature is acknowledged with resignation, it gains strengths of which it had no inkling: it gains its *own* sensuality, frees itself from theses.

6. For this reason, I associate with Christians and other such people without harm to body or soul, and I am superior to them. With the exception of Keller, to whom I am equal on another level. Nevertheless I now confront him (can't you understand this?) *because* I am his equal, because we know that we have nothing in common but this: that we are I. The I is not a gift, but rather a limitation. This is precisely what maturity is.

7. But this still holds: I am only free (sensually), I am only self, when I know my limits. The conscience lives within these limits. They are marked off from nature (even granted that this nature was once conscience) (v. thesis 4).

I cannot know more than this and this illumination is the result of the last three weeks.

The descriptive part: yesterday I went dancing in Littenweiler with Keller, Englert, Manning, Heinle—I didn't care whether I danced well or poorly while they were watching. I came and went as I pleased. Further: there is a growing revolution here and I am confidently in control of it. I am Keller's diametric opposite and liberate people from him after having liberated myself from him. I can do this only because I hold him in esteem—as an artist (not as a Bohemian, for that is not what he is). Here in Freiburg I have proclaimed the slogan of youth. This is what happened:

I had a conversation with Manning in which I said that the one thing separating us from Keller is that he assumes the gestures of a forty-year-old without truly being one. (And other things like this which you could understand only if I were able to describe for you in detail his current state: he is in crisis.) Suddenly Manning, who loved to impress upon me the fact that he had the same experience with Keller, says: but we're young. We really only want to be twenty-one. I: "I have nothing more to say about it, you're saying what I think." I liberated this person in one evening between 10 and 1:30. All at once he looks at me dumbfounded: "How can you say that to me. By doing that, you hold the key to my life in your hands before you even know what it is." . . . Just say the magic word[1] . . . Since that time, I have known that I am an integral part of Wyneken's mission, and return people to their youth. The same evening, I ask Manning: Where do you get this dreadful fear of sentimentality? "Well, Keller crammed that into me too." These are the kinds of answers I get. I give him the courage to be sentimental—he reads out loud from the (truly terrible) diaries he wrote as a fifteen-year-old. All of these people are being liberated so that they will have a chance to form themselves, unsentimentally and soberly, according to ideas, instead of adopting a veneer of gestures.

Young Heinle, with whom I recently had an hour-long conversation about the literati, is a similar case, only easier. I see that these people, at least Heinle, do not come close to holding Keller in as high esteem as I do—because they are still pursuing him.

I hope it did not take autumn to prove to you and me "how totally necessary and beneficial this stage of development was."

For the *first* time in my life, I understand Goethe's words:

> Only where you are let everything be—always childlike
> Thus you are everything—you are invincible.[2]

I know: as a respectable person you have to forget this bit of wisdom (for it is a piece of *wisdom*) infinitely often—and infinitely often again comprehend it. I have comprehended it for the first time.

Whether the semester will produce anything else that is fundamental—not likely. A lot of work. A lot of pleasure.

Yesterday, in Littenweiler, Manning admired my childlike cheerfulness. I will return his to him. Keller and I are currently the only childlike ones here. For this reason we are kindred spirits.

Give my regards to Franz and to Willi.[3] May waves of this beautiful experience also reach him. At the moment I am unable to write him.

And that is why I came here. Only I learned to grasp the experience differently than I thought I would.

Yours, Walter

P.S. Franz should be shown this letter.

1. Eichendorff, "Triffst du nur das Zauberwort," from *Schläft ein Lied in allen Dingen.*
2. "Marienbader Elegie."
3. Franz Sachs and Willi Wolfradt.

14. To Franz Sachs

Freiburg
June 4, 1913

Dear Franz,

I have no classes this morning and want to write letters: the first one goes to you. The "Summer's Night Epistle" is a fine documentation of your rapprochement. Neither of you would have written it alone: you are not *that* sure of yourselves!

Concerning *Der Anfang:*[1] I don't know if you get together with Barbizon[2] all that frequently, but I would appreciate it if you did. Had you added your two cents' worth, then it is unlikely that Heinle's poetic and youthful odes, which Barbizon calls "inappropriate," would have been rejected. If such a thoroughly confident personality were in charge of *Der Anfang,* it might well be that Wyneken would completely remove himself from its day-to-day management. But even as it is he was only supposed to go over manuscripts with a fine-tooth comb. And what's going on with [Wilhelm] Ostwald? I wrote to Barbizon: how is it possible to allow such a notorious "school reformer" and scribbler to write in our *Anfang.* Now the public has what it wants: the comfortable slogan that will allow it to consign *Der Anfang* to the mass grave of "school reform." People and writers like Ostwald are the greatest enemies of our cause, for in the final analysis we do *not* want just school reform but something else that he can't even imagine. Or am I mistaken? If the article in the second issue understands us (I don't believe it!), fine—then it can stay in. Otherwise, serious damage will be done. Therefore, please pay attention to the editing. By the way, I in no way share your judgment of the poems by Eleutheros in the first issue. I, Heinle, Manning—even Keller—found them unusually beautiful. Naturally, it is not possible to judge them in terms of individual lines, any more than this can be done with Goethe's "Mailied." The following poem, however, has the same momentum and, at the same time, the same ponderous, calm ending:

> Lift the hour with strength and pride
> out of the jug of the ages.

Furthermore, it feelingly plumbs considerable depths:

> . . . may not bemoan the fact
> that he only at first *lacking will*
> was carried on high.

You are familiar with my views and know that I approve of this insight. If I had the *Anfang* here, I could analyze the poem more closely. The more often you read the second poem, the more profound it becomes (which is not the case with the first).

I intend to send you a copy of the Heinle odes very soon so that you can see them through the editing. In the *Tageblatt,* I read the trivial criticism by Matthias, who lacks an ear for the rhythm of the poems. I have not yet read the other critics.

Just as I am asking you to take charge of Barbizon, I am also asking you *to take charge of the Berlin Discussion Hall.*[3] This is an important institution that can provide the setting for a fine communality of interest. *Naturally* Wyneken is to have nothing to do with it. Quentin recently wrote an open letter to the Freiburgers,[4] in which he said that Moritz Heimann[5] was planning a Jewish Free School Congregation for Germany. What determination! What do you know or hear about this?

Paul Hoffmann has written me, is interested in us, and wanted to speak to me personally shortly before my departure, but it was too late. I presume that he is from the *Kunstwart* circle, and so handle with care! Don't be too radical.

Tell me about Herbert's talk to the school-reform group.

And now I am approaching the point of my "letter" (whose strange stationery is quite disturbing to me). Wyneken's grounds for abstinence. You call them "wonderful"; my brother writes me almost the same thing: this is the way they must affect everyone who sits there with a pure conscience and *is* abstinent. Not me. What helps you [ending missing]

1. The *Zeitschrift der Jugend,* published by Gustav Wyneken, to which WB contributed under the pseudonym Ardor. The first issue had just appeared.

2. Georg Barbizon (actually G. Gretor), one of the two editors of *Der Anfang.*

3. The Discussion Hall was an organization founded in 1912 by WB and his friends for the purpose of discussing the problems of youth in the spirit of Wyneken. It attracted many students, particularly in 1913 and 1914. Martin Gumpert described the organization in his autobiography.

4. The Free Students' Division for School Reform.

5. The storyteller and editor at S. Fischer Verlag, who took a lively interest in things Jewish.

15. To Carla Seligson

Freiburg
June 5, 1913

Dear Miss Seligson,

I returned from Paris one evening after Pentecost and found, among many others, your letter waiting for me in the mail. I was very happy to receive it. Thank you so much!—Yes, I did go to Paris for fourteen days over Pentecost; instead of having a few isolated memories of this city I could tell you about, I have only an awareness of having lived intensely for fourteen days, as only children do. I was on the move the whole day and almost never went to bed before two. Mornings in the Louvre, in Versailles, Fontainebleau, or the Bois de Boulogne; afternoons in the streets, in a church, in a café. Evenings with acquaintances or in some theater or other: then, above all, every evening on the Grand Boulevard, which in some ways could be compared with Unter den Linden if it were not narrower (cozier!), and if these streets did not wend their way through the entire inner city, whose houses seem made, not to be lived in, but to be stone stage sets between which people stroll. I have become almost more at home in the Louvre and on the Grand Boulevard than I am in the Kaiser Friedrich Museum or on the streets of Berlin. By the end of my stay (I was in the Louvre an awful lot), I only strolled through the exhibits, repeatedly stopping in front of the same paintings I already knew, and which have been indelibly engraved on my memory since they struck me as being more beautiful every day. I have never before understood art so easily. For the first time I got some notion of the French rococo—of Fragonard, who is the boldest and most sensual of these painters. Boucher, Watteau, Chardin, and many less significant painters cover the walls with paintings two meters across. I frequently walk through the gallery; gradually I get used to isolating specific paintings and then, the next time, I can spot them from far away.

The veneration of our time for El Greco is not empty posturing. While walking through art collections, I twice found myself attracted by a painting, and both times it was an El Greco. One time in the Köster Gallery in Berlin (the Free Students are visiting it in June—why don't you go along!), and one time in the Louvre, where his royal portrait of Ferdinand I hangs, melancholy and full of pathos. Of all the painters I know, El Greco can best depict pathos (pathos but, of course, not vacuousness).

By the time I left Paris, I was familiar with its stores, the advertisements in lights, the people on the Grand Boulevard. At the opera, I saw the most old-fashioned ballet imaginable. It is no longer moving as art, but I did admire the discipline of the individual ballerinas, something I had never noticed to this extent in performances at the Berlin Opera. I saw the most beautifully groomed women in the lobby—by the way, in Paris even the most refined women wear make-up.

When I was back in Freiburg again, I felt as if I had been gone for three months—but Paris is behind me as such a wonderfully consummated experience, that I felt no dissatisfaction, but much more the joy that . . . everything had come to a happy conclusion. The following truism can be found in *Brand*. Here, of course, it should not be taken so solemnly.

Happiness is born of loss
only what is lost remains eternal.[1]

In the meantime, a lot had changed here. Primarily, summer. In Paris it was usually cool. Last Sunday it was a pleasure to arrive at the top of a mountain in the heat and suddenly to have the Feldberg before me, a snow-covered vista.

The discussion evenings I wrote you about have also changed. Mr. Keller led them but has withdrawn. Since he attracted many people, we are now pretty much alone and the better for it, because formerly the group was neither big nor small enough to allow us to socialize. Sometimes I give talks about Spitteler or read essays by Wyneken to the group. His new book, *Schule und Jugendkultur,* has now appeared, published by Diederichs. I am ordering it today.

In recruiting for *Der Anfang,* I have won over a new contributor and am fairly confident about the future. It is very important that our ideas finally be liberated from the dogmatism clinging to them on the outside: this is basically what I expect from the journal. I don't know whether people in Berlin are moving in the absolutely right direction—I was taken aback to hear that [Wilhelm] Ostwald (!) is supposed to write a lead article for the next issue. For heaven's sake, what does Ostwald have to do with *Der Anfang!*

Nevertheless, *Der Anfang* has driven me back into the fold of the Free Students. This semester, I must not set my goals too high; as I have already written you, the organization here is precarious. My only goal is that, by the end of the semester, some people will emerge from the division who have understood us to the extent that they will subscribe to *Der Anfang,* even if at first they do so more out of respect (which they should feel in any case) than out of interest. I have only one loyal and capable assistant here.

I also think of our "fellow youth" in the same sense in which you write about them, but my work here is simply more impersonal, more abstract, than it was in Berlin where I knew more, and where I knew younger, people. During the first strange weeks of the semester, I have become acquainted with one young person[2] about whom I will write you. We have been working together since we met. But even our acquaintances are already "mature." They already have too much life behind them, so that they hardly have direct access to ideas anymore. They have, at most, a lot of sympathy for us. But there is the large abstract mass of Free Students, in whose history we must simply *believe,* even though often not a single student proves the value of our work through really understanding us.

Therefore it was difficult for me to decide to reestablish the division, but I am doing it anyway for *Der Anfang* and I am waiting for what will come of it with great equanimity.

Concerning your letter: where are these beautiful words from: "full of spaciousness, happiness, and wind." I remember having read them and have no idea where?[3]

In conclusion: since I am, after all, studying philosophy, you are now going to have to listen to—to be sure, nothing about philosophy (I am reading Kant, Schiller, Bergson for seminars)—but something about philosophers.

Yesterday, for the first time since I've been a student, I found myself in a small group of professional philosophers. I had been invited to a reception at the home of a privatdocent.[4] It was a grotesque spectacle, from both an internal and external perspective. I provide the internal perspective: of course, I am acutely aware that I am not a card-carrying member of the union because, although I do indeed philosophize a lot, I do so in a totally different manner: my thinking always has Wyneken, my first teacher, as its starting point and always returns to him. Even when it comes to abstract questions, I intuitively see the answer prefigured in him. And when I philosophize, it is with friends, dilettantes. Thus I am totally forlorn among these people who speak with somewhat more circumspection (perhaps?) and more knowledge, for they have already completed their studies.

But the external perspective is just as strange. I have hardly ever seen anything so sublimely tragic! In conversation, of course, they conduct themselves more openly, more freely as personalities, each one of them as the thinker he is, and here is where I see the childish impulsiveness with which each one of them begins from the beginning. The "schools" we know about and which I come across in journals disintegrate into all sorts of individual beings fighting each other, happily or vehemently. People who outwardly present themselves in lectures as rationalists say: yesterday, that doesn't make any difference; we need ideas, productive ideas! They see this vivacity and, always associated with it, the striving for "science" but, on the other hand, the impulse to grasp an idea that will further our life today.

I kept very much to myself and take comfort only in this: that I nevertheless have in reserve many an unthought thought, at least among those I know to be *thoughts*. I also found an older student who knew a lot about philosophy and with whom I could make myself understood. But my tragic fate pursues me: he was a history major!

Please excuse this letter that touches on such a variety of topics. But if this variety were to be brought into pleasant harmony, I would have to write you four times a week, as I do Mr. Sachs who yesterday received twenty-eight (!) pages from me.

Also please excuse my bad handwriting—I'm writing on paper to which I am not accustomed—and please don't wait to answer until you have the "Dialog über Religion" [Dialogue on religion]. You will get it, but I have still not found the time to have the second part typed.

Sincere regards.
Yours, Walter Benjamin

1. The concluding verses of act 4 of Ibsen's *Brand.*
2. Heinle.
3. The lines are from the third part of Rilke's *Stundenbuch* [Book of hours].
4. Richard Kroner.

16. To Herbert Belmore

Freiburg
[June 7, 1913]

Dear Herbert!

This letter comes to you from the heights of uneventfulness. That is, after having sent only informational letters this semester (not to mention informative), I finally feel obliged to make things less easy for myself and to respond to you on your level. Thus finding myself in a state of total soullessness, I'll give it a try:

The weather here is very beautiful ——— now it isn't anymore, it's somewhat cloudier. What is the forecast for tomorrow? (Answer immediately!) Recently—at the beginning of June—Gluck's saccharine *Maienkönigin* was still playing at the Municipal Theater. The backdrop was painted by Mrs. Oppler Leyband [?]. Philinth was the best-performed role. Afterward the three sisters Wiesenthal (except for Grete) danced.

Yesterday, however, during a literary evening, I recited some Rilke. Keller and Heinle also read. You still don't know what kind of poetry Heinle writes; listen to his latest:

Portrait

Out of yellow linens rises, tanned and distinct,
The thin throat, erect. But very aware
Of bestowed banquets the singed couple sinks
In beautiful arcs to arched delight.
Like dark grapes the paired lips leap
With sudden ripeness to heaving breast.

This, of course, is in manuscript form! Have you been reading Ludwig Strauß's magnificent poems in the *Freistatt?*[1]

Just *send* me the *manuscript* of your *lecture* in the *Div. f. School R[eform]*. Was it well attended?

Maybe this evening I'll see *Tegernseer Bauern:* the first-place medal.

This afternoon I began to compose a novella with the lovely title: *The Death of the Father.* Outline: soon after the death of his father, a young man seduces the maid. Then: how these two events merge and one weight balances the other (the girl's pregnancy).

The subject matter is from Mr. Manning's life, which I am learning about during the wee hours of the morning, sporadically and in terms of one or the other of its seemingly endless dimensions. At this time Keller is making very slow progress on his new novel, but what he has written, approximately ten printed pages, is good. I recently attended the open house given by the philosopher [Richard] Kroner and felt hopelessly out of my depth in this group of experts. I made the acquaintance of an example of a species that was only a myth to me until now, a Jewish woman, ca. twenty-six years old, who is studying art history and has three categories of artistic judgment: wonderful, sweet, splendid.

[Jonas] Cohn's seminar on the *Critique of Judgment* and Schiller's aesthetics has been chemically purified of ideas. The only thing you get out of it is that you read the texts. Later I'll give them some thought. I also just sit and pursue my own thoughts in Rickert's seminar. After the seminar, Keller and I go to the Marienbad, agree with each other, and believe ourselves to be more incisive than Rickert. All of literary Freiburg now attends his lectures; as an introduction to his logic, he is presenting an outline of his system which lays the foundation for a completely new philosophical discipline: philosophy of the perfect life (Woman as its representative). As interesting as it is problematical.

Downcast, I close in the knowledge that even this letter will contain individual sections that are interesting and informative.

Regards to Willi. Regards. Regards to Franz.

Regards to you,
Your
I: Walter
Benjamin (i.e. I).

1. A Jewish journal. The reference is to the poems in 1:118–20.

17. To Herbert Belmore

[Freiberg]
June 23, 1913

Dear Herbert,

Good manners would seem to suggest that I should write you again,—although *you* were the one to hear from me last. But by writing you, I can use up a few minutes and thus avoid more strenuous work.

We don't have a topic of conversation—do we?—therefore I have to expend an inordinate amount of intellectual energy every time I write you.

This time let the topic be a reference to Hauptmann's youthful and divine drama commemorating the centenary of Napoleon's fall. The only thing that allows me to be reconciled with this anniversary, which did not cause me to suffer, however, is that such an immortal and felicitous creation could come into being and could lay to rest the question of whether Hauptmann is a great poet and independent mind. If you have not yet read this drama, please do so as soon as possible so that you may experience one of the most delightful hours you have ever spent. I have not been so spiritually moved, i.e. so uplifted, by art for a very long time—not since Spitteler, I think. The banning of the play is something beautiful and gratifying: I can't imagine a more historically appropriate insight into its greatness. With its banning, a piece not only of the past but also of the present has been rationalized.

Tomorrow I'll write Wyneken. I will most urgently repeat a suggestion I first made when I heard about the banning and was familiar with only a few lines of the play: to dedicate the August issue of *Der Anfang* to this *Festspiel* by making it a Hauptmann issue. Let young people respond to a politically ossified public. We are busy: Heinle has his article about the *Festspiel* ready (full of pathos and rabble-rousing). Tomorrow I'll write mine: I have already noted the direction my thoughts will take: "The *Jahrhundertfestspiel* or Youth and History."[1] I think I have some essential things to say. I am firmly counting on those of you in Berlin to read the play immediately and energetically support our (Heinle's and my) plan for the August issue. I am not in Berlin right now. But will we have another opportunity in the near future to demonstrate the role that the judgment of young people should play in public life? This issue of *Der Anfang* will contribute to our cause. Above everything else, it will be relevant to our cause, as well as Hauptmann's, and it will sell! Let me know your opinion about the *Jahrhundertfestspiel*. Be as thorough as you can while avoiding technical aesthetic commentary as much as possible.

As I said, I will write Wyneken tomorrow or the day after at the latest; in any event, when I am able to enclose both my article and Heinle's. At that point, I also expect a speedy response from you. You'll get in touch with Wyneken and also with Barbizon. I hope the matter is just as important to you as it is to us.

Yesterday I wrote an article, "Erfahrung" [Experience].[2] Possibly the best thing I have ever written for *Der Anfang*. It is intended for the September issue. Recruit! Recruit! There is no way for us to know *how* much we affect things. *Der Anfang* absolutely must remain a purely intellectual (not aesthetic or some such) publication, yet removed from politics.

I must close; when I tell you that I am currently deeply involved in these things, in conjunction with further thoughts on the ethics of intellectualism, etc., you will be informed about the most important personal things.

What? To Gibraltar in August? Then we'll never see each other again!

Salve, scriba, valeas

Walter.

1. Appeared under the title "Gedanken über Gerhart Hauptmanns Festspiel" by Ardor, in *Der Anfang* (August 1913).

2. Appeared in the October issue.

18. To Herbert Belmore

Freiburg
June 23, 1913

Dear friend, your letter urgently demands a response. So I'll write and will not let it bother me that I already wrote you this morning.

Addresses are not an illusion. Since my previous letter, to which you primarily refer, was addressed to Franz, and not to the indifferent recipient of some learned theorem. I have to mention this so that you will keep in mind that the letter, whose effusiveness and vagueness disturb you so much, was not meant for you. I wrote this letter and these lines to Franz. Moreover, had I communicated these opinions to you at a more mature stage of their development, they would have been formulated differently. Of course I still owe you a justification for these opinions. But why didn't Franz reply? Or did he do so through you? Is he already just as sure as you are? If so, I have deluded myself, since I assumed that he is subject to greater confusion and doubt than you, and is consequently more receptive. To repeat, I would have presented these thoughts for your consideration only when they were at a more advanced stage of development. But that's water under the bridge.

This will probably not be a very long letter since these lines are meant only to clarify the earlier ones. But this letter cannot become "affectionate" (in spite of all of its inherent affection), dear Herbert—instead, it will perhaps be somewhat polemical. After all, I would not want you to be surprised sometime in the fall. Nor would I want everything you ascribe to a bad climate and the terrible distance between us to be a transitory phenomenon. Before I go on, you should know that, having thought about these things, I am not well served by your diagnosis of my "touchy defensiveness." And this must be said about my moods: don't let these initial Freiburg letters have more long-lasting repercussions in your drawer than they had in my brain. Now, for once, I have been very serious[1]—as can be read in the letter to Franz—but I've never been "fatally depressed."

And one more thing: The essay "Romantik" [Romanticism] is now in print, unchanged from when you read it.[2]

To get to the point: I agree with most of what you say about women at the beginning. "The less we are troubled and confused by those awful 'personal' experiences." You'll find out just how well that expresses my own view when you read my essay "Erfahrung." And, as you so nicely put it, "the man must be gentle, must become feminine, if the woman becomes masculine." I have felt this way for a long time. There may also be some truth to your simple formulas for man and woman: spirit-nature/nature-spirit—though I generally avoid speaking concretely on this topic, and prefer to speak of the masculine and the feminine. For both are found intertwined to such a great extent in people! And thus you should understand that I consider the types, "man"/"woman," as somewhat primitive in the thought of civilized humanity. Why do we usually stop short at this division (as conceptual principles? fine!). But if you mean something concrete, then the atomization has to go much further, even down to the last single individual. Europe consists of individuals (in whom there are both masculine and feminine elements), not of men and women.

Who knows what the extent of woman's spirituality actually is? What do we really know of woman? As little as we do about youth. We have never yet experienced a female culture, no more than we have ever known a youth culture. But you, Herbert, demand "absolute affirmation." Who of us is actually the absolutist? Am I the one who says: Ananke will have ordained it, somehow? Am I the one who denies reality, which does not conform to the idea? Or are you the one who has to base his opinion of woman on reality and who then pins the requisite world plan on Ananke? "It would truly be the torment of the Danaids to want to redeem the unredeemable." We know as little about what is unredeemable as we do about what is redeemable. And our redemption comes about through love! But certainly: you may call it the torment of the Danaids. And human existence is surely the torment of the Danaids, which is meant to engender an ethereal spirit whose end is itself—and the death of humanity will come about at some time in the future—or maybe never. Both possibilities are equally bleak. We should have learned from Wyneken that this contingency, the "as if" and the redemption of the unredeemable, is the universal meaning we proclaim.

However, your barely restrained indignation at my views on prostitution runs through your letter—in any case, you should not blame anything other than my thoughts. I am unable to prove these opinions at the moment (and never ever!). But I can show you that you are making do with vagueness, and that we must go beyond the kinds of convenient answers that Franz first, and now you, wrote. It really seems that I have already written what is essential.

What is the moral meaning of a prostitute's life?

Or do you think that we can circumvent this question. For our part, we lay claim to morality and personal dignity—don't we? But we are supposed to dare to stand before prostitutes and call them priestesses, temple vessels, queens, and symbol. You should know that this infuriates me as much as Franz's "sympathy." Much more, even. After all, with this sympathy the prostitute is still a moral individual (a sympathy that remains shabby enough when it comes from the man who sleeps with her—but at least it can be honest). And the man who turns her into a morally bad person has more conscience than the one who makes her inhuman, immoral. To you, a prostitute is some kind of beautiful object. You respect her as you do the Mona Lisa, in front of whom you also would not make an obscene gesture. But in so doing, you think nothing of depriving thousands of women of their souls and relegating them to an existence in an art gallery. As if we consort with them so artistically! Are we being honest when we call prostitution "poetic." I protest in the name of poetry. And we are being infinitely smug when, with subjective self-promotion, we believe we are able to endow the *prostitute's* life with meaning. I would like you to acknowledge the shallow aestheticism of what you write. You yourself do not want to relinquish humanity. Yet you would have us believe that there are people who are objects. You arrogate human dignity to yourself. As for the rest, they are pretty things. And why? So that we have a noble gesture for ignoble deeds.

If we want to be moral and at the same time acknowledge prostitution, then there is only one question: What is the moral meaning of a prostitute's life? In that it has moral meaning, it can have no other meaning than that of our own lives. For you ask all too timidly: "Either all women are prostitutes or no women are?" No: "Either all people are prostitutes or no one is." Well, choose your own answer. But I say: We all are. Or should be. We should be the object and subject of culture. In truth: If we wish to reserve for ourselves this kind of private personal dignity, then we will never understand the prostitute. But if we feel that all of our humanity is a sacrifice to the spirit, and if we tolerate no private feelings, no private will and spirit—then we will honor the prostitute. She will be what we are. Then what you obscurely mean by the words "priestess and symbol" will become true. The prostitute represents the consummated will to culture. I wrote: she drives nature from its last sanctuary, sexuality.

For the time being, let's say nothing about the spiritualization of sexuality. This precious item in the masculine inventory. And we speak of the sexualization of the spirit: this is the morality of the prostitute. She represents culture in Eros; Eros, who is the most powerful individualist, the most hostile to culture—even he can be perverted; even he can serve culture.

I believe that I have now stated my opinion clearly and concisely. You have to want to understand it, in order to understand it, but—. The lamenters [?] speak of the "glorification of prostitution." They have good instincts.

But maybe I'll hear from you that your remarkable balancing act, (one time) poetic, then sacerdotal, basically meant this all along.

Yours, Walter.

P.S. Sire, grant us freedom of thought!

I don't know what you mean by "chaotic shamelessness"—you apparently understood very little of my last letter.

Second P.S. This morning I received a letter from Franz; therefore, all of the above also applies to him. At the same time, I received a letter from Wyneken: "I agree with you as concerns the female psyche: 'as if.' Biologically and psychologically, of course, God only knows."

Think about the writings of Wyneken, who for now is our intellectual better.

I will discuss your letters with him as the occasion arises.

1. Reading uncertain; perhaps it should be "happy."
2. In *Der Anfang* (June 1915).

19. To Herbert Belmore

July 3, 1913

Dear Herbert,

Nothing in my letter was meant to offend you. It was meant neither as an insult nor an honor when I said I would have written you my thoughts only when they were at a more advanced stage of development—rather, it is an intellectual instinct. For god's sake—please don't start any mystery mongering with my letters: now as before, everything I write is meant for all of you. And let that be the end of it!

I cannot spare you this pain: you did not understand my last letter either. But no new refutations. After having given it much thought, I decided to console you with a novella that I am currently writing. If it is a success, you will get it; and perhaps you will understand in very veiled language what seems to be incomprehensible when clearly expressed. That will be better than hopeless explanations in letters. Just one thing: for me it was always a matter of endowing prostitution *as it now exists* with an *absolute* meaning. You may call this premature! But this is just what I think. And now, until we can talk in person or until the novella arrives, let me close with Marion's beautiful words in [Georg Büchner's—Trans.] *Danton's Death* [*Dantons Tod*]: "Everything pleasurable comes down to the same thing; whether it's bodies, pictures of Jesus, wine glasses, flowers, or children's toys; it's all the same feeling; whoever enjoys the most, prays the most."

But: *to be capable of pleasure* and to act as if she were friendly—this is the prostitute's noble virtue. This is how I interpret Marion—apart from that, you may confidently claim her words for yourself.

But how can you think me capable of believing that a man should satisfy himself with a prostitute so he can return to his work refreshed and fortified (as well as peaceful and serene)! Do you take me for a Botocudo?[1]

Get in touch with Barbizon about putting out a Hauptmann issue. After lengthy consideration the pros and cons seem equally compelling to me. You will find that both Heinle's article and my own on the *Festspiel* for the next issue are in Barbizon's possession. My "Erfahrung" article, as well. In any case, the articles on Hauptmann are already the basis of a discussion with Barbizon: I referred him to you—as I did you to him.

Whenever you call to my attention the dirt about Hauptmann or *Der Anfang* to be found in newspapers, I am very glad that I haven't been reading any.

Just a little about Freiburg (out of a sense of duty).

Heinle has finally become the only contact among the students with whom I still have personal dealings. Keller is now neurasthenic—we rarely see each other and, when we do, we are conscious of speaking guardedly. I recently witnessed a terribly embarrassing scene in which Freiburg gossip was aired by Manning, Englert, and Keller—insults, suspicions, etc. Things it is totally impossible to reproduce in writing without a lot of gibberish. The fact that Heinle and I had nothing at all to do with it—but were considered neutral by both sides—may attest to our secure and totally isolated position.

Two older students are among the loyal guests at the literary evening, the school reform evening, and on Tuesday. It is touching to see them seriously and steadfastly beginning to develop their spiritual selves, using Wyneken and us as their foundation. One of them may not even be bright. The evenings devoted to school reform (eight to ten in attendance) are always on a high level. The essential thing is that Wyneken is discussed every evening and that we do not beat about the bush about our unequivocal discipleship—everything will follow from that.

I recently made the acquaintance of a female student from Essen whose name is Benjamin. We took a walk on the Schönberg, which I discovered only this semester and which is one of the prettiest summits I know. I intend to go there at night with Heinle in the very near future.

We talked effortlessly and happily about a lot of things—each time I think about this walk, I note how much I lack human contact in Freiburg. There's just Heinle.

I once took a walk like this with Wolfgang Brandt's sister, who isn't pretty but has a dark-complected delicate face. Two weeks from Sunday I'm going hiking with her (and unfortunately another horror of a female student) on the Plauen.

Are you interested in the fact that there was a meeting about Hauptmann here yesterday? It was disgraceful. A philistine educated in philosophy babble[d] irreverent nonsense. "And especially those of us from Breslau would have wished that . . . (the city of Breslau would also have cropped up as the mother of the movement)," "You don't ignore the anecdotes and memories dear to the people without suffering the consequences," otherwise—and all in all, of course, we're for it. Disgusting!

During the discussion: Keller. In a bad mood—you could tell that he wanted to make an impact. He didn't succeed—people were grumbling. Heinle and I stamp our feet. Surrounded by shuffling feet. Aside from this, Keller spoke the only hopelessly reasonable words. I said to Heinle: "If I knew these people here in the auditorium better, I would surely feel there are as many embittered personal enemies here as there are people present."

In closing: our work progresses—I'm doing some philosophy (unfortunately not very much); I'm reading Heinrich Mann's *Little Town* [*Die kleine Stadt*], which does not allow perfunctory praise; and I'm having a go at my second novella.

Yours, Walter

1. [A tribe of Brazilian Indians who, at this time, were considered extremely primitive.—Trans.]

20. To Carla Seligson

Freiburg
July 8, 1913

My most esteemed Miss Seligson,

Thank you for your letter. It arrived here in Freiburg and did not come as a total surprise. Let me formulate what you have written and I have experienced here as the One Question: How are we to save *ourselves* from the lived experience of our twenties?

You may not know just how right you are—but one day we will really notice that something is being taken from us (not that we had it too long, but they are not going to let us hang on to it anymore). All around us we see those who once suffered the same thing and saved themselves by taking refuge in coldness and superiority. It is not that we fear what we are experiencing, but rather the dreadful result: that after the lived experience we will become numb and assume the same cowardly gesture unto eternity. These days, I often recall Hofmannsthal's lines:

> and that my own I, restrained by nothing
> glided over out of a small child to me
> like a dog, eerily mute and alien.[1]

Is this not true? that the question for us now is whether these lines are to come completely true, and whether we must choose this kind of existence simply in order to defend ourselves from the others, who are also so "eerily mute and alien."

How can we remain true to ourselves without becoming infinitely arrogant and extravagant? People want us to fit in without complaint, and we are completely ridiculous in the solitude we want to preserve—and we cannot justify that.

I felt this when I came here, having let the familiar circle of my Berlin friends; I discovered aloofness, incongruities, nervousness—now I have become acquainted with loneliness for the first time; I turned it into a lesson for myself by spending four days hiking alone through the Swiss Jura—completely alone with my exhausted body.

I am still unable to tell you what kind of tranquility I have achieved with this solitude. But in my first letter to you, when I so fulsomely praised my room with its window looking out onto the church square, it signified nothing but this tranquillity.

I have completely divorced myself from someone[2] who was the reason I came here; because at the age of twenty-two he wanted to be a forty-year-old like many of the most spiritual young people around us. It is quite true that now, at the age of twenty, I have not the slightest guarantee that the life I am leading will be a success: I am very busy supporting *Der Anfang* by organizing the divisions and I am separated from my friends. During the first weeks of my stay in Freiburg, these friends received letters that were uneven, confused, sometimes depressed. For two days, I was thoroughly unhappy here in Freiburg.

So in recent weeks I have worked very quietly for the *Anfang*. You will find my article, "Gedanken über Gerhart Hauptmanns Festspiel" [Thoughts on Gerhart Hauptmann's *Festspiel*], in the next issue, and in the September issue an essay, "Erfahrung."

My father visited me a few days ago, and I was surprised at how very reserved and friendly I was. (Of course my father is opposed to my aspirations.) I assure you that this is so without the least trace of arrogance.

Why is it? Recently I saw a schoolboy on the street. I thought: you're working for him now—and how alien he is to you; how impersonal your work is. Meanwhile I took another look at him. He was carrying his books in his hands and had an open, childish face with only a slight overlay of schoolboy blues. He reminded me of my own school days: my work on the *Anfang* no longer seemed at all abstract, at all impersonal.

I really believe that, for the second time, we are beginning to feel at home in our childhood, which the present wants to teach us to forget. We need only to live in rational solitude, somewhat less concerned about this difficult present and about ourselves. We will steadfastly rely on young people who will find or create the forms for the time between childhood and adulthood. *We* are still living in this period without these forms, without mutual support—in short: alone. I do believe, however, that one day we will be allowed to move very freely and confidently among the others, because we know that the multitude of others are no more "eerily mute and alien" than we ourselves. How do we know that?

Because we wanted to mobilize the openness and sincerity of children who later will also be twenty years old.

Think of the secretive and noble gestures of the people in early Renaissance paintings.

I hope you won't be annoyed if these words, which could be uttered only from my point of view, failed to touch on anything of importance to you, if I made the mistake of keeping my remarks too general.[3] But you will surely agree with me that everything depends on our not allowing any of our warmth for people to be taken from us. Even if, for a while, we must preserve this warmth in a less expressive and more abstract way, it will endure and surely find its form.

My most sincere regards.

Yours, Walter Benjamin

1. *Terzinen 1* ("Über Vergänglichkeit").
2. Philipp Keller.
3. Seligson had undergone a difficult experience about which she wrote in a letter dated July 2.

21. To Franz Sachs

July 11, 1913

Dear Franz,

We certainly all have reason to be pleased with the third issue of *Der Anfang;* I have already given Barbizon my critique. All in all, the issue is very appropriate as propaganda but, at the same time, is more assured and intimate than the previous issues. I agree with your individual judgments, except for the one on Heinle. After all, it is enough that his essay, as you concede, is characteristic—when we were in school, how often did we feel that boundless anger, which was left unsaid but is expressed in Heinle's essay. Heinle's essay[1] is well justified as an expression of this sentiment, theoretically (and hygienically). It offers not facts, but feelings. At the same time, Wyneken's editorial comment is also justified. But you speak of a "tone that needs to be developed" for *Der Anfang*. We are probably in agreement on this point: in general, however, we must guard against bringing to the task too specific a notion of what youth and beginning are. I wrote the same thing to Fritz Strauß[2] concerning his criticism of the second issue.

I am asking Herbert to send me his essay right away if possible; I have high expectations for it and am thinking of reading it to a small group here before it appears in print. *So please have him send it!*

I am really pleased, and I think it is very decent of you to want to take over as the first president[3] in Berlin. I hope you will be elected.

In the farsighted way in which I conduct such deliberations and consider the consequences even for semesters in the distant future, I had no compelling reasons either to reject or to accept. I only know that now I will gain a semester, which I hope to devote to relatively intensive philosophical work. In any case, your sacrifice of one of your semesters replaces my activity there. And from another perspective: it is reasonable that in this way you will for once fill your semester with intense extracurricular activities (since, after all, you do study in Berlin). I will give you one piece of advice, straightforward like that of a western (or better, Greek (?)) wiseman: always be shrewd, and occasionally be bold.

We are now undoubtedly able to represent the Free Students idealistically. More to the point, they are literally waiting for the members of our camp to adopt them. For our part, we will construct a theoretical basis for the Free Students (perhaps in the guise of a specific interest group, v. Kranold and Kühnert, "Wege zur Universitätsreform"[4]). Therefore it would be good if you were occasionally to manifest a shrewd boldness, a well-thought-out radicalism. Basically, we must always have the feeling that you are too rich in ideas (not in moods) to be totally predictable. And when the said university administration receives such an inconclusive but entirely personal impression of you, it will only contribute to your effectiveness. I read your news from the university with great interest, but—as far as I can judge from here—Cohen's candidacy would be very logical to me (apart from your own, of course). She is totally resolute, and if someone were to keep an eye on her relationship with Müller-Jabusch,[5] she would seem to me to be a very viable candidate (as I said, always keeping in mind that I assume your presidency would be best). For one thing must not be forgotten: the said university administration will have a much harder time fleecing a young woman as friendly as Miss Cohen than they would Mr. Saturnus or Schneider. I do not give the administration credit for *that much* adroitness; and they may underestimate the intelligence of a young woman in a way that would be of benefit to us. In addition, of course, I would much prefer to be able to work with her in Munich. I am of the same opinion as you: if only for programmatic reasons, a woman president of the Berlin Free Students is very desirable.

Why has the Deutsches Volk been dissolved? Because of last semester's leaflet?

——In the summer I am going to spend several weeks with my mother in Switzerland or the Tyrol or in Italy. I think I will be in Berlin at the beginning of September or the end of August. I hope we will be together at least during this month.

Please expedite the school reform circular. Also please let me know which Free Students have a Division for School Reform so that I can send it to all of them. The report will probably go out to you tomorrow. Please read it to the division members.

The weather here is not fit for dogs. Spent Wednesday in Basel. I saw the originals of the most famous Dürer prints: *Knight, Death, and the Devil, Melancholia, St. Jerome,* and many more. They happened to be on exhibit. Only now do I have a notion of Dürer's power; of all the prints, *Melancholia* is inexpressibly profound and eloquent. In comparison, the primitive power of Holbein the Elder is a surprise. Finally, the greatest of the paintings there, Grünewald's *Crucifixion,* which moved me even more deeply this time than when I saw it last year. I am getting ever closer to German Renaissance art, just as, when I was in Paris, I observed that the early Italian Renaissance touched me. There's a painter, Konrad Witz, whose figures all look like children in adult costume (with the expression of peasant children, revealing their misery, stuck in the costumes of old people). He paints an inexpressibly happy John who is nonetheless unaware of his happiness: smiling to himself like a child at play. And a Christopher with the silliest smile carrying a butterball of a Christ child, who is suffused by an equal amount of expressionless but fundamentally unconscious seriousness.

Welti, Albert, and Keller. With these names, I have enumerated those who made the greatest or most perfect impression on me. Also Bö[c]klin's splendid *Spiel der Najaden.* I was there for two hours.

Yesterday, at a very nice gathering at the Ungers', I laughed as I haven't in a very long time. Miss Brandt and another stupid lady (but cute), as well as a gentleman, were present. There was a lot of joking around about Unger's bibliophilic library, a lot of white parchment volumes and books with colored spines on black shelves. The atmosphere was cheerful and sexually liberal (as I have rarely, perhaps never, experienced it). Dr. Unger and his wife got engaged when they were students in Freiburg; that is what makes this possible.

I read Heinrich Mann's *Little Town* with sincere human and artistic involvement.

I am reading Bonaventura's *Nachtwachen,* which is much more than just "educational"—and the excellent 1910 *Hyperion-Almanach.* And also an essay by Husserl.[6]

I recently received a letter from Carla Seligson. It was sad (but not despairing), the most beautiful letter anyone has ever written me—one of the most beautiful letters I have ever read. She is a very extraordinary person. You will see the letter in Berlin; since there is virtually nothing factual in it, there is nothing I can report to you. Don't mention that I wrote you about it (should you happen to see her).

Regards.
Yours, Walter

P.S. Please excuse the crumpled envelope: I am including something for Barbizon that he sent me. Give it to him when you see him.

1. Friedrich C. Heinle, "Meine Klasse," *Der Anfang* (1913).
2. A schoolmate of WB who, along with Franz Sachs and WB, spent the first semester in the summer of 1912 in Freiburg. He was born on November 18, 1894, and later moved to Tel Aviv.
3. Of the Free Students.
4. Hermann Kranold and Herbert Kühnert, "Wege zur Universitätsreform = Wege zur Kulturbeherrschung," no. 3 (Munich, 1913).
5. Maximilian Müller-Jabusch (1889–1961).
6. Apparently "Philosophie als strenge Wissenschaft," *Logos* (1910).

22. To Herbert Belmore

Freiburg i.B.
July 17, 1913

Dear Herbert,

I came back from Freudenstadt yesterday evening. I was there on the fifteenth with my parents and my brother and sister. This is why I haven't gotten around to thanking you until today. For the letter and the book. The title struck me as no less daring than it did you: it is a title that gives you the courage, not only to read an unknown book, but also to buy it. Thank you so much for sending me the book: not because it contains good poems; there are very few of those. But because I now own a recently published book by Dehmel—to be sure, some of these "new" poems have been known for a long time. And so—in lawful possession of this book—I have been set at ease to some extent about the conundrum Dehmel. From now on, I will never be able to open up his books with anything but suspicion. Just yesterday evening, I was reading some of the "beautiful, wild world" in the expectation of finally finding the simple, beautiful, unproblematical Dehmel. What I found was largely not even problematical. He is a master of rhythm. His feelings, however, are by no means unrefracted and braced against realities. Rather he develops feelings almost *logically*. But you should not feel the slightest regret at having given me such a present, any more than I regret owning this book. On the contrary, as I said, as a consequence I have a degree of certainty about Dehmel for the first time.

My brother gave me Dehmel's hundred selected poems. I was already familiar with them and decided to exchange them because I had found little of value in them at that time. Well-meaning relatives gave me Kellerman's *Tunnel.*[1] It's supposed to be awful and I may not be able to bring myself to read it. For I am fastidious about reading only good things.

I received two copies of Halm's book[2] (you see: the Fury of confusion assails my library!)—the only other things were: Hueber's *Organisierung der Intelligenz.*[3] Kierkegaard's *Concept of Anxiety*. I will buy some things myself. You are surely reading Kierkegaard in the Diederichs edition; the other translation is indigestible. But even then, it is highly unlikely that you will read the book in a single sitting. It becomes very difficult and dialectical, particularly in the second part—which is where I had to take a break. I believe that such a high degree of artistry in presentation and overall vision is not as evident as a by-product in many other books as it is in Kierkegaard. In his life, he probably forcibly subdued the melancholy cynic in himself, in order to write this *Either*—and above all, the *Diary of a Seducer*.

In Freudenstadt I read my brother some lines from my Hauptmann article. At that moment I regretted that I didn't let the essay settle a while longer but immediately sent it off to Barbizon. I noticed that my personal involvement at the time had kept me from a more broad-based and livelier treatment. Everything seemed to suffice. Heinle is no critic, which is something I miss here. Had I taken more time, a lot of the essay would certainly have turned out better. Wyneken is right. I regret to say—

Please read "Erfahrung," my essay for the September issue. If it is not good enough, and if it can be improved, please send it to me with your comments. After the thirtieth, mail it to Freudenstadt, Villa Johanna. Because Barbizon, who has accepted it, is not at all critical. I want to remain totally receptive to art and philosophy for quite some time, perhaps until I have written a novella. Above all: I do not want to write for *Der Anfang*. There is the danger that thoughts, over whose concrete consequences I still have no control, will become self-evident to me.

I also want to defend Heinle against Wyneken. His poem is hard to understand, as well as being flawed. It manifests something very similar to the license that Goethe takes in *Faust II*. His *Jahrhundertfestspiel* was supposed to be an appeal to hearts and minds and is that. He has made an impression with it, and not only on me. There are no ideas in it, and they do not belong in an appeal, at least not absolutely.

If all of you consider an appeal to be unworthy, if you have contempt for pathos that comes into being groundlessly, then the play is a dubious enterprise. Perhaps this is the way Wyneken thinks. But then it goes against Heinle's *inclination* and therefore a lack of competence cannot be established.

When I am back in Berlin, I will show you some poems by Heinle that may win you over. We are probably more aggressive here, more full of pathos, more thought-less (literally!), and what's more: that's just the way he *is* and I sympathize, empathize, and often that's the way I am too. This is also the reason we were unable to reach an understanding about prostitution. (But beware! Misunderstandings threaten anew—)

What you said to Franz seems to be necessary for him—for me it is downright refreshing. It has been such a long time since I have heard anything like it, since there aren't any moralists at all around here. There are Zionists instead.

The most important thing: won't you at least be in Berlin again toward the middle of September? Because at the beginning of October I have to go to Breslau—or are you coming along?—and will probably be in Berlin only until about the fourteenth or seventeenth. But: in August I am going with my mother to the Tyrol. We may go to northern Italy, specifically Venice, toward the end of August. It would be wonderful—not to mention useful—if we could be in the Academia together. Our plans are still very uncertain; but if I knew you would be in Venice around the twentieth, I would of course meet you there with my mother if at all possible. So let me know!

Let me stop here!

If you want to have some notion of what I have been like in the last two weeks, just picture me in my room, as withdrawn as possible, reading.

Regards to your parents and Helmut.[4]

Yours, Walter

1. A clear-cut bestseller at the time.

2. *Wege zur Musik* (1913). August Halm (1869–1929), Wyneken's brother-in-law, was the music authority in Wyneken's circle.

3. Victor Hueber (Leipzig, 1910). The author belonged to the group around Pfemfert's Aktion.

4. Belmore's brother.

23. To Herbert Belmore

Freiburg
July 30, 1913
(unfortunately!)

Dear Herbert,

This is the last letter you will receive from Freiburg. I am leaving on Friday at 9 A.M.; I will then spend another eight days in Freudenstadt and finally go on a trip with my mother and probably my aunt, Mrs. Josephy.[1] Our first stop will probably be San Martino in the Tyrol. But I am also seriously thinking of Venice as the final stop of the trip even if I will not get to meet you there. By the way, let me congratulate you on having Erich Katz as a traveling companion. On our trip to Italy, I discovered that he is the least moody and most amiable companion imaginable. So as things stand now, in August we will still be quite far apart but—*if I should have the time*—I would like to go to Dresden with Willi and you in September.

I have been daring in planning my reading for the trip. Do you know, I will begin reading the *Critique of Pure Reason* [*Kritik der reinen Vernunft*] with commentaries as soon as possible: thus I have taken Kant and Riehl along. I also want to read *Der Tunnel*—after all—Kurt Pinthus recommended it recently in the *Zeitschrift für Bücherfreunde* and, by the way, as critically as you did. I have also surrounded myself with a few Insel books; you will be glad to know that Stendhal's *Römerinnen* is among them; because it was under this alluring title that I discovered the impossible stories which remain unread among my Reclam books at home. After that I mean to attempt *Der Sturm.*

I have done a lot of reading recently. For one thing, the earlier issues of the *Logos,* especially Rickert's essay "Zur Logik der Zahl,"[2] considered by his students here to be his most brilliant essay, and the one that has to be read. Guy de Maupassant's *Woman's Pastime* [*Notre Coeur*]. A novel containing such inconceivably beautiful sentences, I would have liked to memorize some. Somewhere he writes, "And she, the forlorn, poor, errant being who had no place to rest but was serene because she was young . . ." (!) I can remember this one right now. The story is very simple and narrated almost abstractly. Its psychology sees to the very core of people and, in spite of that, touches them as if with the hand of a kindly old physician. The name Maupassant only now has meaning for me, and I am looking forward to everything else of his I will be reading. I have Hesse's collection of novellas, *Diesseits,* in my room. He knows how to do many things, even if they may all boil down to just this one thing: to depict landscape without endowing it with a living soul, and nonetheless to make it the focus rather than just decoration. His particular way of seeing things is located midway between a mystic's contemplation and an American's penetrating gaze.

You know it is impossible for me to feel bad while reading books like this. But I feel even better than that. I have finally truly grasped that there is sun. You have received a postcard with an old master's depiction of an afternoon in Badenweiler. On the return trip I came across some unwelcome acquaintances. A chatty student (Rudolf Goldfeld) with a certain Miss Seligson who was most disagreeably unladylike. After all, it is a fact that very few young girls can be wittily uninhibited. Käthe Müllerheim is the best example.

Monday evening I had a ten o'clock appointment with Heinle on the Loretto. Heinle wanted to bring another gentleman along. We sat together at the top in semidarkness—Heinle, I, and the gentleman—so that I could not see him properly at all. Rockets marking the finale of a children's festival rose from the other hillside into the skies. I primarily spoke with Heinle—the gentleman mostly listened. (You know that Dr. Wyneken is getting the information on Breslau[3] from the *Frankfurter Zeitung;* thus he is going there.) I discussed with Heinle how to organize some kind of testimonial to Wyneken in Breslau. It cannot be anything at all public; it is time that people for once approach him as something other than the founder of Wickersdorf. It has to be a personal act. Some evening at a small gathering (at most twelve people—but I couldn't even come up with twelve who were very close to him) seems good to me. During the evening, someone would simply speak about him, primarily stressing that, because of him, we had had the good fortune of growing up conscious of the presence of a leader in our lifetime.

In any case, the need to do something should also be obvious to you. And just as obvious is the error made by a public for whom he would always be the unemployed founder of Wickersdorf.

After that we still walked in the woods and spoke about goodness.

Yesterday Heinle came by and brought me two poems, not his own. I read them and said: Surely only [Ernst] Blaß[4] could write that. It was not Blaß, but Müller. We established that the poems meant a lot to us, that they also go much further than Blaß in terms of their metrical freedom (you'll get to see them in Berlin). Müller, however, was the gentleman with whom we had been yesterday. Both of his poems dealt with Gladys who lives in Paris (he rejects the rest of his work and approves of only two poems). He is, however, the son of the man who edits the *Freiburger Boten,* the ultramontane newspaper. He spends the day sitting in the editor's office writing articles—he quit school two years before he could take qualifying exams for the university. Heinle telephoned him yesterday; we wanted to get together with him again. And this evening we will. It is a real shame that we did not find the third person to complement the two of us until now. We do not need to make an effort to get along with him; he does not talk a lot, never indulges in idle chatter, and truly has a radiantly intense feeling for art—also for ideas. Yesterday we climbed around the woods from 10 to 12:30 and talked about original sin—we came up with some important ideas—and about dread. I was of the opinion that a dread of nature is the test of a genuine feeling for nature. A person who can feel no dread in the face of nature will have no idea of how to begin to treat nature. The "idyll" does not represent any kind of pleasure in nature—but rather a pseudo-artistic feeling for nature.

The semester is concluding with the fortissimo of warm active days—I am sorry that I have to start traveling.

Thanks for your parcel. I like your sketches[5] a lot—I am going to show them to Heinle today. I had forgotten to do so earlier. The sketch of the poor black schoolboy is even better than the David; the bizarre landscape is magnificent. But the David is the shrewder choice (for a stamp), also "more positive" (nonsense!). The David may be selected because he has a hard, sleepy expression that is very beautiful. I mediate between Heinle and all of you, just as I mediate between all of you and Heinle. Heinle still feels that your essay lacks rhythm. I would express it in these terms: what is missing for me is the assured, almost classical, way of "establishing" something like an apostrophizing, i.e. exhortatory, tone meant for the individual. What you say seems to be intended more for adults than for young people. The essay is very good (for what I have said above deals only with practical considerations). For the reasons implied above, however, I do not know whether it might not be better for you to choose a more neutral title that more emphatically stresses the programmatic aspect. For example: Concerning (On) Themes and Ideas of *Der Anfang*.

Heinle still needs the essay for propaganda purposes; he is sending it off tomorrow or the day after. That is to say that he is making an effort to establish a Discussion Hall here, but with little hope of success. Vacation has come—as well as the members of the *Wandervögel*, individualists, who are most accessible to him.

Many regards.
Yours, Walter

1. Friederike Josephy, one of WB's father's sisters and the relative who was closest to WB, committed suicide in 1916.

2. In *Logos* 2, no. 1a (1911).

3. The reference is to the first Student-Pedagogical Assembly in Breslau on October 6 and 7, 1913.

4. Ernst Blaß (1890–1939), who, among other things, was editor of the *Argonauten*, which is mentioned later.

5. Belmore was a student of interior design at the Berlin School of Commercial Art. He drew and painted on the side.

24. To Carla Seligson

Freudenstadt
August 4, 1913

Dear Miss Seligson,

The semester is over now. I am spending a few days with my parents, brother, and sister, and then I am going with my mother to the Tyrol until the beginning of September—maybe the weather will be tolerable for our trip to Venice. Saying good-bye to Freiburg—to this semester—turned out to be difficult for me after all. This is something I can't say as easily about any other recent year. My window was there, the one you have heard about, looking out on the poplar and the children at play; a window in front of which you feel mature and experienced, even when you have not yet accomplished anything. Thus it poses a danger, but it is still so precious to me that I plan to live there again should I go back to Freiburg. Mr. Heinle was there, and I am sure we became friends overnight. Yesterday evening I read the poems he wrote this semester, and here, with some distance between us, I find them almost twice as beautiful. Finally, life there also suddenly turned beautiful and summery with the arrival of sunny weather at the end of the semester. The last four evenings we (Heinle and I) were constantly out together past midnight, mostly in the woods. A young man of my age, whom we got to know by chance in the last days of the semester, was also always along. We told ourselves that he was the third person who would complement the two of us. Not a student. He quit school two years before he could take university qualifying exams; he works in the editorial office of his father, who publishes Freiburg's ultramontane newspaper.

Consequently, this semester ended on a pleasant note—I am as sure as I am about nothing else that, while I do not fully grasp it, the semester will bear fruit in years to come, somewhat like my Paris trip may in the coming months.

You may have heard about the pedagogical student congress that will take place in Breslau on October 7. I recently learned that I will be giving a talk there; besides me, [Siegfried] Bernfeld, head of the Academic Committee for School Reform in Vienna, will also give a talk. A third speaker is a Mr. Mann, who is a member of an opposition group. Both orientations represented by the student movement, the one associated with Wyneken and the other with Prof. Stern (my cousin),[1] will confront each other for the first time at this congress. In Breslau we will also for the first time get an overview of our troops (as I believe they can be called), our wider circle of friends. Before the congress meets, another three issues of the *Anfang* will appear; you may put your trust in them, to the extent that I am familiar with the contributions.

As difficult as it is, I must now respond to what you wrote about the form of the new youthfulness. I thought about it until I trusted myself to be able to express with relative clarity what I have always thought. What I have to say is no longer part of our work in the strict sense—it is probably philosophy of history, but what you wrote surely demonstrates its relationship to our most intimate thoughts.

Will what we want take away anything at all from the young person, the individual? (Will we—this question is even more serious—be giving him anything at all?)

But above all: will a new youthfulness, of the kind we want, make the individual less lonely? I do not see how we can answer no to this question, if it is construed in all seriousness. Indeed, I believe that we will not suffer the distress of loneliness (which is certainly a mysterious moon, if not a sun) in what we are trying to achieve; we want to destroy loneliness, eliminate it.

Thus we can say—nevertheless, we may still assert something completely different, something that is apparently its opposite. Because, let's just have a look around in our own time. Somewhere Nietzsche says: "My writings are supposed to be so difficult. I was supposed to think that everybody in distress understands me. But where are those who are in distress?" I believe we may ask, Where are those who are lonely nowadays? Only an idea and community in the idea can lead them to that, to loneliness. I believe it is true that only a person who has made the idea his own (irrelevant "which" idea) can be lonely; I believe that such a person must be lonely. I believe that only in community and, indeed, in the most fervent community of believers can a person be truly lonely: a loneliness in which his "I" revolts against the idea, in order to come to its senses. Do you know Rilke's "Jeremiah," where this idea is wonderfully expressed? I would not want to call loneliness the relationship of the ideal person to his fellow man. Although, to be sure, even this can be a form of loneliness (but this form is lost in the ideal community). Rather, the most profound form of loneliness is that of the ideal person in relationship to the idea, which destroys what is human about him. And we can only expect this loneliness, the more profound type, from a perfect community.

But whatever we may think about loneliness, today neither the one kind nor the other exists. I believe that only the greatest people will ever totally achieve that "other" loneliness. (Of course if they, like the mystics, became totally one with the transcendental, they have already lost it, along with the "I".) The conditions for loneliness among people, with which so few are familiar nowadays, have yet to be created. These conditions are "sentience of the idea" and "sentience of the I," and the one is as unfamiliar to our time as the other.

I must summarize what I have said about loneliness: in that we as individuals want to free ourselves from our loneliness among people, we transmit our solitude to the many who were still unfamiliar with it. And we ourselves become familiar with a new kind of loneliness: that of a very small community in the presence of its idea. (This sounds more arrogant than it is. For in reality there are and will remain in almost every person two kinds of loneliness.)

Your question and your objection are basically the most serious things that can be raised against *Der Anfang*—and not only against *Der Anfang*.[2] And even before this journal appeared I often had misgivings about it. I am writing about this for the first time in this letter, and consequently in a way that is entirely incomplete and fragmentary. People have expressed this objection in more abstract terms and said (or better, *thought*): *Der Anfang* deprives young people of their obvious lack of inhibition, deprives them of what is natural to them—in short, what one might perhaps call innocence. This would be true if young people had innocence *now*. But youth is beyond good and evil, and this condition, which is permissible for animals, always leads a person into sin. This may be the greatest obstacle that the youth of today must overcome: the assessment of them as animal, i.e. as unrepentant innocent, as that which is instinctually good. For people, however, this kind of unaware youth (we see this every day) matures into an indolent manhood. It is true that youth must lose its innocence (animallike innocence) in order to become guilty. *Knowledge,* the self-awareness of a calling, is always guilt. It can be expiated only through the most active, most fervent, and blind fulfillment of duty. I believe that the following does not express it too abstractly: all knowledge is guilt, at least all knowledge of good or evil—the Bible says the same thing—but all action is innocence.

There are some lines in Goethe's *Divan* whose profundity I still can't fathom:

> For real life is action's eternal innocence,
> which proves itself in that it harms no one but itself.[3]

However, the innocent person cannot do good, and the guilty one must.

You really have to excuse me for answering your simple question with a metaphysical discourse. But maybe these thoughts will appear to be just as simple and obvious to you as they do to me. For any person, innocence has to be earned anew every day *and as a different kind* of innocence. Just as the forms of loneliness always surrender to and redeem each other—in order to become ever more profound. The loneliness of the animal is redeemed by the gregariousness of the human being. (This is a third kind of loneliness about which I have not yet written: I call it "physiological."

Strindberg's characters are tormented by it.) The person who is lonely in gregariousness establishes society. And only a few people are still lonely even in a community?

I cannot close without telling you about an entirely different idea with which I will answer your question about the punctilious certainty and great facileness of the coming generation of young people. Please read my essay[4] in the July issue of the *Freie Schulgemeinde*—I will enclose it. In this essay, I try to explain that there is no certainty that a moral education will take, because the pure will that does good for the sake of good cannot be apprehended with the means the educator has available.

I believe that we must always be prepared for the fact that no one now or in the future will be influenced and vanquished in his soul, the place where he is free, by our will. We do not have any guarantee for this; we also should not want one—because good only issues from freedom. In the final analysis, every good deed is only the *symbol* of the freedom of the individual who accomplished it. Deeds, lectures, journals do not change anyone's will, only a person's behavior, insight, etc. (In the moral realm, however, this is completely irrelevant.) *Der Anfang* is only a symbol. Everything it is beyond that which is internally *effective* is to be understood as grace, as something incomprehensible. It would be quite conceivable (and it is surely the case) that what we want will gradually come to pass without the spiritual young people whom we wanted having appeared in their individual manifestations. This has always been the case in history: its moral progress was the result of the free act of only a few individuals. The community of the many became the super- and extra-human *symbol* of a newly fulfilled morality. While the old morality was just as much a symbolic form, constructed by a few free individuals. Were it otherwise, "new" moralities could never have arisen; there are "new" moralities only for those who are immoral and instinctive. Whereas those who are spiritual wanted something that was exactly the same, forever modifying it so that the others who sleep unawares accommodated themselves to that symbolic community. (Everything else was a single act of grace in its particulars.) The morality of the community remains independent of the morality of its members, in spite of their immorality. Thus—from the perspective of the individual—it is only a symbol. But in those who feel the symbolic, impractical value of the community, who founded a community, "*as if*" the individual were moral—only in these creators of communities did the moral idea become *real;* they were free. What an "as if" of knowledge is, is an absolute of action.

Now please keep in mind that I am far from being finished with this line of thought, and that it appeared necessary to me only in order to liberate our idea from everything utopian yet triumph over the most brutal aspect of reality.

Although it has been typed in final form, I will send you my "Dialogue"[5] another time, because I have already unfairly inundated you with philosophy and if it is incomprehensible, please blame that on me and not yourself.

Have a wonderful vacation!

Yours, Walter Benjamin

1. William Stern (1871–1938), a well-known psychologist.
2. Seligson had asked whether modern youth might not be a bit too firmly and surely rooted. "We will miss being alone" (letter from Seligson, July 20, 1913).
3. From "Der Deutsche dankt."
4. "Der Moralunterricht" [Moral instruction].
5. "Dialog über Religion."

25. To Ernst Schoen

San Martino di Castrozza
August 30, 1913

Dear Mr. Schön [*sic*],

In Spitteler's *Der Olympische Frühling,* there is the very lovely story with a small garden called "After All, Why Not," and the street leading to it called "Could I, Would I"; there is no access to this garden.

This is the mythology I would like to contribute to our summertime correspondence, and everything else would be consigned to a metaphysics of silence, writing, and laziness. I was very surprised today when the very first thing I saw was the picture of Trafoi on your postcard. I am happy to confirm that the picture is true to life, because I arrived in Trafoi myself about two weeks ago and stayed there for a week, i.e. I am traveling with my mother and an aunt through the southern Tyrol. Presumably this is happening in order to bring some order into my life and to stabilize a six-month period of inactivity, May to September. Nevertheless, little of this inactivity is voluntary—I experienced much of "fate."

Above all, a time of isolation in Freiburg, which was almost amusing and from which I ultimately gained a good friend and many bad weeks. Then this summer's centenary celebrations of Napoleon, which I weathered in the solitude of the Swiss Jura. I fled to Paris over Pentecost: this was the most beautiful experience, mainly restaurants, the Louvre, and the Boulevard.

In the meantime, maybe you have had a look at *Der Anfang*. If so, you will have seen that "Ardor" is very much in need of some order in his enthusiasm and in the logic of his thinking.

Since even you must be burdened at some point with something—presumably?—you can be sure that you will have something to tell me when you look me up at 23 Delbrück Street. I hope this will be soon. I will be back home on the twelfth at the latest. If for no other reason, look me up to return *Imago*.[1]

Yours, Walter Benjamin

1. By Spitteler.

26. To Carla Seligson

Berlin-Grunewald
September 15, 1913

My dear friend,

You will let me call you that, won't you? I have to address you this way after what you wrote me yesterday and even before that. It would also be tactless if those of us who want to represent a new kind of youth were to speak to each other differently from how we actually feel.

After I read your letter this morning, I walked to where there aren't any more houses but only fenced-off vacant lots. For the first time I thought seriously about what you had asked me: How is this possible? Because formerly my delight in understanding Hueber had been so great that I did not even consider the majority who do not hear what he has to say. For a long time I was unable to think of anything because I was completely consumed by the joy of having found the first person who understands this book the same way I do. None of my friends has yet read it. But then I finally discovered the simple answer: those of us who understand Hueber feel our youth completely only in the presence of his ideas—the others, who feel nothing, are not young. They have simply never been young. They took pleasure in their youth only when it was over, just a memory. They did not know the great joy of its presence, which we are now feeling and which I sensed in your words. I truly believe that this is the reason why things are even worse than Hueber thinks they are. But in every individual who is born, no matter where, and turns out to be young, there is, not "improvement," but perfection from the very start. This is the goal that Hueber so messianically feels is near. Today I felt the awesome truth of Christ's words: Behold, the kingdom of God is not of this world, but within us. I would like to read with you Plato's dialogue on love, where this is as beautifully expressed and with such profound insight as probably nowhere else.

This morning I gave this some more thought: to be young does not mean so much serving the spirit as *awaiting* it. To see it in every person and in the most remote thought. This is the most important thing: we must not commit ourselves to one specific idea. For us, the concept of youth culture should simply be illumination that draws even the most remote spirit to its light. For many people, however, even Wyneken, even the Discussion Hall, will be merely a "movement." They will have committed themselves and will no longer see the spirit where it manifests itself as freer and more abstract.

This constantly reverberating feeling for the abstractness of pure spirit I would like to call youth. For then (if we do not turn ourselves into nothing more than workers in a movement), if we keep our gaze free to see the spirit wherever it may be, we will be the ones who actualize it. Almost everybody forgets that *they themselves* are the place where spirit actualizes itself. However, because they have made themselves inflexible, turned themselves into the pillars of a building instead of into vessels or bowls that can receive and shelter an ever-purer content, they despair of the actualization we feel within ourselves. This soul is the *eternally actualizing soul.* Every person, every soul that is born, can produce the new reality. We feel it in ourselves and we want to project it from ourselves.

I recently inquired about Hueber's address at his publishers[1] in order to offer my services for his cause. I found out that everything is in a sad state of affairs. So whatever you do, do not read the "Wirkung des Aufrufes" with sympathy, but with defiance!

I would like to talk to you about all of this. Please let me know by phone or letter whether you can visit me Thursday or Saturday afternoon. If you prefer, we can go for a walk.

Thank you—for what? For your delight in the book and for having written me. Sincere regards.

Yours, Walter Benjamin

1. Johann Ambrosius Barth, Leipzig.

27. To Carla Seligson

Berlin-Grunewald
September 25, 1913

My dear friend,

You do not have to externalize anything other than what is manifested in substantial deeds. And, of course, you have always done this, more than any of us. For which of us would have had the will you had? If I put almost too much of our thoughts into words, I basically do not externalize anything of myself. Rather, I am saying what I hope at some time to be able to conceive philosophically. Therefore I actually internalize it and then use it to build myself up.

Do not think, however, that I did not understand you. I am saying only that you have already accomplished infinitely more in your lifetime than any of us. And we abstract nothing from our being. Each of us internalizes the spiritual in his life differently: you by studying, I with words. It is not supposed to be easy for any of us. The words should be least easy.

[. . .]

Let me send you my regards with my unspoken greetings.

Yours, Walter Benjamin

28. To Carla Seligman

November 17, 1913

Dear Carla,

I am writing you from the reading room of the Royal Library, which "is reserved for serious professional work," and I have erected a barrier of books around myself. My class has just been canceled and I can therefore write you immediately. Yesterday evening Heinle and I ran into each other on the way to the Bellevue train station. We spoke about trivialities. All at once he said, "There is actually a lot I have to say to you." I thereupon asked him to do so immediately because it was high time. And since *he* really wanted to say something to me, I wanted to hear it and went up to his place at his request.

At first we went round and round about what had happened and tried to explain things, etc. But very soon we realized what was at issue and put it into words: that it has become very difficult for both of us to part. But I realized one thing that was the most important aspect of this conversation: he knew precisely what he had done, or better, there was no longer anything for him "to know" here. He understood our opposition to be just as uncompromising and inevitable as I had expected. He confronted me in the name of love and I countered with the symbol. You will understand the simplicity and abundance of the relationship, which contains both for us. A moment arrived when we both confessed to confronting fate head-on; we said to each other, each of us could be in the other's shoes.

I can barely bring myself to write you about this conversation, but through it we both overcame the sweetest temptation. He overcame the temptation of enmity and offered me renewed friendship or at least a fraternal relationship. I overcame, in that I rejected what I—as you will understand—could not accept.

At times I had thought that, of all the people we know, we, Heinle and I, understand each other best. This way of putting it is not quite accurate. But this is: in spite of each of us being the other, it is inevitable that each must remain true to his own spirit.

I once again recognized the *inevitability of the idea,* which places me in opposition to Heinle. I want the fulfillment that one can only anticipate but that he can satisfy. But fulfillment is something too serene and divine for it to issue from anything other than a burning wind. Yesterday I said to Heinle, each of us has faith but everything depends on how we believe in our faith. I am thinking (not in a socialist, but in some other sense) of the multitude who are excluded and of the *spirit* that is in league with those who sleep and not with those who are brothers. Heinle told me something your sister[1] said: "fraternity, almost again[st] one's better judgment." You will remember that in my policy speech I already stated, "No friendship between brothers and comrades, but rather a friendship among friends who are strangers."

While writing, I realize that maybe this can be said only in person—but you will get my meaning.

The movements proceed with their internecine struggles. Yesterday Heinle and I saw the type of youth movement that paves the way for struggles of the kind we are engaged in. I still do not know of any word to describe my relationship to Heinle, but in the meantime I will take pure delight in the pure struggle. I still do not know much about him, but I will give him some thought. For the goal remains: to push Heinle out of the movement and to leave the rest to the spirit.

Yesterday you were unchanged when I thanked you. But we may also give thanks for the *truth* in these ideas. Indeed, we are obliged to give thanks for it alone.

Yours, Walter Benjamin

1. Rika (Erika) Seligson, with whom Heinle committed suicide after the outbreak of war.

29. To Carla Seligson

[Berlin-Grunewald]
[November 23, 1913]

Dear Carla,

Everything is now completely straightforward again. You want to resign.[1]

The past few weeks had tired me out. I had finally become active in the movement again, but I was exhausted after having spoken at the meeting on Tuesday evening with such a lack of restraint, as if unconsciously, drastically sure of my subject and myself. It was a success, and I was disappointed and depressed. On Wednesday I came across as being at a loss when we were speaking about your sister. The next morning I read:

no feeling is the most remote.

When you talked to me in the afternoon, the word was fulfilled. I have gone farther; if, after these chaotic days, you could only see everything as straightforwardly as I do as a result of what you said.

An intimate, as well as the most remote, feeling allows me to perceive things in this way, and I have never written you, my friend, as uninhibitedly as I do today.

You are not resigning because of your mother, are you? If that were the only reason, a solution could be found. You made the decision entirely on your own. All the words probably tired you out—and you feel all alone whenever things go beyond words.

We must all bear the burden of words. I believe that work helps alleviate this burden, as does the silence of friendship.

But you also find yourself alone and no longer comprehend the certainty of others. You believe unresistingly what people tell you. I am writing you in response to that.

> The rain does not fall for itself, the sun does not shine for itself,
> you too are created for others, and not for yourself. (Angelus Silesius)

None of us could proceed so happily and seriously if we were not aware that friends are watching. Perhaps they are too distant and weak to help us, but they believe in us. In view of this conviction, however, there is no resigning as long as one believes. One gives holy orders to a friend as to a priest who is unable to deconsecrate himself. Consequently, before the friend refuses to excommunicate him, the friend is part of the friendship.

I believe in you without reservation.

Whether you face up to the issue or avoid us, your youth will struggle among us, unmoved by the torment of words or family strife. One day you will join your youth.

It sends you the most sincere regards!

[no signature]

1. From the Free Students or the Young People's Discussion Hall.

30. To Carla Seligson

March 26, 1914

Dear Carla,

To begin with: I hear you are not well. I hope you will soon be free from pain and, above all, that you will be able and allowed to go with us to Kohlhasenbrück after the Discussion Hall on Saturday. In order to obtain permission for you to go, a letter has been written to your mother, and will be mailed at the same time as this one. I hope she will accept it gracefully. My mother considers the letter "impossible."

So much seems not to be working out for you. And yet—isn't it really simple? You have to hope that Barbizon will finally declare some holidays, some days of repentance, and the only thing we want from him as well; that he of his own accord will acknowledge, and thus expiate, the guilt he has incurred because of what happened in the Discussion Hall (even if he personally is innocent ten times over). From that moment on, he will affirm his position in the Discussion Hall. From then on, we will all turn to him as freely as you do.[1]

Guttmann will probably also stay away from the next Discussion Hall, if the whole situation does not change after Guttmann's and Heinle's "explanations" have been sent out. This is supposed to happen on Friday. You would not want to turn to him before he has become peaceable and pure enough to earn your trust. You have a duty to the "cowardice" about which you speak. You are confusing shyness with cowardice. I would certainly not be so quick to call the rejection of Guttmann shyness, but in good conscience I will justify *your* rejection of him with this word. First let Guttmann earn your trust, and until that happens perhaps you will allow me to be a spiritual medium between you and him.

Because of the stress I am under, I hope you will forgive me if this letter does not entirely manage to address what you have in mind. For this reason, however, I ask you to continue to turn to me with your demands. To that extent, I take responsibility for Guttmann before you and the Discussion Hall. I told you that yesterday. It has gotten late, I am tired. Good night.

Walter Benjamin

P.S. Not for a single second did I consider you to be "devoid of character." I am a comrade of Guttmann *and* Barbizon too. I hope Barbizon makes it possible for me to remain his comrade.

[On the envelope] P.S. I'm tormented by the feeling that my somewhat overtaxed brain may be preventing me from telling you everything in the best way possible; I may again have a few words with you about this on Saturday.

1. Many serious disputes had developed in the Berlin Discussion Hall between Georg Barbizon and a group whose spokesmen were Heinle and Simon Guttmann. Disagreements about what the *Anfang* was supposed to look like and efforts to change the editorial board were behind these disputes. WB, who had just been elected president of the Free Students, tried to mediate although he was secretly on Heinle's and Guttmann's side. Many reports and other things were written and the excitement went on for months. Copies have been preserved of a detailed explanation written by Barbizon on March 12, 1914, "An den Kameraden Walter Benjamin" [To the comrades of Walter Benjamin], and of Barbizon's "description" of the events between February and April 1914. The result was a schism in the Discussion Hall to which a number of the following letters refer.

31. To Herbert Belmore

Evening: May 6 [1914]
Grunewald

Dear Herbert,

It seems to be easier to write from London to Berlin than from Berlin to London.[1] I have already attempted the latter at least once without success. For here in Berlin it is impossible to take the measure of my days, and on the other hand, if anyone wanted to write from within their core, everything would sound too rhapsodic. But as much as Berlin is diminished by your departure for London, it still remains Berlin, and nothing remains but to write from within its abundance. What can be said about the Free Students' inaugural evening is that it took place the night before yesterday; that there were far fewer students than friends in attendance in the lecture hall; that the evening, however—because it was, in fact, almost totally removed from the student body—was singularly beautiful, in that friends who had left in search of new recruits unexpectedly found themselves reunited in a strange place. Nevertheless, I know now that my talk moved not a few people who did not know about us before this.[2] The floor was opened to discussion, but with the observation that we would be happy to dispense with it. Consequently nobody raised a hand. Of course, everything just went by some of those in attendance. You will get to read the lecture sometime later on. Dora brought me roses because my girlfriend was not in Berlin. It is true that flowers have never made me as happy as these, which Dora[3] had just brought from Grete.[4] When I think that I was able to have only a quick word with you about Dora and Max before you left and that, at that time, I had seen them only once! Even now, after having spent Thursday evening at their place, I do not know what I should add; I talked; afterward Max read poems and played the piano; then we looked at pictures; and Dora spoke to me about Franz, after we had a conversation later on Monday night. There were others at the table. Dora had proposed the wonderful topic "Help" for the Discussion Hall, and Franz intimidated her with his timorous and trivial objections. Until we so clearly perceived the pure essence of helping, that we understood: we can talk about help, with anybody. Even after such a profound conversation or affectionate gathering, I am unable to tell you any more about the two than I did the last time. I am unable to tell you anything other than what I wrote Grete: that few people have ever seemed to me to be as good and yet to have an equally sure and accurate eye for the clarity or opacity of human deeds and the doer. As you well know, Franz is developing this kind of perception. On the very evening of your departure, both of them spoke with me in passing and told me a lot of things I did not know before. Franz may then have written you about the conversation I had with him on Wednesday. He is ardently and defiantly clinging to his relationship to Genia.[5] So I said: do whatever you want and think is the right thing to do. If, however, you refuse to accept advice (what he does is constantly play the coquette with those who give him advice—and this term is *not* too harsh), then finally take responsibility for your actions. I told him not to speak with *anyone* about his relationship to Genia. He promised. That evening, and before I had spoken like this to him, he read me part of the *scriptum* on the vocation. Who could deny that it contains ideas? But I do not know what honor you wish to bestow on it by calling it Jewish. No—and I demonstrated this to Franz—it is conceived entirely without courage, without ultimate commitment to its subject, with concepts taken out of an entirely alien context, the "Diary";[6] moreover, it seems to me that the style is not compelling and the text evinces a lot of confusion instead of profundity. He retracted it, but I am not completely sure that he is not still working on it. No, Herbert, I am not at all completely sure of Franz. I have always defended him against Dora. But even now, in the days since my last conversation with him, which I wanted to make the first and last we had about him and Genia in every respect, he said things that embody his strange ambiguity. I accidentally learned that he is meeting Leni Wieruszowski, while avoiding the Discussion Hall and wanting to "withdraw" from everything. You know that Dora has greater doubts about his innermost being than those of us who, on the contrary, affirm it have experienced thus far. But if he goes on playing games—and here I am not thinking so much of myself, although I have spoken plainly with him—than of Dora, who wants to extend to him the noblest help he could expect. He nonetheless wrote her a letter expressing his gratitude, which was quite insipid. If he continues to play games here and explains the situation to his own advantage, if he continues to foster uncertainty and indecisiveness, even then there will be people who will help him, teach him, and you may be his teacher—but I will stop at the limit of my ability, and in this case that also means at the limit of my will. To be sure, this final stage of my willingness is one I had never reached before. After a while you will find out whether it is necessary.

The Art Division tours begin on Friday. [Simon] Guttmann is leading them and we will go first to Gurlitt's to view the Schmidt-Rottluff pictures under discussion. Guttmann recently said to me: this morning I received a letter from Herbert B., which did much more than simply please me. And Heinle once told me something similar. There was a Discussion Hall on Saturday. About attitude. Dora may have written you about it. It was flawed, like all of them, but not depressing.

I can hardly believe how long you have been gone. I have a lot to tell you: That I visited [Martin] Buber in a room that was sumptuously furnished in Oriental style. He will come sometime when the discussion of the Free Students deals with a dialogue out of his *Daniel*. Now I have to read it. Write me if you have it here,[7] so that I can borrow it. That classes are not very stimulating, and we are learning only gothically; but that the *Jahr der Seele* is ever more beautiful; that Guttmann wants to read Spinoza with some people as the ultimate and surest basis of understanding among them; and that I am planning to send Grete a still-life that I have been mulling over for a week. It depicts one carton of Cordon Rouge, very long, magnificent cigarettes that I recently discovered at a party; one colored Japanese wood carving (there are good ones at Keller and Reiner for 2 marks, even if they cannot be mistaken for Hokusai); birds and grasses; and a—book, book, charming, beautiful, good, light and small, exotic and familiar, illustrated and in color, expensive and cheap. A book that is so like—there is certainly only one: an ideal book: please tell me if you know of one. One will occur to you when I tell you that one day this paper, on which I am now saying adieu, hoping you will find a good position, and hoping for a letter from you—came from Munich.

Yours, Walter

1. Belmore had been in England since April 1914. He was a British citizen.

2. This was WB's inaugural address as president of the Free Students in Berlin, part of which has been published in *Das Leben der Studenten*.

3. Dora Pollack, née Kellner, WB's future wife. At that time she was married to Max Pollack, who died in 1960. She was an active participant in the Discussion Hall.

4. Grete Radt, to whom WB was engaged at the time.

5. Belmore's sister-in-law. She was a Russian from St. Petersburg.

6. A part of WB's *Metaphysik der Jugend* [Metaphysics of youth], copies of which were circulated among his friends. Scholem's copy has been preserved.

7. Buber's *Daniel: Gespräche von der Verwirklichung* [*Daniel: Dialogues on Realization*] appeared in 1913. The Free Students held a debate between Buber and WB on the book on June 23, 1914.

32. To Herbert Belmore

April [should be May] 15, 1914
Grunewald

Dear Herbert,

You could just now have seen me engaged in an endeavor of a kind in which you have never seen me engaged in all the years we have known each other. I was sitting at the piano, without music, by the way, which I still cannot read, and was playing charming thirds and octaves to myself. You see, the most beautiful thing the summer here could provide me is actually going to happen: Max and Dora will go through the Halm book with me.[1] Between sessions, I want to review it with my sister. Of course, it will be terribly slow going. But perhaps this most modest of beginnings will be the basis on which I can later make progress more independently. We began on Wednesday. That evening Simon Guttmann was also at their place. He brought Dora some wonderful, reddish-black, lustrous tulips. You know that only this year have I found within myself the capacity to notice flowers and take delight in them. I discovered this suddenly when presented with myriad opportunities to do so. Yesterday, for example, Lisa[2] visited me and brought me lilies of the valley. Dora will have written you about the recent evening, how at first Max and Guttmann were in the study for an hour while I was talking to Dora in her room about the Discussion Hall and about Dr. Wyneken, objective spirit, and religion. At this time, the only thing I am at all sure of is that Dora has written you about things here. If I were not convinced of this, but had to think that Franz and Hertha Levin were the only ones writing you, I would consider it necessary to sit continuously at my desk and tell you that everything is happening more clearly, simply, and calmly than you must suspect. At least, that it could be happening that way. And even Dora is not as calm as I would like her to be. She has slept very little for many a night now. But she always comes to feel again what is fundamentally right and simple, and therefore I know that we are of one mind, although I rarely have the time to write (letters Grete and I wrote each other, in which we passed on your regards, crossed in the mail). Thus you will also know about Barbizon's last memorandum, which you will receive in a week, when I can spare it, so that you can read it until you have had your fill. In it he first provides a "description" written on April 20th. After that, in a summary occasioned by Dr. Wyneken's letter and written on May 12th, after he had once again amassed all the evidence, he drops his suspicion "from lack of evidence." He is ready to engage in any new task with anyone who takes a stand based on Dr. Wyneken's letter.[3] Before that, in the paragraph preceding the summary, he assures the reader that he bears me no grudge, that my intentions have been focused on just one dimension. He now understands this: "namely, in the most four-dimensional way." Journalism still allows him to avoid feelings and thought. Yesterday an unsigned invitation to the Discussion Hall arrived, once again demanding in sterile and insolent words "purity of sensual and spiritual instincts" and expecting everyone in the Discussion Hall to be determined to put his best foot forward. It closes with the following beautiful sentence instead of with a signature: "Whoever is there on Saturday will proclaim that he has made this his own cause." Herbert, I am very reluctant to write you about all of this because it is such a confused mess and, through the medium of a letter, you will not get a sense of the certainty and the emotions of those individuals who have liberated themselves, at least not from what I have written here. It can again be said of Franz that he has lost his head and his heart. I will talk to him this evening when the council meets. I will ask him whether he is going to the "communal" Discussion Hall. If he says yes, as I assume he will—on the basis of a recent brief conversation with me, when he knew about the memorandum before I did—I will remind him of the promise he made to me in my apartment after the Discussion Hall before the party at Heine's.[4] I will demand, without discussing it, that he follow your lead and mine and not go. If he refuses—well, Dora and I are now keeping our distance from him because, in the final analysis, he has to make up his own mind to join us. The last few times we got together, as infrequent as this was (probably three times in five weeks), it was always at my request. Dora thinks he is distancing himself from me because it bothers him that Genia is angry at me—naturally, without cause—and that she says provocative things about me while he does not defend me energetically enough. All the same: he ultimately has to do something that is motivated from within instead of having the motives implanted in his soul by somebody else's arguments. Have you ever considered this possibility? Of using Lisa to educate Franz? Yesterday she almost seemed to me to be strong and able enough to do it. Although everything had confused her and she understood little, she told me that she had not gone to the Discussion Hall on Saturday, and that she would *not* have spoken to me because she felt that it was also possible for a skeptic (actually, only for a skeptic) to go to that Discussion Hall, that it does not demand resolve and faith as we do. And I was happy to be able to say to her: Lisa, force yourself not to think about it anymore. In this matter, to arrive at results you must not think. You have to know what the results are. Thinking is allowed only for the purpose of preventing others from thinking, of directing them to the fact that this whole question appears difficult and uncertain only because it touches on assumptions, but to *know* the assumptions is the concern only of those who are aware. The concern of the others, however, is the faith and strength of will not to think on their own (because assumptions are not deducible and are unconscious to those who are unaware), but to obey or—if you are unable to trust to that extent—to stand apart, like Molkentin, but not to judge. And here it is always those who are uncertain who want to judge, to mediate. [Fritz] Strauß and Franz. Or ultimately: to struggle through to awareness. This is the minimum, the least quality of a leader. Not everyone will do it. Had there been one among us who had never thought, he would be the most visible.[5] After that I was able to read some poems by Hölderlin with her, and her departure was as peaceful as her arrival had been agitated. Two days before that, she had already tried to get Franz not to go to the

Discussion Hall on Saturday. But Franz had given a vague response. Out of our group, only Guttmann and Cohrs,[6] who came from Göttingen to spend a few days at Heinle's, might go to the Discussion Hall on Saturday. Guttmann will make a few closing remarks: we are not strong enough to clear up the stubborn confusion of these people; he will also repeat what I said to Lisa yesterday, and then leave. But it is not yet certain: someone else may also speak. There is no sense at all in all of us going back again. Just imagine, it was Lisa's idea that Guttmann had to speak!

Today I am taking the *Daniel* out of your library and I also hope to find Rilke's *Book of Hours* [*Stundenbuch*] there. If not, would you be so kind as to send it to me. Before that I am going to the Graphisches Kabinett. I recently bought a very beautiful reproduction of a Rodin watercolor there for 1 mark. How often have I turned to the graphic arts in my efforts to put together a still-life for Grete! I bet I am going to be lucky and find something very beautiful. Of course the Rodin is splendid, but it does not go with the book and cigarettes. When I thought about this book, given the range of choice, I had such a quiet, superior, and vibrant notion of a book—but, for once, I had no intention of buying such an expensive book, and it was almost too obvious a choice anyway. Then the card came—it was listed. Now the only choice left is between the two editions, Müller's and Bardt's.[7] Now that I am familiar with both of them, I will unhesitatingly choose the one by Müller, a facsimile edition of the first German edition, much more substantial than Bardt's larger, wider volume, which has widely spaced lines and is printed on pure white paper. Both use the translation of the first edition. Therefore, I still need a drawing to go with Müller's edition. This afternoon I plan to look at reproductions of old drawings.

I have moved into the room with the balcony, which is next to the room I had before. It is more livable and has a good desk, which unfortunately has a long mirror hanging over it, so that you cannot look up when you are writing. It could be draped or gotten rid of, but for the time being I am not doing anything about it because I just do not have the time. Journal articles, short novellas, a George volume, a Balzac, and readings from Fichte's *Deduzierter Plan einer in Berlin zu errichtenden höhern Lehranstalt,* his courageous commemorative essay on the founding of the University of Berlin. This is what I am reading at great intervals. It seems a lot—yet it is actually very little. I am reading Fichte's essay because I may want to quote something from it if I am attacked today in the council.[8] It is very closely related to various ideas in my speech. The speech that you, by the way, will probably receive only in a few weeks when I have had the opportunity to make a legible copy. The council meeting today may be very stormy and interesting. You will soon get a report on it from Dora, since she and Max are coming too.

In Weimar[9] I will not give my talk as a formal address to the congress but as part of the congress, because people want to discuss it. Fichte will be of use in this regard, and so will Nietzsche: concerning the future of our educational institutions. In June, I will finally be in Munich.[10] Yesterday I wrote Grete: my relationship to her is the only creative thing in this unbelievably disrupted period of activity. At the moment, she is the only person who sees and comprehends me in my totality. If I were not conscious of this, I could hardly bear the ineffectuality of these days. It does not allow for continuity in any serious activity and leaves no human relationship totally free of the compulsion to discuss and conciliate. This became clear to me only yesterday evening, when Cohrs, Suse Behrend,[11] Heinle, I, and later Guttmann, were together in a café. Thus, the best thing for me still is working on the Halm with Max and Dora. And receiving a letter from you, from an existence that, due to both its remoteness and its immediacy, outweighs our still restless existence a hundredfold. We hear nothing about Willi [Wolfradt], except through Grete, with whom he often speaks.

I have been asked to shower you with all the greetings you so extravagantly distribute in Berlin.

Yours, Walter

1. See letter 22.
2. Lisa Bergmann, who later married Max Pollack.
3. Barbizon's description has been preserved.
4. The social-democrat Wolfgang Heine, a member of parliament, who supported the Free German Youth Movement and the Free Students.
5. The concept of "leadership" in the new youth movement played a significant role in the Free German Youth Movement, particularly in the circle around Wyneken.
6. Ferdinand Cohrs, at that time a student of theology.
7. Probably one of the Sterne volumes in the books of the Thelem Abbey in Georg Müller, *Yoricks empfindsame Reise* (Munich, 1910); J. Bard edition (Berlin, 1910).
8. The advisory council of the Free Students.
9. At the congress of Free Students in June 1914, in which WB participated as president of the Berlin Free Students. See letters 33 and 34.
10. Grete Radt was studying in Munich at the time.
11. Died of influenza in 1918. A close friend of Wolf Heinle.

33. To Ernst Schoen

May 23, 1914
14 Joachimsthaler St.

Dear Mr. Schoen,

Thank you very much for your letter. I would like to respond to what you said about the Free Students. At the moment it is not a matter of civilizing the uncultured mass, but rather of defending the purity of the place where otherwise the worst things take place. Lectures are being given to small audiences that include very few students. These students, however, come back and always listen attentively. In the outside world people are silent, thus showing a certain degree of respect. Basically what we can do is cultivate this respect and the rather modest tone of the lectures, create a cultured kind of meeting. The intended outcome is that vulgarity and bad manners will in the future be less at home in the community of Free Students. And that vulgarity and bad manners will be forced to avoid this circle as a treacherous place that is difficult to comprehend and where people engage in strangely serious endeavors. It is already apparent that this outcome can be achieved. I have never experienced such a peaceful council meeting as the last one and, in spite of that, principled discussions of considerable breadth took place. Once the conditions have been created to make it possible, the question of how the creative fulfillment of this place can be brought about depends entirely on the productive individuals who enter its orbit. Until now there have indeed been pupils, but few teachers. If it is absolutely necessary, I have no choice but to allow myself to be nominated again next semester, so that I can locate someone to succeed me (from among our friends at the gymnasium who are taking the university entrance exam) who will create a ready following for the productive individuals in the Free Students. The only issue is to create a group that acknowledges the leader's moral strength and receives its spirituality from the productive individual by following him. This can come about as a result of the smallest and quietest beginnings and is, moreover, a screen shielded from enmity (if not the crudest kind) by a highly cosseted invisibility; and thus it will come to pass. The same thing Heinle and I succeeded in creating in Freiburg for some people and, not least of all, for ourselves—that is to say, an educational community—is being started in Berlin. All of this leads to the concept of the academy, which—it seems to me—can nowadays be made productive only in this way. We will slowly succeed in attracting productive individuals, and the leadership will then be able to limit itself to organizational matters instead of having to be dynamically active, as it is now. Your friend is already giving me tremendous support by his very presence at lectures and such. The presidium must be highly visible and, so to speak, omnipresent.

At the meeting of the Free Students in Weimar I will be giving a talk on "the new university": I will present a utopian university, such as would be necessitated by a new middle school—in this way it can be made intelligible. In truth, of course, what is at issue is the creation of a new university out of itself, out of the spirit. In Weimar, discussion in an uncomprehending and unprepared group will become chaotic, cowardly, and blurred, like all initiatives that nowadays reach the horrid public. There was no intrinsic reason to expect the unheard-of from the members of the Free German Youth Movement, but it is nonetheless awful that things have taken such an ignominious turn. You know that the group has officially separated from Wyneken (to say nothing of their separation from *Der Anfang* and the Discussion Halls). Wyneken will finally open his school in Triberg—as far as I know, in October. His years of inactivity as an educator have done him extraordinary harm. I became aware of this by seeing how unequal he is to the demanding forms being assumed by the movement in Berlin; surely unequal to the movement's strongest, boldest, and most dangerous expenditure of energy being achieved here. The establishment, or better, the facilitating of a community of young people that is only internally and intrinsically grounded, and not at all politically, has already filled everyone here with the greatest suspense for more than a quarter of a year. Given all of this and precisely because of it, I believe that the most serious of all things is being accomplished here, perhaps the only serious thing. Would you please read *Schule und Jugendkultur* or reread it if you have read it before. And please consider whether something other than perverse motivation is not concealed in the "objective spirit." I at least, as well as some of my friends, am moving farther and farther away from the image of education Wyneken presents there. It is becoming clear to me that he was—and may still be—a great educator and, given the nature of our time, a very great one. His theory continues to lag far behind his vision.

Thank you for returning the book.[1] I am now lucky to have the opportunity of being able to work through it with friends of mine, a married couple. To that end, I am learning how to read music and everything else except how to play the piano, because I still can't find the time for that. I would also like to thank you very much for offering to make my manuscript[2] more generally available to others. Mr. Cohn[3] has just passed it on. Its publication is presenting me with terrible problems. I am having trouble coming up with an appropriate outlet, and am not sure that Robert Musil will accept it for the *Wiener Rundschau*.

The semester is as unsatisfying as ever, but I am making up for this in more remote fields than you: with Stefan George and, as far as I can manage it, with Balzac. He of course should be devoured at a single sitting, but I am forced to read him piecemeal. Martin Buber has written a book, called *Daniel,* which is irksome because it is not well thought out.

Will you be going away over Pentecost? I am going on a walking tour and then from Weimar I will travel to Munich for another week.

With my kindest regards.
Yours, Walter Benjamin

1. By August Halm.
2. The reference is probably to *Metaphysik der Jugend.*
3. Alfred Cohn (died 1954), later the spouse of Grete Radt; a schoolmate of WB.

34. To Ernst Schoen

Berlin
June 22, 1914

Dear Mr. Schoen,

I have not yet thanked you for your letter. It was the first and most welcome of those I received in Weimar. Let me thank you now. From your friend's reports, you will have some notion of how much pleasure I take nowadays in every word of support. Nothing has affected me as much in years as the solid malevolence of this gathering. There was no lack of intelligent individuals from Berlin. But the people who had the votes were for the most part the kind you would usually avoid. Here they were much in demand. I committed the folly of giving a talk to them on the subject of the new university. The talk presupposed a certain degree of decency and a certain spiritual orientation (instead of hitting the audience over the head with this to the point of unconsciousness). This was a huge mistake and made it possible for imbeciles to come to a so-called agreement with me concerning the most basic questions. I wanted to end my talk with the verses from your letter, had I not unexpectedly found myself in the full swing of my concluding remarks. Nonetheless, I may add them to the conclusion of the written version of the talk, which I will put together during the long vacation.[1] After being brutally voted down on a daily basis, the only result is the elevated but lonely stance that our Free Students assume—when showing their face to the outside world—and the respectful awe of the others. There is a lot of secret discontent. The (spiritual) leader of the opposition is personally and materially uncultured. (He declared me "morally immature" during a polite discussion in a café.) The prospects of securing Berlin next semester are quite good. Of course, I still don't know for sure whether I will be here. I suppose there is no question of your spending the winter here?—After the meeting, I went to Munich and found out that the Munich Youth Movement and Free Students—the only ones who went along with us in Weimar—were in the same wretched state.

June 23

(I will probably have to continue writing this letter in bits and pieces because my time is so fragmented.) The Free Students have some good evenings coming up, such as today's discussion with Buber about his *Daniel,* and at a later time lectures by Ludwig Klages[2] and Prof. Breysig.[3] I visited Klages in Munich and found him forthcoming and polite.—As you can imagine, I yearn for the vacation and I will flee as soon as possible at the end of July. Therefore it is questionable whether I will be able to welcome you here soon after your arrival as I had hoped. Since beginning this letter, the Berlin chaos (of the "Youth Movement" and the Free

Students all in one) has begun to stir again, after having been subdued with difficulty and a sense of resignation, and after I had just begun to recover somewhat from this in Munich. Someone I know personally stormed into a gathering that was discussing Buber's book. In a loud voice, he insulted a gentleman who is close to me and did not leave the room, so that the meeting had to be suspended and relocated. This kind of thing is naturally intolerable, but if you are fairly sure of your intentions, you are safe from such things. But on the same day I received one of the most gratifying testimonials I could expect at this time—namely, a letter from a young Viennese who did not know me personally. Much has reached him from Berlin (maybe even my silence in the *Anfang*), with the result that he is asking to correspond with me, appealing to the fact that we are both somewhat removed from the mainstream of the Youth Movement. It is nice to see that a young person in a faraway city can make out the harmony amid all the noise and has been reached by silence (which, in the final analysis, is one of the clearest means of communication). His name is Arno Bronner[4] and at the age of ten he wrote a play, *Das Recht auf Jugend*, which is very courageous and shows talent. I have read it in manuscript.

I will spend the long vacation alone in some remote cabin in the woods, in order to find both peace and work at the same time, i.e. leisure. I am in need of both after the way life has been here, sometimes hellish and, in any case, never leaving me the time to become immersed in anything. I apologize for communicating more complaints than anything else; but since I am so confident that you will understand all good intentions, nothing is left for me, if I am to give you an accurate picture of my life here, but to list the bare facts. I owe a lot to your friend's presence, not only for his practical assistance, but even more for the encouragement resulting from his very presence.

Most sincere regards.
Yours, Walter Benjamin

1. In fact, WB placed George's verses to Hofmannsthal from *Das Jahr der Seele* at the end of his essay "Das Leben der Studenten" [Students' life], which appeared in the *Neue Merkur* (September 1915) and in Kurt Hiller's collection *Das Ziel.*

2. Klages's lecture took place in mid-June. See H. Schröder, *Klages Biographie* 2:602.

3. Kurt Breysig (1866–1940).

4. The author who later became known by the name of Arnolt Bronnen (1895–1955).

35. To Herbert Belmore

July 6–7, 1914, after midnight

I want to write you, dear Herbert. Why just now? when it is so late? and I am quite tired? Perhaps because I just noticed that the Kurfürstendamm exists by night, with cafés, but I am seldom in them. Or perhaps because in the next few days I will again have things to do? I have whiled away the entire evening; I was thinking of vacation. I am looking forward to—I can even say, eagerly—a time in which to work. My series[1] needs to be completed, and I then intend to begin to set down what I am able to grasp of the nature of education. All of this will happen in the solitude of some small place; in Bornholm or the Alps, maybe the Dolomites. Because if I do not go to Bornholm with my mother and sister, I will first spend eight days visiting Grete in Munich and then probably go to the Dolomites with her. She plans to go hiking there with her brother,[2] while I rest.—While thinking about this, the Kurfürstendamm slipped my mind. I was in the Café des Westens to meet some acquaintances, and I waited for a long time but they did not show up. That did not bother me because my thoughts are inclined to come home to roost and can therefore always be left to themselves. (This however does not mean that I was comfortable and had cozy thoughts. Rather, I am scrupulously aware of the weeks coming up.) I was reading a Jewish journal. Then Else Lasker-Schüler saw me and invited me to join her at her table; I sat there between two young people for fifteen minutes without saying a word. There was a lot of crazy joking around, which Mrs. Lasker greatly enjoyed. She knows me as a result of a one-hour conversation we recently had partly due to chance. In company, she is shallow and sick—hysterical. Robert Jent[z]sch[3] went by, [Georg] Heym's friend whom I know slightly. I said hello to him and spoke two words about books I have to lend him. He is a most polite and reticent person. His politeness is very precious. He recently said to me, "The book, which you had the kindness——the book, you most kindly lent me . . ." He prefaces the simplest things with "I would neither be competent nor do I feel called upon to pass judgment on it . . ." He seems highly educated. He conducts himself in a refined and sympathetic manner. You sense he is a precise thinker. I know he is studying mathematics. He is by nature absolutely fastidious about matters of form. I have rarely spoken alone with him. He spends a lot of time with Heinle. Do you know that once again I am not making any progress in my studies? You can imagine. Occasionally I learn something from Heinle for example, when he talks about Platen. I am reading George a lot; I am reading Kleist's prose with great care; and not long ago a drama by Lenz. Sometimes I learn something about Munch or the splendid Karl Hofer from one of Scheffler's essays. I have been to exhibitions: van Gogh, Heckel, Schmidt-Rottluff, and intend to take in the Sezession. Perhaps the only thing in which I have made progress at this time has been my appreciation of the fine arts. I sat with Grete for an hour in front of a Marées (in front of a picture) and could see a lot in it.

The university simply is not the place to study. You are in a position to judge to what extent my being president is at fault. I have not been totally unsuccessful as president, but I have served under almost painful and adverse conditions. And then everything justifiably seems so infinitely trivial to me when, at the Free Students Festival, Wolf Heinle[4] stands next to me wearing his Wickersdorf cap and his imperious, serious expression, and says only a few words about the people meeting there—to me, because I am the person responsible. It was the day before yesterday—a festival good enough to be judged—and judged to be pitiful. Far above other free student festivals, ennobled by the presence of beautiful people, but still self-conscious and ugly, like all festivals—except for Wolfgang Heine's unforgettable one.[5] To me it had pleasant associations because of Wolf Heinle, Wieland Herzfeld[e][6] (to whom I spoke for the first time and who told me a lot of profound things about myself), and because of the unexpectedly nice time spent with Carla Seligson. I will be here in winter, perhaps holding the same office, from which I will resign the moment I see that it will not let me have any more time for myself than I do now. I do not know to what extent I would be conscious of this semester's being agonizingly crammed with wasted time, unfocused activity, and tormenting human experiences, if my consciousness were not, so to speak, suppressed by my days in Munich and comforted by the promise of creativity to come. I am unable to write you any more about these days. The good things here are Grete's letters, my correspondence with Ernst Schoen, some hours spent with my books, very infrequent conversations with Heinle, the summer weather during which it is possible to knock around on your own. Things are good enough for me to remain basically quite healthy, to preserve myself and to keep the most painful events inside myself until your return, which I do not wish to forestall but wish to bring about by sending you my most sincere regards. Wishing you sunshine and someone, another person or yourself, who will preserve your manly serenity for you, something I experienced so late and so happily.

Walter

1. *Metaphysik der Jugend,* which was never completed.

2. Fritz Radt.

3. The mathematician and poet whose poems were published in avant-garde journals of the time. His personality left a lasting mark on WB.

4. Friedrich C. Heinle's younger brother, in whose fate WB took an active interest until his untimely death in 1923. He wrote poems and dramas to which WB at times devoted a great deal of attention.

5. WB wrote a detailed report about this festival, which has not been preserved.

6. Herzfelde (born 1896), later founded Malik Verlag.

36. To Herbert Belmore

[July 17, 1914]

Dear Herbert,

What does it mean that I am unable to write you a letter, to communicate anything to you about what life is like here? There is only one way I can do it—by not writing about this place, but only talking about Grete. But how impossible even that is! You saw the real me when I mutely accompanied you on your walks. My silence is now the only thing by which my friends recognize me. My girlfriend gets to hear the little I have to say about my daily existence—and everything else, after all, comes down to one thing. I experienced my silence as nuanced—but still the one underlying rhythm reaches even those who are far away, Franz and Dora. And everything comes together in the single melody of the weeks that I now anticipate. If only a rigorous life were possible for me here, as it is for you.

I am molded by the incomprehensible love of people. I cannot tell you anything about Grete: innermost silence can find no words. You know me well enough to know what and who I am confronted with. But you may no longer think of me as a single person, and it is as if I had only now been born into a divine age, to come into my own. And the soul of three other women gets to me in a strange way. I know I am nothing, but that I exist in God's world.

Haven't we taken a step on the same path without being visible to each other. I sensed all of this from the few lines you wrote in the most recent *Anfang*. I am going to ask Barbizon if he will let me write a lead article: I will call it "My Farewell." I want to make people ashamed of this publication and ask that it be allowed to disappear. For nothing living any longer blooms in the great swamp of the ACS, the Marburg congress, FG, [illegible]. Recently it was possible to read these words in *Der Anfang:* "the *new* self-respect."

Come and help me here during the winter—since I plan to continue working for the Free Students. I do it sincerely, but without being able to predict its ultimate "success." This work allows me only enough time to read second-rate stuff: a book on the lofty Charlotte von Kalb,[1] Blüher, philosophical essays.

Grete gave me wonderful presents: an orchid, an expensive dark tie that goes very well with the orchid, a book with blank pages that she had bound, *Die deutschen Stilisten,* and a volume of Schäfer's anecdotes. The gifts were accompanied by the most splendid letter. My parents replaced the things I had lost: a canteen and a walking stick. In addition, some large and beautiful portfolios, and Homer, the Greek-German edition, the first half of the *Odyssey*. I received the collection of Italian early Renaissance paintings published by Diederichs.

For the first time in many years, perhaps in more than a decade, I was in Berlin on July 15th. As it turned out, I went to the botanical gardens out of pure joy and there discovered summer as I had previously experienced it in the Black Forest or the Engadine. I had not discovered it so far this year—unless you count the heavy, humid nights.

Herbert, thank you for your good wishes. A falcon has taken flight.

Walter

1. Ida Boy-Ed, *Charlotte von Kalb* (Jena, 1912).

37. To Ernst Schoen

Grunewald
[October 25, 1914]

Dear Mr. Ernst Schoen,

I would like to tell you, courageous person that you are, what I discovered today (for the umpteenth time), each time with ever greater horror. In exchange for which, you must set irony aside in order to find pain as pure form, to the extent that we are capable of this. We have exchanged some letters about this, and it seems to me they require relentless determination. Of course we all nourish an awareness of the fact that our radicalism was too much a gesture, and that a harder, purer, more invisible radicalism should become axiomatic for us.

In the only way I acknowledge as living, you have discovered within yourself that it is impossible for you to go to school, before we even broached the topic. And it has also become impossible for you to follow the prescribed plan and walk into the swamp that the university of today is.

The only salient point—which you know more deeply because you have never experienced it the way I have—is that this university is capable even of poisoning our turn to the spirit. On the other hand, this is the only salient point: that I made the decision to run the gauntlet of the course of lectures . . . and saw the shrill brutality with which scholars display themselves before hundreds of people; how they do not shy away from each other, but envy each other; and how ultimately, they ingeniously and pedantically corrupt the self-respect of those who are in the process of becoming, by turning their self-respect into fear of those who have already become something, of those who have matured early, and of those who are already spoiled. The naked accounting I made of my shyness, fear, ambition, and more important of my indifference, coldness, and lack of education, terrified and horrified me. Not a single one of them distinguishes himself by tolerating the community of the others. I know only one scholar[1] in the entire university, and he is vindicated (perhaps) only for having come so far by his utter seclusion and contempt for such things. No one is equal to this situation, and I understand the total inevitability of your decision; you must eliminate from your own life any possibility of having to face this situation, because the sight of such vulgarity is unspeakably humiliating.

"Oh, if only all of them were great men and I could address them familiarly; it is becoming difficult for me to learn from others." From my friend's notebook.[2]

Yours, Walter Benjamin

1. The reference is to Kurt Breysig.
2. Heinle had taken his own life at the beginning of August.

38. To Ernst Schoen

[January 1915]

Dear Mr. Schoen,

I am very happy to be able to sincerely reciprocate what you wrote me some weeks ago. At the same time, please accept my apology for your having had to wait in vain for Jula Cohn[1] last Sunday. I hope to get together with you at the beginning of February, since by that time I will have completed a gratifying study on fantasy and color.[2] You know, you can find some fine things on this subject in Baudelaire.

Regards and best wishes.
Yours, Walter Benjamin

1. A close friend of WB and Ernst Schoen; the sister of Alfred Cohn.
2. Does not seem to be preserved.

39. To Gustav Wyneken

[Berlin]
[March 9, 1915]

Dear Doctor Wyneken,

With these lines I am totally and unconditionally disassociating myself from you. I ask you to accept them as the final proof of my loyalty, and as that alone. Loyalty—because it would be totally impossible for me to say a single word to the person who wrote those lines about the war and youth,[1] yet I do want to speak to you. I am well aware of never having been able to tell you freely that you were the first person to introduce me to the life of the spirit. Twice in my life, I have stood before someone who pointed the way to a spiritual existence; two teachers have brought me along, and one of them is you. As spokesman for a small number of your disciples—and not of those closest to you—I wanted to address a few words to you in Breslau in October 1913. At the last minute, the servility of some of those disciples prevented this from taking place. The words I had thought of saying are as follows:

"This age does not have a single form that allows those of us who are silent to express ourselves. We, however, feel oppressed by this lack of expression. We reject facile, irresponsible writing.

"We who are gathered together here believe that future generations will come to speak your name. Life has no room for this awareness. Yet it should make room for it for a minute's time. We call you the bearer of an idea, and that is how we expressed it to the outside world; it is true. But as the chosen ones, we experienced something altogether different in this era. We experienced that even the spirit, entirely on its own and unconditionally, constrains the living; that the person transcends the personal; we were given to learn what leadership is. We have experienced that there is pure spirituality among people. Something has become true for us that is endlessly more remote for almost everybody else."

Experiencing this truth made it possible for us to speak these words. I must embrace you in spite of yourself, as the most rigorous lover of this living youth, which is how I still envisage you. You once said about boys and girls: "The memory that they were once comrades in humanity's holiest work, that together they once gazed 'into the Eidorzhann Valley,' into the world of ideas—this memory will constitute the strongest counterweight to the social battle of the sexes. This battle has always existed, but in our time it threatens to burst into bright flames and to endanger the assets humanity has been appointed to guard. Now, when they are young, when they may still be human in the noble sense of the word, they should just once have seen humanity realized. The actual significance of coeducation is to allow them this irreplaceable experience."

θεωρια within you has been blinded. You have committed the awful, horrible treason against the women whom your disciples love. Finally, you have sacrificed young people to the state, which had taken everything from you. The young, however, belong only to those with vision who love them and the *idea* in them above all. The idea has slipped out of your erring hands and will continue to suffer unspeakably. The legacy I now wrest from you is that of living with the idea.

Walter Benjamin

1. "Jugend und Krieg" (1914).

40. To Herbert Belmore

[April 1915]

Dear Herbert,

I have just returned from a visit to Alfred Steinfeld's parents. Their son died at his parents' home on April 6th, of a kidney infection he caught while serving in the army medical corps. As I was leaving, his mother took me into his room, which—perhaps in keeping with Jewish custom—had been left completely untouched, so that I thought I could see the impression of his body on the unmade bed. His uniform and cap lay on an armchair. I believe he died just as his spirit once again confidently took courage; the last time I saw him, months ago, he had already gained ground. I do not know whether you remember him as vividly as I do, as someone who lived as a very noble, yet very undeveloped person in a state of promising sorrow. He endured the few days of his terrible illness in such a way that his parents suspected its nature only when it was already too late. I am unable—not because I have thought about it but because I have seen it—to think of anybody unhappier than they, since I have never known a couple whose life together was so dependent on their only son for its light and blossoming. Therefore, I urge you[1] to write a few kind words to them.

Walter

1. Belmore was in Switzerland.

41. To Gerhard Scholem

Berlin
October 27, 1915

Dear Mr. Scholem,

In the final days before my departure, I was unfortunately so pressed for time that I was unable to look you up. I wish you well in the coming weeks. At my last army physical, I was given a year's deferment and, in spite of having little hope that the war will be over in a year, I am planning to be able to work in peace, at least for a few months, in Munich. As soon as I have a permanent address, I will write you and, at that time, hope to receive favorable news concerning the progress of your affairs.

Until then,
Yours, Walter Benjamin

42. To Gerhard Scholem

Munich
December 14, 1915

Dear Mr. Scholem,

I did in fact assume you were in the military and, under these circumstances, did not want to address a letter to you at random. As it is, your news has made me very happy. Given the orderly, busy, and relatively cloistered life I am leading, I do not have much to report from here. I'm not coming to Berlin over Christmas. For some time to come, I intend to interrupt my stay here only briefly and to devote a solid stretch of time to my work. Another factor is that here—away from my hometown—I have finally found the place I needed. [. . .]

I look forward to hearing from you soon. Once I do, you will again hear from me. Regards.

Yours, Walter Benjamin

43. To Herbert Belmore

Seeshaupt
March 25, 1916

Dear Herbert,

Since finishing the Hölderlin study[1] and the "Regenbogen" [Rainbow], I have begun several new essays, but have not even half completed any of them. This has to do with the magnitude of the subjects that concern me: organic nature, medicine, and ethics. But I definitely would not want to send you any of the things I wrote in the past. I no longer have any confidence in their form and, as important as they are for me in many ways, I would prefer not to speak to you through them. Rather, I believe—even if the European situation were to become more ghastly—that we cannot act other than as two neighbors in a storm who continue to wait for the moment when they are able to go outside the gates and greet each other personally. Nothing I could send you can convey the eagerness of my anticipation. Therefore I have to wait until I can leave Germany to come to you.[2] I am fine.

I sincerely return Carla's and your regards.

Walter

1. In *Schriften* 2:375–400 (written in the fall and winter of 1914). "Regenbogen" has been lost.

2. Belmore was in Geneva from the beginning of 1915. WB and Dora Pollack visited him there in the spring of 1915. When they saw each other again in Zurich in July 1917, they became permanently estranged.

44. To Martin Buber

Munich
4 Königin St.
[May 1916]

My most esteemed Mr. Buber:

The problem of the Jewish spirit is one of the most important and persistent objects of my thinking. Your flattering offer,[1] for which I must thank you, affords me the possibility of giving expression to my thoughts. Yet only in a conversation could I expect the most essential prerequisite to be met, i.e. freeing these thoughts from their larger contexts and defining specific points of departure. Only this could settle the question of our collaboration and the form it would take. For this reason, I would like to ask for an opportunity to talk about this, should you be coming to Munich in the next month, or should I manage a visit to Berlin at Christmas—unfortunately, however, this is very uncertain.

Most respectfully yours, Walter Benjamin

1. To collaborate on Buber's journal, *Der Jude*.

45. To Martin Buber

Munich
July 1916

My most esteemed Doctor Buber:

I had to wait until I had a conversation with Mr. Gerhard Scholem[1] before making up my mind about my basic attitude toward your journal, *Der Jude*. After this conversation, I was in a position to decide whether I could possibly contribute to it. Because, in view of how intensely I disagreed with so many of the contributions to the first volume—especially their position on the European war—my awareness that, in reality, my attitude toward this journal was and could be no other than my attitude toward all politically engaged writing was obscured. The beginning of the war finally and decisively revealed this to me. Moreover, I understand the concept of "politics" in its broadest sense, in which it is now consistently used. Before going on, let me say that I am fully aware that the following thoughts are still inchoate and that, where their formulation might sound apodictic, the reason is that what is foremost in my mind is their fundamental relevance to and necessity for my own practical behavior.

The opinion is widespread, and prevails almost everywhere as axiomatic, that writing can influence the moral world and human behavior, in that it places the motives behind actions at our disposal. In this sense, therefore, language is only one means of more or less suggestively *laying the groundwork* for the motives that determine the person's actions in his heart of hearts. What is characteristic about this view is that it completely fails to consider a relationship between language and action in which the former would not be the instrument of the latter. This relationship would hold equally for an impotent language, degraded to pure instrument, and for writing that is a pitiful, weak action and whose origin does not reside within itself, but in some kind of sayable and expressible motives. On the other hand, these motives can be discussed; others can be juxtaposed to them, and thus the action is (fundamentally) placed at the end as the result of an arithmetic process, tested from all sides. Every action that derives from the expansive tendency to string words together seems terrible to me, and even more catastrophic where the entire relationship between word and deed is, to an ever-increasing degree, gaining ground as a mechanism for the realization of the true absolute, as is the case among us now.

I can understand writing as such as poetic, prophetic, objective in terms of its effect, but in any case only as *magical,* that is as un-*mediated.* Every salutary effect, indeed every effect not inherently devastating, that any writing may have resides in its (the word's, language's) mystery. In however many forms language may prove to be effective, it will not be so through the transmission of content, but rather through the purest disclosure of its dignity and its nature. And if I disregard other effective forms here—aside from poetry and prophecy—it repeatedly seems to me that the crystal-pure elimination of the ineffable in language is the most obvious form given to us to be effective within language and, to that extent, through it. This elimination of the ineffable seems to me to coincide precisely with what is actually the objective and dispassionate manner of writing, and to intimate the relationship between knowledge and action precisely within linguistic magic. My concept of objective and, at the same time, highly political style and writing is this: to awaken interest in what was denied to the word; only where this sphere of speechlessness reveals itself in unutterably pure power can the magic spark leap between the word and the motivating deed, where the unity of these two equally real entities resides. Only the intensive aiming of words into the core of intrinsic silence is truly effective. I do not believe that there is any place where the word would be more distant from the divine than in "real" action. Thus, too, it is incapable of leading into the divine in any way other than through itself and its own purity. Understood as an instrument, it proliferates.

For a journal, the language of the poets, of the prophets, or even of those in power does not come into question. Neither do song, psalm, and imperative, which, on the other hand, may have totally different relationships to the ineffable and may be the source of an entirely different magic. The only thing at issue is objective writing. Whether a journal will achieve it cannot be humanly foreseen, and probably not many journals have done so. But I am thinking of the *Anthenaeum*. I am just as incapable of composing writing designed to have an effect as I am of understanding it. (Intrinsically, my essay in *Das Ziel*[2] was entirely in keeping with the sense of what I have said above, but that was very hard to tell since it appeared in what was a most inappropriate outlet.) In any case, I will learn from what is said in *Der Jude*. And just as my inability to say something clear on the question of Judaism at this point coincides with the journal's inchoate stage, there is nothing to prevent us from hoping that there may yet be a more favorable coincidence in the stages of our development.

I may be able to come to Heidelberg at the end of the summer. I would then be very happy to attempt to enliven through conversation what, at this point, I have been able to express so imperfectly. And, from that vantage point, it might even be possible to say something about Judaism. I do not believe that my way of thinking is un-Jewish in this respect.

Most respectfully,
Yours, Walter Benjamin

1. Scholem was with WB from June 16 to 18.
2. "Das Leben der Studenten."

46. To Gerhard Scholem

Munich
November 11, 1916

Dear Mr. Scholem,

I am very grateful that you supplied me with the information so quickly. A week ago I began a letter to you that ended up being eighteen pages long. It was my attempt to answer in context some of the not inconsiderable number of questions you had put to me. In the meantime, I felt compelled to recast it as a short essay, so that I could formulate the subject more precisely. I am now producing a fair copy of it. In this essay, it was not possible for me to go into mathematics and language, i.e. mathematics and thought, mathematics and Zion, because my thoughts on this infinitely difficult topic are still quite far from having taken final shape. Otherwise, however, I do attempt to come to terms with the nature of language in this essay and—to the extent I understand it—in its immanent relationship to Judaism and in reference to the first chapters of Genesis. I await your judgment on these thoughts, certain that I will benefit from it. I can't send you the essay for a while yet—it is impossible to say when—maybe in a week, and maybe even later than that; as I said, it is not completely finished. From the title, "On Language as Such and on the Language of Man" ["Über Sprache überhaupt und über die Sprache des Menschen"],[1] you will note a certain systematic intent, which, however, also makes completely clear for me the fragmentary nature of its ideas, because I am still unable to touch on many points. In particular, the consideration of mathematics from the point of view of a theory of language, which is ultimately, of course, most important to me, is of a completely fundamental significance for the theory of language as such, even though I am not yet in a position to attempt such a consideration.

I would like to let you know explicitly that the *Neunzehn Briefe,*[2] as well as the translation of the essay by Zeitlin[3] (what does *schechinnah* mean?), are *always very* welcome, precisely in view of my current project. Could you take the trouble of writing the German translation next to the most important Hebrew words in the Hirsch book? I assume that there are only a few of them, otherwise I would not ask you to do it. In the last issue of the *Reich,* there is a seemingly well-informed essay by Hans Ludwig Held: "Über Golem und Schem: Eine Untersuchung zur hebräischen Mythologie" (part 1). I have the issue (and thus can send you the essay); I bought it because of something else in it (which I have, of course, already cut out and bound separately): it contains the first printing of an apparently very late Hölderlin manuscript[4]—in terms of its content, it is *absolutely* powerful, like everything Hölderlin wrote in his later years.

In the last issue of *Kant-studien,* Mr. Zilsel includes an advertisement for his own book. An essay (originally held as a lecture when he received the *venia legendi* in Freiburg[5]) on "Das Problem der historischen Zeit" has appeared in the last or next to last issue of the *Zeitschrift für Philosophie und philosophische Kritik,* and documents precisely how this subject should *not* be treated. An awful piece of work, which you might, however, want to glance at, if only to confirm my suspicion, i.e. that not only what the author says about historical time (and which I am able to judge) is nonsense, but that his statements on mechanical time are, as I suspect, also askew.

My Mexican professor[6] has not yet announced his courses and, for some reason, does not seem to be giving any courses. Because of my current project, I have not been able to finish reading Kierkegaard, but have gotten only halfway through. How did things turn out with your mathematics course?[7]

Regards.
Yours, Walter Benjamin

1. In *Schriften* 2:401–19.

2. Samson Raphael Hirsch, *Neunzehn Briefe über Judentum,* a famous book that appeared in 1836.

3. The reference is to Scholem's unpublished translation of a Hebrew essay on the presence of God in the world, which appeared in 1911 and was seen as significant at the time. It was written by Hillel Zeitlin, a Hassidic journalist.

4. *Das Reich* 1 (1916), pp. 305ff. The reference is to the *Pindar Fragmente* (subsequently called *Untreue der Weisheit* after the first fragment), which were presumably written around 1803. Norbert von Hellingrath had already published these annotated translations in 1910 (*Hölderlins Pindar-Übertragungen*).

5. Martin Heidegger's inaugural lecture on July 27, 1915.

6. Walter Lehmann, whose course on Aztec mythology WB attended.

7. Scholem was the only student in Schottky's four-hour lecture course.

47. To Herbert Belmore

[Late 1916]

Dear Herbert,

I am very happy you wrote me.

But your letter takes the form of an objective report and thus passes over some profound assumptions that my answer must make regarding both of us. If this were not necessary, my answer would not be what it is: an ardent challenge to the kind of objectivity you simultaneously demand and practice.

It has been my experience that it is not bridges and flying that help you get through the night, but only the fraternal step. We are in the middle of the night. I once tried to combat it with words (Thomas Mann had published his abject *Gedanken im Kriege*). At that time I learned that whoever fights against the night must move its deepest darkness to deliver up *its* light and that words are only a way station in this major life struggle: and they can be the final station only where they are never the first.

I can just see myself sitting on my suitcase in Geneva, with Dora and you in the room, as I advocate the idea that productivity, in every sense, must be supported (but criticism, as well) and that life must be sought in the spirit solely with all names, words and signs. For years, Hölderlin's light has shone down on me out of this night.

It is all too great to criticize.[1] It is all the night that bears the light, it is the bleeding body of the spirit. It is also all too small to criticize, not there at all: the dark, total darkness itself—even dignity alone—the gaze of anyone who attempts to contemplate it will grow dim. Inasmuch as the word appears to us on our path, we will prepare the purest and holiest place for it: however, it should dwell among us. We want to preserve it in the final, most precious form we are able to give it; art truth justice: perhaps everything will be taken out of our hands, and it should then at least be form: not criticism. To criticize is the concern of the outermost periphery of the circle of light around the head of every person, not the concern of language. Wherever we encounter it, it means work for us. Language resides only in what is positive, and completely in whatever strives for the most fervent unity with life; which does not maintain the pretense of criticism, of the χριων of discriminating between good and bad; but transposes everything critical to the inside, transposes the crisis into the heart of language.

True criticism does not attack its object: it is like a chemical substance that attacks another only in the sense that, decomposing it, it exposes its inner nature, but does not destroy it. The chemical substance that attacks *spiritual* things in this way (diathetically) is the light. This does not appear in language.

Criticism of spiritual things is to distinguish between the genuine and the nongenuine. This, however, is not the concern of language, or only deeply disguised: as humor. Only in humor can language be critical. The particular critical magic then appears, so that the counterfeit substance comes into contact with the light; it disintegrates. The genuine remains: it is ash. We laugh about it. The rays of anyone who beams excessively will also tackle those heavenly unmaskings we call criticism. It was precisely the great critics who amazingly saw what was genuine: Cervantes.

A great author who saw what was genuine in such a way that he could barely engage in criticism anymore: Sterne. Reverence for words does not a critic make. Reverence for his subject in the presence of what is unpretentiously genuine: Lichtenberg. This is the way, if criticism is to become explicit or take linguistic form. This is solely the concern of great individuals. The concept is being misused: Lessing was no critic.

Sincere regards,
Walter

Do you want to read any of my work? I have written the following essays:

Das Glück des antiken Menschen [The good fortune of the people of antiquity]
Socrates
Trauerspiel und Tragödie [*Trauerspiel* and tragedy]
Die Bedeutung der Sprache in Trauerspiel und Tragödie [The significance of language in *Trauerspiel* and tragedy]
On Language as Such and on the Language of Man[2]

1. The relationship of what follows to the train of thought in letter 45 to Buber is clear.
2. These essays are all preserved, in part only in manuscript form.

48. To Ernst Schoen

Berlin
February 27, 1917

Dear Mr. Schoen,

Thank you very much for your last letter. I continue to hope you will soon come to Berlin. When you do, I will return the book by Jammes you lent me. I found the *Roman du lièvre,* as well as the two stories about the young girls, splendid. Are you familiar with Jammes's books of poems? If you think they are good and happen to have them, I would appreciate your lending them to me sometime. I have known and valued *Existences* for a long time, and recently bought it for myself. At the moment I am busy reading Flaubert: *Bouvart* [*sic*] *et Pécuchet.* As far as I know, this is in every sense Flaubert's most difficult work. A few weeks ago I read Dostoyevsky's tremendous novel *The Idiot.*

I am working on my Baudelaire translation to the extent I can, given my currently very restricted circumstances. I am also giving a lot of thought to a more extensive study I began four months ago and am yearning to continue.[1] I keep suffering from attacks of sciatica.

My existence is so limited that I am unable to tell you anything more about it in writing. Yet I would be sorry if these lines were to make it *seem* I was in even worse shape than is actually the case. The worst thing is that I am staying with my parents while my future wife[2] is here, and I have to endure daily quarrels.

Have you read that Norbert von Hellingrath[3] died in the war? I had wanted to give him my Hölderlin study to read when he returned. The way Hellingrath framed the subject in his work on the Pindar translation was the external motivation for my study. Incidentally, he intended to write a comprehensive book on Hölderlin.

Among the few consistently gratifying things is a correspondence I have conducted almost without interruption for more than a year with someone who is several years younger than I am,[4] and who is stationed at a military hospital, which provides him with the opportunity to think and write. I visited him once in the spring of last year. Correspondence is the only possible form of expression for many things, due to its different premises which, to a certain degree, always allow and vouchsafe the writer's suffering and pathos.

Given your situation, there is nothing better I could wish than for my letters to give you frequent pleasure, and for this one to please you as much as possible too.

Yours, Walter Benjamin

1. The essay on language.
2. Dora Pollack. The wedding took place on April 17, 1917.

3. The publisher of Georg Müller's Hölderlin edition, whom WB valued very highly.
4. Werner Kraft, at that time in Hannover.

49. To Gerhard Scholem

Dachau
May 23, 1917

Dear Mr. Scholem,

I had barely found the time and opportunity to write you when, all at once, a reason to write clearly presented itself. Namely, the collected works of Baader, for which I have been searching for a long time, arrived this morning and because now, of course, I hope to devote myself to my studies with some intensity, I want everything that goes together lined up side by side. This is the only way I can work. And Baader and Molitor[1] go together so well that one of the very first things by Baader I read were two important letters he wrote to Molitor which, among other things, have something important and fine to say about *schechinnah*. So, how do things stand with the copy you were going to inquire about for me. If you have it, would you please send it to me immediately, and let me know how much it cost so I can pay you back by return mail. If not, I will try to find it at the Munich university library. But if this also proves futile, I may decide to ask you to send me your copy on loan by registered mail—if you can spare it. I would do this only if my work makes this research something I cannot do without and if I am unable to get the book in any other way. From time to time, you should be getting excerpts from Baader commenting on the *schechinnah* and maybe some other things as well.

For a few days now, our address has been Dachau bei München, Moorbad and Kuranstalt. It is summer; we have a nice room with a loggia overlooking the verdant garden; and since we are on the second floor, we can occasionally even see the Alps. The food and care is good, but my sciatica nonetheless persists.

I am reading a lot of Friedrich Schlegel and Novalis. In the case of Schlegel, it is becoming ever clearer to me how he is probably the only one of all the romantics (we can surely leave his brother out of consideration in this regard) who has contributed to this school's spiritual development without being constitutionally weak and murky. He is poetically pure, healthy, and indolent. However, a germ of sickness is at the very core of Novalis and Brentano. I still hope to show precisely the nature of Novalis's sickness.

The mathematical theory of truth[2]—or better, its development—is everywhere in good hands. After more than a year, I spoke with my friend (the genius)[3] in Munich who, in the meantime, has gotten his doctorate summa cum laude from Erlangen. He is working on the same problem as you are—even if not explicitly from the perspective of Zionism. I had the *most significant of all* conversations with him about the mathematical theory of truth and how this discipline revealed itself in Europe for the first time among the Pythagoreans. However, I have not yet conceptually penetrated these matters sufficiently to be able to communicate them in the form of a letter. This is also true of some related matters that were laid out for me in that conversation and are most astonishingly bold.

In Munich I bought Kant's correspondence and Scheerbart's lunar novel, *Die große Revolution,* at a used bookstore.—How are you? Please let us know soon. We often think of you and the better we feel, the more we hope the same for you. As far as Lugano is concerned, we are once again waiting for precise instructions from you—as well as for your mother's address.

Best wishes. We hope to hear from you soon.

Yours, Walter Benjamin

1. Molitor was the author of the most important earlier study of the Kabbalah, *Philosophie der Geschichte oder über die Tradition* (1827–53). It could still be obtained through the publisher in 1916.

2. This expression came from Scholem, who used the term for his mathematical-philosophical speculations.

3. WB consistently uses this designation for Felix Noeggerath (1886–1961), with whom he had a lot of contact during the year he spent in Munich, 1915–16, and after 1925.

50. To Gerhard Scholem

[June 1917]

Dear Mr. Scholem,

Without exactly having been conscious of this, there is no doubt that I have always considered a revision of your translation of the Song of Solomon probable (because it was necessary), and I also expected the printed text—I have it with me—to become important to me in evaluating any future new text. I am therefore very willing to take on the critical task you are offering me and I am sure to learn a lot by doing it. Please send me the manuscript as soon as possible.—The Molitor arrived and the money for it will be in the mail today. Since it is being mailed by my wife, who will be in Munich until the day after tomorrow, I am not sure whether she will think of including the 1 mark for postage. In case she doesn't, I will compensate you for it immediately. I was very happy to have the book: like the Baader, it is sure to become rare, valued, and even expensive in keeping with the current trend. Am I right in assuming that it has not progressed beyond the first part of the fourth volume? Please tell me the subject of the second volume, just to get an overview of its general direction.[1] Baader certainly has a lot to do with romanticism and was thus a major influence on Schelling, one that Schelling concealed. I, for one, was referred to Baader by the author of the essay you mention,[2] a young doctor and poet and someone who is also interested in philosophy. I spoke with him at a seminar in Munich and not infrequently elsewhere in Munich. I am familiar with an essay he wrote about Baader, but do not know whether it is the one you mentioned. The dignity of Dr. Pulver's philosophical views is still *very* problematical for me. He submitted a quite confused dissertation on romantic irony and romantic comedy, although it received superb marks. For the first time, I am happily steeping myself in the study of romanticism. Studying Kant, which in some ways would be of paramount importance, must be put off and wait for a more propitious time, because I can deal with him (as well as [Hermann] Cohen who, by the way, is said to be seriously ill) only in the broadest context, which thus requires large chunks of time. To begin with, I will turn my attention to early romanticism, primarily Friedrich Schlegel, then Novalis, August Wilhelm, even Tieck, and later, if possible, Schleiermacher. I will proceed by arranging some Friedrich Schlegel–like fragments according to their *systematic* basic ideas; this is a project I have been thinking about for a long time. It is of course purely interpretative and it remains to be seen what objective value it will have. The limits of this study are also narrowly defined by the limited number of fragments that can be interpreted in terms of the system. But I am indebted to this project for almost everything I understand of early romanticism to date. In addition, I am compiling some corresponding Novalis fragments. The result was more meager than you would have supposed, considering the huge number of Novalis fragments (including the posthumous ones). The core of early romanticism is religion and history. Its infinite profundity and beauty in comparison to *all* late romanticism derives from the fact that the early romantics did not appeal to religious and historical facts for the intimate bond between these two spheres, but rather tried to produce in their own *thought* and life the higher sphere in which both spheres had to coincide. The result was not "religion" but that atmosphere in which everything that was without religion and that was ostensibly religion, burned and disintegrated into ashes. Just as the same kind of quiet disintegration of Christianity was apparent to Friedrich Schlegel, not because he disputed its dogmatism, but because its morality was not romantic: i.e., it was neither quiet nor vivacious enough, because to him it seemed to be turbulent, masculine (in the broadest sense), and in the final analysis unhistorical. These words cannot be found in his works. They are an interpretation. But romanticism *must* be interpreted (with circumspection). Friedrich

Schlegel lived in the ethereal fire of this atmosphere longer than any other person, above all longer than Novalis, who tried to realize out of his practical, in its profound sense, or better, pragmatic genius what Schlegel made inescapable. For indeed, romanticism is the last movement that kept tradition alive one more time. Its efforts, premature for that age and sphere, aimed at the insanely orgiastic disclosure of all secret sources of the tradition that was to overflow without deviation into all of humanity.

In one sense, whose profundity would first have to be made clear, romanticism seeks to accomplish for religion what Kant accomplished for theoretical subjects: to reveal its form. But does religion have a *form*?? In any case, under history early romanticism imagined something analogous to this.

I will write about Novalis's "germ of sickness" another time. I am still giving it some thought. Because of the great difficulties the subject poses for me, I am unable to communicate anything about the genius's research in a letter. [. . .] The theses on identity will soon follow.[3]—The genius's dissertation has not yet been published. A small section that I know from having seen the manuscript is quite plainly *extremely* significant.

You can probably get the volume by Baader, in which I found the passage on *schechinnah,* in the library: references to it are scattered throughout the book and would be tedious to excerpt. Furthermore, I believe that his view may be close to the truth. See the *Collected Works,* published by F. Hoffmann, vol. 4, pp. 343–349. Moreover, the discussion of time and history, pp. 356–57 in the same essay, is very noteworthy. I have not yet understood it. And the concluding paragraph of the previous essay, p. 340, may also be of interest to you. You would be doing me a service if you were able to write me something about the concept of dual creation, in which I am very interested, and with good cause.

Most sincere regards and good wishes from me and my wife.

Yours, Walter Benjamin

P.S. The remittance (16 marks) is enclosed.

1. The second volume was no longer in print.

2. Max Pulver. The work mentioned somewhat later on in the letter is his 1912 Freiburg dissertation.

3. The "Thesen über das Identitätsproblem" [Theses on the problem of identity] has been preserved. It originated in discussions between WB and Scholem at the beginning of 1917.

51. To Gerhard Scholem

Zurich
July 17, 1917

Dear Mr. Scholem,

Allow me to say a few words about your translation of the Song of Solomon. I unfortunately do not have the text in front of me now and could not read it in its entirety during my recent gruelling stay in Dachau: nevertheless these limitations are less important than my ignorance, not only of the Song of Solomon, but also of Hebrew. Consequently, what I say cannot be more than an aperçu, but I think I am on relatively firm ground in what little I do have to say.

What distinguishes the second from the first[1] translation is its thorough and conscientious application of *critical methodology;* the revision is methodically based, and at the same time it is only methodical. And, if I might allow myself a conjecture, this is because, in the medium of the German language, your love for Hebrew can manifest itself only as reverence for the nature of language and the word as such, and thus only in the application of a proper and pure method. This means that your work will remain apologetic, however, because its proper sphere does not include the expression of love and reverence for an object. In principle, it would not be impossible for two languages to inhabit the same sphere: on the contrary, this is the foundation of all great translation and is the basis of the very few great translations in existence. In the spirit of Pindar, Hölderlin discovered the congruent spheres of German and Greek: his love for both became *one.* (I am not sure, but I think it is almost possible to accord equally high praise to George's Dante translation.) Nevertheless, you are not as close to German as you are to Hebrew and therefore you have not been *called* to be the translator of the Song of Solomon. At the same time, you can thank your reverential and critical spirit that you have not become an uncalled-for translator. In the final analysis, I believe you yourself will benefit more from this work than anyone else.

In the spring Insel catalog, I saw the following entry: Buber, Martin, *Die Lehre, die Rede, und das Lied.* This is precisely the linguistic classification of modes of expression I made in a letter to him to which he did not respond. Might his response be concealed behind the title? Perhaps an indication of approval? Perhaps without indicating the person to whom this approval is addressed? I will make an effort to support this contention, at which point you will hear more from me.

We will soon be leaving for the Engadine. Write, soon and often, to this address until you receive the new one. You are often in our thoughts and we sincerely wish we could be with you.

Yours, Walter Benjamin

1. Some copies of this translation were printed in 1916.

52. To Ernst Schoen

St. Moritz
July 30, 1917

Dear Mr. Schoen,

It is a beautiful early morning and the time has come for which I was waiting to thank you for your letter and the book. The letter reached me while I was still in Zurich. I read it lying in bed, while next to me on the night table lay a small, inadequate edition of Maurice de Guérin's works, the only one I was able to get a few months ago in Germany. Before I had even turned a page and read the title of your gift, I *knew* that it was Maurice de Guérin's works. A few days ago I had read *Le Centaure*. By the way, do you have any advice on how I might somehow get a look, even if only a quick one, at the Rilke translation of this book. As far as I know, it was published by Insel, but their last catalog no longer has it listed. The way Guérin penetrates the spirit of the centaur is magnificent; after I had read it, I opened Hölderlin's powerful fragment, "Das Belebende" (at the end of Hellingrath's special edition of the Pindar translations), and the world of Guérin's centaurs enters the larger world of Hölderlin's fragments.

We have been here for a week; I found this spot—if I may say so—after years of struggle, and finally set foot here after the last relationship[1] obscurely entrapping me with things from the past had died away in Zurich. I hope to have absorbed the two years before the war as you would a seed and I hope that everything since then has purified it in my spirit. When we see each other again, we'll talk about the Youth Movement, whose preeminence experienced such a total and precipitous decline. Everything was in decline, except for the little that let me live my life, and to which I tried to draw close in the last two years, and I find myself saved here in more than one sense: not for the leisure security maturity of life, but in having escaped from the demonic and ghostly influences, which are prevalent wherever we turn, and from raw anarchy, the lawlessness of suffering.

For my birthday I received the works of Gryphius in a beautiful, old edition. This man's work is a sign of the great danger threatening us even today: the danger of allowing the flame of life, if not to be smothered, then to grow hopelessly dim; light makes me circumspect in the spirit of the past years.

I am not yet working; when I can get down to work depends on circumstances. If I had a large library at my disposal, I could accomplish a lot; as things are, I hope in time to assemble my small library, and I can only hope that I will always be able to work, now that, after so many years, working once again becomes possible.—I cannot get my essay on language to you right now. The copy in Germany is inaccessible to me at this time.[2] I dare to hope that, when you do read it, it will have progressed beyond the first part. But maybe I can send you brief copies of my notes from time to time?

That's all for today. Sincere regards from both me and my wife.

Yours, Walter Benjamin

1. With Herbert Belmore.
2. Scholem was in the army.

53. To Gerhard Scholem

St. Moritz
[September 1917]

Dear Gerhard,

Permit me to combine my commemoration of your battle and victory with our shift to a first-name basis. In spite of all the pleasure your last letter gave me (and which, as you can see, I am answering right away), I experienced an almost painful sensation at the thought that we won't be together. Is it really impossible? I am convinced that, in a certain respect, in the very circumstances of our existence we have reached an *equality* whose primary color is no doubt gratitude and which would hold the promise of an extremely productive and splendid collaboration. Another reason I wish we could be together is that my wife and I are totally isolated here. Wouldn't it be possible for you, through some modest enterprise, to earn a modest amount of money (in francs) which, added to your monthly income, would guarantee a modest but healthy standard of living? How long would we otherwise have to wait before seeing each other again?

I am going to Bern on business in a few days. I still do not know where I will be studying in the winter. Maybe in Zurich; under certain circumstances, however, I might be forced to choose Basel if it should prove to be more advantageous in terms of getting my doctorate. The extremely liberal Prof. [Karl] Joel is there.—Based on what I have heard about Prof. Bauch's conflict with the Kant Society, it seems to be out of the question for him to do more than transmit some of the minutiae of philosophical research. You will probably get to hear something about this conflict from time to time. As far as I know, Linke is not highly esteemed in phenomenological circles;[1] but I am indebted to one of his essays for some information on the nature of phenomenology, or what he considers it to be. The essay is a polemic against an uncomprehending critique of phenomenology by Elsenhans, and it is in the 1916 issue of the *Kant-Studien*.

At the moment, I am not working but only pondering various things from time to time. This is not the place to do anything else and it was a good choice to spend these few weeks of summer. The landscape is very bracing and it steels the spirit. With its healing power, it prevents the internal solution we have found from being able to convulse us internally to the point of destruction. I am reading Gryphius's *Cardenio und Celinde* to my wife. In doing so, I am reading it for the second time. It is a *very* beautiful play. [. . .]

You may read my essay on the language of Ludwig Strauß to a group, if in return, and if at all possible, I can borrow a copy of his work.[2] I want you to know that it is *very* important to me to become familiar with a study on ethics that you consider to be significant. I can hardly imagine anything more interesting and important, and for this very reason I would like to have a verbatim transcription of the work at my disposal for a while. As far as my work is concerned, I would naturally return the favor for Ludwig Strauß. Please give him my warmest regards. Total mutual trust is a prerequisite for such an exchange of manuscripts.—I am ordering the latest volume of the Hölderlin edition. Unfortunately, I have not yet seen the George poem[3] that Mr. Kraft[4] had also mentioned to me.

September 6

I have received your essay.[5] Thank you. It is very good. I would like you to keep in mind the following observations for any further work you do on it. You write: "All work whose goal is not to set an example is nonsense." "If we wish to be serious: . . . then today, as always, the most profound way—as well as the only way—to influence the souls of future generations is: through example." The concept of example (to say nothing of that of "influence") should be totally excluded from the theory of education. On the one hand, what inheres in the concept of example is the empirical; on the other hand, the belief in pure power (of suggestion or something similar). Example would mean showing by doing, that something is empirically possible and to spur others on to imitation. The life of the educator, however, does not function indirectly, by setting an example. Because I must express myself very concisely, I want to try to elucidate this in terms of instruction. Instruction is education by means of the theory in its actual sense, and must therefore be at the center of all ideas about education. The separation of education from instruction is the symptom of the total confusion in all existing schools. Instruction is symbolic for all other areas of education, because in all of them the educator is also the person teaching. You can, of course, designate teaching as "learning by example," but you will immediately discover that the concept of example is being used figuratively. The teacher does not actually teach in that he "learns before others," learns in an exemplary way. Rather, his learning has evolved into teaching, in part gradually but wholly from within. Thus, when you say that the teacher sets the "example" for learning, under the concept of example you conceal what is characteristic and autonomous in the concept of such learning: that is to say, teaching. At a certain stage, all things become exemplary in the right person, but they thereby metamorphose into themselves and are rejuvenated. Seeing this rejuvenated creative something as it unfolds in human life cycles provides insight into education. I now hope that you would eliminate the concept of example from the final version of your essay and that, indeed, you would want to preserve it in, and elevate it to, the concept of tradition. I am convinced that tradition is the medium in which the person who is learning *continually* transforms himself into the person who is teaching, and that this applies to the entire range of education. In the tradition everyone is an educator and everyone needs to be educated and everything is education. These relationships are symbolized and synthesized in the development of the theory. Anyone who has not learned cannot educate, for he does not recognize the point at which he is alone and where he thus encompasses the tradition in his own way and makes it communicable by teaching. Knowledge becomes transmittable only for the person who has understood his knowledge as something that has been transmitted. He becomes free in an unprecedented way. The metaphysical origin of a Talmudic witticism comes to mind here. Theory is like a surging sea, but the only thing that matters to the wave (understood as a metaphor for the person) is to surrender itself to its motion in such a way that it crests and breaks. This enormous freedom of the breaking wave is education in its actual sense: instruction—tradition becoming visible and *free,* tradition emerging precipitously like a wave from living abundance. It is so difficult to speak about education because its order completely coincides with the religious order of tradition. To educate is only (in spirit) to enrich the theory; only the person who has learned can do that: therefore it is impossible for future generations to live other than by learning. Our descendants come from the spirit of God (human beings); like waves, they rise up out of the movement of the spirit. Instruction is the only nexus of the free union of the old with the new generation. The generations are like waves that roll into each other and send their spray into the air.

Every error in education goes back to the fact that we think our descendants are dependent on *us* in some fundamental way. Their dependence on us is no different from their dependence on God and on the language in which, for the sake of some kind of community with our children, we must immerse ourselves. Young men can educate only other young men, *not* children. Grown men educate young men.

I hope this letter is not too long. I will close with the most sincere regards from both me and my wife, and I hope to hear from you soon.

Yours, Walter Benjamin

1. Bruno Bauch and Paul Linke taught in Jena, where Scholem studied during the winter of 1917–18.

2. An outline (handwritten) of an "Ethics."

3. "Der Krieg."

4. Werner Kraft, with whom WB had been conducting a lively correspondence (unfortunately lost) since 1915, primarily about literary matters. Kraft and Scholem, independently of each other, had become familiar with WB because of the impression made by a discussion that took place in June 1915 and in which all three, among others, had spoken. The discussion was about a lecture given by Kurt Hiller to academicians.

5. A fundamental critique of the work in Jewish education conducted by the Jewish *Wanderbund, Blau-Weiß*. The essay appeared in the league's publication, *Führerzeitung* (Summer 1917).

54. To Ernst Schoen

Bern
September 10, 1917

Dear Mr. Schoen,

I am writing this although I do not have your last letter in front of me. I am writing you in spite of this because everything in this city motivates me to do so, and because I am thinking of how the—perhaps unfortunate—semester you spent here resulted in some nice letters from you which moved me deeply at the time. [. . .] Communication by letter is inadequate for almost everything. I intend to write only what can be expressed without violating the truth, and I intend to remain silent whenever it is impossible for me to be completely clear in writing.

Yesterday we saw a young musician[1] whom I had met several years ago when he first arrived from Wickersdorf. I knew him as a charming and quiet boy who, even then, was completely absorbed in music. I had hoped that both my wife and I would enjoy this reunion—but what I found was a young man who (although certainly not ugly) had lost the singular beauty that had characterized him. He may be unspoiled and malleable. But let me speak frankly: he had developed a hump. The spiritual impression he made on me was concentrated in this *image*. I later talked about it with my wife: this hump suddenly seemed to me to be a characteristic of most modern people who devote themselves to music. It is as if they are internally deformed; as if they were carrying something heavy on top of something hollow. This "hump," and everything connected to it, is a particular form of the Socraticism I despise, a form of the modern, of "beauty in ugliness." We automatically started talking about you and how, given your circumstances, your consciousness of not yet being equal to a total absorption in music does not assume this bitter and futile shape. Your spine will remain straight because you are able to renounce and will *never by any means* express a false exuberance. Aren't you conscious of this yourself, and wasn't this consciousness what sustained you during what was certainly a lengthy crisis?

Free yourself from your most immediate misery.

It now seems to me that your strengths must join the perilous agon.

Bern is a magnificent city even if it may well be impossible to live there alone. I am still not sure how long we will stay here and where we will go then. I have to be patient until I once again have a desk and some work in front of me. But there are a lot of things urgently clammering to be done.

Here is a poem I wrote.

Upon Seeing the Morning Light

Since a person rises up out of mild madness
How could awakening take its own measure?
The sun's incoming tide still fills the ear
until its ebb lost itself in the day
And dream that foretold its self forgotten

Above all however form will first materialize
for him who thrusts a hand into the ancestral preserve
the refuge of sadness the lofty forest
In its treetops a light has ripened
gazing tired and cold from the nights

How soon I will be alone in this world
which creating reaches out, my hand holds back
And shuddering feels its own nakedness
Is after all this sphere too small for the heart
Where will he find a place to breathe in keeping with his proper stature?

Where waking does not part from sleeping
Luminousness makes its appearance, clad like the moon
And yet no brightness threatens him, no mockery
The meadow of man where, dozing, he grazes
No longer suffers in the dream's old darkness
Wakes in the light of the old sphere: God.

Sincere regards. Let me know how you are. Many regards from my wife.

Yours, Walter Benjamin

1. His name was Heymann.

55. To Gerhard Scholem

Bern
October 22, 1917

Dear Gerhard,

I could reply to your last letters, dated September 20th and September 28th, only after some time had elapsed, so that my reply could reflect at least somewhat the fact that I had been able to absorb them and thus continue the discussion. Meanwhile, I have been constantly thinking about what you wrote—except about your thoughts on Kant. I am unable to say the same thing about them because they coincide exactly with what I have thought for the past two years. I have never been more astonished about the extent to which we agree on things than about what you had to say about Kant. I could literally claim it as my own. It is therefore probably unnecessary for me to write you very much about that subject. Although I still have no proof for this, it is my firm belief that, in keeping with the spirit of philosophy and thus of doctrine to which it belongs (that is, if it does not perhaps constitute doctrine in its entirety), there will never be any question of the Kantian system's being shaken and toppled. Rather, the question is much more one of the system's being set in granite and universally developed. The most profound typology of conceiving doctrine has thus far always become clear to me in Kant's words and ideas. And no matter how great the number of Kantian minutiae that may have to fade away, his system's typology must last forever. To my knowledge, within the realm of philosophy this typology can only be compared with Plato's. Only in the spirit of Kant and Plato and, I believe, by means of the revision and further development of Kant, can philosophy become doctrine or, at least, be incorporated in it.

You would be justified in pointing out that "in the spirit of Kant" and "the typology of conceiving doctrine" are very vague expressions. In fact, the only thing I see clearly is the task as I have just circumscribed it, that what is *essential* in Kant's thought must be preserved. I still do not know at this point what this "essential" something consists of and how his system must be grounded anew for it to emerge clearly. But this is my conviction: anyone who does not sense in Kant the struggle to *conceive doctrine itself* and who therefore does not comprehend him with the utmost reverence, looking on even the least letter as a *tradendum* to be transmitted (however much it is necessary to recast him afterwards), knows nothing of philosophy. Thus all adverse criticism of his philosophical style is also pure philistinism and profane gibberish. It is quite true that art must be subsumed in great scientific creations (the reverse also holds true), and thus it is my conviction that Kant's prose per se represents a *limes* of literary prose. Otherwise, would the *Critique of Pure Reason* have shaken Kleist to the core?

I know that I am in agreement with the genius in what I have said here. I do not have his current address, but could probably find out what it is. Let me also note the following: I have come to feel most deeply that an intimate affinity is indispensable for such a profound equivalence in the image of truth that two individuals carry within themselves. It is also indispensable for their community in every sense, and specifically in the sense of the discovery of this truth, because otherwise they cannot go beyond a candid sharing of information and mutual respect. To the extent that we have not yet attained this affinity, it is also the most I could hope for from my relationship to the genius; our methods of working diverge at every point except at this most peripheral point of contact in *intuition* which, for the two of us, flows not only from different sources but probably from antithetical sources; so that we can speak with each other in absolute harmony, but will not be able to work with each other that way. As far as my relationship to the genius goes, I believe I may already take that to be a certainty; as I once said to him, German and Jew stand opposite one another like related extremes. Yet what matters for him and me would still be a serious attempt to work together should the opportunity present itself, and the same may also hold true for you. After all of this, I hardly need tell you how much I would expect *our* being together, in its deepest sense, to advance our self in knowledge.

This winter I will begin to work on Kant and history. I do not know yet whether I will be able to find in the historical Kant the completely positive content required in this regard. Whether a doctoral dissertation will come out of this study in part depends on that. For I have not yet read the relevant works by Kant. I believe I recognize the ultimate reason that led me to this topic, as well as much that is apropos and interesting: the ultimate metaphysical dignity of a philosophical view that truly intends to be canonical will always manifest itself most clearly in its confrontation with history; in other words, the specific relationship of a philosophy with the true doctrine will appear most clearly in the philosophy of history; for this is where the subject of the historical evolution of knowledge for which doctrine is the catalyst will have to appear. Yet it would not be entirely out of the question for Kant's philosophy to be very undeveloped in this respect. Based on the silence that reigns over his philosophy of history, this is what you would have to expect (or its opposite). But I think that the person who approaches it with proper understanding will find enough or even more than enough. Otherwise I will find another area in which to work. The best way to give you some notion of my other thoughts on this subject would be in conversation.

By all means, please read Barthel's "Die geometrischen Grundbegriffe" in the *Archiv für systematische Philosophie,* ed. by L. Stein, new series of the *Philosophische Monatshefte* 22(4), November 1916. I have leafed through the essay and, of course, only partially understood it. You must grapple with it and write me what there is to it.

At the moment, before I can begin reading Kant, I am reading Harnack's three-volume textbook on the history of dogma. I am at the end of the first volume. The book is giving me a lot to think about, in that it enables me for the first time to form an impression of what Christianity is, and constantly leads me to comparisons with Judaism, for which my knowledge is totally inadequate, to express it euphemistically. In spite of that, I have become aware of some specific problems, and to expound them properly would require a separate letter for each one. Let me outline two in the form of questions: 1) Does Judaism have the concept of faith in the sense of an adequate attitude toward revelation? 2) In Judaism, is there somehow a fundamental division and distinction between Jewish theology, religious doctrine, and the pious Judaism of the individual Jew? My intuition tells me that the answer to both questions must be no, and both would then constitute very important antitheses to the Christian concept of religion. Some other time I will write about another important problem of Christianity that became evident. But apropos this observation: a principal component of *vulgar* anti-Semitic as well as Zionist ideology is that the gentile's hatred of the Jew is physiologically substantiated on the basis of instinct and race, since it turns against the physis. This unconsciously drawn conclusion is false, however, for one of the remarkable and essential characteristics of hatred is that, whatever basis and grounds it may have, in its most primitive and intense forms it becomes hatred for the physical nature of the one who is hated. (The relationship between hatred and love would also have to be sought in this quarter.) Thus if in certain cases you can speak of the gentile's hatred of Jews, this does not then exempt you from the effort of seeking intellectual reasons for these cases. In this regard, one motive (to begin with, not for the hatred of Jews and Judaism, but for anger toward them) that must be considered is the extremely spurious[1] and distorted method, now become historical, in which an acknowledgment of the coming Christian centuries and peoples was imposed upon the Old Testament by the oldest Christian churches and congregations. This was, of course, originally done in the hope of wresting the Old Testament from the Jews, and without an awareness of historical consequences, since people lived in anticipation of the imminent end. Because of this, universal and historical enmity of Christians against Judaism had to be created. As I said, this is only apropos.

Nothing has arrived yet from Ludwig Strauß. Assuming that I will get a copy of his essay and once I have confirmed this, you may send him a copy of my essay on language. A second copy can be sent to Mr. Kraft. You can keep the third and, if you have no other use for it, send the fourth to me. Otherwise a fifth copy could perhaps be made for me; but *who* should then get the fourth?—Unfortunately, dear Gerhard, I do not know when your birthday is. My wife and I can send you birthday greetings belatedly, prematurely, but never too affectionately. So please let us know whether the photographs you will receive in the next parcel arrived prematurely or belatedly. They were taken during the most trying time in Dachau and were originally meant to be passport photos, but they will not be used for that purpose. Considering how hard it is to take a picture of my wife, this one is probably not bad.

This next parcel will also contain the transcription of an essay I wrote, entitled "Über die Malerei" [On painting]. It will have to serve as my response to your letter on cubism, although this letter is hardly mentioned in my essay.[2] Actually, it is not an essay at all, but only the outline for one. Now for some observations on the essay: as I wrote you from St. Moritz at the time, after I had thought about the nature of graphic art and had gotten as far as writing down some sentences, which were unfortunately unavailable to me when I was composing the new sentences, your letter, in combination with my earlier thoughts on the subject, occasioned these new sentences. They were the results of my reflection. Your letter was the most immediate impetus for the essay, in that it awakened in me an interest in the unity of all painting in spite of its seemingly disparate schools. Since (contrary to your assertions) I wanted to prove that a painting by Raphael and a cubist painting as such manifest fundamentally congruent characteristics, in addition to those that divide them, I omitted any consideration of the characteristics dividing them. Instead I have attempted to discover the foundation on which all disparity could first of all be brought into relief. You will see how decisively I thus had to refute your trichotomy of painting into achromatic (linear), chromatic, and synthetic. From one perspective, the problem of cubism lies in the possibility of a, not necessarily *achromatic,* but radically *unchromatic* painting (this distinction of course must first be explained and clarified) in which linear shapes dominate the picture—not that cubism has ceased to be painting and has become graphic art. I have not touched on this problem of cubism from this or any other angle because, in one respect, things have not yet become absolutely clear from looking at concrete examples of individual paintings or masters. The only one among the new painters who has touched me in this sense is Klee but, on the other hand, I was still too uncertain about the fundamentals of painting to progress from this profound emotion to theory. I believe I will get there later. Of the modern painters Klee, Kandinsky, and Chagall, Klee is the only one who seems to have obvious connections to cubism. Yet, as far as I can judge, he is probably not a cubist. However indispensable these concepts are for an overview of painting and its foundation, a single great master does not become theoretically comprehensible through just one specific concept. Any painter who, as an individual, can be relatively adequately grasped within the categories of artistic schools will not be one of the great painters, because ideas of art (for this is what notions of artistic schools are) cannot be directly expressed in art without becoming impotent. In fact, I have so far always received this impression of impotence and inadequacy while viewing Picasso's paintings, an impression that, to my delight, you confirm; certainly not because, as you write, you have no eye for the purely artistic content of these things, but because, as you also write, you have an ear for the spiritual message they radiate: and artistic content and spiritual communication are, after all, precisely the same thing! As in these jottings I also allow the problem of painting to flow into the large domain of language whose dimensions I outline in my essay on language.—Purely for the sake of argument, I want to write you that, without even attempting an independent classification of cubism, I consider your characterization of it to be wrong. You consider the quintessence of cubism to be "the communication of the nature of the space that is the world through decomposition." It seems to me that this definition contains an error concerning the relationship of painting to its sensory subject. In analytical geometry, I can certainly produce an equation for a two- or three-dimensional figure in space without consequently overstepping the bounds of spatial analysis; but in painting I cannot paint *Woman with a Fan* (for example)[3] and [*sic*] to communicate the nature of space through decomposition. On the contrary, the communication must under all circumstances relate entirely to the *Woman with a Fan*. On the other hand, it is probable that painting actually has nothing to do with the "nature" of anything, for then it might collide with philosophy. At this time, I am not yet able to say anything about the import of the relationship of painting to its subject; but I believe that the issue here is one neither of imitation nor of the perception of essence. Incidentally, however, you may infer from these jottings that even I could imagine a profound relationship between, for example, cubism and church architecture.

Might I ask you for two favors? For her birthday, my wife wants Franz Hartwig's *Märchenkönigin*. The book must have appeared in the last twenty to forty years of the last century. If a bookstore in Jena can get it, please order it for me. Also please order Stefan George's "Krieg" if by chance you do not own it or are unable to lend it to me. If it is very short, you can just copy it for me. I have to believe everything you say about it, unfortunately, but would nonetheless like to see it once with my own eyes.

I will write some other time about what I wrote to Mr. Kraft on Judaism a year ago. [. . .] Please do not take it amiss that I was not able to deal directly with what you had to say on cubism, but approached it from another angle—and that I was basically inspired to jot down these thoughts. This is in the nature of things; you had paintings in front of you, and I had your words.

I continue to hope for a joyful reunion,

Yours, Walter

After November 1, our address will be 25 Haller St.

1. The word might be *verlegene* (confused), but the reading *verlogene* (spurious) better corresponds both to the context and to WB's use of language.

2. The reference was to a few pages with the title of "Zeichen und Mal" [Sign and mark], which are preserved among WB's papers.

3. This Picasso painting had been shown in the Berlin exhibition of the Sturm in the summer of 1917 and provided the impetus for Scholem's observations.

56. To Gerhard Scholem[1]

December 3, 1917

Since receiving your letter, I often feel solemn. It is as if I had entered a festive season and I must venerate revelation in what was disclosed to you.[2] For it is surely the case that what came to you, you alone, was meant just for you and reentered our life for a moment. I have entered a new phase of my life because what detached me with astronomical speed from everybody and pushed even my most intimate relationships, except for my marriage, into the background, now emerges unexpectedly someplace else and binds me.

I do not want to write you any more today even though this is meant to be your birthday letter.

Yours, Walter Benjamin

1. The letter has no salutation.

2. Scholem had seen the manuscript of the essay on Dostoyevsky's *Idiot* (*Schriften* 2: 127–31) and interpreted it as an esoteric comment on Friedrich Heinle.

57. To Gerhard Scholem

[December 7, 1917]

Dear Gerhard,

Your letter of November 2, 1917, arrived only this morning, on December 7th, "delayed because it was over two quarto sheets long." It would be best if you split such long letters or at least send them special delivery. The first page of this letter was written yesterday and I am now going to append the shorter answers I can give in response to your letter. But as far as the question requiring the longest answer is concerned, i.e., How can I *live* given the nature of my attitude to the Kantian system?, well, I am constantly working to make this life possible through insight into epistemology and, given all my zeal, I must have patience for the immense task this signifies for people who think like us. What I have written thus far is so sketchy that I cannot send it to you without having done a somewhat better job of justifying it. I will tell you just as soon as a certain stage has been reached. After all, my hope to really know and communicate these things someday rests not least of all on my conviction that I will be able to work with you. It was very painful to me that you misunderstood the part of my next to last letter that referred to this: I meant the *precise* opposite. When my wife read the letter, she explicitly drew my attention to the ambiguity of that passage; I seem to recall that I believed the possibility of misunderstanding had been eliminated by underlining a specific word in the passage. Please read it once more: it goes without saying that you are not at all at fault for the misunderstanding, but you will find that the passage was somehow ambiguous; and this is precisely what I meant: that the relationship that exists between us is totally positive and entirely different from the one between me and the genius. I mentioned him because, at the time, you had just inquired about him. From this misunderstanding more than from anything else, you can see to what extent correspondence is an inadequate substitute for being together.

As far as I am concerned, our discussion about Kant must continue to be postponed. Yet two points you make in your letter seem credible to me. In fact, one of them is a certainty: namely, it is necessary to begin by being concerned with the letter of Kantian philosophy. Kantian terminology is probably the only philosophical terminology that *in its entirety* did not only arise but was created. It is precisely the study of this terminology that leads to a realization of its extraordinary potency. In any case, it is possible to learn a lot by expanding and defining immanently the terminology as such. In this regard, I recently came upon a topic that might have something in it for me as a dissertation: the concept of the "eternal task" in Kant (what do you think?). Second, however, is that, having given some thought to it, I have become more familiar with the other point you make in your letter, i.e. that under certain circumstances it is necessary to be a completely independent thinker when it comes to your own thought, above all when ultimate questions are at issue. In any case, there are certain questions, like those related to the philosophy of history, that are central for us, but about which we can learn something decisive from Kant only after we have posed them anew for ourselves.

At the moment, I cannot delve any further into the abundant content of your letter without being superficial, because I would like to mail this letter. I hope we will soon be corresponding across a shorter distance, and this letter may already reach you by the new route. No doubt, we can have a real exchange of ideas about the Torah and the history of philosophy only when we are together again. I recently told my wife something about the decline of Christian concepts in exactly the same terms you refer to it. I have had to take a break from my reading of the history of dogma. This is such a voluminous work and requires so much concentration that you should carefully consider whether or not to read it, since you cannot just interrupt your reading, but have to keep going to the end.—It is very nice of you to let me know about Bauch; again there is some clarity about a philosopher, and it is as good as if I had studied in Jena. I shouldn't wonder that my answer to your question concerning Mr. Kraft's work will now arrive somewhat belatedly.[1] These essays—as you have certaintly recognized and as I expressed it to him in appropriate terms—are the pure spawn of his desperate state and as such neither can, in the external sense, nor may, in the internal sense, be published. I wrote the following to Kraft without receiving a clear answer: Rudolf Borchardt knows him, and is certainly not without influence in the matter at hand. Borchardt *must* do something for him because, if Borchardt is indebted to anybody of this generation, it is to Kraft. He should be indebted to him out of affection, just as he is indebted to him out of obligation.

I *urgently* request your paper on symbolic logic.

[. . .]

Best wishes, and please do not be angry at me for having had to pass over so much in silence.

Yours, Walter

1. Werner Kraft, who was a medic in Hannover at the time, had visited Scholem in Jena.

58. To Gerhard Scholem

[ca. December 23, 1917]

Dear Gerhard,

Due to its abundance, our correspondence is assuming baroque proportions and now, when indeed a letter like the one you mailed on November 19, 1917, arrives out of sequence due to its length (it got to us only in mid-December), I am almost at a loss as to how to treat the many different and quite important subjects without being superficial and without omitting the most essential ones. Let me begin with what comes easiest to me and express my most sincere gratitude for the care with which you see to my requests. I don't believe you have any notion of the pleasure that the arrival of the fourth volume of Hölderlin's collected works provided me. I had been waiting for it so long and so eagerly (you see, I had ordered the collected works in August (!) at a bookstore). Because of my excitement, I was almost incapable of doing anything else the entire day. I am now eagerly awaiting the sixth volume. After reading the *Reich* fragments, I must presume the sixth volume is also inordinately valuable. Another factor is that, at the moment, I need the broadest base imaginable for coming to terms with Hölderlin. It would be wonderful to talk about this in person. The George has been here for quite some time.[1] Please accept my apologies for having forgotten to express my gratitude and to acknowledge its receipt for such a long time. I do have something to say about these verses. What? I have already said it to Mr. Kraft and written the same thing in another letter to Mr. Gutkind,[2] and would not wish to repeat myself.

[. . .]

As far as Kant's history of philosophy is concerned, my exaggerated expectations have met with disappointment as a result of having read both of the main works that deal specifically with this (*Ideas for a Universal History . . .* [*Ideen zu einer Geschichte*] and *Perpetual Peace* [*Zum ewigen Frieden*]). This is unpleasant for me, especially in view of my plans for a dissertation topic, but in these two works by Kant I find no essential connection at all to works on the philosophy of history with which we are most familiar. Actually, I can perceive only a purely critical attitude toward them. Kant is less concerned with history than with certain historical constellations of ethical interest. And what's more, it is precisely the ethical side of history that is represented as inadequate for special consideration, and the postulate of a scientific mode of observation and method is posited (introduction to *Ideas for a Universal History*). I would be *very* interested in knowing whether you have a different opinion. I find Kant's thoughts entirely inappropriate as the starting point for, or as the actual subject of, an independent treatise. What did you and Miss [Toni] Halle have to say about this during your conversation?[3] I can only continue to regret, for the sake of the new plan I have for a dissertation, that you are not here. The plan would at least provide subject matter for the most illuminating conversations. The question can be put something like this: What does it mean to say that science is an eternal task? As soon as you look at it more closely, this sentence is more profound and philosophical than might be believed at first glance. You only had to become clear in your own mind that the subject is an "eternal task" and not a "solution that requires an eternally long time," and that the first concept in no way can or may be transformed into the second.—Some time ago I read Simmel's *Das Problem der historischen Zeit,*[4] an extremely wretched concoction that goes through contortions of reasoning, incomprehensibly uttering the silliest things.

Regarding the question of the problem of identity there is no doubt that we could make real progress only in conversation. I therefore do not attribute any absolute certainty to the following sentences. Nevertheless, the question appears to me as follows: I would deny that there can be identity in thinking, whether identity of one particular "object" of thinking or of one particular instance of "what is thought," because I dispute that any "thinking" is the correlate of truth. The truth *is* "thinkish" (I have to coin this word because none is available to me). "Thinking" as an absolute may somehow be only an abstraction of the truth. The assertion of identity in thinking would be the *absolute tautology.* The illusion of "thinking" arises only through tautologies. No more than the truth *is* thought, does it think. In my opinion, "*a* equals *a*" characterizes the identity of what is thought or, to express it *better* (in the *only* correct way), of truth itself. At the same time, this proposition designates no other identity than that of what is thought. The identity of the object, assuming there were such a thing in absolute terms, would have another form (forms of imperfect identities which, perfected, turn into *one* form of the type "*a* equals *a*"). By concrete object, I understand everything that is not the truth itself and is not concept. For example, the concept is a concrete object. The concept of the concept is an abstract one. This in fact probably leads to the eidos doctrine. Apropos: as far as I know, Linke's reputation is not very great in the rigorously phenomenological school; this of course does not mean anything. I also read Husserl's logos essay several years ago; just as, at that time, I read Linke's dispute with Elsenhans in *Kant-Studien,* after which I seized the opportunity to write my essay on concept and essence as a corrective to it. If I remember correctly, you know this essay.[5]

[. . .]

I recently received another letter from Werner Kraft. It was very depressing not only in view of the actual suffering it expressed, but also in view of the decline of his *internal* power of resistance which, I fear, came through. Have you once again made it clear to him most urgently that it is his duty to himself and to us to approach Borchardt? I do not know of anything else that would be of help. I do not need to ask you to stand by him as much as you can. What is sad—although not at all unexpected in spite of everything you had written—is your latest news. But our trust in you is unending.

For the first time in years, I have read—not counting the unimportant *Crime of Sylvestre Bonnard* [*Le crime Sylvestre Bonnard*]—my very first book by Anatole France, *The Revolt of the Angels* [*La révolte des anges*]. I found the book very good and will read more by him. It is profound and seems to me an indication of his total opus, with which I will attempt to familiarize myself gradually. He has a profound understanding of history and it seems to me that, in this regard, he can be truly stimulating. I am also reading Nietzsche's unsettling correspondence with Franz Overbeck, the first authentic biographical record of his I have seen.

All the best from me and my wife.

Yours, Walter

1. "Der Krieg."
2. Erich Gutkind (1877–1965) in Berlin, a friend of WB and Scholem since 1916; author of the book *Siderische Geburt* (Berlin, 1912).
3. Toni Halle (née Steinschneider, 1890–1964), a friend of Scholem, was writing a thesis on Kant at the time.
4. Berlin, 1916.
5. It is preserved in manuscript form.

59. To Ernst Schoen

[Locarno]
[December 28, 1917][1]

Dear Mr. Schoen,

I received your letter in Bern just a few days before embarking on the trip that brought me and my wife here for a few weeks. This trip was the reason for a delay in my response because, in new surroundings, I was unable to find time to answer immediately. Constant rain now eases the effect on body and soul of this landscape's beauty, for which I have yearned for an eternity. I would have greater difficulty reconciling myself to these rainy days if they had not finally exhorted me to write you and, of course, to respond first of all to your letter with a few words. My wife will later add some words of her own.

What you write is unequaled in its nobility of expression and understanding and it finally illuminates the darkness we are all trying to avoid. My wife and I are making your words entirely our own, especially in the sense that we are all confident of being together again sometime in the future as if for the first time, and are reconciled to understanding this separation, which will have been painful and inevitable for each of us in our own way.

Please allow me to tell you how much I rejoice in the thought of being able to continue this correspondence until we are reunited and can speak face to face. I inferred from your letter that your living conditions have become more tolerable, something that pleases me in every sense, since we are increasingly able to see the relationship between fate and human nature in those who are close to us.

At this time there may be more to say about my work than ever before but, to be sure, the more there is to say, the less there is to write. What I have to say regarding the immediate future is that, if things work out, I want to get my doctorate in Bern so that the road will have been cleared for me to do genuine research. Should difficulties arise in this regard, however, I will interpret them as a sign that the first thing for me to do is to bring my own thoughts into order. Connections with the most far-reaching significance are being revealed to me, and I can say that now, for the first time, I am forging ahead toward an integration of my thought. I recall that you seemed to understand me extraordinarily well when, on the corner of Joachimstaler and Kant streets (we were coming from the direction of the zoo), I shared with you my desperate reflections on the linguistic foundations of the categorical imperative. I have tried to develop further the way of thinking that concerned me then (and the special problem this posed at the time has not yet been solved for me, even today, but has been subsumed into a larger context). Thus what is at issue are problems that I find impossible even to touch on in a letter. The trains of thought I presented to you at the time in a lecture entitled "Das Swastika-problem" [The problem of the swastika] also incessantly concern me. Primarily, for me, questions about the essence of knowledge, justice, and art are related to the question about the origin of all human intellectual utterances in the essence of language. This is precisely the relationship that exists between the two subjects preeminent in my thinking. I have already written a lot about the first train of thought but it is not yet in a condition to be communicated. Do you happen to know my 1916 essay, "On Language as Such and on the Language of Man?" If not, for the time being I can unfortunately let you only borrow it. For me it constitutes the starting point for a more thorough study of the first of the above mentioned problems. By the way, I cannot remember what I sent you the last time, other than the *Centaure.* Please let me know in your next letter.

Without having read anything of substance by Anatole France before, I have now read, one right after the other, *The Revolt of the Angels, The Gods Will Have Blood* [*Les dieux ont soif*], and *Penguin Island* [*L'île des pingouins*]. In my opinion, his books deserve surprisingly high marks considering that they always lack that ultimate knowledge which alone is able to preserve the depth and homogeneity of a work of art. He loses himself in what is insignificant but, for all that, not without being clearly able to give a clear accounting of what is significant. Charles-Louis Philippe's *Marie Donadieu*. You should, by all means, read this book. There is nothing like it, even by Louis Philippe himself. I think it is simply wonderful—profound and true. Nonetheless, after having read it only once, I am unable to form a definitive judgment. Friedrich Nietzsche's correspondence with Overbeck. Maybe you have already read it, or will certainly do so soon. And the fourth volume of the Hellingrath Hölderlin edition is finally mine. I read a lot of Stifter, an author whose inconspicuous exterior and apparent harmlessness conceals a great moral as well as a great aesthetic problem. Which of his works do you know? The only ones I know that are almost *pristinely* beautiful are *Bergkristall* and *Die Mappe meines Urgroßvaters*. Since September I have been reading Harnack's three-volume history of dogma, which has provided me with some very valuable and revealing knowledge; I hope to have finished it soon. I had all sorts of peripheral things to do for the university: to deal very thoroughly with Schleiermacher's sterile psychology, with Bergson, and with Hegel. Hegel seems to be awful!

This is the third day of rain that has flooded the land. No ray of sunshine can be seen in a sky that previously had been deep blue and cloudless. This atmosphere militates against internal expansiveness and consequently this time you have received a letter that is much too concentrated. After all, the distance I have maintained from activity during my current convalescence does not allow me to concentrate on anything specific. Best wishes. Please write soon.

Yours, Walter Benjamin

1. The postmark is not legible. The letter may have been written on February 28, 1918, and may belong after letter 64.

60. To Gerhard Scholem

Bern
January 13, 1918

Dear Gerhard,

In what I believe was my next to last letter, which reached you quickly, I included a copy of a brief note entitled "Zeichen und Mal," which was prompted by your observations on cubism and was supposed to provide some basic principles for a theory of painting. Thus far, you have not mentioned it and it therefore occurred to me that you had not received it, although I could not imagine how this might have happened. But if you have received it, allow me to supplement it with the following important observation: from a human perspective, the draftsman's plane is horizontal; that of the painter is vertical.—You should soon receive a copy of my observations on concept and essence. In return, we are eagerly awaiting your translation and essay on the Lamentations, and I steadfastly hope that you still intend to let me know your thoughts on symbolic logic. On the other hand, for the time being you cannot count on my sending you the dubious philosophical jottings transcribed by my wife.[1] Before I send these off on their long journey, it is imperative that they be well-founded by considerations that, I admit, concern me intensely at the present. I cannot, however, predict the date they will be concluded—even if only in a makeshift way—because of my *total* isolation from anybody on the same wavelength and from you, Gerhard, the only person I can name who is. And before they are concluded, I must refrain from giving you any inkling of them in our letters, because this would not get us anywhere. Sooner or later I hope to be able to unbosom myself to you. Let me also note that, for my part, I am discontinuing our written discussion of the problem of identity: in fact, as we both constantly affirm, progress on this issue can be made only in conversation. These are not the only things, dear Gerhard, that make it necessary for me to return to the topic of the internal and spiritual side of the plight of our physical separation—or rather to broach the topic, in a certain sense, for the first time. To broach its spiritual, not technical, side.

In spite of the effort I made, I did not understand the sentence in your last letter in which you assert your claim to a mission. There is no one there (if I might be allowed to say this: and as far as Werner Kraft is concerned, I certainly have the right)—there is no one there for whom you would have to sacrifice yourself. This is simply the way I see the situation, and this is how it has to be seen. Today, as always, every ***human being*** has nothing but unvarnished spiritual life. How you behave and where you spend your time cannot be regulated and determined by practical pros and cons; the ultimate reasons, through which precisely how you behave and where you spend your time become communicable to your fellow human beings, reside in symbolic and manifest expression. What you are trying to express by where you spend your time is beyond me. I have to reject it. I have to reject it thrice over if you are sacrificing your means of expression and perhaps your life to a mission about which you say that it "may" be yours. It may be that I am exaggerating your words;

I admit that, under some circumstances, it is impossible to talk about this. That should not prevent me, however, from rejecting what you did in fact write about this in your last letter. I know you basically agree with me that, whatever form and force your assistance (your *existence*) has for Werner Kraft, it is governed by precisely this existence whose expression you define from within yourself in every respect.

I share your distrust of Borchardt, in spite of all my appreciation for, and even enchantment with, parts of his work. For that reason, I am eager for a resolution of the internal crisis that Borchardt, for his part, is supposed to effect in his relationship to Werner Kraft. Of course, neither you nor I can write,[2] and there was nothing left for me to do but to impress upon Kraft as urgently as possible that he should do so.

Because of a postal error, your last letter first went to Bonn. *Tristram Shandy* just arrived; the Yorik hasn't yet. You will shortly receive 65 marks, which I ask you to apply to the expenses you incurred on my account. After you get it, please let me know whether I am in the red or in the black. *Is Anatole France still alive?*—My dissertation is causing me horrible difficulty. The entirely hopeless situation of the contemporary university! My own thoughts have not yet matured. I do not want to produce any old historical study—even if someone would just offer me one! And even the only possible thing seems impossible, i.e. writing a few good, well-grounded pages under the supervision of a university professor here. I am writing a paper on Schleiermacher's *Psychologie* for a seminar[3] (I am losing time trying to establish myself in seminars here). This work of Schleiermacher's consists of notes and lectures that are part of his estate. It has no philosophical basis, and the only negatively interesting thing in it is his theory of language. I love Else-Schüler's poem "David und Jonathan."[4] The corresponding poem by Rilke[5] is—aside from everything else—bad.

We are experiencing very mild spring weather. Have you heard anything from Mr. Gutkind? He still has not responded to a rather long letter I wrote him.—I am really looking forward to the next installment of your last letter.

Best wishes from me and my wife.
Yours, Walter

1. This is apparently a reference to "Das Programm der kommenden Philosophie" [Program of the coming philosophy], which Scholem published in *Zeugnisse* (festschrift for Theodor Adorno, 1963) from a copy belonging to Dora Benjamin that he received after his arrival in Switzerland.
2. He means "to Rudolf Borchardt."
3. With Paul Häberlin.
4. In *Hebräische Balladen*.
5. In *Neue Gedichte*.

61. To Gerhard Scholem

[January 31, 1918]

Dear Gerhard,

It is sad but true that words fail me because of the sheer quantity of what I ought to say to you. It is becoming harder and harder for me to write. This time, the cause of my difficulty is the gratitude I must express and, if it were to be expressed in the way I would like, it could only be expressed with you actually here. Therefore, I prefer to remain silent and be quietly content with the happiness your news means to us (my wife and me). Now to your last letter with its query as to whether I consider ethics to be possible without metaphysics. It inspired thoughts in me that, once again, I do not yet consider myself capable of communicating to you. Even though it is painful, I will deny myself because I still cannot make up my mind to let go of anything that is much too amorphous. Rather, I will impose this silence on myself as a spur not to stop thinking about it until I am at the point where I can write you. There will, therefore, be nothing yet on the material reasons for my no. On the other hand, I think that, methodologically, the answer to this question should a priori always be no. If I were supposed to give the rational meaning I would attach to the word *metaphysical*—a provisional meaning until it is more closely defined—I, at least, would say the following: *metaphysical* defines that body of knowledge that a priori seeks to understand science as a sphere in the absolute divine context of order, whose highest sphere is doctrine and whose embodiment and first cause is God. It is also the knowledge that views the "autonomy" of science as reasonable and possible only within this context. For me, this is the a priori methodological basis for deeming ethics, and any other science, without metaphysics, i.e. outside of this postulated context, to be impossible. At this time, I will still say nothing about the profound material reasons for my no.

Here I am harvesting seminar laurels (*laurea communis minor*) with papers on Bergson and on a paragraph of Hegelian phenomenology, and I am doing this for an end that the means truly do *not* justify, and about whose viability I am not yet even sure. In the very near future, I want to speak with the professor[1] about a dissertation. In any case, next semester I hope to be able to work a bit more in fields that are more to my liking than those being plowed through at the university right now but which I just had to participate in once. Maybe I will be able to read *Sieben Bücher zur Geschichte des Platonismus,* a critique of Plato from a Christian viewpoint, by Heinrich von Stein, a professor at the University of Göttingen who died at a young age in the second half of the last century. The author is important and the introduction that I read contains some excellent things. The Hegel I have read, on the other hand, has so far totally repelled me. If we were to get into his work for just a short time, I think we would soon arrive at the spiritual physiognomy that peers out of it: that of an intellectual brute, a mystic of brute force, the worst sort there is: but a mystic, nonetheless.

It would not be any easier to see me if you came from Freiburg—as far as I can tell. Yet, to the extent it is possible, you must avoid entering the zone where you would be in danger of aerial attacks. When is your mother going? As far as we are concerned, the question[2] for you, now as before, is one of tenacity and prudence. We are happy to wait as long as we—and you—have hope.—I am reading *Penguin Island.* I have recently added some new things to my library, among others Stefan George's translation of the *Flowers of Evil* [*Les fleurs du mal*]; Rudolf Borchardt; Hugo v. Hofmannsthal; Schröder's *Hesperus,* an almanac that ought to be valued for Borchardt's contributions and detested for Schröder's; Baudelaire's *Spleen* [*Spleen de Paris*]; Baudelaire's *Artificial Paradise* [*Paradis artificiels*]; Charles-Louis Philippe's *Marie Donadieu,* an extremely important novel that I gave my wife for her birthday. If I read Anatole France,[3] sometime later you will have to read two or three novels by Charles-Louis Philippe (but in French!), and you surely will not come out the loser in this exchange.—You do have the small philosophical book containing the theses on identity in your safekeeping, don't you? What about "Zeichen und Mal"? Did you get it? And the Dostoyevsky? And the 65 marks?

That's all for today. In a few months you may be deluged by a flood of essays that are piling up. No one would be happier about this than I.

Best wishes.

Yours, Walter

P.S. Permit me to add a small picture gallery to the envelope.

1. Richard Herbertz.
2. Of a trip to Switzerland.
3. WB did this after constant urging by Scholem.

62. To Ernst Schoen

[End of 1917 or beginning of 1918]

Dear Mr. Schoen,

Please do not be angry at the lengthy interruption in my correspondence. I want to begin this letter by expressing my hope that you have fared well and that things have turned out better for you, during the time of my silence. You were often in our thoughts. We were extremely busy during this period and therefore I could not write *this* letter any earlier.

In both your last and next to last letters, you spoke about Jula's work.[1] I am responding to this only now because I see that the continuation of our correspondence depends on our being clear about this. I certainly believe that Jula is more or less clear in her own mind that, regardless of all attempts we (Jula, my wife, and I) have made to establish a harmonious and well-founded relationship with each other, were in vain [*sic*]. I believe that Jula is basically no less clear than we are that none of the three of us has truly lost anything by the unraveling of this relationship, as it has taken place in the mutual silence that has lasted so long. This is all I can tell you about this, whether in person or in writing; the only thing that bothers me is being aware that in this way you might learn something that you had not already heard from Jula.

I am finally in the position of being able to keep my promise and send you some of my work. If you are already familiar with my critique of Dostoyevsky's *Idiot,* there is all the more reason for me to ask you to accept this handwritten copy as a gift. I believe that the book itself must be of infinite significance for each of us and I, for my part, am happy if I have been able to convey this. Besides that, I am sending you a brief note on painting that is at such a preliminary stage that we would normally deal with its content only in conversation. I would be very pleased if, whenever it is convenient, you could send me your thoughts in response to these jottings—but only if this won't encroach on your current activity and thought, which are, no doubt, otherwise engaged. In view of the repellent phenomenon that, nowadays, inadequate attempts at a theoretical understanding of modern painting immediately degenerate into contrastive and progressive theories in regard to earlier great art, the primary issue for me was to suggest a generally valid conceptual basis for what we understand by painting. This being the case, I have disregarded modern painting, although these reflections were originally prompted by the false absolutizing of precisely that art. Regardless of this, however, I have been thinking for a long time about where free scope and opportunity for the development and greatness of basic "aesthetic" concepts might finally be found, and where they might be released from their wretched isolation (which in aesthetics is the equivalent of what in painting is mere artistry). I am also enclosing *Le Centaure* and some thoughts engendered in me by Hölderlin's powerful fragment "Das Belebende."[2] Please forgive me for sending everything at once but the whole thing is technically so complicated that it is better to take care of it all at once. I am sure I have already called your attention to Hölderlin's fragments, which appeared last year in the *Reich* under the title "Untreue der Weisheit." Have you read them? "Das Belebende" is the same kind of thing as these fragments and can be found in Hellingrath's first printing of the Pindar translations.

I have gotten to know this university and, since pretty much all universities will have the same attitude to what is essential in my work, I am thinking of getting my doctorate here, to the extent that it is possible to predict anything at all under circumstances that, even here, are becoming more difficult day by day. I visited Dr. [Anna] Tumarkin and told her of my intention, in a preliminary fashion, to treat Kant's history of philosophy systematically. I have attended her, Häberlin's, and Herbertz's[3] lectures and, as I might have predicted, find your silence about them totally justified. I am staking all my hopes on my own work. We are living in a very small apartment in a quiet street near the university. I have most of my books here; you probably know, however, about the sad state of the libraries.

Among other things, I am reading Jacob Burckhardt's *Age of Constantine the Great* [*Die Zeit Constantins des Großen*], an unbelievably splendid book. Unfortunately, the theater has nothing to offer, but from time to time there are good concerts.

Please write us soon about how you are doing. Sincere regards from me and my wife.

All the best.
Yours, Walter Benjamin

1. Jula Cohn was a sculptor.
2. In Hölderlin's *Werke*, edited by Hellingrath, 5:272–73.
3. WB finally received his doctorate under Richard Herbertz.

63. To Gerhard Scholem

February 1, 1918

Dear Gerhard,

The letter you sent special delivery on December 29, 1917, arrived today, after I posted a short letter to you yesterday evening. Now I will add a few things relating to your letter on this card. To begin with, let me ask again whether you have "Zeichen und Mal"? I cannot understand why, but it seems to have gotten lost. Miss Kraker's pronouncement truly delighted me. As far as I know, I have not seen her since my semester in Freiburg in 1913, nor she me. At that time she was a witness to the era in which a friend and I tried to appeal to the Freiburg students. It is the era that contains the deepest roots of the Youth Movement. She was a modest and passive participant in things, yet somehow seems to have a sense of what it was all about.—I can't say anything good about Miss Heymann.[1] For years she has been up to her neck in confusion. Things have gotten steadily worse with her; she seems to have nothing to hang on to and lacks any strength of her own. She is one of those young girls who demonstrate most clearly that only *their* husband, if they can find one, is able to help them. Moreover, they entice you to render all kinds of "help" that leads to nothing. Giving her my Hölderlin study was an instance of this kind of help; at that time she was in a much better frame of mind than when I spoke to her for the last time in Munich about one and a half years ago; that was awful.—I am very sorry to have caused you so much trouble with my inquiry about Barthel.[2] If I had thought about it, I would have had to arrive at the same thing you wrote me, but I did not have enough confidence to give it a try because I did not see that the matter could be disposed of in such an elementary manner. I am grateful to you for showing me where one stands with him. I told my wife about the whole thing and she also declared it to be nonsense. The notion of a finite cosmic *space* is absurd; Gutkind, however, occasionally spoke to me of the finitude of *fulfilled* cosmic space; maybe that is what's implied. This would be a factual question.

If you continue to be so open to the mathematical theory of truth (and perhaps to me), it should not concern me if you seem to be so closed to others. Two other books by Charles-Louis Philippe, *Le Père Perdrix* and *Marie Donadieu,* are artistically even more mature than *Bubu de Montparnasse*. I hope you read it in French? Schleiermacher is no fun, especially since what is at issue are posthumous lecture notes and dictated lectures. It was pure drudgery.—I will write about the "eternal task" in my next letter.—It is virtually impossible to gain any access to the philosophy of history using Kant's *historical* writings as a point of departure. It would be different if the point of departure were his ethics; even that is possible only within limits and Kant himself did not travel this path. To convince yourself of this, read *Ideas for a Universal History from a Cosmopolitan Point of View*. I may be able to write you about this sometime. I am not familiar with Rickert's big book,[3] but I know about his method: it is modern in the worst possible sense of the word, so to speak: modern *à tout prix*. All the best from me and my wife.

Yours, Walter

1. Alice Heymann (1890–1937), who later married the art historian Alfred Schmitz.
2. See letter 55.
3. *Über die Grenzen der naturwissenschaftlichen Begriffsbildung*.

64. To Gerhard Scholem

Locarno
February 23, 1918

Dear Gerhard,

Three years of our continuous yearning for sun have finally brought my wife and me here. You mustn't tell anyone we are here, because it is absolutely imperative that our parents not learn of our whereabouts in some roundabout way. Even this past summer did not provide us with the sun for which we yearned indescribably; the Engadine is at too great an altitude for it to be hot there. At the time, however, what we needed more than anything else was the intensity that emanates from this sublime landscape; we had to submit to a new tension if only not to collapse under the impression of an eternal release. These few words may already make comprehensible to you that my life here is fulfilled by the sonorous and liberated melody of the end of a great epoch in my life now behind me. The six years [that] have passed since I left school have constituted a single epoch, lived through at a monstrous pace, which for me contains an infinite amount of the past—in other words, of eternity. I am now looking at summer's nature, as I have not done since I was last in school—I also spent my last or next to last school vacation in the Engadine.

Now, on one of those days set aside for reviewing what is the same for me and what has changed, I receive your letter (that of February 1, 1918, which was again delayed by the censor), which touched my clarity-seeking spirit as being *infinitely* kindred. My very surroundings, which I do not want to leave at this time, prevent me from alluding to any single point of your letter, especially any with philosophical content; but I have never been more grateful than I was today for the tone of inner peace that is the mark of your letters, and most particularly of this letter. This may assure you that I also thoroughly understand the difficulty of writing, as well as the sense of your words. I am charmed by the style of your lines, i.e. the replete sense of responsibility, the clarity, and the restraint, precisely because it is thoroughly responsive to me. I recently read the following words in Goethe: "A real response is like a sweet kiss."

I must tell you that, in addition to several books that the southern climate here won't tolerate, however useful, indispensable, and good they may be, I have at least one book with me that is on excellent terms with the climate: Goethe's *Maxims and Reflections* [*Maximen und Reflexionen*]. Or, to be more precise, I have part of them in the unsurpassed and rigorously philological Weimar Sophien edition. Detailed involvement with them reinforces me in the old opinion that ours is the first generation to [confront?] Goethe critically, and is consequently grateful to succeed him. The romantics were much too close to Goethe to grasp more than some *tendencies* of his work: above all, they did not understand the *moral* dimension with which his *life* struggled, and they were ignorant of his historical isolation. But I am also becoming convinced that Goethe—at least in his later years—was an extremely pure person who let no lie cross his lips and into whose pen no lie flowed.

At first it was cool here—now it is hot and summery. The culture and language of the region is Italian. Palms and laurel grow in the gardens. There is still snow on the high mountains but there is no doubt that it is melting off day by day. On a steep cliff above Locarno is a famous pilgrimage site: the abbey church of the Madonna del Sasso (on the cliff). The church is a dainty example of Italian baroque, with a facade painted using perspective and color in a playful manner. It contains simply extraordinary small votive pictures as might have been painted by peasants commissioned by people who had been healed and redeemed, and which are among the most beautiful examples of religiously or cultically motivated folk art, which is now being rediscovered by new European painters. What is most eye-catching is a remarkable Madonna. It is completely static and makes an eerie impression: The mother bends down toward her swollen belly; her expression is very somnolent and soulless; she becomes visible as if against her will, and bears signs of physical suffering. I suspect this is related to the primeval, prehistoric ideal of beauty as embodied in a swollen-bellied, fat woman, and which must be mythologically determined in a way with which I am not familiar. (According to the genius[1] this ideal is related to the role the liver plays in mythology.)

I do not want to write about the *Mal* now and I will also put off some other things until later. This letter was intended only to communicate what ought to be communicated from here, and includes the most sincere regards and wishes from me and my wife, which are meant to reach you wherever you may be.

Yours, Walter

1. Felix Noeggerath.

65. To Gerhard Scholem

[March 30, 1918]

Dear Gerhard,

I have been at a loss at how to respond to your three letters dated from February 23 to March 15, and have delayed confirming the arrival of the Lamentations till now. Why is that? It was my attempt to get away from everything for a few weeks in Locarno: to spend lovely days in the sun, bad days in all kinds of diversions. I now notice that you have not even received the card from Locarno you asked for, because I simply am unable to write cards to you; I would have enclosed one in a letter. Since we prolonged our stay as long as possible, after a few days of rain we got to feel the first breath of spring in the valley, and I can't tell you how wonderful it was. We lived inexpensively and pleasantly and the only cosmopolitan aspect of our stay was that quite a few young people I know unexpectedly showed up and we basically were unable to get along with them.

Mrs. Lasker-Schüler was also here. Suspecting that there will be a lot to worry and preoccupy me upon my return, I prolonged the trip as long as I could: and I see that the first confirmation of this fear is that we have been given notice to vacate our apartment at a particularly inconvenient time. It is not absolutely sure we will have to do this, but the threat that we may have to is extremely unpleasant because there is an unbelievable shortage of apartments in Bern (as in Zurich), and furnished apartments are practically impossible to find at a price I can afford. I would leave Bern, however, only if I were absolutely forced to, because I am finally working on my doctorate. Once I have made some headway on the dissertation, it would be easier to leave. Even under the best of circumstances, this is still a few months off; nonetheless, winter in the country continues to be very lonely. I am waiting for my professor[1] to suggest a topic; in the meantime, I have come upon one myself. Only since romanticism has the following view become predominant: that a *work* of art in and of itself, and without reference to theory or morality, can be understood in contemplation alone, and that the person contemplating it can do it justice. The relative autonomy of the *work* of art vis-à-vis art, or better, its exclusively transcendental dependence on art, has become the prerequisite of romantic art criticism. I would undertake to prove that, in this regard, Kant's aesthetics constitute the underlying premise of romantic art criticism.

I will intentionally avoid going any further into your question regarding the "eternal task." It too is one of those questions that cannot really be dealt with in letters—above all, not in this letter, which not only has to serve as a response to three of your letters but may for some time have to take the place of others that should follow if, as may be the case, external circumstances make it impossible for me to write any more extensive and substantial letters. For the time being I will not be taking a class on differential calculus. I will instead concentrate all my energy on finishing my doctorate, i.e. on starting my dissertation. Mathematics and any further grappling with Kant and Cohen have to be put off. The development of my philosophical ideas has reached a crucial stage. As difficult as this might be for me, I have to leave it at its current stage in order to be able to devote myself to it completely and with complete freedom after I have taken my examination. If obstacles to the completion of my doctorate should crop up, I will take that to mean that I should work on my own ideas.

After half a year of frequently interrupted reading, I finished Harnack's history of dogma here in Locarno. You can congratulate me for this twice over: for having done the work, and for having finished it. Once the book has been closed, the benefits derived from this kind of reading are inestimable. To give only one example, I realized how ignorance, among other things, is a strong source of the contemporary neo-Catholic trend, particularly as it has affected intelligent Jews. It is obviously an expression of the romantic movement, which is, of course—I do not know whether I have already given you my view on this—one of the most powerful contemporary movements. Like the romantic Catholicism of an earlier period, it has aspects of both power politics and ideology (Adam Müller, Friedrich Schlegel). While the first has remained unproductive (Scheler represents it; Franz Blei and—even if not as a Catholic—Walther Rathenau, among many others, belong to it), the second has evolved from Schlegel's lethargic and less defined attitude into anarchism through the absorption of social elements (Leonhard Frank, [Ludwig] Rubiner). What I will be able to read in the near future is still uncertain.—I have *much* to say about Goethe—as you might imagine from my biting review of the Gundolf book.[2] I am waiting to hear what your judgment will be.

I read your essay,[3] the one you sent my wife, three times. The third time, we read it together. My wife plans to thank you for it herself. I personally owe you special thanks because, without your knowing that I wrestled with the same problem two years ago, you have made a significant contribution to clarifying it for me. After having read your essay, the problem now appears to me as follows: on the basis of my nature as a Jew, the inherent code, the "completely autonomous order," of the lament and of mourning, became obvious to me. Without reference to Hebrew literature, which, as I now know, is the proper subject of such an analysis, I applied the following question to the *Trauerspiel* in a short essay entitled "Die Bedeutung der Sprache in Trauerspiel und Tragödie": "How can language as such fulfill itself in mourning and how can it be the expression of mourning?" In so doing, I arrived at an insight that approximates yours in its particulars and in its entirety. At the same time, however, I wore myself out to no avail studying a relationship the actual circumstances of which I am only now beginning to divine. For in German the lament appears in its full linguistic glory only in the *Trauerspiel,* which, in terms of what the word suggests, borders on being inferior to tragedy. I was unable to reconcile myself to this and did not understand that this ranking is just as legitimate in German as its opposite probably is in Hebrew. From your essay, I now understand that the question as I posed it and which concerned me at that time must be asked on the basis of the Hebrew lament. In any case, before I have a command of Hebrew I can neither acknowledge your comments as a solution nor tackle the problem on the basis of your translations (which would probably be impossible anyway). In contradistinction to your point of departure, mine had only the advantage of pointing me, from the very start, to the fundamental antithesis of mourning and tragedy, which, to conclude from your essay, you have not yet recognized. I would also have an awful lot of comments to make on your essay which in a letter, however, would necessarily lose themselves in endless subtlety—because of terminological difficulties. I think the concluding section dealing with the lament and magic is really good. On the other hand, I openly admit that the theory of the lament in this form still seems to be burdened by some basic lacunae and vagueness. Your (and my) terminology has not as yet been sufficiently worked out to be able to resolve this question. Let me specifically note that I continue to doubt the clear relationship between lament and mourning in the sense that every pure act of mourning must lead to a lament. The result is a series of such difficult questions that we really must forgo any consideration of them in writing.—Just a short word on your translation. We—my wife and I—have the same thing to say about it that we previously said about your translation of the Song of Solomon. In the final analysis, your translation (of course, I am unable to judge its relationship to the Hebrew, but I have total confidence in you in this regard) has the character of a study in terms of its relationship to German. The issue in your translation is apparently not, as it were, to save a text for German, but rather to relate it to German in terms of what is correct. In this respect, you do not receive any inspiration from German. I, of course, cannot judge whether the Lamentations can be translated into this language in a way that transcends such a relationship to German, and your work seems to preclude it.

I am slightly acquainted with David Baumgardt[4] from Berlin. I always found him very pleasant. But I have not formed any opinion on his particular philosophical capabilities. At some point I will be able to tell you more about Simon Guttmann (maybe when we are both old—should we live to be old!) than about anyone else in the world, except perhaps my wife. Mr. Robert Jentzsch also belonged to the same circle.[5] This young man, who several years ago qualified as a privatdocent in mathematics at the University of Berlin, is already supposed to be famous as a mathematician on the basis of his habilitation dissertation—it was translated by the academy [?]. I know him slightly too. Have you heard of him or can you find out something about him (he is a soldier in the field)? I am very interested in this.[6] Now to two other requests. A letter I wrote to the genius has either not arrived or has not been answered. (The only address I have for him is very old and I have no idea where he is now.) I am extremely eager to see his dissertation now (it must have been published around October 1917) and cannot easily turn to him. Might I ask you to write to the warden of the University of Erlangen, enclosing a stamped self-addressed envelope, and find out from him whether and where the dissertation of Mr. Felix Noeggerath, who graduated from Erlangen in October or November of 1916 with a degree in philosophy, was published. And whether he might know this gentleman's current address. I would be very grateful if you would make this inquiry for me because I would rather not make it under my own name. Finally, I would also like to request the following: that you not order the Langenscheidt translations of Tibullus and Propertius that I put down on my last book list or, if the order has already been placed, that you cancel it, but only if this were to cause you *absolutely* no trouble. You see, I have located them here at a used bookstore, but do not want to buy them before hearing from you—if possible, by return mail—as to whether they have already been ordered in Germany. Also, please let me know anything and everything concerning the books I have ordered. Thanks again for your trouble. (My order for the Langenscheidt translations of Catullus and Pindar still stands and, of course, I want only translations of these authors that appear together under one cover. When they appear separately, these translations do not run to one or several volumes, and I would therefore have to put up with other authors' being mixed in. This also applies to Tibullus and Propertius, should you not be able to cancel the order.) I am familiar with the fairy tale about Fanferlieschen Schönefüßchen[7] but no longer remember which it is of the many fairy tales I have read by him.—My wife will personally deal with the medical information you are providing her.—Did you get the papers from Mr. Kraft? I wrote him. What is the situation concerning your friend's arrival? He will be very welcome.

What you wrote is almost word for word what my friend told me about Buber after his one conversation with him.[8]

This letter is not as totally lacking in coherence as it might seem. It has been dictated by the need to give answers without raising new questions so that, should our correspondence have to be suspended for a while on my part, I will not leave you with too much unsettled business. My greatest regret is that I am still unable to pass on to you any of the philosophical dynamics of my thought; but this is incompatible with a letter. My wife still plans to write you. Please do not let me wait too long for news. My very best wishes,

Yours, Walter

1. Richard Herbertz.

2. The main parts of this review were incorporated into the essay on Goethe's *Elective Affinities* (*Schriften* 1:123–201).

3. "Über Klage und Klagelied" (unpublished).

4. Scholem had become acquainted with Baumgardt in Erfurt. He was later a privatdocent at the University of Berlin.

5. The reference is to the "neopathetic cabaret" around Georg Heym, Erwin Löwensohn, Kurt Hiller, et al.

6. One day before receiving this letter, Scholem (who was studying mathematics at the time) informed WB that Jentzsch had died in the war and told him the news of Hermann Cohen's death.

7. By Clemens Brentano.

8. Scholem had written a vehement diatribe against the cult of experience in Buber's writings from these years.

66. To Gerhard Scholem

April 11, 1918

Dear Gerhard,

Let me exchange news of life for news of two deaths,[1] the second of which I was still unaware and which deeply distressed me. When I found your letter, I had just come home from the clinic where, this morning, my wife gave birth to a son.[2] Both are doing well. Except for the baby's grandparents, you are the first one to hear the news. Best wishes on behalf of the baby and his mother.

Yours, Walter

1. Of Hermann Cohen and Robert Jentzsch.
2. Stefan, died in London on February 6, 1972.

67. To Gerhard Scholem

[April 17, 1918]

Dear Gerhard,

Many thanks from both of us for your good wishes; they just arrived. My wife and the baby are both doing well. We named him Stefan Rafael. The middle name is after one of my wife's grandfathers who died shortly before Stefan was born. Tomorrow for the first time Dora is supposed to get out of bed for a while. Among the most wonderful things to see is what I have observed these past few days: how a father immediately perceives such a small human being as a *person,* in such a way that the father's own superiority in all matters having to do with existence seems very insignificant in comparison. There is a very famous letter in which Lessing says something very much like that.

I am reading a whole *stack* of enormously interesting things and there is more of the same stacked up on my desk; among the former is the Schlegel brothers' *Athenaeum,* a first edition I borrowed (!). Further, an extremely exciting, almost too exciting, and very well documented book by Bernoulli, *Franz Overbeck und Friedrich Nietzsche*. It contains everything relevant to Nietzsche's life, including much that does not appear anyplace else. In addition, Heinrich von Stein's *Platonismus*. Among the latter (i.e. books that are still on my desk) is F. Schlegel's *Philosophie der Sprache und des Wortes,* a collection of his very last lectures (since by this time I have become something of a specialist on the late Schlegel, I will be able to wind up this difficult vocation after having read this book).—At this very moment, I am thinking about many things: I am still unable to write about what I am thinking about most, and I do not yet want to write about what I am thinking about least. At some point you will receive a *bundle* of manuscripts—although, for the most part, they do not exist yet.—Were you able to cancel the order for the Catullus-Tibullus-Propertius translations at Langenscheidt's? What's the status of this? Please let me know very soon.

A sincere and urgent request: my innumerable requests to Werner Kraft that he send me a copy of the letter[1] I wrote him from St. Moritz, which contains my comments on "greatness," have proven futile. I now *really* need these comments but do not want to approach him about them from here. But, if it is too much trouble for him to copy it, may I ask you to please transmit my request, emphatically, quickly, and urgently, that he relinquish the original letter, temporarily if need be, and send it to me by registered mail. I really need it. Many thanks! Have you written Kraft about the birth of my son? If not, please don't; if you have, let me know so that I can write him myself—you see, basically I would rather not encroach on his self-prescribed silence with anything extraneous. Do you happen to know of anything he might like? We would like to send him a book anonymously.—Please write, and really soon.

Most sincerely.
Yours, Walter

1. These comments about Stifter are included in letter 69.

68. To Ernst Schoen

[Bern]
[May 1918]

Dear Mr. Schoen,

I have put off responding to your two letters for so long that I now have to provide you with a response at a particularly busy and harried time. Harried from without, in that the bleak housing situation here is forcing us to move in fourteen days.[1] This is bound up with a number of other unpleasant circumstances. Harried from within by a profusion of duties, because they prevent me from giving completely free rein to my inhibited need to express my own thoughts. In part, my thoughts are still too undeveloped; they constantly scatter before me and those I grasp require the most exact grounding before I would allow myself to express them. For me, certain—as it were, revolutionary—thoughts bear within themselves an urgent need to study their great adversaries very thoroughly so that it is possible to remain steadfastly objective when expounding them. The greatest adversary of these thoughts is always Kant. I have become engrossed in his ethics—it is unbelievable how necessary it is to track down this *despot,* to track down his mercilessly philosophizing spirit which *has philosophized* certain insights that are among the reprehensible ones to be found in ethics in particular. Especially in his later writings, he drives and senselessly whips his hobbyhorse, the logos.

Thus far I have been unable to complete a very important study of epistemology. It has been lying fallow for months. My professor approved my dissertation topic, and he did so most readily. It goes something like this: the philosophical foundations of romantic art criticism. I do have some things to say on this topic, but the source material is proving to be terribly resistant. If [I] want to wrest anything of a more profound nature from it and a dissertation requires you to indicate sources, however, that are almost impossible to find for certain of romanticism's most profound tendencies. I am referring to its historically and fundamentally important congruence with Kant, which under certain circumstances might prove impossible to demonstrate in "dissertationlike" format. On the other hand, if I can do it, this work will bring me the internal anonymity I must secure for myself whenever I write to achieve such ends. I do want to get my doctorate, and if this should not happen, or not happen yet, it can only be the expression of my *deepest* inhibitions. I intend to remain silent about how many obvious inhibitions there are, and it is also unnecessary to tell you about this.—Let me take this opportunity to ask you to send me, in a series of letters, the quotations from the compilation of fragments[2] you have (perhaps divided among three to five letters so that they do not get too long). I ask your forgiveness for the immense trouble this request will put you through. The compilation is indispensable for my work. It is awful that I must also impose on your valuable time.

In both your letters, you refer to two very important things upon which I have deliberated for a long time and which have been subjects of an ongoing conversation I have conducted with Mr. Scholem, who in the meantime has shown up here,[3] i.e. Stifter and Borchardt. I do not want to write you anything about the former today because I have already written something substantial about him. When I get a chance, I will expand on it and then be able to send it to you separately. It would be difficult for you to have a clear notion of the mental images that the name Borchardt conjures up in me. He is an integral part of the unhappy life of a young Jew who is close to me and who is currently a soldier.[4] Mr. Scholem (who got to know him through me while I was here) and I share the grief of knowing that he has been forsaken in Germany. This individual, who honored and honors Borchardt with unrivaled enthusiasm, forced me to come to terms with Borchardt in the most exacting manner and, beyond that, in some respects provided me with an image of Borchardt's nature. Consequently, Borchardt has been on my mind for more than two years. I know his poems and "Villa," his things in *Hesperus* (and the speeches on the war), and finally the famous polemic against the George circle in the *Süddeutsche Monatschefte*. In order to speak about him in a way that is thorough and lucid, I would have to reach far and say things for which there is no room here, in every sense of the word. Therefore, permit me to share with you in only a very suggestive way why I reject Borchardt as a person in spite of all the respect I have for the "qualities" of his work (for he has traits that, in others, could be all there is, nothing more). Borchardt is no longer tragic and problematic to me, no less than Walther Rathenau, even if he is not base like Rathenau. As for the rest, however, they are alike, above all in the single characteristic that defines Borchardt's moral nature, in his *will* to falsehood. He has a heart of stone. Today there is no better example than he of the terribly deceptive nature of isolated instances of beauty, in which his work abounds. As a whole, however, this body of work proves to be an attempt to gain the following for its creator: rank, in intellectual terms; power, in intellectual terms; greatness, in intellectual terms. He consumes himself in portraying for the Germans a type that does not exist among them, that cannot yet exist among them, that they may not achieve through false pretences, and that he senses is a future prospect without comprehending it: the type is that of the public and responsible man of the people, the appointed guardian of the people's intellectual and linguistic heritage. (I am unable to say here what is a future prospect and what is misunderstood about this notion. You will have your own view. To the extent it was possible at the time, he seems to have found a precursor to his aspiration in Jacob Grimm.) His works are the high-handed means to this end, and not a service. What you also find in him is the "inversion of an idea," which, in his last letter to me, Mr. Scholem declared to be characteristic of modern books; objective mendacity, as I call it. In Borchardt, it is directed at history, and it in turn rests on a perversion that seems to me to have become canonical for our time, [on] the misrepresentation of the medium as the voice. He turns history, the medium of the creative person, into the voice of the creative person. This cannot be easily presented, and for precisely that reason Borchardt may today be the only remaining worthy object of *crushing* (the most merciless) polemic (the kind he magnificently attempted against the George circle), if everything fundamentally polemical were not nowadays rejected. At the very core of

Borchardt's work, you encounter a gesture that can shelter and distinguish the human being, but that is an illegitimate mask for the poet, or else his work relies on composing such a gesture. He has placed himself on top of a tower of lies so that he can be seen by the mendacious masses of his time. If I understand you correctly, this feeling is very clearly heralded in your lines.

Please feel free to read my essay on language. I have another request to make of you. In *Kreis der Liebe,*[5] which I could not make use of because of its handwriting, there is a ghazal by Platen. I have now bought Schlösser's (unfortunately incomplete) edition of his poems. Incredibly, the ghazal does not seem to be included in it. What number is it? Where did you get it? Could you send me a copy of it when you have a chance? I am sorry I am unable to comply with your request. We do not have a photo of my wife and me on hand and I am sure [you] will understand if we think your request is not a valid reason to have our pictures taken. Finally, please forgive me for the fact that, while making claims on your kindness and meticulousness in such an important matter as the safekeeping of my papers, I have to make this request belatedly, after Mr. Scholem had made it on my behalf. The entire transfer[6] had to proceed so quickly because of Mr. Scholem's imminent departure. On the other hand, I was still uncertain whether the transfer was necessary at all, so that I first had to wait and see how things turned out. It was especially unfortunate that I had to ask you to send me something even before I could get your consent to the transfer. I hope you will view what I did as excusable due to the circumstances, and I also hope you will do me this *great* service, which is what the safekeeping of my manuscripts means to me.

As you can imagine, I am now studying romanticism and specifically, in addition to reading the *Athenaeum,* I am working on A. W. Schlegel, who so far is the romantic I know least well. Do you know what amazes me about the critical writings of the romantics? It is their great and noble humanity. They have a command of the caustic language needed to take on what is base, but they also have at their command a wonderful generosity of spirit when faced with unfortunates. Goethe and Schiller seem to have been unable to achieve this to the same degree in their criticism. By comparison, A. W. Schlegel's review of Bürger and Schleiermacher's review of Garve[7] are wonderful. In their criticism, moreover, again in complete contrast to Goethe, these romantics have always turned out to be right in the end and therefore have always been right. If you have the time and already know Nietzsche rather well, as well as his correspondence with Overbeck (who is very important), then, but only then, you should probably read C. A. Bernoulli's *Franz Overbeck und Friedrich Nietzsche.* In the final analysis, this book is only a two-volume brochure, but it contains much interesting material. S. Friedländer called Elisabeth Förster-Nietzsche "the notorious sister of her world-renowned brother."

My brother is in a German military hospital, wounded; apparently he has a rather serious belly wound. My wife and I most sincerely return your and Jula's greetings. My wife will write about Busoni later; we heard him the day before yesterday.

Yours, Walter Benjamin

Sincere thanks for your best wishes.

P.S. I feel compelled to express myself more clearly about Borchardt: it is incorrect to say that his work only has "qualities." The *Germania* translation—to the extent I know it—is probably a milestone in the history of the German language's relationship to Latin. It is also incorrect that a will to falsehood is central to him. Rather, he is an adventurer who lusts after the *highest* laurels and who places enormous ability at the service of an absolute will to power. Finally, in an era in which the ultimate absorption and contemplation makes you invisible, he is someone who, for the sake of being visible, distorts and reflects that absorption and contemplation even in the face of the abyss. He is not himself the lie, but the lie takes hold of him each time he defines his relation to the public. He may leave behind much that is great, but it will remind us of the story of the man who wanted to find gold but found porcelain—in other respects, it is not at all a pretty story in terms of its "moral." Searching for fool's gold, something of the sort could befall Borchardt, but since he wants to be a poet, his impure will is the greatest barrier to his possibilities: he will surely not leave any work behind; he will leave behind discoveries, land that has been made arable, things he has discovered of a philological, historical, and technical nature. It is not the lie that is operative in him, but rather what you yourself clearly allude to, impurity.

1. To Muri bei Bern.
2. WB had put together a compilation of Schlegel's and Novalis's fragments in Dachau in the spring of 1917. They were in Ernst Schoen's safekeeping at the time.
3. Scholem was in Bern from the beginning of May until the fall of 1919.
4. Werner Kraft.
5. Poems by Ernst Schoen (unpublished?).
6. Of WB's papers that were with Scholem.
7. In *Athenaeum* 3 (1800), pp. 129ff.

69. To Ernst Schoen

Muri bei Bern
June 17, 1918

Dear Mr. Schoen,

I am very much in your debt for the great trouble and care you took in transcribing the fragments and notes that have now been in my possession for some time. As a token of my gratitude, please accept a copy of both my brief notes on Stifter that are enclosed. Had I not wanted to do you a good turn, I might well not have decided to give you the two pieces for, you see, one of them is only an excerpt from a letter, while the second was originally meant only as a reminder to me of a task I had set myself, an extensive critique of Stifter's style. But I am sending them to you today because it might be a long time before I will be in a position to add anything to what is enclosed (it will be eminently possible to make the good elements of his style just as comprehensible as the bad ones, based on my observations in II). I used my good stationery for the transcription and hope that it will not get such a terrible going over. This is how most letters from Germany arrive, doused with the censor's disinfectant. Since I am now engaged in expressing my sincere gratitude, I would like to return to the gift you gave me for my last birthday in order to tell you that the Guérin book, bound in blue morocco, is one of the most beautiful volumes in my library. I am busy building the library, as best I can. As it turned out, my inner need to have a library (indeed, the mere possibility of being able to have one) chronologically coincided with the extraordinary financial and material difficulties of acquiring one. I have been zealously engaged in building a library for only a little more than two years and am gradually daring to look around for one book or another among those that are intrinsically the most difficult to get. Now is the bleakest time to do this because they have become investments for the rabble. Thus I must do without many books that were affordable a few years ago (when, by the way, I did not have the money to buy them) and that I would now like to own. Perhaps you have heard of the Piloty auction in Munich (a first edition of *Der siebente Ring* went for over 400 marks—I had bid 75 on it, and Alfred [Cohn] bought it for 45 several years ago). My book dealer is just now sending me the only book I succeeded in getting, the correspondence between Goethe and Knebel. Nonetheless, you would see that I have some nice items even now, and I hope to be able soon to combine my wife's library, which is still in Seeshaupt, with the books I have here. I now have most of my books from Germany with me, or at least the better ones. But so many of the really important books I have been ordering from Germany are unavailable, to say nothing of antiquarian books. I intend to write you more about this, my latest acquisitions, at an opportune time if it won't bore you. I really do like to talk about them.

On the other hand, I don't have anything to report about my projects today, and may not have for some time to come. For some time now, I have been reading Catullus with my wife during my evening leisure hours, and we intend to stick with it and later move on to Propertius. There is nothing more salutary than reading the ancient poets to escape the errors in the canonical view of modern aesthetic concepts, in the modern understanding of inspiration, in lyric poetry—in a certain sense, reading the Latins may be even more salutary than reading the Greeks. I borrowed from the library an edition that had been prepared and printed in Paris for the dauphin Louis XV, and has *annotationes* and an *interpretatio* for every poem, the second of which is a strangely clumsy paraphrase of the poem's content in bad Latin.

I hear that Borchardt has published an index of his completed unpublished works in the first issue of *Dichtung*. (I have had a look at it.) An acquaintance made the most fitting pronouncement on it—the index has various sections: translation, drama, poetry, prose, philosophy, politics, etc.—"The 'letters' section is missing." You wrote about [Heinrich] Mann. Are you familiar with *Die Armen*? With this book, he (like his brother with *Gedanken im Kriege*) has given a tribute to our epoch that requires him to be counted among its servants. A book of unprecedented immaturity and carelessness. Maybe you have noticed that my inquiry about the Platen poem was based on my strange misunderstanding that the ghazal in *Kreis der Liebe* was by Platen himself (and that you had inserted it, as it were, as an extravagant act of homage). Now that I know that yours is a paraphrase whose beautiful conclusion I remembered and sought in vain in Platen's works, I have yet another request: send me a copy of *your* poem. Many thanks for your last beautiful poem. My wife and I send you and Jula our most sincere regards and wishes and I, for my part, must once again express my gratitude for the fragments.

Yours, Walter Benjamin

Stifter[1]

I

One delusion about Stifter seems extremely dangerous to me because it leads to error in one's basic metaphysical convictions about what is essential to people in their relationship to the world. There is no doubt that Stifter produced truly wonderful nature descriptions and that he also had wonderful things to say about human life at a standstill, before it has unfolded as fate, namely about children, like in *Bergkristall*. But he himself once voiced his colossal error without recognizing it as such in the prologue to *Bunte Steine*, where he writes about greatness and smallness in the world, and seeks to represent this relationship as deceptive and trivial, even relative. In fact, he lacks a sense for how elemental relationships between human beings and the world are purified and justified: in other words, a sense of justice in the most sublime meaning of this word. While I was tracking down the way he unfurls the *fate* of his characters in his various books, in each instance, in *Abdias, Turmalin, Brigitta* and in an episode from *Die Mappe meines Urgroßvaters,* I found the other side, the shadowy and dark side of this restriction to the small things in life: in that he can by no means resign himself to or satisfy himself with just describing them, but takes pains to introduce this simplicity into the large context of fate as well. However, it necessarily has a totally different simplicity as well as purity, that is to say, one that is simultaneous with greatness, or better, with justice. And as a consequence, a rebellion and eclipse of nature, so to speak, takes place in Stifter's works and turns into something extremely horrible and demonic, and thus enters into his female characters (Brigitta, the colonel's wife). There nature, as almost perverse and cleverly concealed demonic nature, sustains the innocent appearance of simplicity. Stifter knows nature, but his knowledge of the boundary between nature and fate is very shaky and he draws it with a feeble hand, as, for example, in the almost embarrassing conclusion of *Abdias*. Only the loftiest internal sense of justice can provide certainty as to this boundary. In Stifter, however, a spasmodic impulse sought another way to bind the moral world and fate to nature. This way seemed simpler but in truth was subhumanly demonic and spectral. The truth of the matter is that it is a secret bastardization. Upon close inspection, this uncanny characteristic can be found everywhere Stifter becomes "interesting" in a specific sense. Stifter has a dual nature; he has two faces. In him, the impulse of purity has at times become detached from the desire for justice; it has lost itself in what is small, only to emerge uncannily and hypertrophically (this is possible!) in what is great as undifferentiated purity and impurity.

There is no final and metaphysically permanent purity without a struggle to behold the loftiest and most extreme legal principles, and you should not forget that Stifter was ignorant of this struggle.

II

He can create only on the basis of what is visual. This does not mean, however, that he reproduces only what is visible, for as an artist he has style. The problem of his style is simply how he grasps the metaphysically visual sphere of all things. To begin with, the fact that he lacks any sense for revelation that must be *heard,* i.e. that lies in the metaphysically acoustic sphere, is related to this fundamental characteristic. Furthermore, this explains the main characteristic of his writings: quiet. For quiet is first and foremost the absence of every acoustic sensation.

The language spoken by Stifter's characters is ostentatious. It is language used to display feelings and thoughts in dead space. He completely lacks the ability to represent, by whatever means, "emotional distress," which is something human beings seek to express primarily in language. The demonic that characterizes his writings to a greater or lesser degree is based on this inability. It reaches its apparent peak where he feels his way forward on secret paths because he is unable to find obvious deliverance in the liberating utterance. He is spiritually mute, which is to say that his essence lacks contact with the universal essence, language, from which speaking derives.

1. The first of these notes is taken from WB's (lost) letter to Werner Kraft in the summer of 1917. A transcription of part of it that is preserved evidences few stylistic changes.

70. To Ernst Schoen

[July 31, 1918]

Dear Mr. Schoen,

Many thanks for your best wishes. My birthday provides me with a good opportunity to talk about books again. This is because my wife gave me a small library—not that the books had been lined up in a small bookcase, but they did fill one. The first thing you need to know is that, like a true book collector, I have—at least—carved out an area of specialization for myself. My primary consideration in doing this was what I already had and what I could afford. It is an area that, even today, is not of general interest to collectors, and thus one in which a lucky find is still possible (as I, in fact, made a short time ago to my indescribable delight). The area in question is antiquarian children's books and fairy tales, as well as beautiful legends. The bulk of the collection comes from a massive raid I made on my mother's library just in the nick of time. This was also the library of my early childhood. And thus I was given some fairy tales on this occasion: Andersen's, in the relatively good edition just published by Kiepenheuer; Hauff's, in an edition of his collected works. I may have them bound separately. Above all, however, Brentano's, in a rare first edition of 1846. I received the rest of Brentano's writings in the seven-volume collected works published by his brother Christian, the only edition except for one currently being spawned by Georg Müller, along with many others. Except for the fairy tales and *Godwi,* it has all the essential things. I also received the three small volumes of the *Bambocciaden* by the romantic litterateur and linguist Bernhardi, one of the rarest, even if not the most sought after, romantic books, which I have been trying to get for a long time. I still have not read it. Now, having received *Three Tales* [*Trois contes*] and *The Temptation* [*La tentation*], I have all of Flaubert's novels except *Salammbô, Carnet d'un fou* (that is the title, isn't it?), and *Novembre.* A good edition of Eckermann, the Insel edition of the *Decameron,* and Aretino's erotic work in a French translation. Further, a small book of reminiscences about Baudelaire, including anecdotes from his life and a lot of pictures of him and his friends. In a few years I will come to know what some of these books mean to me; in some instances, it may take a very long time. First they will be deposited, as it were, in the wine cellar, buried in the library: I am not touching them. Among other reasons, because I am familiar with the notion of being an exile in a region where I would be dependent on my library. Then I would get to know them. I am reading only Andersen, who is giving me the craving to fathom the nature of sentimentality. There are very few good things compared to how much really perverse stuff there is, but the good and the bad seem to me to be related in a curiously intimate way.

Whenever possible, I read books I borrow from the Bern library which, at least for my areas of interest, is very inadequate. I am currently busy again doing research for my dissertation and I am, of course, studying Goethe's theory of art. I am unable to say anything about it in this letter because it is too far off the topic, but I am discovering some very important things in it. Of course, it is terra incognita. While doing some reading for my dissertation today, I happened to come across the book by a Mrs. Luise Zurlinden:[1] *Gedanken Platons in der deutschen Romantik.* The horror that grips you when women want to play a crucial role in discussing such matters is indescribable. This contribution is truly base. Her evaluation of the romantics, especially of the Schlegel brothers and most particularly of Wilhelm (who surely was not as significant as Friedrich), is also symptomatic of the shamefulness of the principle underlying the systematic study of literature. Some romantic scholarship was certainly unproductive, even more unproductive than that of our own time; but shamelessness in scholarship is a modern phenomenon. Thus, contemporary experts on principle hold translation to be an inferior type of productivity (because they of course do not feel comfortable until they have classified everything according to the crudest criteria) and they consequently dare to speak of the "adoption of others' sentiments" in reference to the achievement represented by Wilhelm Schlegel's translations. This tone has become commonplace.

Your inquiry about how I am doing and about my relationship to the individuals you mentioned (with the exception of Barbizon) can be answered in a letter only with a brief categorical sentence. What I could say about them (but prefer not to) cannot *even be hinted at* in a letter: they do not exist for me, and even if each one of them in his own way has brought this about, it is precisely this lack of any relationship that makes this a matter of indifference to me. I maintain superficial contact with Barbizon.

With very few exceptions, the relationships I had maintained with my contemporaries have come to an end.

[. . .]

My most sincere thanks for the poems you sent me. It may be a very long time before I can send you something of mine again, because at the moment I envision only longer projects coming up in the near future—please let me hear from you soon. I hope you are well. My wife also sends her regards.

Yours, Walter Benjamin

1. Leipzig, 1910.

71. To Gerhard Scholem

Bönigen
September 18, 1918

Dear Gerhard,

What "approximate time span" am I supposed to give you? That of your trip? But you yourself are limiting that to approximately one week and, thus far, I have formed no clearer picture of what it will be like. Please be sure to get here by the 26th because I do not want to put off our ascent of the Faulhorn for too long. It is not yet certain how much longer the Faulhorn hotel, where we may have to spend the night—this is, of course, unlikely—will remain open. If the weather stays good, until the end of October for sure. However, I have made plans for us to climb to the Schynige plateau on the 27th. My wife will probably come along. Then I want to spend the rest of the day up there with her and on the 28th go with you up the Faulhorn (and if possible, come right back down again).

There is no department of demonology at the university.[1] Otherwise, why else would there be an academy of science there? Knowledgeable circles consider it a sure thing that the current rector will be elected *rector mirabilis* for life.

Dora also sends her regards.

Yours, Walter

1. The University of Muri, an imaginary invention of WB and Scholem in commemoration of the three months they spent there together. Both of them zealously composed satirical official documents of the university, among them a course schedule and academic statutes, etc., by WB, and a *Lehrgedicht der philosophischen Fakultät* by Scholem (published in 1927). WB signed himself as the rector, Scholem as the beadle of the School of Religion and Philosophy. For years, a favorite pastime of WB's was inventing titles for the library catalog and reviews of the books in question.

72. To Ernst Schoen

[November 8, 1918]

Dear Mr. Schoen,

Every obeisance paid to convention in one's own life becomes disturbingly noticeable to friends even from afar, that is to say whenever this convention is felt to be nothing more than that. Such is the case with the doctoral examination for which I am preparing. In the last few months, I was busy working on my dissertation and the constant work, combined with the fact that I was waiting, may have played some small role in your not having heard from me for almost as long as I have not heard from you. You will find my preoccupation reflected in this letter too since I have nothing new to report. My reading has been almost entirely limited to what is required for my dissertation. As you know, we have no social contacts here except the young man who, as I wrote you, is visiting me from Germany. Since he doubtless can involve himself in my work, but I am unable to get involved in his to the same extent because he is working on Hebrew things, it is not possible to give you, who are so far away, any news from here. I can only report on our domestic ups and downs. My wife is ill with the flu, but her temperature is already back to normal. She has received your letter and will answer it when she is well; because of her weakened condition we have not been able to discuss it yet. Stefan is well. He is an extraordinarily good child who never cries or screams without visible reason.

This means I have more freedom to go into all the things you wrote me. What gave me the most to think about was what you have to say about my separation from my former friends. The more I thought about it, the more it seemed possible that the kinds of qualities that at that time made, not understanding, but agreement impossible were completely peculiar to your innermost being. You waited—not impatiently but heedless of the time, not blind but not taking note of what was seen—while my friend and I were in the midst of a crisis that had to end in fulfillment or in change. You saw the people who surrounded us in terms of how they appeared and, therefore, you had to reject them. It was my belief that I felt your nature made a claim on us that could not be satisfied in our timeless, bedazzled question: the claim to patient unburdening and unfolding. I am sure that I could not talk to you about that period now if, at the time, we had not been so detached from each other. As a matter of fact, the only person I have talked to about this besides you is my wife. I dare not speculate as to when we might see each other again.

[. . .]

Even though I would never have taken it on without external inducement, my work on the dissertation is not wasted time. What I have been learning from it, i.e. insight into the relationship of a truth to history, will of course hardly be at all explicit in the dissertation, but I hope it will be discerned by astute readers. The work treats the romantic concept of criticism (art criticism). The modern concept of criticism has developed from the romantic concept; but "criticism" was an extremely esoteric concept for the romantics (they had several such concepts, but possibly none as obscure as this one), which was based on mystical assumptions about cognition. In terms of art, it encapsulates the best insights of contemporary and later poets, a new concept of art that, in many respects, is *our* concept of art. My ideas on this are so inextricably intertwined that it is impossible for me to communicate a conception of the whole in a few written observations, as much as I would like to. I have not yet written any of the actual dissertation, but have made quite a lot of progress on the preliminary research. I will first let my major professor know what I am planning. Up till now, my work has been advanced by the closing of the university due to the epidemic; but it will probably soon be reopened. I am running into obstacles everywhere trying to locate the relevant books, and what is available is excruciatingly boring. I have not yet read the main texts, Dilthey's biography of Schleiermacher and Haym's *Romantische Schule,* but may be able to give you a report on them later.

The following day, November 9, 1918

Yesterday, after having written the above, I received news of the proclamation of the Bavarian Republic. Since no papers are coming out in Switzerland because of a twenty-four-hour general strike (as a protest against military call-ups to defend the state against revolutionary agitation), I do not know what developments have taken place in the meantime. In any case, the bids I have asked you to place at the auction will no doubt be void since it is highly unlikely that it will take place.

[. . .]

As you will know, we spent a quiet summer on Lake Brienz in the most magnificent setting. The part of the lake where we were has the most magnificent meadows I have ever seen, rising from its shoreline. These meadows extend very far and are overgrown with groves and glades, in which we often hunted for mushrooms. The most important thing I read this summer was Goethe's *Metamorphosis of Plants* [*Metamorphose der Pflanzen*]. Reading it with my wife gave me a lot of pleasure, although I cannot make the book bear fruit for me immediately, given my inadequate knowledge of botany. Before I get around to Goethe's *Color Theory* [*Die Farbenlehre*], I hope to have another go at meteorology, to which I had already devoted some time. Beyond that, as I said, I have been reading only for my dissertation. It may be a spiritual fixation, but a beneficial one, for me to feel that it must be written just in these times. The only other thing I am reading is Gottfried Keller's *Green Henry* [*Der grüne Heinrich*]. All of this man's books are among the most ambiguous and dangerous literary products. Why? I hope to be able to tell you sometime.

[. . .]

Sincere regards from me and my wife and please extend the same to Jula.

Yours, Walter Benjamin

73. To Ernst Schoen

[Bern]
[January 29, 1919]

Dear Mr. Schoen,

I see from your letters of December and January, but primarily from the second, that worries are getting you down. I want to begin this letter by telling you how much I hope that you will soon succeed in finding a quick way out of all these difficulties; I am certain you will not lose heart while doing so. Indeed, for people like you and me, the changes that have taken place in Germany are unlikely to have opened up any paths other than those that were open to us before. The material circumstances of my life have gotten worse, and during the rather long time in which I have not written you, I have had a lot to think about and some excitement as well.

[. . .]

I have read some nice things. Of particular note is Gogol's *Magician*. Its subject matter (one of the greatest narrative themes, and meant for an epic) is, of course, superior to the (good) way it is handled.—We were recently invited to go hear Wagner's *Siegfried*, and right afterward I read Nietzsche's *Case of Wagner* [*Der Fall Wagner*] only to be completely surprised by the simplicity and farsightedness of what it said. I still have not read his second essay on Wagner (*Nietzsche contra Wagner*), but the first one filled me with enthusiasm, something that, all things considered, I am unable to say about everything I have read by Nietzsche. I read the new book by the Berlin sinologist de Groot, *Universismus*.[1] Just like the title, which presumes to give a name invented by the author to a religion thousands of years old, the text evidences a complete lack of insight, backwardness, and unfamiliarity with the new questions being raised by the systematic study of mythology. Since this man is quite a connoisseur (to the extent it is possible to judge from the book and his scholarly reputation), it is possible to say that ancient China has totally enslaved him and relentlessly holds him in intellectual thrall. Of course, you learn *quite a lot* that is worth knowing from reading the book.—Do you know Dostoyevsky's *Double*? I have read it for the second time and it would be worth our while to discuss the book sometime at greater length. I am now reading—with rapt attention—*Faust II* for the first time.

Last April you wrote me that you were deeply moved by Stifter's *Das alte Siegel* although it did not leave you with an entirely clear impression. I have now read it and it enraged me like hardly anything else by Stifter. With this novella in mind, I have reread the lines about Stifter I sent you previously and find them relevant, almost down to the last word. Today, however, I want to add something else. Some time ago, a critique of Shaw's *Mrs. Warren's Profession* led me to say that is was a mistake to postulate anywhere a purity that exists in and of itself and needs only to be preserved. This tenet seems to me to be important enough to supplement with what follows and to apply it to Stifter. The purity of an essence is *never* unconditional or absolute; it is always subject to a condition. This condition varies according to the essence whose purity is at issue; but this condition *never* inheres in the essence itself. In other words: the purity of every (finite) essence is not dependent on itself. The two essences to which we primarily attribute purity are nature and children. For nature, human language is the extrinsic condition of its purity. Since Stifter does not feel *this conditionality that first turns purity into purity,* the beauty of his nature descriptions is accidental or, in other words, harmonically impossible. For, in fact, it is literarily hardly possible except in connection with the distortedly conceived human destinies that tarnish Stifter's works. As far as *Das alte Siegel* is concerned, where destinies are in the foreground and the issue is not even the purity of children but of adults, it must be assumed a priori that, given this subject, Stifter's false idea of beauty can in no way remain concealed. The plot has some similarity with the classical epic treatment of purity, *Parsifal.* Both protagonists grew up in complete innocence and both maintain a respectful silence when a question would lead to deliverance. But not even this basic theme becomes completely clear in Stifter, and in his novella the hero is never *delivered* from his childhood purity, for this purity is conceived in absolute terms (if you wanted to be severe, you could say it is an integral part of his character). The man grows old with it, but never grows wise. I would have to be thoroughly familiar with the story of Parsifal the fool to be able to develop this comparison which, I believe, is the best heuristic principle on which to base a critique of Stifter's story. In any case, it is already clear that, in every respect, the plot (not to mention the mediocrity of the form) distortedly peers out from the false basic idea, as if from a disease. For in this story the characters always do, *at one and the same time,* what is absurd and what is abhorrent, what is improbable and what is disagreeable. (The servant in his intercession, the young man at the end, the woman in Lindenhaus) Maybe you will write me once whether you agree with my judgment and what I base it on.

At the beginning of January, I had to write a rather lengthy paper on romantic irony that was of absolutely no interest to me. Now I am back to working on my dissertation. Meanwhile, I got a good bookcase that has a back and now, to my delight, the books I have here are in good order. If you could only come and look at them, read them, and talk to me about them!

I hope you will continue to find it possible to live peacefully in Berlin.

Most sincere regards.
Yours, Walter Benjamin

1. J. J. Maria de Groot (Berlin, 1918).

74. To Gerhard Scholem

March 15, 1919

Dear Gerhard,

Mr. [Wolf] Heinle is looking for a place he can go on a regular basis for his midday meal; please be kind enough to write me where you had yours and what it cost.

Mr. Heinle was being treated in Frankfurt by Prof. Goldstein,[1] who claimed he knew you and me as well, by name only (presumably through you). I have been meaning to ask you how you know Prof. Goldstein. He is supposed to be a good man.

Please answer both my questions. When are you bringing the Molitor book? Why didn't you come today?

Sincere regards.
Yours, Walter

1. Kurt Goldstein (1878–1965) had gotten together with Scholem in Heidelberg in 1916.

75. To Ernst Schoen

April 7, 1919

Dear Mr. Schoen,

[. . .]

A few days ago I completed a rough draft of my dissertation. It has become what it was meant to be: a pointer to the true nature of romanticism, of which the secondary literature is completely ignorant—and even that only indirectly, because I was no more allowed to get to the heart of romanticism, i.e. messianism (I only dealt with its perception of art) than to anything else that I find very relevant. Had I attempted to get to the heart of romanticism, I would have cut myself off from any chance of achieving the expected complicated and conventional scholarly attitude that I personally distinguish from the genuine one. But I hope to have achieved the following in this work: to deduce this state of affairs from the inside out.

After taking my exams, I want to learn languages: as you know, to put the European sphere behind me. It would be hard for me to take leave of Europe, especially in Italy. I am counting on the future to make it intrinsically and extrinsically feasible for me to leave Europe.[1] Both are inextricably intertwined and this sometimes weighs heavily on me, because I can't force it; but I see leaving Europe as a necessity I will have to face.

My wife, I, and our son send our most sincere regards.

Yours, Walter Benjamin

1. Scholem had made up his mind to go to Palestine; WB and his wife often considered the idea; see letter 83 to Hüne Caro.

76. To Gerhard Scholem

April 9, 1919

Dear Gerhard,

Stefan will accept your congratulations[1] at six in the evening—but no later—and requests me to kindly invite you to an evening meal at eight. He himself will participate in the meal if the pressing demands of sleep do not keep him away.

Sincere regards from me and my wife.

Yours, Walter

1. On the first birthday of WB's son.

77. To Ernst Schoen

[Bern]
[May 1919]

Dear Mr. Schoen,

Your short letter has given me an intimate sense of what your life must be like. It is sad that we are no more able to communicate and make real for each other our difficulties and suffering than we are total happiness. Total happiness is less common: but it is a matter of being a whole person in one's happiness and seeing the whole person in his happiness. Thus I have seen that you are not happy, yet I feel a kinship with your struggle as well as close to it. Whenever I behold the beautiful drama and see that it does not drag people into self-destructive behavior under the guise of satisfaction, I love the need for freedom about which you write. I was forced to view this kind of self-destruction for two months—for me, it is the most shocking kind, but ultimately also the most chilling. I will put it down in writing for you because I can no longer conceive of fulfilling the desire you expressed some time ago that I introduce him to you: I am referring to Wolf Heinle. The time he spent visiting us resulted in a negative decision for our relationship. Sometime I will no doubt be able to tell you what else was involved in how this all came about.

Alfred [Cohn] has written me. I was delighted to get his letter because it seemed to indicate that he has at least temporarily shelved his totally weird and drastic plan to become a grade-school teacher. This was a decision I had not welcomed as *the first one* of Alfred's new life. He now writes very simply that he is waiting, that he is attending lectures at the university, including Husserl's.

It will be difficult for me to let you know anything about my work right away because, of course, it has been temporarily shelved due to my exams. What I have to do now is simply study in the most methodical way, because the fewer connections I have to the examiners, the more difficult the exam will be for me. If I could talk to you about the dissertation, I would be delighted. It is still too much a part of me to put it into your hands when you are so far away. I have written an esoteric epilogue for it for those with whom I would have to share it as *my* work.[1] At some point I want to give it to you along with this epilogue, once we no longer live so far apart. I also do not have even one copy to spare just now—although I am sending one to my parents. In any case, I am unable to make up my mind to send it yet, and would like to wait. I have just handed in part of it to my professor, who may not pay enough attention to it to be able to spare me difficulties. The structure of the work makes great demands on the reader as, in part, does its prose. Enough of this. You will notice from my letters when I am again involved in my own work.

At this time, you would more readily notice something else from them: My son is very ill. [. . .] In his illness, he is extremely sweet and endearing. Given these circumstances, I am asking you to forgive me for presenting you only with what you now see before you and with something so incoherent. A letter from you would make me very happy.

My wife sends her most sincere regards.

Yours, Walter Benjamin

1. The reference is to the final chapter of the published version, "Die frühromantische Kunsttheorie und Goethe," [Early romantic art theory and Goethe] into which WB integrated many things that at that time gave him food for thought.

78. To Gerhard Scholem

June 15, 1919

Dear Gerhard,

Thursday evening is fine with us. Please come at seven o'clock.

To my great dismay and anger, I heard from Munich today that Noeggerath is in prison charged with high treason.[1] Please, if it's at all possible, get some more specific information about this from your acquaintances in Munich, if you still have any there. Mr. Heinle, who told me about the situation, is not staying on in Munich. Everything else also confirms the existence of a most ominous state of affairs. For example, why don't you take a look at the *Republik,* which does not seem to be exaggerating.

Best regards.
Yours, Walter

1. Noeggerath was for a short time a member of the Lipp government.

79. To Gerhard Scholem

Iseltwald
July 19, 1919

Dear Gerhard,

Many thanks for your birthday greetings. It was a very nice day—we are no longer so terribly worried about Stefan. He still has a temperature but there are hardly any symptoms associated with it. We therefore celebrated to our hearts' content on the 15th, and I was able to enjoy my many lovely gifts. It is hardly necessary for me to single out your gift of the Avé-Lallemant as having particularly pleased me.[1] I am sure to get a lot out of the book. Incidentally, you told me earlier that the linguistic section was missing from the revision or new edition. However, reading the prologue to the entire work, I see that it is still supposed to be published—but with significant changes.

Other books also gave me a great deal of pleasure—Dora presented me with a great many French books. You will of course get to see everything when you come. Please: on Tuesday. Connections: the train to Böningen (change at the Interlaken-East station); from Böningen, a ship. Arrival here at 9:30. Time till 5 in the evening when you'll leave here by steamship to arrive in Bern the same evening (at 10:13). If you leave here at 8 in the evening, you of course won't manage to get to Bern, but you'll still get as far as Thun. (The 8 o'clock ship only sails on Tuesday and

Saturday.) Unfortunately, you can't spend the night with us this time. But please come! Why can't I have the Lessing? I hope that, in the meantime, you have received the Agnon book[2] from Bloch.[3]

Sincere regards from Dora and me.

Yours, Walter

Naturally, you won't mention my exams to your mother![4]

1. The new edition of Avé-Lallemant's work, *Das deutsche Gaunertum* (1914).

2. S. J. Agnon, *And the Crooked Becomes Straight,* translated from the Hebrew by Max Strauß (Berlin, 1918).

3. Ernst Bloch, whom Scholem visited in Interlaken.

4. WB's impending Ph.D. exams.

80. To Ernst Schoen

[Iseltwald]
[July 24, 1919]

Dear Mr. Schoen,

I really enjoyed your last letter. I hope your mood of self-confidence, full of courageous plans, has sustained itself and acted as a charm against the weather, the need to keep body and soul together, and other everyday annoyances. We are being violently besieged by them here, in conjunction with a persistent, oppressive, and humid west wind. My son is not recovering, even though his condition is not getting any worse. My wife is suffering terribly as a result of the pressure she has been under for months, in addition to not getting the rest we hoped for; anemia and severe weight loss. Over the last six months, I myself have developed an aversion to noise and have need of a room with walls covered in leather and with heavy double doors for my work (the ravings of wishful thinking!). Therefore, I have not yet been able to take on important projects that I see clearly before me in terms of their necessity and, in part, in terms of their content. In the past few days, I have turned once more to the Baudelaire translation. I really would like to see some samples from it attractively published in a journal sometime, in order to test their value. This is a wish I may be able to fulfill at some point. Otherwise, the important projects that have been making demands on my time for quite a while without avail are reviews.

We intend to send Stefan to my in-laws as soon as possible so that we can recuperate here for a time in peace and quiet. Since I have been here, I have read only French books. I was seized by a great desire to immerse myself in the contemporary French intellectual movement, but without ever losing the awareness of being an outside observer. I am reading indiscriminately, just to get a feel for things; thus I would be all the more grateful to you for some pointers. First I read Crépet's commendable Baudelaire biography; it is the model of a purely biographical treatment. It opens your eyes to how the man's work surpasses his life in a totally transcendent way (and in a different way than is usually the case). Then I read an extravagant piece of rubbish by Paul and Victor Margueritte. Additionally, Farrère's *Black Opium* [*Fumée d'opium*]. As you see, indiscriminate—reading whatever happens to fall into my lap. But it is necessary to do this for a while in order to assimilate insights and pointers (for which I ask you once more) with that much more understanding. I subscribe to the *Nouvelle revue française*. A lot in it is still opaque to me and has a tendentious obscurity, even though its German analogue might be penetrable to the point of triteness. I am making some progress in clarifying it. I believe that journals are pretty much of value only for the foreigner—Goethe, by the way, acted in accordance with this practical knowledge. Beyond that, however, I hope to discover something plainly and substantially worthwhile. For example, the *Revue* is publishing parts of Péguy's essay on Descartes, that was among his papers. Finally, I am reading with the greatest interest and obvious impartiality what men like Gide have to say about Germany. I believe I am discovering a delightful loyalty among the members of this circle, but do not yet have a clear understanding of it. In the things I have been reading, there is a point of contact for me with some strand of the "present," which I simply cannot attain vis-à-vis anything German.—Are you by any chance familiar with Jammes's latest writings?

In view of your new circumstances, I have a small proposition I would like to make right away. I would be happy if something good came out of it for the participants, especially for you. You will have heard of Mrs. Emmy Hennings,[1] with whom we socialized in Bern. Her thirteen-year-old daughter Annemarie has been painting for two or three years. I consider almost all of her paintings highly interesting as documents. At the very least, our interest in her is like that we take in exact accounts of dreams or in an absolutely precise description of a person's fleeting state of mind. This of course amounts to nothing less than an artistic standard but, for all that, corresponds fairly precisely to the better part of expressionism, which, I believe, is nothing other than just that (and from which, in any case, I must by all means exclude three great painters: Chagall, Klee, Kandinsky). What I mean by this is that these paintings, whose subject is mostly people shown with what seem to be either demons or angels, would at this time be sure to attract extremely lively interest from the public, if I have a relatively accurate notion of the Berlin public's mindset and desire for sensation. Additional factors are, first, the mother's name, which is extremely well known among the literati; second, the child's paintings have been exhibited with other children's paintings in Zurich. A number of paintings were also sold there, among them some of Annemarie Henning's. Under favorable circumstances, they could be exhibited in Berlin with other children's paintings. This is the exoteric, business side of the matter.

The more serious thing (if perhaps the less important in terms of our intentions) is that *some* of these paintings seem to me to be very valuable, even in terms of a strict standard. These paintings not only evince a new documentary content, as is the case with the other paintings, but also exhibit an extremely original self-assurance and precision. Indeed, what they exhibit comes close to being a new and justified technique for certain artistic subjects (ghosts). I am unable to say anything more in writing. With these words, I am not trying to canonize a budding talent before the fact—on the contrary, I consider it problematical whether this activity will last beyond puberty (in some respects, it is already abating). But what there is of it is quite interesting, primarily in comparison with all the other innumerable children's drawings with which I am familiar. We bought fourteen of her paintings, and had to do without some very nice ones that the girl's mother did not want to give up.

Maybe Mr. Möller will organize an exhibition, "Children's Expressionist Paintings." This would prove to be a real draw, wouldn't it? Or else he is interested only in the paintings under discussion. [. . .]

[. . .] As much as I hope you will come, I fear that doing so will not be made easier for you by Mr. [Simon] Guttmann's offer, if you are relying on him for anything other than, for example, removing the difficulties associated with the mail, which are not insurmountable in any case. Should your trip become possible nonetheless, you will somehow manage to find the way to spend more time visiting us. [. . .]

On my birthday my wife delighted me with, among other things, a gift of some very nice books. They are mostly French: France, Philippe, Verlaine's complete works, Balzac (I am very happy that I now own the complete *Scenes of Parisian Life* [*Vie parisienne*]), Suarèz [*sic*], a complete copy of Remarque's journal, of which, as the publisher and sole contributor, he published twelve volumes during the war. I received a kilim carpet, which makes my room look very beautiful. A Persian pillow came with it.

Concluding my studies with the doctoral examination was no problem for me. It was necessary to do so out of consideration for my family. Your situation is doubtless different. But, without being a student, can you use

German libraries, if only within the narrow limits that have been set for students? I don't know. And you would have to consider taking the university qualifying exam purely for the sake of this advantage, if it were impossible to get it any other way. I am unable to judge whether, beyond this, purely social reasons, as well as the practical ones having to do with your need to earn a living, make the title necessary for you. Isn't contemporary society—and thus its codex—very unstable? Are you also thinking of somehow being appointed a university lecturer?

I have never read *Poetry and Experience* [*Das Erlebnis und die Dichtung*] in its entirety. To be precise, I read only the Hölderlin section when I was still in school and gave my talk about Hölderlin in Tonndorf's class. I do not know whether you heard it. And I am not at all inclined to blame you for my unproductive reading. I did have to read Dilthey's *Ideen zu einer beschreibenden und zergliedernden Psychologie* very carefully for my exams and found it completely useless. The most significant things by Dilthey will turn out to be the long treatises in *Weltanschauung und Analyse des Menschen im 15ten und 16ten Jahrhundert*. But thus far I have been able to manage only a cursory look at them. Yet it may well be that such immense erudition is required in order to read him with the necessary control and overall perspective that, on the basis of this immense erudition, somebody would have more important things to say than he does. This is a guess based on my minimal knowledge.

[. . .]

Most sincere regards and many thanks for your best wishes.

Yours, Walter Benjamin

1. Hennings and Hugo Ball lived in the house next door.

81. To Gerhard Scholem

Klosters
September 15, 1919

Dear Gerhard,

I am not in a position to actually inaugurate our correspondence with this letter[1] because of a certain constraint attributable to a misfortune that refuses to abate and to my very uncertain prospects. But, with this letter, I would simply like to propose to you that we begin corresponding. I myself have only one question for you, which is whether you can enlighten me about a problem in number theory that came to mind at the zenith of a night full of worries.

[. . .]

I have been intensively reading the book by [Ernst] Bloch[2] for a week and may publicly point out what is praiseworthy in it for the sake of the author, not the book. Unfortunately, not everything in it is deserving of approval. Indeed, sometimes it leaves me overcome with impatience. The author has certainly already transcended the book. I have again read some things by Péguy. In this instance, I feel that I am being addressed by an unbelievably kindred spirit. Might I be permitted to say that *nothing* written has ever impressed me so very much because of how close it is to me, because of my feeling of oneness with it. Of course a lot of things have shaken me more; this touches me, not because of its sublimity, but because of its kinship to me. Immense melancholy that has been mastered.

Bloch cites the Zohar:[3] "Know that there is a twofold way of looking at all worlds. The one reveals their exteriority, that is to say, general laws of the worlds in terms of their external form. The other reveals the inner being of the worlds, that is to say, the essence of human souls. As a consequence, there are also two degrees of doing, works and rituals of prayer; works must be accomplished for the worlds in regard to their exteriority, but prayers in order to make the one world part of the other and to lift it upward." I have never read anything about prayer that would have been enlightening, as this.[4]

How are you doing? Please write.

Our most sincere regards.
Yours, Walter

1. Scholem returned to Germany at the beginning of September.

2. *Spirit of Utopia*. Bloch and WB met in Bern in 1918.

3. At the end of the book. The passage (first reproduced by Molitor) does not come from the Zohar, but from a work of the Safed kabbalists.

4. Seen in the context of the very sparse use of commas in these early letters, this punctuation proves that the phrase should not be editorially emended to read "more enlightening than."

82. To Ernst Schoen

Klosters
September 19, 1919

Dear Mr. Schoen,

It would be very sad if my last letter to you—written in July—had been lost in the mail. It contained the answers to your various questions: the visit to Switzerland, the matter of the art venture, and gave you some information about me. Or is there another reason for your silence? I hope that no adverse changes have occurred in your circumstances and that it is not "simply" a matter of your not being well.

In any case, nothing will stop me from again writing you a few words about myself, not even the fact that I have not succeeded in completing anything that I would be pleased to report to you. When you always report only bad news about your own external circumstances to certain people, after a while it almost becomes a transgression against them. Internally, however, things look a lot brighter and therefore I want to start with that. I have done a lot of thinking on my own and, in so doing, have conceived of ideas that are so clear that I hope to be able to write them down soon. They concern politics. In many respects—not only in this one—a friend's book has proven useful. He is the only person of consequence I have gotten to know in Switzerland thus far. His companionship was even more useful than his book, because in conversation he so often challenged my rejection of *every* contemporary political trend that he ultimately forced me to immerse myself in these matters, something I hope was worthwhile. I still am unable to divulge any of my thoughts on this topic. The book is called *Spirit of Utopia* [*Geist der Utopie*] by Ernst Bloch. It exhibits enormous deficiencies. Nonetheless, I am indebted to the book for much that is substantive, and the author is ten times better than his book. You may be satisfied to hear that this is nevertheless the only book on which, as a truly contemporaneous and contemporary utterance, I can take my own measure. *Because:* the author stands alone and philosophically stands up for his cause, while almost everything we read today of a philosophical nature written by our contemporaries is derivative and adulterated. You can never get a handle on its moral center and, at the most, it leads you to the origin of the evil that it itself represents.

I have read a few good books. I would be very interested in whether you are familiar with one of them, namely Gide's *Strait Is the Gate* [*La porte étroite*]. Your opinion? What I admire in it is its serious, wonderful animation. It contains "movement" in the most sublime sense of the word, like few books, almost like *The Idiot.*[1] His jewish[2] seriousness speaks to me as to a kindred spirit. Nonetheless, the whole appears refracted as in a dark medium, in the *materiality* of a narrow, ascetically Christian event in the foreground, vividly transcended a thousand times over by the intent of the internal event, which thus remains fundamentally unchanged as if it were not alive. I have also read Baudelaire's *Artificial Paradise*. It is an extremely reticent, nonoriented attempt to monitor the "psychological" phenomena that manifest themselves in hashish or opium highs for what they have to teach us philosophically. It will be necessary to repeat this attempt independently of this book.[3] But its beauty and value lie in the author's childlike innocence and purity, which emanate from this work more clearly than from his others.—Goethe's correspondence with Count Reinhardt, the French ambassador to Germany, is very beautiful because of its human warmth and aristocratic distance, which remained the same for twenty-five years. In this communication between very unequal individuals, totally unequal in terms of their significance, the reader is aware of an amazing, extremely noble and imperturbable confidence in the tone with which they speak about each other and to each other. Various excursuses could be appended to the theme "correspondence." First, one concerning the great extent to which correspondence is undervalued because it is placed in conjunction with the totally slanted concept of the work and authorship, whereas it belongs in the sphere of "testimony" whose relationship to a subject is just as unimportant as the relationship of any kind of pragmatically historical testimony (inscription) to the personality of its author. "Testimony" is a part of the history of how a person *lives on,* and precisely how this afterlife, with its own history, is embedded in life can be studied on the basis of correspondence. The *exchange* of letters characteristically takes shape in the mind of posterity (whereas the *single* letter, in regard to its author, may lose something of its life): as letters are read consecutively with only the briefest intervals, they change objectively, from within their living selves. Their life moves to a different rhythm than the recipients' lives at the time of writing, and they change in other ways too. A second reflection that comes to mind: nowadays there are many people who are losing their sense for letter writing. Letters *by* anybody at all are being senselessly published. Whereas in the middle of the previous century, when important correspondence was sensibly edited, like, for example, the exchange I mentioned or the one between Goethe and Knebel (which I also own), no one provided footnotes. Footnotes cause these documents to lose so much, to lose life, just like a person who is being leeched. They become pale. Nowadays, however, these books are neither being reprinted nor are they appearing in new editions because, as things stand, they are just there and thus are still waiting for the time when they will come into their own.—My most important literary acquaintance, about whom I have probably already written you and with whom I still need to deal much more extensively, is Charles Péguy, an acquaintance mediated by the *Nouvelle revue française*. More about that some other time. Best of all, in a personal conversation. It would be wonderful if we could see each other again. But it is impossible for me to consider a trip to Germany at the present time. Would it be possible for you to visit Austria sometime during the winter? I hope to have, if not my books, at least my manuscripts there. When am I going to hear from you again? I would be grateful for any news.

[. . .]

We both send our most sincere regards.

Yours, Walter Benjamin

1. WB wrote the critique that completes these thoughts at that time. It was published in *Schriften* 2:271–73.

2. WB uses the word here as a categorical designation. He knew that Gide was not a Jew.

3. WB took an interest in this phenomenon years later when he placed himself at the disposal of a doctor he knew, Ernst Joel, for experiments in this area.

83. To Hüne Caro

[Breitenstein]
[ca. November 20, 1919]

Dear Hüne Caro,

In response to your letter, I want to write you a few words immediately, although my correspondence has been suspended because I do not have even my writing desk with me. Your letter reached me in Austria where my aunt[1] owns a sanitorium three hours from Vienna. This is where we all are now. But my wife is in Vienna at the moment, where she is making an effort to get our luggage . . .

We are hardly in a position to announce our plans for the immediate future. The only thing certain is that I will begin my research for my habilitation dissertation as soon as possible;[2] and in any case I am returning to Switzerland in the spring, but—for how long? with my wife? with my son? Even I do not know the answer to any of these questions yet.—Will you be going to Palestine?[3] Under certain, not entirely unlikely, conditions I am ready, not to say determined, to go. The Jews here in Austria (the respectable ones who do not make any money) speak of nothing else.

What will you do if you leave Switzerland? Is your esteemed mother still there or are you alone? I can imagine the conflict you have to live with, whether to earn the bitter bread of exile in Switzerland or to pick up crusts from the street in Germany. This question may also become relevant for us. My son is well, my wife is not. We had some difficult weeks during the summer because of another bout of illness and an entirely unexpected visit from my parents;[4] but at the end we spent some pleasant weeks in Lugano.

We are going to stay up here for another few weeks and then will probably go to Vienna.

I would like to speak with you again. But you will probably not go to Austria under any circumstances; we are unable to invite anybody.

Most sincere regards from me and my wife.

Yours, Walter Benjamin

1. In reality, an aunt of his wife, Dora.

2. Herbertz had offered WB the opportunity to get his postdoctoral degree in philosophy in Bern. This proved to be unrealizable already in 1920 because of inflation.

3. Caro, in fact, later went to Palestine.

4. In Iseltwald.

84. To Gerhard Scholem

Breitenstein
November 23, 1919

Dear Gerhard,

Delighted to receive your letter! And there is a lot to say so that we can again establish contact between our thoughts. Naturally, especially when I write you, I feel that my prospects are wintry, in the botanical sense of the word; in the literal sense, I have not come into bloom because I must somehow close myself off so as not to suffer from my deficient working conditions and various living conditions. I continually wait for books from Vienna; my father-in-law[1] writes me that everything is currently out on loan, and what I had taken along to tide me over has gone astray—a hefty book about Goethe's writings on metamorphosis, my copy of Baudelaire, as well as other things. (Not, of course, my translation.) Who knows how we will extricate ourselves from these difficulties. If the things should fail to show up or if the railroad does not pay a very big indemnity, it will be quite a financial loss. Scheerbart's *Lesabéndio* is also on the missing list. I am telling you about this because I can predict that you, as the person who gave it to me,[2] are interested in its fate, as well as in its deserved resurrection, and I am already asking you if you would be kind enough to look around for its possible "resurrection in the flesh." Spiritually it went through a second metamorphosis with me in that I wrote the prolegomena to a second critique of *Lesabéndio* in Lugano. After that, I wanted to read it again (which is why I took it along when I came here) and then begin the longer essay in which I intended to prove that Pallas is the best of all worlds. The temporary loss of the book has not only impeded this plan but, based on my discussion with Herbertz, I mainly see that I must immediately look around for a project for my habilitation dissertation, which only a short time ago I had not anticipated doing.

Congratulations on the *Billionär*.[3] I was introduced to my father-in-law's library in Vienna. It may indeed have some things on Judaica that would interest you, but it has lost almost all of its previous *glory* (a first edition of Descartes's collected works, among other things) to theft, to the most careless lending practices (!), and to the sale of some items. My father-in-law is making me a gift of the Akademie edition of Kant's works, at least those parts of it that are still to be found in his library. Also a Latin Agrippa von Nettesheim, which, however, I will be able to read only with the help of a German translation.—I have a favor to ask of you, namely, would you be so kind as to inquire immediately at your Munich bookdealer's about Borchardt's Swinburne translation published by Insel and to have a hard-bound copy (ca. 40 marks) sent to my address here as soon as it appears, or immediately . . . Since I would like to give it to Dora as a present, you will be doing me a great service by taking care of this for me. I won't order it in Vienna because, given the laziness of the people there, I fear they would delay until the 600 copies, for which I assume there will be a great demand, are no longer available.—I will make note of *Weltenmantel und Himmelszelt.*[4] By the way, the title had piqued my interest before you mentioned it. How much does the book cost?

During the summer the name of a "Professor" Noeggerath, with a wife and son, from Freiburg, was listed for several weeks running among the names of foreign authors published by Zuoz in the Engadine. I really would like to know whether this (for I cannot imagine it to be otherwise) is the genius who, according to this list, was an adjunct professor or privatdocent in Freiburg.[5] You could probably find this out easily.

[. . .]

I have not worked terribly much the past summer, but have seen some magnificent things. In one day, we made the crossing from Thusis over the St. Bernhardin to Bellinzona by post chaise and thus, on this one day, saw some truly magnificent and beautiful things, since the journey took place during the most magnificent weather. For the most part, everything was also wonderful for us in Lugano. I wrote an essay there, "Fate and Character" ["Schicksal und Charakter"], which I put in the final form here. It contains what I said to you about fate and character in Lungern.[6] I will publish it immediately if the opportunity presents itself. To be sure, not in a journal, but only in an almanac or something similar.—My plan to write a review of Bloch's *Spirit of Utopia,* which had not been realized but was to have been carried out here, has now also come to naught since the book, with all my preparatory marginalia, is missing. By the way, Bloch himself is still in Interlaken and will be in Germany on business for at most a short time.

What is the status of your seminar paper for Bäumker? I would be keenly interested in everything you could, for example, tell me about Lehmann[7] and what kind of things go on in his class. I am amazed that he is still mentally sound. To be sure, his moral character does not seem to be of the highest caliber. Is he giving readings in his apartment again? It is now becoming important for me to know your father's estimate of what it will cost to print my dissertation. On a separate sheet, I have provided you with specifics, which I hope will suffice, and if necessary I would submit a typewritten page. (Francke will presumably publish it. Yet naturally I have to pay for the printing.) I place no value on an especially large typeface. On the contrary, it can be printed in a typeface as small as is respectable. On the other hand, I do want good paper (no glossy paper). I prefer gothic type, especially for the small print of antiqua.

I believe Francke will be agreeable to having 1,000–1,200 copies printed. [. . .]

Please excuse my handwriting. Most of the letter was written while I was lying down. If you could tell me something about Bäumker,[8] I would be very interested. Will something new by Agnon (in translation) appear soon?

That's all for today, except for our most sincere regards.

Yours, Walter

1. Professor Leon Kellner, Anglicist and publisher of Theodor Herzl's works and diaries.
2. The book had been Scholem's wedding present to WB.
3. Another book by Scheerbart, *Rakkox der Billionär*.
4. By Robert Eisler (1909), whom Scholem had met.
5. This was not the case.
6. *Schriften* 1:31–39.
7. Walter Lehmann, the Americanist, who was interpreting Mayan hymns at the time.
8. Clemens Bäumker, a great light in the field of medieval philosophy, under whom Scholem planned to get his doctorate.

85. To Ernst Schoen

Breitenstein am Semmering
December 5, 1919

Dear Mr. Schoen,

Our last letters crossed in the mail; I believe I sent mine from Klosters. Based on the long silence that ensued, neither of us will have concluded that the other is faring well. In my case, this letter means quite precisely that I have finally found a moment to collect my thoughts, because it is only a few hours since I have been in a room that does not interfere with thinking. And how are you? Are you being well taken care of? We were saddened to hear that your hopes had been dashed; people like us are being engulfed by a pregnant darkness. I am confident that we will overcome this and, freed from a nightmare, see it dissipate. I had seen it coming for too long—despite all appearances, even of my own circumstances—as the response of nature (of which contemporary society is only one part) to our life. Now my father is writing me letters full of advice. For the time being, I'll just wait and see.

We are not bad off here as guests at a sanatorium that belongs to one of my wife's aunts. We are not lacking for anything and have a warm room at our disposal, which we made quite livable today. My son is here with a nanny and my wife has time to herself, as well as peace and quiet. But four weeks passed very differently before we were able to look at things the way we do now. After a sometimes perilous trip from the Swiss border to Vienna, we received the news that the carriage containing all the luggage we had not left behind in Switzerland had gone missing. But after four weeks we are again in possession of those things that were not damaged; the carriage had been sent to Budapest by mistake.—We spent some very beautiful, if not always untroubled, days in Lugano. It was a very warm October. By post chaise we crossed the St. Bernhardin pass from Klosters into Tessin via Thusis—the Via Mala—in one day and saw one of the most magnificent Alpine passes under the clearest sky imaginable—this is a region to which there is still no access by rail and which is, therefore, less known. There are some mountains near Lugano with very unusual and wonderful views. We sent a postcard with a picture of the most beautiful of them, the Monte Generose, to Jula. You may have seen it.

I am beginning work on a lengthy review of Ernst Bloch's *Spirit of Utopia;* this book is by someone I got to know in Switzerland and about whom I probably wrote you. I mean to publish the review. Likewise, I hope to be able to publish an essay I wrote in Lugano, "Fate and Character." I consider it to be one of my best essays.[1] I also wrote the prolegomena to my new review of *Lesabéndio*[2] and a review of Gide's *Strait Is the Gate* there. When I think of this and other things, my intense desire to meet with you again is redoubled. I must add that you have less reason than anyone to write me that your friends do not need you; I hope a meeting in the foreseeable future will prove to you in what sense I need you. As long as I am up here, of course, I am inaccessible. Being a guest myself, I am unable to invite anybody. I will write you as soon as I have an opportunity. It is not clear what the immediate future holds in store for me. Contrary to my wildest expectations, the prospect of an opportunity to work for my habilitation has opened up for me in Bern. But I will not be able to accept such an opportunity unless my wife finds a position that is appropriate in terms of the nature of the work and the salary and would enable us to stay on in Switzerland. A ministerial post would be best. You probably never get to hear of such openings? In any case, at the end of winter I want to go to Switzerland, if at all possible with my wife, in order to talk with the professor about my habilitation and the habilitation dissertation, whose topic has not yet been set. On the other hand, my parents want to see our child before long and we are therefore also considering a visit to Germany in the spring. Given these circumstances, for the time being there can be no talk of establishing a permanent household and we are likely to run into difficulties in our daily life.

I also plan to read the Curtius book you mention.[3] After all, at present it is the only thing on the topic. Of course the conjunction of authors mentioned in the title in the same breath as Romain Rolland already shows that it is uninformed. The *Nouvelle revue française* has reprinted a large number of important works that were out of print and I would like to get hold of some of them for myself. A four-act drama by Claudel, *The Humiliation of the Father* [*Le père humilié*], recently appeared in the journal. I haven't the slightest idea of what to make of it. Otherwise I am not familiar with Claudel. I can get all kinds of things here, since Vienna has a really excellent lending library. I am just finishing an extraordinarily splendid novel by Galsworthy, *The Patrician*.

I hope my letter will move you to send me some news of yourself, regardless of your current circumstances. My wife and I send our most sincere regards. Stefan is well.

Yours, Walter Benjamin

1. The essay appeared in the first issue of *Argonauten* (1921).

2. *Lesabéndio* by Paul Scheerbart (Munich, 1913) was one of the latest literary works that WB valued most highly. His review is identical to the unfortunately lost essay on the true politician, which is often referred to in the following letters.

3. Ernst Robert Curtius, *Die literarischen Wegbereiter des neuen Frankreich* (1919).

86. To Gerhard Scholem

Breitenstein
January 13, 1920

Dear Gerhard,

Dora will write *thanking* you for the gift; I would just like to let you know immediately how much pleasure the story has given me. Based on the beauty of both the story and the language, I must conclude that your translation[1] is perfect. I am extremely eager to hear the "remarkable" things you promise to tell me in connection with the story[2] because I did notice that there must have been something special about such sublime material, treated in such an unpretentious and consummate way.—If you only knew Dora's love for all stories about extremely small creatures—or did she tell you the Chinese story about the small hunting dog? What I first admired in the story you sent me was how the poet, without changing Gadiel, succeeds in producing out of Gadiel's initial insignificant corporeality the second powerful one in which Gadiel gains status.—The other fairy tales that turned up here as birthday presents are goyish. They gave us great pleasure nonetheless since we discovered in them a source for our favorite collection of fairy tales, Godin's.[3] It is a work by Arndt, in a new edition published by Müller,[4] probably only the third edition since the first one appeared in the last century. The edition must be very rare, since I had neither heard of it nor seen the book before I held it in my hand and bought it.—We would be happy for every line of your Agnon translations: What is the situation with the poem?[5]

My current project is a lengthy review of *Spirit of Utopia* for a periodical. The review will let the many good and excellent things speak for themselves, but will diagnose the constitutional defects and weaknesses in completely esoteric language; the whole thing will have an academic format, because this is the only way to do justice to the book. In view of the fact that the review may require me to come to terms with expressionism, I read Kandinsky's *Concerning the Spiritual in Art, and Painting in Particular*. This book fills me with the highest esteem for its author, just as his paintings elicit my admiration. It is probably the only book on expressionism devoid of gibberish; not, of course, from the standpoint of a philosophy, but from that of a doctrine of painting.

We will probably be in Berlin at the beginning of March, then after four weeks move close to Munich, where we will stay until the situation in Switzerland has been cleared up, and then leave or stay depending on how it turns out. The decision, at least the provisional one, depends not only (even if to a significant extent) on the question of money but also on how the work on my habilitation dissertation shapes up. All that exists of the dissertation is my intention to work on a particular topic; that is, a research project that falls within the sphere of the larger question of the relationship between word and concept (language and logos). Given the immense difficulties inherent in the project, for the time being I am looking for literature that can no doubt be found only under the rubric of scholasticism or works about scholasticism. In the first case at least, the Latin is going to be a tough nut to crack. I would be *extraordinarily* grateful to you for any bibliographical references you can give me on the basis of this information. Conditions in the Vienna library are so bad that, first, I can get hardly any books and, second, can find hardly any in the catalog. Have you ever given any thought to this topic? If we could just write each other about it, that would be *incredibly* helpful to me. You may share my view that the foundation of logic must be sought among the many abysses of this problem.—Please write me what the story is with the S. Friedländer book.[6] The same about Bäumker; you never tire of announcing upcoming informative reports about him, but I never get to see a single line about him.

We never considered staying in Austria for a whole year and now, of all times, we have confronted the same familiar and deplorable conditions in Vienna, which make staying there difficult. We would not consider staying in Austria, whether in the city or the country, because of the impossible Vienna library alone.—Only our furniture has an apartment in Seeshaupt; we don't.

Many thanks to your brother [Reinhold] for giving me an estimate of the printing costs; should I agree to them—which still depends on several bits of information—I will naturally write him. Best thanks for the issues of *Der Jude.* I now urgently request you to send me a copy of the note on analogy and relationship. I am enclosing "Fate and Character." I must expressly ask you not to pass it on or to read it to anybody. On the other hand, if you want you can keep the carbon copy, which is unfortunately of poor quality.

I must make the following official announcement: Mr. Stefan, cand. phil., has assumed his diplomatic duties and has become the representative of the subjugated peoples of Putzikullen and Abramolchen in peace negotiations at our court. Whatever other subjugated peoples there are, must continue to rely on your representation.[7]

Kraft informed us of his engagement to Miss Erna Halle.[8]

Please write very soon. Most sincere regards.

Yours, Walter

1. S. J. Agnon, "The Tale of Rabbi Gadiel, the Child," *Der Jude* 5 (1920).
2. When translating this story, Scholem had quite unexpectedly come upon its source in kabbalistic literature.
3. Amélie Godin (i.e. Linz) (1824–1904). She published the following collections, among others: *Märchen: Von einer Mutter erdacht* (1858), *Neue Märchen* (1869), and *Märchenbuch* (1874).
4. E. M. Arndt, *Märchen und Jugenderinnerungen* (Munich, 1913).
5. Scholem at this time produced a series of such translations, which were published in *Der Jude*. The translation of an extremely melancholy Agnon poem remained unpublished.
6. *Schöpferische Indifferenz* (Munich, 1918).
7. Scholem was accustomed to present himself as the "representative of subjugated peoples."
8. Toni Halle's sister.

87. To Ernest Schoen

February 2, 1920

Dear Mr. Schoen,

We were very happy to hear you report in your most recent letter that your life has taken a turn for the better. I hope that, in the meantime, you have acquired the peace and quiet necessary to do your own work. Based on what you have intimated, I can hardly wait to know more about it. First, of course, because it is the expression of your thoughts; but also for another reason. Namely, I am very interested in the principle underlying your extensive project on literary criticism: the entire area between art and philosophy per se, which is actually a term I use only to designate thinking that is, at the very least, essentially systematic. There must of course be an absolutely fundamental principle of literary genre that encompasses such great works as Petrarch's dialogue on contempt of the world, Nietzsche's aphorisms, or Péguy's works. This question has now been brought home to me, on the one hand because of Péguy's works and, on the other, because of the process of becoming and struggle through which a young man of my acquaintance is going. Beyond that, I am becoming aware of criticism's primary reason for existence and its primary value for my own projects as well. Art criticism, whose foundations have interested me in this sense, is only a subset of the larger domain.

I am unable to get much done here. This is due in part to my surroundings, from which I am unfortunately unable to isolate myself entirely—more in terms of internal than external factors. But even more because the Vienna library has left me completely in the lurch. I had been counting on the library when I left my scholarly books behind in Bern along with all the others, because for good reason I had no confidence in the shipping facilities. I have completed the only project I tackled here, the review of *Spirit of Utopia* which you mention in your letters, perhaps not entirely without the irony I looked for in what you said, because I enjoy it. Didn't you feel, even mean, that the book makes you suspicious precisely because of its plethora of explanations and because they are facile? I hope you will soon be able to see my review in print:[1] highly detailed, highly academic, highly and decidedly laudatory, highly and esoterically critical. I wrote it—I hope—in gratitude to the author, who pleaded with me to do so. I did it because I am linked to him by a predisposition, the reason for which I also find in some of the book's central ideas, although it is hardly the pure medium of our relationship. For I admit that, as I said, in some of its important explanations it corresponds to my own convictions, but never to my conception of philosophy. It is diametrically opposed to that. But the author transcends his book, more than he knows. Whether he will succeed in expressing himself philosophically in this sense is the crucial question for him. The book's content is everywhere muddied by the author's need to express himself. Therefore, as much as I vouch for its author, I would never want it to come between me and the people who are close to me. In the review, you will see what the positive things are for which I am indebted to the book, as well as the way in which my thinking ultimately distances itself from it. This essay was a project requiring three months of preparation. It was that difficult for me to fathom the book completely.

In the last two weeks I read one of the most magnificent books there is: Stendhal's *Charterhouse of Parma* [*Chartreuse de Parme*]. I hope you have already read it and, if not, will read it as soon as possible.—Have you heard of Odillon [*sic*] Redon, a French painter of the second half of the nineteenth century? And what do you know about him? I came across copies of the corpus of his etchings or drawings at an antique dealer's in Vienna. They were unaffordable. They seemed to me to be, in part, beautiful in a totally bizarre way and better than almost anything by Kubin, but at the same time somewhat similar to his things.

We really will come to Berlin at the end of this month or the beginning of the next. The only bright spot of this trip will be seeing you, Jula, Alfred, and some few others. We won't bring anything other than ourselves, separated as we are from everything with which we surrounded ourselves in the last years for our own sake, as well as that of our friends. In spite of this, I need not mention how much we are looking forward to the trip. You will finally be relieved of the responsibility of safeguarding my papers. Let me thank you now for this service from the bottom of my heart.—If Heinle's brother is in Berlin and has all of the manuscripts Fritz Heinle left after his death, I will finally take all of them into my safekeeping.

I hope you are well. When you find the time, please write me at the address on the envelope. My wife and I send our sincere regards.

Yours, Walter Benjamin

1. After many vicissitudes, this review remained unpublished and was ultimately lost.

88. To Gerhard Scholem

February 13, 1920

Dear Gerhard,

I received your last two letters, as well as "Analogie und Verwandtschaft." Many thanks! As far as Ernst Bloch is concerned, I would give a great deal to be able to speak about the situation with you in person. As long as this remains impossible, let me just say this: I am *totally* in agreement with your criticism of the chapter entitled "The Jews" and have held the same opinion of his views from the very first for, of course, knowledge, which I lack, does not play a major role in it. I have nothing to add to what you wrote about this. In my review, I hope I have made my radical rejection of these ideas apparent in what is, I hope, the most polite way possible. But this, of course, does not resolve the question. With good reason, you will have two questions to put to me: First, what is my stance toward other things that are generally related to this book. Specifically, my stance toward what you most aptly call "incomprehensibility of distance"; I believe this is the same thing my wife very aptly calls "seduction to truth." I remember that the first question you asked about this book in Bern was whether it included an epistemology. And that is precisely the crux of the matter: the book requires a confrontation with the author's epistemology, as well as with his axiomatic Christology. The last nine lines of my review do just that. I will not repeat their content here; you will read them, we will discuss them. It is important that we do so. Therefore, the last nine lines are intended as a rejection of the book's premises regarding knowledge, as a—restrained—rejection en bloc. The actual review, therefore, consists only of a detailed and, when possible, laudatory essay on individual trains of thought. You are right in assuming that there is no lack of opportunity for honest praise. But to be sure: my philosophical *thinking* has nothing in common with that of the book. Having said this, let me put the second question in your mouth: why am I reviewing it, why did I take on the task of doing this review (N.B. an enormous enterprise that took months)? More precisely: why did I respond to the author's request? I hope out of gratitude to him (he still has not seen the essay). More for the sake of what I value in him than in his book (which consequently is not totally without merit); for the sake of the hope I hold for his future development. In this book, he has presented us with something facile and overdone. But in the conversations we had in Interlaken, there was so much warmth and there were so many opportunities to express myself and make myself understood that I am making the sacrifice of this review to my hope.

If you can get me the bibliographical information I asked for from Bäumker, you will be doing me a great favor. I knew nothing of Heidegger's book.[1] On the other hand, I put my name down for a monograph on the linguistic logic of Duns Scotus (by Frey, I think?); I have the precise dates in Vienna. Since finishing the review, my projects here have come to a standstill due to the total lack of resources. No French dictionary. Therefore I could translate only two short Baudelaire poems. Thus I must rely entirely on my own devices and am now sketching out a rough draft for an essay with the charming title "Es gibt heine geistigen Arbeiter" [There are no intellectual workers].[2]

[. . .]

We are presumably leaving Breitenstein in three days and will be in Vienna until the end of February in care of Prof. Kellner, Vienna XVIII, 28 Messerschmied Lane; later at my parents'. [. . .] Our Munich plans have again become uncertain because my parents have ordered us categorically from now on to live at home with them since my father's bad financial situation no longer allows him to support us away from home. Naturally, we are unable to comply with my parents' wishes under any circumstances, but our situation is taking a very difficult turn. Dora may go to Switzerland by herself for a few months so that she can save up some Swiss francs, which we could use in Germany. She would therefore have to take a job there. We would very much appreciate getting some specific information on the cost of living in Bavaria—above all, what the average cost of room and board in the country is. Whatever the circumstances, I am going to try to get the *venia* in Bern so that, even if I cannot put it to use for any length of time in Switzerland, I can try to transfer it to a German university. Given these circumstances, we are not happily looking forward to our stay in Berlin.

Another question is, when will we see you if we do not go to Bavaria in the spring? It would hurt Dora and me to have to do without seeing you and we would like to ask you whether, should the worst come to pass, you would be so kind as to come to Berlin for a time right after the end of the winter semester—that is, around Easter?

We have recently been able to get some real rest here and, to my great delight, Dora is better than she has been for a long time, although she is not sleeping well.

How old is Werner Kraft's bride? Will he still be in Berlin at the beginning of March? His last letter to me was actually more cheerful. Nonetheless, based on the flimsiest information, we are unable to feel any more at ease about him than you are. [. . .]

Are you perhaps going to get your degree with Bäumker? Approximately when? A doctorate under his direction is, after all, quite respectable. Not like . . . Should you still have something in the way of concluding remarks to share on *Schöpferische Indifferenz,* please don't keep them from me.

I hope I will have your response to my important questions very soon.

Most sincere regards from me and my wife.

Yours, Walter

1. *Die Kategorien- und Bedeutungslehre des Duns Scotus* (1916).
2. This essay has not been preserved. It was directed against Kurt Hiller.

89. To Gerhard Scholem

Berlin
April 17, 1920

Dear Gerhard,

You are the last one in your family to receive my attention during my stay in Berlin. I have already consulted with your brother Reinhold and used the opportunity this occasion offered to chat with your father. These consultations have today temporarily come to a depressing end: despite all possible reductions on my part as well as theirs, the publication will cost over 5,000 marks because of recent large increases in printing costs and because the number of pages exceeds the original estimate. In Bern, I will probably petition for a larger subvention or for permission to postpone publication. My first week here has been just horrible.

[. . .]

Therefore, as I already said, I am as unable to assure you that I will visit Munich as I am unable to invite you to come here, because I do not know what the next few days have in store for me. I'm very sorry. I still have not gotten around to my habilitation dissertation because of the pressure of more immediate demands, and have not produced anything except a very short but timely note on "Leben und Gewalt" [Life and violence]. I believe I can say that it was written from the heart.—Does my memory deceive me, or didn't I some time ago refer you to a book, *The Complaint of Nature,*[1] which I actually never laid eyes on? I did not see Max Strauß[2] in Vienna. We heard Karl Kraus. A lot could be said about how he has changed from the way he used to be—but nothing against it. Many thanks for your information on the economics of Munich and its environs.

Your father succinctly pronounced you a genius in a conversation we had—he should know. But may God preserve every father from a genius. If you add to this that he then felt it necessary to explain what the Jews call *tachles,*[3] you can imagine the direction the conversation took. Your father struck me as being *very* content and spoke most kindly of you.

The Gutkinds are coming the day after tomorrow. I regret not being able to show my library to anyone here—it is represented by only a tiny, mixed legation. I found a lot of different things in Vienna, for example a very rare book, *Extrait d'un catalogue d'une petite bibliothèque romantique,* by Baudelaire's friend Asselineau, which, even in his time, only had a printing of 350 copies—it contains a very nice copperplate and the first printing of a sonnet I translated. Charlotte Wolter is among the previous owners of the book! If I tell you further that, my pathetic economic circumstances notwithstanding, I paid a tidy sum to acquire a "tabu,"[4] you will be able to judge what this means and you will also know that I believe myself to be in possession of a real treasure. But, please, let's neither one of us say anything about it. I only learned very late that Wertheim has been selling off the remainder of the [Georg] Müller publishing house for the past two years, which means that you can get good books for next to nothing. Just today, on the morning of our anniversary, I was able to bring some of these books home to Dora, among them Scheerbart's *Asteroiden Novellen* and *Das graue Tuch.* I was recently able to borrow *Rakkóx* in an old Insel paperback.

I hope things are well with you, dear Gerhard.

Yours, Walter

1. By the scholastic Alanus ab Insulis.
2. The brother of Ludwig Strauß and translator of Agnon.
3. A practical goal. Scholem's father used to criticize his son's "unremunerative arts" (pure mathematics and Jewish studies).
4. The term used by WB to denote books in his library that he did not lend out.

90. To Gerhard Scholem

Berlin/Grünau
May 26, 1920

Dear Gerhard,

You will doubtless already have come up with all kinds of explanations for the long hiatus in my correspondence. And you won't be on the wrong track if you assumed that things have almost never been as miserable for me, not in my entire life. I am totally unable to tell you anything about this period—other than in personal conversation—in part because I am unable to fathom the situation per se and it becomes plausible only in the sphere of idle chatter to which we were banished; in part, because it is necessary for me to avoid even the memory of it if I am to be able to surface ever again. I plunged very deeply. It ended in a total split. [. . .] The relationship between me and my parents had seemingly long since been put to the most severe tests and weathered them. That now, after years of relative peace, it disintegrated under the burden of these very tests—this is the one odd, but somehow logical, aspect of the situation. At this time I do not want to talk about the other aspects of the situation that are even worse and senseless.

I would most likely not be able to write you these lines even now if we had not found temporary lodging thanks to the Gutkinds' great kindness. Their wonderful patriarchal hospitality is helping my wife, who has been severely taxed, to begin to feel herself again. For the first time in weeks, we feel very fortunate to be living once again under humane conditions. We had made provisions that would allow us to bring Stefan too, [yet] a room (not at Gutkinds') we had counted on is no longer available to us. The temporary aspect of these arrangements of course cries out to heaven, and there is no way of telling how things will turn out. The only sure thing is that *somehow* we must get an apartment to serve as a base from which we can look around for a way to support outselves. Since the Gutkinds also want to get out of Berlin, we thought of sharing a place and have been looking for one for some time now. Do you know of *anything at all*? Of course, bureaucratic difficulties are supposed to be just horrid in Bavaria. We have already written to Seeshaupt.

My library is now stored at three different locations, all the books packed in crates. In spite of everything, I have recently made some good and very good buys. When will you, when will I, see them? As I said, it is impossible for me to speculate at all about the future before I find an apartment. [. . .]

We recently met Agnon at [Max] Strauß's. I wish you all the best in your acquaintanceship with [Robert] Eisler. I had just started reading his book[1] when I had to pack it away with everything else. I got as far as his treatment of Proserpina in the first volume and find his analysis of the legend of St. Agatha fascinating indeed. I also discovered observations at various other places that were very informative, especially those on the astral significance of fruit and field symbolism.

My next projects are to complete the note on the intellectual worker and an edition of my friend's [Friedrich Heinle—Trans.] works, or to establish an authentic text. Beyond my fondest hope, I have finally succeeded in gathering together all of his papers and have brought them along in order to work on the edition. Then I have to get down to work on my habilitation dissertation. It will retain this designation which, although it does not confer dignity, previously held out so much hope. At most, the dissertation would amount to my earning the *venia* for form's sake. Although my prospects of becoming a lecturer in Bern have come to naught, I will still do this, but only after I am living under halfway humane conditions.

My in-laws are the only support left to us. Even if, on the surface, this support is not very sturdy in material terms, they are willing to make the most extreme sacrifices and insist that I become a bookdealer or publisher. My father is denying me the capital to do even that. But it is very likely that I will have to stop giving the appearance of pursuing my former goals, that I will not be able to become a privatdocent, and, in any case until further notice, that I will have to pursue my studies secretly and at night, while holding down some bourgeois job. On the other hand, I do not know what this job would be. (This month I earned 110 marks by doing three graphological analyses.[2])

I hope to hear from you soon. After which you should also get a happier letter from me (because it will cover other topics). By then I hope at least to have made a lot of progress. I am also really happy about the peace and kindness we are enjoying. You will get "Gewalt und Leben" [Violence and life] once my wife has made a copy of it, which could take some time yet.[3] It is very short.

I am making a great effort to find a position reading manuscripts for a publishing house. Bloch recommended me to S. Fischer. They are looking for someone but they did not give me the job. You know something? I would have a very good list for a publishing house.

Most sincere regards. Please write soon.

Yours, Walter

P.S. At the moment—and evidently only for a few more days—Ernst Bloch is in Seeshaupt at Burschell's.[4]

1. *Weltenmantel und Himmelszelt* (Munich, 1909).
2. WB was an extraordinarily gifted and perceptive graphologist and sometimes gave his friends amazing examples of his talent. In 1922 he even gave private lessons in graphology.
3. It never arrived.
4. Friedrich Burschell (b. 1889).

91. To Gerhard Scholem

July 23, 1920

Dear Gerhard,

This letter is not only meant to make up for the long period in which I left you without news, but also to mark the beginning of another period in which I plan to write you more frequently. As it is, I have never thought of you more often and more affectionately than during the entire time I remained silent when your beautiful letters, all of which I received, kept your presence alive for me now and as a comfort in the future. Perhaps your June letter, which thoroughly grasped my situation, is what led me to start Hebrew—a decision I would not have dared make on my own. Let me now take this opportunity to tell you an anecdote about this. Erich Gutkind took me to Poppelauer and Lamm,[1] where I immediately filled my book bag and a bag from another trip with several books. As I ignorantly yet confidently rummage around among the books, Landau's *Chrestomatie (Geist und Sprache der Hebräer)* winds up in my hands. To his great amazement, Mr. Gutkind was able to buy it for 25 marks. He told me the story of your copy and, through a combination of mystical and inductive inferences, I deduced that I will not own this book before I have a Hebrew pupil. At the time, I bought myself the Fürst book,[2] the small Midrashim, the *Midrash Mechilta,* Mendel Hirsch's *Die Propheten,* and the book by Marcus on Hassidism.[3] Everything I needed to get started. And it cost about 350 marks. I was not able to do anything about getting a Bible because of the exorbitant prices. Erich Gutkind gave me the book *Kusari* as a birthday present.[4]

Dora may already have mentioned many of the things with which she surprised me. I was particularly pleased with an extremely beautiful painting by Klee, entitled *The Presentation of the Miracle.* Are you familiar with Klee? I really love him and this is the most beautiful of all his paintings I have seen. I hope you will get to see it here in September if, in a month's time, I don't have to bury the rest of my belongings in a crate too (and for how long?). For we will stay with the Gutkinds only until the end of August because they want to go to Italy on the first of September. Unfortunately we cannot move into their house for the two months they will be gone because it would then be unlikely that we could still find an apartment in November for the winter. We are diligently looking for one now. Furnished or unfurnished, about four rooms. Do you by chance know of anything suitable through your acquaintances? We also can't continue to remain separated from Stefan any longer. We know he is by no means being cared for the way we would want, because my parents are now taking him to a day-care center while my mother goes on a trip.

[. . .]

Reading the *Lewana* [*sic*], which I am doing now, is making the separation from Stefan especially difficult. This work relieves you of having to make an effort to write about the topic yourself. If you leave aside the effect of the religious and social community, and address only the most intimate relationships of parents to their child, it is impossible to speak with more insight and inspiration about childhood education than Jean Paul does. This is another case of the Germans not knowing how fortunate they are in what they have. He is the most imaginative spirit, yet how strictly, soberly and temperately he knows how to treat the subject of children! (It goes without saying that, in writing this, I am not using the word *strict* in its more narrow, pedagogical sense.)

Now let me get around to thanking you for your absolutely beautiful gifts. I do not know which of them gave me more pleasure and, above all, which will give me more pleasure. For I have not been able to read *Niobe* yet. But any mythological work from you fills me with the greatest sense of expectation. The subject is significant too. I believe no praise would be too high for the Agnon story. Therefore I won't even attempt it. While reading the story, I felt glad to have met Agnon. And my thanks to the translator.

[. . .]

Do you remember my having spoken to you in Iseltwald about Charles Péguy? In the meantime I happened across one volume of his selected works at the Gutkinds'. It has made me even keener than the fragment in the *Nouvelle revue* did to get unabridged versions of his works. For this volume also contains only fragments. Whether I will write an essay expressing my admiring and encouraging approval depends only on whether I finally get to read his most important writings in unabridged versions. I tried in vain to win S. Fischer and Kurt Wolff over to the idea of publishing a translation (by me) of selected essays. The copyright fees demanded by the French publisher are too high.

A few weeks ago, Kraft visited me for a few hours. Even if the visit was too short for any exchange of views, I nonetheless got the impression that his spirit is growing stronger. At the end of the summer semester, I hope I will have a better opportunity to talk to him when he visits Berlin for the second time.

Please write me again as soon as you can.

Since you are finally attempting to clarify the relationship between your graduation and the Kabbalah,[5] I will make the following pronouncement: I will claim to be a great kabbalist if you do not get your doctorate summa cum laude.

Most sincere regards,
yours as always,
Walter Benjamin

1. Dealers in secondhand Jewish books in Berlin.
2. Julius Fürst, *Hebräisches und Chaldäisches Handwörterbuch* (Leipzig, 1876).
3. Verus [pseudonym of Ahron Marcus], *Der Chassidismus* (Pleschen, 1901); a very noteworthy book.
4. A religious-philosophical work by Judah ha-Levi (twelfth century) (Leipzig, 1869).
5. Scholem had thrown himself into the study of the kabbalistic manuscripts in the Munich library.

92. To Gerhard Scholem

[ca. December 1, 1920]

Dear Gerhard,

What almost happened is that nothing would have arrived for your birthday other than these very sincere congratulations—and this "selection of short pieces" with which I part all too easily. For I was sorely tempted to keep everything else for myself, *Das Leben Jesu*[1] with its beautiful translations, as well as *Religion der Vernunft,*[2] which is clearly an extremely remarkable book. Since I remembered the iron rule that I myself impose on subjugated peoples these days, however, these hostages, the noble ones among the children of scriptural authorities, will be sent to you after all, for the sake of justice.

The board of trustees of the University of Muri has a special surprise in store for you in celebration of your birthday. The board has authorized me to inform you that, to celebrate this event, the new building that will house the university will be dedicated, and the board has had the following motto inscribed above the entrance: "Lirum, larum spoon's handle/little children ask a bundle." All the buildings are made of chocolate and we have enclosed a sample.

The apartment is slowly being put in order. The large bookcase is still not finished. And then, of all things, instead of one of my crates of books, we received a crate from the shipping agent that was not ours, but was labeled the same way. The shipping agent wrote us that he has already sent ours off but it has not arrived yet. By the way, this crate seems to contain the following books: Schnorr von Frechheitsberg's collected works;[3] Pontius Pilate's *Hebrew for Prefects;* Noeggerath's *Munich Children's Logic* and *Seven Titanic Cheeses.*

Dora seems to be improving only very slowly. She would rather that there not be a record of the way she has been looking of late. (This as an explanation for our failure to enclose a photograph.) Concerning Stefan's moral theology, the virtues that he, along with the citizens of Marburg, defined as eternal tasks for school have not yet arrived, and the sins are all out of print.

Following a long and serious depression, I myself am starting to become very diligent. Thus I now see myself confronted by a difficult decision. That is to say, it became apparent that it would be impossible for me to succeed in getting my bearings simultaneously in two different areas, scholasticism and Hebrew, which are both so difficult, unfamiliar to me, and at a great remove from each other. This made me think that it will be so difficult to pin down the topic of my habilitation dissertation and actually carry out the work that if I were to throw in some large, heterogeneous project, the dissertation might be pushed even further into the indefinite future. And this cannot be allowed to happen, if only for practical considerations. The result is that, at the very moment when philosophy would demand my undivided attention, I would for the last time have to let Hebrew take a back seat (not until I qualify for a university position, but) until the completion of my habilitation dissertation. There is no alternative, given the state of the job market, as well as current conditions in general. I will continue to compromise as long as possible, but I do not think it will be possible much longer. I have read Heidegger's book on Duns Scotus. It is incredible that anyone could qualify for a university position on the basis of such a study. Its execution requires *nothing* more than great diligence and a command of scholastic Latin, and, in spite of all of its philosophical packaging, it is basically only a piece of good translating work. The author's contemptible groveling at Rickert's and Husserl's feet does not make reading it more pleasant. The book does not deal with Duns Scotus's linguistic philosophy in philosophical terms, and thus what it leaves undone is no small task. Recently one of the three hundred new Cologne privatdocents, [Helmuth] Plessner, gave a talk at the Kant Society on the epistemological significance of linguistic philosophy. It was not on a very high level, of course, but its content was mostly very relevant. In the discussion period, no one said anything except for me and [Arthur] Liebert, who put the speaker down in the name of critical philosophy. I may have been the only one in the audience who could have said something pertinent, but I had to keep quiet in view of Liebert's apparent reasons. Meanwhile, I have again become a member of the Kant Society and was immediately invited to advertise my dissertation in the *Kant-Studien.* My critique of the *Idiot* and my essay "Fate and Character" will now appear in the *Argonauten.*[4] I have received the proofs.—An extremely noteworthy and substantial review of Bloch's book recently appeared, which brings out the book's weaknesses with great rigor. By S. Friedländer.[5] I will probably express my opinion on this in the first part of my *Politik,* which is the philosophical critique of the *Lesabéndio.* As soon as I have a book I need from France, I will proceed with the second part of the *Politik,* whose title is *Die wahre Politik* [True politics] and which consists of two chapters, "The Dismantling of Power" and "Teleology without Ultimate Goal."

I am in the process of completing the translation of the *Tableaux parisiens*. In doing so, I am also improving my earlier translation so that I can search for a publisher with full confidence in my cause.

Please write me how things are going in [Moritz] Geiger's philosophy of mathematics course.—I still do not know whether I will take a [Hebrew] class with Miss [Käthe] Holländer now. You will get the letters and the book by Lewy[6] as soon as my things have been put in order. At this time there is still so much stuff lying around that I have trouble finding things right away.

[. . .]

I hope you are well.
Yours, Walter

Kraft wrote me. However, I can't get around my conviction that he is on the wrong track in wanting to write a dissertation on the *Divan* (certainly the ***most difficult*** topic of postmedieval German literature).

1. Samuel Krauss, *Das Leben Jesu nach jüdischen Quellen* (1902).
2. By Hermann Cohen; appeared posthumously.
3. WB liked to complain that Scholem tried to "cadge" [*schnorren*] the best books from his library. Schnorr von Carolsfeld—the Nazarene painter. The titles are works in the library of the University of Muri.
4. *Argonauten* 10–12 (1921). In *Schriften* 1:31ff. and 2:127ff.
5. In *Das Ziel* 4:103–16.
6. Ernst Lewy, *Zur Sprache des alten Goethe* (1913). WB greatly admired Lewy (1881–1965) and his daring work.

93. To Gerhard Scholem

December 29, 1920

Dear Gerhard,

I have surmised the reason for your having remained silent for so long. I wrote to the Gutkinds even before I had come to a decision, purely because of my agonizing indecisiveness. In response I received their rebukes soon after receiving your letter of the 18th. I replied to these rebukes yesterday. As you will see, my reply also contains my coming to terms with your letter. Because I am unable to improve on what I have already said, there is no better alternative than to copy and send you what I wrote the Gutkinds. "When your letter arrived, the dilemma that had caused me to suffer for weeks had been resolved and, after reading your letter, I thought about it once again and reached the same conclusion. No, there is no other way. I am unable to devote myself to things Jewish with full intensity before having derived from my European apprenticeship what may result at least in some chance of a more peaceful future, family support, etc. I admit that I have been spiritually ready to turn away from things European and to begin a lengthy new apprenticeship approximately since the time of my Ph.D. exams. But I also know that the difficult decision I have nurtured for such a long time will leave me the choice, made freely and calmly, of when to carry it out. As it is, it is true that, as Scholem wrote, the older you are, the more difficult it is to make such a choice, and age can ultimately turn it into a catastrophe, even in the most favorable case. Even if it is a purifying catastrophe. But the decision that has been so long in coming and is firm also has a *settling* effect. Moreover, it will probably be a matter of no more than two years *at the most.* During this time, I intend to carve a project out of the complex of ideas floating in my mind, and write a book on it. This project—although it is important to me—can be defined and limited. The prospect of starting in on Hebrew is *overwhelming.* It is therefore impossible to say something like: First I will learn Hebrew for one or two years and tackle the project only after that. You will have to acknowledge the clear reasons for my decision. So I ask you, please do not postpone your own studies, but wait for me with your heart." Only now, while writing this, do I see the extent to which these lines are addressed to you. The only thing left is to add my promise that, after completing this project, I will truly not allow myself to be detained by anything that may come up, even if Herbertz turns one hundred or celebrates his golden wedding anniversary with philosophy.

Regarding my planned project, I have recently been busy with an analysis of the concept of truth, and it is supplying me with some basic ideas for the project. I was very pleased to hear Ernst Lewy (the language man) approve of my analysis when I recently read it to him. He, of course, is not a metaphysician, but an intelligent and right-thinking man. He was in Berlin for a short time where, incidentally, the full professor of comparative linguistics, Schulz, is making an effort to get him an adjunct professorship. This is unfortunately difficult because of the lack of funds. His personality again made an incomparable, and as always an equally incommensurate, impression on me. It is now truly my greatest concern that you get to know him. He has to go to Argentina to pick up his brother who is seriously ill.

You are deluding yourself about the number of "shorter pieces" I have written, as is proved by the ever-rising flood of your insatiable desires. Because, except for the review of *Strait Is the Gate,* which, incidentally, is not a drama but a novel, the shorter pieces I have produced in the past few years (amounting to almost nothing) have not been transcribed yet, except for the "Phantasie über eine Stelle aus dem *Geist der Utopie*" [Fantasy on a passage from the *Spirit of Utopia*], which I may send you soon.

As far as my "theater criticism" is concerned, I would rather call it "Notes on Dramas." Of these, I can in good conscience recommend for your appreciation the one on *As You Like It*. I plan to continue pursuing the views on Shakespeare I expressed in it.—Sometime, could you give me some idea of why *Das Leben Jesu nach jüdischen Quellen* leads to such unprecedented results? I have not yet been able to look at Gundolf's George book and am waiting for an opportunity to do so. I will probably get one soon.

[. . .]

[Richard] Weißbach in Heidelberg wants to publish my translation of the *Tableaux parisiens* (as a book), "if I do not make any demands he is unable to meet." Drei Masken Verlag in Munich has also asked to see the manuscript. Weißbach will probably pay next to nothing and publish only 250 copies of the thing as a paper-conjuring trick. I will wait and see what comes up. For external reasons and because of my family, it is absolutely necessary that I take advantage of any opportunity to publish.

"The True Politician" has now been transcribed. I hope it will soon appear in print. After the New Year I want to write the next two essays that with it are meant to constitute my *Politik*.—I can get Jeremias's *Handbuch der altorientalischen Geisteskultur* here for 15 marks at a used book store. Is it worth it? Please let me know.

The Gutkinds' address is Meran Obermais, Langegasse Mayaburg, c/o Mrs. Promberger, Italy.

Dora is not going to the office for the time being and is gradually recovering. Certainly not least because of our better prospects.

Please excuse the motley nature of this letter. I will be able to write you more when I have less to tell you. I want to add only that my brother gave me an edition of the letters Rosa Luxemburg wrote from prison during the war. I was touched by their incredible beauty and significance. Kraus has appended an important polemic directed against a "German woman's" shameless attack on the spirit of these letters. In the same (last) issue of *Die Fackel,* he published a national anthem for Austria which, in my eyes, unquestionably shows him to be on his way to becoming a *great* politician, just as *Brot und Lüge* does. It is as if the demonic and deeper side of his nature has died off, petrified, and as if his torso and its eloquent head now had an unshakeable marble pedestal from which to talk down.

Both of us send our sincere regards and hope that we will write each other more frequently than before.

Yours, Walter

P.S. A namesake of your landlord has produced an awful translation of *Amphitryon* for the Fulda Molière edition. We recently saw it performed on stage. I believe that it is still possible occasionally to enjoy the theater in Munich, something that is hardly possible here anymore.

94. To Gerhard Scholem

[January 1921]

Dear Gerhard,

I am writing you today out of apprehension, not that the necessity we discussed the last time we spoke will interpose itself between us, but rather that a period constituting a difficult time of waiting for both of us, although not of course entirely in the same sense, might be spent in close proximity to each other. I know that none of this can be forced and that you, I hope against your will, will have to keep many things from me that we ought to discuss, probably the most important things. You should know that I am very far from somehow expecting the impossible. Thus I am all the more convinced that we should preserve what still remains for us, as surely as you understand the necessity of my decision and believe me. It is often difficult for me because sacrifice, of course, does not always immediately bring about that for which it was made. As a result, I essentially must patiently lie in wait for my new project. To be sure, I have firmed up certain basic ideas, but since every one of them must be explored in depth, it is impossible for me to have any kind of overview at the beginning. Furthermore, the research I have done to date has caused me to proceed with caution and to question whether it is correct to follow scholastic analogies as a guide, or if it would not perhaps be better to take a detour, since Heidegger's work presents, albeit in a completely unilluminated way, the elements of scholastic thought that are most important for my problem, and the genuine problem can somehow be intimated in connection with this. Thus it may be better first to have a look at some linguistic philosophers. At the moment, I am planning to read A. F. Bernhardi's *Sprachlehre,*[1] which has been written and conceived in a monstrously unclear fashion, however, and seems only sporadically to be at all productive. Furthermore, everything is still in the most preliminary stage while I am waiting to finish my work on politics, as well as an essay commissioned by Lederer for which I still have not received all the literature I need to complete it. Nonetheless, in the next few days I should probably be getting Sorel's *Reflections on Violence* [*Réflexions sur la violence*]. I have just now become acquainted with a book that seems to me to be the most significant piece of writing on politics in our time, to the extent I can judge after attending two readings by the author. Yesterday evening, that is, on the occasion of the second reading, Hüne Caro told me he wrote you about the book, Erich Unger's *Politik und Metaphysik.*[2] The author belongs to the same circle of neopatheticists to which David Baumgardt (with whom I once spoke here) also belonged. I became acquainted with this circle from its most disreputable and really corrupting side at the time of the Youth Movement, and in a way that had extremely drastic consequences for Dora and me, in the person of Mr. Simon Guttmann.[3] A Mr. [Karl] Türkischer, to whom you presumably at one time gave a piece of your mind, is also spending time there. You are obviously right to meet the Zionist tendencies of these people[4] with complete indifference. I believe I may presume this without actually knowing it to be so. The Hebraic side of these people goes back to a Mr. Goldberg[5]—to be sure, I know very little about him, but his impure aura repelled me emphatically every time I was forced to see him, to the extent that I was unable to shake hands with him. On the other hand, it appears to me that Unger and Baumgardt are of an entirely different type—and, although I am aware of what I have just said, I believe I can assume the responsibility of recommending Unger's book to you because of my extremely lively interest in his ideas. These ideas, for example those regarding the psychophysical problem, surprisingly have some points in common with my own. I met S. Friedländer during these readings. He has a somewhat overwhelming effect on me, due to his expression of infinite refinement and equally infinite suffering. He talks about his own work with genuine humility.

The Stifter book arrived and made Dora unbelievably happy. She already owns the *Erzählungen* in the same edition and now, at one stroke, we have a very beautiful, almost complete, Stifter. The birthday was very nice and tranquil in other respects as well, as a consequence of a prudent political strategem on the part of the family.

[. . .]

Ernst Bloch's wife, one of our favorite people, died in Munich. You most probably saw her in Interlaken. We have invited him to stay with us, but there is still no answer as to whether he will come. His wife had suffered terribly for many years.

Did I already write you that I am negotiating with Weißbach about the publication of my Baudelaire translations. He wants to publish the *Tableaux parisiens* and in the final analysis, in spite of everything, I would prefer this to having the Jewish publishing house cancel an agreement.

Now that this letter is about to be sent after weeks of quarantine, I still want to add a few things. I have quite a lot to do since I am working on an essay for Lederer, "Critique of Violence" ["Kritik der Gewalt"], which is supposed to appear in *Weiße Blätter*.[6] I am finally at the point of producing a fair copy. Even if it does not appear in print, you will get to read it in any case. I had to deal with the *Ethik des reinen Willens* to be able to write the essay. But what I read there really depressed me. Cohen's sense of the truth was clearly so strong that he was required to make the most unbelievable leaps in order for him to turn his back on it.

[. . .]

My whole library has been installed since yesterday. It was only then that the last bookcases came from the carpenter. It looks very nice and not only we, but also our books, now await your arrival.

Do not be angry if I don't add anything else today. I am impatiently awaiting a letter from you.

Yours, Walter

P.S. At the moment, I do not have Kraft's letter to Kraus within easy reach. I will enclose it if I manage to locate it.

P.S. 2 Well, I will now send this letter off, probably three weeks after having started it. Just let me add my thanks for your letter, which I received yesterday. I beg you to forgive us for not thanking you sooner for the Stifter book. I also want to say that it came at just the right time and occupied a place of pride on the birthday table as the only gift from the subjugated peoples.—Regarding the Friedländer review of *Spirit of Utopia,* I intend to try to send it to you soon. It is a pity that you ordered the Unger book yourself because you could have gotten it from me, the author having made me a present of it.—I have now completed "Critique of Violence" and hope that Lederer will publish it in the *Weiße Blätter.* There are still questions concerning violence that I do not touch on in this essay, but I nevertheless hope that it has something important to say. None of my things that have been accepted, and naturally none of those that have not been accepted, have yet appeared in print, but I am not giving up hope for any of them, although I was especially disheartened that I was unable to find a home anywhere for my review of *Spirit of Utopia.* Although I am indebted to this project for clarifying some important things in my own mind, it was nonetheless meant entirely for publication. It was also to be published in a special issue of *Logos,* until it turned out that there was no money available for such a venture. "Der wahre Politiker" has also not been accepted, since Lederer does not want to publish it, at least for the time being. I am naturally not going to turn to Bloch at this time. Since receiving the news of his wife's death, we have not heard one word from him.—I hope to sign a contract with Weißbach soon. [. . .] The *Tableaux parisiens* are finished and I have, of course, translated all of them except for an early poem ("À une mendiante rousse").

From your frequent reports of illness, we gather with sadness that Munich's climate, which is indeed quite awful, does not agree with you and that your health is not as sound as we would wish. We are therefore doubly sorry if you have not found suitable acquaintances in Munich. And why has Agnon been barred? Only because of a lack of the necessary credentials (supposedly)?—As far as your worthy diversions are concerned, I am curious about what bad things you will have to tell me about [Rudolf] Kassner's lecture course. You know he has also written a book about physiognomy, *Zahl und Gesicht*. I will take a look at it when I get a chance. I recently read an essay by him on Baudelaire which is just as extraordinarily spurious as everything else of his I know. I have reduced him to a formula: he sells the whole truth in return for a half truth. This applies to his *every sentence*.

In what context did I write you about mathematics and language? It has slipped my mind and thus I do not know to what the relevant passages in your letter refer. Thank you very much for the reference to the book by Areopagita.[7] Are you still at [Moritz] Geiger's?

I hope you will write again very soon. Most sincere regards.

1. August Ferdinand Bernhardi's romantic linguistic philosophy (Berlin, 1801–3).
2. *Die Theorie: Versuche zu philosophischer Politik,* first edition (Berlin, 1921), a work that is now almost impossible to find.
3. Guttmann brought about the schism in the Discussion Hall at the beginning of 1914.
4. Unger and Goldberg rejected "empirical" Zionism in the name of an "a priori" or metaphysical Zionism.
5. Oskar Goldberg (1885–1952), author of *Wirklichkeit der Hebräer* (1925), a work that had an important impact (in large part subterraneously, as for example on Thomas Mann).
6. The essay appeared in *Archiv für Sozialwissenschaft und Sozialpolitik* 47 (1921); in *Schriften* 1:31ff.
7. Dionysius the Areopagite, *The Divine Names and Mystical Theology*.

95. To Gerhard Scholem

February 14, 1921

Dear Gerhard,

The only reason I did not answer your letter sooner is because I have rested and calmed myself by thinking about it in this troubled time. I continue to trust that the three of us will be able to work together as a team at some time in the future. I could not imagine Dora and me bound to any other third party in this way, but I am indebted to you for the direction my life and thought have taken and, as a consequence of this, Dora is indebted to you for the restoration of what was best in her upbringing. The expression "troubled time" occurs here because once again hostilities with my family have been renewed. I would rather not write about this, but only say that we have adjusted both externally and internally in such a way that the matter cannot have the same disconcerting impact on us it did last spring.

I have given some thought to philology (even back when I was in Switzerland). I was always aware of its seductive side.[1] It seems to me—and I do not know whether I understand it in the same sense as you—that, like all historical research, philology promises the same joys that the Neoplatonists sought in the asceticism of contemplation, but in this instance taken to the extreme. Perfection instead of consummation, the guaranteed extinction of morality (without smothering its fire). It presents one side of history, or better, one layer of what is historical, for which a person may indeed be able to gain regulative and systematic, as well as constitutive, elementary logical concepts; but the connection between them must remain hidden. I define philology, not as the science or history of language, but as the *history of terminology* at its deepest level. In doing this, a most puzzling concept of time and very puzzling phenomena must surely be taken into consideration. If I am not mistaken, I have an idea of what you are getting at, without being able to elaborate on it, when you suggest that philology is close to history viewed as a chronicle. The chronicle is fundamentally interpolated history. Philological interpolation in chronicles simply reveals in its form the intention of the content, since its content interpolates history. A book has made vividly clear to me what the nature of this way of working could be. This book moved me most deeply and inspired me to interpolation. It is Goethe's *Neue Melusine.* Do you know it? If not, you absolutely have to read this story, embedded in *Wilhelm Meister's Travels* [*Wilhelm Meisters Wanderjahre*], as a separate entity, i.e. *without* the frame that surrounds it, just as I happened to do. Should you be familiar with it, I may be able to suggest a few things about it.—I do not know whether you can make use of my oracular pronouncements about philology. I can assure you that the necessity of finding an approach to this matter other than the "romantic" one is clear to me. (I am just rereading your letter. Chronicle, interpolation, commentary, philology—they all have *one* nexus. If I may say so, it seems evident to me, based on the phenomenon of Agnon, that it is necessary to speak of truth when speaking of him. The wise man, of course, will no doubt focus his philology, not on the last, but on the first element of the series cited above if he is not, for example, dealing with the Bible.)

David Baumgardt visited me recently. He said on the one hand that he was very sorry he had not yet spoken with you at any length, but on the other hand that continuing to prepare for such a conversation would be good for him. He is now reading *More nebuchim*[2] in Hebrew. In any case, he very much hopes to see you in Erfurt, maybe during the summer.

[. . .]

It means a lot to us that we now have a piano in my room and Dora is playing again. Unfortunately, we were only able to get one on loan. [. . .]

Aren't you coming here over Easter? We could tell you a lot of cute stories about Stefan, but that would fill pages and pages.

Keep well.
Yours, Walter

P.S. The business affairs of the University of Muri are piling up to such an extent that I no longer know how to cope with them. Another dispute recently arose that I must submit to you. The professor of history approved a dissertation, but the faculty wants to block its acceptance. However, it is supposed to be very good. The topic is road signs at the time of the migration of the Germanic tribes. Please submit the matter to the board of trustees.

1. Scholem had written that philosophy was beginning to seduce him.
2. *Guide of the Perplexed,* Maimonides' philosophical work.

96. To Gerhard Scholem

March 26, 1921

Dear Gerhard,

I really enjoyed your last long letter. I keep hoping that you will follow through and read Goethe's *Neue Melusine* because this really ought to give us a lot to talk about. I am once again torn between several projects, one of which is sure to be of great interest to you, namely the essay "On the Task of the Translator" ["Über die Aufgabe des Übersetzers"]. This is the projected title of the foreword that I would like to place at the beginning of my Baudelaire translation if at all possible. This foreword is my most immediate concern, because I signed the contract with Weißbach (including conditions that are incredibly advantageous to me), and the book is supposed to appear at the latest in October. But what is at issue is a subject so crucial to me that I still do not know whether I can develop it with sufficient freedom, given the current stage of my thinking and provided that I can succeed in elucidating it at all. As far as my treatment of the subject is concerned, I am lacking a very basic aid: preliminary philosophical studies by authors who wrote on the topic before me. After all, in a critical analysis (of unfamiliar viewpoints) it is often possible to say things you would not yet know how to present synthetically. Could you possibly come up with some references for me? For example, I pored over the Cohen book on aesthetics and failed to come up with anything at all. Besides, you of course have your own ideas on this subject. Thus it would be most useful for me to discuss them with you at some length, especially since in your own translation projects you, of course, must capture an entirely different kind of linguistic tension than I do in mine. I hope that this topic alone will supply us with ample subject matter for discussion during your stay in Berlin. The question now is whether you will decide to come. The question of your being able to stay with us shapes up as follows: three visitors have announced their arrival—of course, all of them for April. But we do not yet know for sure whether any of them will actually come, when, and how long they will stay. Those who have announced their visits are my mother-in-law, Ernst Bloch, and Jula Cohn, a friend of ours. If your situation is such that your visit depends on being able to stay with us, we could give you a definite yes or no if we knew when you plan on being here. For if we knew that, we would first ask my mother-in-law whether she is thinking of coming at that time, and then write you immediately. So please give some thought to what kind of arrangements you might want to make as soon as possible.

[. . .]

There is something really wonderful to be seen here now: the commemorative exhibition of August Macke's paintings, the artist who died in battle in 1914 at the age of twenty-seven. I was attracted early on by the few paintings of his with which I was familiar. The exhibition has now made a wonderful impression on me. I wrote a short essay about these paintings. Should Goltz exhibit anything by Macke in Munich, perhaps you will go see it. Also a new painting by Chagall is on exhibit here, *Sabbath*. It, too, seemed very beautiful to me. I am coming more and more to the realization that I can depend sight unseen, as it were, only on the painting of Klee, Macke, and maybe Kandinsky. Everything else has pitfalls that require you to be on guard. Naturally there are also weak pictures by those three—but I *see* that they are weak.

I recently received my Ph.D. diploma, dozens of copies at once. Therefore, I hope you are aware that, as the owner of a naïvely realistic Ph.D. diploma, I will from now on assume the high office of transcendental beadle of the University of Muri.

I was recently able to get Meister Eckhart's sermons, and some volumes of the large Nietzsche edition for my philosophical library at very little cost. I also bought a wonderful copy of a beautiful, old translation of Theocritus. Regarding your Hebbel,[1] I would like to know whether you call it superfluous in and of itself or because it is a duplicate. I am familiar with the Swift edition you got in exchange for it—and this edition is still available at the publishers. Only recently I discussed with Dora whether I should buy it or not. She advised against it because of the translation. A lot of what I tried to read in that edition was quite tedious in any case because I lack the relevant expertise. But I remember having found great things, particularly in the Irish pamphlets. Especially "A Modest Proposal."

I have heard very little from Bloch since his wife died. I have not even heard anything yet about my "Critique of Violence," which is in his possession. I will ask him to send it to you in the next few days. I am also enclosing "Der wahre Politiker," which you asked for and which I would like to have back sometime (it is my best copy). Could you possibly advise me how to get a press to publish the thing? In this instance, it really is a pressing matter for me, so to speak. [. . .]

What do you hear from Agnon? I intend to buy his new novel[2] as soon as it appears in print—or have it given to me as a present to celebrate the 15th of July.

Yours, Walter

1. Hebbel's diaries.
2. *The Outcast*. It was published as a book in German only in 1923.

97. To Gerhard Scholem

April 11, 1921

Dear Gerhard,

I would of course be glad to do everything possible for you for the pure joy of having you here, and would even provide you with occasional verse in honor of your brother's marriage. Why not let the fountain of your inspiration bubble over with regard to your brother's delicate good sense in marrying on the same day as Dora and I? And what do you plan to give us APROPOS our wedding anniversary? You aren't just going to hang around at your brother's?

Erich Gutkind came down with the flu soon after his return and he is very weak although he has fully recovered. Because of this, Lucie and he have still not been to visit us and as far as I know they do not want to come to Berlin yet. It might also prove to be too distracting if they were to get together with you just when you would be staying with us for the first time. I will discuss it with them and would like to propose that we all meet out there for a whole day. The weather here promises to be absolutely beautiful and everything looks more promising for us than it has looked for a long time. A friend whom we have not seen for many years is coming at the same time as you. She will be staying with us.

Today is Stefan's birthday. He is unfortunately complaining, not without cause, about the rebellious behavior of the subjugated peoples. Specifically, *gens academica* (the Murites) have not yet presented themselves with their leader, Warder the Pious. As part of our precelebration activities we took him to the zoo for the first time yesterday. There we encountered the liveliest sort of confusion. The elephant, of course, was recognized immediately, but soon after that the llama was identified in a warning tone as a "large elephant," and an ibex as a monkey.

I am now reading [Salomon] Maimon's autobiography. I discovered some very nice things in its Judaic excursuses. Other attractions in Berlin include a small Klee exhibition on the Kurfürstendamm and the proofs of "Critique of Violence": in addition, there are my new purchases which you may view gratis, exhibited at 23 Delbrück Street, on the anniversary of the union of the libraries.

Most sincere regards. See you very soon!

Yours, Walter

98. To Gerhard Scholem

Breitenstein
End of June 1921

Dear Gerhard,

I have informed Bloch that he cannot visit his friend[1] here. We will not be able to have him here until the fall. I will therefore meet Bloch in Munich. I will be there at the beginning or toward the middle of next week: Tuesday, at the earliest.—Now I have a question. After my visit to Mrs. Bernhard,[2] it was not entirely clear to me that the room she had offered me (exclusively for sleeping) is right next to the kitchen (and that you can only get to it by going through the kitchen) and is her maid's room. Being so near the kitchen would probably get me up very early every morning and this would not be conducive to a restful and pleasurable visit. (As you know, I really need a rest.) Now for the question: if I do not find anything else, could the arrangement Ernst Schoen has also be made for me.[3] Your answer would not reach me in time. By putting the question now, I am asking you only to consider it.

There is no doubt that Dora has pulmonary apicitis and requires the greatest care and indulgence. After three weeks there, during which she will recuperate on her own, she will come back here until she has completely recovered.

Sincere regards to you and Miss Burchardt.[4]

Walter

1. György Lukács in Vienna.
2. WB's former landlady at 4 Königin Street.
3. With Scholem's landlady, at whose house Schoen also lived at the time.
4. Elsa Burchardt. She later became Scholem's first wife.

99. To Gerhard Scholem

Heidelberg
July 12, 1921

Dear Gerhard,

I still do not have confirmation that you received the diploma. Therefore, an objective and expert judgment on the so-called Miss Burchardt does not seem to be appreciated. I should also add that the tasty oranges were wonderfully well hidden.

Yesterday evening I met little Pflaum[1] at Miss Cohn's. Unfortunately, however, I had completely forgotten the colossal impertinences that you had instructed me to perpetrate on him. He is going to take me to Gundolf's lecture tomorrow. Otherwise, I have not done anything here yet and so far have not been to either Lederer's or Weißbach's class. There is absolutely no doubt that I will remain here for some time and will travel hardly at all. Thus a visit from you will be all the more welcome toward the end of my stay here.

Thank you very much for forwarding my mail. What follows are some new questions and requests. Hasn't there been any confirmation yet from Goltz about the 1,000 marks paid in by Bloch? Did you write Dora a letter? and did you also encourage her to stay in Breitenstein if at all possible? If not, it would be very nice if you would do so without delay and have your young lady write.

My lengthy stay here admonishes me about how *much* work there is to do, and I have nothing better to do than read Rosenzweig. Please do me a great favor and send me the book (at my expense) and if possible let me keep it so that I can use it as my working copy—and you can get a copy from your mother at my expense.

I must very abjectly ask the young lady for bread coupons. I often eat in my room and will soon run out of them.

The weather is magnificent here. The Neckar is drying up and the whole city is aglow. The landscape is southern in many places.

I found the *Geschichte des Index* listed for 65 marks in a local store's antiquarian catalogue, but it had already been sold. On the other hand, I did acquire a beautiful edition of the two volumes of Goethe's correspondence with various romantics, published by the Goethe Society (unfortunately, at a hefty price).

Sincere regards to you and Miss Burchardt.

Yours, Walter

I am going to Landau's[2] the day after tomorrow.

1. Scholem's cousin, Heinz Pflaum (1900–1962); later a professor of romance languages and literature at the University of Jerusalem; a student of L. Olschki and Gundolf.

2. Scholem had advised WB to look up Henryk Landau, a Jewish philosopher.

100. To Gerhard Scholem

Heidelberg
July 20, 1921

Dear Gerhard,

The many gifts that enable me to lead a pleasant life here have all arrived safely: the Rivière for which I thank you very much, and which—

without having yet read the essay on Baudelaire—led me back to my translations. I now work on them occasionally. The Rosenzweig,[1] with which I became reacquainted yesterday, and the bread coupons, which recently arrived and guarantee a comfortable feeling of bourgeois security.

I explained the young lady's [Burchardt's] objections to Dr. Nebbish,[2] who paid little attention to them, however, because he is totally preoccupied with his own relocation. For he is threatening to depart and finally to disappear completely from our sight since he has been called to Muri to lecture on necromancy.

Yesterday I made the acquaintance of a student from Muri in the form of a certain Mr. [Henryk] Landauer (not Landau, as you pointed out to me).[3] Students from Muri are characterized by a conspicuous reticence. From another perspective, however, he is known to be somewhat garrulous. That is to say, this observation originates with a certain young Mr. Friedrich Potschuß,[4] an acquaintance of Miss Cohn and Ernst Schoen, with whom I often get together. Although I was most positively predisposed toward him because of you and Miss Cohn, who is also slightly acquainted with Landauer, this did not prevent him from making a strange, difficult, and not entirely delightful impression on me. I cannot, however, precisely account for this. Maybe the fact that he is so obviously very sickly is to blame for the coldness he seemed to radiate. In any case, I am unable to allow myself to make any kind of judgment and will probably get together with him once again. He promised to write you soon. [. . .]

I went to hear Gundolf and Jaspers—one hour each. And still want to have a look at Rickert and [Hans] Ehrenberg. Gundolf appeared to me to be terribly feeble and harmless in terms of the personal impression he makes, quite different from the impression he makes in his books. Jaspers is feeble and harmless in his thinking, but as a person obviously very remarkable and almost likeable. [. . .] He is a full professor now and, when I heard him, had just very decently stood up for the Russians and Jews, something he is said to have done already when he was a privatdocent. It was Pflaum who took me along both times. He behaves very decently.

I was recently in Neckargmünd and took a long walk through the completely parched countryside in the hours before the rain fell—the first in weeks. The countryside here and especially near Neckargmünd is even more beautiful than I had imagined.

[. . .]

Dora does not write much. In her last letter, she says that she is continuing to gain weight and does not have a temperature. For my birthday, she sent me a magnum opus, *Das Erdbeerbuch,* full of profound paintings and sayings. I have placed an announcement for my dissertation in the last issue of the *Kant-Studien*.

Sincere thanks and many regards.

Yours, Walter

1. Franz Rosenzweig's *Stern der Erlösung* [*The Star of Redemption*] (Frankfurt, 1921).
2. WB's humorous self-designation.
3. The correct name nonetheless was Landau (died 1967).
4. The correct name is Podszus (born 1899).

101. To Gerhard Scholem

July 25, 1921

Dear Gerhard,

It makes me very sad to hear that your firmly established domicile is threatened. It has been a sanctuary in Germany, visible from afar, for all pious animals and poor ekuls.[1] One cannot tell how great the danger really is. The only way the woman's claims could have any chance of being accepted is if she either submits compelling profitability statements or if she taps a rich lode of *risches*.[2] But all that aside, it is, of course, possible for you to be offered a settlement that might still be unacceptable to you. Thus, I really do not dare to look forward to the prospect of your being in Berlin in the winter because it would be against your will and in some respects contrary to your interests. By the way, could this eventuality expedite Miss Burchardt's[3] emigration?

One asks oneself and wonders, what the Angelus[4] has to say about this. I really do not know if I said anything to you about "his greeting." All its wonderful beauty notwithstanding, the language of angels has the disadvantage of our being unable to respond to it. And I have no choice but to ask you, instead of the Angelus, to accept my thanks.

In the meantime, I have been to Weißbach's class for the first time and am going back tomorrow. It is quite pleasant. I still don't know what will come of it. I will be seeing Lederer for the first time tonight at the sociological discussion evening. I have already had the privilege of hearing Mr. Ehrenberg at this event. I have made an effort to get into Rickert's and Jaspers's classes. I rather liked the latter (but I believe I have already written you that). And you probably also know that he has become a full professor. Rickert has become gray and wicked.

Probably neither one of us can yet say anything about our plans, and consequently we are still unable to firm up anything regarding the Lewys.[5] It is nevertheless quite likely that I will go to Breitenstein once more. I would then probably go via Munich again?

Just one other small request: please send me "Der wahre Politiker" immediately. [. . .] You see, I have finally started working pianissimo and have again turned to the subject of politics, which necessitates my having a look at the first essay. I am also giving some thought to my talk on Baudelaire, which is supposed to inaugurate my winter lectures (at the Ewer bookstore?) and which should turn out to be very nice. I received a letter from Rang today, according to which he often gets together with Buber.

There are hardly any books to buy here. But I recently bought the first part of Döllinger's essays on the sectarian history of the Middle Ages (about the Manichaeans) for 10 marks. Have other parts of this appeared in print?

I hope you are well. Sincere regards to Miss Burchardt.

Yours, Walter

1. *Ekul* was the opposite of *Ekel,* something or someone nasty or disgusting, in WB's private language with his wife.

2. Yiddish for *anti-Semitism.*

3. Burchardt went to Palestine at the beginning of 1923.

4. Paul Klee's painting *Angelus Novus,* which WB had procured. Scholem had it hanging in his apartment in Munich for a long time and had composed a poem to it, to which WB often referred. The poem went like this [trans.: Smith]:

Greetings from Angelus

(To Walter on July 15, 1921)

I hang nobly on the wall
Looking at nobody at all.
I have been from heaven sent,
A man of angelic descent.

The human within me is good
And does not interest me
I stand in the care of the highest
And do not need a face.

From whence I come, that world
Is measured, deep, and clear.
What keeps me together in one piece
Is a wonder, it would appear.

In my heart stands the town
Whence God has sent me.
The angel who bears this seal
Does not fall under its spell.

My wing is ready to beat,
I am all for turning back.
For even staying in timeless time
Would not grant me much fortune.

My eye is darkest black and full,
My gaze is never blank.
I know what I am to announce
And many other things.
....
I am an unsymbolic thing.
My meaning is what I am.
You turn the magic ring in vain.
I have no sense.

5. In mid-September 1921, WB and Scholem visited Ernst Lewy for several days in Wechterswinkel, where WB put his plan for a journal, *Angelus Novus,* up for discussion.

102. To Gerhard Scholem

[Heidelberg]
[August 4, 1921]

Dear Gerhard,

If only all of the ins and outs of the universe were everywhere thrown into such bold relief as they are in Dr. Escha's[1] gossip column in the *Halberstädter Nachrichten*. No such outlet is as yet available in Heidelberg. Yet we are still hopeful that the opening in the next few days of St. Burchardt's Brewery (with its well-known escutcheon portraying a porter holding aloft the Kabbalah) will turn out to be a powerful magnet for the meeting of great minds.

All this aside, I have some wondrous things to report. The way has been smoothed for me and the paths have been readied for my feet. [. . .] The Lederers, especially Mrs. Lederer, whom I hold in very high esteem, have been charming to me. Bookstores and used bookstores are being opened up to celebrate my presence. I was the first customer in a used bookstore that had opened up just today and was immediately addressed by name. I went there in order to secure as quickly as possible the five volumes of Görres's *Christliche Mystik,* which were displayed in the show window and priced at 100 marks.

I was naturally very pleased with everything you had to say about the "Critique of Violence." It will appear in the next few days. I am working on the next and final section of the *Politik* to the extent I am getting around to doing any work at all. It will doubtless turn out to be much longer than the previous sections. Soon, however, I will leave behind my many new acquaintances and depart, taking with me pleasant memories and hope. Namely, I will first of all go to visit Dora in Breitenstein again. On the whole, she has been sending me positive reports. She writes that only the demands made on her by her relatives have prevented her from writing you.

[. . .]

Can I visit you in Munich, from approximately the 10th to the 14th of August? Are you sure you'll be there? Please answer me immediately and definitively. When you receive this letter, if you should still not have a clear notion of your plans, things are not at all likely to work out for me, because I will most probably have to make firm commitments. In that event, I might want to arrive in Breitenstein earlier than the 15th. And could you free up most of your time for me while I am there? For we do need a lot of time. For what—and the reason why a second meeting between us this summer is indispensable—is something I will explain now, and it will astonish you. I have my own journal. Starting the first of January next year I will be publishing it through Weißbach. And, of course, it is *not* the *Argonauten* (which, as far as I can tell, will fold). Without the slightest hint from me, Weißbach offered me my own journal after I declined to assume the editorship of the *Argonauten*. Specifically, it will be structured entirely and unconditionally in keeping with my conception of the journal when I first thought of it many years ago (to be exact, in July 1914 when Fritz Heinle and I first seriously considered starting a journal). Thus it will have a very narrow, closed circle of contributors. I want to discuss everything with you in person, and will now tell you only its name, *Angelus Novus*. I want to and must speak with you about your collaboration. As far as I can tell, it is a prerequisite for the *success* of this journal (*in my sense* of the word).

The rumors about Weißbach are false. Of late, I have seen that he has an utterly *resolute* drive, even if he of course lacks clearly defined aims, and that this drive is directing him to place the publishing house on my shoulders for the future. He is also going to publish Fritz Heinle's papers, about which I very recently spoke to him. Everything I have achieved has been accomplished without the least pressure or use of force, even if I have naturally also shown myself to be very intense and prudent. As enthusiastically as I may have seized upon the idea, the journal is the result of his initiative. But he now knows *precisely* what I want and, above all, what I do *not* want.

When I come back here at the beginning of September, I first want to visit Rang, and after that, if at all possible, to arrange a meeting with Ferdinand Cohrs.[2] This is so that I will arrive in Berlin at the beginning of October with the materials on the basis of which I can put most of the journal together for an entire year (four issues, 120 pages each).

"Der wahre Politiker" still has not arrived. If you have not mailed it yet and if our mid-August meeting is going to take place, then there is no need to send it. If we are unable to meet this month, I will just have to plan on it for the beginning of September.—Would you please let me have your letter to the publishers of the new *Buch vom Judentum*[3] for the journal.

With the most extraordinary optimism, I send sincere regards to you and Miss Burchardt.

Yours, Walter

1. Burchardt was called Escha by her friends. Her family originally came from the Halberstadt area.
2. He was a pastor in Lower Saxony at the time; a colleague from the Free Students.
3. Which, at the time, was being planned by a Zionist-socialist group as a continuation of the book published by Kurt Wolff in 1913. It did not, however, materialize.

103. To Gerhard Scholem

August 6, 1921

Dear Gerhard,

You will have taken note of the fact that the Angelus has taken flight. Don't be alarmed. He has landed here in the handsome form of Miss Burchardt from Halberstadt and has pronounced a *broche*[1] over Weißbach and his house.

He flew over Wiesbaden, there looked into the heart of Mr. Czaczke[s],[2] and saw that it would be right and fitting for him to erect the "new synagogue"[3] in the heart of the "Angelus." I have now taken the Angelus to the leading café here where, surrounded by entente diplomats, he slurps nectar and ambrosia that I have selected for him. A large protest meeting will take place this evening in St. Burchardt's Brewery, where the angel will speak on the following topic, "Four Weeks among Turkish[4] Angelologists."

P.S. The angel requests that you not immediately run to Mr. von Kahr,[5] and that you not put an announcement in the *Münchner Neusten*. He will return even without "All is forgiven."

1. Hebrew for *blessing*.
2. Agnon's original surname.
3. A story translated by Scholem.
4. Scholem lived on Türken Street in Munich.
5. Of the Bavarian home guard.

104. To Gerhard Scholem

October 4, 1921

Dear Gerhard,

I wish both you and Miss Burchardt good luck on the occasion of the new year as well as on your new apartment. [. . .]

I would really like to know what the angel's attitude is toward the new year.

> The godchild's wit thinks and means to ask
> Whether he does not perhaps nod and beat his wings?

Based on many a favorable turn of events here, I gather that his arrival will not be long in coming now. Of course, things are still not going right for Dora—at least, as far as her health is concerned. The operation was not entirely without complications, which made it necessary for her to recuperate at home. My father has miraculously completely recovered and will probably be able to get out of bed soon. I must also report on two great events that took place in the last few days, in one of which you figure in a somewhat complicated way. That is to say, your conversation with Dora Hiller[1] brought forth a harvest of blessings thick as hail—specifically, on my own head. [. . .] During my next meeting with [Erich] Unger, when we were planning to discuss the *Angelus,* he preceded a question about my relationship to Goldberg with the observation that his own relationship to him was most intimate. In doing so, he made it obvious in every way possible that he, so to speak, knew the truth and expected only a purely formal explanation that I was "indifferent" to Goldberg. I, however, who after my experiences in Wechterswinkel am unable to look into such an abyss without jumping into it out of fear, spoiled everything—to both my horror and his. In short, there was a total break. In a devilishly clever conversation with Unger, Dora, who in contrast to me immediately recognized the prestige at stake in this whole matter, explained my revulsion in terms of personal idiosyncrasies, thus saving the situation. To be quite truthful, after this conversation Unger, of course, knows even better than before how I feel, but has assuaged his conscience as he had wanted.

[. . .]

The other event is the visit Wolf Heinle paid us, from Saturday until today. [. . .] The more precise insight into his life in Goslar which his stories provided has shown us that we did not know the best part of it. It can briefly be described as follows: the pottery (ceramics) with which he supported himself by extremely strenuous work was a source of not only external but also internal support, on the basis of which his life took on a most decided form. His wife's influence—or at least, his marriage's—

also appears to be beneficial. His situation can perhaps be best described by saying that all other questions and activities took a back seat to specific and clear-cut questions as to how to structure his life. He is hardly doing any writing at all at the moment, but from what I have seen of his latest things, the writing he is doing seems to me to be very good. He is very distanced from his own as well as from his brother's writings. As clear-cut as his relationship to them is, they now concern him very little. All this will be a good basis for an external as well as an internal agreement, and thus I hope, to the extent he does not give me freedom to do as I wish, to be able to come to an understanding with him. It is in this spirit that we discussed the role that his and his brother's writings will play in the journal, as well as my publication of Fritz Heinle's papers. His last letter, written in August, seems to be explicable in great part based on his aversion to the title. He was unfamiliar with the context in which it was chosen but now he likes it just fine. Nevertheless, great care and discretion was required of all of us during our discussions.

The first issue is slowly taking shape. In the next few days, I want to draft the prospectus. To do this, it is quite indispensable for me to know which of the topics we discussed you want to tackle first. The topics were the Lamentations, the Book of Jonah, and the study of Judaism. I also need the precise title of Agnon's second novella.

Ernst Bloch did not come on Wednesday, nor at any other time. He wrote a letter that, I admit, is not exactly a cancellation, but that explains that at the moment he can endure the company only of simple people and irritably enumerates the reasons why he is unable to count me as one of them. Dora intends to help out by writing a letter in this instance as well.

[. . .]

We hope soon to hear how you are. The editor also asks for news of you and appends submissive greetings to Doctor daemonicus.

Yours, Walter

1. At that time, Oskar Goldberg's fiancée, later his wife, who tried to draw Scholem into his orbit. This resulted in a noisy dispute.

105. To Gerhard Scholem

October 9, 1921

Dear Gerhard,

In spite of your wish and my intention, I have no choice but to send you Rang's essay on "Selige Sehnsucht."[1] Since the journal is just being launched, the question as to whether it should publish the essay is so difficult and important an issue that I will briefly summarize how Dora and how I view it, so that you will not be inclined to attribute the problem to a criminal lack of clarity on my part. And if I ask you, must ask you, to read it, I do so only insofar as it is necessary to answer the question that arises from the following judgments. The whole thing, after all, can be read in two hours, and you should be able to spare the time if I assure that you are not being asked to serve in the role of "coeditor." You are only being asked for the advice I need to be of one mind with you when I act on this unusually difficult question. This means that I will follow your advice in this matter regardless.

To be brief, my judgment of the work is

1. The language is intolerable, i.e. full of tasteless things.
2. What he says about the poem—in contradistinction to what a genuine commentator would say—is often said at the expense of the poem.
3. He does not do full justice to essential aspects of this poem, to what is actually poetic about it.
4. He also does not do justice to essential aspects of this.[2]
5. The essay contains extraordinarily deep and very important insights into the poem and especially into the meaning of the *Divan* as a whole, insights that, as far as I know, have never been arrived at before. I consider what this essay has to say about Goethe's religion to be absolutely true.
6. I reject the gnostic metaphysics that appears in the background of the essay as content and in the foreground as form.

What I am unable to determine, and what constitutes the fundamental source of my uncertainty, is the following question: may we (you and I) still view the problems inherent in the language (and which are much more conspicuous there than in the content) debatable? Even if the language is naturally alien to us in a certain sense and does not especially concern you. Of course, I can and should publish things to which, in the final analysis, I have a negative attitude, if they are inherently of enduring value, highly significant, and timely—if they do not try to impress the reader in a way that leaves no room for debate. For to be sure, I can—at most—stand a tone of being nondebatable, of being simply dictatorial or of seeking to impress, only in utterances I espouse down to the last detail (and they are hardly likely to be anything like that, except, perhaps, in statements about art where something entirely different is involved).

Dora agrees with me regaring the above critique of Rang's essay. Her evaluation differs from mine only in that she is much less enthusiastic about what I see as the essay's positive values. Nonetheless, for me the great significance of the essay is inescapable in the sense mentioned above.

I hestitate to sat that the problem the essay presents us with—viewed objectively—is Rang's collaboration. For only its thesis and radicalism are crucial here. But from a personal perspective, the question of whether that is not after all the crucial thing is, of course, an entirely different issue and I fear I might have to answer it in the affirmative.

In no case would I want to put it into the first issue.

Let me close with the urgent request that you take the few hours to read it and write me as soon as possible, because I must write Rang very soon.

Steinschneider[3] was here on Thursday and we really liked him. Dora made quite an impression on him. By the way, she has been doing noticeably better in the past few days, especially in terms of her health.

Sincere regards to you and Miss Burchardt.

Yours, Walter

1. The essay was later published in *Neue deutsche Beiträge* 1 (1922).
2. The poem as such.
3. Gustav Steinschneider (born 1899), a friend of Scholem.

106. To Gerhard Scholem

[October 27, 1921]

Dear Gerhard,

You have truly executed your difficult task well and for that you have my sincere gratitude! You should by no means attribute my silence, which persisted even after I received your letter, to my mulling over its content. Concerns that were in part external, and in part internal, kept me from writing. Therefore, I intend to include all the Berlin trivia I can think of in this letter.

First of all let me confirm that I understood your opinion and that I did not have to resort to interpretation because it is identical to my own, especially when it comes to the editorially important points. What is decisive for me in this regard is, of course, the essay's—almost pathological—dependence on discussion. Thus I do not intend to publish it and have already essentially informed the author of this. I really hope that this will not lead to any disastrous confrontations. In the first place, I will do everything I can to keep my rejection from appearing to be a matter of principle; and second, for some reason Erich Gutkind, whose opinion carries some weight with Rang, is on my side; third, it could be that the incident with [Henri] Borel[1] has shaken his self-confidence about certain things in a *salutary* way. His correspondence having gone throught a critical phase, even with the Gutkinds, Borel's arrival is coming up almost immediately, after the local waiter's strike is over.

It is up to you to hold the well-earned high rank in the angelocracy, that is to say to be legally appointed to the planned ambassadorship at the court of the genius.[2] For you should know that the following maxim obtains in this regard: ambassadorships may only be assumed by proper, official collaborators.[3] Therefore, your manuscript is expected by the Ministry for the Interior so that it can immediately be passed on with the highest recommendations to the Foreign Ministry. So much for the question of promotion. As to the question of whether you can immediately be released from some of your lowlier duties, it must be noted that—as Prof. Ostwald[4] is known to have proven—nothing can be finally and authoritatively brought about in the absence of the assistant angel. The editorial board will, therefore, not be able to come to an independent decision before the honorary angel arrives. We *very much* hope that he will arrive in time to bless a package for Escha Burchardt at this very location.

(He is also supposed to have a sure touch in choosing birthday presents for the degree candidate in cadging.)

I believe Dora will be adding a few words to this letter. Her health has lately had its ups and downs. At the moment it seems to be very good. She may write you at greater length sometime soon, but I do not know for sure.

The relationship between Orpheus S. Fisher and me has taken an unexpected turn for the better due to an amusing business matter involving him and my father. As a result, today I received 2,000 marks from him for the Gauguin pictures, for *Van Zantens Insel der Verheißung*,[5] a matter of five or six hours' work. This was also the occasion for a tough and interesting meeting and it is a pity that I cannot act it out for you.

Have you been to Meyrink's[6] yet? As for me, I looked up Holzmann's cousin [Julian] Hirsch and the sculptor Freundlich. Tomorrow I am going to visit the third person he mentioned. The first two are men of honor, but using them for the *Angelus* is out of the question. Otto Freundlich because of his astonishing immaturity; Hirsch, on the other hand, on absolutely all counts. His book on the *Genesis des Ruhmes*[7] is decked out with a considerable portion of dullness. Freundlich, on the other hand, has good ideas. Some time ago I sent a very good letter to Lewy that was somewhat milder than the one I considered sending when you and I were together. I received an answer that I admit, given his circumstances, was very moderate and pacific in its tone but was undeniably dogmatic in terms of the issue and made my surrender the condition for any further correspondence. Naturally, my response is to keep silent. Besides a number of things that confirmed my view of him and especially of his wife, I heard the extremely interesting story about the end of his university career, for which she is responsible, from Hirsch, who knew him well.

[. . .]

[Erich] Unger is ready to contribute to the journal but I still do not have the contribution he promised, an essay he wrote one or two years ago. He intends to get the thirty-minute doctorate from Erlangen soon.

Yours, Walter

1. A Dutch author (1869–1933) and authority on sinology: close friend of Rang and Gutkind.
2. At Felix Noeggerath's.
3. On *Angelus Novus*.
4. Wilhelm Ostwald, whose philosophy WB liked to mock.
5. A novel by Laurid Bruun (1864–1935), published by S. Fischer.
6. Gustav Meyrink had invited Scholem to Starnberg.
7. Published in 1914.

107. To Gerhard Scholem

[November 8, 1921]

It is only fitting that poetry be dedicated to the original painting,[1] but some prose to its likeness.[2] The publisher is luxuriating in the joys of fatherhood, while I hardly feel like a mother. His estimate is that his youngest will be born in January 1922, while I question every possible birthdate because of a lack of substantial nourishment. The main thing lacking is powerful prose.

So far, I have the following items for the first issue:

Pieces from Fritz Heinle's papers
Poems, etc. by Wolf Heinle
"Karneval" by Rang[3]
"Synagogue" by Agnon
"The Task of the Translator" by me

Of all the contributions that are still outstanding, yours and, after that, Agnon's second story[4] are by far the most important. Since, after careful consideration, I am simply unable to draft a prospectus for the journal[5] before I have the first issue in front of me in all its essentials, this means I am forced to wait for your contribution. Bcause I do not wish to be more general in the prospectus than absolutely necessary, I must refer explicitly or implicitly to what is in front of me. I can only do that if the issue is available to me in its entirety.

I have not felt at all well this last week; I have had to struggle with episodes of depression, which seem to recur with even greater regularity but are, thank God, in no way hopeless. Right now I am definitely at the point of once again coming out of such a depression. I have no alternative on account of all of my urgent projects. I have to complete writing my critique of the *Elective Affinities* [*Die Wahlverwandtschaften*]. This is just as important to me as an exemplary piece of criticism as it is as a prolegomena to certain purely philosophical treatises—what I have to say about Goethe is located somewhere between these two.

I have again made some effort to read the Rosenzweig and have recognized that it necessarily exposes the impartial reader to the danger of overestimating it in terms of its structure. Or only me? It remains questionable whether I will be able to pass judgment on it after having read through it for the first time.

Please make the appropriate arrangements so that I can get what I most desperately need from you before long, and let me know soon when I will get it.

Most sincere regards to you and Miss Burchardt.

Yours, Walter

P.S. I almost forgot to tell you that Lehmann[6] and I celebrated our reunion in grand style and that everything in the lectures I attended started off in the same old style that now, to my great amusement, actually seems to me to be Scheerbart-like.

Scholem does not send the Angelus
To the place where he must go
Gerhard, in his anger, thinks
He does not belong here
Escha acts, doing his bidding,
As if she also knows of nothing
For in this lady's chamber
He is fixed like an advertisement
The Angelus calls himself angel
And quickly flees such strictures
For he does not tarry in the rooms
Of cunning sorcerer-Jews
To Stefanze's[7] dwelling
In his glory he betakes himself
He is bedded on stalks of roses
But he'd rather remain hovering

1. The Klee painting that was supposed to be sent to WB.
2. The journal named after the painting.
3. "Historische Psychologie des Karnevals," later published in *Die Kreatur*.
4. "Rise and Fall" [translated by Scholem as "Aufstieg und Abstieg"].
5. *Schriften* 2:275–79.
6. Walter Lehmann, who had been appointed a full professor in Berlin.
7. WB's son Stefan.

108. To Gerhard Scholem

November 27, 1921

Dear Gerhard,

The new issue of *Der Jude*[1] arrived recently—by mail, and indeed, as is rumored here, the Angelus did not want to accept the issue because the essay on problems in art education seemed so weighty to him. I am unable to imitate his unattainable gestural symbolism, but you must allow me to call it purely and simply a sublime infamy for Buber to place an essay that, in terms of its objective content (and erudition), surely at least measures up to anything previously published in *Der Jude,* right after the teenage drivel of Miss Bileam.[2] *Der Jude* will not gain my goodwill by doing this and it is just as unlikely—even if I had to be at odds with myself over this—that its subscribers will gain my goodwill, and least of all its contributors, who are willing to put up with this kind of thing like sheep.

Furthermore, Solnemann the Invisible[3] has become visible at our house. It would be very nice if he would also become visible in England with Dora's assistance, but this is still completely uncertain.

The Angelus has been assigned the place above our sofa. Everyone was pleased with him. Just as before, he disdains to whisper suggestions—like the oracle. We have therefore fallen prey to distress and helplessness in the face of having to choose a birthday present, since we may not bring shame to his place of residence. Perhaps he has written something about this in the Book of Rasiel.[4]

There are also other doubts that he may not be able to help me overcome. Such as those concerning Rang's collaboration and his whole attitude toward me, and even his own condition. All of this makes me very suspicious that, based on Rang's pronouncements to the Gutkinds, even his Shakespeare study again simply comes down to Christ. (For his part, he still wants to see it in the first issue, along with his essay on the carnival, which I did accept.) I am expecting it in the next few days. But I am looking forward to the Agnon story with much more pleasure. And how far have you gotten with your translation of the Book of Bahir,[5] which is only a retarding element for me at the moment?

What I still have to report—something the Angelus learned as well—is that I was very delighted, albeit silently, with the slight allusion to my "Task of the Translator," which I believed to have discovered in the original version of your "Lyrik der Kabbala." To be specific, the allusion is that, in your words, the true principles of translation have already been established "often enough." I no longer found this thin reed of an allusion in *Der Jude*.

My respects to the water bottle. But before it can prove useful to me, for who knows how long, it still must fill the typewriter and Miss Burchardt with enthusiasm for several more nice letters. Lacking such a propitious occasion, I will have my letters addressed to you by the academic secretary of Muri, a true Solnemann.

Meanwhile, I have been feeling pretty good. The only thing is that I will not have any peace until I finish my essay on the *Elective Affinities*. The legally binding condemnation and execution of Friedrich Gundolf will take place in this essay.

Sincere regards to both of you, also from Dora.

Yours, Walter

P.S. I have very cautiously resumed contact with Bloch. Naturally, in a Machiavellian way. He recently gave me the complete revision of "Münzer" during his first visit here and I have begun reading it.

1. Containing a very long essay by Scholem, "Lyrik der Kabbala?" which was printed in brevier because of space considerations.
2. Ironically, in place of Biram.
3. The novel by Adolf Frey, which Scholem had sent to WB.
4. A book of the Kabbalah on angelology.
5. The subject of Scholem's dissertation (published in Leipzig, 1923).

109. To Gerhard Scholem

[December 2, 1921]

Dear Gerhard,

This letter of congratulations will begin with the Angelus's blessing and the loud acclamation of the subjugated peoples who surround my writing throne. For these peoples have recently been placed under my supervision, since being settled in the wardrobe of the Ethnological Institute of Muri to their general satisfaction. (V. "A New Procedure for Settlement," *Publications of the Muri Academy*.) Even I am finally being taken seriously as someone to be congratulated, which I hope to prove by means of my enclosures and best wishes. These are chiefly meant for your successful completion of the Bahir, to which I hope to see the summa cum laude attached like a dog's little tail wagging to announce its friendliness. They are also meant for the well-being and prosperity of the fertile fields of Hebrew, which are subject to the Angelus, their liege lord. And finally, for the easing of the godforsaken and pitiless regime over the city and people of Halberstadt, in the hope that the tyrant will not some day be struck by it lock, stock, and barrel.

I hope the enclosed book is the one you wanted, the one you came across a while back. Then again: in the first place, you have probably never seen the *Symbolik der Rose,* about which I recently inquired; in the second place, it had already been sold. Aside from the fact that *Selam* was probably what you wanted—but I could not find it recently and therefore confused it with the rose symbolism—furthermore, it made a better impression on me, indeed even a good one—somewhat in the style of the booklets or tomelets cited by France. I would like to see my own things printed *this way* some time.

For good or ill, I must rely more and more on the support of false friends and the archenemy in matters concerning the Angelus, since my true friends are causing me a lot of grief. Rang's extremely wide-ranging Shakespeare study recently arrived and it seems very hard to get into. The first issue is supposed to contain his "Historische Psychologie des Karnevals"—if complications with the author do not thwart this plan.

[. . .]

Sincere regards to you and Escha.

Yours, Walter

Dear Miss Burchardt,[1]

I extended greetings to you in my letter to Gerhard so that he would not know I am writing you separately. Right now, I only want to say this in response to your last letter by express mail: (in the most extreme emergency), cable "Antiochus Epiphanes" and I will be there right away.

Most sincere regards.

Yours, Walter Benjamin

1. This appeared in the middle of the next page of the letter.

110. To Gerhard Scholem

[December 17, 1921]

Since the person who has received the better gifts and, in any case, in a more timely fashion should be the first to express his thanks and since I am that person, I must tell Miss Burchardt and you how very delighted I was with Agnon's story. Its poetic content seems magnificent, just like that of all his most recent stories—and in those instances where my knowledge is not up to the task, namely, regarding questions of translation, the Angelus is supposed to have sung to himself in an inaudible *nigen*[1] that it was good. He read the story eons ago in heaven, where it had fallen out of Agnon's pocket. But perhaps the Angelus only does this on the basis of his connections to Miss Burchardt, which are notorious.

He does not think nearly as much of another manuscript, recently dedicated to him, and he is once again embarrassing me by making me lend my voice to his most secret thoughts. I refer to Rang's Shakespeare study, or better, an excerpt from it that consists of eight translations with commentary. The few sections I sampled seemed to me to be in such urgent need of a categorical judgment, or at least, a more open exchange of views, that I still have not summoned the courage to study it more thoroughly. I am trying to put it off all the more since Rang may come here around Christmastime because he thinks he has some prospects of getting work in the area of culture or education. These prospects are totally chimerical but he believes that the Quakers are going to make him an offer. I am also putting it off because I fear that a confrontation with him based on principles—which will perhaps simply lead to a split—will no longer be avoidable, in spite of all the care I have taken until now to avoid it. Some support will no doubt be available in the person of Erich Gutkind and will mitigate the harshness.

Otherwise, the journal continues to affect my work on the *Elective Affinities*. It is proceeding *very* slowly, and almost too carefully, but there is no doubt that it will ultimately and to my great relief come into being one day. Right now it conflicts with my work on Baudelaire's life, on which I must spend some time. For it is possible that I will be able to hold my oft-planned reading from the translations at a bookstore (maybe at Reuss and Pollak) sometime during the winter. I intend to introduce the poems with a talk about the poet in which I want to combine the greatest precision with some basic pointers, absolutely excluding profundity.

I recently attended a strangely ill-fated and strangely interesting lecture: a bourgeois family in a house in Bendler Street had, for who knows what reasons, contracted a Mr. Lyk[2] to give a lecture. Except for some obligatory bourgeois, the preposterous audience primarily consisted of [. . .] Martin Gumpert, and some young ladies from Berlin's wild west. Mr. Lyk, an incontestably schizophrenic talent, is known (among those who, for their part, are not) as a personality who is pregnant with knowledge, an expert on spirits, world-traveled (!), entirely esoteric, and in possession of all kinds of arcane facts. He could not be much under 45 years old. His religion, origin, and income have yet to be ascertained, and I am not lazy about such matters. This gentleman could be described as a "genius" (Felix N.) who had been transformed by a magic spell into some emaciated thing, skull-like, and not entirely pure. He spoke with the bearing (but not the voice—his voice is very beautiful) of an aristocrat out of the pages of the old *Simplizissimus* about—various things. De omnibus et quibusdam magicis. The debacle was complete. After an hour he was told to be quiet. After another half hour, no one spoke with him, and hardly anyone spoke about him. And now to what is remarkable about the whole thing. What the man said was extremely noteworthy. Now and then, it was unquestionably important, and even when it was wrong, it was significant in every sense. Though extremely clumsy. It appeared as if what he had to say was his life's work, so to speak, and I do not know whether he could have continued to speak much longer than that hour. Unfortunately he did not seem to be a thinker.

Two horrible social lions, bloodthirsty like no one I have ever seen before, [. . .] set upon him and tore him to shreds. The first one's brutality was striking, even taking into account that he was a psychiatrist by profession.

Aside from everything else, the remarkable thing about Lyk is that, based on certain indications, I am able to say that I have most probably discovered in him the ultimate source of *some* theorems of the Goldberg circle. To be sure, not the source of those that are a priori stupid or messy, but only of those (and this, indeed, a priori) that have been blunted and contaminated. The man is, so to speak, a generation older than the members of the Goldberg circle, seems for his part to maintain a great distance from them (at least now), and, beyond that, other personal and factual things point to his role in the circle (Unger's notion of a new migration of peoples). When the person under discussion, totally stripped of authority, finally sat leaning against the stove, thoughtfully weighing everything, I went to him and asked for his address. It will soon become clear what I, or what even the Angelus, can expect from him.

The other things he spoke about can only be suggested: about the prevailing significance of *melos* in language. He also read some remarkable poems.

[. . .]

Dora often asks when we will see you and you will have to appear in person, since no new angel will now be traveling between Munich and Berlin, but only new sleeping cars.[3]

1. Hebrew for melody. Agnon's story was published in *Der Jude* 8 (1924), pp. 38–57.
2. The Baltic German Hugo Lyck. Hans Blüher discussed him in more detail in *Werke und Tage* (Munich, 1953), pp. 22–24.
3. Drawings follow depicting Scholem and Escha Burchardt.

111. To Gerhard Scholem

October 1, 1922

Dear Gerhard,
Dear Miss Burchardt,

Best wishes for the New Year. The old year did not pass without ensuring that our most secret fears had come true. For the Angelus announced his own departure just as yesterday came to an end, as if he wanted to prove one last time what a good Jew he is. He has moved into his old house in the clay-colored sky and the editor's throne of honor in my heart is empty. Enclosed are the preliminary remarks of the person who summons me to the funeral: "I have had to suspend temporarily the setting up of the Angelus because—in keeping with procedures recently introduced to the printing business—I have been asked to pay a very large advance. The Unger book, which will produce considerable income, will not be finished for another four weeks. I hope to be able to come up with the required advance then . . ." The disingenuousness under whose burden his earthly life is now flickering out betrays what is inadequate about even this creature. You are the first to get the news. As much as I fear that Agnon will take the news badly, I believe just as firmly that Escha will be able to arrange an amnesty for me. As for myself, I feel that this turn of events has restored my old freedom of choice. Since from now on I will work on the journal (insofar as there is any question of this at all) only when this does not conflict with other projects, I plan to suspend all work on it for the time being while confronting Weißbach with threatening silence. He still does not seem to want to stop pretending that he is going to publish my Baudelaire.

What I hear from Wolf Heinle seems much more serious than that. He has been confined to his bed for nine months already—because of tuberculosis, as it turns out—and is without hope and money. I think it very doubtful that he will recover. Soon you too will get a solicitation I am circulating even among my most distant acquaintances in order to collect some money for him. It is very difficult to say whether there is anything else to be done to foster his recovery.

This evening we will be at [Moses] Marx's.[1] His prospectus concerning the Hebrew incunabula recently arrived—Dora is helping him with the English translation. I too am busy with books—not only my own—in that I have recently been spending time in an intense search for books I plan to resell immediately. The small book of devotions that I bought for 35 marks in Heidelberg, I sold here at Schönlank's for 600 marks. I recently found a first edition of Nestroy for 10 marks, which I am going to keep, however. For the time being, I am still not making enough profit from these transactions and our situation is bleak because the business with my parents is still completely unclear. The Gutkinds' situation seems to be heading for catastrophe. Since things with his mother remain unchanged, Erich decided a few days ago to become a traveling salesman dealing in margarine in order to support his family. I could not refrain from comparing this decision with my own (in the first days of August 1912) to join the cavalry. His situation is no joking matter. And if he is to succeed, God will have to be selling at his side.

How unattractive the sparse text of your last letter is in contrast with my extensive reportage. And even the greeting card that just arrived, and for which I thank you very, very much, is laconic. Don't you think I would give a great deal to hear what the Frankfurt newspaper has to say about Bloch's book?[2] and [Robert] Eisler about the popes? and Escha about cigarettes. I request her all the more urgently to track down the lost Grand Dukes,[3] which only she—not I—is in a position to do since she is the one who sent them.—You, dear Gerhard, have not been on any book hunts. And you offer only critiques while being sulky and whining, like the one on Unger's book.[4] And you probably have not even begun to read my essay on the *Elective Affinities,* while here great and small alike claim to be waiting for it. I am looking for a new publisher. I could start with the publication of this essay.[5] Do you have any advice?

I hope you are well. Sincere regards.

Yours, Walter

1. Agnon's brother-in-law, who at the time owned a significant Hebrew collection. He published a thesaurus of Hebrew incunabula.

2. *Thomas Münzer* (Munich, 1921). The negative review that appeared there was written by Siegfried Kracauer.

3. Apparently a brand of cigarettes or tobacco.

4. Erich Unger's brochure "Über die staatslose Bildung eines jüdischen Volkes" (Berlin, 1922), sent in by WB.

5. It appeared in *Neue deutsche Beiträge* 2 (1924–25); in *Schriften* 1:55ff.

112. To Florens Christian Rang

Berlin
October 14, 1922

Dear Christian,

It would not have taken me such a long time to respond to your letter and, above all, to express my deepest gratitude if its arrival had not coincided with a time that is crucial for everything on which it touches. My father-in-law, who has been moved by our extremely difficult situation, has been here for approximately one week in order to negotiate with my parents. My father declared some time ago that any further support would be contingent upon my taking a job in a bank. I rejected this and consequently a complete break was imminent, at which point my father-in-law appeared, summoned by my mother. He has been negotiating with my parents since then. I, for my part, agreed to earn my own living, but under two conditions: first, I would do so in such a way I would not be cut off from a future academic career, i.e. under no circumstances would I therefore become a sales representative; second, my father immediately gives me enough money to set up in a used bookstore. For I am determined to put an end to my dependence on my parents no matter what. Because of their pronounced pettiness and need for control, it has turned into a torture devouring all the energy I have to work and all my joy in life. This is not only true for me, but especially for Dora. In the last few weeks, I have made some small deals involving books, and not without some success. If there is no other way, I simply must continue to do this as cleverly and as often as possible. Meanwhile, I must try to finish my habilitation dissertation as quickly as possible so that we do not end up being left out in the cold completely before it is due to be completed. My parents will most probably try to come to an understanding when it is finished. The negotiations are slogging along so that we are prepared for the worst. My parents, whose financial circumstances are very good at this time, are extremely rigid in their way of thinking. As rigid as my parents are, the resolve with which my parents-in-law not only morally but, in spite of their limited means, even financially stand by us is just as extraordinary. Since you adopted our fears for the future in your last letter, I am able to add a more detailed response to the above. I have given careful consideration to the proposal for a lending library. It seems to me that it gives rise to two possibilities: either I establish such an institution in the western part of the city, or in some other part of the city. In the western section, there is competition from the department store and especially from Amelang, with whom no one can compete. This would require an immense amount of capital. Ordinary people, however, not only in the western sector (Schöneberg, etc.) but especially in other areas of the city, patronize only Courths-Mahler and, at the very most, Rudolf Herzog. This is proven by my survey of many such small libraries, undertaken while I was making the rounds looking for books to buy. There would be no room here to develop a feeling for and a knowledge of books. Rather, what would be required would be akin to opening a fish store, with the only difference being that a lending library for the common man has to take into account, first, the possibility of a bad market and, second, the competition for all the stationery stores that have added on lending libraries in the poorer sections of the city. As I mull the matter over, it seems to me that the used book trade offers me the best prospects by far. In terms of its location, and completely in keeping with your suggestion, I have been considering affiliating with a regular bookstore or an antique store, in any case with an already established business. I have not yet discussed this plan with Erich [Gutkind] because I have been tied down in Grunewald by my father-in-law's presence here. On the other hand, I had already proposed the basic outline of such a plan to him earlier, at a time when he thought other opportunities were more promising. In the meantime, these have proven futile—who would have believed that Erich had it in him to be a traveling salesman!

With all of this going on, I am being more diligent than ever in testing the prospects for doing my habilitation. The more obstinate my parents prove to be, the more I am forced to consider acquiring this certificate of public recognition, which will bring them into line. Although Heidelberg is no longer at the forefront of these new considerations, I will be going there anyway at the beginning of November just to make sure. I am naturally very much looking forward to visiting you. If—as almost seems to be the case—my chances might be improved by working outside the area of pure philosophy, I would also consider submitting a habilitation dissertation in the field of postmedieval German literature.—Still no news from Weißbach. I have set my own private deadline for the Baudelaire. If Weißbach fails to meet it, I will ask him for the manuscript back. I hope I will soon be able to report that I have made new connections. But let me ask you to remember the Angelus kindly, on account of its annunciation. In any case, I will remember him this way: this unwritten journal could not be any more important or dear to me if it existed. But today—even if Weißbach were to come to me with a printing press ready to use—I would not do it again. For the time is past when I would make sacrifices for it. And it would all too easily demand the sacrifice of my habilitation dissertation. Maybe I will be able to see the Angelus flying toward the earth at some future time. For the moment, however, a journal of my own would only be possible as a private and, so to speak, anonymous enterprise and, in that case, I would gladly and willingly follow your lead. Furthermore, I would be very glad for Hofmannsthal's occasional collaboration. My only project is still the introduction I am writing to Heinle's collected papers, on whose publication, of course, I no longer count. But the preliminary work is nearing an end and it cannot take more than one month to write the final version.

[. . .]

Most sincere regards from both of us.

Yours, Walter

113. To Gerhard Scholem

Braunfels im Lahntal
December 30, 1922

Dear Gerhard,

I am basically in the midst of an adventurous journey. At least the part that is already behind me has been pretty exciting. But here (at Rang's) I do not have much time to write—furthermore, it will be better telling you in person everything that happened.

I am feeling fine in every respect. I do not know of course if I have good reasons for doing so. But in contrast to my usual mood, when all is said and done I am confident about the future. Not because the *Angelus* will appear—this is unlikely. I am ashamed to admit it, but I cannot deny that I read the final proofs of my prospectus in Heidelberg. And that is it for the moment. I also had some experiences in Heidelberg that, for the time being, do not allow me to consider the possibility of doing a habilitation disssertation there. Lederer did not invite me back after my first visit to his seminar. Surely only because he did not have the time to do anything for me. With all the stories going around, he does not know whether he is coming or going. But the other thing went just as wrong. That is to say, (when, quite unexpectedly, I was given the opportunity to speak, I had to decide to do the first thing that came to mind, and) I gave a lecture on lyric poetry to Marianne Weber's circle: I presented the ideas from the essay I have been working on for the past nine months. I spent a whole week preparing the lecture, working almost day and night, and completed it in draft form. But it failed to make an impression on the audience. I do not blame myself for this because I had no other choice if I wanted to make any kind of showing. At least it was useful for my essay.—The prospects of my doing a habilitation dissertation there have also become less likely because a Jew by name of [Karl] Mannheim will apparently do his habilitation there with Alfred Weber. He is an acquaintance of Bloch and Lukács, a pleasant young man, at whose home I have been a guest.

All I want to say about Frankfurt is that I looked up [Franz] Rosenzweig. Whether because you did not tell me or only told me in passing, or because it seemed unimportant to you, I learned only from his letter and, at the same time, from a third party that he is very seriously ill. The paralysis has reached the speech center so that the only thing he can still do is produce word fragments, which are very hard to understand. His wife, whom I find very pretty, does understand and translates them. I could stay only about three-quarters of an hour. (Toward the end of my visit Mr. [Eugen] Rosenstock arrived, who, on account of the impression he makes, corroborated the reputation that precedes the personalities of the Patmos circle.[1] I was told that Rosenzweig had been on the verge of converting a few years ago; Rosenstock is supposed to be his closest friend, which, by the way, his wife said too. And since I have already embarked on this digression,[2] it is not inappropriate to allude here to the first essay in the most recent issue of *Die Fackel*,[3] "Vom großen Welttheaterschwindel." When I read this essay, it took my breath away. The same experience lies in store for you.) So much for that. I spoke with Rosenzweig about the influence of his book, its significance, the dangers associated with it; intellectually he is completely lucid. It is just that he made conversation difficult by always making me take the initiative when I was not really familiar enough with the book to do so. But then, with considerable vehemence, he brought the conversation around to you. He does not seem to have gotten over the differences that arose at your last confrontation[4] and he seems to see you as a hostile force. Since I was out of time, I had to break off our conversation when he finally got around to your attitude or your behavior (I do not know which he meant) toward compulsory military service, making remarks that struck me as completely cryptic. I would really like to see Rosenzweig again in spite of everything. I was told that what he is suffering from is spinal infantile paralysis,[5] and that it will soon be fatal. I do not know if this is true.

I have been here since the day before yesterday and am resting up as best I can. I am going to Vienna and Breitenstein in a few days.

[. . .]

Sincere regards.
Yours, Walter

1. Authors published by Patmos in Würzburg, among them some of the most prominent converted Jews.
2. On conversions.
3. Number 601–7, in which Kraus wrote about his conversion, apropos his leaving the church.
4. Scholem visited Rosenzweig in the spring of 1922, at which time they had a very passionate disagreement about Rosenzweig's German Jewishness.
5. It was an especially severe form of lateral sclerosis.

114. To Gerhard Scholem

Breitenstein
February 1, 1923

[. . .] I really have nothing good to report about myself. My efforts in Frankfurt also appear not to hold much promise, as might be concluded on the basis of the impenetrable silence emanating from that region. I do not know whether I wrote you that Dr. [Gottfried] Salomon passed my dissertation and the essay on the *Elective Affinities* on to Prof. Schultz[1] under not unfavorable auspices. [. . .] In addition to everything else, it has become even more impossible to remain in Germany and the prospect of my getting away has not improved in any way. My stay here is much too restricted to rest and relaxation for me to be able to keep the gloominess of these observations at bay through some kind of intense immersion in work. As soon as I am back, I will return to my introduction to Heinle's papers with the somewhat bitter feeling of having to bury it in my desk at the very moment I complete it. Then I will finish my habilitation dissertation and, after renewed futile efforts, I will one day worry neither about journalism nor academics and study Hebrew regardless of where I happen to be. When I do that, I will finally be sure to get something out of my efforts. Given these prospects, I remain calm and basically even confident to the extent that this is possible. My fondest wish, however, is still to be able to give up the apartment at my parents' house.

Of course, I am very, very sad that you are going to Palestine soon.[2] My brother-in-law[3] just came from there on a visit to Vienna.

Yours, Walter

Dear Gerhard,

Two hours ago, I received the news that Wolf Heinle died yesterday afternoon, on February 1.

1. Franz Schultz (1877–1950).

2. Scholem went to Jerusalem in September 1923, after he had spent the greater part of the year with WB in Berlin and Frankfurt.

3. Viktor Kellner, Dora Benjamin's brother, cofounder of the Benyamina Village in Israel.

115. To Florens Christian Rang

Breitenstein
February 4, 1923

Dear Christian,

Given the sad news I have to report, let me be brief: Wolf Heinle died on Thursday afternoon, February 1. I do not have any more details about his death as yet. But of course you know how very much I could rely on him. You know my past history well enough to be able to measure the extent of my loss. He and his brother were the finest young men I ever knew.

[. . .]

All the best,
Yours, Walter

116. To Florens Christian Rang

February 24, 1923

Dear Christian,

Our last letters crossed in the mail. I have so much to report and perhaps even some observations to make. It's a good thing that we will see each other soon. I am at the point where I again need *all* my courage to keep my chin up. I am less sure of my path than I would like and, on top of that, there are adversities in the circumstances of my life that sometimes beset me from all sides like wolves and I do not know how to keep them at bay. And on top of that, death: the death of the few people who, in spite of the fact that this is incommensurable, provided the *standards* against which to take the measure of my own life. I recently read in Poe—I do not have the passage at hand—it was at the beginning of a short story—something like the following: that there is a way of thinking that is not sophism; a way of creating things that is not imitation; a way of acting that is uncalculated. These few values stunned me with their reminder that there had been people who had lived whose memory joins things that were very separate for me while they or while one of them was alive, and who really seemed to have come from another world in their youth, which they did not outlive. And just as it is possible that women may unmistakably and classically project beauty, I sometimes say to myself that anybody with inherent knowledge of the noble life would also have known at first sight that it was present in these two young men.

Wolf Heinle did not get to read your letter. It arrived the day before his death and he was already too weak for it to be read to him. But I will read it gratefully when I get to Göttingen. A single, rather large cash remittance in the amount of 90,000 marks arrived for him on his last day as if it were meant to express, even then, his totally cockeyed relationship to contemporary life. It came from someone who once (at the time of the Youth Movement) had been close to his brother.

The date for our planned meeting comes at a very good time for me, as you probably have already gathered from the card I sent from Heidelberg. If it would be on the 8th or 9th of March *in Frankfurt* (not in Gießen), I would be very happy. Thank you for your invitation (which came via Dora in today's morning mail) and I will gladly contribute whatever is in my power and whatever can be reconciled with my guilty reticence in the face of the destiny now making itself felt, overwhelmingly and perniciously. Of course, these last days of traveling through Germany have again brought me to the brink of despair and let me peer into the abyss.

[. . .]

Sincere regards to Helmuth.[1] And most sincere regards to you and your wife.

Yours, Walter

1. Helmuth Rang, born in 1897, son of Florens Christian Rang.

117. To Florens Christian Rang

Berlin
April 2, 1923

Dear Christian,

Your arrival and Buber's are being whispered about all over Berlin and it is only we who are left empty-handed in the midst of such an abundance of news. According to what you wrote the Ottos,[1] we are now counting on your arrival during the second week of April and are looking forward to it. You will find something wonderful here, i.e. the new page proofs of my Baudelaire, which is evidently beginning to appear according to a transcendental standard of time. Given the horrible experiences to which publishers subject you, a thing like this is enough (unfortunately!) for my publisher to regain a grain of the sympathy I had for him. Cassirer has now, in fact, returned my essay on the *Elective Affinities* after studying it for three months. He will not publish it, because of technical difficulties. Nonetheless, I have not despaired of finding an outlet for it.

I received the minutes a few days ago. I was totally unaware that they were being duplicated and distributed. To be perfectly honest, it is not clear to me why this is being done. Of course, the only significant thing about a meeting like the one in Gießen is not to capture and fix, in such a primitive way, the spoken word as it is passed from mouth to mouth. And in resorting to this form of promulgating information, do you not touch on and preserve many things you wanted to avoid, since the distribution of these minutes will soon proceed unchecked. At least what I had to say in Gießen was not intended for this purpose; I shy away from going public with such things in this way, out of conviction. If the minutes of the last meeting in Gießen are also going to be duplicated, as far as I am concerned I must urgently request you to say nothing more than to confirm my presence. As far as I remember, I did not say much of importance anyway.

[. . .] With great pleasure, I have almost finished reading the *Jürg Jenatsch* I borrowed from you. The book is on a high level, but captivates me with the same energy with which seafaring or Indian tales affected me when I was a boy. What I admire about it are its clean lines and restraint, which make it resemble a masterful drawing. I would rather not decide whether, in fact, a trace of bogus "renaissance" does not cling to the passages that touch most closely on actual historical events.

[. . .] Until then, most sincere regards to you and your wife from both of us.

Yours, Walter

1. A married couple, both architects, friends of the Gutkinds.

118. To Florens Christian Rang

Berlin
[September 28, 1923]

Dear Christian,

I want to try to extricate our correspondence from the fate of falling asleep. It appears that everything here is subject to this fate until there is a horrible awakening. In its own way, of course, my long silence also bears witness to the misery into which even we are increasingly being dragged. Dora is the one who must bear the greater burden for the time being. From the first of October on, she will be working for an American journalist and will therefore be tied up all day. As for me, the task of succeeding in Frankfurt will not be an easy burden either. It is a matter of simply forging ahead with a project whose subject matter is refractory and whose argumentation is subtle. I still do not know if I can do it. At all events, I am determined to complete a manuscript, i.e. better to be chased off in disgrace than to retreat. I have also not given up hope that, given the quite obvious decline of the universities, much might be overlooked in order to gain a privatdocent who, in a certain respect, would be welcome. But on the other hand the manifestations of decline have a paralyzing effect. What is certain is that this vigorous attempt to build a bridge for my escape from Germany will be my last attempt and that, if it fails, I will have to try to achieve my redemption by swimming, i.e. by somehow making a success of it abroad, for neither Dora nor I can endure this slow erosion of all our vitality and worldly goods much longer. You see it happening more and more every day, especially in the big cities. For example, where we are, public transportation has almost completely disappeared and Dora has had to try to find an apartment for us in the city, purely for the sake of her job. We spent all of last month looking for an apartment; for the moment, we have turned the search over to the housing office.—The final proofs for my Baudelaire arrived today. It is likely that it may turn out to be among the last German publications to appear for the time being, because everything connected with the book trade is languishing. This book naturally will also be a limited luxury edition. I have thought about what my prospects of getting into the *Neue deutsche Beiträge* might be. I am now ready in every respect to turn to Hofmannsthal with the manuscript of my *Elective Affinities* essay, whether with your help or on my own. I await your instructions.—Scholem left for Jerusalem two weeks ago, where he will most likely sooner or later get a secure position at the library.

I would like to think that time goes by more pleasantly in your seclusion, that things are going well, and that you have better news from Davos. I am worried about the fate of the manuscript you read to an audience in Frankfurt. There is probably no chance of it being published. You probably also know that Buber's anthology will not appear. I had revised my essay for it. I still cling to the idea of a private journal, as we had originally envisioned, without seeing any possibility of its realization. I sometimes think that the "night when no one can have any effect" has already fallen.

Please write soon with some comforting words. Sincere regards to you and your wife from Dora and Walter.

[. . .]

119. To Florens Christian Rang

October 7, 1923

Dear Christian,

It was very comforting to receive such encouraging and detailed news from you, given my anxiety, which had been growing day by day. I expect to be further heartened by your manuscript.[1] I have had the remarkable experience that my attempts to communicate its ideas were nowhere given a positive reception and, what's more, were not understood. I believe there are two reasons for this: first, nowadays every intellectual enterprise, as well as every economic enterprise that has intellectual underpinnings, if it proposes to undertake the improvement of Germany, seems to be encumbered by a bad omen for those who have suffered through the last ten years here in full consciousness; second, the preconditions for your request include personal ties, that it is to say, hardship that has been experienced in common. Perhaps, even probably, your more elemental mode of developing ideas will convince some people where my way of mediating them would fail. I will let you know whether and how I will compose my postscript once I have read your manuscript. It seems to me that it depends on whether I can demonstrate the conviction that allows me to agree with you in such simple terms that the few lines you have allotted me for this purpose would emerge naturally. Right now I must avoid true immersion in the philosophy of politics, all the more because I still have not gotten into my own work as much as I would like. The need to forge ahead with it makes me pause in my work again and again to think of an angle from which I could succinctly formulate everything I had to say. But this angle will not reveal itself very soon, given the refractory nature of the topic. All in all, my original theme, "*Trauerspiel* and tragedy," again seems to be pushing its way to the fore. It would consist of a confrontation of both forms, carried out and concluded by deducing the form of tragic drama from the theory of allegory. On the whole, I will have to draw my citations from the works of the second Silesian school, partly for reasons of expediency and partly so as not to go too far afield. An unpleasant aftertaste lingers from my having to interrupt my project on poetry so soon before its completion, since I was thrown off track in terms of the pedantically neat way in which I usually finish things. Aside from these two things, some earlier concerns unfortunately remain relevant. And unfortunately the primary concern is still

Dora's health. It is uncertain whether she is at all up to the job she has just taken on. Most recently, on top of everything else, public transportation in our area has become almost useless but Dora must depend on it in the winter. [. . .]

I would be really delighted to have a leisurely conversation with you again. For this reason, as well as many others, let me thank you most sincerely for inviting me once again. Of course, I will consider going to Frankfurt only when I have worked out a precise plan for my habilitation dissertation. This is not likely before December in any case. It seems to me that your political prognosis has every likelihood of coming true. Things could turn out differently, but only for the Ruhr and Rhine areas.

You seem to have missed that in his letter[2] Hofmannsthal expresses the desire that you continue to mediate between us for the time being. For this reason, let me ask you to forward to him the manuscripts that I will soon make available to you, and also to enclose a few lines with them on my behalf. I consider it highly advisable to follow Hofmannsthal's lead precisely. A passage in the essay on the *Elective Affinities* is also causing me difficulty. In it I indicate (but carefully and very moderately) my opinion of Rudolf Borchardt, the person who is closest to him. For Hofmannsthal will—and should—not be broadminded in this regard. Very soon, you will receive 1) my essay on the *Elective Affinities,* 2) some things by Heinle, and maybe 3) some things I wrote which have already been published.—Please let me know as soon as you hear something definitive about the publication of your *Deutsche Bauhütte.*

For today, most sincere regards from both of us to you and your wife.

Yours, Walter

1. Florens Christian Rang, *Deutsche Bauhütte: Ein Wort an uns Deutsche über mögliche Gerechtigkeit gegen Belgien und Frankreich und zur Philosophie der Politik,* with responses by Alfons Paquet, Ernst Michel, Martin Buber, Karl Hildebrandt, Walter Benjamin, Theodor Spira, and Otto Erdmann (Leipzig: Sannerz, 1924). For WB's response, see letter 123.

2. See "Hugo von Hofmannsthal und Florens Christian Rang: Briefwechsel, 1905–1924," *Neue Rundschau* 70 (1959), pp. 402–48, esp. pp. 419ff.

120. To Florens Christian Rang

Berlin

[October 24, 1923]

Dear Christian,

The package I sent by registered mail—containing the "Critique of Violence," an issue of the *Argonauten,* the essay on *Elective Affinities,* and a selection from Fritz and Wolf Heinle's writings—has probably reached you by now and I hope it has been forwarded to Hofmannsthal along with a few requisite lines. As I have said, I resorted to this way of getting things to him as a means of complying with his wish that nothing be "simplified." I hope this parcel will not disappear into the mythic hell of editors, but that there will soon be a friendly echo in response. I must add that I need all of these pieces back—except *if need be* the "Critique of Violence." Each of these items represents the only, or last, copy I have. I think that six weeks will surely be enough time for him to look at them at leisure; after that, I would like to have them back in my possession. I thought it would be better to wait before sending a sample of my sonnets.[1]

I still have not heard anything from you about the Berlin manuscript of your book. I am impatiently awaiting it. Has the publisher come to a decision about its publication in the meantime? Otherwise, how are things going at home and with your writing? [. . .] I, for my part, am as busy as can be with my work—to be more precise, busy doing the relevant reading for it. I certainly do not intend to slack off and will finish the project, one way or another. Yet the difficulties associated with a scholarly position are evident in the context of such a decadent way of life and living conditions and they strike me as inexorable and unavoidable. Even now, these difficulties unceasingly occupy my thoughts. The idea of rescuing the independent and private essence of my existence, which is inalienable to me, by fleeing this demoralizing interaction with what is empty, worthless, and brutal is gradually becoming self-evident to me. The only problem is how? And at the moment I have come upon a truly unexpected and, for me, feasible way of doing this. But I am not going to say anything about it, precisely because I am pinning so much hope on it. By the way, at the moment Berlin in particular is totally unbearable; its people are as bitter as they are helpless and, in the last few days, both their bitterness and helplessness have increased because of a widespread and sudden shortage of bread. (The Gutkinds are again occupying a defensive position, part of a Siegfried line in front of the Lützowplatz, and I hope it won't end with a Versailles treaty.) Apropos things French, I remain unflinchingly and cunningly at my post for the sake of expanding my library. Even now, given the truly horrid economic conditions, I managed to get a whole slew of things by Stendhal and Balzac in a trade. Also the first German Dante translation (into prose) by Bachenschwanz in 1768. My study of the baroque is also bringing bibliographical oddities to my attention on an almost daily basis. Otherwise there is again precious little good news to report. Dora's health keeps me in a constant state of suspense. At the moment she does not want to hear anything about taking it easy because we are financially dependent on her job. But maybe a solution will present itself, since her boss seems inclined to reduce the number of hours the office is open, in which case Dora's job would only require a half day's work.

Please send news about everything of concern to you and us as soon as possible. Did I already write you that my Baudelaire has appeared? I have not yet received my author's copies.

Most sincere regards to you and your wife.

Yours, Walter

1. On the death of Friedrich C. Heinle and Rika Seligson; the manuscript seems to have been lost.

121. To Florens Christian Rang

Berlin
[November 8, 1923]

Dear Christian,

I received your manuscript only yesterday. But now a new deplorable state of affairs has arisen. Given the present state of my project, it is absolutely impossible for me to finish reading your manuscript in just a few days as you expected. For reading always makes problems come terribly alive for me. What is more, my habilitation dissertation is making such heavy demands on my concentration that I could do what you ask of me and really get something out of it only during my free time. Anything else would just be idle "note taking," which would make no sense. I do not know whether your plans make it possible for you to do without this copy for a while yet. Let me ask you to arrange for me to keep it a while longer if at all possible. As you know, this is very important to me, not only so that I can get a clear picture of what you have written, but also so that, with your permission, I will be able to discuss one or another important passage with close friends.

That is my first request. I must reluctantly follow this with another request, the reverse of the first one. A few days ago, I heard from Frankfurt that someone in a position of influence is again asking for my essay on the *Elective Affinities*. Even earlier, a few days before I sent you the manuscript for Hofmannsthal, I had requested the return of my other copy by registered mail (the third and last copy is in Palestine in Scholem's possession) from an acquaintance in Heidelberg. It still has not arrived. I have requested it again, but I must fear the worst (especially in view of the scandalous state of the postal service). There is nothing left for me but the following: if the Heidelberg manuscript does not get to me right away, to my most profound chagrin I would be forced to ask Hofmannsthal to send his copy, temporarily and in my name, to:

> Prof. Franz Schultz, University of Frankfurt a. M.,
> German Department, by *registered mail!*

And indeed, I must again ask you to be the intermediary. Should this become necessary, you will get a telegram containing only the word *manuscript*. Since there is *really* a lot at stake for me in the timely arrival of my essay in Frankfurt, I unfortunately cannot let myself be swayed by consideration for you or for Hofmannsthal. This mishap is naturally very unpleasant for me. If necessary, please write to Hofmannsthal after you have received the telegram, making it absolutely clear to him that I really do beg his forgiveness.

That's all for today. I am waiting to hear what you want me to do about the *Bauhütte*.

Most sincere regards.
Yours, Walter

122. To Florens Christian Rang

November 18, 1923

Dear Christian,

I had originally intended to limit this communication to a postcard too. But in considering your latest letters and the affectionate concern all of them express, I decided to write you at greater length. Even though I really would have liked to have had your letter to Erich [Gutkind] at hand while writing you. I have read it, of course, but my memory is too much like a sieve. To begin, let me admit that my situation is not the same as Erich's in every respect. Let me now take a closer look at the context and put it in a nutshell: Erich has probably never experienced what is positive in the German phenomenon. Rather, long ago and most regrettably, he carelessly dedicated himself in his first books, which he has now outgrown, to what was European. He did this in a way that would necessarily one day reveal itself, and had to reveal itself, as a mistake to anyone with eyes to see. For me, on the contrary, circumscribed national characteristics were always central: German or French. I will never forget that I am bound to the former and how deep these ties go. I will be all the more unlikely to forget this given my current project, for nothing takes you deeper and binds you more closely than the attempt to "redeem" the writings of the past, as I intend to do. When I think about all the experiences in my life, I conclude that I do not owe anyone a word of explanation, least of all you who are so familiar with them. Now, however, I must mention some instances that you do not seem to consider in terms of their importance for me. Let me begin with the current situation of Germanness. Nowadays, of course, you represent genuine Germanness (indeed, at the risk of annoying you, I would almost like to say that, because of the great impression made on me by my unfortunately somewhat spotty reading of your *Bauhütte,* you are the only one who does). But this is not the first time you have heard me say that it is with enormous reluctance, with the most profound reservations, that I increase the number of your followers by one person, with my Jewish self. These reservations are the result not of opportunistic considerations, but of a compelling insight of which I am constantly aware: only those who belong to a people are called on to speak in the most terrible moments of that people. No, even more: only those who belong to this people in the most eminent sense, who not only speak the *mea res agitur,* but may also express the *propriam rem ago.* Jews should certainly not speak out. (The profound inevitability of Rathenau's death has always been clear to me, while the death of Landauer, who had not "spoken" but "screamed," is a much graver accusation against the Germans.) Should he have his say *as well?* This too is one of the questions, indeed, objectively the most important one, that your request to contribute a response awakens in me. And shouldn't I be allowed to say, in this context in which it belongs, that any piece of writing whose effect will be measured with such finely calibrated weights, as needs must happen with yours, does itself an injustice in [. . .] admitting Martin Buber into its entourage. Here, if anywhere, we are at the core of the current Jewish question: Jews today endanger even the best German cause for which they stand up *publicly,* because their public German expression is necessarily venal (in the deeper sense). It cannot produce a certificate of authenticity. Secret relationships between Germans and Jews can be maintained with an entirely different kind of legitimacy. As for the rest, I believe that my principle is true and apt: nowadays everything having to do with German-Jewish relationships that has a *visible impact* does so to their detriment; furthermore, nowadays a salutary complicity obligates those individuals of noble character among both peoples to keep silent about their ties.—Returning to the question of emigration, it is relevant to the Jewish question only in the sense of this defensive answer to your attempt at commitment. Otherwise, it is not. Rather, for the moment its demands on me come down to one thing: to learn Hebrew. Regardless of where I wind up, I will not forget what is German. Although this too must be said: the obdurate spirit with which this people outdoes itself at this very hour in prolonging its prisonlike solitary confinement will gradually, if not bury alive its intellectual treasures, then make them rusty, difficult to manipulate and to move. We know of course that the past consists not of crown jewels that belong in a museum, but of something always affected by the present. Germany's past now suffers because the country is being cut off from all other life on earth. Who knows how long it can continue to be understood here as a living entity. For my part, I have already reached the limit of being able to do so. And without dwelling on the spiritual problems, let me turn to the material problems. I do not see any possibility, even as far as my habilitation is concerned, of devoting anything approximating my undivided attention to my endeavors. Hunger poses a most serious threat to anyone seriously engaged in intellectual pursuits in Germany. I am not yet talking about starving to death but what I am saying is nonetheless based on Erich's and on my (in this regard, very similar situations and) experiences. Naturally, there are many ways of going hungry. But none is worse than doing so in the midst of a starving people. Here everything consumes and nothing nourishes any longer. My mission could not be fulfilled here, even if it were here. It is from this perspective that I view the problem of emigration. God willing, a solution can be found. I may go on a trip in just a few weeks—to Switzerland or to Italy. Once I have finished making my excerpts, I can work better and live more cheaply there. But, of course, this is not a solution. *Vague though they are,* let us save the possibilities that occur to me for when we can talk face to face. As far as Palestine is concerned, at present there exists neither the practical possibility nor a theoretical necessity for me to go there.

Dora is considering the possibility of America. For the time being, she is just scouting out the territory and has written to inquire about her chances of getting a job there. She lost her job after the Americans reduced the staff here. Her health has recently improved. She has finally been able to borrow a piano and to play at home for the first time in years. This has made us very happy. For some time now, I have had a small room here, c/o Ruben, Gartenhaus III, 6 Meierotto St. My work has been progressing much better since I have begun to enjoy such extraordinary peace and quiet. This presents me with two problems and what you have to say about them would be of immense importance to me. Let me state both of them as succinctly as possible. The first concerns seventeenth-century Protestantism. I ask myself, to what should you attribute the fact that the Protestant writers in particular (the Silesian dramatists were Protestants, indeed, emphatically so) exhibit a wealth of ideas that are *medieval to the highest degree:* an extremely drastic concept of death, an atmosphere permeated by the dance of death, a concept of history as grand tragedy. Of course, I am familiar with the differences between this and the Middle Ages, but I still ask, why is it that precisely *this* highly medieval range of concepts could have such a spellbinding effect at that time? That was one question. Your comments would be very important to me. I suspect that the state of Protestantism at that time, which is not accessible to me, would shed light on this question. The second question concerns the theory of tragedy about which I cannot refrain from expressing myself. I know from our conversations that you have clearly defined views on this. Is there a way you could let me know what they are, at least their most important aspects? I remember that we were very much in agreement regarding this question, but unfortunately not with sufficient clarity concerning details (such as the relationship between tragedy and prophecy, among others).

I was delighted with the first lines from Hofmannsthal. I am eager for what may follow.—Regarding the Heinle poem, the text of the typewritten version is the correct one. When I come to Braunfels (when? I am still uncertain whether this will be in December), I may be able to bring you some of Wolf Heinle's things that will give you a new insight. I am thinking in particular of the fairy tales with which you are probably still unfamiliar. I am looking forward to the page proofs of your *Bauhütte*. The manuscript was not easy to read. I hope I will soon have your answer to some of the things I touched on in this letter. Let me add most sincere wishes for Helmuth's recovery and regards to you and your wife.

Yours, Walter

123. To Florens Christian Rang

Berlin
November 23, 1923

Dear Christian,

Response[1]

I would like to think of the response form you proposed as a written dedication to you, rather than as a postscript to what you have written. For it would be frivolous of me to use the impression made on me by the lecture and the few page proofs as the occasion for my own comments. No matter how urgently you feel they are required, glosses might also easily damage the singular beauty of what you have written. Of course this beauty is not what is essential. But no subject responsibly addressed by a philosopher can disavow its relevance. It would diminish in importance if subjected to an analysis that stresses one thing but ignores others. Yet, in the final analysis, the hope of being effective rests on this somewhat elevated style of speech, which was meant to disappear. You know that I do not share that hope. But some of the doubts, which I was not the only one to feel, are belied by what is written here, as well as by its having been published. Other things will prevail. But this text, before which the brutal thoughtlessness of public debate is exposed, will also prevail. Anyone who was crippled by the alternative either of being captured by those who pussyfoot through a splendid refutation of the Clarté movement or of disavowing his best intellectual convictions in pacifistic conventions will now see himself delivered from these alternatives. He will also be able to talk to a foreigner without deception and without bonhomie. For this work respects intellectual borders between peoples in the same measure as it makes their closing contemptible. What was needed to achieve all of this was nothing less than the work of a lifetime, which stands behind these lines. For they corroborate the fact that, while the truth is indeed unambiguous, even in the political realm, it is not simple. I was pleased to find that you cited Machiavelli, Milton, Voltaire, and Görres. But not, of course, in the sense in which they appear to me here: as patron saints of a classical polemical treatise, like the ones they wrote. Even you will consent to accept them as landmarks of a realm in which the uneducated party politician is incompetent. This is unlikely to disconcert him. An appeal to his conscience will disconcert him even less, for he will not be at a loss for an ethical principle with which to parry this appeal. A lack of conscience and a lack of imagination combine to strangle the moral abundance of ideas with the obscure generality of principle. You may be pleased to see that I, for my part, emphasize that nothing in your deliberations is derived from what we could call philosophical principles, precisely because they are not deduced from theorems and concepts but are born from an interplay of ideas—ideas of justice, of law, of politics, of enmity, of the life. Among lies, there is none that is more essentially a lie than unrepentant silence. You, on the other hand, have done whatever rigor and humility are capable of doing. To all the wishes that accompany you on your undertaking, let me add just this modest wish: that it cause you no distress.

Yours, Walter Benjamin

1. See letter 119.

124. To Florens Christian Rang

November 26, 1923

Dear Christian,

Even though we have heard more from you in the last few days than I could answer in a single letter, I am nonetheless glad that I did not write sooner, but instead repeatedly put off sending you the letter I had already finished, because it can now be absorbed into a new letter. There are two specific tasks that recently cost me almost a whole day's work with infinitely inconspicuous results: the enclosed "response" and today's even more skimpy letter to Hofmannsthal. You know too much about the makeup of writers for me to have to describe the extent to which Hofmannsthal's lines delighted me (since they are able to do this without appealing to my vanity in any way). What is special about them is that they do so without that ancillary tone that is almost unavoidable when somebody famous writes about somebody unknown: as if only the former's praise could legitimize the latter's accomplishment. I believed it necessary to keep my response as grateful as it was formal . . . In fact, what he says about your political work is unexpected and extremely charming. Given his way of thinking and his past, a position like the one he espouses here would be of extreme and positive significance for him. It would speak for him as almost nothing else could. Concerning my response, let me note the following: it arose out of the need to thank you in my own way, or better, for my part, for what you achieved, and to avoid any suggestion that I am leaving you in the lurch. The response says almost everything I have to say on this occasion. To put it mildly, it would be inappropriate to touch, for example, on the Jewish question in this connection. A major concern I had to consider *before writing it* was the unsettled matter of my habilitation in Frankfurt. The sensitivity of some faculty members regarding the matters under discussion cannot be exaggerated. Another factor was that my particular sponsor is on the *far* right and that the book may become known, especially in Frankfurt. I have not so much overcome these reservations by writing, as set them aside by sending them off in the mail. Out of a need to give you an unqualified sign of my allegiance. The reservations you may harbor *before publication* are another matter. One thing above all else I would like to impress on you: nothing would do a greater disservice to what you have written than if a tiny troop of people, going off in all different directions, came marching in at the tail end of those following the flag bearer. Disregard this image; it isn't any good. What I *mean* is something *very* serious. What you have written cannot bear 1) attenuations and reservations (Natorp!), 2) to be made banal, 3) drivel about politics. Yes, dear Christian, I admit it: my faith *in the tact* of your followers is not unlimited. There may be individuals among them whom I consider capable of doing immeasurable harm to the cause, well-meaning though they may be. At the risk of being called conceited, the fellowship I feel requires me to give my opinion here. Better to have no responses at all than those that say yes in words, and disavow by their tone. There is also the question of the *number* of responses. The minimum to march behind this banner would seem to be seven. Seven *upright* citizens. It cannot be otherwise. In my opinion, fewer are *absolutely* too few! Furthermore: of this number, how many may be Jews? Not more than one-quarter! This is my firm conviction. Not just because of the impact on outsiders, but because otherwise it would be better to omit the responses and to let the book's impact take its course instead of anticipating what it will be in a distorted and inadequate way. Sequitur: you will get my response, but I ask you to consider very seriously what I have said before you publish it. If it seems to you that you can easily dispense with it, please omit it and accept it as just another personal letter. Be assured of my membership in the *Bauhütte*. For the time being, of course, that is all you have. Our financial situation is bleak, and in approximately one year at the latest, but possibly much earlier, we will be on the brink of ruin. If my academic plans do not soon come to a head, I will go into business, probably in Vienna. As I have most likely already written, Dora has lost her job because the staff at her office was cut back. Whether she will go to America and whether we will separate at all for a longer time is still open. My in-laws will always provide Stefan with a place to stay. By the way, the financial situation is critical even for Lucie and Erich [Gutkind], right down to the question of getting enough food. As I put it to Lucie only yesterday, food is surely a particularly high priority for Erich's physis. Even with the best of intentions, everyone is now hard pressed to meet this priority . . . I would now like to add a few words about your last letter to Erich, while saving your platonic reflections for a later time, if and when I am able to get a handle on their coherence. This is not very easy to do in a letter. Basically, I think it best to save them for a conversation, for these thoughts are on the border of where correspondence fails and conversation begins. Concerning your letter to Erich, I would like to say the following: there is one thing in it with which I agree completely, and another with which I disagree. What you say about the "style of professing" seems to me to be entirely true and appropriate. I feel the same way about it, and I know that a person would need totally unambiguous authorization nowadays before saying anything at all different on the subject of a profession of faith, as opposed to keeping quiet. To me, everything you write about different peoples comes from the heart. For me, a love for different peoples, languages, and ideas is part and parcel of the same thing. This does not preclude that it may sometimes be necessary to distance myself in order to preserve this love. As far as Germany is concerned, my love for it is of course so ingrained because of all the significant life experiences I have had there, and thus it cannot be lost. Yet I do not want to become a sacrifice to this love. What you say about a person's profession of faith seems just as true to me as something else you say seems unclear. That is, why you would circumscribe the continuing dependence on God with the concepts of life and death, as if dying partook of the presence of God and life has fallen prey to being godforsaken. It is much more likely that posing the question in this way has led us to a genuine area of conflict between Jews and Christians. From a Jewish standpoint, it seems to me unlikely that the Torah could be more easily understood as a mystery of death than as a promise of life. I think it is very important for us to speak sometime about the question of έδνη. Until now, I have viewed this only from the perspective of language, the perspective from which I began to deal with it in my introduction to the Baudelaire translation. I am very grateful to you for your comments on Protestantism. I found them very illuminating. I have not gotten back to the theory of tragedy in the last few days . . .

125. To Gerhard Scholem

Berlin W.
[December 5, 1923]

Dear Gerhard,

I have chosen this day on which to write you, since it was impossible to calculate when I had to send off a letter for it to actually reach you on your birthday. I congratulate you doubly, and with double the affection due you, on account of your marriage and your birthday. I hope that now you need to apply these good wishes to your hopes for only your external situation; I sincerely hope and believe that your internal situation is peaceful and lucid. That is why I am all the more eager to get some specific information about your impressions and your immediate plans soon. I happen to be in Germany myself just now and less than half my heart is in this visit; I am in need of a separation, of an outside source of energy. On the other hand, because of the general state of affairs, our financial situation has become so bleak in the last few months that a few weeks abroad would see me return home financially ruined—but perhaps not dejected. By waiting here I am using up what remains of my resources. But if the enormous drop in prices predicted for the coming days actually occurs, I will be left with a grain of hope that I will be able to support myself until the spring, and thus have better weather for a trip. Otherwise I will leave around Christmas, but my destination is still quite uncertain because, if at all possible, I would rather not be completely alone. Ernst Schoen may go to Holland. I have even thought of Paris. On the other hand, I have also thought of going south. Enough of these uncertainties and—on to others. My prospects in Frankfurt have improved considerably, but the future of the university is the object of skeptical rumors that, of course, must also be viewed with skepticism. Korff[1] is gone. The matter of my habilitation just came up in a faculty meeting and no objections were raised. They are waiting for my dissertation. The extensive literary research I have been doing with great intensity will be completed by Christmas. I will then get down to the actual writing. I am still unable to say for sure whether this piece of work will meet my standards. I believe I can take it as likely that it will be adequate for its purpose. What is more, the Baudelaire has also appeared. I will send you a copy as a gift.

The book turned out well and looks impressive, but it seems that Weißbach has harmed me with his tricks to the extent that I will not get an honorarium and only seven author's copies. This has left me desolate. The first installment of my essay on the *Elective Affinities* will appear in the next issue of Hofmannsthal's *Neue deutsche Beiträge*. Rang sent it to Hofmannsthal, who then expressed his boundless admiration for it in a letter to Rang. In the next few days, a political work by Rang will also appear in print, the very one he read from on the day you met in Frankfurt. I think very highly of it. Among the "responses" appearing with it, you will find one by me.

[. . .]

Thank God, Stefan is in very good health. I see him twice a week—since I do not live at home—and always have a lot of time for him when I am there. Otherwise I am living a very solitary life, so much so that it has even caused my work to suffer. I never have an opportunity to really talk. I frequently see Ernst Schoen and tomorrow, after a very long hiatus, I will see Bloch.

I hope to hear a lot from you soon. In conclusion, let me repeat most sincerely what I said at the beginning.

Yours, Walter

P.S. Upon the occasion of the fifth anniversary of the founding of the University of Muri, which is scheduled to be celebrated in the coming year, a festschrift will appear, "Memento Muri," for which contributions are requested.

1. Hermann August Korff was offered the position of full professor at Gießen in 1923.

126. To Florens Christian Rang

December 9, 1923

Dear Christian,

Thank you from the bottom of my heart for the loyalty you demonstrated in urging me to reexamine my position in regard to my "response." I acted on your suggestion and got in touch with Frankfurt directly. You may have deduced from my previous silence that I received confirmation from that quarter too. To be sure, I do not have confirmation from an "official" source but it did come from [Gottfried] Salomon, who is familiar with the situation, and this will have to suffice. I have not received any more galleys in the mail recently: is this because I have already sent you the response? or because the publication of the work is now imminent? I hope it is the latter, for I am not only impatient to get a sense of the impression it will make as a whole, I have also done all I could to awaken the most intense interest in it here. I do not know whether in my previous letter to you I mentioned the good and profound impression Hofmannsthal's support of your appeal made on me. I only hope that he abides by the promise contained in his words. This would be very important in my estimation, particularly for him and how he is judged. This morning I started to read *Das gerettete Venedig* for my treatise on tragedy. This is something he wrote years ago based on a book by Thomas Otway, *Venice Preserved.* Are you familiar with it? Meanwhile, of course, I have answered him in the affirmative and sent him the Baudelaire, which is now in print. All those who are close to me—and thus of course you, above all—are blessed with the dubious privilege of having to wait for this gift that is their due. It is really beginning to seem that Weißbach (because of legal shenanigans of the first magnitude (a written description of which is not feasible)) intends to cheat me out of almost all the author's copies and the entire honorarium. Things should soon come into clearer focus for me. Once I sent it, my letter to Hofmannsthal raised doubts in me as to whether it had turned out to be too formal, given all the respectful gratitude it expresses. To be specific, in my first letter I still had reservations about saying anything concerning Heinle's papers, not having wanted to appear insistent because Hofmannsthal, of course, had made no mention of them. Should he fail to bring this up with either you or me sometime soon, could I request that you ask him about it when you get a chance. And in another regard, might I also ask you to resume for a moment your role as mediator—and please do so *with your next letter.* Your role would be to get back to me 1) the *Argonauten* essay and most especially 2) my essay on the *Elective Affinities,* which I must have back before it goes to press. That is, I do not have it here, either in manuscript form or in any copy, and *urgently* need to consult parts of it for my current project. As regards this current project, it is strange that, for a few days now, it has been plaguing me with the very questions your last letter to me presented as the result of your own confrontation with these ideas. In any case, suffering as I am from a kind of loneliness into which I have been thrust by my living conditions and by the subject of my project, it would be extremely worthwhile for me to be able to go into this with you in person. To be specific, what has been preoccupying me is the question of the relationship of works of art to historical life. In this regard, it is a foregone conclusion for me that there is no such thing as art history. The concatenation of temporal occurrences, for example, does not imply only things that are causally significant for human life. Rather, without a concatenation such as development, maturity, death, and other similar categories, human life would fundamentally not exist at all. But the situation is completely different as regards the work of art. In terms of its essence, it is ahistorical. The attempt to place the work of art in the context of historical life does not open up perspectives that lead us to its innermost core as, for example, the same attempt undertaken with regard to peoples leads us to see them from the perspective of generations and other essential strata. The research of contemporary art history always amounts merely to a history of the subject matter or a history of form, for which the works of art provide only examples, and, as it were, models; there is no question of there being a history of the work of art as such. Works of art have nothing that could connect them in a way that is comprehensive and fundamental at the same time, while such a comprehensive and fundamental connection in the history of a nation is the genealogical relationship among the generations. There remains an intense relationship among works of art. In this respect, works of art are similar to philosophical systems, in that the so-called history of philosophy is either an uninteresting history of dogma or even philosophers, or the history of problems. As such, there is always the threat that it will lose touch with its temporal extension and turn into timeless, intense—*interpretation*. It is true as well that the specific historicity of works of art is the kind that can be revealed not in "art history" but only in interpretation. For in interpretation, relationships among works of art appear that are timeless yet not without historical relevance. That is to say, the same forces that become explosively and extensively temporal in the world of revelation (and this is what history is) appear concentrated in the silent world (and this is the world of nature and of works of art). Please excuse these sketchy and preliminary thoughts. They are intended only as a starting point for our discussion: these ideas are the stars, in contrast to the sun of revelation. They do not shine their light into the day of history, but work within it invisibly. They shine their light only into the night of nature. Works of art are thus defined as models of a nature that does not await the day, and thus does not await judgment day either; they are defined as models of a nature that is neither the staging ground of history nor a human domicile. The night preserved. And in the context of this consideration, criticism (where it is identical with interpretation and the opposite of all current methods of art appreciation) is the representation of an idea. Ideas' intensive infinitude characterizes them as monads. Allow me to define it: criticism is the mortification of works of art. Not that consciousness is enhanced in them (romantic!), but that knowledge takes up residence in them. Philosophy is meant to name the idea, as Adam named nature, in order to prevail over those that have returned to their natural state. I am adopting Leibniz's concept of the monad for a definition of ideas. You also invoke him in equating ideas with numbers—because, for Leibniz, the discontinuity of whole numbers was a phenomenon crucial for his theory of monads. In its totality, therefore, Leibniz's concept seems to me to embrace the summa of a theory of ideas: the task of interpreting works of art is to gather creatural life into the idea. To define.—Forgive me if all of this does not make sense. Your basic concept truly got through to me. In the final analysis, it is manifested for me in your insight that all human knowledge, if it can be justified, must take on no other form than that of interpretation; further, that ideas serve as the means to a definitive interpretation. What is important now is to establish a theory of the kinds of texts. In the *Symposium* and the *Timaeus,* Plato defined the compass of his theory of ideas as being delimited by art and nature; the interpretation of historical or sacred texts may not have been anticipated in any previous theory of ideas. I would be very pleased if these reflections allow you to comment on them in spite of how sketchy they are. In any case, we will have to return to this subject often.—What I once predicted about [Eugen] Rosenstock's failure has now come true. I never welcomed having to look at his name at the beginning of the text. He has crossed it out himself now, in moral terms. Our sincere regards to you and Helmuth.

Yours, Walter

127. To Florens Christian Rang

Christmas 1923

Dear Christian,

Allow me to reciprocate your Christmas greetings in a special way in keeping with the "religion of love" we share. This is the felicitous phrase employed by a Christian in the greetings he sent me yesterday although neither one of us had ever touched on our religions in conversation, as we so often do in ours. I am able to reciprocate in a special way this year, because this may have been the first year in which I became so absolutely aware of our bond and of the innumerable things I owe to it or, to be frank, to you. It also may have been the first year in which I became aware that the "you" with which we address each other has grown into a most indispensable form within me. In our conversations, your knowledge of different fields, which is so much more difficult to acquire for the thinker than for the mathematician, has repeatedly had an enormously significant impact on me. I am referring to my realization that I am on firm ground in taking an incomparable step forward in my thinking and that I am not arbitrarily peering in just any direction. And this year, during which we have spoken less with each other, the conversations we did have have come to be extremely vivid in my memory. I have been in dire need of the encouragement I derived from them, and they will come to be more and more indispensable to me. For the forced isolation of thinking people seems to be spreading rapaciously, and it is hardest to endure in large cities where it is necessarily quite involuntary. But what is remarkable about such a greeting is that, given all the childhood memories of Christmas, which are denied broader scope by our conscience, it touches upon the one memory among the three or four indefeasible ones of my life, by which my life was perceptibly formed. I can't remember how old I was, maybe seven, maybe ten years old. Just before the presents were to be passed out, I was sitting alone in a dark room and thinking about the poem "alle Jahre wieder," or maybe reciting it. I do not know what actually happened then, and any attempt to describe it would result only in a distortion. In short, even today and at this moment, I can see myself sitting in that room, and I know it was the only time in my life when a religious verse or any religious saying took shape in me, regardless of whether this shape was invisible or only visible for a moment.[1]—I hope that these weeks, when some of your worries about Helmuth's well-being may be alleviated, will mark the beginning of a good period for you and I hope you will have a pleasant and contented holiday.

As for me, I again agree completely with what you have to say about Hofmannsthal. You are now probably about to get in touch with him again. Therefore let me ask you once more to bring up my request that he send me back my manuscript as soon as possible. I have not yet gotten in touch with him, but must consult certain parts of the text now. Please do not hold it against me if at the same time I make two additional requests for letters. I wanted to comply with your earlier request to return the letter from Hofmannsthal, which gave me so much pleasure; in the meantime, it occurred to me, especially during some conversations, how much influence this letter could have in terms of facilitating my literary negotiations. Therefore, I would be extremely pleased if you would once again send me the original letter when you get a chance. I would put it away for safekeeping and, if necessary, will make very discrete use of it. The second request concerns my last letter on the "Ideas" in which, for the first time, I sketched some thoughts to which I may have to refer in the course of my work. Let me also ask you to keep this letter for me for when I may have to use it . . . What is frightening—totally apart from the material hardship—is how the isolation of intellectuals visibly continues to grow. Storm signals.

I wish you the solemn music of winter storms. I also hope that the year will come to a good and productive end before I again put in an appearance with best wishes for the New Year. Our sincere regards.

Yours, Walter

1. Cf. *Schriften* 1:626ff.

128. To Florens Christian Rang

January 10, 1924

Dear Christian,

I suspect that the latest hiatus in our correspondence is not due only to my situation. It is much more likely that you too are absorbed in your own work. This is true of me only to a limited degree. On the one hand, the project that is due constrains me; but since, in fact, it sometimes constrains me more than it arrests me, I suffered a setback in the form of various diversions. Since I have recently called myself to task, I will not be able to rest now until it is finished. What has been piling up during months of reading and repeated reflection is now ready, not so much as a mass of building blocks, than as a gigantic heap of kindling to which I am supposed to carry the spark of first inspiration from some other place, and in a ceremonious manner to boot. The work of writing it down will thus have to be quite substantial if it is to succeed. My foundation is remarkably—indeed, awfully—narrow: a knowledge of some few dramas, by no means all the relevant ones. An encyclopedic reading of these works in the tiny amount of time available would have inevitably evoked an insurmountable *dégoût* in me. An examination of the relationship of the work to its first inspiration made clear to me all the particulars of the current project and leads me to the following insight: every perfect work is the death mask of its intuition.[1]

As regards your own work, I hope it is not being burdened too much by your publisher's apparent negligence. As things stand, the book is basically much more likely to make a stir now than if it had appeared earlier. As far as my Heidelberg employer (!) is concerned, he has not fulfilled my worst expectations, perhaps because I informed him soon enough about my new patron, Hofmannsthal. He now seems to want to resolve the question of the honorarium in good faith. He has unfortunately taken a different position on the question of the author's copies that are due me. But the appropriate saying for this situation is that time brings wisdom and, if my closest friends will be a little patient, I will be able to come up with the volume, even if belatedly. Now that it exists, I see that in the final analysis it is more important for an author to go public with the works he considers problematical than with those he considers successful, insofar as the author needs to be liberated from the former much more than from the latter, and this liberation is achieved through publication. I no longer have any doubt about what is extremely problematical about my translation. It completely fails to take anything related to meter into account; there was no real thought given to meter. You pointed this out to me earlier, if only very tentatively. Naturally, this was something that could not be mended. The only appropriate thing for me to do would be to start over from the beginning. I hope this may one day turn out to be possible. In some ways I am reassured to see that Hofmannsthal has similar reservations about the translation, and I intend to write him along these lines. What I have left is my total satisfaction with *parts* of the translation. Please return the enclosed letters from Hofmannsthal. They of course gave me the greatest pleasure.

Scholem has written me at great length. He has a position at the library in Jerusalem and later is supposed to be appointed head of its specialized Hebrew division. He has married and seems very happy in his new country. The Gutkinds are seriously entertaining plans to leave, i.e. to emigrate. But it is extremely doubtful that they will be able to come up with the money.

In spite of intense *tsores,*[2] I have been feeling pretty good recently. The only thing that occasionally depresses me is my library, which is getting rusty, as it were, because I am unable to make any new acquisitions. My last, and even irresponsible, extravagance was to buy an old edition of Hofmannswaldau's works at an auction.

I am writing this letter in the Café Bauer, one of the few genuine, old-fashioned cafés remaining in Berlin. In a few days it will be closed and relocated.

Most sincere regards from me and Dora to you and your wife.

Yours, Walter

1. Cf. *Schriften* 1:538: "The work is the death mask of its conception."
2. [Yiddish for *troubles* or *sorrows.*—Trans.]

129. To Hugo von Hofmannsthal

Berlin
January 13, 1924

My most esteemed Mr. von Hofmannsthal:

While your letters filled me with joy and gratitude because of the warm and deep interest you show in my work, my reply has only complicated your task as an editor. This contrast embarrasses me, and I sincerely ask you to forgive me for the uncertainty into which Mr. Rang's last letter plunged you, through my error. Please allow me to put off making a few comments about external matters until the end of this letter, and to begin with what concerns me most. It is very important to me that you clearly underscore the conviction guiding me in my literary endeavors and that, if I understand you correctly, you share this conviction. That is to say, the conviction that every truth has its home, its ancestral palace, in language; and that this palace is constructed out of the oldest logoi; and that the insights of individual bodies of knowledge remain subordinate to truth grounded in this way, as long as they haphazardly resort to things from the sphere of language, like nomads, as it were, caught up in the view of the symbolic nature of language, which marks their terminology with the most irresponsible arbitrariness. Philosophy, in contrast, knows the blessed efficiency of an order, by virtue of which its insights always strive for very specific words whose surface has been hardened in the concept but dissolves when it comes into contact with the magnetic force of this order, revealing the forms of linguistic life locked within. But for the writer, this relationship signifies the good fortune of possessing the touchstone of his intellectual power in the language that unfolds like this before his eyes. Thus, years ago, I tried to liberate two ancient words, *fate* and *character,* from terminological enslavement and actually to recapture their original life in the spirit of the German language. But it is precisely this attempt that today reveals to me in the clearest way possible the difficulties that every such venture has to confront and that have yet to be overcome. That is to say, when insight really proves inadequate to dissolve the petrified conceptual armor, it will find itself tempted not only to excavate but to mine the linguistic and intellectual depth at the bottom of such attempts, so as not to revert to the barbarism of formulas. The unsophisticated pedantry of such forced insights is preferable, of course, to the sovereign allure of their adulteration, which is almost completely prevalent today. But the very fact that the insights are forced definitely detracts from the essay in question. Please believe I am sincere in locating the origin of certain obscurities in the essay within myself. (Exactly the same thing holds true for the beginning of section 3 in my essay on the *Elective Affinities*.) If I were to return to the problems of this earlier project, as might be indicated, I would not dare to make a frontal attack on them this time. Instead, I would confront matters in digressions, as I did the problem of "fate" in my essay on the *Elective Affinities*. Illuminating them from the perspective of comedy today strikes me as the most obvious thing to do.

In the spirit of our growing mutual understanding, the possibility of which you so pleasantly invoke, I will venture to include some words on my Baudelaire. For, in the context of this understanding, it is just as important to share my attitude toward my work in a brief note as it is to share the work itself. Nine years passed between my first attempts at a translation of the *Flowers of Evil* and the book's publication. This time allowed me to make many improvements but also, toward the end, afforded me insight into what was inadequate but, nonetheless, not amenable to "improvement." What I have in mind here is the fact, as simple as it is important, that my translation is metrically naïve. By this, I do not mean only the verse form of the translation itself but also that meter had not posed itself as a problem in the same sense as the literalism of the translation did. My introduction attests to this. In the meantime, I have become so clearly conscious of the problem that I am given sufficient incentive to undertake the translation anew. I am convinced that ultimately only by giving more thought to the meter would another translation of the *Flowers of Evil* approximate Baudelaire's style more closely than mine does. In the final analysis, it is the style that fascinated me more than anything else and that I would be inclined to call baroque banality in the same sense that Claudel called it a mixture of the style of Racine and that of a reporter of the 1840s. In short, I would like to journey forth once more in order to attempt to set foot in those linguistic realms in which the fashionable expression confronts the allegorized abstraction (spleen and ideal). At the same time, I would like to achieve the same kind of metrical clarity in that realm that I believe I hear in the Greek epigram, as conveyed by the new Öhler translation of the songs of Meleager of Gadara.[1] I spent some time on it months ago when I was doing research for an introduction to the papers of the two Heinles.

Regarding my manuscript[2] and its publication by the Bremer Presse,[3] I had let Mr. Rang know of my desire to have another look at the manuscript. But I failed to inform him immediately what you had said in your first letter, and therefore he was not in the picture. Should I now be unsuccessful in getting a second copy from Frankfurt, I would turn to Dr. Wiegand in the way you suggested. It is less ticklish a request than one might think, since I need only the third part of the essay for a short time, and there is probably no rush to typeset it. By the way, Dr. Wiegand's parcel did not contain the transcription of the Heinle poems. I do of course have several copies of them and will be relieved when I know they are in your hands. The section headings of the *Effective Affinities* essay are not meant for publication.[4]

Let me close by again assuring you of my grateful devotion.

Yours, Walter Benjamin

1. *Der Kranz des Meleagros von Gadara* [The wreath of Meleager of Gadara], edited and translated by August Öhler (i.e. August Mayer) in *Klassiker des Altertums* 15, series 2 (Berlin, 1920).

2. The essay on *Die Wahlverwandtschaften*.

3. *Neue deutsche Beiträge*, published by Hofmannsthal, appeared in a handpress printing published by the Bremer Presse, which was founded in Bremen in 1910 by Willy Wiegand and Ludwig Wolde, and was directed by Wiegand from 1921 to 1939 in Munich.

4. The headings are preserved in the manuscript of the essay (in Scholem's possession). The dedication to Jula Cohn was also omitted when it was published, since Hofmannsthal allowed no dedications.

130. To Florens Christian Rang

Berlin
January 20, 1924

Dear Christian,

After a lengthy break, the first day on which I energetically turn away from my literary research and return to my own work, to my own reflections and ideas, immediately brings me back to your contributions to these ideas. And thus to literature, even if only indirectly. That is to say, it is very important for me to find out what evidence there is to support the derivation of tragedy from the agon beyond that suggested by the word *protagonist.* It is also important for me to find out whether the meaning of this word, as you understand it, has been secured for the actor. Another related question is whether the sacrificial altar that was at the center of the stage of antiquity, and the ancient redemptive ritual of escaping from and circling the altar, are viewed as facts in current scholarship. Further, if you happen to be knowledgeable about this topic, what has the generally accepted scholarly view of this evidence been up till now if it is different from your own—something I consider possible. Another of your contributions that I consider particularly important is the concluding sentence of your note "Agon und Theater," a copy of which you sent me. Based on this sentence, I would be inclined to deduce that the conclusion of a tragedy is still somehow removed from the sure triumph of the person-salvation-God principle, and that even there a kind of non liquet lingers as an undertone. Of course, I want to deal only briefly with the theory of tragedy (which, for better or worse, will have to be ours), but I have to strive for precision precisely because of this brevity. I have no idea what the completed product will look like. The only sure thing is that I will have to devote all my energy to it in the near future.

A short time ago I wrote Hofmannsthal at great length. I hope you received my letter so that I can expect to hear from you soon.

Most sincere regards from both of us to you and yours.

Yours, Walter

Agon and Theater

(from the diary of Florens Christian Rang)

The agon has its origin in a sacrifice offered to the dead. The person to be sacrificed may escape if he is fast enough. Since then, the belief that the deceased offers loving benedictions has once again triumphed over the dread fear of the deceased who demands the survivor as a sacrifice. Or, if not the fear of this particular dead person, then of an even loftier one. Thus the agon becomes God's judgment of man, and man's of God.

The Athenian-Syracusian theater is an agon (cf. the word *agonist*), indeed, the kind of agon in which a higher redeemer-God is prayed for in the judgment against God. The dialogue is a speaking competition, that is to say, a race. Not only between the two voices accusing and defending the person, or the god, but also between the two of them racing for the common goal to which they escape. This is the last judgment over gods and people. In the theater, the agonistic run is also still a sacrifice to the dead; see the sacrifice of the *archon basileus*. In the theater, the agonistic run is also a court, for it represents the last judgment. It cuts in two the amphitheater for a race of arbitrary duration and fixes the spatial boundary of the stage. The agonists come running from the door of damnation on the left. They run in unison—through the medium of chaos—through the half circle of the congregation gathered around the sacrificial altar and end up entering the door of salvation—at the right. As last judgment, this race absorbs the human-divine past; the run concludes with the image of the noble dead who have already completed the run. The congregation acknowledges the sacrifice, the death, but at the same time decrees victory to the human being as well as to the god.

131. To Florens Christian Rang

January 1924
[Rang's birthday: January 28]

Dear Christian,

Your somewhat lengthy silence might have alarmed me already if I had not recently heard about your letter to Grünau and that it contains such gratifying news about Helmuth's condition. Thus it seems to me that by far the most important of the wishes we all had for your birthday is close to being fulfilled. I am much less concerned about the fulfillment of another: my wish that you continue to enjoy the strength and wealth of your ideas for years and years to come, so that the crop of ideas may continue to be brought in on a wagon piled just as high as it has been thus far. The gift we present to you might be something like a team of two horses. I believe these horses are very much alike and will therefore behave peaceably and decorously when working. The team might also possess a quite satisfactory, if also little-known and quite mature, [at]traction. It is not our fault that the one small horse has so much free play in its yoke. This was the only condition in which it was available.

But I had a fantastic experience during the excursions I made while looking for the present. Bernhard[1] made a suggestion after I asked for his opinion. He thought that a good edition of a scholastic work could possibly be of use to you. So I proceeded to the large Herder bookstore. Not five minutes had passed before the gentleman in charge was able to give me the reliable information that there was no scholastic work in stock, either in Latin or in German! Consequently the whole firm is full to the rafters with novels and small pamphlets.—I also heard from Bernhard that your children originally had wanted to give you the Baudelaire. But, of course, this is and will remain up to me and I will see to it in the near future.

Forgive me if I devote space to my everyday philological concerns even in this congratulatory letter. But I am so eager to get on with my project that everything I had indefinitely postponed now suddenly demands to be completed. And I am and remain dependent on you alone in questions concerning the Greek theater. I would really like to know whether there is any demonstrable relationships, of a historical or of a purely factual nature, between the dianoetic form of dialogue, especially that of Sophocles and Euripedes, and Attic legal procedure and, if there is, how it is to be understood. I have not found anything at all about this in the literature. I am unable to resolve the question, based on my own lack of expertise, and yet it is an obvious question. As for the rest, I have compiled almost all of the great mass of background material and will very soon begin to put things down on paper. This will be a difficult task. [. . .]

Again, all the best to you and your wife, and a happy day to you all.

Yours, Walter

Theater and Agon

[Reproduced from Rang's letter to Walter Benjamin dated January 28, 1924]

You are correct in saying the following about the concluding sentence of my note, "Agon und Theater": "Based on this sentence, I would be inclined to deduce that the conclusion of a tragedy is still somehow removed from the sure triumph of the person-salvation-God principle, and that even there a kind of non liquet lingers as an undertone." This is definitely my opinion. The tragic resolution discovered each time is of course redemption, but a problematical one, postulated in prayer, but not realized in such a way as to preclude it from again producing conditions that would require a new resolution = redemption. Or—to express it in terms of the race—reaching the god of redemption ends one act, but this is not the final goal of the running soul; each time it is a momentary, fated act of grace, but not a guarantee, not complete rest, not the gospel per se; anger, the demand for sacrifices, and the soul's flight from its destiny can also always begin anew under his sway. Thus the trilogy or tetralogy of antiquity; it depicts phases of the redemptive run.—I have no evidence for the derivation of tragedy from the agon in terms of literary references. But aside from the word *(prot)agonist,* let me call your attention to the *wagon* of Thespis, the *car naval* that follows the celestial revolution of the constellations, not in the fixed (astrological) order, however, but in the dissolution of this order (in the time of transition) so that here ecstasy can forcefully emerge from fear; so that the free word (dictamen) can transcend the law; so that the new god (Dionysius) can overcome the old ones. In this context, allow me to refer you to my essay on the carnival. *Tragedy is the breaching of astrology* and consequently the escape from the destiny determined by the course of the stars.—Unfortunately I am unable to tell you whether the discipline devoted to the study of archaeology and the history of religion is cognizant of all this and whether it can substantiate it on the basis of words from antiquity; but I very much doubt it . . . On the other hand, you too will be aware of the fact (which has, of course, been proven in detail by architects on the basis of the Pyramids, the Babylonian stepped temples, and the gothic cathedrals) that the structure of religious buildings in the cultural sphere of astrological religion (which embraces all Europe) is Uranian: in some sense, a reflection of the cosmos. Of sealed fate. Now, on to the circus—which is nothing other than the architectural fixing of the circular run, as at the grave of the lord, of [?] at the altar as a sacrifice to this specific person who [?] frees himself from his destiny as a sacrifice in that, at the point of transition, he wins over to his side as a god of *redemption* the same god (ancestral god, heros) who initially confronted him as damnation, as a demanding, death-bringing god—I say that the theatrical half circle that provides an exit *from* the circle is close to the circus that already acknowledges redemption *within* the sphere of astrology or of fate. This life and death race of the human sacrifice is already an agon: a contest between those fleeing and those pursuing; but it becomes this completely only if it results in the possibility of freedom, if its conduct is predicated on the possibility of freedom. The person who makes it to the altar *within* the astrological circus is, to be sure, not sacrificed, but now his life is in thrall to the god until his dying day; the one who has escaped *from* it—in the theater half circus—is a free person. This, however, is the sense of the Greek agon at a stage that is no longer astrological: humanity's consciousness of victory over hieratic petrifaction. However, I fear that specialized architectonic studies have not yet sufficiently plumbed theological areas to contribute to a history of the origin of the architectural structure of the theater of antiquity, of the half circus.

I, unfortunately, can also answer only in very general terms your question in today's letter as to the nature of the relationship of the dramatic dialogue, particularly in Sophocles and Euripedes, to Attic legal procedure, without having more precise information about the details and references. A trial in antiquity—especially a criminal trial—is a dialogue, because it is structured on the dual role of accuser and accused (without an official procedure). It has its chorus; consisting in part of sworn associates (because, for example, in Old Cretan law the parties began their presentation of proof with "compurgators," i.e. with character witnesses who vouched for the loyalty and justice of their party's cause—originally also in armed combat, i.e. by ordeal); in part, of the gathering of the accused's associates who beseech the court for mercy (cf. Plato's *Apology*); finally, in part, of the people's assembly that passes judgment. This dialogue, in fact the entire trial as such, was originally a passage of arms, the *pursuit* of justice; the injured party goes after the person who caused the injury with a sword (and it makes no difference whether it is a civil or criminal matter); justice becomes the law of the people only as a result of self-help (of clan against clan). What is actually processed however, the *pro-cessus*—and what distinguishes justice from revenge—is the placing of this legal course into the course of the constellations. The "thing" of Germanic law—which, however, is Old Indo-Iranian and also holds true for Hellas—can only be in session from sunrise to sunset; sentencing must be postponed until the sun goes down because the savior, the champion, could still make an appearance. The "genuine thing" also complies with the course of the moon; it is held monthly (I believe, at new moon). I do not know Attic-Roman legal process down to the last detail; but surely the legal process there is also constrained by religion through the course of the stars (thus certain constellations result in *feriae,* days on which court may not be held, and so forth). But the important and characteristic thing for Attic justice (on which Roman justice is based) is even here the Dionysian breakthrough, or, to use the language of my carnival essay, the triumph of the extraordinary over the ordinary—that is to say, that the drunken and ecstatic word was allowed to break through the regular encirclement of the agon—that humanity oppressed by ceremonies (often in similarly almost inhuman ceremonies) was allowed to burst forth wildly—that a justice grew out of the persuasive power of living speech that was higher than that which grew from the processus of the clans doing battle with weapons or with formulaic language in *verse*. Here the ordeal is liberated by the logos. At bottom, this seems to me to be the relationship of the legal process to theater-drama in Athens. Because the drama, too, is the celebration of the mystery of midsummer animated by Dionysius. Sophocles and Euripedes, however, are not of fundamental importance here; they only continued what was already in place. Development begins with Aeschylus.

1. Bernhard Rang, the son of Christian Rang.

132. To Gerhard Scholem

March 5, 1924

Dear Gerhard,

I do not think that the long period I allowed to pass this time before answering you should become the standard interval between our letters. The various reasons for it, to be sure, in the final analysis all go back to the pernicious influence of the atmosphere here. It is still my most vital intention to extricate myself from its frustrations. Weißach's endless delaying tactics also contributed directly to the situation. At first, I was able to get very few author's copies from him. I have now finally succeeded in getting him to send me some, and you will probably get the book at the same time as this letter, belatedly but still bearing just as much goodwill as otherwise. Let me first thank you for your last letter. I am sure that my lengthy silence did not reveal to you how very captivated I was by the immediacy of the descriptions in your letter. I was delighted to find my fondest hopes for you so reliably fulfilled. In the meantime, you will certainly have seen things in your surroundings that are new, more precise, and just as worthy of being passed on; I hope our correspondence will find a tempo that will ensure that we do not cheat each other out of too much that is significant. My letters to you are less prey to that danger because of the unspeakable sluggishness of things here and the growing lethargy of the people. Your letters to me are probably more prey to it for diametrically opposed reasons. Thus, this time too, I can summarize the few events of the past three months in just a few words. First, on the negative side, I still have not begun my Frankfurt project although I long ago brought it to the point of being able to set things down in writing. The élan that brings about the transition to actual writing simply does not seem to want to make an appearance, and I am planning to complete most of the work abroad. At the beginning of April I intend—by hook or by crook—to get away from here and, to the extent that it is in my power, to complete this matter from a somewhat superior vantage point and quickly, under the benign influence of a more relaxed life in more spacious and freer surroundings. This will be made possible and even promoted by the eccentric meticulousness with which I have completed my research for the project (just to mention one thing, I have at my disposal about six hundred quotations and, in addition, they are so well organized that you can get an overview at a glance). Finally, because of the tempo of the project's origination and its *relative* isolation from my earlier work, this project has always had something of the nature of a reckless escapade which naturally must by all means provide me with the *venia*. Given the increasing gloominess of my financial situation, it also represents my last hope of being able to take out a loan once I have been appointed a privatdocent. My situation also depends entirely on what happens in Frankfurt in other ways. It is still not clear to me how I will finance a stay abroad under these circumstances. In the most extreme case I am even ready to sacrifice some books from my library. To be sure, for the time being I am anesthetizing the pain of this readiness by making occasional daring purchases. Thus to my great delight, a half hour ago I managed to get the *Enfer de la Bibliothèque Nationale* for 3 marks, the catalogue of hidden books that was published in 1914 by Guillaume Apollinaire and others. I truly believe this was a *mezzie*.[1] My passion for baroque emblematica (just between us, as soon as I am free to do so, I intend to publish a rather lengthy illustrated work on this subject because of the considerable income such a publication could generate) also led me to make an acquisition in this field. I now have two emblem books, neither of which is in the library here. In other respects, however, it is precisely this library that I have to thank for a basic overview of this literature. No doubt there are many connections between the illustrations in older children's books and those of the emblem books. [. . .]—To continue with my memorandum about the last few months, Rang's work on the question of reparations has appeared. *Deutsche Bauhütte: Philosophische Politik Frankreich gegenüber*. With this book, he has for the first time recognizably marked a piece of his writing with his intellectual physiognomy, and the book's significance is a function of this. At some point, I will give you a copy and you will find a dedication to the author in it, written by me. It would be a great comfort to me if this book were understood by an occasional foreigner, but they are likely to be very few in number. Rang turned sixty in January.—Parts 1 and 2 are currently in press in the *Neue deutsche Beiträge* and, as I have already read the first proofs, will constitute the main part of the next issue. The third part will be published in the following issue. From an author's perspective, this mode of publication in the most exclusive of our journals by far is absolutely invaluable. From an academic perspective, another mode of publication would perhaps have been more beneficial but not quite as likely. As far as its publicity impact is concerned, however, this is just the right outlet for my attack on the ideology of George and his disciples. If they should find it difficult to ignore this invective, it may well be due to the uniqueness of this outlet. The noteworthy thing is that Hofmannsthal did not conspicuously take umbrage at an unmistakable remark [concerning] his principal collaborator[2] on the *Beiträge*. He subsequently even wrote me two more letters about other things [of] mine in which he specifically mentions the "Task of the Translator" with the greatest approval. These extensive Hofmannsthal autographs have for now resulted in a small annuity from my parents, which is in no way enough to get us back on our feet. For the rest, *libelli mei* are beginning to experience *sua fata.* A short time ago, I heard that all the printed copies of my dissertation that remained in Bern had been burned. I will therefore give you an invaluable tip by letting you in on the fact that there are still thirty-seven copies in stock. If you were to get hold of them, you would be assured of a regal position in the used book trade. End of editorial section.—I find what you write about [Hugo] Bergmann[3] terribly interesting and exciting. I once met somebody in Breitenstein, a certain engineer by name of Langweil from Prague, a fairly shabby being, who described himself as a boyhood friend of Bergmann. How did Bergmann attain to his position?—The Gutkinds are seriously contemplating abandoning the local scene. Their financial situation does not appear at all propitious, either as it now stands or in terms of future prospects. Under Flattau's[4] guidance, they seem to be studying not only more zealously but, above all, more objectively and more modestly. In any case, I have the impression that Flattau is not displeased with their progress. Of course, he is also devoting himself to them with an exclusivity that sometimes seems to me to be harmful for him in terms of the progress of his own attempts to get his bearings in Europe. The more I see of him, the more I like him.—There have been reports circulating here about the danger of pogroms in Russia, which sound unbelievably threatening. Do you know whether there is any truth to them? My father-in-law wrote me that you met each other at a party. If you come across other people who are also on my horizon, I would be happy if you would present them to me.—Given its current stage of development, I am unable to respond to your interest in the progress of my work with any written information. At the very most, I can give just an indication of its status. The beginning and the conclusion (which in some way are ornamental asides) will contain methodological observations on the systematic study of literature, in which I want to introduce myself with a romantic concept of philology, to the best of my ability. Then the three chapters: On History as the Content of *Trauerspiel;* On the Occult Concept of Melancholy in the Sixteenth and Seventeenth Centuries; On the Nature of Allegory and Allegorical Art Forms. In the best case, the work will still bear traces of its origin, which was not unforced and not unpressured by the demands of time. I am still unable to predict how long it will be. I hope to be able to keep it within reasonable boundaries. The last chapter will quickly treat the philosophy of language, insofar as it deals with the relationship of written sign to basic meaning. Of course, neither what the work is intended to achieve, nor the rhythm of its genesis and development, allows me to develop my own ideas on this subject in an entirely independent manner. This is something that my years of thought and study would seem to call for. But I do intend to present historical theories about this subject, arranged in such as way that I will be able to prepare the way for and suggest what I think. Johann Wilhelm Ritter, the romantic, is really amazing in this regard. In the appendix to his *Fragmente eines jungen Physikers,* you will find statements about language whose tendency is to establish the written sign as an element that is just as natural or revelatory (both in contrast to the conventional element) as the word has always been for linguistic mystics. Specifically, his deduction does not proceed, for example, from the logographic and hieroglyphic nature of writing in the usual sense, but from the principle that the written sign is the sign of the *sound* and not, for example, the unmediated sign of the denotated objects. Furthermore, Ritter's book is incomparable because of its preface, which for me sheds light on what romantic esotericism is really all about. Novalis is a popular orator compared to him. I deduce from your letter that you are working on a concordance to the Zohar, as well as on the Arabic publication.[5] Is this correct? then are you working on something that will keep you busy for years?—You will of course know that Buber was given the lectorship in Jewish religious philosophy in Frankfurt; thus succeeding Rosenzweig. [. . .]—There is a new book by Bloch, basically consisting of things that had been published before, gathered together under the nice title, reminiscent of Karl May, *Durch die Wüste*. There is nothing to say about its content. What may be amusing is its conspicuously bloody execution of all critical reviewers. Otherwise, I have odds and ends to report from Muri. [. . .] But this will have to await an official report. On the other hand, the following might be reported "from the halls of knowledge" here. A gentleman I know from the local library told me that recent attacks on Wilamowitz (by Kurt Hildebrandt) have somehow come to the attention of the library. In short, they wanted to find out something more about this and sent the gentleman, my acquaintance, to the university to ascertain whether these invectives had originated with "*a son of the Rhenish poet George,*" as they had heard!

I will close today with that decline of the West. The sooner you can write, the happier I will be. Most sincere regards and best wishes for Escha's good health.

Yours, Walter

1. Yiddish for *good buy*.
2. Rudolf Borchardt.
3. Director of the Jewish National Library in Jerusalem, later a professor of philosophy at Hebrew University.
4. Gutkind's fellow lodger and Hebrew teacher, Dov Flattau from Vilnius.
5. *Das Buch von der Palme des Abu Aflah aus Syrakus: Ein Text aus der arabischen Geheimwissenschaft* (Hannover, 1927).

133. To Gerhard Scholem

Capri
[May 10, 1924]

Dear Gerhard,

Since I have now escaped the events detailed on the other side, I take this card home as my only prize and intend to dedicate it to you with a short description of the occasion. As far as I am concerned, the entire affair was not necessary to convince me that philosophers are paid the worst because they are the most superfluous lackies of the international bourgeoisie. What I had not seen before was that they everywhere display their inferiority with such dignified shabbiness. They all came to the seven-hundred-year anniversary[1] of the University [of Naples] (and I have just noticed that this card refers only to that; what I am speaking of, however, is the International Congress of Philosophy connected to it) and were to some extent totally isolated in the auditoriums where their sections met, while the noise of the agitated student body raged in the university. There were also a few plenary sessions. The important thing was that not one philosopher with any kind of reputation delivered a paper. As a matter of fact, there was almost not a single one present. Even Benedetto Croce, Italy's leading philosopher who, on top of that, is a professor at Naples, participated in the event from a conspicuous distance. To the extent I heard them, the lectures, which apparently were limited to a half hour, were all at a very low level, intended for popular consumption. There never seemed to be a question of addressing other scholars. Thus, the entire enterprise very quickly fell into the hands of Cook's Tours, which hauled the foreign visitors all over the country on countless "bargain tours." I left the congress to its own devices on the second day and traveled to Vesuvius. In the afternoon I saw Pompeii surrounded by the tasteless but very colorful hustle and bustle of a student festival, and yesterday I visited the magnificent National Museum of Pompeii.[2] The city once again overwhelmed me with the rhythm of its life.

In all probability, I will try to stay here longer than I had originally planned. I am making preparations to begin writing my habilitation dissertation here. The Gutkinds will probably not stay much longer. An extended stay will also be a financial burden for me. However, since this would also be true if I were at home and at least here I can live more cheaply, I would rather take on the same burden here. For the time being, please write me at the address indicated on the other side, and as soon as possible.—My dissertation, which had been consigned to the flames, now seems to be taking off: in an essay entitled "Neuere Strömungen der Literaturwissenschaft"[3] the dissertation is discussed in great detail, and it is supposed to have received an excellent review in a Dutch journal.[4] [. . .]

In addition to the great delight I took in reading it, I got a lot out of your last letter. Every subsequent letter will be eagerly received. It goes without saying that all writing, special editions, etc., would also be most welcome whether promoting my work or not. Rang's book may be on its way to you within the next few days. I now had better quote the following sentence from your last letter back to you: "I am also thinking of publishing a note (polemical) in *Der Jude* on the translation of Hebrew poems. It is intended to expose the anti-Zionist slant in the assassination of Hebrew literature found among the ideologies of the philosophy of history (with reference to Rosenzweig, et al.[5])." Let me kindly ask you to return this sentence to me with some elaboration. Otherwise, I will consider accusing you of having a Humboldt- or even Widow Boldt–like attitude. If the latter, difficulties might arise for you in Muri.

Most sincere regards to you and Escha.

Yours, Walter

1. Cf. *Schriften* 2:77.
2. Should be Naples.
3. The reference is probably an error on the part of WB.
4. H. Sparnaay in *Neophilologus* 9:101ff.
5. A reference to Rosenzweig's translations of the hymns of Judah ha-Levi, which had appeared at the time.

134. To Gerhard Scholem

Capri
June 13, 1924

Dear Gerhard,

Things have again gotten to the point where I can fabricate a letter to you. The pretext for this letter is that I must ask you to send part 3 of my essay on the *Elective Affinities* to me at this address. For I do need a pretext. Otherwise, I would have had so much to do that it would have been almost impossible for me to take the time to write a letter. If only I could do that much! It is becoming hard for me to work on my habilitation dissertation. There are several reasons for this. The first is probably that, on the one hand, it is difficult to work under time pressure whatever the circumstances; on the other hand, I am increasingly inclined to monumental caution in my thinking and writing. Just as those subjects that require such an attitude, i.e. philosophical ones, are becoming increasingly more important for me. And here is another obstacle. It is difficult [to formulate][1] my philosophical ideas, especially the epistemological ones, in this study, which has to present a somewhat polished facade. It will get easier in the course of my presentation, as the subject matter and the philosophical perspective draw closer together; it will remain difficult to do the introduction.

I am currently writing it and must give some evidence of my most intimate hidden motives, without being able to conceal myself completely within the confines of the theme. You will again find something like an epistemological effort here, for the first time since my essay "On Language as Such and on the Language of Man." Unfortunately the haste with which it had to be written down marks it as premature in many respects, since years or even decades of working on it in peace would be required to produce a mature work. As for the rest, I only hope that I will be able to get a firm enough hold on it for it to be finished before the due date, which has basically provided me with ample time. All in all, the same anguish is reappearing during the writing phase as was called forth in me during the planning phase, when I was correct in proceeding from the premise of having to enter into a compromise between what was for me the essential argument and the purpose of the project. It will not surprise you to hear that such anguish then invoked the demons of laziness. And finally, not only the grand aspects of life here occasionally cause the tempo to slow down, but also its small inconveniences, which on the face of it are very minor. [. . .]

I began this letter yesterday in the café where I was sitting near Melchior Lechter, whom I met here a few days ago. A friendly, very sophisticated old gentleman with a round, red, child's face. He walks on crutches. In the course of time, especially since the Gutkinds left, I have gotten to know one person after the other in the Scheffel Café Hidigeigei (except for its name, there is nothing unpleasant about it). In most cases, with little profit; there are hardly any noteworthy people here. A Bolshevist Latvian woman from Riga[2] who performs in the theater and directs, a Christian, is the most noteworthy. This brings me to the question of whether you talk to anybody there who knows Flattau's girlfriend. She arrived one day after endless complications. Because of the circumstances of her arrival and the way she is, she unleashed a catastrophe of such force that its repercussions influenced the rest of Gutkind's trip. Then she abruptly disappeared again, without getting in touch with anyone, not even Flattau. The event was definitely memorable. The girl made a strong impression on me. Her name is Chawa Gelblum and she may now be in Kaunas. On the whole, the entire duration of the Gutkinds' trip was memorable, characterized as it was by a conspicuous tendency toward misfortune. Even on the return trip, having had their ticket changed for a different route, they were involved in a train accident near Bologna in which, to be sure, no one was killed but Erich was hurt, right on the knee that had been causing him problems for some time, even before the accident. I think they are now in Grünau. I have not had any news since

Bologna.—[Adolf von] Hatzfeld (the person whose poems I saw at your place) has been here for many weeks.

Today is the third day I have been writing this letter. I spoke with the Bolshevist until 12:30 and worked until 4:30. Now, in the morning, under a cloudy sky with the wind coming from the sea, I sit on my balcony, one of the highest in all Capri, from which you can look far out over the town and onto the sea. By the way, it is striking how often people who come here for a very short time cannot make up their minds to leave. The grandest and oldest incident of this kind involved Tiberius, who on three occasions started back to Rome only to turn back before reaching his destination. The weather here also does not make for conversation, something I would also like you to convey to Escha. Since I have been here, it has rained four times at the most, and then very briefly.—For a short time now, I have again had a little money and I will go to Naples once I have managed to come to terms with my conscience—maybe even as far as Paestum.

I will enjoy looking through a travel guide to Palestine. I intend to do this as soon as I have the opportunity. Until then, however, do not worry about anything in your letters being incomprehensible. What I do not understand when I get one of your letters, I will understand later, and it will be all the more enduring for that. You say very little about Safed. Isn't there still a school there devoted to the study of the Kabbalah? I imagine all sorts of things about the considerable number of incredible types whom you seem to run into there, as I gather from your vivid descriptions—I imagine above all that, even in much of Palestine, things proceed in a very human and a less Jewish fashion than someone who is ignorant of Palestine might imagine. And in order to inspire you to be more resolute in communicating, there follows a report from the intellectual center recently inspected by me, namely from Muri. (Where, by the way, I was terribly sorry not to run into you.) A number of interesting items can be found in the acquisitions catalogue of the library: vol. 1 of the *Documents of the Vocational Counseling Society: The German Honorary Ph.D. in Word and Picture*—Elisabeth Förster-Nietzsche, vol. 6: *Burial and Perpetual Care*—Dietrich Schäfer: *The German Question: Chammer*[3] *or Anvil?*—*The Perfect Hohenzollern,* alphabetical in two small volumes; vol. 1: Abdication to Kicking up a row; vol. 2: Lamb vultures to Z[C]ivil list—Ludwig Ganghofer: *Jewish Army Chaplain and Wood Imp* (collected novellas). From the dissertation section: *Prolegomena to a Theory of Viewpoints*—*Something New from the Early Years of Frieda Schanz*—*The Church Mouse since Luther*. From the Department of the History of Dogma: A. von Harnack's *The Easter Egg: Its Advantages and Dangers*. By the way, are you familiar with the "Regulations for the Proceedings of the Academy"?

[. . .]

Hark and be amazed! Yesterday I subscribed to the *Action française,* the royalist paper managed by Léon Daudet and—primarily—by Charles Maurras. It is written in a wonderful style. As infinitely flawed as the foundations of their politics surely are in many essential respects, their perspective ultimately seems to me to be the only one from which it is possible to view the details of German politics without being stupefied. My work schedule is responsible for me even raising the issue of such a superfluous observation, because the schedule benefits from the considerable amusement I get from reading this paper. In the afternoon, I regularly spend a few hours in the café.

Most sincere thanks to you and Escha for the photographs. I was delighted to get them. I am in a position to agree with you absolutely and completely about your dehumanized expression in the photograph with books, but it is unfortunately impossible for me to agree with the other comments you took the opportunity to make about my library. As much as it is honored at having awakened your disinterested greed,[4] should it be at all possible for me to keep the library intact (right before my trip here I had to sell some good books—no important ones), it would be Stefan to whom I would very happily leave my books as the material epitaph of my existence. He would have to adopt the most irregular attitude toward books for me not to do so. Whether I will be able to keep my library depends on many things and is still, unfortunately, not at all certain. It often seems to me to be almost impossible.—I hope that the poorly concealed lachrymose nature of these observations will dissuade you from further attempts at robbery.

In conclusion: Bloch reviewed Lukács's *History and Class Consciousness* [*Geschichte und Klassenbewußtsein*] in the March issue of the *Neue Merkur.* The review seems to be by far the best thing he has done in a long time and the book itself is very important, especially for me. Naturally I am unable to read it now. Yesterday I was told that he got a very good deal renting his house for a year and is going to travel extensively.—Let me ask you once again for part 3 of my essay on the *Elective Affinities.* Send it by registered mail.

I hope that this long letter is not directed to someone unworthy of it. Your response will determine this.

All the best to you and Escha.

Yours, Walter

1. Something is missing here, and "to formulate" is interpolated.

2. Asja Lacis.

3. Yiddish for *ass.*

4. Scholem had asked whether WB might not leave his books to the Jerusalem library "after 120 years."

135. To Gerhard Scholem

July 7, 1924

Dear Gerhard,

Despite its vitality, it seems you have decided—out of some kind of mythical complexes or atavisms—to abandon our newborn exchange of letters to the paper mountain of your neglected correspondence. But even the ready explanation based on myth breaks down when I ask myself why I have not received the manuscript of part 3 of the *Elective Affinities.* If you still have not sent it off, just keep it: I do not need it at the moment.

All sorts of things have happened here that could only really be communicated in person, that is, if I were to take a trip to Palestine or if you were to take a possibly more legitimate trip to Capri. What happened was not for the best in terms of my work, which was dangerously interrupted; also, perhaps, not for the best in terms of the rhythm of bourgeois life, which is indispensable to every project; absolutely for the best in terms of a vital liberation and intense insight into the actuality of radical communism. I made the acquaintance of a Russian revolutionary from Riga, one of the most splendid women I have ever met.

Otherwise I have had some bad luck that does not carry much weight, however, in comparison with the internal energy accumulating with increasing force because of my three months on this soil. The duration of my stay is absolutely critical. In the first place, until yesterday I had been living for three weeks in such catastrophic financial straits that a similar situation in Germany would have brought me to the very brink of what can be endured. A lot of things are easier here because of how helpful people are and the benign climate. Then, at the beginning of June, the *Frankfurter Zeitung* published Stefan Zweig's extremely bad review of my Baudelaire book and placed it in the most conspicuous section of the paper—right in the Sunday feuilleton. I saw what was coming as soon as I heard that, through an editorial conspiracy, the book had been snatched away from the reviewer who had originally been chosen and sent to Zweig, who had published the third-worst German Baudelaire translation fifteen years ago. But I was unable to do anything about it. The review is obviously petty—but . . . He disposes of the foreword with the following parenthetical comment: . . . "translation (the difficulties of which the author was aware, as the foreword demonstrates)." The person ultimately responsible is the well-meaning, crude, big-mouthed Siegfried called Kracauer. Relying on his political colleagues who are not up to scratch, he declares himself willing to pay reparations he is unable to muster.—Dr. Ernst Simon at 27 Gaisberg St. in Heidelberg responded to my request for the Jonah[1] with a card notifying me that it is being sent. Yet the manuscript has still not arrived (after three months). Could you ask him to send it to Grunewald? Please!

I am not sure how long I will be here or where I might wind up going. Since yesterday I have had a new room, the likes of which I have probably never had to work in before: in terms of its proportions, it has every monkish refinement and a view overlooking the most beautiful garden in Capri and to which I have access. A room in which it does not seem natural to go to bed and which is obviously intended for toil. Furthermore, I am the first person to have lived in it—at least in a long time, but I believe the very first. It was a storeroom or laundry room. Whitewashed walls, bare of pictures, which will remain so.

What do you have to say about the Muri things I wrote you about? Most sincere regards to you and Escha. I hope you are both well and that you will continue to have the most momentous experiences in the land.

Yours, Walter

1. An (unpublished) work of Scholem on the biblical book of Jonah.

136. To Gerhard Scholem

Capri
September 16, 1924

Dear Gerhard,

The completion of the letter that follows–after such a long silence—will be marked by the onset of a day of great political pomp and ceremony, because Mussolini set foot on this island at noon today. All kinds of festive decorations failed to deceive anyone about the coldness with which the people received the event. People are surprised that the man came to Sicily—he must have urgent reasons for doing so—and tell each other that he is surrounded in Naples by six thousand secret agents whose job it is to protect him. He does not look like the lady-killer the postcards make him out to be: corrupt, indolent, and as arrogant as if he had been generously anointed with rancid oil. His body is plump and unarticulated like the fist of a fat shopkeeper. Let me begin by chronicling some of the other things that have taken place in Capri. Since I last wrote, the time has passed when the place was full of noisy Neopolitans with their children and wives, dressed in unimaginably colorful and ugly garb; some Egyptians (who had come earlier in great numbers for the bathing season) were also still here. And now the slimy Germanic wave has rolled in just as it did in the spring, and among the first to be cast up were Ernst and Linda Bloch (something I welcome). Having left to travel in Spain, Tunisia, and parts of the Orient–and who knows whether he would not have sought out Palestine as well in order to bring you the reports you fear so much—the fares charged by the Mediterranean steamship companies forced him to moderate his travel plans. [. . .] He is showing a friendlier, even a radiant and more virtuous, side of himself for the first time in a long while, and his conversations are sometimes truly worthwhile. [. . .] He is still unequaled as a storyteller, if I disregard the slippery area of Jewish humor and bear in mind that he draws more than ever on the comedy of Valentin from Munich. [. . .]

Those dangers about which you raised the alarm do indeed pose a potential threat to my work. While just a few days ago I believed them to have been exorcised and enjoyed almost cloudless days here for an entire week, a new turn of events has once again caused the sky to become completely overcast. But my conscious will, quite tough even in this matter, will not desist at any price and has not desisted. Thus, during these months, which have not always been easy, I have completed the epistemological introduction to my book; the first chapter, "The King in the *Trauerspiel*"; and almost the entire second chapter as well, "*Trauerspiel* and Tragedy"; I still have to write the third chapter, "Theory of Allegory," and a conclusion. Consequently, the project will not be finished by the original due date (November 1). Nonetheless, I hope that handing it in around Christmas, when the academic-diplomatic situation might of course have changed somewhat, will not seriously endanger its success. As for the value of the book, I will be able to delineate its features more clearly and arrive at a judgment once I am engaged in producing the fair copy with its more nuanced formulations. There is a new book dealing with the same subject, *Deutsche Barockdichtung,* written by an up-and-coming Viennese docent by name of [Herbert] Cysarz. After looking through it, my opinion that my work is packed from beginning to end with passages that illuminate the subject in a most surprising way was confirmed. Neither Cysarz's documentation nor his particular viewpoints are in error. Yet all in all his book completely succumbs to the vertiginous attraction this material exerts on the person who plants himself before it for the purpose of describing it. Therefore, instead of shedding light on the subject, the only thing that emerges is again a little bit of postbaroque (with one *r*!); or: it is an attempt to part the hair of the degenerate boor, which is what expressionistic reporter's style is, with the comb of the exact sciences! It is quite characteristic of baroque style that anyone who stops thinking rigorously while studying it immediately slips into a hysterical imitation of it. The fellow sometimes comes up with very apt epithets, and in this regard I can learn from him. I am still lacking some mottoes, while other magnificent ones are at the ready.

Let me now formally petition you to be allowed to table the competing problem of present-day communism. The material aspects are not yet ripe for a decision and the personal motives involved are not yet ripe for transmission. Perhaps, or probably, I wrote you that several references converged: a reference to Lukács's book joined one of a private nature. While proceeding from political considerations, Lukács arrives at principles that are, at least in part, epistemological and perhaps not entirely as far-reaching as I first assumed. The book astonished me because these principles resonate for me or validate my own thinking. [. . .] Regarding communism, the problem with "theory and practice" seems to me in effect to be that, given the disparity that must be preserved between these two realms, any definitive insight into theory is precisely dependent on practice. At least it is clear to me how in Lukács this assertion has a hard philosophical core and is anything but bourgeois and demagogical claptrap. Since I am unable to fulfill this most difficult prerequisite at the moment, I must also to some extent table the material aspects. But I will most likely only table them. By the way, I want to study Lukács's book as soon as possible and I would be surprised if the foundations of my nihilism were not to manifest themselves against communism in an antagonistic confrontation with the concepts and assertions of Hegelian dialectics. But, since I have been here, this has not prevented me from seeing the political practice of communism (not as a theoretical problem but, first and foremost, as a binding attitude) in a different light than ever before. I believe I have written you that much of what I have arrived at thus far in thinking about this subject was greeted with very surprising interest by those with whom I discussed it—among these individuals was a wonderful Communist who has been working for the party since the Duma revolt. I also believe I have written you that my "Beschreibende Analysis des deutschen Verfalls [Descriptive analysis of the German decline],[1] certain passages of which I have since expanded, is supposed to appear this winter in Moscow in the *Rote Garde*. You will hear from me as soon as I can give serious thought to the matter. The general tendency of my reflections was indicated by my last card in a rather distorted way, and these lines present it in a very piecemeal fashion. But time will pass and then—or sooner—you will also get to hear the things surrounding this moment that can be communicated. But first it would be to my benefit and advantage if you would share with me something about the practice of communism of which you seem to be uneasily aware and which you keep tabs on. This is all the more important since I doubt that these subjects will become truly alive for me in information coming from the German-language area.

I am enclosing Zweig's review. Please return it to me in your next letter. At the same time or soon, I will send you the issue of a journal[2] in which you will find some new Baudelaire translations. At the moment, I am not in a position to send you an issue of the new journal *H*. More out of weakness than as a favor to its publisher [Hans Richter], I translated for the first issue a blague by Tristan Tzara[3] with a verve that commands respect. I have translated the first volume of *Ursule Mirouet*[4] over weeks of terrible drudgery. Let me ask you to fulfill your obligation and send the issue of *Kiryat Sefer*[5] you mentioned to my address by return mail. You report that your introduction to the Bahir is nearly finished—I am sure you have completed it in the meantime. Do I assume correctly that, within the philological realm, it gives the reader a perspective on your most intimate insights into this text? Do you still intend to publish things in German?

Rang has been so seriously ill since returning home that I do not know if there is any hope of ever seeing him again. He first thought his illness was something like rheumatism. Then it began to look like neuritis. Since I last heard, however, it has completely resisted diagnosis and has finally developed into almost total paralysis accompanied by constant fever. If you have had the time to read his book, I am certain it has drawn him even closer to you. He once spoke very warmly of you when he was here. His death would truly affect me, just as his illness distresses me. I have not written him at all for some time because as far as I know he is no longer capable of understanding letters. I expect to hear from his wife again. She has been afflicted by misfortune in other ways as well: their son has become ill again. After treatments in Davos and some serious operations, he finally seemed to have miraculously escaped from the clutches of the tuberculosis with which he was infected in the war.—I did not know about the terrible thing that happened to Agnon[6] until you wrote me about it. I cannot even begin to imagine reaching the point of being able to endure such a thing, much less of being able to overcome it.

Bergmann is probably not back from London or America yet. Is there anything new you can tell me about the status of the plans for the university?[7] I had already received the news of [de] Haan's murder.[8] But what is almost more terrible than that, is what you have to say about the effect this event has had. I recently spoke with a Russian Jew from the Kiev area, a farmer who came directly from Palestine. I do not remember his name. He did not look like just any Tom, Dick, or Harry and attracted my interest since he firmly believed he had seen me in Palestine. He has also seen you and heard of you, without having spoken with you.

You can imagine that in the course of time I have seen a lot here, and if I make an excursion to Positano, south of Sorrento, tomorrow—which remains to be seen—I will have gotten to know all the famous spots in the region except for Ischia. The impact the temple ruins in Paestum made on me was unequaled. I was alone when I saw them on an August day in the malaria season, when people were avoiding the area. The cliché

I had associated with the words "Greek temple" on the basis of pictures I had seen does not even come close to the reality. The area in which the ruins are located is as splended in terms of its landscape as it is barren in terms of its civilized configuration. The narrow, burning blue ribbon of the sea is visible not that far from the temples. They are supposed to be the most imposing that can be seen outside Athens. All three—but only two are very important—are more or less in the same style and belong to the same period and even now exhibit almost glaring, perceptible differences because of their vitality. Since they are very close to each other, the confrontation is unnerving. I saw Salerno on the same day. And Pompeii for the second time, and Naples for perhaps the twentieth time. I have collected a lot of material on Naples, noteworthy and important observations that I may be able to develop into something. I saw Pozzuoli, Amalfi, and Ravello. Fireworks are set off all summer on the beaches here, night after night, one display better than the other, with constantly new colors and shapes.[9] I must have written you about this. The vineyards are also among the miraculous nighttime sights here. You will surely have experienced the following: fruit and leaves are immersed in the blackness of the night and you cautiously feel for the large grapes—so as not to be heard and chased off. But there is much more to it than that. Maybe the commentaries on the Song of Songs will shed some light on this.

I can hardly believe—and the more anxiety-ridden I become, the harder it is for me to believe—that I intend to and will leave here in twelve days in order to see something more of Italy. I want to spend October traveling, to see, not so much Rome, but Florence, Ravenna, Assisi, and Ferrara, and I will then go to Paris if no difficulties arise. But I do not know whether this will be possible, on account of my visa. I intend to be in Berlin on November 1. Please send your letters to my home address from now on. They will be forwarded to me from there.

In Naples I seized the opportunity to buy some new French books as long as my money held out. Thus, only a few. Among them, the splendid exegesis of the *lieux communs* (two vols.) by Léon Bloy;[10] a more embittered critique, or better, satire, of the bourgeoisie than this could hardly have been written. By the way, in terms of the philosophy of language, it is a well-grounded commentary on the way they talk. Bloy was a (royalist?) Catholic. I have a number of things he wrote. Then a beautiful, rare German children's book came into my hands in Naples. Why not in Jerusalem? Keep an eye out! The book of my Berlin competitor, a master in the field and ungrudging promotor of my collection, has now appeared. Karl Hobrecker's *Alte vergessene Kinderbücher*. I recently received the review copy.[11] The old gentleman writes in an avuncular style and displays an ingenuous humor that sometimes comes off like a flat soufflé. His choice of pictures is somewhat problematical, but they are quite respectable insofar as they are in color. I have told you that the editor was desolate at not having given me the commission when he became aware of my collection and its life with me.

In your letter, you make an allusion I do not understand to [Richard] Willstädter having been invited to teach in your place.[12] I do not know whether you are talking about Munich, Berlin, or Muri: if the latter, we are prepared to increase the emoluments to the maximum limit of Mr. Wilhelm II's annual emoluments, so that your valued energy, etc.

I think that your magnifying glass can take a holiday today.[13]—I contracted blood poisoning from the food here. I first saw signs of it on my leg, then on my arm, and it is now again a painful threat to me. An unpleasant story. For a short time now, I have been using nets to protect myself against the mosquitos, which had chewed me down to the bone every night for two months, and I hope things will be better now, because the bites probably promoted infections.

I hope you will not imitate my silence but will soon provide me with a vivid and delightful report about what is happening with you. Most sincere regards to you and Escha.

Yours, Walter

1. WB had given this manuscript as a roll of parchment to Scholem on his departure. Another version appears under the title of "Reise durch die deutsche Inflation" [A tour of German inflation] in *One-Way Street* ("Kaiserpanorama" [Imperial panorama]).

2. *Vers und Prosa* 8 (August 1924), pp. 269–72. It was published by Franz Hessel.

3. "Die Photographie von der Kehrseite," *Zeitschrift für elementare Gestaltung* (June 1924).

4. This Balzac translation was published by Rowohlt (Berlin, 1925).

5. A journal published by the Jerusalem library, edited by Scholem, in which his first Hebrew essays appeared.

6. The house in which Agnon lived in Homburg von der Höhe burned down, and his manuscripts and library were destroyed.

7. The founding of the Hebrew University in Jerusalem.

8. With a political background. The story of the man and his murder is the subject of Arnold Zweig's novel *De Vriendt kehrt heim* (1932).

9. See *Schriften* 2:77.

10. WB published samples of the exegesis in his translation and with an introduction in the *Literarische Welt* (March 18, 1932).

11. The review appeared in *Das Antiquariatsblatt* 22 (December 1924).

12. Willstädter had resigned his chair as professor of chemistry at Munich when an important appointment was rejected by the faculty for anti-Semitic reasons. His resignation caused great comment. The word at the time was that efforts were being made to get him an appointment at Jerusalem.

13. The letter is written in somewhat less microscopic handwriting than most other letters from WB.

137. To Gerhard Scholem

October 12–November 5, 1924
Rome and Florence

Dear Gerhard,

It is my turn to be at a loss: I do not know why you haven't answered my last letter. Since I now must, as it were, use my last report as a starting point, it is paradoxically twice as hard to pick up the "narrative thread" again. A few lines from you would have erected a sylphidic bridge over the chasms that are part and parcel of any journey. For at the eleventh hour, that is what has developed: a journey. During which I move along alone but unbound on a golden road. I left Capri on the 10th of October; I was in Positano and then—once again longer than planned—in Naples, and have now been in Rome for a week. Not quite with the secure feeling of having a finished product in hand. Part 3 and the conclusion of the book are still not done, but they are ready to go since I have organized my data down to the last detail. Capri no longer provided firm ground and I had not gotten past part 2, which I will have to complete in Berlin as quickly as possible. I will be working on material with a lot of potential when I get down to producing a fair copy. It is here that my real involvement in the project begins, and I hope to have the serenity that is indispensable for this task. Many passages will not require any changes at all.—The news for which I have been preparing myself for the past two weeks, but which is only now slowly getting through to me, arrived on my last day on Capri: Rang is dead. It is good that his image will also be preserved in you, thanks to your brief meeting. I was not exaggerating when, in a letter in which I tried to convey how very attached I was to him, I wrote his wife that, odd as it may seem, I was indebted to this man not only for his support and validation, but also for whatever essential elements of German culture I have internalized. Not only the main subjects of our steadfast reflection in this area were almost all the same. But also I have seen the life that dwells in these great subjects humanely manifested only in him. It burst forth from him with all the more volcanic force when it lay paralyzed under the crust of the rest of Germany. There was not only harmony in our thoughts when we spoke, but also the opportunity for me, weatherproofed and athletic, to test myself on the impossible, battered massif of his thoughts. Often enough I made my way to a pinnacle that afforded me a broad view onto the region of my own unexplored thoughts. His spirit was shot through with madness, just as a massif is with crevices. But, because of his morality, madness could not gain power over this man. I, of course, was familiar with the wonderfully humane climate of his intellectual landscape: it constantly had the freshness of sunrise. But it is also clear to me how ossified this landscape is after the sun has set, and I have been worrying about the fate of his writings without seeing any prospect of a solution. Who is up to taking them on? The Shakespeare project has probably been mostly completed. His wife has had to suffer a hard lot. Their third son (one died in the war), who finally seemed to have recovered from tuberculosis some months ago, has to have a second operation. She lives all alone in a small town in which her husband had not established any social contacts.

Did I write you—I think I probably did—that I spent a lot of time with Bloch on Capri? Cassirer is publishing a yearbook for which he needs publicity for Bloch. By sending telegrams and the like, I have finally succeeded in placing my review of *Spirit of Utopia,* which will belatedly receive its due in Cassirer's yearbook, earning 1,100 lire in service of my trip. You will get an offprint of the complete essay on the *Elective Affinities* in one or two months. Today recent Baudelairiana, comparable to the kind of things done by Lotte Wolff. I do not know whether you have met her. Then, as soon as I have finished a fair copy, "Naples" ["Neapel"] will be published in Latvian and perhaps in German.[1] I still have not bid farewell to this city, even with my stay in Rome. The restrained cosmopolitan atmosphere of Rome left me cold, especially after the highly temperamental way of life in Naples. Only now can I really judge how oriental a city Naples is. I was primarily looking for early Christian monuments here. I am so ignorant of antiquity that its ruins, which come alive only under archaeological observation, make the requisite imposing impression on me. And today I became drastically aware how very much I miss having a relationship to the Renaissance that is not mediated by study. This happened when, visiting the Borghese Gallery, I saw not a single painting from before 1400. I compared my walk through its deserted halls with my visit to the Vatican Gallery where I stopped in front of every painting [like] a snail before every small rock. I will go back again tomorrow. The first rooms contain splendid paintings of the Sienna school and other schools of the trecento. Just think what I have to look forward to when I get to Florence. I do not intend to write anything about Michelangelo's Sistine Chapel other than that, the first time I looked at it, it dealt a death blow to my neutrally ignorant expectations. It is unspeakably beautiful and powerful. I am simply unable to write anything about it at the moment. (A terrible thunderstorm is descending on the city.) I do not know what to make of Raphael's paintings.

So much for news from Rome, where I wrote the above on approximately October 12.

Today is November 5. My childish remark about Raphael (childish, even if it is accurate) put me in such a bad mood that I stopped writing the letter. Meanwhile something amusing happened, namely that here—in

Florence—I was truly moved to stop in front of a panel labeled, "Raphael?" This is of course quite typical for me, but in a way the question mark was the reason I stopped. The panel portrays an eerie-looking young man. By the way, Burckhardt's remark about "demonic religiosity" in Raphael's paintings was not just pulled out of the air. But it is precisely this that begins to make me feel uneasy. You are probably familiar through reproductions with the painting of John as a young boy with one finger raised, a gesture that speaks volumes. Yet the similar intent of the boy depicted in the Sistine Madonna affected me differently.

Since the aforementioned storm, I have traveled mostly under an unsuitably gray sky but have always been able to see the landscape in sunlight for brief periods, except for Assisi. There a dense autumn fog descended which was not unsuitable for St. Francesco's fortresslike structure. But on the particular day I was there, I could hardly see anything of the frescoes in the vault of the church, which is dark in any case, regardless of the weather. As a result, I was better able to study Giotto's frescoes in the main body of the church. Considering the loneliness of my ramblings, in the final analysis I looked at too many paintings yet did not have enough time to be able to concentrate on architecture. For my inductive way of getting to know the topography of different places and seeking out every great structure in its own labyrinthine environment of banal, beautiful, or wretched houses, takes up too much time and thus prevents me from actually studying the relevant books. Since I must dispense with that, I am left only with impressions of the architecture. But I do come away with an excellent image of the topography of these places. The first and most important thing you have to do is feel your way through a city so that you can return to it with complete assurance. Your first limited stay in such places cannot help but be somewhat inferior if you have not most thoroughly prepared for it. I came away with more clearly defined notions, or at least, questions from only a very few painters. Especially from Signorelli, who painted one part of the cathedral at Orvieto with frescoes whose intrinsic affinity (there may also be some direct influence) to those of Michelangelo in the Sistine Chapel, which were painted one hundred years later, has long been acknowledged. Incidentally, I have not written you anything about the illuminated manuscripts of the Vatican library, which are kept in display cases. It is worth becoming a cardinal just to be able to leaf through them. But maybe the stages of your career will elevate you to a position that will allow you to do this. (Naturally I am not thinking of missals and miniatures but of the oldest extant manuscripts of the Bible, Virgil, and Terence.) Fascism presented me with too much of a good thing in Florence. During my few days here, there have been no fewer than three holidays featuring the greatest display of power.

Processions that lasted for hours confined me to a small quarter in which there was nothing to see. Whether out of resignation or in an attempt to break out, I joined the throng of people lined up in rows. I did so each time at the crucial moment, the one for which those who were more knowledgeable had waited during many long hours of standing at their post. Since I had pushed forward into the first row out of impatience, I recognized the moment as a completely hopeless constallation that I had to salute, however, given my exposed position. I at least got to see the military cap of the king, who is very short. This is the same way in which I was given the opportunity on another occasion to see Del Croix, a man who was completely ruined in the war and now plays a leading role in Fascist politics. To say nothing of the youth parades in which all young people participate as soon as they have been weaned from the maternal breast. The same thing happened to me in Perugia: there was a large body of men there also—the Fascist militia taking an oath to the king—in short: if I were the Italian correspondent for the *Action française* instead of just a reader, I could not have acted any differently.

My original plan was to go from here to Genoa and from there to Marseilles by ship and then on to Paris. But this is not possible for various reasons. I had to limit myself to buying French books in Naples, Rome, and Florence, mostly new editions. I can highly recommend the writer Jean Giraudoux, whose *Juliette au pays des hommes* I have read. I will be going to Berlin tonight and I hope to hear from you soon.

Sincere regards.
Yours, Walter

1. It was published in the *Frankfurter Zeitung* (August 19, 1925).

138. To Gerhard Scholem

Berlin
December 22, 1924

Dear Gerhard,

This magnificent paper is appropriate for the late hour in which I am beginning this letter, and you may also read "baroque" shapes out of the hammered handmade sheets—this is what they are called. I do not believe I have written on this kind of paper in years. After my long drawn-out silence, this captatio benevolentiae will not seem superfluous to you and I hope it will not be in vain. The reason: this time it is essentially the need to finish my project at all costs. I therefore made arrangements a few days ago to do so. I finished the first draft of the section I plan to turn in. It is the main part. I have put off tackling the introduction and the conclusion, both of which are devoted to methodological questions.

I have gradually lost my perspective on what I have done. I would have to be mistaken, however, if the organic power of the allegorical realm were not to emerge vividly as the fundamental source of the baroque. Yet what surprises me most of all at this time is that what I have written consists, as it were, almost entirely of quotations. It is the craziest mosaic technique you can imagine and, as such, may appear so odd for a work of this kind that I will probably touch up the fair copy in places. Some intrinsic defects are clear to me. Calderón is essentially the subject of the study; in some passages, my ignorance of the Latin Middle Ages has required me to be profound when precise knowledge of the sources would have made this unnecessary. And yet if a work such as this were to be based exclusively on original sources, it might never come into being. I would like to believe that it is nonetheless worthy of having come into being. Yet I dare not predict with complete assurance whether "allegory"—the entity it was my primary concern to recover—will momentarily burst forth from the whole in its totality, as it were. The book will probably look something like this (excluding the introduction and conclusion): *The Origin of German Tragic Drama* [*Der Ursprung des deutschen Trauerspiels*] as the title. 1 "*Trauerspiel* and Tragedy." 2 "Allegory and *Trauerspiel*." Both parts are divided into three sections, headed by six mottoes. No one could have collected any more valuable or rare mottoes—almost all of them are taken from baroque texts that are almost impossible to find.—The following items have appeared in print: a favorable (glowing) review of my Baudelaire in the *Neue freie Presse;* my review of a book, *Alte vergessene Kinderbücher,* by Hobrecker, a Berlin book collector I know, in a rare-book journal; another review of the same book in the *Leipziger illustrierte Zeitung*.[1] [. . .] Now, after having completed the rough draft, a first-rate book has fallen into my hands whose title I will give you—and the Jewish national library, should this still be pertinent. It is the last word on an incomparably fascinating area of research: Panofsky's and Saxl's *Dürers Melancholia I* (Berlin Leipzig, 1923; Studies of the Bibliothek Warburg). You should get it immediately. It is unlikely that I will be able to consult the well-known, infamous Rosicrucian book[2] before I have finished the fair copy. I hope I can take all the more delight in doing so afterward. I was properly purged by *The Plaint of Nature*. However, I had taken up the Alanus de Insulis long ago and noted that he has nothing to do with my subject.—The book will not be published by Arthur Scholem, but produced by . . . Jacques Hegner. Finally, a gothic typeface, which strikes me as uniquely appropriate for the text, has also been beckoning. All of this because a week ago I signed an inclusive, two-year contract with a local, newly established publishing house, for which I am concurrently assuming the position of publisher's reader (but without any obligation or honorarium). Otherwise the publishing house will pay a suitable fee based on specific circumstances. It will also subsidize an annual trip abroad, about which I am supposed to inform the public by keeping a travel diary. I cannot say what will come of this enterprise. But the head of the firm, a trained bookdealer who is ten years my junior, does not make a bad impression.[3] A plan for a journal has been added—my plan for it is in every respect the complete and diametric opposite of the one I had for the *Angelus,* and with this cryptic remark I will let the matter drop for now. Regardless of whether it materializes or not, you will hear about it and, should it appeal to you, please consider yourself as having received the best sort of invitation to collaborate on it. My work is keeping me busy enough for the time being. It is more urgent for me to tell you that I hope to bring Muri to the attention of the public within the framework of a pastoral fantasy. I am preparing (as a private printing or as a publication to be offered for sale) "Plaquette für Freunde" [Plaques for friends]. (In France, a *plaquette* is a narrow, brochurelike, short, special issue containing poems or something similar—a bookdealer's terminus technicus). I intend to collect my aphorisms, witticisms, and dreams in several chapters, each of which will carry the name of someone close to me as its only heading. And Muri would unfold under your name.—I am probably obligated to write my essay on the *Neue Melusine* next year. [. . .] I am expecting you to send me *Kiryat Sefer,* "Alchemie und Kabbala." To my horror, I have been unable to find your translation of the Song of Songs since I returned home. On the other hand, [Ernst] Simon had sent me the Jonah manuscript. I have not been able to read it yet. When can I expect to get copies of your publications? I think you will receive the conclusion of my essay on the *Elective Affinities* in February. If I am not mistaken, the writer's block about which you write must often be purely a symptom of intense and momentous immersion in one's work. And if you and, I hope, Escha completely recover your health, we can rest assured that it signifies or signified nothing else. But precisely for this reason, I would really welcome hearing more about this matter and in greater detail.—Still, to get back to my trip, people in Berlin are agreed that there is a conspicuous change in me. The exaltation with which I prepared for it in the spring by fasting and similar exercises and with which, not without Dora's support, I struggled to achieve this change, both externally and internally, was not in vain. I hope some day the Communist signals will come through to you more clearly than they did from Capri. At first, they were indications of a change that awakened in me the will not to mask the actual and political elements of my ideas in the Old Franconian way I did before, but also to develop them by experimenting and taking extreme measures. This of course means that the literary exegesis of German literature will now take a back seat. This exegesis is at best essentially meant to conserve and to restore what is genuine in the face of expressionistic falsifications. As long as I do not manage to approach texts of a totally different significance and magnitude from a stance that is appropriate to me, that of commentator, I will generate a "politics" from within myself. And in view of this, my surprise at the various points of contact I have with radical Bolshevist theory has of course been renewed. It is really a shame that I still do not anticipate producing a coherent written statement about these matters, and that, until I do, I may remain the object of your speculations on the elective affinity between Walter Benjamin and Werner Scholem.[4] What is much more regrettable, however, is that we are unable to speak in person. For regarding this particular subject, I do not have any other means available of expressing myself. It is remarkable and could not have been anticipated, but the core of our international social set on Capri has again gathered here, somewhat diminished by the absence of Ernst Bloch, who is still living in Positano. [. . .]

Erich Unger and Adolf Caspary have published a thirty-page essay arguing against school reform and for a humanistic gymnasium.[5] The parlor magician Erwin Löwensohn[6] has written a metaphysics of the art of lecturing for an anthology in honor of Ludwig Hardt.[7] David Baumgardt[8] has finally become a privatdocent after handing in his fourth habilitation dissertation on *Baader und die romantische Philosophie.* I have not read any of the works cited here, but urgently recommend them and am willing to get them for you for a 30% surcharge.

I do not have a picture of Rang: I will see if I can get one for you. I had intended to tell you a long time ago that on one occasion in a conversation on "the mills at the edge of the precipice"[9] he referred me to the Edda, where the mill plays a role as a symbol of the underworld.—Yesterday, on the first night of Hanukkah, Stefan received a train set, as well as a splendid Indian costume, one of the most beautiful toys to have come on the market in a long time: colorful feather headdresses, axes, chains. Since someone else happened to give him an African mask for the same occasion, this morning I saw him dancing toward me in a grandiose getup.—Please write very soon. As soon as I have completed my project, my letters will again become more frequent. Please write me about Agnon[10] as well.

Best wishes and take care.
Yours, Walter

1. In the Christmas issue.
2. By Hargrave Jennings.

3. His name was Littauer.

4. Scholem's brother who was a Communist representative to parliament at this time and was locked out in 1927 when the German Communist party was Stalinized.

5. "Die Vergewaltigung des Gymnasiums durch den Geist des praktischen 'Lebens'" (Berlin, 1924).

6. See H. Tramer, "Berlin Frühexpressionisten," *Bulletin des Leo Baeck Instituts* 6: 245–54, for information about Löwensohn (born 1888 in Torun, died 1963 in Tel Aviv). He lived a very withdrawn life.

7. "Ludwig Hardts Rezitation: Eine neue Kunstgattung," in *Ludwig Hardts Vortragsbuch* (Hamburg, 1924).

8. Baumgardt died in 1963 in the United States. A privatdocent in Berlin until 1933. Of the four individuals mentioned above, Unger, Löwensohn, and Baumgardt were acquaintances of WB.

9. A metaphor that appears in the Zohar.

10. Agnon had returned to Palestine and lived in Jerusalem.

139. To Hugo von Hofmannsthal

Berlin
December 30, 1924

My most esteemed Mr. von Hofmannsthal:

I do not want to let the waning year go by completely without gratefully calling to mind that with your support it validated my work. I hope you will not find it unseemly if, out of this sense of gratitude, I wish you a happy year to come.

The past year fulfilled wishes I had harbored for a long time. One was my lengthy stay in Italy, the other the establishment of a more solid relationship with a publishing house (for which I indirectly have the *Neue deutsche Beiträge* to thank). In retrospect, therefore, I myself could call the past year a happy one had it not taken my friend Christian Rang from me. Mrs. Rang has written me that you were informed of his death by one of his sons. Now that some time has passed, I would like to share with you, my esteemed Mr. von Hofmannsthal, the memory of this man and his very bitter and very untimely death, even if Mrs. Rang had not requested that I inform you of his death. He would never have been thought of as someone whose life had been "consummated," but he struck me as someone who was destined to reach old age and to renew his dignity at a time in which it had been lost in almost all respects. On Capri, where we were last together and where he was collecting his thoughts while resting, he spoke of his intention to leave Germany, to avoid the political questions it urged on him, and to live in Switzerland (he had Zurich in mind), where he would devote himself to purely philosophical and theological projects. It seems particularly difficult to salvage the extensive prolegomena to these works in the form of a collection of his "papers." Because of this, your publication of "Selige Sehnsucht"[1] acquires a special significance for those who were intellectually close to him. His death would be even sadder for these people if they had to tell themselves that this man had never had an opportunity during his lifetime to express the thoughts most important to him. You have deflected this fate that almost came to pass.

I am eagerly looking forward to the next issue of the *Beiträge;* among the pieces in the previous issue, I found Burckhardt's[2] notebooks, which you promised to continue in the upcoming issue, particularly fascinating.

I remain most respectfully yours,
Walter Benjamin

1. In the first issue of *Neue deutsche Beiträge.*

2. Carl Jacob Burckhardt, "Kleinasiatische Reise." Cf. *Hugo von Hofmannsthal und Carl J. Burckhardt: Briefwechsel* (Frankfurt am Main, 1956), pp. 168ff.

140. To Gerhard Scholem

Frankfurt am Main
February 19, 1925

Dear Gerhard,

In a letter you sent me on Capri, which I have often thought about and even quoted, you wrote that you were following my situation with the greatest concern and that you had the impression that my internal resistance to getting my habilitation would gain the upper hand now that things were getting easier for me in terms of external factors. Your diagnosis is correct. The prognosis, I hope, is incorrect. In spite of everything, the part of the thesis I plan to submit now exists in rough draft, and two-thirds of it in a handwritten fair copy as well. Only now do I see that it just barely reached completion and safe harbor. I fear that, like the Argo, this small explorer's craft in quest of the golden fleece of baroque allegory will also take its sign from two islands knocking into each other (they are probably called the Cyclades), and the powerfully planned and well-built bibliographical tail end and rudder will have to pay the ultimate price. Not that it is meant just to be dropped completely. That is naturally out of the question. But I will have to polish it up to make it more accurate in terms of the page numbers, book titles, etc. of the references. Otherwise I will never finish, given the quixotic way in which I wanted to do honor to the philological part of the work. As it is, I will not meet the publisher's deadline for submission—the first of March—by quite a ways. After all, just like most of the introduction, which I will not be submitting to Frankfurt, the conclusion has not been written yet. This introduction is unmitigated chutzpah—that is to say, neither more not less than the prolegomena to epistemology, a kind of second stage of my early work on language (I do not know whether it is any better), with which you are familiar, dressed up as a theory of ideas. To this end, I also plan to read through my work on language once more.[1] Be that as it may, I am glad I wrote this introduction. Its original motto was "Jump over sticks and stones, but do not break your bones"—while now a maxim by Goethe appears in its place (from the history of his *Color Theory*), the kind that will make people's jaws drop. Then there are two parts, 1 "*Trauerspiel* and Tragedy," 2 "Allegory and Tragedy," plus a concluding section dealing with methodology. 1 and 2 are each subdivided into three parts with a total of six mottoes, which are not likely to be considered a laughing matter by the reader. The conclusion's motto is from Jean Paul,[2] but the six middle ones are all taken from the most incredible, old, baroque works of popular fiction. Reading a few short sample passages out loud turned out to be impressive. To be sure, I have lost all sense of proportion in the course of working on this project. It now also has a new theory of tragedy; in large part, it derives from Rang. It cites Rosenzweig extensively, much to [Gottfried] Salomon's[3] displeasure, who maintains that everything that Rosenzweig has to say about tragedy has already been said by Hegel. And this may even be possible. I have not been able to go through the entire *Aesthetics*.—But this project marks an end for me—I would not have it be a beginning for any money in the world. The next project I promised the publisher is on *Die neue Melusine*. In it, I intend to go back to romanticism and (perhaps already) go on to political things; I want to work in a polar climate. This would be very different from what has become for me the all too temperate climate of my baroque project, although it may well not affect others as quite so temperate. But for the moment I must breathe the tepid air: that is why I came here, and immediately picked up the nicest flu and sniffles. It is still questionable whether I will be able to turn anything in to Schultz before he leaves; the typing has just now begun. In any case, I will present myself to him very soon. The situation is not unfavorable: Schultz is a dean; and in other respects as well, some things are positioned to practical advantage. I dread almost everything that would result from a positive resolution to all of this: I dread Frankfurt above all, then lectures, students, etc. Things that take a murderous toll on time, especially since the economical use of time is not my long suit: multifarious dealings with publishers, my own work—Melusine and then the book on politics—have to be done, and finally, if ever, I soon have to start taking seriously my study of Hebrew. For the time being, I am keeping an eye open for any opportunities that may arise locally and finally have applied for the editorship of a radio magazine or, to be more precise, a supplement. This would be a part-time job, but it probably will not be so easy for me to get because we are having trouble agreeing on the honorarium. The situation is that Ernst Schoen has had an important position here for months now. He is the manager of the Frankfurt "broadcasting" station and put in a good word for me. All the university professors here blather away on the radio, etc.

I accidentally learned of your father's death when I saw the obituary in a newspaper. Will this cause a change in your situation?—I now want to turn part of my attention to your letter, and part to my work. As far as Agnon is concerned, I am planning to commemorate *Rabbi Gadiel* in the essay on *Die neue Melusine* by hook or by crook, the way we once considered doing in Frankfurt. This should be done in a way that will do him good even if it cannot be very detailed. And Muri [. . .] finally: regarding my book on the baroque, you can imagine how impatient I am for you to have it. Strictly speaking and just between us, with Rang's death it has lost the reader for whom it was intended. For who will be able to participate fully in these esoteric and forgotten issues? As the author, I may be the last one to be able to do so today (but, in the negative sense, will not). But enough remains to which it would be extremely important for me to have your response. And sometimes I begin to be confident that the whole thing—if it only existed—has turned out to be globular and peculiar. A heavy ball with which you can hit all nine pins, and then it is all over. Unfortunately I am no longer able to consider Rosicrucian factors.

[. . .]

Otherwise, I have been reading very little. *Incredibile dictu:* Thomas Mann's new book, *The Magic Mountain [Der Zauberberg],* is fascinating purely because of its sovereign workmanship. Beyond that, there is André Gide's *Corydon*—hesitant and sanitized dialogues on love between young boys who, however, are all too lacking in Attic spice. [. . .] Lukács has produced a book called *Lenin*. Are you familiar with it? Bloch writes from Carthage. So go and climb the watchtowers of Jerusalem and look about you.

My bibliomania is strangely—but explicably—receding. I have not bought anything for months. I intend to put aside the money I am able to save, not much so far, for travel and add to it when I can. But my last buy was epochal. Von dem Werder's *Der deutsche Tasso von Paris* (Frankfurt a. M., 1624).

I have said everything I wanted to say for now. Written with "sympathetic" ink, regards—and best wishes—will cover the rest of the page. Threats are appended in the event that I should have to wait for your answer.

Yours, Walter

1. In fact, sentences from his essay on language, which was then unpublished, were included in the *Trauerspiel* book word for word, primarily in the concluding section.
2. This concluding section was omitted from the fair copy.
3. Salomon (1892–1964) was at this time a privatdocent in sociology at Frankfurt.

141. To Gerhard Scholem

Berlin
April 6, 1925

Dear Gerhard,

Even though there is not much news and this letter will—I hope—cross yours in the mail, I nonetheless want to let you hear from me again. Frankfurt was a dreary weight on my shoulders, partly because of the mostly mechanical work of dictation, bibliography, and other technical things I had to do there; partly because of the urban life and cityscape, which I find particularly loathsome there; finally because of the not unexpected, but nonetheless unnerving, unreliability of the authority deciding my fate. This professor Schultz, who is insignificant in the world of scholarship, is a shrewd cosmopolitan who probably has a better nose for some literary matters than young coffee house habitués. But I have exhausted all there is to say about him with this blurb on his pseudo-intellectual cultural pretensions. He is mediocre in every other respect, and what he does have in the way of diplomatic skill is paralyzed by a cowardliness clothed in punctilious formality. I still have not heard anything about how my work has been received, or more precisely, anything good. When I gave him the second part a week after having submitted the first part, I found him cool and critical and, by the way, evidently not very well informed. He had probably gone through only the introduction, the most recalcitrant part of the work. After that I came here, and meanwhile he has either been away as well or has been immersed in wary seclusion out of which not even [Gottfried] Salomon is able to ferret him. Although he gave me clear cause to hope—even if he did not make a binding promise—that he would endorse my receiving the habilitation in the field of literary history if I produced an original and suitable habilitation dissertation, he has now backed away from this, even before the work has been submitted, and is pushing me to get my habilitation in aesthetics. Of course, if that is how it goes, his vote will not have quite the same authority. Be that as it may, there is no question of my getting my habilitation unless he most vigorously supports me. Even though my incredibly accurate scholarly apparatus caused him to marvel, I am not assured of that kind of support, for in the final analysis, thousands of factors play a role, including resentment. As he said to Salomon, and with fitting self-irony at that, the only thing he has against me is that I am not his student. Salomon is thus far the only one who is familiar with the work in its entirety. He also is not averse to my view that six people could be awarded the habilitation on the basis of my dissertation. I handed in only the second, tamer half of the epistemological introduction. Although the demands of symmetry and other formal aspects of the structure would speak for it, the plan I was originally determined to carry out will probably not be realized, namely, to have a similarly constituted conclusion parallel the unofficial introduction. The climax reached in the conclusion of the main part could not be surpassed. Another several months of work would be necessary to endow the methodological section, which I had planned to devote to my ideas on "criticism," with the power it would need to follow on the heels of this conclusion. The weight of what would result might easily crush the entire edifice. Furthermore, the manuscript finally has to go to the printers. This must happen in a few days.

You haven't seen Bloch around. Understandable: he has been back here for four weeks, ever since the person who is renting his house and who was to finance Bloch's stay in Africa by paying exorbitant rent pulled out of the commitment. Thus you have to be satisfied with [Ernst] Toller. By the way, just as not a single one of your letters tends to be without a promising riddle, the four dots representing the reviewer of *Durch die Wüste* have also kept me in suspense. For a moment I suspected it was you. I hope this will not turn out to be like an earlier conjecture I made, to which I was led by mysterious remarks about Karl Kraus and Zionism. I bought the famous (or infamous) August issue of the 1924 *Fackel* and instead of a fictionalized letter from you to K.K., what I discovered were some cowardly and mediocre jokes about Palestine. I was very happy to receive "Alchemie und Kabbala." When will the conclusion appear? I have probably written you that I was no longer able to incorporate anything on the Rosicrucians into my own book after the copy deadline. Furthermore, I have carried the scholarly or bibliographical effort too far, surely due not to high standards or the "profundity" of my deliberations, but to a scrupulous accuracy deriving from twisted hidden motives. Fantastically enough, I have also been put at the mercy of the seductions of the splendid spring sun. The traveling bug I injected into myself last year is now—one year after I started out—stirring again and I am making further plans to travel. But it is not certain that they will work out. At the same time, I may have—and, in spite of everything, do have—pressing work ahead of me. My essay on *Die neue Melusine* has to be gotten ready. Hofmannsthal requested my private, personal opinion of *Der Turm,* his published version of Calderón's *Life's a Dream;* I am planning to produce it in conjunction with a written opinion for publication. A new review of literary criticism being published by Rowohlt wants regular contributions from me and I am thinking of starting out by submitting a review of *Der Turm.*[1] [. . .] Thomas Mann published a short essay on Goethe's *Elective Affinities* in the last issue of *Neue Rundschau.*[2] I have not read it yet. But it caught my attention because recently I have repeatedly come upon this author's work. I hardly know how to begin telling you that this man, whom I hated like few other writers, has essentially gotten very close to me because of the last novel he wrote, which I happened to read, *The Magic Mountain.* What was unmistakably characteristic of this novel is something that moves me and has always moved me; it spoke to me in a way that I can accurately evaluate and acknowledge and that I must, in many respects, greatly admire. However charmless such analyses are, I can only imagine that an internal change must have taken place in the author while he was writing. Indeed, I am certain this was the case. I still do not know whether he knows my essay on the *Elective Affinities.* In any case, I can no longer see anything purely arbitrary in his current observations about the book. Beyond that, I must [let] the subject drop: it is not suitable for a letter. The evening before yesterday in Frankfurt, the director of the Bremer Presse, Dr. Wiegand, looked me up in order to persuade me to compile an anthology of selections from the works of Wilhelm von Humboldt. I told him I was under contract and that I could not allow myself to plunge into these depths of German classicism. I intend to begin taking Hebrew lessons in the near future. A variety of circumstances makes it impossible for me to contact the Gutkinds about this. Having said this, I hope to have urgently requested you to give me the name of someone reliable, not only in Berlin but also in Frankfurt, someone to whom I can turn. Regardless of whether this is the person who will actually do the teaching or the person who would be responsible for finding an appropriate teacher. If at all possible, please send me some names by return mail.

[. . .]

I hope you will respond to my letters and also give me some information about the opening of the university.

Most sincere regards.
Yours, Walter

1. The review appeared in the *Literarische Welt* (April 9, 1926).
2. April 1925, pp. 391–401. It was not influenced by WB's ideas.

142. To Gerhard Scholem

Frankfurt am Main
[ca. May 20–25, 1925]

Dear Gerhard,

I am again sitting in Frankfurt during one of the endless waiting periods into which the local academic enterprise is divided, if not dissolved. My formal application for the habilitation has been before the college faculty for a week. My chances are so slim that I put off my application until the last possible moment. Since it was finally and irrevocably deemed impossible for me to be granted the habilitation in German literary history due to my "preparation," I was forced into "aesthetics" where the threat of [Hans] Cornelius's opposition again looms. For he has a teaching position in "general aesthetics," which with aesthetics is considered a single field. Another factor is Schultz's unreliability. He naturally does not want to reveal his weak point to me. Thus he let drop a few short, forced words of great appreciation for my habilitation dissertation, but does not want to put himself out. Thus at the moment there is no one who can say what will come of it. I am able to identify a number of benevolently neutral gentlemen on the faculty, but I do not know anyone who would actually take up my cause. I will know in a few days if my application is turned down right away. It is more likely that a committee will sit on it until the end of the semester and that I will have to be thankful if the matter is decided before summer vacation. Given these circumstances, it is of course hardly likely that I will spend the entire time waiting around here. Instead I will serve the time in Paris, if at all possible, otherwise in Berlin. From whatever perspective I look at it, the situation remains dubious, even from a material standpoint. For a thousand reasons, it is becoming less and less likely that I will enter upon a university career. Moreover, "aesthetics" is one of the worst beginnings for such a career. And the only thing you can ultimately count on is a monthly "subsidy" of 180 marks. But after having essentially lost any importance for me, it all became somewhat important again due to the miserable turn for the worse in the circumstances surrounding my assets, or better, my income. That is to say, my publisher went bankrupt before having published even a single book. His considerable debts amounted to 55,000 marks, none of which was covered. Others were swindled worse than I was. At least I received some payments from him, whereas they lost their money to a reckless young man who could have achieved something with some luck but, having none, lost his head to such an extent that, after publicly declaring bankruptcy, he looked for a sanatorium entirely *comme il faut*. A few weeks later, Dora was let go from a tolerable and profitable part-time job she held in addition to her main job. All of this is just terrible bad luck.

Nothing better seems on the horizon as yet. Given all of this, something more minor hardly makes a difference: thus in a few weeks you will be able to read in *the Frankfurter Zeitung* an essay entitled "Naples." I wrote it with a female acquaintance of mine from Capri and it is now in press.[1] Starting in August, Rowohlt will publish a journal, the *Literarische Welt*, as a weekly magazine. I am involved in it, not only as the contributor of a regular column on recent French art theory, but also by having claimed it as a publication outlet for Muri. The holdings of the library will be submitted to it along with the other "books submitted for review" and, indeed, will in some cases be accompanied by reviews I will write for this purpose.[2] These reviews, as well as some of the titles, will be new to you. For example, I am starting with a Däubler-like travel report, "Athos und Atheisten"—which proves that the so-called atheists were not people who denied the existence of God, but an age-old pious community of monks from the holy mountain of Athos. The final section of my new book will appear during the summer under the title "Konstruktion der Trauer" [The construction of mourning], in a yearbook published by Cassirer, where my review of *Spirit of Utopia* also appears. I am currently translating a curious work, *Anabasis* [*Anabase*], written under a pseudonym by a young French author.[3] Rilke was originally selected for the job of translating it, but I have taken his place. Although he admires the poem, he is no longer interested in doing the translation and just wants to write an introduction for it when it comes out. I consider the thing to be of little importance. The translation is extraordinarily difficult, but it is worth doing because this short "prose poem" will be very respectably remunerated. Insel is scheduled to publish it. Hofmannsthal intervened on my behalf in Paris to get the translation for me. (He was in Tunis during the spring and returned via Paris.) On one of the last days of my previous stay here, the head of the Bremer Presse came to see me (under instructions from Hofmannsthal, so to speak). [. . .] This meeting was extremely rich in opportunities for me, but I let it go by without exploiting it. And—feeling confident on account of my by now useless contract—I even dared to go much too far in my conversation and in my criticism of Hofmannsthal's intentions. I did this in such a manner that, now that a renewal of relations has become enormously important to me, my chances of doing so are not very good and I do not know how successful the various efforts I plan to make in this regard will be. This is one of the not all that frequent stupidities of my life and I truly regret it. I intend to offer the Bremer Presse an essay I plan to write on Tieck's "Der blonde Eckbert" for the next issue of their journal—it will probably be only a few pages long.

[. . .]

So much for the profoundly depressing collision of my literary with my economic plans. I am nearing the jubilee anniversary number of one thousand in the list of books I have read. I have been keeping this list ever since I graduated from the gymnasium.[4] The last entries were Thomas Mann's *Magic Mountain: History and Class Consciousness,* an extraordinary collection of Lukács's political writings; Paul Valéry's *Eupalinos, or the Architect [Eupalinos ou l'architect]*. Except for the originals, this is the only beautiful and significant work I know in the form of the Platonic dialogue with Socrates as the central figure. I am going to announce its publication in the *Literarische Welt*. For me, everything depends on how things shape up in the world of publishing. If I have no luck there, I will probably hasten my involvement with Marxist politics and join the party—with a view of getting to Moscow in the foreseeable future, at least on a temporary basis. I would take this step sooner or later in any case.[5] The horizon of my work is no longer what it was in the past and I cannot artificially keep it so narrow. To begin with, of course, the primary thing to happen will be a mighty conflict among powers (my individual powers). That must be a factor, along with my study of Hebrew. Also, I do not foresee making a fundamental decision, but instead must begin by experimenting with one thing or the other. I can attain a view of the totality of my horizon, more or less clearly divined, only in these two experiences.

I have allowed several days to elapse before starting this part of the letter. There has been no progress as far as my personal situation is concerned. The issue may be raised in a faculty meeting this evening. I am lowering my hopes appreciably; the question of who has jurisdiction weighs too heavily. If these very circumstances had obtained two years ago, I would have mustered the most fervent moral indignation. Now I can see too well through this institution and how it works to be able to do that. At a party a few days ago I met Professor [Joseph] Horovitz, with whom you, of course, have spoken in Palestine. I was unable to speak with him at length, but little of what he had to say about the inauguration of the university was close to the information in your report. Your revelations really interested me, especially your remarks about the conflict between the socialist settlements and American financial supporters. I will always be grateful to you for any further reports that consider events from this point of view. It is also important to me in every sense to hear how you will judge further developments as you await with apprehension the effects of intense capitalist colonization. Your observations on the "seemingly dead" transmitted language, which, as the Hebrew living and being transformed in the mouths of the new generation, threatens to turn against those who speak it, are not clear to me in every respect. Perhaps you could say something more on this topic. Please comply with this wish, even if I am unable to comment on the "Wahrnehmungsproblem" [The problem of perception][6] by return mail. For one thing, I have not worked on it for a long time. I recently wanted to read a book by Moritz Schapp[7] that you may know (from the Linke period), *Zur Phänomenologie der Wahrnehmung,* but I did not have the time. I would also need to know which passages you believe are in most urgent need of explication. And finally, I will not be wrong in suspecting that the human expression of your skeptical consideration and weighing of what I have written in part 3 is also inherent in your thirst for knowledge. Let me once again ask you to admit to this unflinchingly.—*Please do not keep the glosses to "Rabbi Gadiel, the Child" from me.* If the conclusion of *Alchemie und Kabbala* has already appeared, please have a copy sent to me. I read the first part with care; since the book is philological, I naturally did not get all that much out of it; its substance is outside my sphere of competence. But I would like to own it. The (so to speak "synthetic") reflections on the Bahir, from which you thought to create an introduction to the book, have probably taken temporary refuge in the folder labeled "Audible Sighs of Relief"?

I am going to send the manuscript of my *Trauerspiel* book to Hofmannsthal sometime soon.—Currently, besides the translation from French and other tasks that occasionally come my way, I am working on the fairy tale in preparation for my projects on "Der blonde Eckbert" and *Melusine.* I secretly entertain the opinion that there must be new and surprising things to say about the beauty of fairy tales. Hardly anyone has as yet delved into this matter. In addition, this particular form of intellectual productivity is beginning to fascinate me. Poor and rocky soil is revealed for the most part when you undertake a panoramic overview of the expanses of secondary literature that must be plowed through for the project. Do you know of any books on this subject that are more productive? Wesselski's magnificent collection, *Märchen des Mittelalters,* which was published in Berlin two years ago, is extremely praiseworthy in terms of its subject matter, but lacks any theoretical dimension. I would indeed be grateful to you for giving me the names of any *noteworthy* theoretical works on the fairy tale.—As you may well imagine, I am very pleased at your bringing up the prospect of a visit. I hope that by then you will be enjoying the fruits of your appointment as docent. As far as my own appointment is concerned, the most I can expect from it is a fiery-red, late cactus blossom. This expectation notwithstanding, I will probably leave Frankfurt at the end of the week, regardless of whether a negative decision has been reached by then or whether my academic star will have to begin its journey through the labyrinth of committee meetings.—I did not go to hear Buber's lecture in Berlin. Was it noteworthy? Your comment, of course, leads me to conclude it was. I reciprocate Escha's best wishes many times over. Let me wish you a rich haul for your mysterious folder and close with sincere regards.

Yours, Walter

Ernst Schoen also sends his sincere regards.

1. *Schriften* 2:72–82.

2. The only thing to appear was the anonymous "Büchereinlauf," in *Literarische Welt* 1:2.

3. St.-John Perse.

4. Only works that WB had read in their entirety were entered in this list, which he took great care to keep.

5. He never did. See letter 203, dated April 17, 1931.

6. One of WB's older manuscripts.

7. The author's name was Wilhelm Schapp (published 1910).

143. To Hugo von Hofmannsthal

Berlin-Grunewald
June 11, 1925

My most esteemed Mr. von Hofmannsthal:

Your last letter made the appearance of the new issue of the *Beiträge* doubly welcome because of the announcement of the publication of *Der Turm* and because of your kind encouragement to write about my impressions of this work. Your letter has now been here for weeks. One of the reasons for my responding only now is that I just heard of your return from Africa a short time ago. I also had to go through the drama many times in order to achieve the distance necessary to give an accounting of it that would go beyond the profound impression reading the text made on me. Please indulge me if I confess to being of the opinion that I am somewhat better prepared to give this accounting than some other, arbitrarily chosen, reader. Consequently, I might be permitted to confide to you my joy in seeing in the drama an intellectual realm that reveals itself to me ever more clearly. My most recent studies brought me into very close proximity to this realm. In fact, I see your work as a *Trauerspiel* in its purest, canonical form. And at the same time I sense the extraordinary dramatic energy of which the best examples of this genre are capable, contrary to accepted educated opinion. A comparison with your other works is not appropriate at this point, but perhaps I have seen things correctly if I view this last work as the crowning glory of the renewal and rebirth of the German baroque form and as an extremely authoritative work for the stage. The point—to name just one—at which Sigismund recoils from his mother while standing in front of the alcove in the hall would have to be one of the greatest moments for a great actor. And I immediately want to mention Julian, who should also be able to inspire anyone to become a real actor because of the way that, having been miraculously summoned by the doctor's Latin epigram, he maintains his nocturnal nature throughout the entire play. What touches me most deeply in this figure is the splendid interplay between profound weakness and profound loyalty. A loyalty that involuntarily derives only from weakness and is nonetheless wondrously reconciled with it. For this man is heading straight for the liberating decision yet remains fixed where he stands as the eternal servant of what has been decided. I myself feel how my words fall terribly short of expressing the character's mystery. I would be hard pressed to come up with kindred spirits for him in the realm of drama. Basilius, who appears to me to be a genuine brother to King Claudius, is a different matter. How wondrously the grand description of the evening landscape on the day of Agidius issues from the lips of this forlorn individual: how truly dramatic and how far removed from a lyrical intermezzo it becomes when it issues from the lips of this man. Who could speak these lines today? More than ten years ago, I heard Paul Wegner read King Claudius's prayer in a way neither he nor anyone else would probably be able to manage today.—Study and reflection have brought me to the point of believing that I may assume, with a certain degree of assurance, that you share and wanted to share with Calderón no more than the pure content of the legend. Therefore no words of comparison seemed very appropriate. I might, however, be permitted to tell you that I deciphered Calderón's highly remarkable and philosophical procedure in this drama, which he uses in almost all his dramas: he crystallizes what is most profound in a formula, almost in the same way morality plays do; he turns it every which way and a very carefree, facile, and hastily constructed play is reflected as something significant in the faceted essence. In a word: Calderón takes from the content nothing but the formula he used for the title. This formula is of course treated more philosophically than could be imagined possible without him, but his drama could no more be equal to what is dramatic in the material than any "play" could. It is the stuff of "Trauerspiel" and the Sigismund of your drama is a "creature" in a much more radical sense than Calderón's "courtier of the mountain," indeed in a much more radical sense than any hero of baroque drama I could name. Am I mistaken if I see that, in him, the author has pushed to the sober center of the stage of *Trauerspiel* what in Shakespeare constituted the colorful edge of what is comical, under the name of Caliban, Ariel, a half animal–half man, or any kind of primal spirit? For the question of how the child-king draws close to this prince at the end is resolved for me precisely from that perspective. It is, of course, a childlike nature that distinguishes the young human creature from animal progeny, and in the case of Sigismund it has been denied protection. The condition of being a child now grows within him, sometimes fervently, sometimes to gigantic proportions, sometimes fatefully, because he lacks the redeeming moderation that derives from contact with one's parents. He consequently becomes a judge who is incorruptibly and terrifyingly pure. It is all too clear that he cannot have anything to do with women. But it is also a certainty that the muffled ghosts of his early years in the tower must ultimately fell this gigantic child. His battle for language is a prelude to this. I found all the dramatic clues to it quite extraordinary; I recognized a basic motif of the *Trauerspiel* explained in these passages, not only in an incomparably decisive manner but in a way that was theatrically comprehensible for the first time. And it is precisely among these passages that the powerful scene with the organ in the third act belongs; since, of course, the music of a *Trauerspiel* always projects in song the elegaic tone of the human voice, liberated from meaning and words. Thus music has the last "word" here too, in the sounds of the trumpets. The prince must of course succumb. Does he not basically succumb only to the recurrent power of dead things, of the pig, which he feared to become? In the adjuration, which is usually nothing more than an intermezzo in the *Trauerspiel,* this child who childishly treats it as his last resort destroys himself. The spirits that are obligatory for the *Trauerspiel* here unite most intimately with the creature.

It would be painful for me if these few words were to strike you as alien; if the ideas in my new book that are reflected in them were to have encountered the spirit of your work in an unseemly way. I hope this is not the case and that these ideas will not prevent you from glancing at the manuscript, which I am also sending you today, when you have a chance. I would not trouble you with a typewritten copy if the prospects of it being printed were definite. My technique of piling one quotation on top of the other may require some explanation; but here I would like merely to observe that the academic intent of the work was nothing but an occasion for me to produce something in this style. Indeed, this was an occasion of which I ironically took advantage. You may keep the manuscript for as long as you like. Please believe me when I say that it is quite clear to me that I can make no claims on your time by sending you the manuscript.

But now, my esteemed Mr. von Hofmannsthal, I must above all express my warmest thanks for the kindness with which you thought of me even while traveling. I learned through a friend who was visiting Paris, Mrs. Helen Hessel,[1] that I have you to thank for my having been entrusted with a translation of St.-J. Perse's *Anabasis.* I am currently working on it.

Let me assure you that I will do my best to do honor to the recommendation you made in Paris. What you did for me was all the more providential since a pleasant, but very brief, relationship with a new publishing house came to an end at precisely that time, when difficulties forced it into liquidation.

The situation concerning the slender manuscript of aphorisms is somewhat different from that of the *Trauerspiel* book, which will accompany or follow it. I would be greatly obliged if you would cast a friendly eye on the aphorisms, to see whether you might want to fill an empty page of the *Beiträge* with one or another of them as you see fit. I know that they include some personal things that would be made to seem highbrow if they were published this way. All the same, let me ask you to accept that this is only an inquiry made in all modesty. It was occasioned by a social call from Dr. Wiegand in Frankfurt. I have rarely had the opportunity to speak about literary and journalistic matters with a man who is as noble as he is farsighted. We came to speak of the *Beiträge* and Mr. Wiegand spoke about your continuing editorial interest in my projects. I would also like to express my thanks to you for this.

Some time ago I approached Mr. Wiegand with a proposal. His answer arrived just this morning. The proposal concerns German legends, which are consuming a lot of my time. My starting point is a series of questions I intend to address in conjunction with a work on Goethe's *Die neue Melusine*. I have been planning this project for years. In it, I do not intend to treat the literary theme against the background of Goethe's person, as I did in the essay on *Elective Affinities,* but to bring increased visibility to this artistic fairy tale within the context of the folk tale. In doing this, I must investigate the form of the fairy tale in particular. For I envision a definition of the fairy tale that will derive many essential aspects from the specifics inherent in its form. And it is here that the comparison with legends most forcefully suggests itself to me. I envisioned the style of the legend—in many ways different from that of the fairy tale—to cite Grimm, its "epic integrity," as one of the most sublime and undervalued possessions of the German language when I wrote to Mr. Wiegand proposing a collection of legends. Based on this perspective, the collection would bring together a number of them as documents of a perfect entelechial prose. What I have in mind is that just the shorter, more ordinary pieces—etymological legends or ghost stories, transmitted in shy and hurried whispers—would come into their own only in such a context. It might perhaps be justified in an epilogue. Mr. Wiegand delighted me by telling me that he plans to discuss the matter with me. I hope to see him, either here or in Frankfurt. That is to say, I may go to Frankfurt again at the end of the month. The decision about my academic plans and, consequently, the framework, however fragile, for my immediate future is due to be made at that time.

I have already taken too much of your time with all this talk of myself. On the other hand, please allow me to add that Rang's papers are currently in Gießen, where a professor of English[2] will undertake to complete the Shakespeare book.—Please attribute the length of this letter to the fact that I count on your friendly and benevolent interest in what I do.

Let me assure you of my continuing gratitude and devotion.

Walter Benjamin

1. Known as an author under the name of Helen Grund; Franz Hessel's wife.
2. Theodor Spira, a privatdocent in Gießen at the time.

144. To Rainer Maria Rilke

Berlin
July 3, 1925

My most esteemed Mr. Rilke:

Allow me to express my sincere gratitude for the kindness with which you demonstrated your confidence in me by wanting to entrust me with the task of translating the *Anabasis*.[1] Before I began the actual translation, I read the book again and again and am now intimately familiar with it. Enclosed you will find seven chapters. Mrs. Hessel and, recently, Mr. von Münchhausen[2] have assured me that you have been so kind as to declare yourself willing to assist me should I run into difficulties. There is no lack of them. I have singled out very few passages with a question mark in the margin, but that should be understood as an invitation to you to indicate in the margin whenever you happen upon something you find objectionable. Aside from the four passages I have marked, some other passages strike me as too tentative. In such passages, the correct solution may be possible only for somebody who knows the author's ultimate intentions and is thus saved from doing violence to the text. Otherwise, I trust that faithfulness to the text and study have for the most part spared me from egregious errors. During the past few weeks, I have gained a clearer understanding of the atmosphere in which—in a broader sense—the work originated. The way language enters the realm of dreams by conquest, authoritatively and normatively, is what particularly moved me about surrealism (and some of its goals are surely also unmistakable in St.-J. Perse). It is the faster pulse of this prosodic action that I have primarily tried to capture in the German.

Thanks to your kindness, I am very pleased to be able to contribute in a small way to furthering the bond between German and French literature. Translation as the path to this goal, particularly the translation of such a recalcitrant text, is certainly one of the most difficult of paths, but it is also probably much more legitimate, perhaps, than that of commentary, precisely for that reason.

As a sign of my grateful devotion, I am venturing to send you my most recently published essay, on Goethe's *Elective Affinities,* by the next mail.

I would like to assure you in advance that you will have my full attention and sincere gratitude for every suggestion you make to improve my text.

With highest esteem and the greatest respect, I am

Your most devoted, Walter Benjamin

1. Rilke had originally been chosen as the translator. WB took his place at Hofmannsthal's suggestion. The edition, translated by WB in collaboration with Bernhard Groethuysen, was announced for 1929 and Hofmannsthal had written a foreword; it was not published then, probably at the request of the author, who allowed a new edition of the poem in French to be published only in 1945. The translation appeared in 1950 in a version "reviewed and revised by Herbert Steiner," in *Das Lot* 4 (Berlin, October 1950).

2. Thankmar, count of Münchhausen, a friend of Rilke.

145. To Gerhard Scholem

Berlin
July 21, 1925

Dear Gerhard,

This time it has taken me inhumanly long to write. I was extremely grateful to receive your letter of June, with its observations on how things are going in Palestine and on the status of your work. It has now remained unanswered for a long time. It seemed as if my unsettled situation was not coming to a resolution and I therefore put off writing you. Now the time has come: I hope you have not become angry in the meantime and that you will be compensated if I now write at length and in detail. To be sure, I cannot bring myself to write at great length about the first point I want to touch on, the wreckage of my Frankfurt plans. Things were at the point where I was supposed to take my fourth or fifth trip to Frankfurt at the beginning of July, when a letter from [Matthias] Friedwagner, a specialist in Romance languages, reached me by way of my in-laws. He reported to Vienna the total hopelessness of the steps I was taking. His friendship for my father-in-law had moved him to explore the lay of the land, at which point it became evident that the two old crocks, Cornelius and Kautzsch,[1] the former perhaps well-disposed, the latter more likely hostile, claimed not to understand anything of my dissertation. I immediately turned to Salomon for more precise information. He was unable to find out anything other than that it was generally thought advisable for me to withdraw my application as quickly as possible in order that I might be spared an official rejection. Schultz (as dean) had, of course, assured me he wanted to spare me that in any case. He remained incommunicado. I have very cogent reasons for assuming that he behaved in extremely bad faith. All in all, I am glad. The Old Franconian stage route following the stations of the local university is not my way—to be honest, after Rang's death, Frankfurt is the most bitter wasteland. Meanwhile, however, I have not withdrawn my application, since I am inclined to leave the risk of a negative decision completely up to the college faculty. Everyone is totally in the dark as to how things will proceed now. Naturally, any chance of my revising it to make it acceptable is probably completely out of the question although the field of literary history is currently very understaffed due to some recent changes in the faculty. If I were given the chance to revise it and it were accepted, the first thing I would do would be to take a leave of absence in the winter. So much for the final stage of this endeavor. One of its prerequisites after another has disappeared in the last year. First there was my parents' refusal to increase my stipend once my habilitation dissertation was approved; then my conversion to political theory; and finally Rang's death. This does not change the fact that this kind of base trifling with my efforts and accomplishments would truly irritate and embitter me if I still were attached to the project. It is quite unheard of that a project like mine could be authorized and then ignored in this way. Because—I remember this much of the penultimate stage of the process about which I must have written you—when all is said and done, it was Schultz, who, before the faculty, opposed my getting a degree in literary history and thus brought about the current situation. Given these circumstances, an expert recommendation like the one I recently received is doubly valuable. Hofmannsthal has a copy of my dissertation and has shown it to the professor of German in Vienna, [Walther] Brecht. He was the teacher of a certain Cysarz, who is my immediate forerunner and occasionally my obvious opponent in this area of literary history. Brecht is now supposed to have received the work with the greatest approval and is ready to intercede on its behalf by recommending it to any publisher whatsoever. Hofmannsthal has volunteered to do the same thing in his very helpful and positive letter. I may send you a copy of it when I get the chance. He speaks of how his own essays were most deeply affected by my conclusions. He has many nice things to say about the book and states that it demonstrates "absolute mastery in many sections." I am very eager to hear that it is in your hands and whether you are able to make something of it.

Meanwhile, I have not done a lot and, to the extent that I have devoted any time to literature, I have done so by reading. I have read mainly the latest things from France: on the one hand, the splendid writings of Paul Valéry (*Variété, Eupalinos*); on the other hand, the dubious books of the surrealists. Confronted by these documents, I must gradually familiarize myself with the technique of criticism. I have taken on all sorts of tasks as a contributor to a new literary review that is to appear in the fall—I think I have already told you about this—primarily, a regular column on new French art theory. And that is exactly where I will introduce in brief reviews the best items in the catalog of the Muri library. You will then receive these and other tomfoolery. For today, all you will get is an excerpt from the *Berliner Tageblatt*. Because of the way they were printed, the theses[2] have lost much of their impact. For they were meant to be printed in two facing columns whose individual lines were intended to be read with the corresponding, adjacent lines, but could also be read from top to bottom as a whole, especially the second column. To top it all off, I remain unable to present this scrap of paper to you. Instead I must ask for it back because the "Theses" appeared only in the stop-press edition of the *Tageblatt* and only a few copies were still to be found in Berlin by the time I was informed they were in print, a week after the date of publication. I have made some preliminary sketches for a future book of aphorisms in the style of these theses. My preliminary research for the fairy tale book, however, has not gotten very far. "Naples" still has not appeared in the *Frankfurter Zeitung*. Another short piece, a trivial thing, was recently accepted there.[3] My preliminary research for the fairy tale book is overlapping with my plans for another project, in whose problematical execution I am now engaged. What I have in mind is an anthology of legends, German legends. It would be based on two approaches: 1) The formulation of a motif, always in the most laconic manner, combined with its most important *linguistic* variations. What concerns me here is the mystery of the *formulas* of legends, and the different and significant way in which legends know how to intimate things. 2) A selection of eccentric and somewhat more obscure motifs, regardless of whether they are authentic or not. In short, what I have in mind is an attempt to approach, for the first time since Grimm (as far as I am aware), the entire complex, not bound by local or historical limitations, and to do so by proceeding from the linguistic nature of the legend. And additionally to strike sparks from the many stones that people after Grimm continued to chip out of the mountain of legends. It seems to me that my planned structure and brevity would work wonders and provide objectively compelling clues to an interpretation. Yet I would write an epilogue, not so much for the purpose of interpretation, as to write something on the prose of the legend. I still do not know whether it will materialize.—You will have heard the name of Marcel Proust. I recently decided to translate the main novel in his lengthy cycle of novels, *Remembrance of Things Past [A la recherche du temps perdu]*. I am to translate the three-volume work, *Sodom and Gomorrah*. The remuneration is not at all good but it is good enough for me to believe that I had to take on this enormous task. If the translation is a success, I can count on being securely accredited as a translator, like, for example, Stefan Zweig. We may have occasionally spoken about Proust and I have asserted how close his philosophical perspective is to mine. Whenever I read anything he wrote, I felt we were kindred souls. I am eager to see whether this feeling will be maintained now that I will be intimately involved with his work. For a pittance, I previously agreed to translate Balzac's *Ursule Mirouet* for Rowohlt. It will appear in three weeks. Since the money was not worth the time I had to spend on it, I passed on the translation of the second part to someone else and only looked it over. I believe I already wrote you that, at Rilke's behest, I have translated a brand new poem from the surrealist school: *Anabasis* by St.-J. Perse (this is a pseudonym—I do not know who the person behind it is). I have sent samples of the translation to Paris.—The Bremer Presse recently turned to me for the second time with the request that I undertake to put together an edition of selections from Wilhelm von Humboldt's works. I accepted the second offer for many reasons, whereas I had rejected the first. Precise details still have not been worked out: I will probably meet soon with the director of the Bremer Presse to discuss everything. Maybe you will be able to give me some useful references on Humboldt—after all, you have most likely studied some of his works. The offer particularly pleased me because it meant I had been chosen over Spranger, Litt, and other university professors who had also been under consideration.

My hope to be able to take a long trip soon is based on my literary income. I am planning to travel by freighter from Hamburg via Spain and Italy to Sicily. The freighter docks at all the major Spanish ports, even if usually for only a few hours. This is supposed to be a relatively cheap way to travel and this way I hope to be able to fulfill my burning desire to bask again this summer in the glow of the August and September sun that shines upon the southernmost tip of Europe. I assume I will be alone.—Bloch is in Riga to deal with matters concerning an inheritance. —The Gutkinds have been invited to Holland in August. I have seen very little of them recently, but will go to visit them soon.—I have not in fact written to Kraft. At the time we were in Italy, it appeared conceivable to me that we would get together once again. And in the same spirit, it is conceivable to me even now that I would not be averse to chance's bringing us together. But I am incapable of creating this chance myself.

Have you actually read Lukács's *History and Class Consciousness?* And is the "finishing off"[4] of Lukács's book by Deborin or whomever also available in German or some language other than Russian?[5] I would really love to read it. Maybe you can give me the bibliographical reference.

Ernst Schoen was extremely pleased to receive your greetings. He is still in Frankfurt, but is trying to get from there to here any way he can.—By the way, if you were twelve years younger and still a budding student of history, I would recommend Werner Hegemann's *Fridericus* to you. It was recently sent to me and contains the most radical attempt imaginable to dispose of the "greatness" of this monarch. It is also superbly well written and impresses the reader as being highly reliable. To be sure, its form is that of an uncouth dialogue extending over five hundred pages, but even that has style and it reminds you of the philosophical conversations of the English (Hobbes's *Leviathan*). Beyond that, one thing or another manages to turn up in my library—although I have really bought next to nothing for a year, since I am compelled to consider putting my assets to other uses. My brother gave me the first volume of selections from Lenin's works in German. I am impatiently awaiting the second volume, which will contain his philosophical writings and will soon be published. I agreed to review some things by Kafka that are among his papers.[6] Just as I did ten years ago, I still consider his short story "Before the Law" ["Vor dem Gesetz"] to be one of the best German short stories. I have also received the collected works of Poe in German translation. Besides the Schreber book and the book containing tables and charts which we acquired in Munich, a new paranoid system for world and state government has recently entered my library: Whole-Earth-Universal-State. A work that need not be ashamed to appear in public.[7]

I am eagerly waiting to get what you have written. It seems totally unbelievable to me that it would be hard to find a publisher for your *Die physiognomischen Traditionen der Kabbala*. I should say, incredible. Aren't you still in touch with [Moses] Marx—and isn't he still in touch with the Euphorion Verlag? Of course, I know nothing about Jewish publishing houses. But could you simply consider the consortium of publishers of scholarly works (W. de Gruyter)?[8] Otherwise: Buber has connections with the new Marcan publishing house in Cologne. Regarding the topic as such, perhaps a work on physiognomy in Old French literature might interest you. I have not read it yet myself. It is in a 1911 publication (volume 29) of the *Romanische Forschungen* published by Vollmöller.

Did I write you that two of Rang's friends from Frankfurt want to put together a selection of his letters that, at the same time, is intended to trace the course of his life. Based on information in a letter from Mrs.

Rang that arrived yesterday, it seems that this needed and felicitous enterprise is less certain than I had hoped.

Please write soon. You now have a fairly detailed overview of what I am doing (or, if you prefer, of what I am not doing). What do people in Palestine think, and what do you think, about the Zionist congress soon to take place?

Send letters to this address.

Most sincere regards.
Yours, Walter

P.S. I must add that I ran into Ernst Lewy on the street two weeks ago. We greeted each other and he spoke to me. His *first* words to me were that he is now a professor. (Since, for some time, he has been re-habilitated in Berlin—but most likely only as an honorary professor.) All this just occurred to me while I was reading about Humboldt's writings on the philosophy of language in Steinthal's annotated edition.[9] It contains an exquisite essay on Humboldt's style which reveals where the affinity between Lewy and his favorite author lies. Steinthal writes about Humboldt's "depth" with exemplary candor.

1. Rudolf Kautzsch (1868–1945).
2. "Dreizehn Thesen wider Snobisten" [Thirteen theses contra snobs] *Berliner Tageblatt* (July 10, 1925). In *Schriften* 1:538ff.
3. Presumably "Sammlung von Frankfurter Kinderreimen" [A collection of Frankfurt children's rhymes] (August 15, 1920).
4. Scholem had used the expression ironically.
5. A. Deborin, "Lukács und seine Kritik des Marxismus," *Arbeiter Literatur* 10 (Vienna, October 1924), pp. 615–40. The review "exposed" the "idealistic and even mystical tendencies" of Lukács's book.
6. This is the first indication of WB's interest in Kafka, which WB maintained until the end.
7. There was a small collection of writings by the mentally ill in WB's library. He devoted much attention to them. The reference is to Daniel Paul Schreber, *Die Denkwürdigkeiten eines Nervenkranken* (Leipzig, 1903).
8. The book remained unpublished, because Scholem came to doubt the validity of its theses.
9. Berlin, 1883.

146. To Hugo von Hofmannsthal

Berlin
August 2, 1925

My most esteemed Mr. von Hofmannsthal:

Just as I was getting ready today to extend you my sincere gratitude for your continuing interest in my work and my situation and for the undiminished warmth with which you demonstrated it, your letter of the 31st arrived. I am pleased that you are once again so kind as to offer me entrée to the *Beiträge* and this makes me all the more indebted. I trust you will understand and detect no false note in my words if I, privately as it were, express my long-nourished hope of sometime, at a propitious moment, being able to express in person not only my appreciation but also, and above all, the gratitude with which your constant solicitude fills me. That is precisely how I might characterize the remarks and suggestions in your penultimate letter, insofar as they refer to my Frankfurt endeavor. I talked to Dr. Wiegand about it two days ago. In the meantime, they have as good as arrived at a negative decision and it has been proposed that I voluntarily withdraw my application for the habilitation. Looking back on the twisted course of this affair, I have every reason to be glad about the internal and external conviction that increasingly kept me from respecting the contemporary university as a place for productive and, above all, disinterested activity. In any other situation, the kind of treatment to which I was subjected would have aroused in me much unproductive indignation and spleen. After all, I was led to write and to submit my work on the *Trauerspiel* with the agreement of a university professor in Frankfurt only after I had most carefully sounded out the situation, mainly by initially submitting my essay on *Elective Affinities* three years ago. To be sure, it would seem worthwhile (and is even obviously so) to be able to stand in front of young people and win them over with living speech: but it is not irrelevant where this takes place and who these people are. And as surely as no one outside the university today would vouch for the fruitfulness of the enterprise, it seems just as sure to me that the university itself increasingly muddies the clarity of its pedagogical sources. Thoughts of this kind—which I have only intimated—can console me for the fact that even the kind of benevolent intercession you envisioned would have achieved nothing in Frankfurt today, or even earlier. At the same time, my esteemed Mr. von Hofmannsthal, you indicate you are inclined to interest a publisher in my habilitation dissertation. At the moment it is still with Rowohlt in Berlin. My friend, Franz Hessel, a reader for Rowohlt, recommended it to them. For my part, the idea that it would be easier to find a publisher who puts out books of general interest than one who does purely scholarly books, in the narrow sense of the word, also played a role in choosing Rowohlt. For a "scholarly" stance, in the contemporary sense, is certainly not the main thing in my study. From the perspective of a clearly scholarly publisher, therefore, that could diminish the value of the text, whereas it is precisely where its interest for me lies. Be that as it may—because of what you had to say, I will inform you of the outcome of my negotiations with Rowohlt; I know that Rowohlt is well aware of your own opinion of my book. Regarding the manuscript, I beg you to continue to do with it whatever seems useful. In particular, I would be happy for it to be made available to Professor Brecht[1] for a while.

When he was here, Dr. Wiegand discussed with me the selection of Humboldt's works planned by the Bremer Presse. It is with gratitude and conviction that I will take part in the project that Dr. Wiegand briefly outlined for me: to attune and prepare students to use the large editions of collected works, which nowadays do not reveal but keep hidden our great thinkers and authors. My work on Humboldt takes me back to my years as a student when I read his writings on linguistics in a seminar under the guidance of a man who was extremely strange in human terms and who was almost grotesquely of one mind with the contemplative genius of the late Humboldt. I might perhaps be permitted to mention this because you may possibly know the individual in question (I am almost sure you do) as the author of a slender volume on *Die Sprache des alten Goethe*. It is Ernst Lewy, at that time professor of Finno-Ugric languages in Berlin.

My idea for a book on legends still needs time to ripen and it must first be sufficiently developed in terms of the material I am gathering. That, should I be on the right track, I will find the most obliging and encouraging assistance from Dr. Wiegand at the proper time—I do not have the slightest doubt about this. When he was here and we had our first long conversation, I once again realized the value of the trust you asked me to have in him.

In the letter you wrote at the beginning of July, there is a reference to a collection of "sad" puppet plays from lower Austria. You name Kislick (?) and Winter as the publishers. I was unfortunately unable to get the book[2] here. Should you have more precise information available, I would be very grateful if you would pass it on to me, when you have a chance. I recently read in a Berlin newspaper that sensational peasant dramas are still performed among the Tirolean farmers. An excursion to such a performance was featured as a part of Prof. [Arthur] Kutscher's seminar in Munich.

With gratitude and devotion, my esteemed Mr. von Hofmannsthal, I remain

Yours, Walter Benjamin

1. Walther Brecht, prematurely pensioned off in 1937 for political reasons; Hofmannsthal's friend and the executor of his estate.

2. *Deutsche Puppenspiele,* edited by Richard Kralik and Joseph Winter (Vienna, 1885).

147. To Gerhard Scholem

Naples
September 21, 1925

Dear Gerhard,

The rainy season seems to be starting here. I fled into a café where I am writing this letter. But the weather plays no role in this letter. It was due today—actually overdue—even if it were hot and the sun were shining. If I am to follow procedure, I will have to encumber it with news of my journey. You will have received my card from Cordoba or Seville. During the few days I spent there I used all my energy to soak up all I could of the architecture, landscape, and customs of southern Spain. In Seville I discovered a powerful baroque painter who would not have been ignored in the dedications of *Flowers of Evil* if Baudelaire had known him! Juan Valdez Leal,[1] who has Goya's power, Rops's mentality, and Wiertz's subject matter. The terrible bout of illness that afflicted me in the final hours of my stay unfortunately prevented me from getting any reproductions. We passed very close to Gibraltar and saw the coast of Africa. After three [days] we docked in Barcelona, an untamed port city that quite felicitously imitates the Parisian Boulevard on a small scale. Every place I have been, I have seen cafés and working-class neighborhoods in extremely out-of-the-way areas, partly because I went wherever my constant meandering took me, and partly by sticking close to the captain and the "officers." (This is what the upper ranks are called in the merchant marine.) These people were the only ones with whom I could speak. They are uneducated but not without independent judgment. And they also have a sense for the difference between people who are well- and ill-bred—something not so easily found on land. The captain did not want to let me get away in Naples and because of this I imagine that the man, who naturally has no inkling of what I am writing, wanted to get hold of some of it. He will get my translation of *Ursule Mirouet,* which may have finally appeared in print during my absence from Berlin. Then we docked in Genoa and Livorno. I went to the Riviera for one day and walked along the beautiful shore road that goes from Rapallo to Portofino. I seem to have the impression that you are familiar with this area. We were in port in Livorno for a long time and I had time to go to Pisa and Lucca. For there is nothing in Livorno itself and by looking at the city you would not think it had its Zohar,[2] any more than, by looking at any kind of bibliopolis, you would think it had a crown. I was greeted by the most memorable annual market on the evening of my solitary arrival in Lucca. I now make note of it instead of keeping a travel diary, since, thanks to Littauer's collapse, I am able to make this trip without having any literary obligations. To be sure, the Proust translation is looming. Or didn't I write you that for the next month I have undertaken the task of translating his three-volume novel, *Sodom and Gomorrah,* for a modest fee? I intend to complete this task in Paris if possible. In October—toward the end of the month—I would like to go there via Marseilles. I still have no idea of how tricky a task the translation will turn out to be: this is the only way I could have taken it on. The most thankless task imaginable, and justifiably so, after the response to the best thing I have ever done, but a task from which I may reap a lot of benefits. I will go to Capri for only a few days this year and I do not intend to stay even here much longer. The city has again completely filled the entire space in my heart that it occupied last year. Yesterday, on a hot Sunday, I walked around and circumnavigated the city from a different perspective. I find its very topography a fascinating study in cartography. Incidentally, my efforts will probably be in vain if I do not get a relief map. I am paying 10 lire for a very modest but clean room to sleep.—A copy of "Naples" finally reached me here in the mail. It appeared in the August 15 issue of the *Frankfurter Zeitung,* and a few days before that the paper carried another short piece I wrote. At the moment, I am unable to send either of them to you because only a single proof copy was sent to me here. Later.—Write me and let me know whether anything important happened at the congress in Vienna. I do not know anything about it. Two hours before I left for the train station, I signed a contract with Ernst Rowohlt Verlag in Berlin. It guarantees me a fixed income for the next year and Rowohlt will publish *The Origin of German Tragic Drama,* my essay on Goethe's *Elective Affinities,* and "Plaquette für Freunde." The third work is a slender volume of aphorisms. It is not yet certain whether it will be able to live up to its planned title. [. . .] I wrote you about the joy with which I received your Mendelssohn,[3] as well as the *Rivière.* Please do not get behind in sending me all the things you have published. I am supposed to write some reviews here. The place I intend to claim under my own name in the *Literarische Welt*—much of what I write will appear under a pseudonym, but in a terribly unpredictable fashion[4]—will be staked out by my review of Unruh's *Flügel der Nike.*[5] This review must turn out to be simply formidable. The book, of course, is the dross of German republican literature.—Your last letter accompanied me on my trip; I am reading it once again and will adopt the concept of the "lesser immortality," the door to which—who knows?—was closed in my face by the Frankfurt concierge. The approval it awakened in me was as great as the deep disapproval my brief theses versus prehistoric man/Negroes/idiots/art awakened in you. Why? Except for *one* highfalutin and low-down thesis, everything there is clear as mud. "Man without shadow" had an even more devastating effect. I promise that I will soon deliver the papers of my shadow to the lesser immortality with a visa that is good for the trip both there and *back*. For the word is the greatest affront beneath this sun. And thus the morning sun of my fame casts such a long shadow that it arrives before me in Jeruscholayim. Quod felix faustumque sit!

All the best,
Yours, Walter

1. Succeeded Murillo as president of the Academy of Seville (1622–90).
2. WB had often seen a six-volume edition of the Zohar from Livorno at Scholem's.
3. The first edition of Moses Mendelssohn's *Jerusalem*.
4. WB preferred the pseudonyms A. Ackermann and Anni M. Bie (an anagram), and later E. J. Mabinn.
5. No. 21 (May 1926).

148. To Rainer Maria Rilke

Riga
November 9, 1925

My most esteemed Mr. Rilke:

I hope you will be so kind as to forgive me if you did not receive an immediate response to your telegram; it reached me in Naples only after taking a long and circuitous route and its arrival also coincided with preparations for my temporary move here. I was very grateful and pleased to receive this invaluable sign of your interest in my translation. It is clear to me that many passages are problematical because of the nature of the text and the difficulty of deciding on a translation. Before it goes to press, I hope to get some further information and advice about certain details, whether in the form of a tip from you or even by simply going through the text with friends during my upcoming stay in Paris. The latter might indeed not take place until February and you may have set an earlier deadline to get it to the printer. I would be interested to know whether there is already a publishing agreement and with whom. If I understood Mrs. Hessel correctly, you will write a foreword for the German edition. I recently received Larbaud's foreword for the Russian edition from Mr. von Münchhausen.—If I might be permitted to add one more thing, all of my time is devoted to the translation of *Sodom and Gomorrah*. The deeper I delve into the text, the more grateful I am for the circumstances that caused it to be entrusted to me! What I have gained from having been so deeply involved with this great masterpiece will in time become very tangible for me.—Finally, let me be permitted to express to you, my esteemed Mr. Rilke, my hope that your health has improved and that you might acknowledge me with a few lines when you have an opportunity.

[Ending missing]

149. To Hugo von Hofmannsthal

Berlin
December 28, 1925

My most esteemed Mr. von Hofmannsthal:

Thank you so very much for your kind lines from Aussee. This time, I cannot act immediately on your suggestion that I expound for you my ideas about Shakespeare's use of metaphor. I deeply regret this. Whenever I have completed a major project, it remains impossible for me to return to related themes and ideas for quite some time, and without doing that it would be impossible for me to begin to deal with the issue: for a reason that, I confess, is not likely to excuse the cause for my delay. I am not actually all that familiar with Shakespeare, but have confronted him only sporadically. On the other hand, of course, I learned what it means really to know Shakespeare through my contact with Florens Christian Rang and I would have approached him long ago with the topic you broached if he were still alive. I do not know whether the juxtaposition of Shakespeare and Calderón would be as revealing in this instance as it so often is in other instances. In any event, Calderón's use of metaphor is dazzling and seems to me quite different from Shakespeare's: if this were the case, they would certainly be revealed as two distinct and significant poles of the figurative language of the baroque (Shakespeare's metaphor being the "image and trope" of the action and the individual, Calderón's the romantic intensification of speech itself). But for now I have to call a halt to this; if I ever get around to carrying out an old plan to write a commentary on *The Tempest,* I believe your question would be the focus of my study. I am currently paying close attention to Proust's use of metaphor. In an interesting controversy with Thibaudet about Flaubert's style,[1] Proust simply declares metaphor to be the essence of style. It is perhaps common practice among great writers to take their metaphors from what is close at hand and of no consequence to the current state of affairs. I admire how Proust adapts this practice and, as it were, mobilizes a whole complex of trite, universally known relationships in the service of more profound expression. Thus Proust brings to the most feeble perceptions a beautiful, belligerent laconicism, in that he enlists them in the service of metaphorical expression. In addition to working on the translation, I am busy writing criticism; but the more inclined I am to deal with some topical subjects, especially books by the Parisian surrealists, the more aware I become of the difficulty of finding a place somewhere for my ephemeral, although perhaps not superficial, considerations. In this regard, I must somewhat lower the hope I placed in the appearance of *the Literarische Welt.*—I hope and I wish, my esteemed Mr. von Hofmannsthal, that you will begin the new year in good health and well motivated to work. Should a new issue of the *Beiträge* appear in the first third of the new year, sometime before the end of March or the beginning of April, the publication of my chapter on *Melancholia* there would certainly be the first time it appeared in print, and no objections would be raised (either by Rowohlt or by me).[2] In any case, I am always at your disposal should you want the exact text of Andreas Tscherning's "Melancolei redet selber" (in *Vortrab des Sommers deutscher Gedichte,* Rostock, 1655).[3] I believe I have selected the strongest—in a poetical sense, as well—passages in the text, which is somewhat clumsy in places. Yet on the whole it is beautiful and remarkable. There are more likely to be reservations because it was reproduced in a worthless anthology of baroque poems that was published some years ago in Berlin.—I read [Ernst] Cassirer's book on *Die Begriffsform im mythischem Denken*[4] some time ago with great interest. But I remained unconvinced that it is feasible not only to attempt to present mythical thought in concepts—i.e. critically—but also to illuminate it adequately in contrast with what is conceptual.

All the best. Your devoted,
Walter Benjamin

1. *Nouvelle revue française* (January 1920). Cf. Marcel Proust, *Tage des Lesens: Drei Essays* (Frankfurt am Main, 1963).
2. The chapter was published only in *Neue deutsche Beiträge* 2, no. 3 (August 1927), pp. 89ff.; the book appeared in 1928.
3. The poem is repeatedly cited in the *Trauerspiel* book.
4. Leipzig, 1922.

150. To Gerhard Scholem

Berlin
January 14, 1926

Dear Gerhard,

I had been meaning to write you for a long time. Your letter to Dora just arrived today. She plans to answer you herself. I believe I am at liberty to reveal that she was very pleased to get it. A more detailed report on Stefan will most probably be included in her letter. He is of course learning Hebrew now—but probably not much is accomplished in his elective courses and the only thing he really likes are the Bible stories, which are taught by another teacher. Speaking of this, I would really like to know whether you know of a Jewish reader (with German text) that I could go through with Stefan. I read aloud to him for a few hours, if not every day, then certainly every week and in doing so wander aimlessly through a fairy tale edifice, something urged upon us by our books. Instead of this, I would like to read Jewish history or stories to him, something that, in the final analysis, would also be more appealing to me—regardless of my imminent involvement with problems relating to the fairy tale. But I do not know whether there is anything that would meet such vague goals. There has recently been a hailstorm of festivities, for Stefan too; Hanukkah (after that, Christmas at my parents') and Dora's birthday, and he received more gifts than his still sparsely furnished room can hold. Naturally he has had his own room for a long time now: Grete has the room next to the kitchen, in which my brother used to live. In a few days he will be marrying a likable young woman,[1] a friend of my sister, whom he trained to be a communist. His Christian in-laws, therefore, have a doubly bitter pill to swallow. By the way, has your brother Werner been "expelled" from the party, as you once seemed to predict?[2]—I have written down my son's "opinions and thoughts" in a notebook since the day he was born. Needless to say, because of my many absences it is not terribly long, but nonetheless lists a few dozen unusual words and expressions. I am thinking of having it typed and one of the few copies would be intended for you. Ernst Schoen was in Berlin over Christmas. He spoke up and began to predict great things for Stefan. Incidentally, my old puppet theater was dragged out for Hanukkah and a spectacular fairy play by Raimund was performed in high style for him and an elite circle of the children who are his friends. We were busy behind the stage, three deep.

Hardly anything of mine has appeared recently, except for an essay on revues and theater in *Der Querschnitt,*[3] written in collaboration with an acquaintance, the director Bernhard Reich. I will soon be sending you a small bundle of such trifles that I have recently written. The proof copies of my baroque book and my essay on the *Elective Affinities* are being printed. I recently read a sinful amount of things and did not work on the Proust translation even once. In compensation, I can now say that I am *au fait* in current French affairs: it only remains for me to weave this threadbare fact into a solid context. Other than that, I read Trotsky's "Whither England?"—I finally finished a very good book, *Sodom and Gomorrah,* not to mention a ponderous tome that heavily fell onto my desk, C. A. Bernoulli's *J. J. Bachofen und das Natursymbol.* It is more relevant to me—in terms of the *fairy tale.* A confrontation with Bachofen and Klages is unavoidable; of course, there is much that says that this can be strictly conducted only from the perspective of Jewish theology. This, of course, is where these important scholars scent the archenemy and not without cause. Bernoulli has already proven his talent for sensational scholarly rubbish in the Nietzsche-Overbeck book and has learned nothing and forgotten nothing. Nonetheless, the huge tome is educational and the "European Institute" (?) of the University of Jerusalem should procure it. Apropos of this: start reserving a nice blank page in the catalog for me under *B*. [. . .] You will know about what befell [Robert] Eisler recently—probably better than I. The Institut de Coopération intellectuelle[4] (or whatever it is called) has nominated him to represent Germany,[5] along with Schulze-Gävernitz. And you can imagine what German scholars are saying about this. In any case, he is in Paris and I will look him up if I get there at the end of February (as planned).

I am looking through your letter now and see that I am telling you old news—at least, as concerns Eisler—and, on the other hand, I have left a bunch of questions unanswered. So: Stefan attends a regular school—not the Jewish school. Emil Cohn seems to have nothing to do with his religious instruction. I am unable to support [Heinz] Pflaum's Proust theory at such a remove: I believe I have detected that his books contain much that comes from the best tradition of French scholasticism, from Cartesius to the sensualists. For the rest, the subject is much too complicated for written communication. These books certainly contain quite significant views and theses. The whole thing may become more problematical the more deeply you go into it. How is Pflaum otherwise?[6] You might not get far when you read my Proust translation. Some unusual things would have to happen for it to become readable. The thing is immensely difficult and there are many reasons why I can devote very little time to it, the primary reason being how poorly I am paid. At some point, I intend to publish some observations on him, "En traduisant Marcel Proust" [On translating Marcel Proust], in the *Literarische Welt*.—I had been looking forward to including in this letter a prospectus for *Die Wirklichkeit der Hebräer*.[7] But I would have gotten there *post festum*. I will read the thing. Let me urgently ask you to make the basic concepts of your review available to me. This is naturally of great importance to me. This book will be more interesting than Unger's *Gegen die Kunst* (Leipzig: Meiner, 1925), which is ingenious nonetheless. I am also terribly eager to read the pronouncements you made in the style of your ripe old age, as contained in your inaugural address,[8] and I hope your wife will soon get started on the translation. My congratulations and best wishes to you on this undertaking.

Well. For diplomatic reasons, I do not intend to issue a bulletin today on the battle of the spirits that interests you so greatly, since the benevolent spirits have withdrawn from my command for a time through passive resistance. But, in a special meeting, they have decided to participate in these most sincere regards to you and your wife.

Yours, Walter

1. Hilde Benjamin, who later became well known as minister of justice in the GDR.
2. This did happen one year later.

3. 1925, pp. 1039–43.
4. Of the Völkerbund.
5. Actually Austria. The hue and cry was the same.
6. Pflaum had lived in Jerusalem since 1925. For information on his personality, see Scholem's elegy to him in *Romanica et Occidentalia: Études dédiées à la mémoire de H. Peri (Pflaum)* (Jerusalem, 1963), pp. 7–11.
7. By Oskar Goldberg.
8. As a lecturer at the Hebrew University in the fall of 1925.

151. To Hugo von Hofmannsthal

Berlin
February 23, 1926

My most esteemed Mr. von Hofmannsthal:

It was very kind of you to send me a copy of the letter you sent to "Schmiede."[1] Let me express my most sincere gratitude for your kind information (which promises to become crucial for the publisher and his stance toward my Proust translation). More than a week ago—after it had been sent off—I was shown a copy of the publisher's letter to you about the Proust business. Needless to say I was dismayed, not so much because demands relating to the entire affair were made on you as because of the way in which these demands were made. Certain passages made me almost think that I needed to assure you outright that I am very far from agreeing with the "principles of translation" stated in the letter. In other respects, the debacle the publisher suffered due to this incompetent first attempt at a translation[2] makes my participation in the Proust translation even more of a responsibility and riskier. Without reflecting on the difficulties of translation in general, the limits of what can be achieved (which Sch[ottlaender] naturally did not examine) seem to me to be most strictly fixed in this instance. This is because Proust's long, drawn-out periods account for a good part of the original text's character, due to the tension that exists between them and the linguistic spirit of the French language as such. It seemed to me that they cannot have a similarly allusive and startling effect in German. Consequently, it is hardly possible to translate into the reader's language what just might be the most important thing for the German reader when it comes to Proust. To be sure, there is plenty left that is characteristic, for, of course, he depicts life in an entirely new way insofar as he makes the passage of time its measure. The most problematical side of his genius is his total elimination of what is moral, along with the most supreme subtlety in his observation of everything physical and spiritual. This is perhaps—in part—to be understood as the "experimental procedure" in this immense laboratory where time is made the subject of experiments with thousands of reflectors, concave and convex reflections. In the midst of translating, I cannot hope to achieve any real clarity about the profound and ambiguous impressions with which Proust fills me. But for a long time I have nurtured a desire to collect some of my observations under the title "En traduisant Marcel Proust." They would be in the form of aphorisms, the way in which they come into being while I work.—The kindness with which you once again recall my prospectus for *Der Turm* made me feel very good. I am extremely pleased to write down the few things I am able to say within the prescribed limits of a prospectus. My only fear is that its pragmatic nature might, perhaps, retreat too far from the thoughts your drama evoked in me. Meanwhile, I can only hope that the prospectus achieves its purpose without any allowances having to be made for the dilemma posed by where it appears. The *Literarische Welt*'s almost panicky fear of every utterance that does not simply lose itself in whatever is topical is grotesque. Before I could have any idea that this was the paper's inclination, the first thing I did when it was founded was to go to the publisher with the request to be allowed to write a prospectus announcing the publication of *Der Turm*. My request was deferred, like so much else. My appearing to be more hesitant when Haas then took it upon himself to approach me is a precautionary gesture [. . .] and it would not even be worth mentioning if now it might not have led (without your obliging patience) to new confusion on the publisher's part.—My most sincere devotion.

Yours, Walter Benjamin

P.S. I recently read the "natural adventures" of the poor man in Tockenburg[3] for the first time, and was moved by its beauty and the incomparable ending. Are you familiar with the author's observations on Shakespeare? Based on the evidence of his autobiography, they must be quite remarkable.

1. A Berlin publishing house that published the first, incomplete translation of Proust into German. After the first volume, translated by Rudolf Schottlaender, the translation was passed on to WB and Franz Hessel. Their translation of *À l'ombre des jeunes filles en fleurs* [Within a budding grove], *Im Schatten der jungen Mädchen,* was published by Schmiede in 1927; their translation of *La côté de Guermantes* [The Guermantes way], *Die Herzogin von Guermantes,* was published by Piper in 1930; the manuscript of *Sodom und Gomorra* seems to be lost, if it was ever completed.

2. Willy Haas had initiated a survey on Schottlaender's translation in the January issue of the *Literarische Welt*. The results of the survey were not very flattering for Schottlaender.

3. Ulrich Bräker, *Lebensgeschichte und natürliche Abenteuer des armen Mannes im Tockenburg* (1789).

152. To Jula Radt

Paris
March 22, 1926

Juliette, *bien-aimée, au pays de l'homme*[1]

ce qui signifie; mari en ce cas. Please forgive me for this—to be sure, enticing—beginning, which must necessarily remain incomprehensible for the time being. Under no circumstances should you ask anybody for an explanation; if you so desire, I will send the translation in my next letter for 50-pfennig worth of stamps. Well, I'm in Paris and I intend to inform the R. family[2] of this officially in the coming days. Now I will lower my voice even more, something expressed in a figurative sense here by my writing in pencil.

The following waystations mark the course of my coming and arrival: Hagen, from whence I departed at five o'clock in the morning; train trip with poker, played by a Spaniard, an Egyptian, a Berliner, and me; splendid arrival with [Thankmar von] Münchhausen at the train station; then, two hours later, the Café du Dôme (in Montparnasse, where Russians have now established a new Bohemian quarter—as opposed to Montmartre, where I am writing this); dinner with a few people; and right after that a wonderful dancehall, known to very few people, called *bal musette,* which has no counterpart in Berlin. For men and women and for men among themselves. There is a small street with these narrow barrooms and dance halls in which there wasn't a single foreigner to be seen except for us. Etc. Finally, at four, we were in a honky-tonk. Since with this I had immediately absorbed Paris right down to my fingertips, I was able to sit down with my translation the very next day. I have not gotten up this early in years. But there is nothing to be done about it. I must get up early if I want my evenings free. Naturally I have no time left over to indulge my curiosity for things generally educational. When I am not busy writing, I can do only fun things. That is to say, I approach the city only in terms of its externals: the location of streets, public transportation, cafés, and newspapers are what concern me. I was at the theater once and saw one of those nice, clean, unchallenging comedies that do not exist in Germany. On the average, lunch costs as much as it does where you are, but there are more courses—very well prepared, in a roadhouse next to my hotel. I have not bought a single book; if you consider that there are streets full of books, that says a lot—of course, the sheer quantity of books is also part of the reason why I have not bought any. I have paid somewhat more attention to paintings. I had an invitation to the opening of the "independents"—these are local unjuried shows—but the paintings were horrid. On the other hand, I saw some nice things in many of the galleries. While I walked along the street that specializes in art galleries, I went into each for three minutes.

I will not move out to the Hessels' in Fontenay. Instead, I will continue to live in comfort in a nice—if cold—small room in order to be able to sample the pleasure of living in a hotel for once. Please write a nice letter to this address so that I can tell you more. There is, indeed, a lot to tell—e.g. a great Punch and Judy show in the children's theater. Leave my head[3] nicely wrapped up! Adieu. Affectionate greetings, Jula, and best wishes. My address is 4 Avenue du parc Montsouris, Hotel du Midi.

Yours, Walter

1. A reference to the title of Jean Giraudoux's book, *Juliette au pays des hommes,* which WB valued highly.

2. Jula Cohn had been married to Fritz Radt for a few months (1925).

3. A sculpture Cohn made of WB at the beginning of 1926.

153. To Gerhard Scholem

Paris
April 5, 1926

Dear Gerhard,

After a rather total if not profound silence, I believe I can predict that our correspondence will now be more dependable. If, that is, my plan somehow to establish myself here proves successful. At the moment, the prerequisites for my doing so already exist in the form of a wonderfully clean and pleasant hotel room and a steady, albeit inferior, job. I have been here for a little over fourteen days now. I hope that your mother will have passed on to you my modest collection of manuscripts at approximately the same time, and that you will have accepted it graciously, or not so graciously. Rowohlt is postponing the publication of my pieces until the fall, so that you cannot count on me making more imposing donations to your library at the moment. I hope to be able to send you the volume of aphorisms in October to make up for this. The majority of my observations in this volume will be new to you. In it, an earlier aspect of my character intersects with a more recent one. This does not benefit the volume's overall persuasiveness and clarity, but it does make it all the more interesting for you—if this is not saying too much—the quiet and shrewd observer. Otherwise, nothing much has appeared in print. Most worth mentioning is the ten-line foreword to the *Trauerspiel* book, which I wrote to take a dig at the University of Frankfurt and which I consider to be one of my most successful pieces. I received a curious commission that will soon force me to eke out three hundred lines. The new *Soviet Encyclopedia* wants to hear from me with that many lines on Goethe from the viewpoint of Marxist doctrine. The divine impudence inherent in the acceptance of such a commission appealed to me and I think I will manage to concoct something appropriate.[1] Well, we shall (or they shall) see. An enormous number of shorter, still unpublished pieces—a Bachofen review,[2] an Unruh review, a Hofmannsthal review—are all sitting at the *Literarische Welt.* Now as before. My meager Parisian library consists mainly of a few Communist writings: the Lukács dispatches in *Arbeiter Literatur* (which I still cannot make head or tail of) and *General Tectology,*[3] or the doctrine of organization as a new basic science that is supposed to take the place of all former "philosophy." It was written by Bukharin, a professor in Leningrad. I recently studied his first attempt at a Marxist universal history, *Developmental Forms of Society and Science.* It was a very fragmentary and unpalatable.

I am naturally doing everything I can to get myself oriented here. I go to hear papers read and discussed in small, intimate groups and I am gradually getting to know the important people. [. . .] It remains to be seen what will come of all this. The most important thing is that I soon plan to locate an educated young man and assign him the task of conversing with me several times a week on scholarly topics, because there is a lot to the language that I have not yet mastered.

Bloch has indicated that he may come here in the next few days. At the moment he is in Sanary in southern France. I will give him the Bergmann review then. My sincere thanks for Escha's contribution! When can I expect her translation of your inaugural address?[4]—A few days ago [Hans] Driesch was received at the Union intellectuelle. He made a good impression. People will soon be able to look forward to the same experience with Scheler.

Did your debate with Agnon take place? How would Agnon react to the possibility of some of his things being translated into French. If he were to agree to it, I could very well keep it in mind. Might he agree to having something of his published in *Commerce,* a poetry review? Perhaps you can sound him out on this when you get a chance.

Please send me Eisler's Paris address or tell me where I can get it.

Do you know whether Marx is still involved with the Euphorion Verlag? I recently got hold of Bethge's disgusting *Ägyptisches Tagebuch*[5] published by Euphorion. Let me now, however, go on to something really good that you should read and about which you should inform people in Jerusalem. The book is called *Der Russe redet*[6] and was published by Drei Masken. It consists of bits and pieces from conversations between Russian soldiers and stories told by them. These are presented without any footnotes, dates, or names, just the way a woman from Samaria who was at the front took them down one after another. It may be, and probably is, the most candid and positive book the war has brought forth.

[. . .]

Sincere regards to you and Escha.

Yours, Walter[7]

I would like to retell the fairy tale of Sleeping Beauty.

She lies sleeping in her thorn hedge. And then, after so and so many years, she awakens.

But not because of the kiss of a lucky prince.

The cook woke her up when he boxed the ears of the busboy. The blow, resounding from the conserved energy of so many years, echoed throughout the castle.

A beautiful child sleeps behind the thorn hedge of the following pages.

If only no fortune-hunting prince in the blinding armor of scholarship approach it. For it will bite back during the bridal kiss.

Instead, as head cook, the author has reserved the right to awaken it himself. The blow that is meant to echo shrilly throughout the halls of academia is long overdue.

Then this poor truth that pricked itself on the old-fashioned distaff when it illicitly thought to weave a professorial gown for itself in the attic will also awaken.

Frankfurt am Main July 1925
(Foreword to the *Trauerspiel* book)[8]

1. The original German text of WB's article on Goethe is preserved in the later revised, more detailed version.

2. The reference is to the review of Bernoulli's Bachofen book; it appeared on September 10, 1926.

3. A. A. Bogdanov, *Allgemeine Organisationslehre, Tektologie* Vol. 1 (Berlin, 1926).

4. The address was published only in Hebrew.

5. Reviewed by WB in the *Literarische Welt* (June 11, 1926).

6. By Ssofja Fedortschenko (1923). Reviewed by WB in the *Literarische Welt* (November 5, 1926).

7. The following is on a separate page.

8. The foreword was not published.

154. To Jula Radt

Paris
April 8, 1926

Dearest Jula,

My last letter did not have much in it. All of its energy went into the wording needed to clear up a misunderstanding. You misunderstood me when we talked on the telephone: now that I am writing to you, I hope you will understand me better. [. . .]—I have been alone in Paris for some time now. I do not count Mrs. Hessel because, first of all, she is very involved in her own affairs. When she happens to make an appearance, there is usually nothing in it for me other than an exercise in social maneuvering, which is not always fun, even when it comes off right. In the meantime, she exhibits the amusing inclination to flirt with me and I derive at least as much pleasure from stiffening my resolve not to respond in kind. I get on much better with Münchhausen; we had a goodly number of pleasant suppers, daytime and nighttime walks, and, finally, a splendid automobile excursion to Chantilly and Senlis (all in the company of his local flame, a not terribly significant but not at all irksome painter whose husband melts into the background in a way beyond description). This stationary still bears witness to the Hôtel du Grand Cerf in Senlis. I wrote you about the shock I had in Senlis when Münchhausen told me in the cathedral that the Germans had been in it in 1914. And then you must remind yourself what it means to begin the retreat from Paris, which is a half day's march away.—It appears that chic *goyim*[1] are currently my cup of tea. It was always most pleasant when we were together as couples. But it will not go on like this: the friendly and by no means chic Mr. Hessel is coming. Furthermore, no sooner had Bloch heard I was here, then he announced his arrival in Paris. In the meantime, however, he is overdue. Happily enough, he intends to come without his wife, who will continue to paint in Sanary. Münchhausen did not leave without establishing some contacts for me. For example, he introduced me to Count Pourtalès. I am supposed to hear a lecture at his house in fourteen days. It will be in French, about M. Stefan George. He has a salon with expensive furniture, adorned by a sprinkling of ladies and gentlemen with the most wicked physiognomies, the likes of which you can find only in Proust. I recently attended my first lecture there—the event takes place around three o'clock in the afternoon. The effect it had on me was that I almost fell asleep in the midst of the most wonderful snobbery while somebody was reading something by Dante Gabriel Rossetti. Münchhausen who was sitting next to me, kept himself awake with difficulty only by flirting. I was recently also at a breakfast in one of the foremost Parisian restaurants. It was given by Princess Bassiano for seven people, including Münchhausen and me. It began with huge portions of caviar and continued in this way. The cooking was done at a stove in the center of the room and everything was displayed before it was served. There was even a genuine Italian revolutionary among those present at this gathering. Also present was the editor-in-chief of the *Nouvelle revue française*, who makes an excellent impression and, among others, [Bernhard] Groethuysen, who sat next to me. I believe Alfred [Cohn] heard him lecture in Berlin.—By the way, I am being very diligent, at least as far as translating is concerned, and the most amazing thing is that it is becoming very easy for me. Of course, I have discovered a regimen that magically entices the goblins to help out. It consists of my sitting down to work as soon as I get up in the morning, without getting dressed, without moistening my hands or body with a single drop of water, indeed without even drinking any. And I do nothing, much less eat breakfast, before finishing the task I set myself for the day. This induces the strangest side effects imaginable. I can then do what I want in the afternoon or just stroll along the streets. I often saunter along the quays in a state of complete relaxation; real finds have become very rare there and the sight of countless ordinary books gives me a certain sense of satisfaction. All this strolling along the streets also makes it easy to get out of the habit of reading for a while, or so it seems to me. I have been to the theater to see this and that—I simply go wherever a complementary ticket may take me. Thus I have just come from a performance of [Georg] Kaiser's *Kolportage*. It is the only play of his I can stand. It flopped here in Paris. In the first place, it is inaccessible to the French and, in the second place, it was not a very good performance. Its first performance in the Lessing theater was better. What I have seen of avant-garde theater is pitiful. It was a surrealist soirée in a small private theater in Montmartre before an invited audience. But nothing is better than the annual fairs, and the best thing about all the art and all the activity of this city is that it does not rob the luster from the little that remains of what is original and natural. These fairs drop like bombs on one or the other quarter of the city: if you want, you can find some boulevard every week where you will see the following lined up next to each other: shooting galleries, silk canopies, butcher's stalls, antique stores, art dealers, waffle stands. I bought some of those wonderful snow globes at the *foire aux jambons et aux ferrailles* (ham and old-iron market), and sometime this week I will go to the *foire aux pains d'épice* (gingerbread market). At the *foire aux pains d'épice,* I will buy you a nice gingerbread house, which will stand on my desk until we see each other again. Not on a "writing" table, but on a wonderfully solid piece of furniture, probably the only real table to be found in the whole hotel. Dear Jula, I intended to write you a proper letter, with pages covered from top to bottom. Something you could hold in your hand and put down on the table and pass around. If you are satisfied, please write and keep in mind that this kind of hot, holiday sun does not shine upon me every day as you might conclude on the basis of this letter. How are things going with the exhibition?

All the best.
Yours, Walter

1. A play on the Yiddish expression "schikkere [e.g. drunken] goyim."

155. To Jula Radt

Paris
April 30, 1926

Dear Jula,

With these words I have performed a double christening: of a new fountain pen and of these sheets of paper which, to be sure, I use as stationery only when writing you—otherwise they serve as my most valued manuscript paper. They are in a shade I have been looking for for a long time and it coaxes my best ideas from me. We have not seen any sun in quite a while, but a summer sultriness hangs over the city after weeks of ice-cold weather. With the arrival of warmer weather, I am once again very gradually surfacing in the city and in life. I was terribly depressed the last few weeks. This is, of course, one reason why you did not hear from me. And yes, I have not been to the *foire* yet (the gingerbread market) and there still isn't any gingerbread on my desk waiting for you. It rained for days on end and going there was simply out of the question. But everything will have been properly taken care of by the time you read this letter. I must, however, say that the gingerbread structure I had in mind was intended to be understood more as something plastic and monumental and less as something to be gobbled up (yes, that is what I said: gobbled up) as you did: it is not a sign of my imminent return (it did not make any difference to me if it was as hard as a rock by the time you got it). I often think of you and, more than anything, I often wish you were in my room. It is not at all like the room in Capri yet it would seem plausible to you—and you would seem *very plausible to me* in it. But for the time being, I do not intend to return. Instead, I very patiently want to test the efficacy of a persistent courtship of this city. Such a courtship will turn time into its ally. Indeed, this patience makes me almost too indolent. I get to see almost nothing of all those things that simply "must be seen." I get around less than I might, and so far I have not been getting much more done than the work on my translation. With some exceptions, to be sure. I know my way around the Hôtel des Ventes as well as any Parisian (this is the large municipal auction house in Paris, an institution that has no counterpart in Berlin). I have attended many book auctions (which are held there, as well as other kinds) and I learned all the more since I bought so few things. And then, when things were at their worst for me, I pushed everything having to do with Proust to the side and worked entirely on my own projects. I wrote some brief notes of which I am very fond: above all, a magnificent one on sailors (the way the world looks at them), one on advertising, another on female newspaper vendors, the death penalty, annual fairs, shooting galleries, Karl Kraus[1]—nothing but bitter, bitter herbs, the like of which I zealously cultivate in a *kitchen* garden.—Now, like a princess out of the Thousand and One Nights, you have mounted Gundolf's head and mine on your castle's battlements[2] and behind them you are up to your old tricks (and without interrupting you at this, I will quickly give you a kiss). Maybe now, however, you will get around to telling me something about Gundolf's stay in Berlin (naturally I am not shameless enough to ask you to reveal confidences and, in all modesty, ask only for a few nice lies). I would just go ahead and call you, but our technology is not yet sufficiently advanced to make a long-distance call from Paris to Berlin. [. . .]—I have begun to take French conversation lessons with a student at the École normale, but they are too expensive for me and I will probably look around soon for someone else. Right now it is important to me to find out something about how these students live (they are in their early twenties). Therefore, I am continuing with the lessons. I may tell you about them some other time. I have acquired a need for solitude here, the likes of which I have never experienced before. As strange as it may sound, this is of course only the other side of my being alone. Hessel's pleasant, as well as Ernst Bloch's problematical, company naturally changes nothing. Bloch is an extraordinary individual and I revere him as the greatest connoisseur of my writings (he knows what they are about much better even than I because he is thoroughly acquainted not only with everything I have ever written but also with every word I have ever spoken, going back for years). However, while I must surrender completely to the phenomena of Parisian life, for him Garmisch is and will always be what he constantly yearns for. Various other personages have of course made an appearance. The day before yesterday I spoke to Valeska Gert, who will be dancing here one evening next week. Karl Kraus was here. I did not bother myself with him. [. . .]—My comments, which [Eugen] Wallach sent you, appeared in the *Frankfurter Zeitung*.[3]—Jula, please write me a really serviceable letter that I can show around in Paris. And when can I take you around? (By the way, can you give me some hint as to what I can give you as a wedding present. It is of course not easy for this scoundrel to give something meant for both of you. Please make a suggestion.) [. . .] The sun is shining on this page and I will now close this letter, which emerges from the overcast Paris of the past few days. Let me close by extending you a mawkish, may-flowery greeting:

Yours, Walter

1. All pieces from *One-Way Street*.
2. Cohn had also produced a sculpture of Gundolf's head.
3. "Kleine Illumination" [Small illumination] (April 14, 1926).

156. To Gerhard Scholem

Paris
May 29, 1926

Dear Gerhard,

As you can already gather from the format, I am gearing up to write a long and detailed letter. Nevertheless, I confess that I am somewhat uneasy at barely being able to respond to your most urgent questions. For this very reason, I would like to make my unworthy effort to do so right at the outset. It is basically very difficult for me to have to give a hypothetical account of myself, since my book on these matters (should it ever materialize) has not yet matured. What there currently is of it increasingly seems to be giving signs of attempting to leave the purely theoretical sphere. This will be humanly possible in only two ways, in religious or political observance. I do not concede that there is a difference between these two forms of observance in terms of their quintessential being. Yet I also do not concede that a mediation between them is possible. I am speaking here about an identity that manifests itself only in the sudden paradoxical change of one form of observance into the other (regardless of which direction), given the indispensable prerequisite that every observation of action proceed ruthlessly and with radical intent. Precisely for this reason, the task is not to decide once and for all, but to decide at every moment. But to *decide*. These realms may share (and surely do share) another identity beyond that of pragmatic sudden change, but this other identity will lead those of us who would seek it here and now terribly astray. If I were to join the Communist party some day (something that, in turn, I am making dependent on one last twist of fate), my stance would be to behave always radically and never logically when it came to the most important things. Whether it would be possible for me to stay in the party would be determined simply through experimentation. What is more interesting and more debatable than whether I will join the party is how long I would stay a member. The brazen weapons of certain irrefutable insights (such as, for example, that materialistic metaphysics or, indeed, even the materialistic conception of history is irrelevant) may in an emergency achieve just as much in practical terms, and perhaps even more, acting in concert with communism rather than against it. If it is true, as you claim, that I have actually gotten "behind some principles" that I knew nothing about in your day, I have gotten "behind" this one above all: anyone of our generation who feels and understands the historical moment in which he exists in this world, not as mere words, but as a battle, cannot renounce the study and the practice of the mechanism through which things (and conditions) and the masses interact. Unless in Judaism such a battle organizes itself for this purpose in a completely different and disparate (never hostile) way. This does not alter the following: radical politics that are "just" and, precisely for this reason, are intended as nothing but politics will always work on behalf of Jewry and, what is infinitely more important, will always find Jewry actively in support of them. But once this kind of thesis has been put forward, you are already at such a remove from the concrete that it becomes embarrassing. I implicitly assume that you are much more at home in the realm of the concrete, because of the life you now lead and the decisions you must make, than I am, because of my life and my decisions. Precisely because of this, if I am not mistaken, you must nonetheless be able to appreciate my few comments: particularly, why I am not thinking of "renouncing" the things that I supported; why I am not ashamed of my "early" anarchism but consider anarchist methods to be useless, Communist "goals" to be nonsense and nonexistent. This does not diminish the value of Communist action one iota, because it is the corrective for its goals and because there are no meaningfully *political* goals.

To be sure, neither you nor anyone else can be expected to infer such ongoing reflections from a few book reviews or travel notes (a false construction, but okay!). What you will find enclosed or perhaps in the same day's mail, is not to be seen as enigmatic but simply as information on how I plan to earn some pocket money. To be sure, I worked diligently on the Unruh review last year in Capri. It did not appear until now (in somewhat abbreviated form) because Heinz Simon[1] himself intervened with the *Literarische Welt,* making dreadful threats because of a much tamer attack that had appeared there. It took six months before I could push through the publication of this review, which may cost me my job as a contributor to the *Frankfurter Zeitung.*

Now on to the external circumstances of my life. I am not in Paris with a firm, clearly delineated plan but because of a number of external circumstances. First of all, to finish and go over the Proust translation. It is, of course, easy to find the means to facilitate this task here. It is also possible to live on a half or a third of the money needed in Berlin. I admit, however, that what I have in mind is to make a reputation for myself here through some of my work, if at all possible. Since, however, I have not succeeded in attaining a command of French that is adequate to be published *tel quel,* I have had to rely on translators and this makes the whole thing so difficult that success is doubtful. My contacts are neither good nor bad. Instead, as is usually the case when first you are in foreign surroundings somewhere, there are as many people as you could possibly want to socialize with pleasantly for a quarter of an hour, but no one who is terribly eager to have anything more to do with you. Giraudoux is press secretary in the foreign office and I really like him as a novelist. I once consulted him about something having to do with my passport and had good results. I later consulted him about something to do with translation and had no luck. This is an indication of how things are. In order to get on the most intimate terms with the language, I even arranged to have regular conversations with a student at the École normale, a state institution for students, founded during the reign of Napoleon I, where an elite lives on the premises at state expense. What I need, however, is a tempo and a temperature that are possible only when language is unforced. This did, in fact, come about a few times in conversations I had with [François] Bernouard, a local publisher and printer who, among other things, is publishing deluxe bilingual editions of the complete Talmud (!) and the Bible. They have been in the works for years. I am planning to write an essay on Proust ("En traduisant Marcel Proust"). It remains to be seen whether I will succeed in getting it into print here, as well as some other things I have already completed. Even without that, however, my material circumstances are satisfactory for the time being because I have been getting a monthly stipend from Rowohlt for my books for the brief period of a year, starting back in January. At the moment, my translating fees have been coming in on top of that.

Except for the translation, which may well be completed in preliminary form no later than mid-July—reading proof will be a formidable chore—I am working only on the notebook that I am reluctant to call a book of aphorisms (leaving aside lesser things like a Keller prospectus that I now have to write[2]). The latest title—it has already had quite a few—is "Street Closed!" While I am at it, let me get back again to the articles for Russia—in addition to Goethe, there are some more recent French writers about whom I am supposed to write brief pieces—let us both just wait and see what comes of this. To the extent I am familiar with it, "literary history," at least the more recent kind, has so little cause to crow about its methodology that a "Marxist" treatment of Goethe is just another reason to improvise. I have to decide for myself what such a treatment consists of and what it teaches. If "literary history" in the strictest sense has as little reality from the Marxist point of view (as I am very much inclined to assume) as it does from any other reasoned point of view, this does not preclude that my attempt to treat a subject from such a perspective, a subject I would not otherwise treat, may result in something interesting enough to be safely rejected by the editorial board, if worst comes to worst.

It was rather painful to come across the remark "not of general interest" when you reported on your projects. Even if my interest is totally incompetent and ineffective, it is an interest in *your* projects as such and not some general interest. Therefore, when you have a chance, you might want to give me more information about them. Out of a sense of devotion, I recently had Hugo Bergmann's review of Bloch translated for me because I erroneously believed that you had written it. You can imagine how astonished I was at first. The signature reassured me. [. . .] The translator was Meir Wiener, who now lives here.[3] He does not think much of Bergmann's Hebrew and, therefore, takes all the more pleasure in recalling the pedagogic lashings you gave him in *Der Jude*. Regarding Buber, the *Frankfurter Zeitung*[4] carried a review of his Bible translation by [Siegfried] Kracauer, which quite simply appeared to hit the mark, insofar as it is possible to judge this without a knowledge of Hebrew. The review also incorporated some of the things I said to him in person on the subject. I will have a look: if I still have it, I will enclose it. If not, I will tell you where to find it along with the (pointless) reply and rejoinder.

I am unable to create a Lilliputian state with this letter. To compensate, however, I want to tell you that I discovered the Book of Esther written on a sheet of paper in the Hebrew section of the Cluny Museum. It contains not quite half the extant text. Perhaps this will hasten your visit to Paris.

Now for my most sincere congratulations on the nice and momentous things your letter reports about you. Indeed, the future could not have smiled more kindly upon you. At the moment, I dare not look any further into my future than the publication deadline of my writings—probably in October. As soon as I can get to my own work, I will start on my fairy tale book, which has doubtless been haunting my letters for years.

After the announcement in my last letter, it probably will not surprise you that Bloch is in Paris. Likewise Hessel, with whom I have been in somewhat closer touch these days on account of the Proust translation, his knowledge of the city, and a multitude of shared reactions. Ernst Schoen left yesterday; he was here with his wife for a few days over Pentecost. I am really not in need of people who are not all that close to me. All of this is the reason I have not yet been able to make up my mind to look around for Eisler. Bloch's condition in particular gives me no joy at the moment. [. . .] Whatever may happen: God knows, you cannot count on me for a "system (!) of materialism."

As you see, a long and wonderful letter like your last one is not wasted on me. I really hope to hear from you again soon, and in ever greater detail; maybe then we might come to see through each other, even without public pronouncements.

Most sincere regards to you and Escha.

Yours, Walter

1. The owner of the *Frankfurter Zeitung*.
2. *Literarische Welt* (August 5, 1927).

3. Historian of Hebrew and Yiddish literature (1893–1941). Scholem's essay in *Der Jude,* "Lyrik der Kabbala?" was directed against a volume of expressionistic translations from Hebrew. See letter 108.

4. On April 27 and 28, 1926; reprinted in Kracauer, *Das Ornament der Masse* (Frankfurt am Main, 1963), pp. 173–86.

157. To Gerhard Scholem

Agay (Var)
September 18, 1926

Dear Gerhard,

Your letter from Safed[1] reached me today via Berlin. I was pleased to receive it for—at least—three reasons. First, you are seeing Safed for yourself—with your own eyes. Second, you are not strictly and without exception adhering to the principle of writing only in response to a letter received. This is the principle we have hitherto observed in our correspondence. Third, at the very moment I was about to start a letter to you, yours arrived. Should this digression and its mathematical character appear to be and strike you as something new in my correspondence, you can attribute it to my immersion in the third book of *Tristram Shandi.*[2] At the same time you will have observed that sooner or later I do follow up on your suggestions on what to read; I hope you are not trying to calculate (but should you be, that you will not turn out to be right in your calculations) when it will be time for me to start reading Steinheim,[3] given that the ratios remain constant. This letter and, even more, the stationery on which it is written should tell you that I have also come to some sudden decisions. Thus, I have no intention of waiting until I am back home to unstack and put in proper order the events that have piled up. Instead I will start right here at the beach. To begin with, I retreated here and to *Tristram Shandi* because my nerves are in a bad state (prospects of recovery are doubtful) and I needed some peace and quiet. Yet I cannot stay here very long in any case, and must be back in Berlin by mid-October at the latest. Therefore, please write me there for the time being. For the moment, my health prevents me from formulating more precisely my vague plans for the winter. But it has become very likely that my elliptical lifestyle, Berlin-Paris, will continue next year because this is how things are shaping up as far as I can tell: Hessel and I will do the complete German Proust (Franz Hessel, who may sound somewhat familiar to you because of his books or my letters, is my valued, pleasant, and friendly collaborator). We will probably translate the first volume over again [!]. The original translation, by someone else, resulted in a lot of bad publicity and a great critical fiasco. We finished the second volume a month ago. We will translate the third volume (which was done by yet another person) over again because the translation submitted to the publisher cannot be published (it is too awful). The manuscript for the fourth volume, which I translated, has been at the publisher's for a long time. Every one of the "volumes" I mentioned actually contains two or three volumes as a library would define them. One could say a lot about the actual work. Let me add, 1) that, in a certain sense, it makes me sick. Unproductive involvement with a writer who so splendidly pursues goals that are similar to my own, at least former, goals occasionally induces something like symptoms of intestinal poisoning in me. Let me add, 2) the material advantages of the enterprise are, however, worth mentioning. The advantages of the honorarium are debatable and the work is not tied to a specific place (*à la rigueur,* of course, it is always necessary to return to Paris), but it is very pleasant to present yourself as a Proust translator in France. I have also been contemplating writing something called "En traduisant Marcel Proust" for who knows how long and just now *Cahiers du sud* in Marseilles promised to publish it. It will take quite a while just to get it written. It will basically not contain very much about translation; it will deal with Proust.—

On this occasion, allow me to interject what I still have to say, or rather ask, about the Buber dispute. I would like to know what your position is based on. This is naturally the most important thing for me. It goes without saying that I consider myself, not to mention Kracauer, as not competent in this matter. I can only make conjectures about something to which I have no strategic access (that I am unable to grasp). Instead, I see it spread out before me at a distance and from above, from only *one* perspective—from that of the massif that is the spirit of the German language. [. . .] I have no idea what might be involved in, or who in the world could legitimately be concerned about, a translation of the Bible into German at this time. Now of all times—when the potential of Hebrew is being newly realized; when German, for its part, is at a highly problematical stage; when, above all, a productive relationship between the two seems to me to be only potentially possible, if at all—won't this translation result in a dubious display of things that, once displayed, will instantly be invalidated in light of German as it now is? As I said, this question becomes even more urgent for me on the basis of the passages from the text with which I am familiar. It would be nice if you could at least give me some indication of what you had to say on this subject at the time.[4] [. . .] Everything having to do with Frankfurt strikes me as being a complete mess: my Unruh review apparently fell on deaf ears, unless you want to mention the one response that a friend of that nobleman is soon supposed to publish in the *Literarische Welt,* accompanied by my rejoinder, even though the response has already been deflated because of its pure stupidity. It will, however, be very difficult for me to say anything about the whole thing a second time. It might be more gratifying for you to receive a brief note I wrote on the hundredth anniversary of Hebel's death. By the time you get this letter, it will already be available to you in the *Literarische Welt.* At the same time, I wrote yet another note on the same subject for publication in the press.[5] The most important news is that my book *One-Way Street* [*Einbahnstraße*] is finished—I have already written you about it, haven't I? It has turned out to be a remarkable arrangement or construction of some of my "aphorisms," a street that is meant to reveal a prospect of such precipitous depth—the word is not to be understood metaphorically!—like, perhaps, Palladio's famous stage design in Vicenza, *The Street.* It is supposed to appear by Christmas. I hope it does. In violation of our contract, Rowohlt has repeatedly postponed the publication date of my essay on the *Elective Affinities* and of the baroque book, which I, of course, have been eager to have you read. A firm date for its publication is supposed to be set in October. Therefore, as you can see, the publication of almost all of my writings is pending (the only thing you might possibly still get before Christmas is Proust's *Within a Budding Grove* [*A l'ombre des jeunes filles en fleurs*]), whereas your writings, thank God (and unfortunately), are probably pending only in terms of my receipt of them. For I still do not have your Beliar essay or your article about the Cohen brothers' compilation of demons[6] (should it meanwhile have been published). Please send me everything you have finished right away, to Berlin. I am particularly eager to receive "Kontemplation und Extase in der jüdischen Mystik," if this lecture is to be published in a language directly or indirectly accessible to me. You did give it as planned, didn't you? Also please send me your review of the individual who desecrated the Kabbalah (Pauly?) as soon as it appears.[7]—I intend to hold fast to my hope that we will be able to spend some time together in Paris. In case of emergency, will you still be able to come up with the money for this, as if it were for research travel? By the time we see each other, I hope the *Trauerspiel* book will be out. The foreword is giving me trouble. I rejected the only practicable approach, as suggested by you, i.e. definitive objective comments, because I withdrew the book (probably very foolishly!) in order to escape "rejection." And therefore I continue to remain undecided about what to do because now I would really not want it to appear without any comments on its origin and early fate.

[. . .]

One of the things on my agenda, should I get to Berlin, is a general reorganization of my library on the basis of the card catalog, which must finally be brought up to date. I want to discard a lot of things; I basically want to limit myself to German literature (recently with a certain preference for the baroque, which is made very difficult because of my finances), French literature, theology, fairy tales, and children's books. There are not many new publications in the last-mentioned category, but I believe that almost all of them are worthy of your interest. Especially three horror novels from the fifties—with colored illustrations!—enormously beautiful and rare. I recently acquired two of them in a trade. Specifically, I traded the first edition of Burckhardt's *Age of Constantine the Great* for them. —Last Sunday I was in Aix-en-Provence. If you should travel to France via Marseilles, you really must take the two-hour trip by streetcar in order to look at this unspeakably beautiful city that has been frozen in time. A bullfight I watched outside the city gates during the afternoon seemed quite inappropriate and was rather pathetic.—In conclusion, I want to tell you that the same post that brought your letter also brought a request from the *Literarische Welt* to review Buber's "Rede über das Erzieherische" and *Das Buch Namen* (??) and Rosenzweig's *Die Schrift und Luther*. I do not have to tell you that I will be sure to decline and that I therefore expect to receive instruction and news from you all the sooner.

Sincere regards to you and Escha.

Yours, Walter

1. WB wrote "Saafed." Safed in Galilee, the holy city of the kabbalists. Scholem spent his summer vacation there.

2. The spelling is a mixture of *Shandy* and the spelling used by Bode in his German translation, *Schandi*.

3. S. L. Steinheim, *Die Offenbarung nach dem Lehrbegriff der Synagoge*, a primary text of Jewish religious history. The four volumes of the German text were published between 1835 and 1865.

4. In a long letter to Buber in April 1926. Scholem's reservations were of an entirely different kind. For more information, see Scholem's discussion of this translation in his *Judaica* (Bibliothek Suhrkamp, no. 107), pp. 207–15.

5. *Schriften* 2:279–83.

6. Essays Scholem wrote in Hebrew.

7. A review of Paul Vulliaud, *La Kabbale juive* (Paris, 1923), which Scholem had published in the *Orientalische Literaturzeitung* (1925), col. 494ff. Jean de Pauly was the author of the French Zohar translation, which Scholem also did not think much of.

158. To Hugo von Hofmannsthal

Berlin

October 30, 1926

My dear and most esteemed Mr. von Hofmannsthal:

With each one of your letters, you renew the encouragement I receive from the awareness of being able to count on you to support my work, both in terms of what is essential and what is peripheral. Your last letter, however, encourages me even more since, in spite of my silence, which ultimately oppressed even me, you find such kind and, as you know, such cheering things to say about me and my book. Things did not go well for me this past summer and even if I seem to have momentarily overcome the worst, a long stretch of troubled days left behind a diminished sense of well-being. My father died in July. I was prevented from writing you these last few weeks by obligations connected with this event, even though it became increasingly urgent for me to write with every passing day. And when all is said and done, I would have replied more quickly to your extremely important proposition concerning the matter of publication if Rowohlt had not been away the whole time I have been back. Above all, please accept my most sincere thanks for the helpful encouragement your proposition contains. I cannot quite make up my mind at the moment, without having had another talk with Rowohlt. I still owe him one last ultimatum. (My desire to have all my things appear with the same publisher, to the extent that this is possible, also plays a role: my new book of observations or aphorisms would not readily be accepted by a publisher of scholarly books. Rowohlt, on the other hand, took it on.) The crucial factor, however, continues to be that the baroque book must, without fail, be published in a few months. If Rowohlt is unable to make a firm commitment, I would gratefully and confidently entrust my next step to your judgment. In this regard, please extend my thanks to [Walther] Brecht.

In September I went to Marseilles via Paris and was able to enjoy that marvellous city, the even more splendid Aix, and fourteen days on the Mediterranean. I have been here for some time and intend to stay until Christmas. I will be busy translating for another month or two, but then I will turn my back on that activity for quite a while. I am also organizing, revising, and sorting out my library and making some surprising discoveries in the process, as usual. Thus I was amazed to learn how literary history was still written around the middle of the last century. To my surprise, I discovered how powerful Julian Schmidt's three-volume *Geschichte der deutschen Literatur seit Lessings Tod*[1] is; and what clear contours it has, like a beautifully structured frieze. It is possible to see what has been lost when books of this kind are structured as reference works, and that the (unimpeachable) demands of more recent scholarly techniques are incompatible with achieving an eidos, a vivid image of a life. It is also amazing how the objectivity of this uncompromising chronicler's mentality increases with historical distance, while the measured and lukewarm manner of expressing judgments, which is typical of more recent literary histories, cannot help but appear as the insipid and indifferent expression of contemporary taste, precisely because it lacks the personal element that might act as a corrective. It so happens that, in the past few days, I had to write a review of Walzel's *Wortkunstwerk*, a typically modern work in this respect but one of the better ones. I attempted to express these thoughts as well as some others in my review.[2] The project that is the reason for my return to the writing of Germany literary history in one specific period is as much an enticement as it is a responsibility and difficult: I am supposed to write the article on Goethe for a Russian encyclopedia. To be sure, I would view it almost as a miracle if I were able to succeed in painting in a relatively small space a picture of Goethe that would just happen to leave its mark on today's Russian readers; in principle, however, this strikes me as not only possible but also as highly productive.

My book of observations will probably benefit from the unwarranted delay of its publication, for better or worse, and has accommodated quite a few new ones written both here and in Marseilles. It is not entirely without anxiety that I think of it in your hands some day, soon, I hope. For it presents something heterogeneous, or rather polar. Certain lightning bolts may perhaps emerge from this tension as too harsh, and certain explosions as too blustering. (I only hope that you will not encounter the artificial sound of stage thunder anywhere in the book.)

I am happy that the plan to publish a preview of the *Melancholia* chapter is on again, not only for my own sake but also because I see this as a good omen for the likely continuation of the *Beiträge*. It will not be difficult to make the chapter conform to editorial requirements regarding length. If you would be so good as to send me the manuscript at the appropriate time, I will get it back to you immediately with deletions that will leave what is essential in my train of thought and the citations intact. —I hope you will not think me vain if I say that I was most deeply delighted by the phrase in which you praise my style. I did "put a lot of effort" into writing it, first of all because it was impossible for me to do otherwise; then, however, acting on the maxim that a plan for a minimalist style that is strictly executed usually complements the successful execution of a plan that is maximalist in the realm of ideas. Finally, your letter astounded me by its reference to the actual but very obscure core of this work: with its literal reminder of a youthful three-page effort called "Über die Sprache in Trauerspiel und Tragödie" [On language in *Trauerspiel* and tragedy], my explanation of picture, text, and music is the germ of the project. A more profound treatment would of course require me to leave the domain of German and enter that of Hebrew, which, in spite of my best intentions, I have yet to set foot in. It is fortunate, and I am not even permitted to thank you for it, that you are conducting the creative experiment of analyzing one phase of German drama that belongs to the past (but only apparently and superficially). With redoubled impatience,

I am waiting for *Der Turm* to be performed and thus for its new final version. What you write, therefore, is the sympathetic response I almost thought would be denied me. To tell you the truth, back when I was writing the book, I knew that the only one of all my friends, even my closest ones, who would wish to acknowledge its "mea res agitur" was Rang. I am also indebted to his letters for many of the book's particulars. When he died, I at first wondered, not who would read it, but who would really appreciate it. I am indebted to you for the answer to this question. And because of you it will by all means reach, if not many people, yet all those people whom it is intended to and can reach. Later I may also be able to hope for the interest of the Hamburg circle around [Aby] Warburg in addition to the sympathy of [Walther] Brecht. In any case, I would first expect to find academically qualified and, at the same time, sympathetic reviewers among the members of that circle (with whom I myself have no contact); as for the rest, I do not expect very much goodwill, particularly from the official representatives of the scholarly profession.

Sincere regards. Your grateful and devoted,

Walter Benjamin

P.S. I will send this by registered mail because I do not know whether the address is quite accurate.

1. Published under this title starting with the fifth edition (1866).
2. It was published in the literary supplement of the *Frankfurter Zeitung* (November 7, 1926).

159. To Jula Radt

Moscow
Sadovaia Triumfalnaia
December 26, 1926

Dear Jula,

I hope you get this letter. If you do, answer it nicely. I have not dared to write until now because I just had my first news from Germany since arriving. I had therefore thought that all my letters were getting lost. But the mail seems to be reliable. I have already written you a card. You must not think that it is easy to report on things from here. I will have to work for a very long time on what I am seeing and hearing before it takes on some kind of shape for me. The situation here—even if only ephemeral—is of extraordinary value. Everything is in the process of being built or rebuilt and almost every moment poses very critical questions. The tensions of public life—which in large part have an almost theological character—are so great that, to an unimaginable degree, they seal off everything private. If you were here, you would probably be even much more amazed than I am; I remember some of the things you said about "Russia" during the summer in Agay. I am unable to evaluate everything; basically, these are conditions on which you can and must take a position while you are in the midst of them, and in many respects this position may even be one of skepticism; from the outside, you can only observe them. It is impossible to predict what the upshot of all this will be for Russia. Perhaps a true socialist community, perhaps something entirely different. The struggle to decide this question continues without interruption. To be objectively associated with these events is extremely productive—because of fundamental considerations, it is not possible for me to get involved in them. It remains to be seen, however, to what extent I will be able to establish substantive connections to developments here. Various circumstances make it likely that, from now on, I will be contributing more substantial articles to Russian journals from abroad and my involvement in the encyclopedia may be expanded. There is much to be done here and an unimaginable dearth of contributors with expertise in the humanities.—On the other hand, I still do not know what I will write about my stay here. I probably already told you that I have been compiling a lot of material in the form of a diary.[1]—I escaped my dread of Christmas Eve by listening to the lovely hum of a samovar. There were other nice things: a sleigh ride through the Russian winter woods to visit a pretty little girl,[2] and in doing so I got to see a first-rate children's clinic. I have been going to the theater a lot—the most monstrous notions have been circulating about it. The truth is that, of all the things I have seen so far, only Meyerhold's productions are really significant. Even when it is as cold as it gets (down to −26°), walking around the city is very pleasant if I do not happen to be exhausted. But I often am because of my difficulties with the language and the rigors of daily life. A stay here at this time of year is extraordinarily good for your health and, when all is said and done, I have not felt this well for a long time. But things are unimaginably expensive. Moscow is probably just about the most expensive place on earth. When I get back I will fill you in more on the details. Did you have Stone[3] photograph the head? How are you doing? Was Ilse[4] in Berlin? How is Fritz? Please give me all the answers by neatly writing them down on several sheets of your illustrious onionskin stationery. You may write the address in the Latin alphabet. But do send a charming answer by return mail. I wish you benevolent demons for the New Year.

Yours, Walter

1. The diary has been preserved.
2. The daughter of Asja Lacis.
3. Sascha Stone, a famous photographer, had also done the cover for WB's *Einbahnstraße*. The photograph of the head has been preserved.
4. Ilse Hermann, a friend of Jula Cohn-Radt. Cohn-Radt had her Berlin studio in the house of Ilse Hermann's parents.

160. To Gerhard Scholem

Berlin
February 23, 1927

Dear Gerhard,

Tomorrow it will be three weeks since I have been back in Berlin. I really have a lot of work to do. I am not getting it done fast enough; every little thing I manage to get done is packaged in a great deal of idleness. Having just recovered from the flu I caught upon my arrival, I am busy working on an article about Moscow.[1] You will have already seen a few tiny essays by me in the *Literarische Welt,*[2] or you will be able to find them in the next issue you receive; it is very difficult to write anything fairly coherent without sliding into the abyss of idle chatter, which gapes almost everywhere you tread in pursuit of such a project. Certain specific details over which I had no control at times adversely affected my freedom of action in Moscow, so that I did not get around as much as I would have wished. But two months in which, one way or another, I had to struggle in and with the city have given me some understanding of things that I would not have achieved in any other way. I quickly determined this to be the case from this vantage point and on the basis of conversations with people here. It is possible that I will succeed (although I am not sure I will) in making some of these things clear for averse readers like you in my notes on Moscow, on which I am now working.

I had very little luck with my Goethe article for the *Soviet Encyclopedia.* The fact that it will not be published can, of course, be explained in another way. The kind of exposé contained in the article I submitted was, so to speak, too radical for these people. Confronting the European scholarly world, they are shaken by fear and pity, in fine Aristotelian fashion. They want a standard example of Marxist scholarship, but at the same time want to create something that is meant to elicit sheer admiration in Europe. Nonetheless, I believe that this exposé turned out to be so interesting that, given the right conditions, it could be published somewhere else sometime in the future.

[. . .]

Sincere regards from Dora and me.

Yours, Walter

1. *Die Kreatur* (1927), pp. 71–101. In *Schriften* 2:30–66.
2. In the issues of December 3, 1926, and February 11, 1927.

161. To Martin Buber

Berlin
February 23, 1927

My esteemed Mr. Buber:

My stay in Moscow lasted somewhat longer than I had expected. After finally arriving in Berlin, the first thing I had to contend with was a case of the flu. I have been at work on the project for a few days now, but still will not be able to send you the manuscript by the end of February.[1] Would you be so kind as to write me when you are going to leave Germany? I will make every attempt to get the manuscript to you approximately eight days before then. The work by Wittig to which you referred me is valuable and convincing. One thing I can promise you for sure—something negative—my presentation will be devoid of all theory. I hope I will succeed in allowing what is "creatural" to speak for itself, to the extent that I will have succeeded in comprehending and seizing this very new and disorienting language that loudly echoes through the acoustic mask of an entirely transformed environment. I intend to present a picture of the city of Moscow as it is at this very moment. In this picture, "all factuality is already theory" and therefore it refrains from any deductive abstraction, any prognostication, and, within certain bounds, even any judgment. It is my unshakable conviction that all of these things taken together can, in this case, be conveyed only on the basis of economic facts and not at all on the basis of "spiritual" data. Even in Russia, very few people have a sufficiently broad grasp of these facts. In schematic form, Moscow, as it appears at this very moment, reveals the full range of possibilities: above all, the possibility of the revolution's utter failure and of its success. In both instances, however, there will be something unforeseeable whose appearance will be vastly different from any programmatic painting of the future. The outline of this is today brutally and clearly evident in the people and their environment.

That is all for today. With best wishes, I remain your devoted,

Walter Benjamin

1. "Moscow" for *Die Kreatur.*

162. To Hugo von Hofmannsthal

Pardigon
June 5, 1927

My most esteemed Mr. von Hofmannsthal:

I believe it has been almost a year since I last wrote you. I have been to Russia in the meantime. I did not write you during the two months I spent in Moscow because I was unable to report anything while this strange and intense existence was making its first impression on me. Later I put off writing because I had hoped to be able to enclose my attempt at a description of my stay in Russia in my first letter to you. However, although the galley proofs have been done for quite some time, it still has not appeared in print. In this work, I made an attempt to depict the concrete phenomena of daily life, which affected me most deeply, just as they are and without any theoretical excursuses, even if not without taking a personal stance toward them. Because I did not know the language, I was of course unable to get beyond one specific and narrow stratum of society. But I concentrated even more on rhythmic experiences than I did on visual ones. As far as the rhythmic experience is concerned, I found that the time in which the people over there live, and in which a primeval Russian tempo is intertwined with the new tempo of the revolution to produce a whole, was much more incommensurable by Western European standards than I had expected.—The literary project I thought of as a very peripheral aspect of my trip proved to be unfeasible. The editorial board of the *Soviet Encyclopedia* represents an organization consisting of five final authorities. It includes very few competent scholars and by no stretch of the imagination is it in a position to carry out this immense enterprise. I saw for myself the ignorance and opportunism with which people here vacillate between the Marxist scholarly agenda and the attempt to win prestige in Europe. But the difficulties and rigors of a stay in Moscow during the depth of winter, like this private disillusionment, are no match for the powerful impression made by a city, all of whose inhabitants are still reeling from the great struggles in which everyone was involved, in one way or another. I concluded my stay in Russia with a visit to Sergievo Lavra, the second oldest monastery of the empire and a place of pilgrimage for all the boyars and czars. For more than one hour, with the temperature at -20, I walked through rooms filled with jewel-encrusted surplices; with illuminated gospels and prayer books, ranging from the manuscripts of the monks of Athos to those of the seventeenth century, arrayed in unending rows; and with innumerable icons from every period, with gilt facings from which the heads of the madonnas peer as if from Chinese neck irons. It was like a freezer in which an old culture is being preserved under ice during the dog days of the revolution. During the following weeks in Berlin, my work basically consisted of extracting from the diary I kept on this trip those things that can be communicated. It was the first time in fifteen years I had kept a travel diary and it went into great detail. When I returned to Germany, my translation of Proust's *Within a Budding Grove* had appeared and I confirmed that the publisher had it sent to you in my absence. If you have had a chance to glance at it, I hope it did not put you off. It was well received by the critics. But what does that mean? I think I have come to understand that every translation that is not undertaken for the highest and most urgent practical goals (like biblical translation, as a prime example) or for the sake of purely philological research must have something absurd about it. I would be satisfied if this were not all too obviously noticeable in this instance.—At first glance, the length of this letter, my esteemed Mr. von Hofmannsthal, will have cautioned you to put it aside until you have some time to spare; with this in mind and being aware of your genuine interest in me, I will take heart and tell you even more about myself. My work at the moment is mainly devoted to consolidating my position in Paris. I will try to support my stay here by reporting on literary subjects and with other more minor projects—at the moment I am with my wife in Pardigon near Toulon for a few days over Pentecost. To be sure, the validity of my first experience, which you yourself so emphatically corroborated, was repeatedly confirmed for me: it is extraordinarily rare to achieve the kind of emphathy with a Frenchman that would make it possible to converse with him for more than fifteen minutes. But with the passage of time I have been tempted to get close to the French spirit in its modern form as well, completely aside from the fact that it incessantly preoccupies me in its historical guise, and I firmly intend to speak my piece on this sometime, i.e. on its older manifestation. I sometimes think about writing a book on French tragedy as a counterpart to my *Trauerspiel* book. My plan for the latter had originally been to elucidate both the German *Trauerspiel* and the French tragic drama in terms of their contrastive nature. But something must be added. Given my activities and interests, I feel that, in Germany, I am completely isolated among those of my generation. In addition to all this, there is something else. In France individual phenomena are engaged in something that also engages me—among authors, Giraudoux and especially Aragon; among movements, surrealism. In Paris I discovered the format for the notebook. I sent you some excerpts from it a long time ago, very prematurely. I hope to be able to publish some excerpts from it here in translation, as well as parts of my report from Moscow. But then I am not terribly satisfied with the way things are going in Germany. Rowohlt has so ruthlessly violated the idealistic aspects of our contract that, at the moment, I cannot decide whether to award him the imprimatur to the book on the baroque. I know that these eternal delays can ultimately prove fatal. But I have to decide soon whether I will stay with Rowohlt or look for another publisher. In the meantime, several weeks ago I received the first proofs of the *Melancholia* chapter for the *Beiträge*. At the same time as I took care of that, I sent Mr. Wiegand a long letter. I find it inexplicable and, in the long run, unsettling not to hear one word from Mr. Wiegand. I do not know how to interpret his silence. Here in Pardigon I am working on a piece I have been planning to write for a long time; it announces the publication of the critical edition of Keller's works. (While working on it, I accidentally came across some lines he wrote about French tragedy: they are distinguished by their great insightfulness from everything that it was fashionable to say about the topic at the time.) I am really deriving a lot of pleasure from working on this project and I intend to send it to you as soon as it appears, in the hope that it can also provide some pleasure. I would like to close by assuring you how much it would mean to me to hear from you, however brief your words might be. With sincere esteem and regards, I remain,

Your very devoted, Walter Benjamin

163. To Martin Buber

Paris
July 26, 1927

My esteemed Dr. Buber:

You will not have thought well of me: it has been a very long time since you have heard from me. For several months I did not know where to reach you. In the meantime, you are sure to have returned from Palestine. Then, when the issue appeared, I wanted to write you a few lines about it. It took a long time for me to assimilate it. It is a whole that gradually assumed precise, definitive features for me. I do not have to tell you how happy I am to appear next to Rang in this issue. This letter[1] is one of the most concentrated confessions of his I know. It is a matter of infinite regret to me that the confrontation between his mature spiritual experiences and my most recent material experiences—cultic versus Communist activity—will remain unrealized. This confrontation has by no means been settled in my own mind. This man—and I have known this for a long time—would have been the only one of my friends who would have quickly and decisively resolved these questions in conversation with me. "Moscow" would have more clearly assumed those more personal accents you mention in your last letter if I could have gone to him with the things that moved me before, during, and after my stay there. Nonetheless, I hope it has become clear to some readers that these "visual" descriptions have been introduced into a grid of ideas. If you have heard any opinions expressed about "Moscow," I would really like to know whose and what they were.—The work by Wittig is very remarkable, or should I say disturbing, in the truth of its findings and the questions they raise. I believe it has been a very long time since it has been possible to express these simple but infinitely hard to grasp experiences in a way that is new and convincing. I would be interested in knowing whether Rang and Wittig knew each other.—I would like once more to assure you explicitly that I stand ready to contribute to *Die Kreatur*. I will let you know if I spot a topic in connection with my own work that might be considered appropriate.—Scholem will be coming to Paris with his wife in the next few days.

Best regards.

Your very devoted, Walter Benjamin

It would be even better if you would happen to have a suggestion.

1. To Walther Rathenau.

164. To Hugo von Hofmannsthal

Tours
August 16, 1927

My dear and most esteemed Mr. von Hofmannsthal,

I was delighted to receive the kind words you sent from Mendola. But the puzzled reserve with which you reacted to my plan to write on Keller was also important to me and, I believe, understandable. In the meantime, the essay has appeared in the first August issue of the *Literarische Welt* and you may well get to see it sooner or later. Today I want to do the best I can to say a thing or two about it: it is of course always hardest to talk about a project you have just completed. I can no longer remember exactly what first caused me to be attracted to Keller; by the time I went to Switzerland in 1917, my love for him was already clearly established (I happen to remember this because of a very animated conversation I had with my wife a few weeks after my arrival there). Then there was a meeting of minds between Ernst Bloch and me concerning Keller's writings and I remember that our involvement with *Martin Salander* put the seal on it for both of us, at different times and perhaps even for different reasons. Reading *Green Henry,* I experienced all of the antipathy the name Keller evokes in you, but in *Martin Salander* I thought I could see another pole of this world, which has an entirely different intellectual climate. (Only after I had finished the essay did it occur to me while reading it that it makes absolutely no mention of *Green Henry*. This appeared to me to be the acid test, if I may express it in this way. For the Philistines' love of this author gathers around *Green Henry* as around a banner.) Yet I continue to be aware of the need to make manifest in an entirely different way the unity that results from the intertwining within this man of what is limited and unloving with what is far-reaching and loving, in a way that is genuinely Swiss. To my mind, what I wrote was only the prolegomena—it points to another, overlooked Keller and does not reconstruct this author out of his two, apparently so disparate, halves. For the time being, I do not dare to start on such a project. I hoped to be able to find the resolve to do that after the essay was finished, if only by creating a contrasting mood through reading the little Insel book on Keller by Ricarda Huch,[1] but my antipathy to this unctuous, puny pile of sentences was so great that I got nothing out of it.—I am writing these lines to you from Tours. Without really knowing anything about the country's official holidays, I felt within myself the centrifugal force that Paris communicates to its inhabitants at this time of year (the feast of the Assumption is celebrated on August 15), and I fulfilled my long-nourished plan to go into the interior of France. Since reading a few lines by Péguy on Orléans and the Loire region several years ago, a place within me has been receptive to these images. Now, of course, they fill that place much more beautifully and vividly than I could ever have imagined. Especially the city of Tours, which does not usurp the river's green banks and islands, but indeed truly seems to caress the river with its bridges. Insofar as being a solitary visitor does not deprive one of the criteria for this kind of thing, I also believe that I am slowly developing an eye for cathedrals in that I am pursuing the hidden beauties of each one, whether they be unique or typical, without for the time being striving for anything more. Thus the choir of the cathedral of Orléans, which otherwise has nothing splendid about it, will remain unforgettable to me. It rises from a low, gently climbing pedestal as from a pillow. What struck me about the castles was the felicitous reserve with which they approach Renaissance forms: they rarely flaunt the playful element, at least on the facade, and private and military life-styles coexist without any mediation. When I return to this area, which I hope will be very soon, I hope to know more and to be better equipped. In fact, I will be spending some time on French culture of this era (the sixteenth and seventeenth centuries) in order to see whether I am getting any closer to writing a work on French tragedy, to which I believe I alluded in my last letter. For today, my most sincere regards and best wishes for a pleasant autumn in Austria. This time, I plan to come to Vienna in the winter, should my intention to give a lecture there work out. I would be delighted if this would bring us together and finally make it possible for me to tell you of my gratitude and devotion beyond the confines of my letters.

Yours, Walter Benjamin

1. *Gottfried Keller* (Leipzig, 1914).

165. To Max Rychner

Paris
October 18, 1927

Dear Sir:

Let me extend my sincere thanks for your proposition. Most remarkably, it goes right to the heart of my own intentions. It seems to offer me a chance to comment in your journal in context on the current state of German fiction.[1] This is precisely what would allow me to get beyond certain misgivings that have thus far kept me from publicly formulating my great reservations about this fiction. I have been familiar with your journal for a long time and value it highly. I also value highly the opportunity it will provide me to write for a Swiss audience, which fundamentally has a more open and more critical view of German intellectual movements. The only qualm I have to express concerns the deadline. Aside from the fact that I currently have a lot of demands on my time because two of my books are going to press, an essay of the kind you have the right to expect requires a certain amount of free time. Thus I would like to ask you if you would be willing to wait for it until around the end of the year.

May I add how much I valued your response to my Keller essay and how much it pleased and encouraged me to hear of the impact you say it had. I lived in Switzerland for two years and believe I know it fairly well. In some passages, you certainly could read between the lines what it is about the nature of the Swiss that moved me. If I might be permitted to express it in this way, what I attempted was a small but intelligible adjustment of the border in favor of Swiss-German soil versus that of the German empire.

I saw [Ferdinand] Hardekopf here and we spoke about you. I read your poem in the September *Querschnitt* with much pleasure. I will be going to Berlin in the next few days. Please send your kind response to my address there: Berlin-Grunewald, 23 Delbrück St.

Most respectfully and devotedly yours,
Walter Benjamin

1. The journal is the *Neue Schweizer Rundschau*.

166. To Hugo von Hofmannsthal

Berlin-Grunewald
November 24, 1927

My dear and most esteemed Mr. von Hofmannsthal,

The post office mistakenly forwarded to Paris the parcel from the Bremer Presse in which your letter was enclosed. It remained in my hotel there for a week before being returned. You would have heard from me earlier in spite of this but for the fact that I was unfortunately stricken by a case of jaundice after my return. It continues to bother me even now. For this reason, let me ask you to be so kind as to forgive me for this belated letter—I just received the card you wrote on the 22d.

Aside from my illness, things are looking up. It finally seems as if the *Trauerspiel* book will be in print shortly before Christmas. And now that I am, in a certain sense, dismissing it, allow me to extend to you once more my sincere gratitude for the support you gave me during a waiting period that was at times discouraging. I do not know where the book would be today—and I almost do not know what my attitude toward it would be—if I had not found in you the first, the most understanding, and the most favorably disposed reader, in the best sense of these words.

[. . .]

It is nonetheless with some hesitation that I now present you with my Keller essay (it is being mailed at the same time as this and you may have already noted its presence). I would consider it almost a lack of candor if, at this point, I were to withhold from you this profile of a terrain that for years has repeatedly attracted me. I would like to know that it is in your hands, even if you would rather pass over it in silence.

[. . .]

For today, my most sincere regards. I hope I will soon be able to send you something new.

Your devoted, Walter Benjamin

167. To Hugo von Hofmannsthal

Berlin-Grunewald
December 4, 1927

My dear and most esteemed Mr. von Hofmannsthal,

Please accept my sincere thanks for the text of your Munich lecture[1] and the note you enclosed with it. I was deeply affected by your depiction of the German type on whom you focus in the lecture. I believe I can see Rang's qualities in him, as well as many other things. What you say in the lecture has, therefore, renewed my intention to become familiar with the figure of Alfred Brust. Everything you designate as the cognizant and foreboding aspect of this type of person is intensified in him to the point of agony. I know Brust not only from the *Neue deutsche Beiträge*. As you must know, Rang corresponded with him toward the end of his life. The first thing I want to do is read *Die verlorene Erde*.[2] (The welcome occasion for doing so is a survey of the most important novels of the last few years, which I am to write for the *Neue Schweizer Rundschau*.) But then the wonderful piece by Passarge in Borchardt's landscape book again directed me to things Nordic. I will send you a review of this book[3] very soon.

[. . .]

Wishing you a pleasant new year. Sincere regards from your devoted,

Walter Benjamin

1. "Das Schrifttum als geistiger Raum der Nation" (Munich, 1927).
2. Leipzig, 1926.
3. The review of *Der Deutsche in der Landschaft,* edited by Rudolf Borchardt (Munich, 1927), appeared in the *Literarische Welt* (February 3, 1928), p. 5.

168. To Gerhard Scholem

Berlin
January 30, 1928

Dear Gerhard,

This letter may well turn out to be interminably long. You should view it as chain lightning to be followed in a few days by a long, rumbling clap of thunder in the form of an imposing package of books. How long you will have to wait for it will be a direct function of the distance from the eye of the thunderstorm to the Holy Land. May the package find a resounding echo in the mountain valleys of your excellency's head!

It simply would not have done to write yet again to "announce" the publication of my books. And luckily it was the end of January before both of them were available. Now I can simply say, "Here they are." In your role as protector of the university library, you will receive at the same time a second copy of both works and, in your not less important role as protector of my career, a third copy of the *Trauerspiel* book with an inscription for Magnes.[1]

Whatever else there may be in the way of bibliophilic fringes protectively surrounding these gifts is affectionately intended for you and is interlaced with all kinds of good wishes.

Because this will not suffice, let me announce a supplementary package with some essays from the *Literarische Welt* that will appear soon; "Moscow"—for Magnes—which I still have to get from Buber; and the Andrian issue of the *[Neue deutsche] Beiträge* that you requested. At the moment I do not have a copy of it either. On the other hand, I am terribly sorry to have to disappoint you as regards my *Elective Affinities* essay. My personal copy is absolutely the only one I have. I do not expect that my effort to provide Magnes with a copy will succeed. Let me please ask you to come to my aid by lending him yours. I am also unable to send you "On Language as Such," since I have only a single copy of this essay. I really regret this, because it is very important in the context of our concerns. In the final analysis, of course, I could have a copy made if you consider it to be a crucial factor (which I doubt, given the number of other works and their relationship to the foreword of the *Trauerspiel* book).

And now, right at the beginning, let me talk about what I have planned in this regard. This is perhaps my last chance to devote myself to the study of Hebrew and to everything we think is connected with it. But this is also a very propitious time for it. First and foremost, in terms of my being ready for the undertaking, heart and soul. Once I have, one way or another, completed the project on which I am currently working, carefully and provisionally—the highly remarkable and extremely precarious essay "Paris Arcades: A Dialectical Fairy Play" ["Pariser Passagen: Eine dialektische Feerie"]—one cycle of production, that of *One-Way Street,* will have come to a close for me in much the same way in which the *Trauerspiel* book concluded the German cycle. The profane motifs of *One-Way Street* will march past in this project, hellishly intensified. As for the rest, I am still unable to tell you anything about it, and do not even have a precise conception of its length. In any case, it is a project that will just take a few weeks.[2]

I must say that Rowohlt offered to extend my contract, but under such unfavorable conditions that I have provisionally rejected the offer. On the other hand, Hegner is interested in entering into an exclusive contract with me. But I would only do this if I were up to my neck in water. Because, as you must understand, the basic Catholic tendency of this publishing house (Buber notwithstanding!) really goes against the grain.

Now that the way ahead is clear, therefore, nothing would be more obvious for me than to make the decisive move to commit myself to Hebrew. I am free but, unfortunately, in the twofold sense of the word: free of obligations and of income. If you and Magnes are currently engaged in serious discussions about me, explain to him exactly how things stand: that I need a subsidy or, to express it better, security if I am now to jump off the cart that, although slow-moving, is traveling the career path of a German writer. And if things get to the point where he asks you about a figure, tell him 300 marks a month for however long an accelerated course of study would take. He himself will be best able to estimate the duration of such a course of study, predicated on my total independence from other ties and interests.

So much for that. It is important enough and the situation is such that I would like to know what his position is on this matter, and the sooner the better. I am trying to drag out my negotiations with publishers as long as possible because I basically do not want that, *but rather Hebrew.*

I am therefore interested in getting a response very soon so that I do not forfeit my chances here, because under certain circumstances I may yet have to rely on them. In spite of this, it seems to me much more important that you proceed exactly as your judgment dictates, even if this means that I have to live with uncertainty a while longer.

Thank you very much for your notes on our conversation about the concept of the symbol. At the moment I am in no position even to attempt to put together the concordance along with my other writings. I must therefore file it away, but you will get to see it someday. I hope it will be as part of a trade in which I will get your commentaries on Job and Jonah. Apropos the commemorative volume for Buber's fiftieth birthday.[3] I recently was given a description of a submission by—it is unlikely you know him—Dr. [Ernst] Joel. He is contributing to the festschrift an epileptic's observations on experiencing a revelation. They appear to be quite remarkable.

I myself know the individual in question from my days as a student in Berlin, when he was the presiding officer of the so-called social welfare office.[4] I formally declared war on him in the lecture I gave in May 1914 upon assuming my presidency. He and another one of my opponents from that time, through God's—or Satan's—intervention, have miraculously transformed themselves and have become caryatids on the gate through which I have now entered the realm of hashish on two separate occasions. That is to say, both of these physicians are conducting experiments on narcotics and they wanted me to be their subject. I agreed. The notes I made, in part independently, in part relying on the written record of the experiment, may well turn out to be a very worthwhile supplement to my philosophical observations, with which they are most intimately related, as are to a certain degree even my experiences while under the influence of the drug. But I would like to be assured that this piece of information will remain locked in the bosom of the Scholem family.

Allow me to say in passing that, as far as the family's Berlin branch is concerned, I have been given reason to be displeased. Your brother [Erich] had me show him all my stuff and then took it away with him only to disassociate himself from it as much as possible. At the eleventh hour, of course, he redeemed himself by sending over some things that he had printed privately in his shop. But I still have seen nothing of your *Alphabet,* which he absolutely wanted to publish, nor of the galleys that were supposed to be sent to me.[5]—Franz Blei is nowadays putting out a new, awful, soi-disant, satirical journal. To my great regret, he has not published the Muri manuscript, but will publish some excerpts with attribution.

I still do not know how my books were received. [. . .] You will be interested to hear that Hofmannsthal, who knew I was interested in establishing a connection to the Warburg circle, sent the issue of the *Beiträge* containing the preview of the *Trauerspiel* book to [Erwin] Panofsky with a letter, perhaps somewhat prematurely. This kind act, meant to be of some use to me, has—*on ne peut plus—échoué* (gone awry, and how!). He sent me Panofsky's cool, resentment-laden response to his parcel. Can you make head or tail of all this?

In the past few days I had a delightful experience. André Gide was in Berlin and I was the *only* German journalist he agreed to see. He granted me a *two-hour* interview, which was enormously interesting. You will probably get to read an account of it in the *Literarische Welt.*[6] Of course, the account will have been drastically censored for public consumption. You will be unlikely to be able to infer from it that the interview was wonderful. You also will not be able to infer what it implies. Namely, Gide does not consent to be interviewed even in France. During this conversation, he asked me on two or three occasions to stay a while longer and told me how much he enjoyed our meeting. He later even said as much to others. In addition to a lengthy description of our conversation, I also wrote up the interview for the *Deutsche Allgemeine Zeitung* in compliance with Gide's special request (for certain sensible reasons, Gide specifically wanted this paper). He had not held the press conference for which he had come here in the first place and wanted to introduce himself to the public in another, quasi-official way. The interview appeared today. I hope that this interview will greatly enhance my standing in Paris (where I will return in any case, perhaps in April; I can learn Hebrew there just as well as here).

Two months ago Wolfskehl visited me, prompted by Hessel. It was very charming, *sans aucune importance.* A few days later I saw him once again at Hessel's, where we had a nice conversation.

Escha's critique of Goitein[7] was of great interest to me. Indeed, it greatly enlightened me, to the extent I can assert this without knowing the work under discussion. The fate of Dora's book still has not been decided. But she is doing a lot of writing and is currently giving a series of radio lectures.

I believe I have redeemed myself through this long and detailed report. Just for good measure, let me mention that I have known and valued Hegemann's *Fridericus* ever since I can remember and that the same author's *Napoleon,* recently published by Hegner,[8] is supposed to be not nearly as good.

I commend to your keen eye and into your care everything reported and considered in this letter, but above all its main topic. I expect timely and respectful thanks for the parcel mentioned at the beginning and send you my most sincere regards.

Yours, Walter

1. Judah L. Magnes (1877–1948), chancellor of the University of Jerusalem, whom Scholem had brought together with WB in Paris for a productive discussion.

2. Hebrew ultimately lost out in its conflict with the *Arcades* project. The *Paris Arcades*, WB's uncompleted major work, is mentioned here for the first time (but was called this already in a conversation in 1927).

3. *Aus unbekannten Schriften* (1928).

4. Of the Free Students.

5. "Amtliches Lehrgedicht der philosophischen Fakultät der Haupt- und Staats-Universität Muri" by Gerhard Scholem, beadle of the Religious-Philosophical Institute. Second edition, revised according to the latest, certified achievements of philosophy. It was privately published (Berlin, 1928).

6. February 17, 1928. In *Schriften* 2:296–304.

7. S. D. Goitein's Hebrew drama, *Pulcelina*. The essay was published in the *Jüdische Rundschau*.

8. *Napoleon oder Kniefall vor dem Heros* (1927).

169. To Hugo von Hofmannsthal

Berlin-Grunewald
February 8, 1928

My dear and most esteemed Mr. von Hofmannsthal,

You are now sure to have both my books.

While *One-Way Street* was being written, I did not really feel I could write you about it and, now that you have the actual book before you, it is even harder for me to do so. I do, however, have one request that is very close to my heart: that you not see everything striking about the book's internal and external design as a compromise with the "tenor of the age." Precisely in terms of its eccentric aspects, the book is, if not a trophy, nonetheless a document of an internal struggle. Its subject matter may be expressed as follows: to grasp topicality as the reverse of the eternal in history and to make an impression of this, the side of the medallion hidden from view. Otherwise the book owes a lot to Paris, being my first attempt to come to terms with this city. I am continuing this effort in a second book called *Paris Arcades*.

I am enclosing two clippings with this letter. I would be delighted if my review of *Der Deutsche in der Landschaft* gives you and Mr. Wiegand some idea of the joy and profit I derived from reading the Borchardt book.

As you surely know, Gide was in Berlin. I sat across from him for a two-hour-long, wide-ranging, and fascinating conversation, unfortunately a one-time event. Since he spoke rather candidly about all the literary matters on which we touched but, on the other hand, since his position in France is so precarious, only bits and pieces of our conversation could be published and I had to hold back for my personal notes many of the significant things he said. The enclosed clipping is a version of the interview I wrote up at Gide's request for the *Deutsche Allgemeine Zeitung*. I will send you a detailed description as soon as it appears in the *Literarische Welt*. Gide has a thoroughly dialectical nature, characterized by an almost confusing profusion of reservations and barricades. Talking with him in person sometimes intensifies this impression, already projected by his writings in their own way, to the point of sublimity, and at other times to the point of being problematical.

Otherwise I spent last week under the dominating influence of reading Leskov. I can hardly put him down since having begun to read him in the new edition of his collected works published by Beck. [. . .]

Thank you for sending me Panofsky's odd letter. I was aware that he is an art historian "by profession." But based on the nature of his iconographic interests, I thought I could assume that he was the same kind of man as Émile Mâle, e.g., someone who would be interested in important things, if not to the same extent, even if they have nothing to do with his profession in all of its manifestations. Now there is nothing left for me to do but to apologize for my untimely request. [. . .]

Yesterday I saw the final version of *Der Turm* for the first time. I have not read it but in connection with this task am looking forward to being able to deal again with the drama in the *Literarische Welt*.

Most sincere regards. Please extend my regards to your daughter Christiane as well.

I remain, as always,
your devoted Walter Benjamin

170. To Hugo von Hofmannsthal

Berlin-Grunewald
February 24, 1928

My dear and most esteemed Mr. von Hofmannsthal,

I fear that your stay here might be coming to an end and that Berlin has so imperiously asserted its demands in the last few days that you will not have one free hour left to visit me in my room in Grunewald. I would like to forestall this with these lines and ask you to call me in the next few days, should you have the time, so that we can arrange a meeting.

[. . .]

That is all for today. Sincere regards,

Your devoted and grateful, Walter Benjamin

171. To Gerhard Scholem

Berlin
March 11, 1928

Dear Gerhard,

Thank you for your excellent letter, to which I will respond in great detail. The vitally important thing for me about your letter is that, but also how, the Jewish things it touches on are made concrete. That is to say, what struck me as the most felicitous thing in your letter is the notion that, for the time being, I should not deprive the Jewish world inherent in my thought of its defenses, if and to whatever extent it should manifest itself. Furthermore, that I should surround it with the protective cloak of my instructive preoccupation—or whatever you may want to call it—with things French and German. This corresponds entirely to my own deepest desire. I must confess that I was unaware of it myself up till now, and I am grateful for the perspicacity and delicacy with which you broached my situation.

I will now immediately make the leap to the purest formalities and can again thank my lucky stars that you have already given Magnes some indication of the questions that might arise in securing academic references for my scholarly qualifications. Let me begin, however, with something positive. Hofmannsthal can be counted on. I have met him personally since the last time I wrote. He was in Berlin for a short time and we saw each other twice, the second time here at my place. Motivated by considerations that have nothing to do with the practical ends we are now discussing, I had decided at the outset to say a few words to Hofmannsthal about my relationship to Jewishness and, thus, to the question of Hebrew. And this was not the only time it became clear to me that he picked up on what I had in mind with amazing speed and genuine concern. (I was even more surprised at this when I began to speak about my *Paris Arcades* project—an essay that might turn out to be more extensive than I had thought and for which the passage on "stamps" in *One-Way Street* timidly sets the tone.) It is almost impossible for me to indicate to you in a letter how difficult my situation sometimes became. It was a situation that allowed for the confluence of so much genuine understanding and goodwill on his part and so much indefeasible reserve on my [part], in spite of all my admiration for him. An additional factor is that he sometimes almost has something of the old fogey about him when he sees himself completely misunderstood by everybody. This is particularly the case when he talks about his best things, the things that are dearest to him. I also must tell you in person about his own extremely illuminating plans. He told me about them when we were talking about my *Arcades* project. Given that the situation becomes clearer, I will write him tomorrow or the day after in Rodaun where he now is.

[. . .]

Sincere regards from Dora.

Yours, Walter

172. To Hugo von Hofmannsthal

Berlin-Grunewald
March 17, 1928

My dear and most esteemed Mr. von Hofmannsthal,

Now that, as I hope, you have returned to Rodaun in good health and spirits, let me pick up our conversation at almost the precise point we had to interrupt it. I am now doubly glad that I seized the opportunity to tell you something about my inmost intentions, and to speak about external matters that seem to be taking shape more quickly than I had imagined. In short, the University of Jerusalem intends to add an Institute for the Humanities in the near future. And I must say that they have in mind to appoint me professor of modern German and French literature. The one condition is that I acquire a solid command of Hebrew in two to three years. This should not be understood as implicitly intended to fix my area of specialization. Instead, the goal is to introduce me to things Jewish in a very organic way and to leave the degree to which this occurs completely open. As for me, I find myself being able to speak of the rare case in which my desires, which in this form were still almost unconscious, were identified for me from one perspective. Nothing would intrinsically appeal to me more than initially to deal as a learner with only the problem of language, that is, with a technical problem, protectively surrounded by my former projects, and to leave everything else in abeyance.

Last fall my friend Scholem, who is a professor of the philosophy of the Kabbalah at the University of Jerusalem, arranged for me to meet the permanent rector of the university, Dr. Magnes. We had a very comprehensive conversation, after which my plan to devote myself to Hebrew for the first time took on the definitive shape in which you became acquainted with it and encouraged it. Dr. Magnes is now very much inclined to obtain a subsidy for me through one of the usual channels for such things. This would require me to study Hebrew; however, as in all cases of this kind, he needs some references attesting to my qualifications, and quite aside from the question of the subsidy, he also needs them in order to be able to entertain my future appointment as a professor. Dr. Scholem writes me that your opinion would be extremely valuable and he suggests that I give Dr. Magnes the go-ahead to make written inquiries of you concerning my qualifications. Let me now ask for your permission to do this. I do so with the internal conviction that I am asking for more than a service, indeed for truly significant help. I am also convinced that you will therefore be all the more certain to fulfill my request. I assume that you will receive a brief letter from Dr. Magnes in the near future.

The question of academic references in the narrowest sense of the word presented me with difficulties. Thus I allowed myself to list Professor Brecht, in addition to some other Germanists and philosophers.

[. . .]

I continue to think about the things you said to me concerning the *Paris Arcades* project when you were here. What you said drew on your own plans and was supportive and lent precision to my thinking, while making what I should most emphasize ever clearer to me. I am currently looking into the sparse material that thus far constitutes all efforts to describe and fathom fashion philosophically: into the question of what this natural and totally irrational, temporal measure of the historical process is all about.

There was one thing I terribly regretted having failed to do when you were here. I would have really liked to speak with you about Alfred Brust. Not only because I know from the *Neue deutsche Beiträge* and from [Willy] Haas that you are interested in and sympathize with him, but because we would probably have also touched on the friendship between Rang and Brust—who, to be sure, most likely never met. Yet his work is alien to me, and will probably remain so forever. I have begun to read *Jutt und Jula*,[1] and acknowledge that this man is owed the greatest respect. I also sense the energy that was operative in the book, albeit as dangerous and inimical. It may be that I saw such energy harnessed and turned into true genius only once, specifically in the configuration that was Rang.

Let me ask you to receive with indulgence the few lines about *Der Turm* enclosed with this letter.

Most sincere regards.
Your truly devoted, Walter Benjamin

P.S. The kind words you wrote in Rodaun with the delightful news about [Walther] Brecht have just arrived. Please give him my thanks when you have the opportunity—or even better, I may take the opportunity to establish contact with him myself after the publication of his review. But forgive me—the one does not, of course, exclude the other.

Best wishes for bounteous and blessed weeks of spring.

1. WB's review of the book was called "Eine neue gnostische Liebesgedicht" [A new gnostic love poem], *Literarische Welt* (March 30, 1928), p. 5.

173. To Alfred Cohn

Berlin
March 27, 1928

Dear Alfred,

I will now, belatedly though it be, show up at your vacation haunt through a small package. Here are the requisite instructions on how to use it: first and foremost, it is recommended that you study the elementary [?], after which I hope you will add it to your library with redoubled delight. Then take up the French scribblers and send them back to me after you have finished celebrating your acquaintanceship with them. If you feel like it, put a letter of recommendation or a Uriah letter into Jouglet's[1] maw so that I will know what I am supposed to think of him and whether he is really important enough to merit discussion. That is just what I did with Benda's book and, in spite of this, what I wrote about it[2] will appear, if at all, in an embarrassing place, should you happen to see it.

Write me what you are doing and how you are.

Similar information coming from me might include the kind request, spoken eloquently enough, that you return the 10 marks as soon as you can.

Too bad you're not here: I am writing this to you during the evening of a day on which I was once again able to look into the jaws of Berlin as the capital of the empire. This is how it came about: Last evening Kraus read *La vie parisienne* as the fourth and last installment of his Offenbach lecture series. It was the first time I heard him read an operetta and I am all the more loath to write you about the impression it made on me because it has at this very moment precipitated a whole mass of ideas—you know from which area—making it difficult for me to keep track of my own. Among the stanzas he added was a couplet with the concluding verse, "From every city I bring the scoundrel—out." It was obvious that the reference was to Kerr. Shortly before the first intermission, Kraus, standing, read out a short text whose drift was "I am publicly calling Kerr a scoundrel in order to see whether this way I will be able to force him to sue. I have proof in hand that Kerr denounced me in 1916 to the highest military authorities as an author who was guilty of high treason and defeatism." As I have said, some things occurred to me at this lecture about which I absolutely wanted to write. Naturally, I did not want to conjure away this "incident" but instead briefly present it as the evening's dynamic core. The result of a morning's effort was my discovery that a report of this lecture would not find an outlet anywhere. I will not give up writing my brief report because of this, but I have little hope of seeing it published.[3]

That's Berlin.

Otherwise Kraus made a stronger impression on me than ever before. That is to say, now that he has found suitable subject matter, he has grown more comfortable in his own skin and has become more honest and relaxed.

Unfortunately, I still have a lot to take care of this evening and I must close. A bookstore on the Potsdam bridge set up a window display today featuring my writings with Jula's head right in the center.

Sincere regards to you and Grete.

Yours, Walter

1. Probably René Jouglet, *Le nouveau corsaire* (German translation published in 1927).

2. Probably *La trahison des clercs*. The review was published in the *Humboldt-Blätter* (May 1928).

3. A version, in which the sections about Kerr were censored by the editorial board, was published in the *Literarische Welt* (April 20, 1928).

174. To Max Rychner

Berlin
April 22, 1928

My esteemed Mr. Rychner,

In the rainy quiet of a Sunday morning, I will master my embarrassment to the extent of being able to write you. It should have been immediately clear to me that the honorable and enticing proposition you made to me last fall would have a demoralizing effect on me because of its magnitude. I have been so dilatory in conceiving a plan that—please forgive me for saying this—I am unlikely to get to a theme that is representative in the actual sense of the word, that is, to write about German literature of the past two years for a readership that has for a long time seemed to me to be the most important among all the audiences of German language journals.

On the other hand, I see it as an established fact that—given your eventual agreement—my first important piece of work that is not already spoken for will go to the *Neue Schweizer Rundschau*. What I have in mind are some parts of an essay, *Paris Arcades,* on which I have been working for months and which must be completed by the time of my impending return to Paris.

Should you, my most esteemed Mr. Rychner, get to Paris during June, it would be invaluable to me to be able to make your acquaintance. I have just now read [with] great delight your observations on Holitscher and Keyserling. My Paris address is Paris XIVe, 4 Avenue du parc Montsouris, Hôtel du Midi. On the other hand, it is possible that I may go to Switzerland in the fall. By then I confidently hope to have made amends to you for my literary unreliability.

Most respectfully yours,
Your devoted, Walter Benjamin

175. To Gerhard Scholem

Berlin
April 23, 1928

Dear Gerhard,

I now have your letters of March 22d and April 12th. Also the special issue of *Der Jude,*[1] to which I subscribed through the Ewer bookstore as soon as you mentioned it in your letter. I do not have the *Jüdische Rundschau* with your note on Agnon.[2] Please send this to me, immediately if possible. It is already impossible to get it in the local stores. Why don't you take my good example to heart. I never bibliographically "refer" you to where you can find something of mine in the *Literarische Welt.* Instead, I provide you with anything halfway important *in natura.*

This applies today as well. You will see from the essay by Haas, which I am mailing at the same time, how my editor thought to honor me. Notwithstanding some highly questionable omissions, it is possible to be pleased with this review. It seems to me that it has some very clever things to say toward the end. By the way, the first review to speak out for the *Trauerspiel* book came out of Hungary. A gentleman whom I had not heard of previously gave me an excellent review in a philological journal published with the support of the Academy of Sciences. The publisher of this journal informs me that he is already recommending the book in his lectures in Budapest. As you know, some important voices are yet to be heard from. Among them, that of Mr. Richard Alewyn, whose verdict can be expected to appear in the *Deutsche Literaturzeitung.*[3] The name will be just as new to you as it is to me, but he is held in high regard here.

I was delighted at the letter from [Fritz] Strich.[4] The closer the matter gets to its critical stage, the better. I will be in Paris at the beginning of June. Please send me a letter of introduction to the chief rabbi or some other authority who might be able to recommend a Hebrew teacher. I really hope to hear from Magnes before I leave Berlin. In any case, I will arrange things in such a way that I will see him at the meeting of the board of trustees. In keeping with your suggestion, I will travel to Paris via Frankfurt, should Buber not come here in May. I will write him soon. The next issue of the *Literarische Welt* will contain a brief prospectus for the book *Aus unbekannten Schriften,* in which you and your contribution are prominently mentioned.[5] I, Amhaaretz,[6] have no more honors to bestow. On the other hand, it really seems as if, behind closed doors, I might and must wrinkle my brow at the special issue of *Der Jude.* But your essay, of course, appears in it to unwrinkle it again.[7] It is really good. I thought of our conservation in the Café Versailles near the Gare Montparnasse where I heard these bells for the first time. I believe this essay is a junction in the railway net of your thinking; at least I sense that navigable routes radiate in all directions.

Quant à moi, I do not want to omit mention of the fact that I am still working on the *Paris Arcades.* I have probably occasionally mentioned or written to you how slowly the work is taking shape, and about the obstacles it faces. But once I manage to get everything under control, an old and somewhat rebellious, quasi-apocryphal province of my thought will really have been subjugated, colonized, managed. There is still a lot missing, but I know precisely what is missing. I will finish it in Paris, one way or another. And then I will have put to the test the extent to which it is possible to be "concrete" in the context of the philosophy of history. Nobody will be able to assert that I made things easy for myself.

In the meantime, a letter has arrived from Moscow. People there suddenly seem to have reconsidered and are offering me the job of writing the article on Goethe for the *Soviet Encyclopedia* with quite acceptable conditions. It is to be one printed sheet long. Naturally I'll accept.

Let me add another word concerning the festschrift put out by *Der Jude.* I read the genial article by Magnes. On the other hand, I really disliked Max Brod's article. And I find it incomprehensible how anyone could possibly have come up with the unfortunate idea of publishing Rosenzweig's letters. They surely touch on things for which it is impossible to give a public accounting *in this way.* I have yet to find the courage to read the piece by Ludwig Strauß. I will see whether I understand [Ernst] Müller's essay on Hebrew and by then I will probably have had enough.

It would be nice if you wrote or if you had already written Saxl.[8] As far as [H. H.] Schaeder is concerned, I would prefer to wait until his review of my book has appeared in the *Neue Schweizer Rundschau.* That is the right moment to make my presence known by means of a letter. It will probably be too late to have any influence on Cassirer. But I see no viable way to do that in any case. Therefore there is nothing for me to do but wait. Please write as soon as you hear something from that quarter.

Write soon in any case. Sincere regards to you and Escha.

Yours, Walter

1. In honor of Buber's fiftieth birthday.
2. "Über die Erzählungen S. J. Agnons" (April 4, 1928).
3. It was never published.
4. Magnes was soliciting letters of recommendation from Germanists in support of the plan to get WB an appointment at the University of Jerusalem.
5. April 27, 1928.
6. Hebrew for "ignorant."
7. "Über die Theologie des Sabbatianismus"; reprinted in *Judaica* (1963), pp. 119–46.
8. Fritz Saxl, director of the Warburg Library and coauthor of the work on Dürer, *Melancolia I.*

176. To Hugo von Hofmannsthal

Berlin-Grunewald
May 5, 1928

My dear and most esteemed Mr. von Hofmannsthal,

Thank you so much for your card. I am delighted that you now have the matter in hand and hope it will turn out the way we want. Prof. [Fritz] Strich in Munich has also been approached for a letter of recommendation and he is supposed to have said some very kind things. It is quite possible that Magnes will also approach Brecht. I do not, of course, have the details. But I do list his name, among others, at the end of a curriculum vitae in which I have to provide scholarly references.

I continue to work almost exclusively on the *Paris Arcades.* I have a clear idea of what I want to accomplish, but this is precisely where it becomes extraordinarily risky to want to evoke the happy unity of a theoretical perspective with ideational fittings. Indeed, I must not only invoke experiences but verify some crucial insights into historical consciousness in an unexpected light; if I may be permitted to say this, I conceive of your "seminarian's" journey through the centuries as an arcade.

I now only have to fit in a review of a book that is not entirely alien to this project before returning to it. The book struck me as quite noteworthy when I first took a quick glance at it: Mirgeler's *Geschichte und Dogma,* which has just been published by Hegner.[1]

The wonderful early summer we are now enjoying, as well as the state library, are keeping me here and I do not know when I will get away this year. With the most sincere regards, I remain as always,

Your devoted, Walter Benjamin

1. This review was not published.

177. To Gerhard Scholem

May 24, 1928

Dear Gerhard,

I am enclosing a copy of my vita and the exposé I am sending to Magnes in London today. I hope you will find it satisfactory. You will see from my letter to Magnes that nothing is happening with Paris and I do not know myself if and when anything will happen this year. I am finding it difficult to leave Berlin. First, there is my room, specifically, a new one because at the moment I am not living in Grunewald but in the depth of the Tiergarten—In den Zelten—in a room into which nothing but trees peer at me through both windows. It is wonderful and, in addition to everything else, ten minutes away from the state library, the other focal point of the ellipse that keeps me here. The work on the *Paris Arcades* is taking on an ever more mysterious and insistent mien and howls into my nights like a small beast if I have failed to water it at the most distant springs during the day. God knows what it will do when, one of these days, I set it free. But this will not happen for a long time, and though I may already be constantly staring into the housing in which it does what comes naturally, I let hardly anyone else have a look inside.

In any case, it gives me no respite. Thus it was with mixed feelings that I learned that Soviet Russia has searched its conscience and, in the eleventh hour, commissioned me to write the Goethe article for the encyclopedia after all. Even this is reason enough to stay here for the time being. I really cannot let myself think for a moment about all the deadlines I have for projects over and above this one, especially some long articles about French literary developments. The *Neue Rundschau* recently asked me for a contribution. I have already had to beg off doing a lengthy review of recent German literature that I had taken on for the *Neue Schweizer Rundschau,* one of the most respectable periodicals around.

I am delighted that Hofmannsthal's reply was so apt and to the point. It was a very lucky coincidence that, within certain limits, he was in the know—obviously only in terms of my plans for *Hebrew*—as a result of the conversations we had during his last visit to Berlin. And on top of that I just got the excellent response from [Walther] Brecht. Many thanks!

I have firmly put an autumn visit to Palestine on my agenda for the coming year. I hope that Magnes and I will have reached an agreement about the financial terms of my apprenticeship before then. Thank you so much for your invitation. I would naturally be very happy to stay with the two of you for a few weeks, if this can be arranged.

I do, in fact, intend to bring actual production to a temporary halt once I am finished with my current project, in order that I may *just* learn. I hope to be able to apply an early advance Rowohlt gave me for a projected book on Kafka, Proust, etc. to the *Arcades* project. By the way, as is my wont, I came upon Max Brod while working on this project. He appeared in the form of a small book, *Über die Schönheit häßlicher Bilder*, published in 1913. It is remarkable how fifteen years ago he first ran his fingers over a keyboard for which I am trying to write a fugue.

That your first Kafka book has turned out to be such a godsend for you is all the more edifying for the fact that I—a German author—had to buy one volume after another in a bookstore and therefore still do not own *The Castle* [*Das Schloß*] or *Amerika*—to say nothing of the rare, out-of-print *Meditation* [*Betrachtung*]. This is the only early Kafka work I still do not have.

Hessel and the Gutkinds send best thanks (in good Swiss German) for receipt of your *Alphabet*. Your brother also put an adequate number of copies at my disposal.

Gutkind advertised a debate on "paths to ritual" here in various Jewish circles and I have been blacklisted because I still have not taken my place in line. There will be another gala evening tomorrow and I will attend the Jewish magic show if I have not been given a theater ticket to a new play.

Enclosed are some trifles from the *Literarische Welt*. Please write soon and, by the way, to Delbrück Street. I will be moving there again at the beginning of June.

Sincere regards to you and Escha.
Yours, Walter

178. To Gerhard Scholem

Frankfurt am Main
June 2, 1928

Dear Gerhard,

My mother's uncle, the mathematician [Arthur] Schönflies, has died. I have seen him often in the past few years and have gotten along really well with him. As you may know, I also lived with him while the Frankfurt business was going on. I came here for the funeral. It took place on May 31.

In keeping with the reminders in your letters, I was in Heppenheim yesterday, on June 1. A conference of some kind of religious socialist group is being held there at this very moment. It was not convened by Buber, but he seemed interested in it. Thus he had very little time for me. But this may have actually made things easier. Our half-hour conversation in his apartment was very definitive and very positive. There is surely no real reason for me to doubt that Buber will in fact support my cause, just as he assured me he would. He went so far as to ask me about the money involved. I was particularly pleased at this, and I quoted him the sum of 300 marks, which had so often come up in conversations between you and me.

Magnes intends to be in Heppenheim on June 17. Since Buber (who is not participating in the meeting of the board of trustees) will not return from a trip to Switzerland until around the 20th, however, it still has not been decided whether they will meet. By the way, generally speaking, Buber was somewhat better informed than I thought he would be.

Magnes's plans being what they are, I hope to speak to him in mid-June when he comes through Berlin. I will tell him then that it is very important for me to have a firm commitment on the basics by fall.

Do not be put off by my handwriting. It is early morning and I am writing in bed using bad ink. My nerves are in a rather bad way. I went to Königsstein for a day because I was feeling so low. It is very beautiful here, and my only regret is that I must be back in Frankfurt this evening.

I will probably stop off in Weimar on the way back, where, to further the progress of my encyclopedia article, I will reacquaint myself with the Goethe collection, which I have not seen for more than ten years.

Please write soon. Sincere regards to you and Escha.

Yours, Walter

179. To Gerhard Scholem

Berlin
June 18, 1928

Dear Gerhard,

You may have already learned the outcome of our discussions in Berlin from Magnes before receiving this letter. My mother suffered a stroke right after his visit here (Dora and Stefan had just left for Pardigon, where we had been last summer). The initial symptoms have receded somewhat, but she still has weakness in her limbs and her speech is still severely impaired. I am now living in Grunewald again (I am subletting my room to Ernst Bloch) and during my first days here I, of course, did not find the peace I needed to do any writing.

Our conversation lasted approximately half an hour. Magnes had a strenuous day of making the rounds and of missed appointments behind him and for a while I was worried whether I would reach him at all. When we finally did get together, he was very friendly and very precise. We arrived at the following: First, Magnes neither wants nor is able to make a commitment on behalf of the university as such, either as a source of funding or as a scientific institute. But he did say that my letters of recommendation were excellent and that he is absolutely counting on the likelihood of getting me a teaching position of some kind if the Institute for the Humanities, whose foundation was laid at the London conference, makes as much progress as expected in the next two years. Second, he promised, on his own and without further ado, to provide me with a stipend to study Hebrew. [. . .]

He appeared to consider it most important that I discuss the matter here with [Leo] Baeck,[1] and promised me he would have him get in touch with me. I am surprised that nothing has happened yet. Should I take the initiative? [. . .] Magnes told me that you hold Baeck in high esteem. [. . .]

So much for that. I hope that my conversation with Magnes does not pose a problem for you. I would, of course, write him myself if I did not know that he now wants to discuss these matters with you. [. . .]

After my return from Weimar, I wrote a very short piece, "Weimar," which I hope you will soon see and, to be sure, somewhere else than in the *Literarische Welt*.[2] And then I turned to the Soviet Goethe with the death-defying attitude of a person spurred on by a fast-approaching deadline. I do not have to explain to you the insoluble antinomy of writing a popular Goethe from the materialistic perspective on a single printed sheet. It is not possible to wait too long before beginning such a project. The threatening copy deadline is, indeed, my only muse. Otherwise, I have once again turned to my favorite book on Goethe, the unspeakable, three-volume study by Alexander Baumgartner, SJ, which I am going through with even more mature returns and more carefully than I did when I wrote the essay on the *Elective Affinities*. Brandes's grotesque *Goethe* is also on my desk and Rowohlt will have to make me a present of Emil Ludwig's. We will not distill a nectar from such fermented juices from hell, but probably a flat bowl of top-notch, middling sacramental wine to scatter before Lenin's mausoleum.

One book has deeply moved me in the past few days: Anja and Georg Mendelssohn's *Der Mensch in der Handschrift*.[3] Having read it, I am about to get back my feeling for different kinds of handwriting, which I lost about ten years ago. This book goes in exactly the same direction I anticipated when looking at handwriting, yet obviously did not discover. Both intuition and reason have never before been advanced further in this field. It contains a confrontation with Klages, which is as brief as it is pertinent.

I hope all is well with you. I have not heard anything from you for a long time. Please write soon. Sincere regards.

Yours, Walter

1. A rabbi in Berlin.

2. It was published in the *Neue Schweizer Rundschau* (October 1928). In *Städtebilder* (Frankfurt am Main, 1963).

3. WB reviewed the book in the *Literarische Welt* (August 3, 1928).

180. To Gerhard Scholem

Berlin
August 1, 1928

Dear Gerhard

My trip to Palestine is a settled matter, as is my intention to strictly observe the course of study prescribed by Your Hierojerusalemitic Excellency. Let me moreover avow that the awestruck undersigned will be able to read the alphabet common to the country before he sets foot on the soil of Eretz Israel. On the other hand, in return for some donations to the authorities, he has in mind to take advantage of the assistance of public scribes at first. According to the reports of travelers, these scribes exist in the Orient and can be found everywhere, especially in the neighborhood of Mea Schearim[1] in Jerusalem. With the help of such a scribe, he plans at the very start to direct a request to Professor Magnes for a partial stipend, whether for one or several months, leaving the amount the undersigned will receive to Magnes's judgment.

So much, dear Gerhard, for the official part of this letter. Now to the pertinent details. First the date of my arrival. It may have to be delayed until mid-December. This will depend first of all on whether I can make up my mind to complete the *Arcades* project before I leave Europe. Second, on whether I get together with a Russian woman friend in Berlin in the fall.[2] Neither question has been decided as yet. The former will be clarified in Paris in a few weeks. That is, I intend to go to France in about ten to twenty days, at first as a tourist spending two weeks in the Limousin—Limoges, Poitiers, etc.—and then I will go to Paris. That is where I will probably learn how to read Hebrew. Please write me an introduction to the chief rabbi that I can use for this purpose. Send it, and all other mail as well, to my Grunewald address.

Since I intend to stay in Jerusalem for at least four months, and probably even longer, the date of my arrival does not of course have the same crucial importance it might have if I were staying only a few weeks. If necessary, I might have to resign myself to arriving while you are in the middle of the semester. The question of all of these dates should be clarified in a few weeks.

Regarding my financial situation, I must point out that I can still count on a small income from the *Literarische Welt,* in addition to the stipends from or via Magnes. But I must also take into consideration the fact that Dora has no fixed income of any kind at the moment and it is still unclear how her material situation will shape up. You probably know that the "Bazar," where she worked for a year, has folded. I do not expect anything from Rowohlt for the time being. Therefore please have Magnes send something on September 1st. When we spoke here, that is the date on which I asked him to begin making payments.

What you said about *One-Way Street* in your penultimate letter to me validated my efforts in a way hardly anyone else has. It coincided with occasional comments that were made in periodicals. I am gradually starting to come more and more frequently upon passages by young French writers who, while pursuing their own trains of thought, betray only fluctuations, aberrations, yet the influence of a magnetic north pole that discombobulates their compass. And I am steering straight for it. The clearer the susceptibility of my contemporaries to these influences becomes to me, in other words the more I become aware of the strict relevance of what I intend to do, the more urgently I hear within myself the warning to hasten its completion. What is truly relevant always arrives in good time. Or rather, the party does not begin until the last guest has arrived. Perhaps this brings us to a historicist arabesque around that wonderful Prussian saying, "The later the evening, the more beautiful the guests." But all of this does not delude me about the fact that I am taking a greater risk with this project than I have ever taken before.

Your news about Saxl and about Hofmannsthal's letter was extremely delightful.[3] I have to wait for Dora's return to enjoy its details and its finesse. She intends to be here in a few days with Stefan. They are returning from Austria, where they were with my in-laws. The desire you expressed to be kept up to date about critical opinion of my books does me honor. Regarding this request, I can do no more now than promise to present myself in Jerusalem with my complete dossier (for I am gathering everything). In anticipation, however, do let me say this: the *Frankfurter Zeitung* is publishing a lengthy review of both books in the literary supplement of July 15, and the *Vossische Zeitung* is publishing an extensive review of *One-Way Street* in its August 1 issue. The former is by Kracauer,[4] the latter by Bloch.

The last-named author will shortly marry for a third time. He is divorced from his second wife, whom you most likely knew, and is now marrying a very young Jewish woman from Lodz.

À pure titre d'information, let me report that Proust is again starting to stir, but probably only to breathe out the weak living remnants of his German incarnation in the narrow passage of a trial. To express it more soberly and more carefully: Schmiede has sold its rights to the work and their manuscripts of the translation to Piper publishing house. He treated us so badly (rudely and shabbily) that we are trying to make him see reason by disputing the transfer of rights. On the one hand, this means that I will not get any money out of it in the foreseeable future. On the other hand, the project has an intense effect on my own writing because it is inherently so immensely absorbing. Given this, my disputing the transfer of rights is an expression of my desire to go back to the project only on terms that are not likely to be met or else my desire not go back to it at all.

There are two books I still want to mention. One, because of the curious fact that I have not been this disgusted in years by anything in print; the other, because it is splendid and I want to recommend it to you. First, Alfred Kleinberg's *Die deutsche Dichtung in ihren sozialen Bedingungen.*[5] It is the first sizable, materialist literary history. The only thing dialectical about the book is that it is located precisely at the point where stupidity begins to turn into baseness. I had to read this repulsive mixture of banal idealism and materialist abstruseness because of my "Goethe." And have recognized once again that this—that is, my article—is something with which no one can help and that it cannot be produced at all other than with felicitous imperturbability. Consequently, I continue to be far from my goal of completing it.

I will speak to you in person about the concluding paragraph of your "Cardozo."[6] A misunderstanding on the part of the uninitiated, in fact syntactically conceivable—but I would never have thought of it myself. It was sufficient for those who are in the know, and just these few concluding lines, of course, could not be aimed at anyone else.

Finally, I know nothing more about the Gutkinds or what is happening in the ritual and devotional branch. A card from them came from Vilnius. I believe I have correctly deduced that they visited Flattau. Ten days later I called them in Grünau and was told that they were in Paris. Under the palm trees I will tell you about a memorable debate between Gutkind and Unger[7] if I have not already done so on the snowy fields of my stationery by then.

Please give my respectful regards to Escha, my future instructor. And sincere regards to you from the dean.

Yours, Walter

1. The quarter in which Scholem lived.
2. Whose appearance on the scene had more to do with the developments of the next two years than was evident in the letters to Jerusalem.
3. To Magnes; Scholem had sent him a copy of the letter.
4. In *Das Ornament der Masse,* pp. 249ff.
5. Berlin, 1927. The second book, which he forgot to name, was apparently by Kommerell.
6. Scholem's essay, mentioned in the letter dated April 23, 1928, whose last lines contained a polemical reference against Oskar Goldberg.
7. Over ritual in the Torah. Erich Unger represented the views of Oskar Goldberg.

181. To Gerhard Scholem

Berlin
October 30, 1928

Dear Gerhard,

I am lying in bed in order to stave off an attack of jaundice before it is too late. Let me list the props for the still-life I pose, at least on the outside: There is a desk pad called *Geschichte und Dogma* by Mirgeler, which finally demands to be glossed. There is a mountain of books erected around the double massif of Julien Green's two books, *Mont-Cinère* and *Adrienne Mesurat,* which would not let me rest until I had saddled myself with a promise to review both of them.[1] Now I am at my wits' end. And finally, in honor of my not being well, there is a true-blue novel, *Joseph sucht die Freiheit,* by Hermann Kesten, who some claim is important.

But I believe I have already called your attention to Green and none of my friends can avoid *Adrienne Mesurat* (whom, of course, I did not discover and who is already famous in Europe). Since we are now on these topics, I hope that my putting a complete halt to all publishing in the last few months has been appreciated on all sides. This would be all the more desirable since I can no longer hold to this decision in spite of all my good intentions. I recently approached the editors of the *Literarische Welt* with some manuscripts just as this gang was busy manufacturing a time bomb intended for me.

I still do not know when and how some of the things I have completed will be published. Nevertheless, I am still counting on the following being published: the Soviet Goethe; "Marseilles" (a very brief series of sketches);[2] a cryptic report from Marseilles that you will receive personally some day; a review of the new edition of Goethe's *Color Theory;*[3] a new theory of the novel that lays claim to your highest approval and a place beside Lukács.[4]

I will absolutely refrain from initiating any sizable projects in the near future. My way is clear to begin Hebrew lessons. I am waiting only for the arrival of my friend because the decision as to where I will be in the next few months lies with her. It will not necessarily be in Berlin. The actual break that Hebrew, of course, must make in my more select projects will now affect my work on the *Arcades.* But, oddly enough, this converges with another circumstance. An all too ostentatious proximity to the surrealist movement might become fatal to the project, as understandable and as well-founded as this proximity might be. In order to extricate it from this situation, I have had to expand the ideas of the project more and more. I have thus had to make it so universal within its most particular and minute framework that it will take possession of the *inheritance* of surrealism in purely temporal terms and, indeed, with all the authority of a philosophical Fortinbras. In other words: I am putting off the project's projected date of completion way into the future, in spite of the danger that the manuscript may experience a pathetic time lag similar to that of the *Trauerspiel* book.[5] I believe that enough of it exists now and in a sufficiently imperfect state for me to be able to accept the great risk that accompanies slowing down the pace of the work while expanding the subject matter. [. . .]

"Weimar" is being sent at the same time as this letter and I am also sending the "Goethe" to you on special loan for an indefinite period of time (with the proviso that, if need be, I might ask you to return the copy). It will probably not see the light of day in either Russia or Germany in the form in which you will be lucky enough to see it. I will make sure that your excellent Goldberg letter[6] is honorably received, by first ceremoniously circulating it. I am specifically thinking of Frankfurt because I may soon be there for some time.

I now think I will be coming in the spring of next year. The climate is basically not a factor. Therefore, let's simply ignore anything having to do with the climate that would militate against that date. But do write me about anything else that would be a factor when you get a chance. There is plenty of time until then.

Regarding Kraus-Kerr[7]—yes, things are pretty lively, *et moi-même j'y suis pour un tout petit peu.* Meanwhile, a new and grotesque twist has been added (the case of the Czernowitz madman—Paul Verlaine–Zech[8])—a monumental one and predicted by your devoted servant, even if I did not estimate the diluvial extent of Kraus's embarrassment. (And, in his honor, let it be said that it is a deserved embarrassment.) For quite a while, a new note on Kraus has been among my additions to *One-Way Street.* It is the counterpart to the "War Memorial"[9] and an attempt to sketch his Jewish physiognomy.

That's all for today. Sincere regards to you and Escha.

Yours, Walter

1. Both reviews appeared in the *Literarische Welt* (November 16, 1928) or the *Internationale Revue* 2 (1928), p. 116.

2. *Neue Schweizer Rundschau* (April 1929). In *Schriften* 2:67–71.

3. In the *Literarische Welt* (November 16, 1928).

4. It is unclear to which work he is referring.

5. "Conceived in 1916, written in 1925."

6. "An einen Leser von Oskar Goldbergs *Wirklichkeit der Hebräer*" (unpublished).

7. The controversy between Karl Kraus and Alfred Kerr that was conducted in *Die Fackel* and the *Berliner Tageblatt.*

8. Kraus had published poems that a doctor in Czernowitz had found in the possession of an inmate of an insane asylum, and had given some of them the highest praise. The true authors soon revealed themselves, not entirely to Kraus's delight. See *Die Fackel,* nos. 781–86 and 800–805.

9. In *One-Way Street.*

182. To Max Rychner

Berlin-Grunewald
January 15, 1929

My most esteemed Mr. Rychner,

Enclosed is the *editio ne varietur* of my small pamphlet "Marseilles."

Your question about Proust embarrasses me. I am embarrassed for Germany, for the circumstances that caused this project to rest in uncaring and ignorant hands from the very beginning (and even if it should now find itself in new hands, there still will be no better minds to accompany them). You are sure to understand that I am speaking of the publishers. The reading public really can't be reproached with anything, for it still has not laid hands on these things. First was the volume translated by Schottlaender, a ridiculous debut. Then the volume Hessel and I translated, in an entirely different and not necessarily skillful way. There are therefore two volumes that, as a translation, evidence neither external nor internal continuity. After that, everything comes to a complete halt. As you may know, a new publisher has recently appeared who is just as incapable as his predecessor of understanding that Proust can succeed in Germany only as a complete oeuvre, and not as individual volumes. Considering that our translation of his work up to and including *Sodom and Gomorrah* has been finished for years, you will understand how very much we sympathize with your displeasure and how grateful we are to you for having established the *Rundschau* as almost the only arena in which Proust is referred to again and again. There is of course no end to what remains to be done. And it is just as much a matter of course that I have already thought of making a contribution to the interpretation of Proust. But I am still too close to the entire project, and it still looms too large. I will wait until I can see details. I will then use them as handholds to climb up on. German Proust scholarship is sure to have a different look to it than its French counterpart. There is so much to Proust that is greater and more important than the "psychologist" who, as far as I can tell, is almost the exclusive topic of conversation in France. If we can be just a bit patient, I am certain that one day you will be just as glad to receive as to publish a comparative study of German and French Proust commentaries, from whatever source.

For today, let me close with my most sincere compliments.

Your devoted,
Walter Benjamin

183. To Alfred Cohn

[February 1929]

Dear Alfred,

I do not want to let even a single day go by without congratulating you immediately on the things you mailed. They still have not been given to the editor, but they will of course be published. I will take responsibility for this as if they were my own. Don't be angry if I tell you that the reviews are even better than I had a right to expect, even considering my most steadfast confidence in your perspicacity and power of expression. I am happy finally to have a fellow exile in the inconsolable banishment that is the *Literarische Welt*.

The review of the Luxemburg biography in particular is a consummate piece of work.

Please accept my apologies for the fact that the promised book by Panferov, *The Association of Have-nots,*[1] has not arrived. I originally put my name down for it and finally received it because my Russian friend is on very friendly terms with Panferov. She has been here for a while and intends to tell me all sorts of things about him that I would like to use to advantage in a review.

Ever since I have known that you are meant to get the parchment book, I have been much more diligent, at least in this regard, and am crisscrossing it with writing.[2] Indeed—to stay on this topic for a moment—I am referring to the sizable notebook with flexible parchment binding you gave me in Mannheim. Using it has produced in me a shameful weakness for this extremely thin, transparent, yet excellent stationery, which I am unfortunately unable to find anyplace around here. Do you know of a source from which I can order it *en gros?*

I intend to see to it that the editor will now send books to you directly and on as regular a basis as possible. I would like to propose to the editors that they publish thirty lines from Flaubert's *Dictionary of Platitudes* [*Dictionnaire des idées reçues*][3] in the second issue devoted to France. I will be writing you about this. If you are interested in the essay on surrealism,[4] the best thing for you to do is to wait until it has been published in its entirety and to read it then. That is to say, the installments could not have been divided anymore absurdly than they were.

That is all for today. Let me close with best wishes for your good health and sincere regards to Grete and the children.

Yours, Walter

P.S. I know nothing about anything by Burschell actually titled "Rubric" in the *Literarische Welt*. Please send me more details. As for the rest, I hope that with time everything will take care of itself.

1. Appeared in 1928. The German translation, *Die Genossenschaft der Habenichtse,* was reviewed by WB in the *Literarische Welt* (March 15, 1929).

2. This book, with a parchment binding, is in Scholem's possession. It was among Alfred Cohn's papers.
3. From *Bouvard et Pécuchet*.
4. In the *Literarische Welt* (February 1, 8, 15, 1929).

184. To Gerhard Scholem

Berlin
February 14, 1929

Dear Gerhard,

I want to begin by confessing that I find your last letter, to which I am now responding by return mail, quite decent—in view of my scandalous behavior, for that is how this behavior must look to you in any case.

Now for an explanation of the conditions that produced it. Among these, the most important are the weeks of conflict resulting from my assurance to you (and to myself) that I would come to Palestine in the spring. And now I am not following through. I am now putting off my arrival for the second time and have to reckon with the danger of your no longer taking me seriously. Of course, two very urgent considerations are currently making themselves felt. Let me begin right away with what is the lesser consideration in your terms, but the greater in mine. This is that the *Arcades* project, which I have attempted to circumvent with a hundred tricks (to which the enclosed attests), will no longer allow itself to be pushed aside. I still do not know whether this points to a direct and immediate completion, and I do not even believe it does. But I must firmly hold on to what is now taking shape within me if this entire enterprise is not to end in failure.

There is therefore no other course but for me to begin immediately with the study of Hebrew in Berlin, as pure language learning, and to accomplish both tasks at the same time; namely, the most intensive language study and the most intensive writing. I am fully aware of the many reservations that stand in the way of this. But each of my two plans on its own is already so inherently fraught with unforeseeable risk that carrying them out concurrently again embodies my understanding of the crisis. Please let me know by return mail to whom I should turn for Hebrew instruction in Berlin. I know that you have already done this once before, but I am unable to locate the letter.

The external reason is my mother's severe illness—she had a stroke three months ago, and for a few days now her condition has taken an ominous turn for the worse. Since she might die, I have every reason not to be too far away and not to be gone for too long.

My future plans include a trip to Palestine in the fall, if at all possible with you, when you return there from Europe. Between now and then, I plan to spend several weeks in Paris. Otherwise, absolutely no trips are planned.

Now to your work. I read "Entstehung der Kabbala"[1] with the greatest interest (alas, if I could only also say, "with profit," but God knows, I do not yet have the right to make this claim). What you have accomplished is to establish the concept of chaos out of which your paper simultaneously arises. And then I hope to have been of some use regarding your extraordinary letter about Goldberg. Encouraged by the great success I had reading it to Hessel, I passed it on to someone you are sure to know, Dr. [Leo] Strauss[2] of the Jewish Academy, to be copied and further distributed *in partibus infidelium*. I won't deny that he awakens my trust and I find him sympathetic. I will soon intercept him once again at the state library, at which time I hope to get his reports from the theater of war. By the way, the Goldberg people have channeled their activity into an orderly groove and advertise themselves weekly on kiosks as a "philosophical group," inviting the public to their Tuesday events.

I have some further bibliographical information to pass on about my writings, namely that a "Weimar" essay has appeared in the *Neue Schweizer Rundschau*. It most charmingly presents the side of my Janus face that is turned away from the Soviet state. But I probably already sent it to you. If not, please ask me for it. The face will show itself in its entirety, if only *en miniature,* after the appearance of "Marseilles," which I would like to see published in the same outlet for the sake of symmetry. This may well happen. It will become fairly clear to you what other things have recently drawn my attention when you read "Surrealismus," an opaque screen placed before the *Arcades* work. Among the articles I am working on is one with which I hope to cause some offense: "Tiefstand der literarischen Kritik in Deutschland" [The nadir of literary criticism in Germany]. Furthermore, the undersigned has translated a long novella by Jouhandeau, *Le marié du village*. Its fate is still unknown.[3] *En demeurant,* he believes to have already called your attention to this author, to whom visions appear in the oppressive atmosphere of small French sacristies before which the shrewdest saints from next door would take to their heels. You will find further trivial pieces—sad to say—in a second issue devoted to France.

What does the *Jüdische Rundschau* want to know about me? And why are you keeping yourself out of it? But I know the answer very well, and may God bless you for it.

[. . .]

With the greatest humility, I would like to ask you for your observations on [Karl] Kraus and Halakah. I somehow think I have not seen them. I do not consciously remember having heard anything from you about them. He betrays such a clumsy hand in his Berlin maneuvers, starting with the large *Fackel* issue directed against Kerr, that it is unlikely anything will come of his plan to move here.

I have now written extensively, if not necessarily to your delight, and I will continue to do so. Please answer as soon as you can, no matter how briefly. Sincere regards to you and Escha.

Yours, Walter

[. . .]

1. In *Korrespondenzblatt des Vereins zur Begründung einer Akademie für die Wissenschaft des Judentums* (Berlin, 1928), pp. 5–23.

2. 1899–1973. Later professor of political science at the University of Chicago.

3. Appeared in 1931 under the title "Der Dorfbräutigam" [The village bridegroom] in the *Europäische Revue* 7:105–31.

185. To Gerhard Scholem

March 15, 1929

Dear Gerhard,

I was delighted to hear that you will probably not come to Europe. This may make it possible for me to begin my trip to Palestine even before fall.

I spoke to Buber yesterday. I explained the situation to him in detail and learned from him that Dr. Magnes is not here at the moment but is expected back in a few days. I will turn to him. Weltsch[1] has already left for Palestine. Buber told me that he recommended me as someone to give lectures at the School for Jewish Youth. For the time being, however, I more easily see myself sitting at one of its desks than standing at the rostrum.

Optime, amice you ask about what might lie hidden behind my essay on surrealism. (I believe I sent it to you in its entirety. Please let me know if you have received it.) This work is, in fact, a screen placed in front of the *Paris Arcades*—and I have many a reason to keep secret what goes on behind it. But I will nonetheless reveal this much just for you: the issue here is precisely what you once touched on after reading *One-Way Street:* to attain the most extreme concreteness for an era, as it occasionally manifested itself in children's games, a building, or a real-life situation. A perilous, breathtaking enterprise, repeatedly put off over the course of the winter, not without reason—also because of the terrible competition with Hebrew—thus sometimes paralyzing me, and as I have discovered, it was just as impossible to postpone as it is to complete at this time.

I will consequently a tempo take up Hebrew and at the same time make enough progress on the *Arcades* project that I can again put it on a back burner in Palestine without any harm coming to it. The best thing would be for it to come to a sudden conclusion. But I am unable to count on that. I will write to Magnes as soon as I have started my lessons.

I have produced a pack of reviews for the next French issue of the *Literarische Welt* and am currently hatching some arabesques on Proust.[2] The surrealism piece has earned me a delightful, delighted, even enthusiastic, letter from Wolfskehl, as well as one or two friendly notices. I also hope soon to be able to send you a piece called "Marseilles" and something else called "Kurze Schatten" [Short shadows].[3] But let me know as soon as possible which of all these or of my other things you consider part of my "experimental demonology."

[Leo] Strauss, whom I mentioned previously, has disappeared from sight. But I will send out a warrant for his arrest since he took with him an extensive bibliography on the nature of the fairy tale. This may advance the cause of your Goldberg letter, which is also still in his possession. By the way, the Goldberg circle is establishing a regular Tuesday activity in Nollendorfplatz. Lecture evenings: I only enjoy them as they appear on posters and for me they are only a photomontage of serious *tsores* on wretched *ponems*.[4]

I in fact find the haste of the Jewish community in Berlin regrettable.[5] *Que faire?* The starting line has now been drawn. You must keep your lane in view. You will continue to get a running account of what is happening.

All the best.
Yours, Walter

What you wrote about Parliament and the Arab question[6] struck me as illuminating and was probably much needed. Do continue to make your presence felt by sending me such things. First, I would like to urgently request your note on the origin of Kraus's language in mosaic style—the Halakah dispute.

1. Robert Weltsch, editor-in-chief of the *Jüdische Rundschau.*

2. Appeared in the *Literarische Welt* between June 21 and July 5, 1929. In *Schriften* 2:132–47.

3. *Neue Schweizer Rundschau* (November 1929). In *Schriften* 2:13–22.

4. Yiddish for "serious worries on ugly faces," meaning that genuine problems are being addressed by dishonest people.

5. This is no longer comprehensible.

6. In an essay in the *Jüdische Rundschau* (February 8, 1929).

186. To Gerhard Scholem

[June 6, 1929]

Dear Gerhard,

I am answering your letter by return mail.

My letter to Magnes, of which I am enclosing a copy for your information, will be sent tomorrow as soon as it has been typed.

I unfortunately am in no position at all to counter your reproaches; they are absolutely justified and I am up against a truly pathological inclination to procrastinate in this matter. I have unfortunately occasionally experienced this inclination with regard to other matters. To be sure, it does seem that you misinterpreted the brevity of my last letter. It resulted from my haste to let you know that this business had *finally* gotten started.[1] And this, of course, is all the more significant, the more complicated my inhibitions were. (By the way, you have only an incomplete picture of their nature and scope and, insofar as they are of a purely personal nature, I must wait to fill you in on the rest until I can do so in person.)

My coming in the fall depends strictly on my material circumstances. On nothing else, given good health. On the contrary, you may rest assured that now that I have begun, I will absolutely go on with Hebrew, here or over there, quite independently of when I leave for Palestine.

Subject to the reservations incumbent on anyone with very limited experience, I must, however, conclude that I am in the mood to learn and that, even if Hebrew is not easy, it also is not as fantastically hard to learn as I had feared. Within certain limits, I am even having fun doing it. I believe that Mayer's[2] method is very good: a lot of written work and translation *into* Hebrew.

As I said, I have daily lessons and I have my grammar book with me at all times. For the time being, we are still confining ourselves to it. But Mayer soon plans to move on to reading. [. . .] You must admit that, although I have owed you news about these matters for a long time, it is now as complete as is currently possible. Let me turn to something else. [. . .] I am working on "Die singende Blume oder die Geheimnisse des Jugendstils" [The singing flower, or the secrets of *Jugendstil*] for the *Frankfurter Zeitung*.

I have made some noteworthy acquaintances. To name one, a close acquaintance with Brecht (about whom and about which there is much to be said). To name two, an acquaintance with Polgar, who is part of Hessel's intimate circle. Hessel's *Spazieren in Berlin* has appeared.[3] I will see to it that he sends it to you.—Schoen has become the artistic director of Frankfurt broadcasting and an important man.

I will stay in Berlin at least until August 1st, perhaps somewhat longer.

My original plan is then to go to Paris for a few weeks, and from there to Palestine via Marseilles.

Please keep me informed about your decisions. Give Agnon all the best; I will write him. I was delighted to hear from him.

Let's talk about the Baader again in the fall. I will try to hang onto it until then.[4]

I am working an awful lot. You will regularly receive things from me from now on, as soon as they appear in print in the *Literarische Welt*. With this letter, but primarily with my previous ones, I hope to have cleared the air of our correspondence, and promise a continuing and constant east wind.

beracha gam le[5]—Escha.

Yours, Walter

1. Hebrew lessons.
2. WB's teacher, Max Mayer (born 1887); went to Palestine in 1932, lived in Haifa.
3. Reviewed by WB in the *Literarische Welt* (October 4, 1929).
4. A reference to WB's copy of the works of Franz von Baader, which Scholem wanted to acquire for the university library in Jerusalem.
5. Written in Hebrew letters. ("Regards also to . . . "). He discontinued his lessons in July and this was essentially the end of his study of Hebrew.

187. To Max Rychner

Berlin
June 7, 1929

My most esteemed Mr. Rychner,

I should probably have responded to your kind words in April with a brief "agreed." At least I assume this from the fact that I have not yet received any proofs. However, I certainly do—agree. And it is precisely in the context of these notes that I do not place any critical value on "Schönes Entsetzen" [Delightful terror][1]—as dear as it is to me because of the experience from which it derives. So that, however, we do not imprudently invoke the nine Muses for these shadows, I am now sending you a new one to fill the place that has become vacant, and we will keep it at ten.

You would certainly have heard from me sooner if I had not entered into a new round of activity that has claimed all my time and energy on account of my study of Hebrew. I have to find time for my other projects whenever I can snatch a few moments. I will be in Berlin at least until the beginning of August. But since you are unable to hold out any hope that you will appear on that particular soil, you should know that I will be in Paris for a short time after that.

Kind regards, and special thanks for the C. F. Meyer you had sent to me and which has come to mean a lot to me.

Yours, Walter Benjamin

1. A piece in "Kurze Schatten."

188. To Hugo von Hofmannsthal

Berlin-Grunewald
June 26, 1929

My dear and most esteemed Mr. von Hofmannsthal,

Perhaps this letter will reach you at the same time as the cordial greeting I asked Mrs. Wiesenthal to extend. The chasm of my silence would be better bridged in that way than by the various things you will find enclosed here.

I have been saving these slight pieces for you. I was always happy when I was able to put aside something of which I could say that you might actually read it at some propitious moment. My Proust essay is intended to serve as a recommendation for all the other things. I hope I have good cause to assume that it will give you some idea of what absorbed my attention years ago in Paris, and in which you were also interested. It is for this reason that I waited until it was published before letting you see it. "Surrealismus" is a companion piece to this essay, and contains some of the prolegomena to the *Arcades* project we once discussed at my place. "Weimar" is a by-product of my "Goethe" for the *Soviet Encyclopedia.* I do not know whether it will ever appear. The only sure thing is that it can get into the encyclopedia only if it has been distorted beyond recognition. I was in Weimar a year ago. The impression the city made on me benefited some passages of the article for whose sake I went there in the first place. I tried, however, to capture its essence on these two pages without the encumbrance of a descriptive context. "Marseilles"[1] is a companion piece to all of the aforementioned. It is probably weak, but dear to me for the least compelling of all reasons, which is that I had to do battle with this city as with no other. You could argue that it is harder to wrest a single sentence from it than it is to get a whole book out of Rome.

For the last two months, I have finally been putting my plan into practice: I am learning Hebrew. I was unable to make this crucial turning point in my work an equally crucial and marked turning point in the external circumstances of my life, as you so convincingly advised me to do in our first conversation on the topic. I was unable to leave Berlin. Yet I have found a really excellent teacher here, an older man with an admirable understanding for my situation yet with the necessary authority to force me to assimilate vocabulary and linguistic forms. On the whole, the only difficulty for me in my current situation is the constant switching between language learning and literary activity. I could imagine a series of the most beautiful days spent doing nothing but grammar. All the more so since at the moment I am unable to return to the *Arcades* project I mentioned. In the months since I last saw you, however, it has grown a lot in terms of material and its foundation, and I can leave it alone for a few months without endangering it.

It seems I will be leaving in September to spend a few months in Palestine. I will wind up things in Berlin on August 1st, when I will unfortunately also give up the nice room in which I was able to receive you. The first thing I will do is go to Paris.

My dear Mr. von Hofmannsthal, please consider this letter not only an accounting, but also an expression of my desire to remain alive in your memory.

Sincere regards from your devoted,
Walter Benjamin

P.S. "Weimar" and "Marseilles" are not enclosed. I asked Rychner several months ago to send them to you directly.

The publication of Proust III has been delayed for a long time, and thus the mailing of these lines as well. Now I can add some more specific information. I am leaving from Marseilles for Jaffa, via Constantinople and Beirut, on September 17. I want to be in Jerusalem by the beginning of October, where I will devote three winter months exclusively to the continuation of my study of Hebrew. It makes such great demands on me even now that I am unable to consider taking on a big project, and it is taking me longer than usual to complete the small ones. Nonetheless, in a few more weeks I hope to be able to send you a very brief study of *Jugendstil* that is supposed to appear in the *Frankfurter Zeitung*. After that, I will work on an essay on the question, "Why the art of storytelling is coming to an end"—i.e. the art of oral narrative.

Again, my most sincere and devoted regards.

W.B.

1. *Neue Schweizer Rundschau* (April 1929). In *Schriften* 2:67–71.

189. To Gerhard Scholem

Volterra
July 27, 1929

Say what you like: all in all, my letters are not that infrequent, and rarely brief. And what I took the liberty to say to you about the state of my European correspondence should only have shown the virtues of my international correspondence to better advantage. One of these virtues is how tirelessly I attempt to present you with rare and changing dates. At least in this sense, even the letter now before you may demand your attention. For it comes from a center of Etruscan culture, let us say from its limbo, to the extent that I have just atoned for thirty-seven years of being ignorant of these things with a three-hour visit to a museum. From Volterra. Unknown, and not without reason; even praised in song by D'Annunzio without suffering any damage; extremely grand, situated in the middle of a kind of snowless African Engadine—the huge wastelands and bald mountains of its environs are that clear.

Straight up above me, the weather vane of the old, fortresslike *munizipio* moves about like a roofer.

This is how I wound up here. [Wilhelm] Speyer invited me to drive to Italy with him. He is staying with friends in Forte dei Marmi. We are planning to drive back together the day after tomorrow. I accepted his offer. It was made three days after Dr. Mayer had left for the spa at Bad Eibing to take the cure. We arranged that I would regularly send him my written work. I have begun to do this, but long-distance instruction continues to be somewhat precarious. In short, I was in San Gimignano for a week and came here today. Tomorrow I am going to Sienna. Time will be rather tight there. But Speyer's arrangements are flexible. [. . .]

I will not write you anything about San Gimignano. I also believe that this will not be the first time you have heard the name. I may write something about it later.[1] Under the worst circumstances, you will have to make do with pictures of Derain; under the best circumstances, you would have a look at the place personally and would be the only person from Palestine there, just as surely as I am the only German.

Now for my upcoming arrangements. I have been given to understand that I may be invited to spend time in Pontigny from mid-August to the beginning of September. An invitation to the so-called second decade; that is, the annual gathering of the most famous French authors, begun by Gide, which attracts most of the great novelists and poets. Unfortunately, there are some purely technical difficulties. [. . .] My plans have become even more doubtful on account of the legal proceedings[2] and because of my mother's health. We fear the worst for her. *Sauf imprévu,* however, I would like to embark in Marseilles in September, on the Lamartine, and arrive in Jaffa on October 3d. I would therefore go to France very soon after my imminent return, and not return to Berlin before my departure.

Hofmannsthal's death saddened me. I am not sure whether before his death he received my package containing a sizable selection of my writings. It had been sent two weeks before the catastrophe, but it was the custom in Rodaun to dole out the mail to Hofmannsthal based on his condition. The insolence of the German obituaries was repulsive.

Please write and let me know what you are working on. In San Gimignano my hands were flayed by the thorns of a rose bush in George's garden that was in surprisingly beautiful, partial bloom. I am referring to the book, *Der Dichter als Führer in der deutschen Klassik.* The author's name is Kommerell and the title of my review is "Wider ein Meisterwerk" [Against a masterpiece].[3]

I will now get on the bus and by the time I am again in Berlin you may already have received these most sincere regards to you and Escha.

Yours, Walter

1. In the *Frankfurter Zeitung* (August 23, 1929). In *Schriften* 2:83ff.
2. WB's divorce.
3. In *Schriften* 2:307–14.

190. To Gerhard Scholem

Berlin-Grunewald
23 Delbrück St.
August 4, 1929

Dear Gerhard,

At the very moment when, engulfed by clouds of dust and surrounded by mountains of crates, I am busy vacating my residence of ten or twenty years and leaving this apartment, I come across the manuscript of the *Trauerspiel* book. It is not pretty to look at,[1] and perhaps not even quite complete. But the book has its mistakes too, and it is in this regard that they belong together. And since with these words the manuscript clears its throat on your threshold and shakes off the collected dust of years, I hope you will accept it kindly. I will write more as soon as I have survived these days and have an overview of my plans for the next few months, or more specifically my trip to Palestine. Mail sent to Grunewald will be forwarded to me.

All the best.
Yours, Walter

1. The manuscript is in microscopic handwriting, with many things crossed out.

191. To Gerhard Scholem

Berlin
15 Friedrich Wilhelm St.
c/o Hessel
September 18, 1929

Dear Gerhard,

Yesterday I sent you a radiogram meant to serve as an additional team of one hundred horses pulling this letter. It fixes my arrival for November 4th. I can now candidly state that events there[1] played no role in this month-long delay. This has to do with my profound mistrust of what I read in the paper. But your letter forces me to admit that, in another sense, my mistrust was unfortunately misplaced this time. No, the real reason for the delay was the court date I had already mentioned, and beyond that a project with Speyer—Wilhelm Speyer, the novelist and dramatist—that might be of some financial importance for me. I will not voluntarily stray from this new date. My mother's condition is also somewhat improved.

I do not know whether I already wrote you that a friend, Mrs. Lacis, has been in Germany for approximately one year. She was just about to return home to Moscow when, the day before yesterday, she was again stricken by an acute attack of encephalitis. At least, that is what I think it is. Yesterday, with her condition barely allowing for it, I put her on the train to Frankfurt where [Kurt] Goldstein, who knows her and has treated her in the past, is waiting for her. I too will soon go to Frankfurt, if possible before my trip to Marseilles where I embark. In the past few weeks I have lectured over Frankfurt radio on three or even four occasions. Of all of these lectures, the longer one on Julien Green is probably the only one that is important and it will be among the papers I bring along to show you, if it has not been published before then.[2]

I have recently done an extraordinary amount of work, just not any Hebrew. Without a teacher I am unable to force myself to work on Hebrew, given the things I am doing, which are both intrinsically and extrinsically pressing. After Dr. Mayer's departure, it did not seem worth finding a new teacher for four weeks. I have initially decided to stay in Palestine for three months, during which time I basically want to do nothing but learn grammar.

Please write me whether you still want to buy the Baader. I will send it immediately if you do. You can wait to pay me until I arrive.

I will send you two of my short pieces at the same time as this letter or soon thereafter. I did not write anything about Hofmannsthal and am unable to; I will tell you why in person. I recently wrote a new "Hebel," my third, for the *Frankfurter Zeitung*.[3] Under the title of "Die Wiederkehr des Flaneurs," [The return of the flaneur], I published a short piece made up of associations from the *Arcades,* which was occasioned by a review of Hessel's Berlin book. I have written a hostile essay on Robert Walser[4] and a novella. I am now engaged in the final editing of the long review I was working on in San Gimignano. It deals with the most astonishing publication to have come out of the George circle in the past few years: Kommerell's book, *Der Dichter als Führer in der deutschen Klassik.*

Meanwhile the "season" has opened to howling and the chattering of teeth. There was an indescribable, eastern Jewish play by Mehring, produced by the ill-advised Piscator with a great deal of bravura; this play is actually as abysmally bad as I made his chansons out to be in a review I wrote for the *Frankfurter Zeitung*[5] and probably sent you. Not much honor has been garnered by Brecht's new play either and whatever else there was to see has not yielded any complimentary tickets.

I picked up the *Jüdische Rundschau* for the first time during the days of violence. It seemed to me that there was a lot of terribly timid and officious maneuvering going on, but I was perhaps too naïve to be able to read the paper with proper understanding. The last and latest report in the Berlin papers was in the *Tageblatt* and seemed more disturbing. Your letter was of course extremely instructive. I imagine that anyone on the side of reason is in the minority, even among Jews, and so your position may be difficult.

I will close with a list of my current reading. What I am doing is, in Marxist terms, partially "reflected" in it: Krupskaya's *Memories of Lenin;* Cocteau's *Holy Terrors* [*Enfants terribles*] (very much from the neighborhood of the *Arcades*); Goncharov's *Oblomov.*

Please note that this time I was very quick to respond and reward me for this.

Yours, Walter

1. The severe unrest in Palestine in August 1929.
2. Appeared in the *Neue Schweizer Rundschau* (April 1930). In *Schriften* 2:152–58.
3. In the literary supplement (October 6, 1929).
4. Appeared in *Tagebuch* (1929), pp. 1609ff. In *Schriften* 2:148–51.
5. June 23, 1929.

192. To Max Rychner

Berlin
November 21, 1929

My esteemed Mr. Rychner,

Let me first of all thank you for your kind words about my Hebel essay. I am so terribly indebted to my years in Switzerland for my understanding of the Allemanic character that I could perhaps dare to try and repay it once by attempting to fumigate dry wraiths like Ermatinger and his ilk with sulfur. I was especially pleased that you found Ermatinger to be so clearly targeted. This man's nature became apparent to me years ago as a result of an insignificant experience associated with my studies. It was when I was working on my "Keller"—to be precise, first in Berlin, and then in Paris. Eager to familiarize myself with the latest research, I worked with Ermatinger's edition of Keller's life and letters while in Berlin, and only became acquainted with the Bechthold edition in Paris, where the other one was not available. Then everything that had previously remained unclear and hazy suddenly became clear to me—I do not know myself what organizational elements, footnotes, or aura in the Ermatinger book might have caused this.

Have you read the second of the poems by Gertrud Kolmar in the last *Inselalmanach*?[1] I first came across it there and it really impressed me.

Please have a look at what I have enclosed. This manuscript[2] is the reason why the completion of my essay on "the novel and the short story" has been delayed and may continue to be delayed for a while. I would be truly surprised if you were not familiar with the phenomenon of Julien Green and if you had not considered him important for quite some time. I would therefore be delighted to see my attempt to describe this phenomenon in all its profundity find a home with you.

Cela dit, might I perhaps tell you that another outlet (one I find much less appealing than yours) is again interested in this manuscript. This is the reason that—with considerable reluctance—I ask you to let me know your decision as soon as possible.

I am eagerly awaiting the publication of Schaeder's Hofmannsthal book.

That is all for today.

Sincerely yours, Walter Benjamin

1. Kolmar was WB's cousin (on his mother's side).
2. "Julien Green."

193. To Gerhard Scholem

Paris
January 20, 1930

Dear Gerhard,

You will probably think me crazy, but I find it immensely difficult to end my silence and write you about my projects. I find it so difficult that I may never manage it without resorting to French which for me is a pretext for writing this letter.

I cannot delude myself any longer that the question I have been putting off for so long threatens to turn into one of my life's most serious failures. Let me begin by saying that I will not be able to think about my trip to Palestine at all until my divorce becomes final. It does not look like this will happen very soon. You will understand that this subject is so painful to me that I do not want to speak about it.

[. . .] I think I must definitively give up my hope of learning Hebrew as long as I am in Germany for two reasons. On the one hand, offers of work and urgent requests for contributions are coming in from all quarters and, on the other hand, my economic situation is too precarious for me to reject all of them.

At the moment I am in the process of looking back on the last two years, namely, the time I was away from Paris, and am coming to a realization of what has been accomplished during those months. There are two main things: first of all, I have already carved out a reputation for myself in Germany, although of modest proportions. The goal I had set for myself has not yet been totally realized, but I am finally getting close. The goal is that I be considered the foremost critic of German literature. The problem is that literary criticism is no longer considered a serious genre in Germany and has not been for more than fifty years. If you want to carve out a reputation in the area of criticism, this ultimately means that you must recreate criticism as a genre. Others have made serious progress in doing this, but especially I. This is the situation. I soon hope to be able to submit my work for publication. Rowohlt is inclined to publish a selection of my essays as a book, something you were kind enough to suggest in one of your last letters to me. I am preparing two new essays for this book, specifically, one about *Jugendstil* and one about the state of criticism and theory.

But what I primarily want to talk about now is my book, *Paris Arcades*. I am truly sorry that a personal conversation is the only possible way to deal with anything having to do with this book—and, to tell you the truth, it is the theater of all my conflicts and all my ideas, which do not at all lend themselves to being expressed in correspondence. Let me therefore limit myself to noting that I intend to pursue the project on a different level than I had previously planned. Up till now, I have been held back, on the one hand, by the problem of documentation and, on the other hand, by that of metaphysics. I now see that I will at least need to study some aspects of Hegel and some parts of Marx's *Capital* to get anywhere and to provide a solid scaffolding for my work. It now seems a certainty that, for this book as well as for the *Trauerspiel* book, an introduction that discusses epistemology is necessary—especially for this book, a discussion of the theory of historical knowledge. This is where I will find

Heidegger, and I expect sparks will fly from the shock of the confrontation between our two very different ways of looking at history.

My actual stay in Paris will be rather brief, that is, I will return to Berlin at the beginning of February. The day after tomorrow, I will go to Frankfurt for two days. I have been renewing contact with a few more or less important people here. I have also met many other people I did not know previously. What worries me is that it does not look like I will meet Gide this time. Among those I did meet, the most interesting are Emmanuel Berl and Marcel Jouhandeau. I believe I have already spoken to you about the latter. He writes studies of Catholic daily life in the French provinces; they are all imbued with a formidable mysticism and "reek a bit of a fagot," as someone said to me the other day. In these tableaux, in which the same characters always recur, there is in fact a kind of intermingling of piety and vice that is close to Satanism. I recommend the following books most highly: *Les Pincengrain, Prudence Hautechaume, Opales, Astaroth.* Berl made his debut in surrealism, and he is not entirely cut off from it. He wrote novels with which I am not familiar and which are probably not very important. The distinctive thing about him is that he has a quite rare critical acumen, which he exercises above all in a book called *Mort de la pensée bourgeoise.* This book is destined to be the first in a series of pamphlets, the second volume of which, *Mort de la morale bourgeoise,* has begun to appear in the review *Europe.* These writings come astonishingly close to my own point of view. But since he rigorously restricted himself to a "critique," the author seems to have remained unaware of the difficulty that arises as soon as you try to build on this basis. In any case, he is Jewish.

I did, however, see Green again. Have you read *Adrienne Mesurat*? An essay I wrote on Green will appear in one of the next issues of the *Nouvelle revue suisse.* I then intend to submit for publication excerpts from my Paris diary that I diligently kept for the *Literarische Welt.*

I arrived in Paris just in time to be able to follow closely an unsavory quarrel that erupted among the surrealists and whose victim appeared to be one of their main leaders, André Breton. You will find my observations on the entire affair in the *Literarische Welt.*

I end this letter with a feeling of oppression almost equal to the one that weighed on me at the beginning. Let me ask all the more urgently that you respond soon, and give me some idea of what you are currently working on.

When will you be coming to Europe? All the best.

Walter

194. To Gerhard Scholem

Paris
January 25, 1930

Dear Gerhard,

I just returned from a short trip and found your last letter, which had been forwarded from Berlin. As you see, it has restored my ability to use my mother tongue. What I mean by this is that, until this morning when I read your letter, I had never been so aware of the extraordinary thoughtfulness and the great friendship you have shown me in this whole affair for a year or actually more. And you should not interpret this to mean that I was not aware of it earlier.

Having heard that you will say some words on the occasion of [Franz] Rosenzweig's death, I feel doubly secure in the decision I communicated just yesterday, in Frankfurt, to the *Frankfurter Zeitung*. They invited me to write about Rosenzweig's range of ideas, and even offered me particularly favorable financial terms. I decided to turn down the invitation. Yesterday I realized what a huge effort such a project would have cost me. An additional factor is that it lies completely outside my current sphere of interest. I also gave some thought today to what the result would be and how shabby it would have looked next to your speech, which is made of whole cloth. I would of course have liked to have heard it, even without being able to understand it. And isn't there any possibility of a German translation?[1]

I gave two radio lectures in Frankfurt and now, having returned, I can devote myself to somewhat more useful things. The first thing I have in mind is a review of Franz Mehring's literary criticism. Otherwise, I hope very soon to be able to cut down as much as possible on the work I do simply to earn a living, at least the journalistic work. You know what this is in aid of. I am quite pleased that I have already succeeded in somewhat divorcing myself from organizational and technical matters in that I no longer write out most of the things that must be considered as work done simply to earn a living, whether for periodicals or the radio. Instead, I simply dictate things like that. You understand that this way of doing things is morally liberating, in that my hand is gradually being reclaimed as one of the nobler parts of my body.

I have not told you anything yet about my most memorable evening in Paris. It was the one spent in the company of M^{on} Albert. M^{on} Albert is the counterpart of Marcel Proust's Albertine.[2] I had dinner with him. Our conversation was marked by many a memorable moment but nothing that can compete with the first sight of the man I had in the small homosexual bathhouse in the rue St. Lazare, which M^{on} Albert runs from a podium. On the podium is a table covered with bathing paraphernalia, *pochettes-surprises,* and admission tickets. Even though I began to keep a handwritten Parisian diary three weeks ago, the material for it has since proliferated to such an extent that I will probably be able to continue it only with the help of my secretary. I will have a carbon copy made of the evening with M^{on} Albert, exclusively for you and as a gift without which I—without the promise of which I—would not want to send this letter off to you.[3]

That is all for now. Are you interested in hearing that Ernst Bloch is in Vienna visiting Lukács and is trying to renew old, seemingly rather fruitless debates with him under very different circumstances?

All the best.
Yours, Walter

1. Scholem's eulogy was published only in Hebrew, but the ideas it contains were in part incorporated in another essay (*Judaica,* pp. 226–34).

2. It is more likely that he may have served as the model for Jupien in Proust's novel.

3. This report, "Abend mit Monsieur Albert" [An evening with Monsieur Albert], has been preserved. An abridged version appeared in the *Literarische Welt,* nos. 16–17 (April 1930). The visit took place on January 21, 1930.

195. Gerhard Scholem to Walter Benjamin

Jerusalem
February 20, 1930

[. . .] It is perhaps just as well that we clarify our respective positions since in your last few letters, but especially the first of them, you broached the serious issue between us in a way I found quite unmistakable and which awakened a very rare feeling of anxiety in me. Three years ago you thought, and I agreed, that you had gotten to the point where a productive confrontation with Judaism seemed the only way of making real progress in your work. On the basis of this insight, about which we both seemed certain, I did what I did with a view to finding the means for you to realize your intentions.[1] Three years having elapsed since that time, the question that now seems to answer itself on the basis of your position and your work is this: haven't you long since outgrown the view of yourself that you held in the past and that you described and represented to Magnes? Indeed, you prove *in actu* that, on the one hand, the complex of problems with which you have become engaged and, on the other hand, the position that you have attained as a leading literary critic or that I am in any case certain you can attain, will continue to be productive and fulfill you in a thoroughly positive way, contrary to your own interpretation, and entirely outside the Jewish world we were thinking of at that time. It would be well to be clear about this, if only so that I will not be put in an awkward position here in Jerusalem. For I cannot easily assert year after year that you are on the verge of something you will never actually do, which seems ever more likely to me. Since, however, as we both know all too well from long experience, it is your internal inhibitions that first elicit your external reservations, the question for us is, aren't the inhibitions that have now determined your position on these matters for about twelve years, even if in a different spiritual or physical form in each epoch of your life, obviously so fundamental that it would be better to confront the reality of your existence outside that world head on (for me still an oppressive, but at least an unambiguous, reality) instead of indulging in false illusions about coming to terms with Judaism? This is something that can never really happen, but we have taken it to be our common cause for almost fifteen-years now. It is evident from the questions now absorbing you that you will come upon yet others. It is also evident that the opinion you expressed three years ago has been revealed to be exaggerated and wrong; namely, that if you did not take the path that leads to Hebrew, the only one that would remain conceivable to you as sufficiently clean would be one moving away from literature and to pure party politics. Finally, it is evident that it is impossible to conceive of the *inevitability* of taking the path of Hebrew, specifically from the perspective of your presumptive position as the only genuine critic of German literature. With these considerations in mind, I would like to have you not only come to terms with yourself—I have the impression, one you will hardly contradict, that you do not enjoy doing this as far as this issue is concerned, above all not with passion—but also explain your position to me with the same candor I have shown you. I believe I have a right to expect more candor from you with regard to this question than any other, so that whatever happens we will not deceive each other with a personal apocalypse about the divergencies of our autobiographies. I am surely someone who will be able to accept with composure and, perhaps, with some comprehension if you reveal that you can no longer, and will no longer, in this life consider a true confrontation with Judaism that lies outside the medium of our friendship. I sometimes believe that, when speaking about these matters, you do so with more consideration for me than for yourself—as paradoxical as that may sound, I truly believe it to be an accurate description of your attitude in some instances and I would not feel the way I do about you if I did not suffer on account of this situation. I occasionally say, Walter does not dare to give a clear accounting of his situation out of friendship for me. He avoids "getting to the heart of the issue, comprehending it"[2]—but I assure that you this can and should not be a valid reason, in either a moral or symbolic sense. It is much more important for me to know where you really are than where you perhaps hope to venture at some future time since, of course, given how your life is constituted, it is certain that you, more than any other person, will always arrive someplace other than where you intended. If I should be totally mistaken in thinking this—I, of course, do not believe this to be the case—well then, all the better that I have managed to put it into words. For your biography has given sufficient grounds for such mistakes in the last ten years in any case, even among your friends. We must therefore hope all the more that the crisis in the external circumstances of your life,[3] which I must deduce from hints in your letters without of course having the power to intervene, will at least clarify for you not only where you belong but where you are.

I have written this in the spirit of friendship and from the bottom of my heart.

Yours, Gerhard

1. Scholem had secured a scholarship for WB that was meant to make it possible for him to devote himself exclusively to the study of Hebrew for one year.
2. Quoted from one of WB's essays.
3. WB's divorce.

196. To Gerhard Scholem

Berlin
9 Meineke St.
April 25, 1930

Dear Gerhard,

I am once again rereading the last page of the letter you wrote on February 20. And I must once again put off giving a definitive answer to the question it asks. Not, to be sure, for much longer. And not without telling you that in one respect—in the respect that concerns our relationship—it is insoluble in its alternative form. I have come to know living Judaism in absolutely no form other than you. The question of my relationship to Judaism is always the question of how I stand—I do not want to say in relation to you (because my friendship will no longer depend on any decision)—in relation to the forces you have touched in me. But whatever this decision may depend on, it will be made soon—however much, on the one hand, it is embedded in circumstances that seem to be totally alien to it and, on the other hand, in that procrastination that has been stretched to the limit and that is second nature to me when it comes to the most important situations in my life. Having begun to loosen the extremely tangled knot of my existence in one place—Dora and I have since gotten a divorce—this "Gordian knot," as you once justifiably called my relationship to Hebrew, will also have to be unraveled.

Since I was after all unable to construct my entire life on the splendid foundation I laid in my twenty-second year, after seven years of procrastination, I at least had to be sure to start a new life before I was over forty. I am therefore completely immersed in this new beginning, starting with where I live to how I earn my living, forced into a makeshift existence. I have been without a library for almost a year (it's in storage) and I see considerable difficulties ahead of me, of which the legal ones may well turn out to be the least. In any case, I do not intend to take these things into consideration, at least as far as where I decide to go is concerned.

In view of how provisional everything is, let me ask that you kindly think of this letter as preliminary. Everything is coming down to a decision that cannot be put off much longer. If the outcome is positive, this can only mean that I will come to Palestine before the end of the year and initially, of course, for an indefinite period of time.

I have sent you some printed matter. [. . .]

My contract with Rowohlt for a collection of essays has been finalized. I still have a fair number of pieces to write for it and am currently working on a "Karl Kraus"[1] which should turn out to be about as long as the Green essay. Studying all aspects of the literature on Kraus is most interesting. My most recent short piece bears the title of "From the Brecht Commentary" ["Aus dem Brecht-Kommentar"][2] and I hope it will appear in the *Frankfurter Zeitung*. It is the first product of my recent very interesting association with Brecht. I will send it to you as soon as it has appeared. We were planning to annihilate Heidegger here in the summer in the context of a very close-knit critical circle of readers led by Brecht and me. Unfortunately, however, Brecht is not at all well. He will be leaving very soon and I will not do it on my own.

At this point I remember with horror the huge new tomes weighing down my desk. You will have some notion of what I mean if I mention that Watson's *Behaviorism* is on the left, and Klages's *Geist und Leben* on the right.

What about your work?

Whatever happens, for my part I hope that the two last months will have been the last long interruption in our correspondence. I will close with those words, which contain a very carefully packaged request.

All the best.
Yours, Walter

1. Appeared in the literary supplement of the *Frankfurter Zeitung* (March 10, 14, 17, and 18, 1931). In *Schriften* 2:159–95.

2. Appeared in the literary supplement of the *Frankfurter Zeitung* (July 6, 1930).

197. To Gerhard Scholem

Sopot
August 15, 1930

Dear Gerhard,

Yes, your book[1] reached me in Berlin and I thank you for it. You have now occupied the actual fortresses of philology, the footnotes, with your name and from now on you can let your thoughts prosper and be nourished with all assurance in the vineyards and fields of what is printed in capitals.

Will you again produce something in German in the foreseeable future? So that the, so to speak, cold shame I feel when I receive your Hebrew writings will once again be followed by the hot shame I experience upon reading your work.

It is early morning and the sea is roaring outside my window. I have reached the final or penultimate stage of my journey—that is, Sopot. As pleasant as the long journey now behind me was—all the way over the Arctic Circle and into northern Finland—it was too lonely to have fully restored me; I also worked on many things while on board ship. Here, however, I am together with a friend and his wife[2] and am slowly beginning to recover. It seems to me as if for the first time in years. The editors are grumbling because I am not doing anything. But I have to take advantage of the few opportunities I have to be lazy. This does not prevent me from struggling with all kinds of minor things. I produced a cycle, "Nordische See,"[3] which you will, of course, get to see very soon. I translated Jouhandeau while on board ship. And then for the entire trip I devoted myself to the most recent *mythologicis*. You probably already have one in front of you, [Erich] Unger's *Wirklichkeit, Mythos, Erkenntnis*. On the other hand, I do not know if Klages's major work, *Der Geist als Widersacher der Seele,* is already being discussed in Jerusalem. As for me, I took a rather perfunctory look at the first volume; to study it thoroughly would take many weeks. It is without a doubt a great philosophical work, regardless of the context in which the author may be and remain suspect.[4] It would be quite futile for me to attempt to give you some indication here of what it is about. I also have not yet taken any "position" on what is in the book. I would never have imagined that the kind of clumsy metaphysical dualism that forms the basis of Klages's book could ever be conjoined with really new and wide-ranging conceptions. Since taking up residence here, I have spent time on Unger's book and have now managed to choke down two-thirds of it. I am thoroughly and completely disappointed: I have seldom come across so much clumsiness combined with so much dryness in a philosophical study. It may not, of course, be impossible to make a systematic confrontation with criticism the basis for a conception of the mythical world, but it is such an abstruse procedure that the philosophical concept reaches its goal like a hunger artist who is making an unspeakable effort searching for the Hesperian gardens in order to demonstrate his art there. Stylistically, the book is beneath criticism. After the book has succeeded in discharging the formalities, it is never possible to ignore how eager the author is to begin his magic and thus to make up for lost time as best he can. In comparison with Unger's earlier writings, this book does not seem to contain anything new. But those earlier works were as a rule more concise and original. Having the public in mind, he did not allow those qualities to be demonstrated here. [. . .]

I would like to hear from you soon, especially about the books mentioned above. I would also like to hear whether you have managed to work on any other German things since the repulsive drivel put out by [Friedrich] Wolters.[5] Now that I have mentioned Wolters—naturally, I did not measure up to your heroism in reading him in his entirety—let me say that the only useful thing in it for me—I must admit, from very strange sources—was the remarks about Schuler. I also had ordered a small volume of fragments[6] that I could gaze at in secret. The bulk of his papers is in Klages's hands.

Sincere regards to you and Escha.

Yours, Walter

1. A description of Kabbalah manuscripts in Jerusalem.
2. Fritz and Jula Radt.
3. In the *Frankfurter Zeitung* (September 18, 1930). In *Städtebilder,* pp. 47–54.
4. WB was entirely aware of his anti-Semitism. See letter 150.
5. *Stefan George und die Blätter für die Kunst* (Berlin, 1930).
6. Among Alfred Schuler's papers.

198. To Gerhard Scholem

Berlin
66 Prinzregenten Street
[October 3, 1930]

Dear Gerhard,

A situation report from the silence, just so you will not think it the silence of forgetfulness. It is more likely to be the silence of various preparations and troubles. To be sure, even the latter are being played out before the backdrop of pretty walls bathed in sunshine, such as those that enclose my new apartment, which will unfortunately probably be quite temporary. I believe I have not yet written you from here. It is the first time that life has landed me in a studio. It is, however, both climatically and optically totally free of the cold that formerly made this kind of habitation suspect for me. In addition to every conceivable advantage, above all that of the most profound silence, it has some remarkable architectural neighbors, both inside and out. On the one hand, there is a new synagogue on the street, which I took to be the offspring of the Protestant theological spirit in church architecture until Rosh Hashanah[1] consecrated it; on the other hand, a cousin of mine–a doctor[2]—and his wife, with whom I am on very good terms, are down the hall from me.

[. . .] Many years ago, you were so intimately involved in my projected *Angelus Novus* that you are the only outsider in whom I would like to confide something that, I hope, will not cross your lips prematurely. A new journal is at issue, and indeed the only one to have overcome my firmly rooted conviction that I could never again get involved in anything like it, at least not in the form it assumed in the planning stage. I cleared the way for the plan's acceptance by the publisher Rowohlt by appointing myself the representative of the journal's organizational and substantive features, which I worked out in long conversations with Brecht. Its formal stance will be scholarly, even academic, rather than journalistic, and it will be called *Krisis und Kritik*. I have thus completely won Rowohlt over to the plan; now the large question arises as to whether it will be possible to unite people who have something to say and enlist them on behalf of an organized, and above all supervised, project. Beyond this is the difficulty inherent in working with Brecht. I, of course, assume that I am the one who will be able to deal with that if anyone can. In order to add some spice to these bland allusions, I will enclose for you a page from a new and as yet unpublished book by Brecht,[3] which is meant exclusively for your (and Escha's) information and which I must ask you to send back to me by return mail.

"Karl Kraus" is slowly maturing into a full-term baby. I am sure that you already have the last issue of *Die Fackel* containing his correspondence with the *Literarische Welt*. In it, Haas provides us with the example of a truly German war that is meant as a deterrent. Let me add that, as I write this, Kraus is beginning his reading of selections from Offenbach, which I almost attended. But I will console myself by attending a reading of *Timon* that will be broadcast over the radio in November. I am counting on it for considerable enlightenment about both Kraus and Shakespeare. [. . .]

Your reference to [Max] Picard struck me as curious. I will get his book. Furthermore, he may be the same Picard whose very remarkable editorial recommendations were published a few weeks ago in the literary supplement of the *Frankfurter Allgemeine*. I am currently writing the same kind of thing fairly often for Rowohlt. To be precise, I am making final recommendations on manuscripts recommended to him by his regular reviewers. This must be kept strictly between us; I am primarily writing you about it because that was how I came across a German translation of the autobiographical reminiscences of Shmarya Levin.[4] But only fragments were available to me. If possible, please tell me something about the character and value of this book.

[. . .]

This is a lot of news in brief and deserves to be answered as soon as possible with a situation report from Palestine.

All the best to you and Escha and best wishes for the New Year. May they endure for as many years as the number of days they are late.

Yours, Walter

1. The Jewish new year.
2. Egon Wissing, later in Boston, and his wife, Gert, née Feis.
3. *Versuche* 2 (1930).
4. *Childhood in Exile.*

199. To Gerhard Scholem

Berlin
November 3, 1930

Dear Gerhard,

I was very happy to hear from you. The offprint of your essay on prophecy as self-confrontation arrived with your letter.[1] You can't imagine how I feel watching you deal with Goldberg's work. I read those few pages with true excitement. What really exhilarated me was the level-headed way in which the sources you write about account for the mystical facts or open them up to debate. I have not yet taken the pages in question to the Central European Office for Self-Confrontation,[2] but am planning to do so in the next few days.

In my next parcel, you will receive the announcement and bylaws of a new journal called *Krise und Kritik,* which is to be published bimonthly by Ihering through Rowohlt. My name appears on the title page as coeditor, along with Brecht's and two or three others. [. . .]

I must now tell you that my mother died yesterday after a long and severe illness and my circumstances have thereby arrived at the *stretta,* during which a decision about the future must be reached. [. . .]

I am reading about you and your reader in Tunis. How nice and well done by both author and reader. The only people who ever write me are crazy. I read your observations on the end of the Balfour policy[3] with considerable care. They have intensified my long-standing supposition, which was only strengthened by Escha's reports: namely, the suspicion that you have taken up residence in the only corner of Zionism that is permanently sheltered. This brief but cordial note will be it for today.

Yours, Walter

1. In *Monatsschrift für Geschichte und Wissenschaft des Judentums,* 1930.
2. Ernst Bloch, in whose *Spirit of Utopia* this concept played a role.
3. The English government's efforts to sabotage Zionist politics in Palestine, inaugurated by England in 1917, began officially in 1930.

200. To Bertolt Brecht

Berlin-Wilmersdorf
[end of February 1931]

Dear Mr. Brecht,

You will have already heard from Brentano that I have resigned from the coeditorship of the journal. I would of course have liked to discuss everything with you once more. But after asking [Bernard von] Brentano for the first manuscripts the day before yesterday—Brentano's "Der Generalangriff," Kurella's "Der Kongreß von Charkow," and Plekhanov's "Idealismus und Materialismus"—I informed him of the critical reservations I felt upon reading them. He thought I had to communicate my decision to Rowohlt immediately so as not to give him a pretext to use against the enterprise at a later date.

You will surely remember the conversation we had shortly before my departure in December, during which I discussed with you my intention to withdraw my name as a coeditor. The reasons I gave at that time seemed plausible to you, given my position. But I naturally wanted to wait to see what direction the journal took before taking any further steps. After reading the manuscripts that have been submitted, however, any further delay would have resulted in equivocation. When I compare the stance of these manuscripts with that which arose from the original premises of the journal, the following becomes clear.

The journal was planned as an organ in which experts from the bourgeois camp were to undertake a description of the crisis in science and art. This was meant to demonstrate to the bourgeois intelligentsia that the methods of dialectical materialism are dictated to them by the necessities most characteristic of them—necessities of intellectual production and research, and the necessities of existence. The journal was meant to contribute to the propaganda of dialectical materialism by applying it to questions that the bourgeois intelligentsia is forced to acknowledge as those most particularly characteristic of them. I also told you how obvious to me this tendency is in your works. At the same time, I told you how much your works prove to me that the production of essays that represent something fundamentally new within German literature is hard to reconcile with the demands of journalistic reality. Now these demands have made themselves felt even more. The first issue is supposed to appear on April 15 and not a single one of the three essays submitted can claim to have been written by an expert authority, regardless of how valuable they may be in other respects. The one by Plekhanov was able to make such a claim at one time, but that was twenty-five years ago.

I continue to be entirely willing to work on the journal. I heard from Rowohlt that he considers it important to have me in the first issue; thus I will write something for the first issue. But given the way I work, I would unfortunately need much more time to be able to give the journal the kind of essays I have in mind. As long as I am not in a position to contribute this kind of fundamental essays and as long as they are not forthcoming from others, my coeditorship would amount to signing a proclamation. But I never had anything of the sort in mind.

Kind regards.
Yours, Walter Benjamin

201. To Max Rychner

Berlin-Wilmersdorf
March 7, 1931

Cur hic?[1]—This *hic,* my dear Mr. Rychner, is uncharted terrain; I am not sure that you will see me emerge in the sector you have in mind on account of Brentano's piece. My own sector is rather more opposite Brentano's but, of course, still within the same sphere. I would have to go well beyond the limits of what is possible in written communication were I to attempt to explain to you what led me to use a materialistic approach. And were I to succeed, the real nature of this approach would remain an open question. Nonetheless, I immediately want to bring up one thing for discussion: the strongest imaginable propaganda for a materialistic approach came to me, not in the form of Communist brochures, but in the form of "representative" works that emanated from the bourgeois side over the last twenty years in my field of expertise, literary history and criticism. I have just as little to do with what academics have accomplished here as I do with the monuments erected by a Gundolf or Bertram—and Marxist ways of thinking, with which I became acquainted only much later, were unnecessary for me to demarcate myself early and clearly from the horrid wasteland of this official and unofficial enterprise. It is rather the basic metaphysical tendency of my research that I have to thank for this. My book *The Origin of German Tragic Drama* was the test case for just how far strict adherence to purely academic research methods leads a person away from the contemporary stance of the bourgeois and idealistic scholarly enterprise. This is borne out by the fact that not a single German academician has deigned to review it. This book, of course, was certainly not materialistic, even if it was dialectical. But what I did not know at the time I wrote it, soon thereafter became increasingly clear to me: namely, there is a bridge to the way dialectical materialism looks at things from the perspective of my particular stance on the philosophy of language, however strained and problematical that bridge may be. But there is no bridge to the complacency of bourgeois scholarship.

Cur hic? —Not because I would be an "adherent" of the materialist "worldview"; instead, because I am trying to lead my thinking to those subjects into which truth appears to have been most densely packed at this time. Today those subjects are neither the "eternal ideas" nor "timeless values." At one point in your article you very kindly refer to my Keller essay in a way that does me honor. But you will no doubt agree with me: in this essay too it was precisely my concern to legitimize an understanding of Keller on the basis of understanding the true condition of our contemporary existence. It may be a truly unmaterialistic formulation to say that there is an index for the condition of historical greatness, on the basis of which every genuine perception of historical greatness becomes historicist—not psychological—self-perception on the part of the individual who perceives. But this is an experience that links me more to the clumsy and caddish analyses of a Franz Mehring than to the most profound paraphrases of the realm of ideas emanating today from Heidegger's school.

You must understand that I could not remain silent in the face of your slight challenge, although I am well aware that every attempt at written communication in the inconclusive form of letters must expose just as many weak points as it contains words. This cannot be helped. Perhaps I may also assume that, when you asked me the question to which all of what I have said here is very loosely related, you did not do so without at least having quietly considered some solutions for yourself. Of those, the one most familiar to me would be to see in me not a representative of dialectical materialism as a dogma, but a scholar to whom the *stance* of the materialist seems scientifically and humanely more productive in everything that moves us than does that of the idealist. If I might express it in brief: I have never been able to do research and think in any sense other than, if you will, a theological one, namely, in accord with the Talmudic teaching about the forty-nine levels of meaning in every passage of Torah. That is, in my experience, the most trite Communist platitude possesses more *hierarchies of meaning* than does contemporary bourgeois profundity, which has only one meaning, that of an apologetic.

While asking you for forgiveness for this improvisation—the one advantage it has over silence is that of politeness—I might be permitted to say to you at the same time that you may find more reasoned answers to the question you asked than I *expressis verbis* was able to give to you today between the lines of my essay "Karl Kraus," which should appear soon in the *Frankfurter Zeitung*.

Kind regards.
Yours, Walter Benjamin

1. WB sent a copy of this letter to Scholem with the following preamble: "I wrote this to the publisher of the *Neue Schweizer Rundschau* after seeing his article "Kapitalismus und schöne Literatur"—a review of Brentano's essay with the same title. The article was sent to me with the motto *Dic, cur hic?* Walter."

202. Gerhard Scholem to Walter Benjamin

Jericho
March 30, 1931

Dear Walter,

I am spending a week in Jericho, busy at being idle and similar things, as preparation for next week's scheduled visit of my mother and brother to Jerusalem; tomorrow morning I am taking a short trip to the Dead Sea, where I have never been in all these years. Your copies of the two letters to Brecht and Rychner, which thus take the place of an "original letter," have reached me in my idleness. The letter to Brecht bears out what I have suspected all along, namely, that nothing can come of the journal about which you wrote, although I was not able to say much about it, not knowing the details. On the other hand, I would like to say something about the other letter, which I feel is to some extent also directed to me as coaddressee. I really regret being unfamiliar with Rychner's essay, which may well contain some real insights. But what can be said about your letter presumably does not depend on that—the question *dic cur hic*? is in any case well put. I will ask you to consider my abbreviated observations in the same spirit of benevolence that you were justified in expecting from the reader of that letter.

Since I have become aware of the more or less extensive experiments coming from your pen that look at literary matters in the spirit of dialectical materialism, I have been clearly and surely confirmed in my view that you are engaging in an unusually intent kind of self-deception in this enterprise. Moreover, your admirable essay on Karl Kraus (which I, unfortunately, do not have with me here) most significantly documents this for me. The expectation you expressed, that a reader who is as understanding as Mr. Rychner appears to be would know how to find, in some sense or other, a justification of your sympathies for dialectical materialism "between the lines" of this essay, seems totally deceitful to me. It is much more likely that the exact opposite is the case, by which I mean the following: it seems to me that it would be clear to any impartial reader of your writings that in the last few years you have been trying—forgive me for saying so, but desperately trying—to present your insights, which are in part far-reaching, in phraseology that is conceptually close to Communist phraseology. It also seems clear, however—and to me this is what seems important—that there is a disconcerting alienation and disjuncture between your *true* and *alleged* way of thinking. That is, you do not attain your insights through the strict application of a materialistic method, but entirely independently of it (in the best case) or (in the worst case, as in some of the essays of the last two years) by playing with the ambiguities and interference phenomena of this method. As you yourself quite aptly write Mr. Rychner, your own solid knowledge grows out of, to be brief, the metaphysics of language. This is the most appropriate subject in which you, having achieved undistorted clarity, could be a highly significant figure in the history of critical thought, the legitimate heir of the most productive and most genuine traditions of Hamann and Humboldt. On the other hand, your ostensible attempt to harness these results in a framework in which they suddenly present themselves as the apparent results of materialistic considerations introduces an entirely alien form element from which any intelligent reader can easily distance himself. It also stamps the work from this period as adventurous, ambiguous, and underhanded. You must know that I do not use such a demonstrative expression without the greatest reluctance. But when, for example, I call to mind the simply fantastic and gaping discrepancy that exists between the actual method and the method suggested by the terminology in a magnificent and pivotal essay such as the one on Kraus; and when I consider how everything suddenly starts to limp along *because the insights of the metaphysician into the language of the bourgeois,* let us even say, into the language of capitalism, artificially and in a way that is, all too simply, transparent, *are identified with those of the materialist into the economic dialectic of society,* in such a way that it might seem as if they grew out of each other!—I am so dismayed that I must say to myself that this self-deception is possible only because you desire it, and more: that it can last only as long as it is not put to the materialistic test. The complete certainty I have about what would happen to your writing if it occurred to you to present it *within* the Communist party is quite depressing. I almost believe that you desire this state of suspension and would nonetheless have to welcome every means to end it. It would become unambiguously and explosively clear that your dialectic is not that of the materialist whose method you try to approach, at the very moment you were unmasked by your fellow dialecticians as a typical counterrevolutionary and bourgeois. This moment would be inevitable. As long as you write about the bourgeois for the bourgeois it can be all the same, I might even say totally irrelevant, to the *genuine* materialist as to whether you have the desire to surrender to the illusion of being in agreement with him. On the other hand, in dialectical terms, he should actually have every interest in strengthening you in this illusion, since your dynamite could presumably be, to him as well, recognizably more potent on "that" terrain than his. (Excuse the parallel, but this is, for example, comparable to how he [the materialist—Trans.] encouraged certain psychoanalytical Bolshevists à la Erich Fromm in Germany when he would immediately have sent them to Siberia had they been in Moscow.) He has no use for you in his own camp since the purely abstract identification of your spheres would necessarily be exploded there with the first steps you took toward the center. Since, to a certain extent, you yourself are now interested in a state of your illegitimate relationship that would remain, as it were, *in suspense,* you are all getting along very well; to put this in seemly terms as well, the only question is how long the morality of your insights, one of your most valuable possessions, can remain healthy given such an ambiguous relationship. For it is *not* the case, as you may see it, that you are asking yourself how far you can get experimenting with the stance of the materialist, since you evidently have never in any way assumed this stance in your creative method. As an old theologian, I believe I may say that you are also entirely incapable of successfully doing so. I believe I can assume that, in this specific instance, you have a certain degree of robust decisiveness. Therefore it is quite conceivable that you will project the knowledge that, as you so aptly put it, has been attained in theological activity onto materialistic terminology with some unavoidable dislocations to which nothing in what is to be represented corresponds—*dialectica dialecticam amat*—you can therefore go on together this way for a long time, namely just as long as circumstances allow all of you to remain in your ambiguity. Given the prevailing historical conditions, this might be for a very long time yet. I disagree that, as you claimed to Rychner, something led you to apply the principles of the materialistic viewpoint and that what you produce actually makes no genuine contribution to this. I understand just as well, however, that you have come to the self-deceptive conclusion that the introduction into metaphysics of a certain tendency and terminology in which classes and capitalism appear, even if hardly their opposite, will make your observations into materialist ones. I can, of course, only ironically recommend to you the sure way of proving the complete truth of my view, which would be for you to join the German Communist party. The test of how far a strict adherence to genuinely materialistic research methods leads away from the ideal stance of the metaphysical-dialectical scholarly enterprise (to vary your formulation)—I am, as your friend, not capable of advising you without further ado to conduct this test, as it can only end as the *capitis diminutio* of your existence. I am much more inclined to assume that this connection will one day end just as unexpectedly as it began. If I am mistaken in this, I fear that the high cost of this error will be borne by you. This is, of course, paradoxical but it would only be fitting for the situation that would then result: you would, of course, not be the last but perhaps the *most incomprehensible* sacrifice to the confusion of religion and politics, whose true connection no one could have been expected to work out more clearly than you. But, as the old Spanish Jews used to say, what time can accomplish, reason can do as well.

I will write about other things another time. I am always waiting for letters from you. This one will perhaps transport your fountain pen into a state of polemical rotation!

All the best wishes.
Yours, Gerhard

203. To Gerhard Scholem

Berlin-Wilmersdorf
April 17, 1931

Dear Gerhard,

It is just as impossible for me to answer your long letter today as it is to leave its receipt unacknowledged any longer. I admire the generosity revealed by its being handwritten; this tells me that you did not even preserve a copy of this document for yourself. I will therefore take all the more care to preserve it. Please do not interpret this to mean that I will "conceal" or "bury" it. No, it is much more the case that I must proceed systematically if I am to have any chance at all of doing justice to the task this letter sets for me. And to do that, the first step must be to go through what you have written with some people who are close to me. These include, first of all, Gustav Glück, whom you do not know as yet. He is not a writer, but a senior banking official. In addition, possibly Ernst Bloch. My base, which has always been narrow enough, could otherwise be broadened if you would take a good look at the ensemble of Brecht's *Versuche*. Kiepenheuer published these essays and will be visiting me in the next few days. I will then try to wangle a copy for you. By the way, you have not commented on the highly significant essay about opera I sent you some weeks ago and which appeared in the collection. I refer to these things because your letter penetrates my own position without intending to go beyond ad hominem arguments and lands like a projectile squarely in the center of the position currently occupied here by a small but most important avant-garde group. Much of what led me to ever greater solidarity with Brecht's production is precisely what you bring up in your letter; but this refers to much that is in the production itself and with which you are not yet familiar.

You will note from the tone of these words that your obvious expectation that your letter would provoke a polemical utterance from me cannot be fulfilled. Your letter will be unable to evoke any expansive or emotional reaction at all from me, because my situation is much too precarious for me to afford anything of the sort. Nonetheless, not even in my wildest dreams does it occur to me to claim infallibility for it, or even simply correctness in any sense other than that of necessary, symptomatic, productive falseness. (Little is accomplished by such sentences, but I must try—since you have so clearly seen from so far away the big picture of what is happening here—to give you an idea of the smaller as well, of the reflexive upper registers, so to speak.) In particular, you should not think that I have the slightest illusions concerning the fate of my writing within the party, or concerning how long a possible membership in the party would last. But it would be shortsighted not to consider this circumstance as capable of changing, even if the conditions would have to be nothing short of a German Bolshevist revolution. Not as if a victorious party would at all change its attitude to my current writings, but it might make it possible for me to write differently. That is, I am determined to do my thing regardless of the circumstances, but this thing is not always the same thing under every set of circumstances. It is instead something that corresponds to the circumstances. And it is not within my nature to be able to respond correctly to false circumstances, i.e., with something "correct." This is also not something at all desirable as long as you exist and are determined to exist as a distinct individual.

Something else must be expressed just as conditionally: the question of surroundings. Where is my productive base? It is—and I have not the slightest illusions about this—in Berlin W. WW, if you will. The most advanced civilization and the most "modern" culture not only are part of my private comforts but are in part simply the means of my production. That is, it is not within my power to relocate my productive base to Berlin east or north. (I would be able to emigrate to Berlin E. or N., but only to do something different from what I do here. I admit that this might be called for because of moral reasons. But for the time being I will not acquiesce in such a request; I will say that it is made most immensely difficult for me in particular, as well as for many others in my position.) But do you really want to prevent me, with my small writing factory that is situated in the middle of the west purely out of imperious necessity, from distinguishing myself from the surroundings that I must tolerate with good reason—do you want to prevent me from hanging the red flag from my window with the comment that it is nothing more than a tattered piece of cloth? If someone is already writing "counterrevolutionary" pieces—as you quite properly characterize those I have written from the perspective of the party—must that person also explicitly put them at the disposal of the counterrevolution? Should the person not rather denature them like alcohol and make them definitely and dependably unpalatable to the counterrevolution, with the danger that they will become unpalatable for everyone? Can there ever be too great a clarity with which an individual is differentiated from his promulgations, and with which language is differentiated from the people producing it and whom you increasingly learn to avoid in life? Is it not more likely that this clarity is insufficiently pronounced in my writings and can it be strengthened by moving in any direction other than that of communism?

If I were in Palestine, it is quite possible that things would look completely different. Your position on the Arab question proves that there are totally different methods of unambiguously differentiating yourself from the bourgeoisie there than there are here. No such methods exist here. Not even one exists here. With some justification, you could call what I call unambiguous the height of ambiguity. Good, I am reaching an extreme. Someone who has been shipwrecked, who carries on while drifting on the wreckage, by climbing to the peak of the mast that is already crumbling. But he has a chance of sending out an SOS from up there.

Please think all of this through very carefully. If you can, make me a counterproposal.

I do not want to make you wait any longer, so that's all for today. Most sincere regards.

Yours, Walter

204. Gerhard Scholem to Walter Benjamin

Jerusalem
May 6, 1931

Dear Walter,

Your short letter causes me some embarrassment, since at the end you ask me to take a position on what you presented. I am in no position to do so. You once again describe your situation. Well—that is not exactly what I wanted to discuss. I disputed neither the special nature of your situation in a bourgeois world, nor your (self-evident) right to side with the revolution in terms of historical decisions, nor the existence of the sad phenomena of your surroundings or weakness or whatever you may wish to call it. And you are, of course, correct in saying that your letter provides no answer to the issue I raised: namely, not that you are fighting, but that you are fighting under a disguise; that you issue a currency in your writing that you are increasingly simply incapable of redeeming, incapable precisely because of the most genuine and most substantial thing you have or are. I, of course, do not dispute that a person could possibly write like Lenin. I am attacking only the fiction of pretending to do this while doing something totally different. I would maintain that it is indeed possible to live in the tension of this ambiguity (indeed, this is precisely what I fear) but, to express it very harshly for once, the person who does so will be destroyed because—and this is a point on which I place the most weight as it pertains to you—the morality of any insights achieved in such an existence must degenerate. This commodity happens to be of vital importance and cannot and will not be neutralized in any case. You write that my letter concerns not only you but also some other people with whom you are inclined to discusss it. Well, I can only welcome this, and it is also evident to me that the letter refers to Ernst Bloch, as you may already be able to tell from what I wrote you about his book [*Spuren*]. You write, make a counterproposal. I can only suggest that you acknowledge your genius, which you are currently so hopelessly attempting to deny. Self-deception turns all too easily into suicide, and God knows your suicide would be too high a price to pay for the honor of correct revolutionary thinking. Your desire for community places you at risk, even if it is the apocalyptic community of the revolution that speaks out of so many of your writings, more than the horror of loneliness. I am indeed ready to put greater stake in that than in the imagery with which you are cheating yourself out of your calling.

All the best.
Yours, Gerhard

205. To Gerhard Scholem

Berlin
July 20, 1931

Dear Gerhard,

I want to make use of a calm Sunday evening and an even calmer state of mind to let you hear from me again. I am a bit troubled, of course, by the prospect that you will once again complain about elliptical and laconic turns of phrase, inadequate information, and threadbare arguments. Although I do not have your last letter in front of me right now—however, I will read it once more before mailing this one—I do remember that it is shot through with disgruntled references to such deficiencies in style and thought. Regardless of what the truth about these things may be—for the moment let us assume that it is exactly as it appears to you—you must nonetheless be perceptive enough to say to yourself that these are relationships and developments—the product of living conditions and of years—that are infinitely difficult to maneuver from a distance and can only be projected into the distance with infinite difficulty. God knows I am not saying this in order to withdraw behind a screen of control, much less to withdraw from your friendship. I will remain ready to give an account of myself to the very end. But it is no more possible to do so in writing—as any child should know—than it is a matter, for my part anyway, of pure points of view. Instead a development is at issue, indeed, one that is going on amid the most difficult tension. I am referring much less to internal tensions of a private nature (no, as far as that goes, I have rarely been granted as much internal peace as in the past few months), but rather to the tensions of the political and social environment. No one, least of all a writer, can ignore these in his work, much less give an adequate notion of them in a letter of three or four pages. Just today, I made sure that Brecht's *Versuche* had been mailed to you. I will answer your question as to what they might have to do with the subjects of our correspondence, by referring to the fact that we cannot expect real results from a formal debate conducted through correspondence. We must start out as much as possible with honest, objective information and, therefore, the information in Brecht's *Versuche* has a very special significance. The reason is that these essays are the first—to be precise, of the poetic or literary essays—that I champion as a critic without (public) reservation. This is because part of my development in the last few years came about in confrontation with them, and because they, more rigorously than any others, give an insight into the intellectual context in which the work of people like myself is conducted in this country. Add to this the fact that you can have only an incomplete notion of the social and political conditions under which we must work here. Not to mention the material circumstances that over time have made my existence—with no property and no steady income—a paradox, in view of which even I sometimes fall into a stupor of amazement. In brief, it is surely high time that we see each other again and, given your trip to Europe, I hope the prospect for this will be better during the coming year than you suggest. In the meantime, it would be highly desirable if you would at least have copies of the things you write in German sent to me; I have not received anything for an eternity.

[. . .]

At the moment I am testing my mettle on a review of the volume of Kafka's posthumously published writings. It is an unusually difficult task. I recently read almost all of his works—some for the second time, some for the first time. I envy you your Jerusalemite magicians in this regard; this would be a point about which it seems profitable to quiz them. Perhaps you will send me a hint. You will also, no doubt, have occasionally had your own independent ideas about Kafka.

[. . .]

It is a great pity that the university has no money. If I had some—I have now settled my former relationships to such a degree that a decision to emigrate to Palestine would be no more difficult for me than to walk out the door. It would be the right time. But the times that are "right" for me unfortunately almost always divide my destined path from the outside, in keeping with the law of the Apollonian section. If I could leave Germany, I believe it would now be high time to do so. According to everything I know—and the information I get is usually very accurate—I consider it very doubtful that we will have to wait longer than fall for the start of civil war. If you have things to take care of in Germany, it would probably be good to take this into consideration. Whether or not Germany will get a loan of two billion is likely to change things very little, since the sum is much too small.

What is one to think of the last Zionist Congress? I got to see the news in the *Frankfurter Zeitung* only because it gave me a complimentary subscription.

Since I have now come to the ridiculous details of my existence, I want to close for today. I hope to hear from you very soon.

All the best.
Yours, Walter

206. To Gerhard Scholem

[October 3, 1931]

Dear Gerhard,

I understand completely: I must finally let you hear from me so as not to put you in a justifiably bad mood. The times are such that circumstances are, of course, making things increasingly difficult for people. On the other hand, your most recent letters present plenty of subject matter on their own. The information you provided in response to my question about the condition of Zionism moved me greatly; it was a letter *media in vita,* from the midst of life, in which the close-up view of what has become real is already visible in the long-range view of what is planned, and in which the long-range view of what has been planned is still visible in the close-up view of what has been realized. Before I finish writing this, I will read it once again. I was given an oral account of things by [Heinz] Pflaum, whom I met at the library one day. His account cannot compare with the clarity of the written information I have had from you during the last few weeks—or is it months already? [. . .]

Then a few days ago, after I received a Hebrew parcel for which I thank you very much, your paper on Rosenzweig arrived.[1] I read it with the greatest interest and, if I might use this expression as an *am haaretz*, in complete agreement. If I am not mistaken, it may be appropriate to make these kinds of summary observations, in which it is highly likely that the leaven from the years of your German apprenticeship will always be present and available to German readers even if the observations do not deal with German books. I also made available to Leo Strauss something you mailed earlier, a piece in which you discuss a mystical examination of the Kabbalah by a later—I believe, English—scholar. You, unlike me, probably know Hans Kohn personally.[2] He now reports on Russia for the *Frankfurter Zeitung*. It seems to me that his last report on the situation of religions in Russia was devoid of salient ideas.

If you would come to Berlin soon for ten to twelve days, you would perhaps come across no fewer remarkable sights than others come across in Moscow. But they are more somber, from an overall perspective as well as from my own. The economic order of Germany has as firm a footing as the high seas and emergency decrees collide with each other like the crests of waves. Unemployment is about to make revolutionary programs just as obsolete as economic and political programs already are. To all appearances the National Socialists have actually been delegated to represent the unemployed masses here; the Communists have not as yet established the necessary contact with these masses and, consequently, the possibility of revolutionary action. On the other hand, the task of the fantastic army of reserves in representing the workers' interests is, in every concrete sense, becoming one of reform and could probably be addressed no differently by the Communists than it is being addressed by the Social Democrats. Anyone who is still employed is, as a consequence of this simple fact, already a member of a workers' aristocracy. A huge class of pensioners, naturally microscopic in stature, is apparently emerging among the unemployed; an inactive class of petit bourgeois whose element is gambling and idleness and whose day passes with the same Philistine precision with which moderate gamblers spend their day at spas.

[. . .]

To my great satisfaction Piper, the publisher who finally attained the rights to the Proust, has gone bankrupt. It was impossible to work with these people and my dilatory conduct has now come out on top. I am therefore inclined to work at knocking out some short pieces like reviews and am just reading Theodor Haecker's *Vergil,* which Hegner published after being reorganized by Goldmann, who published Wallace.[3] As much of the history of redemption as possible is packed into this slender volume; some profane passages where the author speaks frankly for those who are less pious and gifted are thus all the more delightful. The proofs of Shmarya Levin's *Childhood in Exile* are also at my side, naturally in German translation. Do you want me to give them to you? While you're at it, please write me what I am supposed to do with them *en attendant?* Review them? Read them? (Let me ask you not to consider these last two questions as alternatives.) Unfathomable bibliographical research led me to the following reference: A. Scholem, *Allerlei für Deutschlands Turner* (Berlin, 1885). I would really like to know whether this is a posthumous encounter with your father?[4]

In conclusion, since we are on bibliographical matters, let me pass on a delightful fact that, however, must be treated with the utmost discretion: the greatest German Lichtenberg collector is paying me a monthly stipend for completing a Lichtenberg bibliography he started but has not finished. You should see the card catalog I have assembled. At least one of my Jewish passions—unfortunately, the least significant—has come into its own through this and, you must admit, on the basis of the most worthy of subjects. I believe the catalog will turn out to be a miraculous work that can be publicly displayed among Jews like, for instance, a synagogue made of straw. Probably nothing more has to be said to make the library subscribe to a copy, for which I would promise to provide a worthwhile dedication.

There is still a lot of space on this sheet, but the postscript also needs room to breathe.

Sincerely yours, Walter

P.S. Man thinks—but never long enough. Since I am now about to get to the postscript by way of once again reading your last letter, the sheet I had already started is at home and now only this one is available. Thus, if nothing else, you will receive a notion of the two extremes between which my stationery lies.[5]—I understand what you write about Kafka. I also had thoughts very close to yours during the weeks in which I became more intensely involved in the subject. I tried to put together a provisional summary of them in a short note, but put the thing aside because I did not have the energy to finish it at the time. It has meanwhile become clear to me that I will probably get the final push from the first and bad book on Kafka, which a certain Johannes Schoeps,[6] a member of the Brod circle, is supposed to be writing. A book would certainly make my explanations easier; the worse it is, the better. Brecht's thoroughly positive attitude to Kafka's work took me by surprise in some conversations we had during the weeks in question. He seemed to devour even the posthumous volume, whereas some things in it have resisted my efforts to the present day because my physical torment while reading them was so great. I am otherwise lacking anything pleasant to read and—leaving aside some visits with Stefan—all other pleasant things.

[. . .] The constriction of the space in which I live and write (not to mention the space I have for thought) is becoming increasingly difficult to bear. Long-range plans are totally impossible. Every longer essay is the product of concentration that hardly seems to be in proportion to its value, and for days and weeks I am at a total loss at what to do.

I interrupted myself to read your characterization of the situation of Zionism once again. I read it with the greatest interest and, I believe, with as much understanding as you could wish for. In any case, I view these lines you wrote[7] as a kind of historical document. I would be surprised if every rather detailed piece of information I received from you did not better define my agreement with your position.[8] Indeed, I can readily imagine that these issues would lead us to a surprising meeting of the minds regarding the other issues that only seem to have nothing to do with the former, and which have been a sore point between us for some time. Let me ask you most urgently to let me know as often as possible about your experiences with these things, whether by letter or even only by sending me documents.

And now, once again, let me cordially wish you all the best.

1. A review of *The Star of Redemption* that has been reprinted in Scholem's *Judaica*.
2. Kohn lived in Jerusalem until 1933.
3. Reviewed by WB in the *Literarische Welt* (February 5, 1932). In *Schriften* 2:315–23.
4. It was in fact. Scholem's father had for years been very active in the Berlin Athletic Club until anti-Semitism came to prevail there.
5. Very beautiful handmade paper, extremely thin and transparent.
6. Hans Joachim Schoeps, later professor at the University of Erlangen.
7. It was an extremely long letter, almost the only one of which a copy has been preserved—except for the three printed above, letters 195, 202, and 204.
8. Scholem was an active member of a group in Palestine that consisted of old Zionists but was working for a reorientation of Zionist politics toward the Arabs and was consequently exposed to severe attacks.

207. To Gerhard Scholem

[October 28, 1931]

Dear Gerhard,

Your last letter, dated the 20th, affected me so intensely and pleasantly that the result is this response by return mail—something sensational indeed in our correspondence. You are, of course, a connoisseur of my work and, above all, enough of a bibliographer to be able to imagine my relationship to my own work and especially to the nature of my publicity, even without my ever having made mention of it to you. The scruples, sometimes disturbing even to me, with which I view the plan of some sort of "Collected Works" correspond to the archival precision with which I preserve and catalog everything of mine that has appeared in print. Furthermore, disregarding the economic side of being a writer, I can say that for me the few journals and small newspapers in which my work appears represent for me the anarchic structure of a private publishing house. The main objective of my promotional strategy, therefore, is to get everything I write—except for some diary entries—into print at all costs and I can say that I have been successful in this—knock on wood!—for about four or five years. You are probably the only one who knows the totality of my writings, if you disregard Ernst Bloch [. . .]. Therefore the sincere appreciation you have mustered for the most unlikely thing—these few epistolary notes—is of incomparable value to me as validation.[1] Could this validation be intensified, it would occur as a result of your observations on what is didactic and the crisis this introduces into my means of representation. To be sure, the reference to the *Arcades* project is painful—you recognized that my essay on photography[2] developed from prolegomena; but what more can there ever be than prolegomena and paralipomena; I could conceive of bringing the project to fruition only if I were guaranteed two years of uninterrupted work. For months now, I have not had this guarantee for even that many weeks. In spite of this, of course—and in spite of the fact that I do not have the slightest notion of "what's to come"—I am fine. I could say—and my material difficulties certainly have a share in this—that I feel like an adult for the first time in my life. Not just no longer young, but grown up in that I have almost realized one of the many modes of existence inherent in me; that I have had my own apartment for a short while is also part and parcel of this. I have reached one of the (probably brief and transitory) moments when there is no one I have to consult and when I stand ready to follow any number of different orders to mobilize. Its current manifestation is nothing other than the ridiculous variety of projects I have undertaken simultaneously. The series of letters is to be continued; there is a somewhat more detailed physiognomic attempt to describe the connections between Kant's feeblemindedness (in old age) and his philosophy;[3] additionally, a shattering review of Haecker's *Vergil;* a position as a judge in an open competition for sound film scripts, for which I am reading and judging approximately 120 drafts a week; a short study of Paul Valéry,[4] which you will find in my next parcel; and I do not know whether the list is complete. If you add to this that solitude is the privilege of the rich or, at least, of economically secure beings, you will understand that my free evenings are rarely pleasant, and my booked evenings not always. (The person I have been closest to for approximately one year has been Gustav Glück,[5] the director of the foreign division of the National Credit Society. You will find a kind of portrait sketch of him—to be taken *cum grano salis*—in "The Destructive Character" ["Der destruktive Charakter"], which I sent you. You did not mention it?)

Since we are now on the topic of physiognomy, I would like to see what a connoisseur would make of the pictures displayed in my apartment. Not everything is up yet, but to my horror I already have to answer for the fact that only saints' pictures are hanging on the walls of my Communist cell, if you disregard a small painting that was a birthday present from Stefan: the old three-headed Christ, which you know; a reproduction of a Byzantine ivory relief; a trick picture—three different representations of a saint depending on the perspective from which you view it—from the Bavarian forest; a Sebastian; and the *Angelus Novus* as the only messenger of the Kabbalah; not to mention *The Presentation of the Miracle;* which is also by Klee. It might be a good idea for you to prepare Mr. [Chanoch] Reinhold[6] for this. Otherwise, he will be very well received. It has been a very long time since anyone has come to see me who has been so well recommended. Perhaps he will also be able to tell me something worthwhile about the situation of Zionism, but more than anything, it is your reports that are assured of my most avid attention. As for the rest, you perhaps no longer remember your report pertaining to the matter in your penultimate letter; it went very deeply into the subject. I would be prepared to send you a copy of it: I could conceive of its having importance for you. Enclosed is a copy of my answer to Rychner—please return it; I hope that the Haecker review will contain all the relevant ideas, but in more concise form.

In the meantime, midnight has come and I want to close. You will again find this letter to be very brief. But you should see how slight the volume containing your letters, and how fat the one containing mine, will look in the hands of someone working for the *Frankfurter Zeitung* a hundred years from now when he pores over no. 999 in the series of letters that make up our correspondence.

All the best.
Yours, Walter

1. At issue were the first "letters" in the *Frankfurter Zeitung,* later collected in the volume *Deutsche Menschen* [German people].

2. Published in the *Literarische Welt* (September 18, 1925, September 25, and October 2, 1931. In *Das Kunstwerk im Zeitalter seiner technischen Reproduzierbarkeit* (Frankfurt am Main, 1963).

3. "Allerhand Menschliches vom großen Kant" [Various things of human interest about the great Kant], *Literarische Welt* (December 11, 1931).

4. *Literarische Welt* (October 30, 1931).

5. Later a member of the board of the Dresdner Bank in Frankfurt am Main.

6. Later general director of the educational ministry of Israel. Reinhold had visited Scholem in Jerusalem.

208. To Gerhard Scholem

[December 20, 1931]

Dear Gerhard,

The Christmas season is upon us once more, or however we might designate this time in terms of the Jewish calendar, and a lengthy hiatus has interrupted our correspondence, contrary to my best intentions. Nonetheless, in order to be able to make even such intermundia [!] between my reports informationally arable, you may go ahead and assume that they are the scenes of a heightened struggle for existence. Moving into my own apartment has, in fact, confronted me with some economically difficult tasks. While my bedroom still does not look the way I would want it to—previously, when [Eva] Boy,[1] from whom I took over the apartment, still had her light furniture in it, it was prettier than it is with the antique and dark furniture, some of it borrowed, with which I had to furnish it—well, to get to the study, it too is not yet completely finished but it is pleasant and livable. All of my books are here now and, even given these times, their number has increased over time from 1,200—although I certainly have not kept all of them by a long shot—to 2,000. The study does have some peculiarities: first, it has no desk; over the years, due to a series of circumstances—not only because I have become used to working in the café a lot, but also because of some notions related to the memory of what I wrote at my old desk—I now write only while lying down. I have a sofa inherited from my predecessor. It lends itself most wonderfully as a place to work because of its qualities—it is quite useless for sleeping. I once heard from her that it had been built for an old woman who was crippled. This, therefore, is the first peculiarity, and the second one is that it has a panoramic view of the old, filled-in bog or, as it is also called, Schramm Lake—almost *l'atelier qui chante et qui bavarde*—and now that it is cold, a view of the ice-skating rinks and a clock is in sight in all seasons; as time goes by, it is especially this clock that becomes a luxury it is difficult to do without. The rent for the apartment is unfortunately such that it seems as if all of these optical furnishings were included in the price.

It is nothing short of an infernal irony that I had hardly written these lines when a piano, never heard before today—perhaps it has only been there for a short time—begins to make itself heard directly below my study. This is simply horrible. But as disconcerted as I am, I can do nothing but continue to write. The first thing I will do is refer a book to you and ask you for your opinion of it as soon as possible. I have put aside everything in order to make time for this book in the last two or three days and have gotten to the final pages. The book will probably be available over there by the time this letter reaches you. It is called *Der Untergang des Judentums*. The author, Otto Heller, works here in the editorial offices of the Communist paper, *Berlin am Morgen*. Aside from this, I do not know anything about him but you may. Although the book is impeccably orthodox in terms of party ideology, the official authorities are said to be making every conceivable difficulty for the author. Whatever opinion you may have of the book, in this case you will find me justified in having violated my abstinence from Jewish reading. The absurdity and abstruseness of its materialistic analysis of Jewish religion, which comes as part of the bargain, are ultimately evident even to me. For me, this is compensated for by the way the book illuminates the latest development of Jewish politics in Soviet Russia, in that it not only gives completely new insights into Jewish events but also into Russian matters. It even goes into matters of geography in terms of cartographic material. It is clear that the author has completely left out all questions concerning the cultural politics of the Jews, not to mention their spiritual commitment; on the other hand, there is much in his prognoses and statistical data on the population—certainly not new—to give the reader pause. I believe that these questions and doubts will suffice to introduce the book to you if it is not already in your hands.

To continue with the topic of brief episodes of writing and reading, I came across one of the most splendid and moving *documents humains* through its publisher, who sent it to me: the life of Pestalozzi as seen through the eyes of people who knew him personally. It is surely difficult to speak about bourgeois education without calling this physiognomy to mind. I was told that almost nothing of it is evident in his famous pedagogical novels; on the contrary, however, everything about it is evident in his personal impact and his misfortune—he compared himself to Job at the end of his life.

On another note, however, I must now ascertain that you—as opposed to both Jewish and Christian long-suffering souls—are insatiable and are already screaming for a commentary from me, after just having received your Brecht books (which I now, retroactively, solemnly declare to be birthday presents) thanks to countless interventions on my part. At the risk of providing your offensive snobbery with the utmost satisfaction, I will in fact enclose in my next parcel to you (to be sure, with a request that you send it back by return mail) the manuscript of my essay on epic theater, which has been at the *Frankfurter Zeitung* for nine months. Rejecting any further requests of this kind, I will nonetheless refer you to the first volume of Brecht's *Versuche* since it, along with my long handwritten commentary, is at your disposal at any time in my library. I also intend to send back a copy of your letter on Zionism and thereby request further information on the matter.

Today, however, I would like to address your thoroughly drastic formulation of the problem concerning the relationship of Communist dogma to the research findings of mathematical physics only with the comment that I have been aware of the problem ever since my devastating experience in Riga, when I tried to get hold of Bukharin's primer on communism. I do not have an answer since, of course, the usefulness of vulgar materialism for certain aspects of popular enlightenment is not a sufficient answer. And how dialectical materialism can spin that vulgar materialism into such fine thread that even strange birds such as you and I are caught in it—I don't know. I think sometimes that the "four gray women" of *Faust II* are weavers who also get the coarsest flax to be fine spun.

And with that, let me wish you all the best for the twelve heathen nights!

Yours, Walter

1. Eva van Hoboken, née Hommel, who as an artist took the name Eva Boy.

209. To Gerhard Scholem

[Ibiza]
April 22, 1932

Dear Gerhard,

I have no doubt that this envelope will astonish you, especially if you can decode the cancellation. At the very moment when you are turning to European metropolises,[1] I have withdrawn to the most remote outpost. In keeping with something you aptly perceived long ago, to wit, that most of what concerns me comes about in a surprising way, my being here also came about that way. It is first and foremost the result of my economic situation, which has been so remarkably nourished by unexpected income and lengthy periods of drought. In short, the economics of my Goethe year unexpectedly provided me with the opportunity to earn a few hundred and, at the same time, I learned about this island from Noeggerath, who was planning to make an exodus here with his entire family. Thus on April 7, I again—as I did six years before—boarded the freighter *Catania* and embarked on a trip to Barcelona. It lasted eleven days and was initially very stormy. From there I came here, where I found Noeggerath. How adventurous my arrival was; how the final impetus to make the journey came to both of us from a man who presently turned out to be a con man, wanted by the police, who had rented Noeggerath a house on the island that he did not even own—this was not without serious and unpleasant consequences for Noeggerath and me as well—these are all things that are better communicated sitting in front of a fireplace than in a letter. Be that as it may, today is my third day here and I would ask you to write to me as soon as possible at the address below.

How the rest of my summer will turn out will in all likelihood basically depend on economic factors. In any case, this was my only opportunity to escape the ignominy of the wheeling and dealing in Berlin, which, in the final analysis, was a strain of inconceivable proportions. The trip could not be put off for even a single day for fear of diminishing my meager resources, not to mention bureaucratic difficulties. You will understand if I tell you that I am living on my own in a house, with three meals of a very provincial kind included and with every kind of *goût de terroir*—on the whole, however, they are quite delicious—and pay 1.80 marks per day for everything. It is obvious from this that the island is really far removed from international trade and even civilization and that it is therefore necessary to do without every kind of comfort. This can be done with ease, not only because of the inner peace given by economic independence but also because of the composure the landscape provides; the most untouched landscape I have ever come across. Farming and animal husbandry are plied here in a very archaic fashion. Not more than four cows can be found on the island, because the farmers firmly hold onto their traditional goat-based economy. There are no farm machines to be seen, and the fields are watered by well wheels turned by mules. The interiors are likewise archaic. Three chairs along the wall of the room opposite the entrance greet the stranger with assurance and weightiness, as if three works by Cranach or Gauguin were leaning against the wall; a sombrero over the back of a chair is more imposing than a precious Gobelin tapestry. Finally, there is the serenity and beauty of the people—not only of the children—and, on top of that, the almost total freedom from strangers, which must be preserved by being extremely parsimonious with information about the island. The end of all these things is unfortunately to be feared because of a hotel being built in the port in Ibiza. It is nowhere near being completed, however, and we are not in the island's capital but in a small and isolated spot. Noeggerath is here with his wife and daughter-in-law, as well as his son, who is writing a dissertation for

Gamillscheg [?] on the dialect of the island. After the con man's swindle was discovered, which did not take very long, Noeggerath obtained permission to live rent free for one year in a stone farmhouse. It is almost in ruins and he has to put it to rights at his own expense. His retinue is very nice and not at all troublesome. He himself has lost something with the years.

I will probably begin to work tomorrow. I have been affected by the aforementioned criminal in that I had rented him my apartment; now it is empty—because the criminal police are after him—and I have to come up with the rent myself. How long I stay in part depends on my opportunities to work. I should perhaps not overestimate them, at least as long as I remain housed in the vicinity of a smithy, which is my current situation. Everything that has recently appeared in print will be sent to you at the same time as this letter; you must also take note of two long radio talks: "Was die Deutschen lasen während ihre Klassiker schrieben" [What the Germans were reading while their classical authors were writing] and "Ein Radau um Kasperl" [A big to-do about Kasperl]. Both were produced with great success. Now I have been commissioned by Berlin Broadcasting to produce a "Lichtenberg." I intend to have it start out on the moon crater named after Lichtenberg (for such a crater is surely likely to exist). I find it strange to have to write everything by hand again but, as you can tell, I will complete my training by writing unending letters.

It is not yet hot here; the real heat is not supposed to start until August. I believe you will be in Berlin then and perhaps we will see each other there. Otherwise I could well imagine that we could arrange a rendezvous someplace between Turin and Nice or even in Turin itself sometime in June. Why doesn't Barcelona have any kabbalistic manuscripts at all? In any event, write immediately what your plans are.

I am now completely exhausted from the clanging of a hammer and the crowing of a rooster and will close with the most sincere regards, on the condition of being able to add a PS.

Yours, Walter

P.S. Dear Gerhard, I was only now able to reread your last letter and it weighs on me that you again had to wait so long for one in Rome. If only you could imagine the difficulty of this, my final, detachment from Berlin and how even my last hour before leaving had to be given over to my editorial work for the *Literarische Welt* in order to take care of necessary business. Yet I continue to hope that my sincere wish for you to have a *good* trip will not reach you too late. I hope it will turn out to be good for both of us. What should I expect when I approach the remarkable Mr. Oko[2] and the miraculous Schocken.[3] I am reading *The Charterhouse of Parma* for the second time. I hope that you will also be able to treat yourself sometime to a second reading of this book. There could hardly be anything nicer.—But twilight is descending. I want to close before the candles arrive, if there are any available.

1. From April to November 1932, Scholem was touring Italian and west European libraries that held Kabbalah manuscripts.

2. Adolph Oko (1883–1944), a bookdealer in Cincinnati, who had visited Palestine at this time and spent time in Europe.

3. Salman Schocken (1877–1959), the owner of a large chain of department stores and an important Jewish collector who had just begun to build up Schocken Verlag, which later played a significant role in Jewish publishing.

210. To Gretel Adorno

[Ibiza]
Spring [1932]

Dear Gretel Karplus,

It is something, how things have a way of turning out. Twelve hours after I had sent my last letter to you, I received yours and therefore feel infinitely relieved. Perhaps it is only my inability to absorb a series of cloudless days just as they come that leads to the kind of anxious questions haunting my last letter. It will, of course, take a long time to adjust to such a climatically strange situation if a certain degree of hotellike comfort does not mediate between the country and us. And you can tell how far removed we are from that here by the small picture that is enclosed. After weeks of work, my acquaintances brought this house back to life again after years of ruin and have succeeded in making of it something thoroughly habitable. The most beautiful things are the view from the window giving onto the sea and a rocky island whose lighthouse shines into my room at night. There is also the privacy the inhabitants maintain toward each other by a clever arrangement of space and walls that are almost a meter thick, through which no sound (and no heat) can penetrate. I am leading the kind of life that centenarians confide to reporters as their secret: rise at seven o'clock and take a swim in the sea. Far and wide, there is not a single person to be seen along the shore, at most only a sailboat on the horizon at eye level. Then, leaning against an accommodating tree trunk in the forest, I take a sunbath whose salutary energy spreads to my head through the prism of a Gide-like satire (*Paludes*). And then a long day of doing without countless things, less so because they shorten life than because none of them is available or, when they are, they are in such bad condition that you are glad to do without them—electric light and butter, liquor and running water, flirting and reading the paper. Having a look at the copies of the *Frankfurter Zeitung* that arrive a week late is of a somewhat more epic character. If you add to this the fact that all my mail goes to Wissing—who up to now has not sent me a single piece of writing—you will see that I have not exaggerated. I led a sedentary existence with my books and my writing for a long time; I have emancipated myself only in the last few days from my shore patrols and taken some long and lonely marches into the even larger and more remote areas. Only then do I become clearly aware of being in Spain. These landscapes are surely the most inhospitable and most untouched of any habitable landscapes I have ever seen. It is difficult to convey a clear idea of them. If I finally succeed in doing so, I will not keep it a secret from you. For the time being, I have not made very many notes with that in mind. On the other hand, I surprised myself by again employing the descriptive form of *One-Way Street* to deal with a number of subjects that are related to the most important topics of that book. I may be able to show you some of this when I am back in Berlin. We can also talk about Corsica then. I think it is really nice that you have seen it; there is something very Spanish about the landscape over there; but I believe that the summer there is still far from carving such severe and powerful features into the country. I hope you also spent a few days in the wonderfully quiet and old-fashioned Grand Hotel in Ajaccio. You must also give me the details of how Wiesengrund did in Marseilles. I believe I will again be passing through Marseilles in the next few weeks, but I can never make up my mind about the precise dates. You will understand this when you keep in mind that I can live here for a small fraction of what I need in Berlin; I am therefore extending my stay here for as long as possible and will not be back before the beginning of August. But I hope very much to hear from you before then.

Indeed, encouraged by your letter, which really delighted me, if I might request a small gift it would be that you send me a small bag (envelope) of smokable tobacco as a "tax-free sample"—[. . .] There is hardly any smokable tobacco on the island.

I too (have) received a letter from Daga and one from her mother [Asja Lacis], shortly before my departure. I was otherwise totally immersed in things Russian for fourteen days; I have just read Trotsky's history of the February Revolution and am about to finish reading his autobiography. I think it has been years since I have consumed anything with such breathless excitement. There is no question but that you must read both books. Do you know whether the second volume of the history of the revolution—the October Revolution—has already appeared?[1] I will soon pick up Gracian again and will probably write something about it.

All the best.

Yours, Walter Benjamin

1. It was not published until 1933.

211. To Gerhard Scholem

San Antonio, Ibiza
June 1, 1932

Dear Gerhard,

I note with anxiety that you have started a section on Catholic theology in your library. This leads me to suspect that little good is in store for what remains of my library after the famous "rental" of my apartment. If I am not mistaken, there are some things there that I would not like to have exposed to your persuasive desires. Since, however—under the admonitory sign of July 15 (which will admit you into the honorable and perhaps exclusive society of Stefan if you take note of it)—it may be imprudent to reveal any obstinacy, I would rather express my concerned and honest uncertainty as to when and how we might together inspect the books in question and as to how any personal negotiations between us might be gotten under way this summer. It was perspicacious of you to understand that this is an economic issue. Only a look at my finances could give you some idea of just how critical an issue it is.

[. . .]

Let us for a change turn to the "minor questions" you raise with a stubbornness worthy of this parliamentarian genre: Collenbusch's letter[1] is in print. As I said, of those you do not have, it is the one thing that I am unfortunately unable, or not yet able, to put at your disposal. This is a shame because in it you would find some strange information about Collenbusch.

[. . .]

I did not find the Nietzsche experience you had in Jerusalem at all astonishing. I have not had any time to deal with the question of what meaning can be wrested from his writings in an emergency. If I were inclined to deal with the question, I would read up on what Klages calls "Nietzsche's psychological achievements." *En attendant,* in the review you mentioned[2] I did not commit myself as regards my own opinion on Nietzsche.

I must now say that the news about your small house is sensational, as is the news of Noeggerath turning up, but in a completely different way. Let me extend you my most sincere congratulations. If I had a *broche* to recite over the house, it would contain the wish that it, along with its books and its friends, outlive the next world war. All on its own, it will of course probably be able to resist the end of the world coming in the form of taxes, bankruptcies, etc.—I think I have now effectively countered your suspicious grumbling about the absence of manuscripts and will close with most sincere regards.

Yours, Walter

1. Samuel Collenbusch's letter to Kant was viewed by WB as one of his greatest discoveries in the field of correspondence as literature; he read it to Scholem in 1918 with inimitable facial expressions and, in parts, with a raised voice. See *Deutsche Menschen* (1926), p. 26.
2. In the *Literarische Welt* (March 18, 1932).

212.* To Gerhard Scholem

Nice
July 26, 1932

Dear Gerhard,

While you were in Milan, writing the lovely letter that reached me here, I was still on Ibiza. My stay there ended up lasting a week longer than planned. Indeed, a somewhat impromptu celebration even materialized, which owed its élan not so much to those characters in the repertoire, with whom you are acquainted, but to two French people who have recently arrived on the scene: a married couple[1] I found quite delightful. Since this affinity was reciprocal, we stayed together—with only slight interruptions—until my departure. Their company was so captivating—right up to midnight of July 17th, when my ship was to sail for Mallorca—that when we finally arrived at the quay, the gangplank had been removed and the ship had already begun to move. I had stowed my baggage on board in advance, of course. After calmly shaking hands with my companions, I began to scale the hull of the moving vessel and, aided by curious Ibizans, managed to clamber over the railing successfully.

Thus, at this very moment I am on my way to Speyer. There, in Poveromo, I will learn whether I must return to Germany in August or whether there is any way for me to extend my stay abroad. Even taking into account the circumstances you are familiar with, you still cannot begin to imagine just how averse I am to returning. To do so, you would need not only to have before you the letter in which the building-safety authorities demand I give up my apartment—because its condition fails to meet certain regulations—you would also need more than just a clear idea of how the reactionary movement you allude to has affected my work for radio.[2] Above all, you would have to grasp the profound fatigue that has overcome me as a result of these very circumstances. That brings me to the important insights contained in your birthday letter.[3] They require no commentary—other than on the concept of the "counterrevolutionary." I hope you will find occasion to enlighten me as to its precise meaning as a characterization of my deeper insights.[4] I can indeed imagine what this concept might mean; all the same, I find it ambiguous. I preface my remarks with this qualification only in order to accord full weight to the expression of my complete agreement with your remaining observations. Your remark that the chances of what you wish for me actually coming to pass are the smallest imaginable thus gains in significance. We would both be well advised to face up to these facts—in view of which the failure of your Palestinian "intervention" was indeed fateful.[5] And if I do so with a grimness verging on hopelessness, it is surely not for want of confidence in my resourcefulness in finding alternatives and subsidies. Rather, it is the developing of this resourcefulness, and the productivity that corresponds to it, that most seriously endangers every worthwhile project. The literary forms of expression that my thought has forged for itself over the last decade have been utterly conditioned by the preventive measures and antidotes with which I had to counter the disintegration constantly threatening my thought as a result of such contingencies. And though many—or a sizable number—of my works have been small-scale victories, they are offset by large-scale defeats. I do not want to speak of the projects that had to remain unfinished, or even untouched, but rather to name here the four books that mark off the real site of ruin or catastrophe, whose furthest boundary I am still unable to survey when I let my eyes wander over the next years of my life. They include the *Pariser Passagen,* the *Gesammelte Essays zur Literatur,* the *Briefe,*[6] and a truly exceptional book about hashish.[7] Nobody knows about this last topic, and for the time being it should remain between us.

So much about me. This hasn't told you anything new. Perhaps by seeing the relative equanimity with which I can, on occasion, lucidly describe my situation, it might appear to you in a new light and give you something to think about.

You will be pleased to learn that I briefly met the cousin you mentioned[8] at the state library and gently but firmly gave him the cold shoulder, recalling how frowningly you wrote of him. I now find it very amusing to discover him in the gallery of Goethe mavens circling the earth this year. Even more momentous is the establishment of the photography section of your Kabbalah archive, for which I send my most sincere congratulations. I include here Ernst Schoen's address to whom you should of course convey my kindest regards: Südwestdeutscher Rundfunk. Eschersheimer Landstrasse 33. You will also come across many other remarkable people in Frankfurt, perhaps even Theodor Wiesengrund, the *privatdocent* who conducted a seminar on my *Trauerspiel* book last semester.

Write as soon as you can, c/o Wilhelm Speyer, Casa Mesquita, Poveromo (Marina di Massa).

I will be prompt in claiming my present. All the best.

Yours, Walter

* Translated by Gary Smith. See Note on Sources, p. vii above.

1. Jean Selz and his wife. Selz published his recollections of their time together on Ibiza in *Le dire et le faire* (Paris: Mercure de France, 1964), pp. 52–72. [Cf. Selz, "Walter Benjamin in Ibiza," in G. Smith, ed., *Walter Benjamin: Critical Essays and Recollections* (Cambridge, Mass.: MIT Press, 1988), pp. 354–66.—Smith]

2. Franz von Papen's so-called gentlemen's club, which deposed the Prussian (Social Democratic–led) government in a sort of coup d'état only days before this letter was composed, had formed its reactionary cabinet on June 2, 1932.

3. My letter had been written for WB's fortieth birthday on July 15, 1932.

4. Strangely enough, WB had already forgotten our exchange of letters between March 30 and April 17, 1931, in which he had termed my characterization of his writings as "counterrevolutionary" from the Communist party's perspective as "quite correct."

5. Cf. the chapter "The Failed Project" in Gershom Scholem, *Walter Benjamin: The Story of a Friendship,* trans. Harry Zohn (Philadelphia: Jewish Publications, 1981), pp. 136–56 [hereafter, Scholem, *WB*].

6. WB has in mind the collection of German letters (with brief introductions) that subsequently appeared in 1936 under the title *Deutsche Menschen* [Lucerne: Vita Nova Verlag]. The letters were first published in the *Frankfurter Zeitung* during 1931 and 1932.

7. The materials WB collected for this book appeared in 1972 under the title *Über Haschisch: Novellistisches, Berichte, Materialien* (Frankfurt am Main: Suhrkamp). [Cf. *Schriften* 6:558–618.–Smith]

8. Heinz Pflaum.

213. To Theodor W. Adorno

Poveromo (Marina di Massa)
September 3, 1932

Dear Mr. Wiesengrund,

I have had to wait for your letter for so long and, now that it has arrived, it has brought me great pleasure. Mostly because of how closely certain sections of its text coincide with the design of the concluding section of the "Naturgeschichte des Theaters,"[1] which is a truly crowning and validating achievement. Let me thank you most sincerely for your dedication. The entire sequel proceeds from a highly original and truly baroque view of the stage and its world. Indeed, it might be said to contain something like a "Prolegomena to Any Future History of the Baroque Stage" and I am especially pleased that you shed so much light on this subterranean thematic relationship in your dedication. It is hardly necessary for me to affirm that it is precisely this piece that has turned out to be a consummate success. There are, however, also some very nice things in the "Foyer" sequel, like the image of the two clock faces and the very sagacious thoughts about fasting during this interlude. I hope that I will also get to see your essay in the Horkheimer archive[2] very soon—and, if I might be permitted to express another variation of this wish, I hope that, along with the essay, I also receive the first issue of the archive, in which I naturally have a lively interest. We have a lot of time to read here. I have already almost gone through the small library I brought with me when I left five months ago. You will be interested to hear that it once again includes four volumes of Proust,[3] in which I often read. But now to a new book that came into my possession here and of which I would like (to make) you aware—Rowohlt has published a history of bolshevism [*Geschichte des Bolschewismus*] by Arthur Rosenberg,[4] which I have just finished reading. It seems to me that it cannot be ignored under any circumstances. Speaking for myself, at least, I must say that it opened my eyes to many things, including those areas in which political destiny affects private destiny. Various circumstances, as well as your recent references to Cysarz,[5] give me cause to think about the latter. I would be not at all loath to establish contact with him. Yet I still do not quite understand why he has not taken the first step to approach me—whether directly or through a letter from Grab[6]—if he indeed wants the same thing. I have no doubt that, in an analogous situation, I, for my part, would do so in his place. Otherwise, it is naturally not reasons of prestige that make me hesitate but rather my experience that errors at the beginning of a relationship tend to be proportionately magnified in what follows. I imagine that Cysarz's influence, for example, would be great enough to get me an invitation for a lecture from some appropriate group or institute in Prague. You might be able to inform Grab of this when an opportunity arises. Meanwhile, however, let me express my most sincere gratitude for the invitation you append to the report on the meetings of your seminar.[7] I know there is no need to assure you either of how glad I would be to come or of the great value I place on the opportunity to have a look at the documents that demonstrate how things have proceeded thus far. It would, of course, be highly desirable if we could do this together. At the moment, however—and this also relates to the chances of my presence in Frankfurt—I am less than ever master of my decisions. I know neither when I will return to Berlin nor how things will shape up there. I will almost certainly be here for several weeks yet. After that I will probably have to return to Berlin: on the one hand in order to take care of housing problems: on the other, because Rowohlt seems to be insisting on publishing my essays after all.[8] As such, the temptation to stay in Germany for any length of time is certainly not very great. There will be difficulties everywhere and those emanating from the radio will probably make my appearances in Frankfurt even rarer. If you happen to know how things are going for Schoen, please let me know. I hear nothing from him. That is all for today. The only thing I would still like to say is that I am working on a series of sketches having to do with my early memories.[9] I hope I can show you some of them very soon.

Most sincere regards.
Yours, Walter Benjamin

P.S. To my great delight, I discovered your "caricature."—Wolfskehl's saying in my review goes like this: "Should we not say of the spiritists that they fish in the *Beyond?*"[10]

1. See Theodor W. Adorno, "Das Foyer: Zur Naturgeschichte des Theaters," *Blätter des Hessischen Landestheaters* 8 (Darmstadt, 1932–33), pp. 98ff.; see also his "Zur Naturgeschichte des Theaters: Fragmente," *Blätter des Hessischen Landestheaters* 9 (1932–33), pp. 101ff., and 13 (1932–33), pp. 153ff. The manuscript of the concluding piece, which remained unpublished at that time, contained a dedication to WB. Cf. the complete text in Theodor W. Adorno, *Quasi una fantasia*, vol. 2, *Musikalische Schriften* (Frankfurt am Main, 1963), pp. 94–112.

2. "Zur gesellschaftlichen Lage der Musik," *Zeitschrift für Sozialforschung* 1 (1932), pp. 103ff., 356ff.

3. WB told Adorno "he did not want to read one more word by Proust than was actually necessary for him to translate because otherwise he would become addictively dependent, which would be an obstacle . . . to his own production" (Theodor W. Adorno, "Im Schatten junger Mädchenblüte," *Dichten und Trachten: Jahresschau des Suhrkamp-Verlages* 4 [Frankfurt am Main, 1954], p. 74.)

4. Berlin, 1932.

5. Cysarz later revealed himself as one of the most convinced Nazi party followers among German university teachers. Even today, his name is frequently found in connection with radical right-wing organizations and publications.

6. Hermann Edler Grab von Hermannswörth, Ph.D., J.D., sociologist and musician; a close friend of Adorno, who introduced him to WB.

7. As a privatdocent, Adorno held a seminar on new works about aesthetics in the summer semester at the University of Frankfurt. Among them was WB's book on tragedy.

8. The edition did not materialize.

9. The reference is to the texts of *Berliner Kindheit um 1900* [Berlin childhood around 1900].

10. See WB's review of Hans Liebstoeckl, *Die Geheimwissenschaften im Lichte unserer Zeit* (Vienna, 1932) in the literary supplement of the *Frankfurter Zeitung* (August 21, 1932). This printed version divests the saying—which is also ascribed to Friedrich Gundolf—of its point because of a typographical error: instead of "im Drüben" (in the beyond), it reads "im Trüben" (in the gloom).

214.* To Gerhard Scholem

[Berlin
January 15, 1933]

Dear Gerhard,

I gladly confirm that your last letter contains much that is worth knowing. Yet it leaves much to protest against: that I learn much too late what I should have known long ago, such as your news of Seidmann-Freud, which you brazenly kept to yourself while I unsuspectingly sent you my reviews of her books;[1] that so much worth knowing breaks off before my hunger for it is quite appeased, as with your innuendos about Magnes, of whose adversaries—who they are, what they want, and where they live[2]—I would like to be able to form a clearer picture.

What—despite such grave faults—graced your letter in my eyes are the truly edifying and apposite sentences you write on my *Berliner Kindheit*. "Apposite," of course, is not meant to refer to the praise you award it, but rather to the place you reserve for this series within my work, and also to the very special thoughts you devote to the piece on "Sexual Awakening."[3] Your thoughts have convinced me and I shall proceed accordingly. Moreover, you could hardly have said anything more encouraging than that in fact now and again certain passages seemed to bear on your own childhood. Your letter, then, is not among the least of the reasons why I have taken up the work again, in order to add several pieces. Yet here, where I lack the tranquility of a vast beach and a secluded place to stay, [I] must proceed with twice the care.

There is some chance that the *Frankfurter Zeitung* will soon start printing the complete series.[4] Incidentally, changes are in the offing there, whose course I cannot predict. I have therefore recently tried to establish new contacts, and have in the process hit upon the *Vossische Zeitung* on the one hand and the Frankfurt *Zeitschrift für Sozialforschung* on the other. The latter has given me a few assignments and promised me others. I will soon receive a large volume to review on the social relations and the ideology of the baroque, written by a certain Borkenau, who is rumored to have done some very remarkable work.[5] Furthermore, several restrained remarks I heard you make about Wiesengrund won't deter me from drawing your attention to his newly published *Kierkegaard*.[6] I only know the book in excerpts thus far, but have already found much in it of merit. What's more, the author's case is so complex as to defy treatment in a letter. When I disclose that he is continuing to use my *Trauerspiel* book in his seminar for the second semester running, without indicating this in the course catalog, then you have a small cameo that should serve for the moment. But you should definitely take notice of his book, all the same.

For my part, I am very eager to receive your open letter on *Jewish Faith in Our Time*. At the same time I wish to thank you very much for sending me the "Kabbalah." Though no judgment can arise out of the abyss of my ignorance in this area, you should still know that the rays of your article did force their way even down there. Otherwise, however, I have to content myself with cobweb-thin esoteric knowledge; at the moment—for the purpose of a radio play about spiritism.[7] I am about to cast a glance over the relevant literature, not, to be sure, without having constructed, slyly and for my private pleasure, a theory on these matters which I intend to put before you on a distant evening, over a bottle of burgundy. You should regard some of my more recent products, like "Das Taschentuch" or the—pruned—"Kaktushecke" [Cactus Hedge][8] as originating from the same evident motives as the spirit revue. I only send them to you to honor your archive, if even at my own expense.

By no means consider this letter short. Besides, it's been written very quickly. Tell me all that transpires in the struggle for your professorship and accept—not for it[9]—my kindest regards.

Yours, Walter

1. Tom Freud took her life after the death of her husband, Jakob Seidmann. WB's very positive reviews of three of her books are printed in *Schriften* 3:267–74, 311–14.

2. Albert Einstein was the most important opponent facing Dr. Judah L. Magnes, the chancellor of the Hebrew University. Einstein was close to him in views and Zionist politics, but challenged his ability to administer a university.

3. I urgently advised him to delete this section because it was the only one in the whole book in which Jewish matters were explicitly mentioned, thus creating the worst possible associations. There would have been no point in leaving out this section if his Jewish experiences had been voiced in other sections as well, but it would have been wrong to have kept it in this isolated position. Adorno, who did not know about this correspondence, printed the section in the first book edition of the *Berliner Kindheit um 1900* anyway, and that is why it is now contained in all editions to date.

4. Publication began on February 2, 1933.

5. Franz [von] Borkenau, *Der Übergang vom feudalen zum bürgerlichen Weltbild,* Publications of the Institute for Social Research, vol. 4 (Paris: Librairie Félix Alcan, 1934).

6. Theodor W. Adorno, *Kierkegaard: Konstruktion des Aesthetischen* (Tübingen: J. C. B. Mohr, 1933), the first German book written under WB's decisive influence. It was Adorno's habilitation dissertation. *[Kierkegaard: A Construction of the Aesthetic,* trans. Robert Hullot-Kentor (Minneapolis: University of Minnesota Press, 1989).—Smith]

7. As far as I know, none of WB's notes on this subject have been preserved.

8. *Schriften* 4:741–45, 748–54.

9. Perhaps this should read: "not *solely* for it."

215.* To Gerhard Scholem

Berlin
[February 28, 1933]

Dear Gerhard,

I'm using a quiet hour of deep depression to send you a page once again. The immediate occasion is receipt of your utterly remarkable article in Das [Bavarian] *israelitische Gemeindeblatt,* which I received only this morning—from Miss [Kitty] Marx from Königsberg, along with your letter of introduction and the announcement of her arrival. The rest of the day was taken up with work and the dictation of a radio play. "Lichtenberg,"[1] which I must now send in, in accordance with a contract the better part of which has long been fulfilled and which facilitated my flight to the Baleares.

The little composure that people in my circles were able to muster in the face of the new regime was rapidly spent, and one realizes that the air is hardly fit to breathe anymore—a condition which of course loses significance as one is being strangled anyway. This above all economically: the opportunities the radio offered from time to time and which were my only serious prospects will probably vanish so completely that even "Lichtenberg," though commissioned, is not sure to be produced. The disintegration of the *Frankfurter Zeitung* marches on. The editor of its feuilleton page[2] has been relieved of his duties, even though he had demonstrated at least some commercial aptitude by his acquisition of my *Berliner Kindheit* at a ridiculously low price. Heinrich Simon[3] now seems to be in charge there. Publication of my work has now been stopped for more than a fortnight.

Prospects of seeing the work published as a book are minimal. Everyone realizes it is so superb that it will be called to immortality, even in manuscript form. Books are being printed that are more urgently in need of it. By the way, as of last week I can consider the text finished, if I wish: with the composition of the last piece—serially the first,[4] for as such it has become a pendant to the last, "Das bucklige Männlein"—the number of thirty has been reached, not including the one deleted on your advice.

When not captivated by the fascinating world of Lichtenberg's thought, I am absorbed by the problems posed by the next months. I don't know how I will be able to make it through them, whether inside or outside Germany. There are places where I could earn a minimal income, and places where I could live on a minimal income, but not a single place where these two conditions coincide. If I report that, despite such circumstances, a new theory of language[5]—encompassing four small, handwritten pages—has resulted, you will not deny me due homage. I have no intention of having those pages published and am even uncertain whether they are fit for a typescript. I will only point out that they were formulated while I was doing research for the first piece of the *Berliner Kindheit*.[6]

Even without being familiar with Schoeps's work, I think I can discern the horizon of your observations, and I am in complete agreement that nothing is more necessary than to finish off those hideous pacesetters of Protestant theologoumena within Judaism. But that is a minor matter compared with the definitions of Revelation given in your text and held by me in high esteem: "The absolutely concrete can never be fulfilled at all."[7] These words (putting aside the theological perspective) say more about Kafka, of course, than that man Schoeps will ever be capable of understanding. Max Brod is just as incapable of understanding this, and I think I have discovered here a dictum possibly embedded in the earliest and deepest layers of your thought.

It would be quite nice to hear from you soon. I am sending this short letter with the reassuring certainty that it will be complemented anecdotally by the stories Miss Marx will relate.

With all the best,
Yours, Walter

Glancing through your last letter, I see that I must oblige with a small postscript. I am doing it on that noblest of papers, which I bought fifteen years ago in a small shop I discovered in Sarnen—on a walking tour—and which was sold to me by a Mr. Narziss von Ach, whose memory is much dearer to me than that of a psychologist of the same name.[8] As this paper is usually reserved for my deepest meditations, please consider it a mark of esteem.[9]

My essay on Kafka is still unwritten, for two reasons. First, I really wanted—and still want—to read the essay announced by Schoeps before I start working on mine. I expect Schoeps's essay to be a codification of all misguided opinions that can be distilled from a specifically Prague-bound interpretation of Kafka, and, as you know, such books have always inspired me. But the publication of this book is not unimportant to me for a second reason as well: it is obvious that I could only undertake the work such an essay would involve if it were commissioned. And where should such a commission come from, out of the blue, unless you obtained one for me in Palestine.[10] The best way to get such a thing done in Germany would be to write it in the form of a review of Schoeps's work, but then again, I don't know whether the book will be published or not.[11]

As to your other requests for your archive, i.e. my works for the radio:

Even I haven't been successful in collecting them all. I am speaking of the radio plays, not the series of countless talks, which [will] now come to an end, unfortunately, and are of no interest except in economic terms, but that is now a thing of the past.[12] Moreover, most of these radio plays were written together with others. Notable from a technical point of view perhaps is a piece for children, which was broadcast last year in Frankfurt and Cologne; I may be able to secure you a copy at some point. It's called "Radau um Kasperl."[13] If you don't receive the *Kierkegaard* from Wiesengrund within a reasonable time, I'll be honored to dedicate to you a copy of the page proofs which is in my possession.[14]

1. *Schriften* 4:696–720. The radio play was not broadcast.
2. Werner Diebold.
3. Part owner of the *Frankfurter Zeitung*.
4. The "Tiergarten" piece was published in the *Frankfurter Zeitung* (February 2, 1933).
5. "Über das mimetische Vermögen," *Schriften* 2:210–13 ["On the Mimetic Faculty," in WB's *Reflections: Essays, Aphorisms, Autobiographical Writings,* ed. Peter Demetz, trans. Edmund Jephcott (New York: Harcourt Brace Jovanovich, 1978) (hereafter *Reflections*), pp. 333–36], a text that will be mentioned frequently in these letters. The reference might also be to the longer alternate version, "Lehre vom Ähnlichen," *Schriften* 2:204–10 ["Doctrine of the Similar," *New German Critique* 17 (Spring 1979): 65–69], but I consider this unlikely, since this version probably wasn't written before the spring of 1933, on Ibiza. The first manuscript version, which is still extant, indeed consists of no more than four and a half small handwritten pages, though he sent me only the first text.
6. This sentence has remained a riddle to me. If it means that WB was writing down notes that led to the formulation of this philosophy of language before he wrote down the "Tiergarten" piece, the relation is not clear. To establish a connection between philosophy of language and the "Weihnachtsengel" piece would be just as difficult.
7. Thirty years later I incorporated these remarks—with small modifications—into an Eranos lecture. They can be found in the volume *Über einige Grundbegriffe des Judentums* (Frankfurt am Main: Suhrkamp Verlag, 1970), p. 110. ["Revelation and Tradition as Religious Categories in Judaism," *Judaism* 15, no. 1 (1966): 23–39.—Smith]
8. Sarnen, on the way from the Brünig pass to Lucerne. Narziss Ach was, at the time, professor of psychology in Göttingen.
9. It is a page in duodecimo, which belonged to a tear-sheet notebook I often saw on WB's desk. Many more pages, closely covered with writing, are still among his papers. The paper is indeed of excellent quality.
10. I was instrumental in helping WB secure such a commission from the *Jüdische Rundschau* in Berlin, which was the official publication of the German Zionists.
11. The book did not appear.
12. This denigratory assessment of WB's radio work, which has only been partially published and is for the most part housed in the GDR literary archives, must be interpreted in the context of his negative attitude toward much of the work he did for money. Yet most of these texts also contain sediments of his decidedly original way of seeing. His Berlin lectures were mostly for the children's radio, where he had a quarter of an hour at his disposal. [The several dozen radio texts in East Berlin are in *Schriften,* vol. 11.—Smith]
13. In *Schriften* 4:674–95.
14. I did indeed receive the book in this form only.

216.* To Gerhard Scholem

Hotel Istria
Paris
March 20, 1933

Dear Gerhard,

So here we are again, about to inaugurate a new chapter in our correspondence, one that will definitely not proceed uniformly on my part, as far as postmarks and addresses are concerned. What you hear about me these days from Kitty Marx will certainly provide you with an accurate image of my internal and external circumstances before they were assailed by events that once again entirely transformed them. But before I tell you more about this, I mustn't neglect to point out how lamentable it was that a farewell visit—if I may call it that—should constitute the beginning of an acquaintance whose potential I considered very attractive. Since this letter will follow close on the footsteps of her arrival in Jerusalem, I wish to place a modest welcoming bouquet for her atop the heavy freight of news the letter itself holds.

I doubt whether you have already spoken with people who left Germany after, say, the 15th of March. Only especially reckless people would have sent you news by mail. It can be very risky to write from there without a carefully contrived disguise. Since I have my freedom, I can express myself clearly and all the more succinctly. A sense of the situation there is better conveyed by the totality of the cultural state of affairs than by the particulars of individual acts of terror. It is difficult to obtain absolutely reliable information about the latter. Without any doubt there are countless cases of people being dragged from their bed in the middle of the night, and tortured or murdered. The fate of the prisoners may be of even greater significance, but harder to probe into. Horrifying rumors are circulating about this, and one can only say that some of them have turned out to be untrue. Otherwise, matters stand as always in times like these: for the few cases that were subject to exaggeration, there may be many you never hear about.

In my case it was not these conditions—more or less foreseeable for some time—that prompted me barely one week ago to transform what were ill-defined wishes to leave Germany into a hard and fast decision. Rather, it was the almost mathematical simultaneity with which every conceivable office returned manuscripts, broke off negotiations either in progress or in the final stages, and left inquiries unanswered. Every attitude or manner of expression that does not fully conform to the official one is terrorized—a reign of terror that has reached virtually unsurpassable heights. Under such conditions, the utmost political reserve, such as I have long and with good reason practiced, may protect the person in question from systematic persecution, but not from starvation. In the midst of all this, I had the good fortune to rent my place for a year to a reliable man. Only through elaborate arrangements did I succeed in raising the few hundred marks that will enable me to live on Ibiza—where I plan to go next—for a few months. What will come after that, however, may one day be as completely closed to me as it is now open. I can at least be certain that I did not act on impulse, out of panic: the German atmosphere in which you look first at people's lapels and after that usually do not want to look them in the face anymore, is unbearable. Rather, it was pure reason, which bid all possible haste. Nobody among those who are close to me judges matters differently.

However, not that many of them were still in Germany at the time of my departure: Brecht, Kracauer, and Ernst Bloch left at the right time—Brecht one day before he was to be arrested. Ernst Schoen was arrested but then released. They presumably took his passport away, as in most such cases. Mine unfortunately expires in August of this year, and one can obviously not count on its being renewed under present circumstances.

These lines are intended to inform you with broad strokes about my situation and the measures I have taken. The details can wait until later. I must ask you to address your reply to me in Paris, even though I won't be here long—if need be, mail will be forwarded. Please give Miss Marx my kindest regards, and tell her that the books she has from me should remain with her in Jerusalem, for the time being. Later on, I'll give her an address where she can send the proofs of [Brecht's] *Mother* [*Die Mutter*]—only after you've subjected them to detailed study, I hope.

Did I tell you that I wrote a small and perhaps peculiar text about language—eminently suitable to adorn your archive?

Answer as swiftly as possible and share my most cordial regards with Escha,

Yours, Walter

P.S. I found a reference to Hubert Grimme's *Althebräische Inschriften am Sinai* among my Berlin notes, which [I] came across here. I am sending you this title—I don't even know whether it's the title of a book or an article—because I read a truly noteworthy iconographic decipherment of the *Sistine Madonna* by this author some years ago.[1]

1. Hubert Grimme (1864–1942) was professor of semitic studies in Münster. The work in question, which unleashed considerable controversy, appeared in 1923. WB confuses Grimme with the art historian Hermann Grimm.

217. To Gretel Adorno

San Antonio, Ibiza
April 15, 1933

Dear Felizitas,[1]

I would have liked to have told you something about me and my situation a long time ago, if only I could have found a moment's rest during the past ten days, sleeping aside. And I would not be getting around to writing even now if I did not have the courage to begin in spite of the most miserable lighting in the world—namely, not candles but a wretched electric lamp suspended from an unreachably high ceiling. I spent eight days traveling here from Paris—stopping in Barcelona and in Ibiza—only to become immediately involved in moving right after arriving. Last year's house, which had played no small role in my fantasies this winter, had been sublet by the Noeggeraths a few hours before my arrival. And even if they had kept it, there would have been no place in it for me due to some remodeling that had since been carried out.

Thus the ceiling with the wretched lamp is in a different house. Compared with the old one, it has the advantage of one-quarter or one-eighth more comfort but, on the other hand, the disadvantages of an inconvenient location and architectural banality. It was built on the edge of San Antonio by the local doctor, who had to move, and is three-quarters of an hour away from the beautiful section of forest in which I spent the previous summer. This, however, is only the scaled-down version in my private life of the great changes taking place in my public life. That is to say, despite the not very graceful construction going on in San Antonio, there are hardly any accommodations to be found at the moment. Prices have consequently risen once again. And thus the changes in the economy and the change of scene that have taken place since last summer balance each other out. In relationship to the fantastically favorable niveau in its totality, of course, both things are not overly painful. The arithmetical growth of the region is an entirely different matter. The isolation of last summer is made difficult not only by topographical circumstances, but also by the appearance of "summer guests" among whom it is not always possible to distinguish precisely between the high season and the twilight of life.

It is not really necessary anyway, because it is sometimes possible here to learn more about the origins and nature of people in days than it is possible to learn in Berlin in years. If you come in a few months, I can therefore promise you a fairly instructive tour through the local park of destinies. As for the rest, a new conjunction of various entanglements is in the process of being formed in that a Frenchman—the brother of the married couple I told you about—is opening a bar in Ibiza, right in the harbor. Its gradually emerging three-dimensional model promises to provide very pleasant quarters.

I received a quite detailed letter from Max [Horkheimer] which he wrote in Geneva and from which I can at least gather that the journal is being continued and that he continues to count on my contributions. It goes without saying that a sociology of French literature, which I am expected to produce next, is just the kind of thing that is not very easy to write here. Nonetheless, I laid the groundwork for it in Paris as best I could.[2] It seems that I can count on getting some reviews to do later. At the moment, I am also writing some for other outlets without having any illusions about the uncertain editorial fate of the manuscripts. May I make a request in this regard? I told my maid to forward to me from Paris the review copy of the collection of Dauthendey's letters the *Frankfurter Zeitung* had sent me.[3] It has not yet arrived and it is important that I get it very soon. Could you perhaps call and ask about it? By the way, I received a letter informing me that my review of Wiesengrund's book appeared on April 2 or 9 in the literary supplement of the *Vossische Zeitung*.[4] I have not received the offprints and would be especially grateful to you if you could send me two copies or have the offprints that are probably waiting in my apartment forwarded to me.

It goes without saying that I very soon hope to get some precise information about what you have been doing since April 1. Not only about that, but also about your health. And finally about how Wiesengrund's projects have been coming along. I am almost certain that he will meanwhile be inclined to accept my most recent oral proposals. You must tell him that Max asked about him with some concern in the aforementioned letter. The pivotal point of your activities for me is the question of your trip this summer and what its destination will be. I would be very depressed if you were to lose sight of the perspectives of our long conversation in the West End. But I am sure that you will manage everything as cleverly and precisely as I have always known you to do. Write me and give me exact details about this.

I have seriously begun to learn Spanish with the help of three different systems: an old-fashioned grammar, the basic thousand words, and finally a new and really sophisticated suggestive method. I think that this will produce results in the near future. Tomorrow is Easter—I am planning to take my first walk of some length into the country. But shorter walks have already convinced me that the old beauty and solitude of the region can only be found a half hour's distance from the houses and I hope that this time I will not have to make all my exploratory journeys by myself. Otherwise, it is sometimes very hot during the day but still cool during the nights, just like a year ago.

Since beginning this letter my impression of the new house had already begun to take on some clarity. I am being accommodated in quite genteel fashion in a room containing a kind of dressing room, in which it is even possible to take a hot tub bath after heating the boiler for a long time: for Ibiza, this is like something out of a fairy tale. It is also useful because there is hardly any prospect of my being able to bathe in the sea before four to six weeks have gone by. Furthermore, the furnishings include a bookshelf and a wardrobe so that I can very neatly arrange my few things and papers around me.

Many thanks for Ernst's [Bloch] address. I will send him a card in the next few days. Since being here I have still not heard much from the outside world. I am waiting to be compensated for this as well by your next letter.

For today, all the very best,
Detlef[5]

1. The form of address WB used for Gretel Adorno during his emigration.

2. Cf. "Zum gegenwärtigen gesellschaftlichen Standort des französischen Schriftstellers" [On the contemporary social position of the French writer], *Zeitschrift für Sozialforschung* 3 (1934), pp. 54–77.

3. Max Dauthendey, *Ein Herz im Lärm der Welt: Briefe an Freunde* (Munich, 1933). WB's review of the book was published under a pseudonym in the literary supplement of the *Frankfurter Zeitung* (April 30, 1933).

4. The review appeared on April 2.

5. [WB adopted the pseudonym Detlef Holz to publish *Deutsche Menschen* in Germany during the advent of fascism. Individual letters from *Deutsche Menschen* were introduced by WB under this pseudonym in the *Frankfurter Zeitung* beginning in 1931.—Trans.]

218.* To Gerhard Scholem

San Antonio, Ibiza
April 19, 1933

Dear Gerhard,

If I'm not mistaken, you must have already received confirmation from Paris that your letter to Berlin reached me there. A few days ago I received the first letter you addressed to Ibiza. To dwell for a moment on the first one, I wish to turn your news about Steinschneider's stay with you into the object of a small inquiry. As you will have read, among the grains of sand that the awakening Germany rubbed from its eyes was—besides Herr Rotter[1] and his wife—Hanussen, the clairvoyant. According to a press report, his real name was supposedly Steinschneider. Please, by all means, let me know if he, too, should turn out to be a member of Gustav's already remarkable family.[2] If Gustav were to share the talent of that putative member of his family, then I foresee a significant boom in your kabbalistic studies, since it would presumably eliminate the costly business of photographing manuscripts.

Your news about Schoeps and Blüher was extremely valuable to me, as I may already have told you. Under the circumstances, I am now doubly impatient to receive his book on Kafka. For what would be more in character for the angel who looks after the destroyed part of Kafka's works than to hide the key to it under a dungheap? Whether comparable enlightenment can be expected from the latest essay on Kafka, I cannot say. It can be found in the April issue of the *Nouvelle revue française* and is by Bernhard Groethuysen. Once I have seen it, you may have it, in exchange for something else to read.

Even though a modest house library of thirty or forty volumes has been assembled here, partly from Noeggerath stock and partly from what I left behind here last spring, it is still only a meager base. As irony will have it, this is precisely the moment I am supposed to write an essay on the sociology of contemporary French literature, commissioned by the *Zeitschrift für Sozialforschung,* which managed to escape with its funds and equipment to Geneva. And I have to write the essay, since I can at least count on being paid by them. The essay, which in any case is sheer fakery, acquires a more or less magical mien by virtue of the fact that I have to write it here, with next to no source material of any kind. It will boldly exhibit that visage in Geneva, but keep it hidden in your presence. I don't know anything more about this yet. On the other hand, I now especially praise the impulse that made me give Brecht's book (and, if I'm not mistaken, several other books on loan[3]) to Kitty to take with her, since by doing so I hope they will return into my possession before too long. It will amuse you to know, by the way, that at the last moment I was suddenly seized by the idea of packing an enormously provocative and well-written work of Brecht's into my suitcase, after I had meticulously sifted through my archive, which means that I have only a fraction of it at my disposal here, and only totally innocuous pieces politically. The Brecht text is unpublished and exists only in galleys. It is entitled "The Three Soldiers"[4] and will also have found—or soon find—its way to Palestine.

By the time your prognoses regarding the fate of German Jewry arrived here, they had been fulfilled. Needless to say, they concur with mine. It was three weeks ago that I asked Dora to send Stefan, if at all possible, to her brother in Palestine. For the moment, however, she does not seem to be contemplating this course of action. I dwell upon my own situation only reluctantly. After having implemented the last option I had—that is, by moving here, to reduce my living expenses to the European minimum of about 60 or 70 reichsmarks a month—I feel incapable of indulging in too much activity for the moment. Not every literary association with

Germany has been dissolved as yet: an essay or a review might still sneak through every now and then. However, the foundation of a "writers' union" that excludes Jews from its ranks and from the press, has to be imminent. I am extremely skeptical about the prospects of securing a livelihood for myself in France, unless émigré organizations were to provide me with a framework within which I could work. With this in mind, I am making use of every opportunity during my stay in Paris, introducing myself in various places. A return to Paris, however, even if it should seem to be the right course to take, poses not only a financial but a legal problem, since my passport won't be valid after this summer. And it is highly unlikely that it will be extended. Needless to say, I will not return to Germany under any circumstances. I only wish that Stefan were already out, as well.

Kitty Marx sends me a congenial postscript, which has not so bewitched my eyes, however, that they would lose the image of the letter she promised, especially since her Cyprian greetings did not reach me at all. Give her my kindest regards, and convey such to Steinschneider as well. I return Escha's greetings and yours most wholeheartedly.—I'll copy the text on language for you. Even though it turned out to be very short, I am sure manifold thoughts and objections will stay my hand and hold it back as I write, and that you will not come into possession of the two or three pages for many weeks.

Yours, Walter

P.S. Your letter of the 13th arrived at this very moment. I can only confirm that I received it, and KM's postscript as well. I have also tried to reflect on the implications of events in Germany for the future history of the Jews. With very little success. In any event, the emancipation of the Jews stands in a new light. Nothing new from Dora. But she lost her job.

1. The director of a Berlin theater.
2. [He was a distant relation of the Steinschneider family.—Trans.]
3. Robert Musil's *Der Mann ohne Eigenschaften,* 2 vols. (Berlin: Rowohlt, 1930, 1932). [*The Man without Qualities,* trans. Eithne Wilkins and Ernst Kaiser (1953; New York: Perigee, 1980).—Smith]
4. First published in *Versuche,* vol. 6, no. 14.

219. To Kitty Marx-Steinschneider

Ibiza
May 1, 1933

Dear Miss Marx,

You laid down conditions before you were inclined to write me. Any discussion of them results in their being fulfilled because this discussion can, of course, only take place in correspondence. Because of all of this, you may believe that the first lines of this letter are already evidence of my submission. But the further you read, the more likely it is that your brow will be furrowed in annoyance when you notice where even my generosity reaches its limit. For one thing, at the bottom of this page. Furthermore, when it is confronted by my irreproachable memory, in which an obelisk stands with old hieroglyphs of your promise to write, which is, however, not set on a pedestal of conditions. Third, at the suspicion that the hard fist of GS is concealed behind your behavior. He will welcome having won a confederate for the acts of violence with which he exacts his tribute from me in the form of letters.

Since I hope that these foregoing explanations have reduced your satisfaction at my letter to a minimum, I might be permitted to ask that you pay all the more heed to the beautiful stationery that I have been ordering from Paris for years whenever I get a chance. It has not been acknowledged even once by GS. Regarding your letters, which are henceforth to be sent to me by return mail, I for my part would be prepared to forgo a special examination and certification of your stationery under the condition that they contain:

Complete information about your arrival and accommodations in the Holy Land—your impression of the Jews in general and of GS in particular—a promise to return *The Mother* very soon—information about what you thought of it—a description of your daily activities that is just as graceful as it is honest—a weather report.

The latter as a consolation since it is ice-cold here as a rule (and, therefore, I hope where you are as well). For the rest, I sincerely wish you better living and working conditions than exist here, in this noisy house shaken by gusts of wind. I have not yet been able to tackle any larger projects, but am quietly planning a commentary on Gracian,[1] for which I have collected some editions of and writings about him. He was a Jesuit about whom GS, if asked, will hold a small speech for you over a cup of tea. You should stick to that for the time being, for it is still uncertain as to what will come of the commentary. I am currently busy writing a quite curious piece about the novel, which, once it is printed, may yet arrive in the harbor of the Scholem archive—probably as one of the last ships to do so.

I am now reading the second volume of Trotsky; this is my only entertainment except for walking. For a sensible word can rarely be heard here, much less advanced. The rare high points of social life consist in chess matches. So, my dear KM, cheer me up as quickly as possible.

Yours, Walter Benjamin

1. On Gracian's *Truthtelling Manual*.

220.* To Gerhard Scholem

San Antonio, Ibiza
May 23, 1933

Dear Gerhard,

Your letter of May 4th has arrived. I have all the more time to answer it, because exchanges with German correspondents turn out to be increasingly sparse. Understandably, the people there are not anxious to put themselves in danger for the sake of an exchange of views. On May 4th you had not yet seen my last inquiry, but did have the somber news about your brother. You write that you are unable to imagine why he behaved as he did. I feel the same way about my brother. I spoke with him on the telephone before I left. At that time rumors of his death had already surfaced twice in Wedding, where he lives. Meanwhile, the rumors I asked you to help me check have turned out to be basically true. He fell into the hands of the SA five weeks ago and since that time has been held prisoner in the state hospital. I don't know anything about the nature of his injuries. [. . .]

Tell me if you are able to find out anything else—which I doubt. Today I exchanged a few words with someone newly arrived from Germany. On the whole, all one knows and suspects is confirmed. A week ago I urged Dora once again—insofar as this is possible in a letter—to send Stefan out of Germany. As long as he is still inside, I must proceed with the greatest caution imaginable in what I allow to be printed.

My constitution is frail. The absolute impossibility of having anything at all to draw on threatens a person's inner equilibrium in the long run, even one as unassuming and as used to living in precarious circumstances as I am. Since you wouldn't necessarily notice this if you were to see me, its most proper place is perhaps in a letter. The intolerability of my situation has less to do with my passport difficulties than with my total lack of funds. At times I think I would be better off if I were less isolated. Nonetheless, the choice of this place was naturally a clever one. The odd letter gives me hope now and then that acquaintances might put in an appearance, although experience of course teaches me not to set great store in their plans. Even last year, nobody actually showed up. When I let more than a week pass—as I have now—without seeing my Parisian friends in Ibiza, it puts me in a dismal state. By the way, the husband is absorbed in his ambition to translate small sections of the *Berliner Kindheit*. He doesn't know any German but is capable of following my paraphrases with excellent comprehension.[1]

Since I must assume that the new press law being drafted in Germany will deprive me of the last remnants of my journalistic opportunities there, Paris would offer me the only remaining base for my work. And isn't this formulation utterly optimistic! But since the most I could earn in Paris would just suffice to cover my living expenses *here,* a dilemma presents itself for which I see no solution.

So much in answer to your kind inquiry.

In the meantime, I apply myself to my ongoing projects as best I can, isolated from all means of production. Both these tasks and my living conditions, which differ somewhat from last year's, have conspired to keep me away until now from what matters most to me: continuing the *Berliner Kindheit.* Did I manage to send you "The Little Hunchback," the concluding piece, or did that first come into being after I had sent you the rest? Once I am done agonizing over my extended study on the state of contemporary French letters, which I'll soon have ready, I will devote myself again to the subject of the novel, which I recently explored in an essay that regrettably hasn't yet been printed.

At about the same time I will probably exchange my present quarters for quarters in a lonely mill—without windows: they will probably make a hole in the door. There things will either become bearable[2] (and then I might remain indefinitely) or (and this is at least as likely) become unbearable, in which case I may leave San Antonio for Ibiza, or leave the island altogether.

I am very much looking foward to *The Mother.* If you want to read the Musil you may keep it, though only for the time being. I have lost my taste for it and have taken leave of the author, having come to the conclusion that he is far too clever for his own good.

And now for something that will line your brow with furrows. But it must be said. After further misgivings about the plan of sending you my recent jottings on language, I realized that this project, hazardous as it is, would only be viable if I could first conduct a comparison of these notes with my early "On Language as Such and on the Language of Man."[3] The latter, however, is of course out of reach, since it is among my papers in Berlin. But I know you possess a copy. I therefore urgently request you to send it as soon as possible by registered mail to my present address—which remains valid even if I move to the mill. Don't lose any time: you will receive my new notes all the sooner. Incidentally, I am waiting for just a few more mailings of printed matter from Berlin before I send you another package to supplement your archive of my writings. I must really congratulate myself now on the conscientiousness with which I have attended to this archive. I hope to hear soon, however, that the largest and most current part of my own archive is secure in a Paris safe; somebody wants to take charge of having it transported there.[4]

Kitty Marx received a long letter from me, sent from here. I honor and welcome an occasion that must have eclipsed this shining event in her eyes, but I can only tell her that once she has paid even slight tribute to it. Be quick about ordering her the *One-Way Steet,* before the German booksellers have read it.

What kind of position did Kraft have in Hannover? And is he still among your correspondents? And what has happened to him?[5] What will become of him?

Write without delay! Adorn your letter once more with enclosures like the *Jüdische Rundschau,* for which I am indebted. Kindest regards to you and Escha.

Yours, Walter

1. These translations, which went through many stages, are printed as an appendix in *Schriften* 4:979–86. Tillman Rexroth, the volume's editor, reports on their origin on pp. 969–70.

2. WB did not want to stay at the Noeggeraths' any longer.

3. [See *Reflections,* pp. 314–32.—Smith]

4. Although this person's identity is not known to me, it could most likely be ascertained from the letters to WB that are in East Berlin.

5. He came to Palestine in 1934 and is still living in Jerusalem.

221.* To Gerhard Scholem

June 16, 1933

Dear Gerhard,

A few days have passed since your letter of the 23d arrived—it, too, took a long time to get here. When it finally did come, I happened to be away for a few days, as I take every opportunity to turn my back on San Antonio. If you take a hard look at things, then you realize that there are no peaceful spots left—let alone peaceful moments—in its vicinity, which has been smitten with all the horrors accompanying the activities of settlers and speculators. Even the cheapest place becomes too expensive if the price is the sheer possibility of getting any work done, and my relocation to the city is only a matter of days, as difficult as it is to find a place both affordable and bearable on Ibiza.

Meanwhile, I am using this situation as an impetus for extended exploratory hikes into the heart of the island. I undertook one recently in the very pleasant company of a grandson of Paul Gauguin, who bears his grandfather's name. We had a lobster fisherman drop us off at a deserted spot on the coast—not before watching him at work—and marched from there into the mountains. Yesterday I was away with my French friends for fourteen hours. As soon as one is out of earshot of the blastings and hammer blows, the gossip and debates that constitute the atmosphere of San Antonio, one feels the ground again beneath one's feet. My long-held mistrust of the whole business of developers, which I first experienced in

Grünau as a guest in the Gutkinds' house,[1] has been all too drastically confirmed here in the Noeggeraths' house. Add to this the very unpleasant nature of the villagers. In short, I already yearn for those saturated shadows with which the wings of bankruptcy will bury this whole glorious paradise of narrow-minded shopkeepers and vacationers within a few short years.

Ibiza also has its drawbacks, although such an atmosphere is not among them. Keep writing to me here, anyway, before you find out my address over there. All my mail will be forwarded.

I want to backtrack to my last letter once again and tell you how very definitely I hope to get my hands on your copy of my manuscript on language, so that I can go through it and then transcribe my new essay and have it sent off to you. Besides this imminent expansion of your holdings, a lesser acquisition will have reached you by now—at least I sent you an envelope of new material a week ago, containing the first pieces written by Detlef Holz. But even his obligingness has its limits. I must forgo his assistance on an essay I am working on at the moment, because it would immediately compromise his name, the way his [predecessor's] name has been compromised.[2] Two review copies are forcing me into the disagreeable position of having to speak about Stefan George, now, before a German audience. I believe I have understood this much: if ever God has smitten a prophet by fulfilling his prophecies, then this is the case with George.

I most likely wrote you that I finished an extended study on "Die gegenwärtige gesellschaftliche Stellung des französischen Schriftstellers" [The present social position of French writers], and to my credit have found a place for it in that very Frankfurt archive which escaped to Geneva. They have presented me with yet another commission, which will perhaps be more demanding and certainly less pleasurable.[3] Most peculiar, though, are the requests for my contributions that keep arriving from Germany, from offices that showed little interest in me in the past. The *Europäische Revue,* for example, asked me for suggestions about possible contributions.

But I am jotting down these brief bits of information for you mostly to give you some idea of the condition of my budget, or rather to demonstrate the utter impracticability of drawing up a budget at all. Since leaving Berlin, I have averaged a monthly income of about 100 reichsmarks,[4] and this under the most unfavorable conditions. I don't wish to imply that I might not manage to earn even less than this tiny sum. But presumably not in the long run. On the contrary: I assume my earnings would increase in the long run, that is, if I am not completely severed from every means of production, as I am here. I could say more—but only tentatively—if I knew more about the impending German press laws.

And with that I have contributed to the discussion I learned of through your letter. I won't deny that I have more to say about it. To begin with, I should state that such a discussion does not leave me indifferent, by any means. It is of tremendous importance to me. But I would not be forty if I did not approach with extreme caution the idea of the mere possibility of change it contains. I tell myself that I might appear at this new shore in an ambiguous light. Thousands of intellectuals have made their way to you. One thing distinguishes them from me—and this seems to work in my favor at first glance. But thereafter—as you well know—the advantage becomes theirs. Precisely this: they represent blank pages. Nothing would have more fateful consequences than an attitude on my part that could be construed as though I were attempting to cover up a private calamity with a public one. This is something that has to be considered, since I have nothing and am attached to little. In such circumstances, one must shy away from every doubtful situation, since it can bear disproportionate consequences. I would be glad and fully prepared to come to Palestine, if you, or others concerned, assume that I could do so without provoking such a situation. And as far as I can tell, the same proviso can be couched in the question, is there more room for me—for what I know and what I can do—there than in Europe? If there is not more, then there is less. This sentence needs no explanation. And neither does this final one: if I could improve upon my knowledge and my abilities there without abandoning what I have already accomplished, then I would not be the least bit indecisive in taking that step.

My brother is in a concentration camp.[5] God only knows what he has to endure there. But the rumors about his wounds were exaggerated in at least one respect. He did not lose an eye. I recently found this out from my sister. I only learned of Erich Baron's death from you.

I allowed KM's greetings to take effect on me. The story of her first letter to me seems to be unfolding in the purest *Tristram Shandy* style.[6] With this observation we also best do justice to the utter uncertainty as to whether the letter will ever come into being.

All the best for today,
Yours, Walter

1. 1920–21. See letter 90.

2. This explains why he chose a new pseudonym ("K. A. Stempflinger") for the review he subsequently refers to, which was of two books on Stefan George. [Cf. *Schriften* 3: 392–99.—Smith]

3. This may well refer to the essay on Eduard Fuchs, which WB was not keen on writing from the outset.

4. About seven English pounds in those days in the valid currency of the British Mandate of Palestine.

5. Georg Benjamin was in Sonnenburg concentration camp. The discrepancy between the date in this letter and the date in Hilde Benjamin's *Georg Benjamin* requires explanation, since she fixes the transfer from prison to the concentration camp as not taking place until September. Could it be that his sister, Dora, who is referred to as a source for at least some of the particulars, was imprecise?

6. An allusion to the way imbroglios are portrayed in Laurence Sterne's novel.

222. To Max Rychner

San Antonio
June 25, 1933

Dear Mr. Rychner,[1]

I have thus far owed you thanks for your very kind words of May 9. However, I wanted to accompany my thanks with a contribution, no matter how short. But a few days after I had written you, I had to go to Geneva for a short time. I have therefore still not gotten around to the essay I have been planning to write on "Romancier und Erzähler" [Novelist and storyteller].

I hope the enclosed short piece[2] will earn your favor because of its brevity.

And now let me use this letter to bring up yet another question: Is it editorially feasible for you to spur on my collaboration by now and then sending me new books? Or may I occasionally take the initiative in this regard? For example, in the last few days I was sent quite a lengthy volume, *Die Stellung der Sprache im Aufbau der Gesamtkultur,* by Leo Weisgerber (Heidelberg: Winter Universitätsbuchhandlung, 1933). Even though it does not exactly fall within the purview of any of your permanent reviewers, it might be an appropriate book to review.

I would sign my contributions with the name you find at the head of the enclosed manuscript, a name that has already on occasion come away with honor.

Because of my departure, the copies of the February 25 issue in which you published "Kurze Schatten" did not reach me. For you surely must have sent them. I would most happily be indebted to you if you were willing to send me one or two copies of the issue for my archive.

Hoping to hear good things from you soon. Sincere regards,

Yours, Walter

1. Feuilleton editor of the *Kölnische Zeitung*.

2. Most likely "Chinoiserie."

223. To Gretel Adorno

[June 1933]

Dear Felizitas,

I am letting a slight musical breeze rock the peak of the pine tree under which I sit and draw a four-leaf thank you at its feet. You may pluck it in return for your last letter. I would have preferred to wish you a few thin, prickly straws from the Baltic Sea dunes for Pentecost. Yes, I am sad that you must duck your head under the bear's paw[1] rather than dip it into the waves. Let me know soon when you might dare show it again.

But it is comforting that the proxy for the bear child has sided with the problem child's. If only in so doing the one meant for you will not be completely lost. [. . .] Something you could actually do from time to time for your own enlightenment, and for whomever you are now seeing after the problem child disappeared. This last maxim is meant to convey my sincere gratitude for the author's copies of the *Kierkegaard;* also please note that the editor eliminated an important paragraph of the review—toward the end.[2] I still have not heard anything from the *Europäische Revue.*

I have been working hard and have written an essay, "Der gegenwärtige gesellschaftliche Standort des französischen Schriftstellers," which is forty typewritten pages. While writing it I had to rely on the hospitality extended to me by people in the city of Ibiza. In the meantime every kind of topographical unpleasantness in San Antonio, which had been long heralded, has now made itself felt to the extent that my moving into the city has become a closed issue. There will unavoidably be somewhat greater expenses there than the ones incurred here. But after having exhausted, not without considerable ingenuity, all technical possibilities that might have made for a place where I could work halfway undisturbed, I had to reach a decision, since not a single one panned out. I am already looking forward to expounding for you in person the physiology of this house and the secrets of the colonizing atmosphere that has gradually developed in San Antonio.

To me it is the most hateful of atmospheres and therefore, for some time, I have been seizing upon any pretext to get away. One of the most beautiful and remote parts of the island was recently revealed to me in that way. I had just gotten ready for a solitary moonlight walk to the highest point of the island, the Atalaya of San Jose, when a passing acquaintance of the family with whom I am staying showed up. He is a Scandinavian fellow who only rarely makes an appearance in areas where there are foreigners and lives in a hidden mountain village. Furthermore, he is a grandson of the painter Paul Gauguin and has exactly the same name as his grandfather. I became more closely acquainted with this character the next day. He was definitely just as fascinating as his mountain village, in which he is the only foreigner. We went out with a lobsterman at five in the morning and first spent three hours together at sea, where we received a thorough grounding in how lobsters are caught. Of course, the spectacle was predominantly melancholy, since in all only three animals were caught in sixty creels. They were of course gigantic and there are of course many more on other days. We were then put ashore in a hidden bay. And there we were presented with an image of such immutable perfection that something strange but not incomprehensible took place within me: namely, I actually did not see it at all; it made no impression on me; because of its perfection, it existed at the very brink of the invisible.

The beach is undeveloped; there is a stone hut in the background, standing off to the side. Four or five fishing boats had been pulled well up onto the shore. A few women were standing next to these boats, who were completely draped in black with only their serious and immobile faces uncovered. It was as if the miraculous nature of their presence had come into balance with the strangeness of their procession so that the indicator, as it were, was on zero and I did not notice a thing. I believe that Gauguin was in the picture; one of his characteristics, however, is that he hardly talks at all. And thus we had been climbing in almost complete silence for over an hour when, shortly before coming to the village that was our destination, a man came walking toward us carrying a tiny white child's coffin under his arm. A child had died in the stone hut down below. The women draped in black had been keeners who, in spite of their duties, had not wanted to miss an unusual spectacle such as the arrival of a motorboat on this beach. In short, in order to find this spectacle striking, you must first understand it. Otherwise, you would look at it with the same kind of indifference and thoughtlessness as you do at a painting by Feuerbach. When looking at such a painting, people remotely think that tragic figures on the rocky shore would make it just right.

In the heart of the mountains you come upon one of the island's most cultivated and fertile landscapes. The earth is covered with deep-cut canals, which are, however, so narrow that they often become invisible for large stretches under the high grass, which is of the deepest green. The roaring of these waterways produces an almost sucking sound. Carob bean trees, almonds, olive trees, and conifers grow on the slopes, and the valley floor is covered by corn and bean plants. Outlined everywhere against the cliffs are blooming oleanders. It is a landscape of the kind I fell in love with once before in *Jahr der Seele*. Today it permeated me even more deeply with the pure and fleeting taste of the green almonds I stole from the trees the next morning at six o'clock. You could not count on getting breakfast; it was a place removed from all civilization. My companion was the most perfect one imaginable for such a region. Just as uncivilized and just as highly cultivated. He reminded me of one of the Heinle brothers, who died so young, and he has a stride that often makes it seem as if he will disappear at any moment. I would not have so readily believed anyone else who asserted that he was struggling against the influence that the paintings of Gauguin had upon him. In the case of this young man, I was able to understand precisely whereof he spoke.

Turning to something entirely different: the serialization of the book in which a certain Trax Harding deals with a Colonel Fawcett who disappeared in the Brazilian primeval forest in 1925 has been appearing in the *Züricher Illustrierte* for about three weeks. I read the beginning of it and believe that the tramp and cowboy who claims to have written this book—and probably did, in fact, write the book—is a very important and uniquely gifted author. If you have read the first chapter, which must have appeared in one of the first May issues or the last April issue, you will be in the picture. You will get hold of the issues of the *Züricher Illustrierte* in question, read the series with breathless excitement, and then send it to me. Right?

In return, you will receive a copy of my Bennett review[3] as soon as I have offprints.

I repeatedly have cause to be grateful to you for the money orders that are paid out punctually and at the relatively favorable exchange rate of 2.7. For me, each of them represents a small model of a secure existence and they may have the same significance as architectural scale models, which often look much more charming than how life in the real buildings afterward turns out. And now you already want to think about my birthday. I have given it much thought and would like to put you in touch with my fondest desire. To be sure, Mac Orlan says that for a man who is forty years old there can actually be no greater celebration than to put on a new suit. So far so good—but I am now turning forty-one and at that point comfort is more essential than celebrations. Indeed, I would like to have blue smoke coming out of my chimney on that day. But no blue smoke has curled over my roof for a long time now and the pictures I enclosed in my last letter to you were the last ones formed by smoke. If you were to put some noble logs on my hearth, you would be associated with my best hours and the plume of my smoke above the house would blow over to you on the 15th.

My dear Felizitas, that is all for today. You should by all means keep my books. Please pass out only the manuscripts; these, for the sake of simplicity, in their entirety. Unless you happen to value one of them particularly. But that would offend the other pieces and this would therefore hardly be welcome.—My stationery is gone and I am unable to obtain the kind of envelope that has become dear to me—and, I hope, to you as well. Nonetheless, please kindly accept these lines which play more clumsily into your hands.

Yours as always, Detlef

P.S. A kind letter just arrived from the *Europäische Revue*.

1. The trademark of the glove factory where Gretel Adorno was working.

2. This paragraph was restored when the review was reprinted in *Dichten und Trachten: Jahresschau des Suhrkamp Verlages* 20 (Frankfurt am Main, 1962), p. 47.

3. The review of Arnold Bennett's *Konstanze und Sophie oder die alten Damen* (Munich, 1932), which appeared in the *Frankfurter Zeitung* (May 23, 1933).

224. To Jula Radt

[Postmarked July 24, 1933]

Dear Jula,

I was truly delighted to receive your letter. For it appeared right on my birthday and, arriving like that, was naturally even nicer than if you had remembered the birthday. For it turned out that your unconscious played into the hands of the World Postal Union in my honor.

But what you had to say was also welcome. Everything you are doing at this time to put down roots in the sandy soil of the Brandenburg March is admirable, as inappropriate as it may be for everyone to imitate. But if you were to or could look over my shoulder while I am writing this, you would find the shadows of pine needles playing over this Parisian stationery, which I have favored and been using for a long time. You would not be able to distinguish these pine needles from the ones in Brandenburg and if you looked straight ahead you would not catch sight of the sea, although it is only three minutes away from my summer hideaway.

That is to say, I have again moved into such a place with my lounge chair, since having succeeded in reclaiming last year's almost undeveloped shore after a less than happy debut on the developed shore on the other side of the bay. Until this, my way of life had been more unsettled, divided between the unsatisfactory working conditions of San Antonio and the diversions of Ibiza, which were in part quite noteworthy. Then a trip to Palma that was necessary for business reasons created a break in my stay here. I got to know Mallorca more extensively this year by hiking and taking car trips. But as beautiful as the island is, the things I got to see there nonetheless reinforced my attachment to Ibiza, which has an incomparably more reserved and mysterious landscape. The paneless window frames of my rooms cut the most beautiful pictures out of this landscape. My room is the only livable one in a shell construction that will still be worked on for quite a while and that I have all to myself as the only tenant until it is completed. By moving into these quarters, I have reduced what I need to live and my living expenses to a bare minimum below which it would seem impossible to go. The fascinating thing about all this is that everything is quite habitable and if I am lacking anything it is much more noticeable in the area of human relationships than in that of human comfort.

These relationships that constitute the chronicle of the island are mostly very fascinating for me, but sometimes also disillusioning and dissatisfying. In this worst case, of course, they leave me all the more time for my projects and studies.

My *Berliner Kindheit um 1900* [Berlin childhood around 1900], of which you unfortunately understood so little and in which there is so much to understand, is growing by some few but important pieces. An essay on Stefan George—perhaps the only one to appear on the occasion of his sixty-fifth birthday—expresses what I had to say on this occasion on behalf of my closest friends. I think it will have come to your attention. But I hardly dare hope that the ideas that once brought us together have matured in us due to the same kind of experience; to be sure, your particular comments would mean so much to me in terms of resolving this uncertainty that I must request you to share them with me.

I continue to read [Arnold] Bennett, in whom I increasingly come to recognize a man whose stance is very much akin currently to my own and who serves to validate it: that is to say, a man for whom a far-reaching lack of illusion and a fundamental mistrust of where the world is going lead neither to moral fanaticism nor to embitterment but to an extremely cunning, clever, and subtle art of living. This leads him to wrest from his own misfortune the chances, and from his own wickedness the few respectable ways to conduct himself, that amount to a human life. At some point you should also get hold of the novel *Clayhanger,* which was published in two volumes by the Rheinverlag.

You can well imagine that I receive very little mail that is pleasant. Thank God, the best so far has to do with Stefan, who is at the moment on an automobile trip with my wife that will take him through Austria and Hungary into Siebenbürgen and Rumania. The news from friends in Paris is depressing and the situation is so hopeless for one or another of them that they have already completely stopped writing. What might await me in Paris is extremely problematical. In any case, a masterly translation of *Berliner Kindheit,* being undertaken by a Parisian friend with my assistance, would constitute a not inauspicious beginning. But it is making very slow progress.

It is possible to read between the lines of your letter that Alfred is still asserting himself in the old, masculine way. I would like to have him here; he is one of the few people whom I could imagine under the island's difficult but not unproductive conditions. But it would be better if you were to say nothing to him about this and only give him my sincere regards, and Fritz as well.

As far as the two of us are concerned, letters may well constitute the best opportunity we have for ourselves. You are therefore receiving this most cordial letter along with a sincere request for your next one.

Walter

My review of *Konstanze und Sophie* appears with the title "Am Kamin" [At the hearth] in the *Frankfurter Zeitung* of May 23, 1933.

225.* To Gerhard Scholem

San Antonio, Ibiza
July 31, 1933

Dear Gerhard,

The mere sight of this stationery should suffice to make you, as the unchallenged authority on my letter writing, realize that something is amiss.[1] And that fact exonerates me for at least part of the three weeks I let go by without thanking you for the beautiful letter you sent me for my birthday. In particular, it covers me for the continued nonappearance of the notes on language you are entitled to.

You see, I have been ill for about a fortnight now. And because the outbreak of the illness—not very serious in itself—coincided with the first fits of July heat (perhaps no coincidence), I had my hands full to keep myself somewhat going under such difficult circumstances. I did so, on the one hand, by drawing upon all available reserves of detective novels, and, on the other, by intensively resuming my work on the *Berliner Kindheit um 1900*. A new section, which I fitted into the existing ones, had me sequestered from all other work for a while. A few pages have come into being under the title "Loggien" [Loggias], and I can only say very good things about them and add that they contain the most precise portrait I shall ever be able to give of myself. I hope you will see the piece in print in the near future.[2]

With it, of course, the Detlevian Holz[3]—which I have thrown upon the flame of my life—will flare up for more or less the last time. The new press laws are already taking shape, and after they go into force, my appearances in the German press will require a far more impenetrable disguise than heretofore.

And of course, probably more seldom. This would have left the future completely overcast had not a somewhat more hopeful perspective become visible over the last few days. It was imparted in a letter promising me free living quarters in a house that Baroness Goldschmidt-Rothschild has reserved in Paris for refugee Jewish intellectuals. Speyer made use of his connections with the world of Jewish finance,[4] apparently with success, in that a dispatch arrived here yesterday making the invitation official. But even this—a free place to live—is an extremely unstable foundation in an expensive city like Paris. However, I do not want to rule out the possibility that the same route that has led me this far may take me somewhat farther still, for this invitation undoubtedly also implies a more or less far-reaching introduction. Furthermore, the steps I took in the matter of my passport have been rewarded with success because of a fortunate constellation for which I may also claim some of the credit. I am now the owner of a new passport, even before my old—supposedly lost—one has expired.

I can of course only regard the Paris invitation as a happy intermezzo; in no way do I see that it opens up any long-term prospects. And precisely because the matter our last letters warily touched upon—the Palestinian options—deals only with the long term, whatever we are able to discuss in this regard must definitely take precedence over short-term European combinations. Yet you have a sufficient picture of my situation in your mind's eye to know how reassuring even a mere breathing spell must be for me. At any rate, I would have faced a winter on Ibiza only with unmitigated horror.

With regard to my poor health, I have a very unpleasant inflammation of a wound on my lower right thigh. Luckily it started up just when I happened to be in the town of Ibiza for a few hours. In San Antonio, my situation would have become grotesque. I live here in a hotel room at one peseta a day—the price indicates what the room looks like—and I drag myself through the town for unavoidable errands. If the situation doesn't improve in the next two or three days, I will be forced to keep myself completely immobile. A German doctor whom I have unearthed here delights in painting daily pictures of my chances of dying, should a complication arise.

I am separated from all books and papers, since they are in San Antonio. If I had the necessary books, I could at least start work on a commission from the *Frankfurter Zeitung* to write something for the two hundredth anniversary of the death of Wieland,[5] whom I hardly know at all. But I have been supplied only with pitiful occasional pieces. The French translation of the *Berliner Kindheit* is, by contrast, making progress. We work on it every day. The translator doesn't know a word of German. As you can imagine, the technique we use is not to be trifled with. But the results are nearly always outstanding.

As I told you, the truly hot spell has begun here. The Spaniards, who are familiar with its effects, speak of "August madness" as a very common occurrence.[6] I find it quite amusing to observe its manifestations in foreigners. Their numbers are growing, and, as you might easily imagine, there are some quite remarkable specimens among their ranks.[7]

I was interrupted here by the doctor, who told me that they will probably have to make an incision. That means an imminent return to San Antonio is out of the question. Nonetheless, send mail only to that address.

Even though you will now have to wait a while longer for the theory of language, I hope to receive a copy of your Schocken manuscript very soon, all the more as I have been exemplary in replacing with substitutes all those items you were kind enough to let me have from your archive of my material. Moreover, my essay on Stefan George should also be in your hands by now. If I can believe what I am told, there must have been a few bright lights who knew what to think of "Stempflinger." I would like very much to know what you think of the article.

So much for today. With kindest regards,

Yours, Walter

1. The letter was written on irregularly sized, grayish-blue paper, of a kind he never used.

2. "Loggien" first appeared in the *Vossische Zeitung* on August 1, 1933 (*Schriften* 4: 294–96).

3. [The German means "wood."—Smith]

4. Wilhelm Speyer, who himself had been baptized, came from a Jewish banking family in Frankfurt, which in its time was as well known as the Goldschmidts.

5. *Schriften* 2:395–404. It appeared in the national edition of the *Frankfurter Zeitung* (September 5, 1933).

6. Days later (August 12 and 13), WB was to write the autobiographical note "Agesilaus Santander," which I published in the volume *Zur Aktualität Walter Benjamins,* ed. S. Unseld (Frankfurt am Main: Suhrkamp Verlag, 1972), pp. 94–102. [English translation by Werner Dannhauser in Scholem, *On Jews and Judaism in Crisis* (New York: Schocken Books, 1976), pp. 204–8.—Smith]

7. Since WB kept all, or nearly all, of the cards and letters sent him during that time, it might be possible—if one had access to his papers in the East Berlin Academy of Arts—to identify the people he had in mind here.

226. To Gretel Adorno

[undated]

Dear Felizitas,

An envelope containing some printed matter was sent off to you in Rügen yesterday. It is mainly important that you make the acquaintance of my "Rückblick auf Stefan George" [Retrospective of Stefan George].

I am so sorry that I must append even to this meager parcel the qualifying request that you send the "Rückblick" back to me; I do not yet have a copy of it.

You know that I am indebted to you for so much that this letter would have been difficult to begin had I started it with an expression of gratitude. The parcel mentioned at the beginning is certainly not intended as such an expression. Rather, I am hopeful that I will ambush you with my gratitude someplace in an out of the way Parisian bistro when you are least expecting it. I will then see to it that I am not wearing the very suit you gave me and which may more readily provide me with the freedom to do many things other than express this gratitude. In the meantime, however, please accept the gratitude that comes in the weatherproof packaging of these few words.

I am glad you are on vacation and hope that it will be a very pleasant one. However, as far as Paulus [Paul Tillich] is concerned, you will wait entirely in vain for my sympathy; even if I previously mustered it inexhaustively for a similar case, in this case—which is so very different because of his background—I find that envy is much more to the point. The pleasure of now taking him to task strikes me as not the worst item on a vacation agenda. Nonetheless, I hope there are better items on the agenda, and that one of them is the public reading of "Tom."[1] I would naturally be delighted if I were able to have a look at the manuscript. Not that there is a shortage of things for me to read here: but I am very interested in it.

As far as the aforementioned "reading" is concerned, my inclination to read is sometimes in inverse proportion to its urgency. For example, Frankfurt thought of me for the commemorative article on the two hundredth anniversary of Wieland's birth and I had to have a good part of his opus sent to me in the Reclam edition. I was not familiar with any of his works before this and it will take even more luck than understanding to say something decent on the subject in the short time available—and naturally also in the shortest space. Before I completely disappear into this reading, however, I still hope to complete yet another piece for my *Berliner Kindheit,* called "Der Mond" [The moon]. The similarity you noticed between "Loggien" [Loggias] and "Fieber" [Fever] does, of course, really exist. But both pieces are close to me in very different ways: the first-mentioned piece, which I see as a kind of self-portrait, is much closer to me than the earlier one. I will probably put it in first place in the book instead of the piece on photography included in the *Mummerehlen*. The French translation is progressing slowly, but very surely.

My most sincere thanks for the effort you made to get me copies of some of the "Briefe." [. . .]

In conclusion, let me return once more to the small parcel that preceded these lines and say that the "Chinoiserie"[2] is precisely the little story about which Elisabeth[3] spoke to you. Knowing full well that it would merit another title, I nonetheless gave it the one that was printed. Things are much more complicated and less gratifying as concerns "Schränke" [Cabinets]. A name for the author was arbitrarily chosen and even I got to see the text very late.[4] If I did not have growing and more detailed knowledge of how much secrecy is now particularly warranted for studies like those in the *Berliner Kindheit,* the fate of this series' publication would have meanwhile driven me to despair. Now, however, things are at the point where this fate only reinforces my conviction that the cloak of secrecy is necessary for this kind of thing to be developed. This conviction in turn helps me to resist for the time being the temptation just to finish the work. The remarkable thing is not so much that pieces that were planned long ago are being added, but rather that they are most often the kind of pieces I thought of only shortly before I started working on them. Given the letter I received yesterday about the matter of accommodations in Paris, I will hardly be likely to leave here before September 15. You can well imagine that I will leave for Paris without any illusions. As of now, the intellectual situation does not include many elements that could be beneficial for an appreciation of my work. [. . .]

I hope to hear from you again very soon. And I hope that your vacation will bring you the kind of serene days that I sometimes spend in my hiding place in the bushes where I work.

Most sincerely yours, Detlef

1. Theodor Adorno's *Tom Sawyer,* an operetta text whose score was never finished.
2. *Kölnische Zeitung* (July 22, 1933).
3. Elisabeth Wiener, a friend of Gretel Adorno.
4. The text, part of *Berliner Kindheit,* appeared under the pseudonym C. Conrad in the *Frankfurter Zeitung* (July 14, 1933).

227.* To Gerhard Scholem

Paris
October 16, 1933

Dear Gerhard,

Even if these wishes arrive far too late for Rosh Hashanah, they will at least reach you in time for the long-sought and now official establishment of your academic duties, not to mention the title of professor.

Before I touch on this or anything else from our last exchange, let me just sketch out my situation. I arrived in Paris seriously ill. By this I mean that I had not recovered at all while on Ibiza, and the day I was finally able to leave coincided with the first in a series of very severe attacks of fever. I made the journey under unimaginable conditions, and, immediately after my arrival here, malaria was diagnosed. Since then, a rigorous course of quinine has cleared my head, even though my strength has yet to be fully restored. It was considerably weakened by the numerous hardships of my stay in Ibiza—not the least of which was the wretched diet.

You won't be surprised to learn that I am faced here with as many question marks as there are street corners in Paris. Only one thing is certain, that I have no intention of making a futile attempt to earn my living by writing for French journals. If I could place something in a representative journal (*Commerce, NRF*) once in a while—although even this seems unlikely—I would welcome it because of the attendant prestige. But to try to make a French literary career my means of subsistence, so shortly after a series of still lingering setbacks, would soon rob me of what's left of my no-longer-unlimited power of initiative. I would prefer any occupation, even a menial one, to whiling my time away in the editorial antechambers of the street tabloids. Probably the best I can hope for right now is a chance to earn something doing part-time bibliographical or library work.

I have hardly been out of my bed, and hence have been unable to activate my local contacts. I would welcome any assistance toward broadening them in a fruitful way. Is Robert Eisler by any chance in Paris?[1]

Friends have transported the major part of my archives[2] to Paris, at least the manuscript section. The Heinle papers are the only manuscript material of any importance still missing. The problem of securing my library is mainly a question of money, and that by itself presents a formidable enough task. Add to this that I have rented my Berlin apartment out furnished and cannot simply remove the library, which is an essential part of the inventory. On the other hand, the person renting it pays only what the landlord demands.

I am still waiting with a certain sense of uneasiness for acknowledgment that you've received the notes on language I sent you in typescript from Ibiza. You should have gotten them shortly after the 19th of September, the date of your last letter. I myself am looking forward to your contribution to the Schocken *Almanach*. I read your poem on the *Angelus Novus* again with undiminished admiration. I would place it among the best that I know.—I reread the dedication in *One-Way Street* with sympathy enlivened by recent written news from KMS. Please convey to her my kindest regards the next chance you have and assure her that a letter will soon notify her when I have regained my strength somewhat.

Haas is editing a journal in Prague called *Die Welt im Wort*. I would much rather send you the first issue—which has just reached me—if you wish, than comment about it at great length. Please consider even these three lines confidential.

Whether or not I will be able to move into the quarters Mrs. von Goldschmidt-Rothschild promised me has become rather problematic because of a series of oversights and delays far too complex to recount here.[3] It is also gradually becoming clear that the apartment is by no means free of charge.

Take it to heart that this is the first long letter I have written since my illness, and let me hear good news from you soon and at length.

Yours, Walter

1. On Robert Eisler, see Scholem, *WB*, pp. 131–32, and *From Berlin to Jerusalem: Memories of My Youth* (New York: Schocken, 1980), pp. 127–32. At that point Eisler had already been back in Austria for some time.

2. By "my archives" WB evidently meant something other than the totality of his papers and correspondence, most of which were lost.

3. It didn't work out in the end.

228. To Kitty Marx-Steinschneider

Paris
October 20, 1933

This letter would still be long delayed if I were to take such pains with the salutation as you perhaps believe I do, my dear addressee. I do not, however, want it to come to that even if only because you gave me such stouthearted information in your last letter concerning things about which I would not even dare to ask Gerhard. I will naturally not conceal the fact—if this must still be stated—that my approval of Brecht's production represents one of the most important and most defensible points of my entire position. I have been able to paraphrase it quite often in literary terms at least approximately, if never comprehensively. And I would further like to assume that these imperfect paraphrases are more likely to be looked on kindly in Palestine than the substantial collection of essays, *Versuche,* to which they refer. You have access to the former. I unfortunately do not assume that they will have any more influence over you than over Gerhard. They were able to move him only to a very meaningful silence and, if I am not mistaken, not to acquire the texts. Our confrontation about them has probably been only postponed and, indeed, absolutely ought to be postponed as far as I am concerned.

I am sure, however, that you have the same thing in mind as I do, to wit, that we not take the matter up on our own. And I would therefore confidently turn to some observations on Paris if only they were to turn out halfway pleasant. This cannot be said to have been true thus far. Instead I am much more inclined to express my appreciation to your emotions for the magical powers they evidently command for their gratification. For isn't my extremely pitiful arrival in this city not the work of the "slight envy" of which your last letter assures me? I arrived with a severe case of malaria. I have recovered from the fever, and the exhaustion with which it left me allows me enough strength to be aware of my desperate situation, but by no means enough to overcome it, since I am unable even to climb the stairs of the cheap hotels I had to choose for my accommodation. You can perhaps best describe what is being done here by Jews and for Jews as negligent benevolence. It combines the highest degree of humiliation with the prospect of alms—which are seldom accepted—and it is eternally eventful for former members of the bourgeoisie to study the detached forts of this benevolence that are concerned with Jews. And right now this is also the most obvious preoccupation of your humble servant who, moreover—in spite of a highly promising correspondence with Jewish high finance—has gotten not one penny, nor one mattress, nor one stick of wood from it to the present day.

I avoid seeing Germans. I still prefer to speak with Frenchmen, who of course are hardly able or wish to do anything, but who have the considerable charm of not talking about their fate. This behavior is even more unforgivable, however, when it claims to be caused by an attempt to overcome distance and I therefore do not intend to continue speaking about my fate.

We must therefore simply be patient until anecdotes have once again assumed their place in my life. And until then, I assume there will be all kinds of time and opportunity for you to think of me with a word of greeting.

Most sincere regards,
Yours, Walter Benjamin

229. To Gretel Adorno

Paris
December 30, 1933

Dear Felizitas,

These greetings will reach you—if not by the New Year, then surely—the very moment you return to Berlin. For I think you will still be in Frankfurt for New Year's. I again need to thank you for many things—for your admonition about Frankfurt, not to mention other, more important things. I had already taken certain steps regarding those things. I still have not heard anything and have every reason to assume that they have been in vain, which could have been predicted from the very beginning. Having predicted it naturally does not make the attendant consequences any easier to accept.

It cannot be denied, therefore, that I am not only at the end of the old year but also at the end of my wits. To be sure: as I probably wrote you, I recently won my first commission here, an essay on the royal governor Haussmann,[1] who rebuilt Paris under Napoleon III. I also have odds and ends to do. All of this cannot balance out my dismal prospects and the even more dismal loneliness that now surrounds me. The decision to be made would be the one to leave here and I would primarily have to find the strength to make it. I still have to wait for some things to happen. I am still hoping—above all else—that you will come. I still dread the Danish winter and having to rely completely on one person in Denmark, which can very easily become another form of loneliness. I also dread having to rely on a language that I do not know at all, something that is depressing if you have to manage all of your daily chores yourself.

The new educational law makes me concerned for Stefan.

My work lacks almost all validating force for me at the moment because I cannot afford to work on the project that attracts me most—the continuation of *Berliner Kindheit.*

I will write about "Tom" next time. I read "Vierhändig"[2] with much pleasure. As strange as it may sound, I should of course also venture into similar reminiscences at some time. I have even made some preliminary studies for such a project, but it has not reached that point.

[. . .]

Write as soon as possible. And my very best wishes to take you into the New Year.

Yours, Detlef

1. Contracted by *Le Monde,* but nothing ever came of it. See, however, *Zeitschrift für Sozialforschung* 3 (1934), pp. 442ff., and *Schriften* 1:419–22.

2. An essay by Theodor W. Adorno, "Vierhändig, noch einmal," *Vossische Zeitung* (December 19, 1933).

230.* To Gerhard Scholem

Paris
January 18, 1934

Dear Gerhard,

This obstreperous format is giving me the courage to prepare a longer letter. First of all, thank you for your letter of December 24th and for the book. You know the exceptional interest with which I read all of Agnon's writings that are accessible to me. I have just finished this volume, and I will often refer back to it. For now, I bring it into the conversation whenever possible. I have yet to find anything more beautiful in his works than "The Great Synagogue," which I regard as a tremendous masterpiece. And then the story about the guardian of books seems to me to be of great significance. Agnon displays mastery in every piece, and if I had become "a teacher in Israel"[1]—but I could have just as easily become an ant lion—I would not have been able to refrain from a lecture on Agnon and Kafka.[2] (By the way, should I ever regain possession of my library, Kafka's *Trial* [*Der Prozeß*] will be missing from it. It was stolen a long time ago. If you could come up with a copy, then the worst devastations the con man subjected my place to in his day would be repaired. I managed to wrest the other irreplaceable piece—the first edition of Brecht's *Hauspostille,* of which there are only twenty-five extant copies—from the author in the course of difficult negotiations.) I cannot predict, by the way, what will become of my library. It would require sixteen pages to set out the facts. But there is hope that I may get it back. I may be able to say more (or less) about it in the near future.[3]

Mentioning Kafka causes me to tell you that I have struck up an—albeit reserved—relationship with Werner Kraft.[4] He spotted me in the Bibliothèque Nationale and approached me afterward, in writing. I was surprised to read several texts of his from which I can withhold neither agreement nor respect. Two of them are attempts at a commentary on short pieces of Kafka's, subdued and definitely not without insight.[5] He has undoubtedly grasped much more of the matter than Max Brod. Among the maxims and reflections that have been discovered among Goethe's papers after his death (and one can guess why he never published the most important ones), one reads the following interesting sentence: "A child once burned is twice shy; an old man many times singed is afraid to warm himself."[6] I allude to it to convey in a few words the kinds of moods with which I have to struggle—often for weeks on end—to bring myself to take some initiative aimed at getting my writings printed somewhere. Overcoming these moods has, in the recent past, hardly ever resulted in anything other than having my inhibitions confirmed. They turned out to be justified in an especially uncomfortable way in the case of Max Brod, to whom I sent an essay at your urging, even referring to you by name. Not only did he reject it, but he was brazen enough to pass it on to Willy Haas without first getting my permission. Since the latter fellow has not sent me any remuneration at all up to now, for two contributions—one of which must be in your possession by now—I will consider myself fortunate if I ever get back the manuscript.[7] I think you will permit me to refrain from listing similar attempts that came to a similar end. It seemed more interesting—even if hardly more promising—to send the *Berliner Kindheit um 1900* to Hermann Hesse, which I did just recently.[8]

Did I write you that my brother was freed from Sonnenburg concentration camp around Christmas? But for all I know, proceedings on charges of high treason are still pending. If it comes to the worst, he and his one-year-old son[9] can be supported by his in-laws. Anyway, I consider it practically certain that he will resume illegal work in one way or another. This in strictest confidence, of course. You may also infer from this passage that it is by no means fear of censorship—what censorship?—that makes me occasionally speak of my own affairs in a laconic manner. Rather, the fault lies with the decidedly depressing conditions—and I am not speaking only about the external ones. I have hardly ever been as lonely as I am here. If I were seeking opportunities to sit in a café with émigrés, they would be easy to find. But I avoid them. Just call to mind how exceptionally important—and at the same time exceptionally small—the circle was that shaped my existence during my last years in Berlin. None of those who were at the center of it are here now, ever since Hauptmann, Brecht's secretary, went to America. And only two people who belonged to its periphery are around.[10]

I am postponing the trip to Denmark, and not only because of the time of year. As close as I am to Brecht, I do have my reservations about having to rely solely on him once I am there. Moreover, it is good to be able to seek the anonymity that a large city has to offer when you are completely destitute. Moreover, steps have been taken on my behalf at the Israélite alliance universelle, and they may provide me with some support for a short period, even though my information suggests that it cannot come to very much. I may have written you that I made contact with the magazine *Le Monde*. I am going to write a long article for them, a critical exposé of Haussmann's actions in Paris, about which I have already collected interesting materials over the years.

Your news about the Mani manuscript has made me curious. I will try to get the relevant academy report. Besides the work just mentioned, I am currently working on the philosophy of language. I had the *Zeitschrift für Sozialforschung* assign me an extensive survey of that field—and this gives me the opportunity to write about it. Are you familiar with Heinz Werner's [*Grundfagen der*] *Sprachphysiognomik*, which Barth published in 1932? I am studying it at the moment.

If you are in Rehovot again, pass on my fondest regards. And to Escha as well. Write soon.

Yours, Walter

1. A Jewish expression (taken from Hebrew) of highest honor.

2. That was a very broad hint to me. I had once written that a revision of Kafka's *Trial* takes place in Agnon's writings. [In "Das hebräische Buch: Eine Rundfrage," *Jüdische Rundschau* 33 (1928), p. 202.—Smith]

3. WB did in fact get "the more important half" (even if the smaller half) of his library, as he wrote to Brecht (letter 232).

4. WB and Kraft had not been in contact between 1921 and 1933.

5. The reference is to Kraft's essays "Über Franz Kafkas 'Elf Söhne'" and "Der Neue Advokat," both of which WB read in manuscript. (They were reprinted in Kraft's *Franz Kafka: Durchdringung und Geheimnis* [Frankfurt am Main: Suhrkamp Verlag, 1968], pp. 13–16, 49–62.)

6. Maxim 931 in 9:620 of the Artemis edition. Also in Max Hecker's edition of the 1907 *Maximen und Reflektionen,* republished as an Insel pocketbook, p. 168. The maxim can be found in both editions under "Aus dem Nachlass: Über Literatur und Leben" and is called "Ein gebranntes Kind . . ." [*The Maxims and Reflections of Goethe,* trans. Bailey Saunders (New York: Macmillan, 1893).]

7. The two contributions, "Erfahrung und Armut" [Experience and poverty] (*Schriften* 2:213–19) and remarks on Johann Peter Hebel's *Schatzkästlein* (*Schriften* 2:628), were in fact published in Haas's journal *Die Welt im Wort.* Because the journal failed, it defaulted on the payments, and the two pieces WB sent to Brod did in fact get published in the *Prager Tageblatt* (*Schriften* 4:757–61), as originally intended.

8. WB's letter of January 13 and Hesse's very positive reply have been printed in a Suhrkamp publication on Hesse (1975), pp. 83–84. Hesse was among the very few writers who tried to do something for WB. He tried to interest two publishers, S. Fischer and Albert Langen, in WB's work, and he later brought WB to the attention of an émigré publishing company in Holland.

9. Michael Benjamin, born December 27, 1932.

10. I don't know whom WB might have had in mind. In Klaus Völker's book on Brecht, the reader can find out who the people at the center of Brecht's Berlin circle were.

231. To Gretel Adorno

Paris
March 3, 1934

Dear Felizitas,

I finally have a few easier days and weeks ahead of me.

And I have you to thank for that. But gratitude—above all, when it comes from so far away—is a weak expression. How much longer are we going to have to depend on it? You helped me get out of a really horrible situation. I can see from the help you gave that you understood the situation and wanted to spare me a more detailed description.

I will now expend the new sense of initiative I gained because of you and Teddie in two directions. I will write you in more detail about one of them at another time—the *Arcades* project, in which I am once again very involved. The other depends on someone wanting to offer me the use of a—very small—art salon for some lectures. I would hold a lecture series there based on the things I have worked on, for a French audience and in French; that is, I would talk about Kafka, Ernst Bloch, and some others in the framework of a self-contained lecture series. It of course remains to be seen whether this will actually come to pass. I can only say that I really hope it will and am trying to mobilize all the connections I have here to make it happen.

The average experience I have thus far had with old French acquaintances has done little to encourage me to resume my former relationships. I must nonetheless push my reservations aside purely in the interest of furthering the plan for a lecture series. And I will turn to the oldest acquaintaince I have here in the next few days. I do not know whether the name of the former publisher François Bernouard[1] means anything to you. He has come into possession of a press again after experiencing all sorts of ups and downs. He also has again created for himself an—indeed, somewhat problematical—literary situation in that he appointed himself the *animateur* of a literary club—the Amis de 1914. I will most likely have to put in an appearance there some Tuesday; but before I do that, I have to determine in a private visit which way the wind is blowing.

With the same kind of thing in mind, I recently looked up Sylvia Beach, Joyce's publisher, whom I have mentioned on occasion. She has an English-language lending library here in the Quarter. Only—at least this is what she tells me—there aren't any Englishmen in Paris anymore. Her shop was in fact rather quiet and I had all the peace and quiet in the world to look at nice portraits and autographs of Walt Whitman, Oscar Wilde, George Moore, James Joyce, and others, which are hanging on her walls. The English milieu reminds me to tell you that I hope you really enjoy reading the Maugham detective stories I will send you tomorrow. I recently happened to read in the *Lu* this old man's autobiographical retrospective. He is now in Nice, looking back on his many successes. And the retrospective sounds very melancholy. You are nonetheless able to deduce from it that he worked for the intelligence service and accordingly drew his Mr. Ashendon from life.

Many thanks for the list of books you are planning to send. By the way: might not the *Trugbilder* and one or two other books of the same sort also be in your possession? No—I am looking at the list again—I am only missing the *Trugbilder* (a book with funny optical illusions on colored plates.) Also, it is not terribly important.

I am happy that Agnon is so close to you. Yes, my two favorite stories are "The Keeper of the Books" and "The Great Synagogue." The latter was supposed to be among the contributions to the first issue of my *Angelus Novus* (the journal I had planned to publish) about fifteen years ago.

[. . .]

Thus even old friends fall by the wayside and the value of the very few who remain becomes ever more tangible. With that, however, I have returned to the starting point of this letter and the only thing remaining for me to do is, in conclusion, to remind you to be good and follow Zian and write me very soon.

Wishing you all that is old and dear,

Yours, Detlef

1. WB published an article about Bernouard in the *Literarische Welt* (June 21, 1929).

232. To Bertolt Brecht

Paris
March 5, 1934

Dear Brecht,

Hauptmann[1] wrote me a letter in which, aside from greetings for you, there are also some lines having to do with you. Above all, as concerns the poetry volume:

"Has the volume[2] already appeared? I really need it terribly. Out of pure desperation, *Kuhle Wampe*[3] is still playing here. Brecht could be big here but I do not have anything of his with me. If he were to come over, he would have no difficulties in prevailing quickly and on a fairly broad basis."

Wissing is back from Berlin. [. . .] Nonetheless, this much is certain: my books have been shipped—what is at issue is about half of the library, but the more important half. I hope that it is already under way at this time. Please be sure to let me know immediately when the shipment arrives in Svendborg. The entire shipment has been paid for; at the most, there might be some unloading fees to be taken care of in Svendborg. I would be very grateful if you were willing to put up the money for this should the need arise. I hardly need to say that the books are at your immediate disposal.

As for the piece on Haussmann, the situation is that I could not resolve to write it for *Le Monde*. The people impressed me as being all too unreliable during my second meeting with them. On the other hand, I have absolutely all the material I need for this piece so that I can write it anywhere without having to look at any books. But I have hit upon another idea to get some income.

I am announcing a lecture series, "L'avantgarde allemande," [The German avant-garde], in the French circles accessible to me and some other ones as well. A series of five lectures—people will have to subscribe to the whole series. I will select only one figure from the various areas of literary activity in whom the current situation is authoritatively revealed.

1) le roman (Kafka)
2) l'essay (Bloch)
3) théâtre (Brecht)
4) journalisme (Kraus)

There will be an introductory lecture to precede these, called "Le public allemand."

So much for my current projects.

Did you get the Weill interview I sent you?

All the best for your work with Eisler. Sincere regards,

Yours, Walter Benjamin

1. Elisabeth Hauptmann, one of Brecht's collaborators.
2. Presumably *Lieder, Gedichte, Chöre* (Paris, 1924).
3. A film by Brecht.

233.* To Gerhard Scholem

Paris
May 6, 1934

This, my dear Gerhard, does not represent the first attempt to reply to your letter. But if the repeated endeavors point to a difficulty, that difficulty does not lie in the content of information you request, but in the form of your request. You dress it up as a—perhaps rhetorical—question: "Is it intended to be a Communist credo?"

Such questions, it seems to me, tend to absorb salt on their way across the ocean and then taste somewhat bitter to the person who has been questioned. I do not deny that such is my case. I cannot imagine what really new things the essay in question could have taught you about me. It leaves me utterly amazed that you seem to want to find a summa—or a credo, as you call it—precisely in this text.

We both know from experience the kind of circumspection necessitated by the meaningful correspondence we are wresting from a long-standing separation. This circumspection by no means precludes touching on difficult questions. But these can only be treated as very private ones. To the extent this has happened, the letters in question have definitely been filed—you can be sure of that—in my "inner registry." But I cannot promise this for your last question: it seems to me to be born more out of a controversy than out of our correspondence.

It should be apparent that we cannot maintain a correspondence in the manner of a controversy. And when items appear in the course of our exchange that suggest such a treatment, there is—it seems to me—no other course for its partners than to turn to the vivid image each carries in himself of the other. I believe that my image in you is not that of a man who easily and needlessly commits himself to a "credo." You know that my writings have certainly always conformed to my convictions, but that I have only seldom made the attempt—and then only in conversation—to express the whole contradictory grounds from which those convictions arise in the individual manifestations they have taken.

And a survey of French literature is supposed to have offered me the rubric under which to do so!?—As far as I can remember, I was actually once given the opportunity to write something under that rubric. At least, it could have been considered as such, since it occurred in the context of a controversy. I found it in the form of a letter Max Rychner wrote to me several years ago. It wouldn't surprise me if I sent you a copy of my answer at the time.[1] If not, then I cannot make up for it now: that letter is among my papers in Berlin.

But what could even that letter tell you which would be new?! That, among all the possible forms and means of expression, a credo is the last thing my communism resorts to; that—even at the cost of its orthodoxy—my communism is absolutely nothing other than the expression of certain experiences I have undergone in my thinking and in my life; that it is a drastic, not infertile expression of the fact that the present intellectual industry finds it impossible to make room for my thinking, just as the present economic order finds it impossible to accommodate my life; that it represents the obvious, reasoned attempt on the part of a man who is completely or almost completely deprived of any means of production to proclaim his right to them, both in his thinking and in his life—that it is all this and much more, though in each case nothing but the lesser evil (see Kraus's letter to the female landowner who declared her opinion of Rosa Luxemburg)[2]—is it really necessary to say all this to you?

I must say I would naturally be dismayed if you found anything in these words even remotely resembling a retraction. The evil—compared to those that surround us—is of so much less that it should be affirmed in every practical, productive form, except for the unpractical, unproductive form of the credo.

And this practice—a scholarly one in the case of the essay you accuse—leaves the theory (the credo, if you like) a much greater freedom than the Marxists suspect. Alas, you seem to approve of their innocent ignorance in this case.

You force me to state that the alternatives which are obviously the reason for your concern do not possess the merest glimpse of vitality in my eyes. These alternatives may be fashionable—I do not deny a party's right to declare them—but nothing can move me to accept them.

If the significance of Brecht's work—and it is to his work that you allude, but, as far as I know, without having ever passed judgment—can be characterized for me, it is rather this: it advances not *one* of the alternatives that do not matter to me. And the not insubstantial importance to me of Kafka's work resides not least in the fact that he doesn't take up *any* of the positions communism is right to be fighting.

So much for your question. And this is the right point for a transition to the ideas contained in your letter, for which I thank you very much. I need not say just how important a commission to write about Kafka would be to me. But if I had to treat explicitly his position within Judaism, I could not do so without pointers from other parties. I cannot encourage my ignorance to improvise in this case. Of course, word from Weltsch has not as yet been forthcoming.

I am sorry for both of us that your efforts with Schocken were futile, without finding this surprising. Nor was I surprised by your portrait of Reiss, about whom I knew nothing, although I do now, and—as I freely admit—it was precisely the image that I had awaited of him. I have heard nothing more from him on the subject since.

I would certainly be glad to work for the small series edited by Spitzer; it is just that no suitable idea has occurred to me as yet. On the other hand, I will spare us both from a recitation of the many attempts—some of which were certainly inferior—to create a basis for my existence here. They did not keep me from writing a longish essay, "The Author as Producer" [Der Autor als Produzent] which comments on current questions of literary politics. I don't yet know if it will appear in print.[3]

Green's *Visionnaire* was a great disappointment to me. At the moment I am busy with a *wretched* study of Flaubert's aesthetics, published by Klostermann in Frankfurt in a very pretentious form, and written by a certain Paul Binswanger.[4] I am by contrast enjoying Brecht's new political drama *Roundheads and Peakheads* [*Die Rundköpfe und die Spitzköpfe*],[5] which I received a few days ago in the final manuscript form. Incidentally, I am now getting quite a few books, since a number of the larger publishing houses have accorded me a sort of *service de presse*.

I must ask you to at least hint at the designs you associate with your suggestion that I look up Lev Shestov. What I have read of his, e.g. in *Die Kreatur*,[6] doesn't give me enough background to make such a step. I cannot find any concrete facts about him in my memory.

Might I add a postscript concerning Weltsch at this point? Besides the essay on Kafka, it would be most desirable by far if the ***Rundschau*** would entrust me with a regular book review section, preferably one that finds its expression in the remittance of review copies. And I say this less in the interest of my library than from the experience that such sections tend to become the smoothest part of editorial operations. Such a regular section need not appear frequently. I would be very pleased if you could put this suggestion to Weltsch. That also seems the only course to take in the long run, because the Jewish link would then at least be thematically established.

The whole question is not without a certain importance, since the discrepancies between contributing to journals published in Germany and contributing to émigré journals are becoming more and more insurmountable, even for the writer who is flexible. Even pseudonyms can offer no more than a brief subterfuge. I myself am trying to put off the decision for as long as possible, as is understandable in my position; but indications have been accumulating that this decision will have to be made in the foreseeable future.[7]

I am truly disheartened to learn from your letter of Escha's poor health. I hope very much that you will soon have better news to report, and I ask you in the meantime to convey my genuine wishes for a speedy recovery.

And fondest regards!
Yours, Walter

1. [See letter 201 and Scholem's reply (letter 202).—Trans.]

2. Kraus's dazzling reply to the "Antwort an Rosa Luxemburg von einer Unsentimentalen" in *Die Fackel* 554 (November 1920), pp. 6–12.

3. This essay was one of the most outspoken Marxist texts WB ever wrote. It was a lecture he finished on April 27, 1934, and which was supposed to be held (but never was) at the Institute for the Study of Fascism, a Communist-front organization. He later abandoned efforts to get the text printed at the time (*Schriften* 2:683–701, 1460–61). [In *Reflections,* pp. 220–38.]

4. *Schriften* 3:423–25.

5. Brecht's advance copy of the play for *Versuche,* vol. 8 (1933), only the proofs of which are extant, reads: "The play 'Die Spitzköpfe und die Rundköpfe oder Reich und Reich gesellt sich gern' is the 17th of the *Versuche.*" The play was first published by Malik Verlag in London in 1938. It is published in Brecht's *Gesammelte Werke,* vol. 2 (Frankfurt am Main: Suhrkamp Verlag, 1967).

6. The quarterly edited by Buber, Viktor von Weizsäcker, and Joseph Wittig from 1926 to 1930, to which WB also contributed.

7. WB did in fact succeed in placing contributions in the *Frankfurter Zeitung* until June 1935 under the pseudonym Detlef Holz.

234. To Robert Weltsch

Paris
May 9, 1934

My most esteemed Dr. Weltsch,

With deep gratitude and by return mail, I acknowledge your letter of May 4, which only arrived here yesterday via my old address.

I am very grateful for your invitation, but am especially indebted to you for the suggestion that I make known my views on Kafka.[1] I cannot imagine a more desirable topic; to be sure, I also am not unaware of the special difficulties that must be taken into consideration in this case. I consider it fair and appropriate to point these out very briefly.

The first and most important is of a factual nature. Years ago when Max Brod was attacked by Ehm Welk because he did not respect certain stipulations in Kafka's will, I defended Max Brod in the *Literarische Welt*.[2] This, however, does not prevent me from having an entirely different stance from that of Max Brod toward the *interpretation* of Kafka. In particular, I do not wish in any way to adopt as my method the straightforward theological explication of Kafka (which, as I well know, suggests itself quite readily). Rest assured that I have not the least intention of burdening the article you propose with polemical explanations. On the other hand, however, I believe I must point out to you that my attempt to approach Kafka—something that was not begun just yesterday—led me to paths that in some respects differ from those of his "official" reception.

The second and third difficulties have to do with technical matters. A lot depends on when it goes to press. If what I have said in the preceding lines does not prevent you from entrusting me with this project, I would ask you to please postpone my deadline as long as possible. An essay of this kind presents me with not inconsiderable bibliographical problems because I unfortunately do not have my library at my disposal here. The problem would of course be drastically simplified if you, my most esteemed Mr. Weltsch, would deem it possible to make available to me through the editorial offices of the *Jüdische Rundschau* on short-term loan certain works that are almost impossible for me to get here—*The Trial*, "The Country Doctor" ["Der Landarzt"], *The Metamorphosis* [*Die Verwandlung*], *Amerika*.

I am not a member of the National Writers Guild. Just as I have not been struck from the relevant lists: that is to say, I have never been a member of any authors' organization.

Hoping to receive your response as soon as possible,

I remain with the greatest esteem your devoted,
Dr. Walter Benjamin

1. WB's essay appeared in the *Jüdische Rundschau* (December 21–28, 1934). The complete version is in *Schriften* 2:196–228.

2. "Kavaliersmoral" [A gentleman's morality], *Literarische Welt* (November 22, 1929).

235. To Bertolt Brecht

Paris
May 21, 1934

Dear Brecht,

It has taken a very long time for me to be able to get a perspective on things here. I wanted to tell you something decisive and for this reason put off writing again and again. I did not even write you about *Roundheads and Peakheads,* which I consider uncommonly important and a complete success.

[. . .]

A few days ago I saw Hanns [Eisler]. He thought that I would have to write you explicitly about how important a London production of the play seems to me. I think that the importance of this is self-evident in view of the fact that there is no more enlightening, interesting, and comprehensible description of the subject for the public than the one you provide. In saying this, I am passing over all the other qualities of the play, which are, of course, included in this state of affairs.

Are you familiar with Go, a very ancient Chinese board game? It is at least as interesting as chess—we should introduce it to Svendborg. You never move any pieces in Go, but only place them on the board, which is empty at the start of the game. It seems to me to be similar to your play in this regard. You *place* each of your figures and formulations on the right spot from whence they fulfill their proper strategic function on their own and without having to act. I believe that the extremely light and certain touch in evidence when things are done in this way will make a much greater impression on the audience—and especially on an English audience—than the strategies with which the theater usually pursues similar goals.

I got to hear some of the new songs and I really like them.

Under the title, "The Author as Producer," I tried in terms of subject matter and length to create a companion piece to my old work on epic theater. I will bring it along for you.

I will see you very soon. Sincere regards.

Yours, Walter Benjamin

236.* To Gerhard Scholem

Svendborg
July 9, 1934

Dear Gerhard,

I just received the lines you sent to Paris on June 20th. The first thing I gleaned from them is that my memory seems to have a vulnerable point. Indeed, the letter of inquiry you refer to seems to have slipped it altogether. That is regrettable, even though it can be explained. A memory that has to digest impressions imparted by unforeseeably changing living conditions will rarely be as reliable as one sustained by continuity. On the other hand, questions can be repeated. Whether that would be the right approach here is of course not for me to decide. For I can't guarantee you that I am in a position today to answer them in written form. And you will share my view that it would be unwise to lessen the prospects of a—though perhaps still distant—oral exchange of views through inadequate attempts at written explanation.

There are, besides the direct ones, numerous indirect avenues of approach for us to take. And thus—treading one of these paths—I don't shy away from repeating my request that you tell me something of your reflections on Kafka, despite your last refusal.[1] My request is all the more justified since my own reflections on this subject are now before you. Even though I have articulated their principal features, they have further preoccupied me since my arrival in Denmark and, if I am not mistaken, will continue to do so for a while. You are the indirect cause of this work; I see no subject more perfectly suited to our correspondence. And it doesn't seem to me that you can refuse my request.

Otherwise, I must get busy working on things that have little in common. Because one goal of my activities in Paris is to come out next winter with an article in the *Nouvelle revue française,* and since they suggested Bachofen as the theme to this end, I shall have to study Bachofen.[2] Other subjects are slated for the *Zeitschrift für Sozialforschung,* and it looks as if I won't be able to sidestep the study on Eduard Fuchs indefinitely, no matter how bitter I may find it.

I have part of my library here, as you know, and it is well housed with my neighbor. Still, it amounts, in total, to just under half of my books. But it isn't only my books that will make my work easier over the next few months; rather, the very fact that I have this neighbor has relieved me of my most immediate worries and I can once again catch my breath. Mrs. Weigel,[3] to whom I must ask you to address my letters, is as friendly as can be imagined; her husband, unfortunately, entered the hospital shortly before my arrival and is still there. The two children, aged ten and three, are quite charming, and we have become fast friends.[4]

Two of the four parcels in which I am sending you the Baader are being sent with the same mail as this letter. The work stood in my library for nineteen years; may it occupy a more secure berth in Israel, be it in the Jerusalem library or in yours. See what you can do and be assured of my gratitude in any case. What is so special about Shestov? I would like more precise information. Can you refer me to some of his books? Perhaps lend me some, should the need arise? I will make an effort to obtain a copy of the play you ask for as soon as my neighbor is home from the hospital. I am sure that it can be obtained, one way or another.

Your question about the *service de presse* brought on a dream in which mine was revoked; let me therefore hasten to provide you with the explanation while I still enjoy its benefits. There are various kinds of *service de presse:* one whereby certain critics or editorial offices are sent every new publication—but that is not the case for me—and one whereby the publishing house agrees to make its new titles available to the respective tabloid or reviewer upon request: this is how it works for me.

So much for today. I must ask you to remain patient a little longer concerning "The Author as Producer"; I had too few copies made, so I don't at present have any at my disposal.

Please write as soon as possible. With kindest regards and all the best wishes for Escha's further recovery.

Yours, Walter

P.S. The first volume of the Baader, which I sent you care of the Hebrew University Library, includes the—of course extremely rare—invitation to subscribe to the series, which I came across by chance long after I acquired the Baader itself. It may be of some use to you if you have to show the copy to a third party.

1. I had set forth such reflections in my letter of August 1, 1931, which WB had with him in Paris among his Kafka papers but which must have slipped his memory as well. It is printed in Scholem, *WB,* pp. 170–71. In 1928, when he began his "Notizen zu Kafka," he had already decided to dedicate his projected work "to Gerhard Scholem" (*Schriften* 2:1190).

2. The Bachofen essay, written in French, was rejected by the *Nouvelle revue française* and was first published many years after WB's death (*Schriften* 2:219–33, as well as pp. 963–67 in the editorial apparatus).

3. Helene Weigel, Bertolt Brecht's wife.

4. Stefan and Barbara.

237.* From Gerhard Scholem to Benjamin

Rehavia, Jerusalem
July 9, 1934

Dear Walter,

I hope you received my lengthy letter, which I still sent to Paris, assuming that it would be forwarded to you. In the meantime, I was in Tel Aviv for a week, to spend a few weeks doing nothing after the semester's end, and upon my arrival I found your shipment with the Kafka article, along with your request for its immediate return. I freely admit that this request was a great disappointment: on the one hand, I can't count on the [*Jüdische*] *Rundschau* printing the essay completely unabridged (unless it decides in favor of four installments), and, on the other hand, I don't know how I am supposed to comment on your findings if you demand its return, and, third, I am of the opinion that it definitely belongs in the archive kept here anyway and why do you begrudge me this copy?

Some months back, I gave a theological didactic poem on *The Trial* to Weltsch, who wanted to print it together with your essay. We will present a most pleasant contrast because, as utterly distanced as I feel from the somewhat harmless-idiotic quotations of the "theological" interpreters you mention,[1] I am still firmly convinced that a theological aspect of this world, in which God does not appear, is the most legitimate of such interpretations. Since one doesn't know when the *Rundschau* will be presenting us in brotherly unity, I don't hesitate to present you with this product, which I composed some time ago for Kitty Marx's theological instruction. It appears to me that we meet in some areas, despite the different directions from which we clearly approach the matter. Your portrayal of the preanimistic age as Kafka's seeming present—if I understand you correctly—is really quite piercing and magnificent. The nullity of such a present seems to me to be very problematic, problematic in those final points that are also decisive here. I would like to say that 98% of it makes sense, but the final touch is missing, which you seem to have sensed, since you moved away from that level with your interpretation of shame (you definitely hit the mark there) and of the Law (which is where you get into difficulties!). The *existence* of secret law foils your interpretation: it should not exist in a premythical world of chimeric confusion, to say nothing of the very special way in which it even announces its existence. *There* you went much too far with your elimination of theology, throwing the baby out with the bathwater.

But that requires greater elaboration. I send you this in haste for now, and to express my most sincere gratitude.

And one question: Who is actually the source of all those stories? Does Ernst Bloch have them from you or you from him? The great rabbi with the profound dictum on the messianic kingdom who appears in Bloch[2] is none other than *I* myself; what a way to achieve fame!! It was one of my first ideas about the Kabbalah.

My kindest regards,
Yours, Gerhard

[enclosed on a separate sheet]
With a Copy of Kafka's *Trial*

Are we totally separated from you?
Is there not a breath of your peace,
Lord, or your message
Intended for us in such a night?

Can the sound of your word
Have so faded in Zion's emptiness,
Or has it not even entered
This magic realm of appearance?

The great deceit of the world
Is now consummated.
Give then, Lord, that he may wake
Who was struck through by your nothingness.

Only so does revelation
Shine in the time that rejected you.
Only your nothingness is the experience
It is entitled to have of you.

Thus alone teaching that breaks through semblance
Enters the memory:
The truest bequest
Of hidden judgment.

Our position has been measured
On Job's scales with great precision.
We are known through and through
As despairing as on the youngest day.

What we are is reflected
In endless instances.
Nobody knows the way completely
And each part of it makes us blind.

No one can benefit from redemption.
That star stands far too high.
And if you had arrived there too,
You would still stand in your way.

Abandoned to powers,
Exorcism is no longer binding.
No life can unfold
That doesn't sink into itself.

From the center of destruction
A ray breaks through at times,
But none shows the direction
The Law ordered us to take.

Since this sad knowledge
Stands before us, unassailable,
A veil has suddenly been torn,
Lord, before your majesty.

Your trial began on earth.
Does it end before your throne?
You cannot be defended,
As no illusion holds true here.

Who is the accused here?
The creature or yourself?
If anyone should ask you,
You would sink into silence.

Can such a question be raised?
Is the answer indefinite?
Oh, we must live all the same
Until your court examines us.

*[This letter is printed only in part in the German edition of this book. The complete letter presented here in translation was first published in the posthumous collection of Scholem's essays and miscellany on Benjamin. *Walter Benjamin und sein Engel,* pp. 193–95.—Smith.]

1. This had to do with a number of quotations from articles by Max Brod and Hans Joachim Schoeps, as well as their jointly composed afterword to the first edition of Kafka's posthumous *Beim Bau der chinesischen Mauer* [Berlin: Gustav Kiepenheuer Verlag, 1931; see also the typescript found among WB's papers, "Franz Kafka: Beim Bau der chinesischen Mauer," *Schriften* 2:676–83.—Smith].

2. In Ernst Bloch's *Spuren,* the same sentence ascribed by WB to a "great rabbi" (*Schriften* 2:423) is quoted from a "truly kabbalistic rabbi." But in 1932 WB had already borrowed the sentence verbatim in the version originating from me, in his text "In der Sonne" (*Schriften* 4:419): "Everything will be as it is here—only slightly different." I learned from this what honors one can garner for oneself with an apocryphal sentence.

238.* To Gerhard Scholem

Skovsbostrand per Svendborg
July 20, 1934

Dear Gerhard,

Yesterday the long-awaited confirmation that you received my "Kafka" arrived. I prized it immensely, above all because of the enclosed poem. It has been years since I felt such discomfort at the limits imposed on us by our (solely) written communication. I'm sure you understand this sense of limitation and do not assume that I might be able to forgo the manifold experiments in formulation only conversation makes possible, and still say something decisive about the poem. Only the question of the "theological interpretation" is relatively simple. Not only do I unhesitatingly recognize the theological possibility as such in the poem, but also maintain that my essay has its own broad—though admittedly shrouded—theological side.

I aimed my remarks against that unbearable posturing of the theological "professionals," who—you won't deny—have held sway over all Kafka interpretations to date and whose smuggest manifestations are yet to come.

To sketch my position with regard to your poem—whose language concedes nothing to that on the *Angelus Novus* which I rank so highly—in at least a little more detail, I only want to name the stanzas with which I unreservedly identify: 7 to 13. And several that precede those. The last stanza raises the question of how one has to imagine, in Kafka's sense, the Last Judgment's projection into world history. Does this projection turn the judge into the accused? And the proceedings into the punishment? Is it devoted to raising up the Law on high, or to burying it? Kafka, so I contend, had no answers to these questions. But the form in which they presented themselves to him—and which I tried to delimit through my comments on the roles of scenic and gestural elements in his books—contains indications of a state of the world in which such questions no longer have a place, because their answers, far from being instructive, make the questions superfluous. Kafka sought—and sometimes glimpsed as in a dream—the structure of this kind of answer that renders the question superfluous. At any rate, one cannot say that he found it. And that is why insight into his work is, among other things, bound up with the simple realization that he failed. "Nobody knows the way completely / And each part of it makes us blind." But when you write: "Only your nothingness is the experience / It is entitled to have of you," I may relate my interpretive effort to precisely this passage with the following remarks: I endeavored to show how Kafka sought—on the nether side of that "nothingness," in its inside lining, so to speak—to feel his way toward redemption. This implies that any kind of victory over that nothingness, as understood by the theological exegetes around Brod, would have been an abomination for him.

I believe I wrote you that this essay promises to hold my attention for a while yet. And that is also the main reason for requesting that you return the manuscript. The one you have in hand has already been superseded at important points; for the essay, as I already wrote you, has continued to preoccupy me here. I am prepared, however, to promise you a manuscript of the final version for the archive.[1]

Since we will now, to my delight, be appearing together in the *Jüdische Rundschau,* this circumstance might afford you the opportunity to prevail upon Weltsch as to the form of the essay's printed version—an opportunity you are assured by virtue of the fact that you are the initiator of my essay. An examination of the definitive version—which I'll send you after you return the copy now in your possession—will convince you far more than any general considerations just how unsatisfactory its abridged publication would be for me. The fact that the *Jüdische Rundschau* is published twice weekly is at least some sort of basis for the prospect of having the essay appear in installments. Please give some thought to whether you could accomplish something to this end with Weltsch.[2]

The question, as you can imagine, is also important for me as regards the fee.

I hope to receive word from you very soon that the Baader has arrived. On the one hand, I would be pleased to see it preserved for me in your library, at least *in my imagination,* but, on the other hand, economic considerations are at present so terribly relevant, that any higher figure which might result from a purchase through the library would be exceptionally important to me. A small measure of support provided by German friends, thanks to which I had a bit of leeway in recent months, has failed to come, apparently in the wake of the events in Germany.[3] Since I made use of the last of my funds to have my Paris books shipped here, so as not to lose hold of my library by virtue of its being spread throughout Europe, I am left without even a drop of reserves for the time being, which means I am dependent upon B.'s hospitality to a degree that might someday turn out to be precarious.

I believe I wrote you that I began working on an essay on Bachofen for the *Nouvelle revue française*. This means that for the first time I shall get to read him myself; up to now I have always relied on Bernoulli[4] and Klages.

Among Svendborg's superior amenities is a radio, which one now needs more than ever. Thus I was able to listen to Hitler's Reichstag speech, and because it was the very first time I had ever heard him, you can imagine the effect.

So much for today. The origin of the stories in "Kafka"[5] remains my secret—one you would only succeed in unraveling by being present in person, in which case I could promise you a whole series of even more exquisite ones. Convey my regards to Kitty Marx and point out that I am still carrying the arrow in my breast which she fixed there by not replying to my last letter.

Most sincerely,
Yours, Walter

1. I did indeed receive the new version. It is conceivable that I did not save it if the typescript didn't contain any handwritten emendations, once it had been published in *Schriften*. [The English text appears as "Franz Kafka," in *Illuminations,* ed. Hannah Arendt, trans. Harry Zohn (New York: Harcourt, Brace and World, 1968), pp. 111–40)]. In any case, I am no longer able to find it among my papers.

2. I intervened without success.

3. An allusion to Hitler's purge of Ernst Röhm and other SA leaders, and its consequences. It may be possible to ascertain the identity of the "German friends" on the basis of the letters addressed to WB kept in East Berlin. My conjectures would include Fritz and Jula Radt.

4. C. A. Bernoulli, *Johann Jakob Bachofen und das Natursymbol* (Basel: Benno Schwabe, 1924).

5. From Pushkin's *Anekdoten und Tischgespräche,* ed. Johannes von Günther (Munich: Allgemeine Verlagsanstalt, 1924), p. 42.

239. To Werner Kraft

Svendborg
[end of July 1934?]

Dear Mr. Kraft,

Sincere thanks for your two letters and the enclosure.

While I am here, where world politics is in the forefront of people's interest, it is truly worthwhile for me to be informed by you about literary matters from Paris. Thus, what you wrote about Jouhandeau caused me to look around for *Images de Paris.* By the way, regarding this poet, let me once again recommend the novella *Leda,* which should be in the volume *Prudence Hautechaume.*

[. . .] You will not be surprised to hear that I am still preoccupied with Kafka—without damage to any other primary concern. My correspondence with Scholem, who has begun to discuss this work with me, provides the external stimulus. These considerations are still too much in flux, however, for me to be able to come to a definitive judgment. Nonetheless, you will be interested to know that he has set down his view of the matter in a kind of theological didactic poem, which I will certainly share with you should we see each other in Paris. In a very different way—as you can well imagine—I was able to consult with Brecht on the same subject, and my text also reflects these conversations.

Otherwise, such or similar consultations are not all that frequent at the moment, since the evenings we spend together are completely consumed by listening to the radio. I am still under the influence of Starhemberg's governmental declaration that was broadcast yesterday at midnight and represents a grandiose mockery of the entire body of satiric literature from Juvenal to Kraus. Moreoever, quite well-founded but, nonetheless, almost unbelievable rumors about Kraus's position are making the rounds, to the effect that he has accepted the politics of Dollfuß as the lesser of two evils. (For all that, the assurances that this is so are not unassailable, so that I must ask you to keep this strictly to yourself!)

This seems to me to be just the place to say a word about a formulation in your last letter. You admit that for the time being you do not want to accept communism "as the solution for humanity." But of course the issue is precisely to abolish the unproductive pretensions of solutions for humanity by means of the feasible findings of this very system; indeed, to give up entirely the immodest prospect of "total" systems and at least to make the attempt to construct the days of humanity in just as loose a fashion as a rational person who has had a good night's sleep begins his day.

So much for that. I am delighted that you like the "Käuferin."[1] I am extremely eager to have your judgment on *The Three-Penny Novel* [*Der Dreigroschenroman*], which has just been completed. To conclude with just a word about what I am doing, at the moment I am primarily busy studying Bachofen. Those of my books that are available to me here are first-rate for this purpose. This man is a fascinating phenomenon; I would be quite happy to have the opportunity to portray him in the *Nouvelle revue française*.

[. . .]

1. A poem by Brecht.

240.* To Gerhard Scholem

August 11, 1934

Dear Gerhard,

I am making use of the moment, in which I am putting what are probably the finishing touches on the "Kafka," to return explicitly to some of your objections and to append some questions concerning your position.

I say "explicitly," because the new version implicitly does just that in some respects. It has been revised considerably. As I said before, the manuscript in your possession has been superseded. I expect it any day. For technical reasons, I cannot possibly send you the revised one before I have the original in hand.

First off, several urgent requests: 1) if at all possible, give me access to Bialik's "Halakah and Haggadah" as soon as possible; I need to read it. 2) Send me the letter to Schoeps you reminded me of, as background to our pending discussion.

Now the few major points:[1]

1. I wish tentatively to characterize the relationship of my essay to your poem as follows: you take the "nothingness of revelation" as your point of departure (see 7 below), the salvific-historical perspective of the established proceedings of the trial. I take as my starting point the small, nonsensical hope, as well as the creatures for whom this hope is intended and yet who on the other hand are also the creatures in which this absurdity is mirrored.

2. If I characterize shame as Kafka's strongest reaction, this in no way contradicts the rest of my interpretation. On the contrary, the primal world, Kafka's secret present, is the historical-philosophical index that lifts this reaction out of the domain of the private. For the work of the Torah—if we abide by Kafka's account—has been thwarted.[2]

3. It is in this context that the problem of the Scripture [*Schrift*] poses itself. Whether the pupils have lost it or whether they are unable to decipher it comes down to the same thing, because, without the key that belongs to it, the Scripture is not Scripture, but life. Life as it is lived in the village at the foot of the hill on which the castle is built. It is in the attempt to metamorphize life into Scripture that I perceive the meaning of "reversal" [*Umkehr*], which so many of Kafka's parables endeavor to bring about—I take "The Next Village" ["Das nächste Dorf"] and "The Bucket Rider" ["Kübelreiter"] as examples. Sancho Panza's existence is exemplary because it actually consists in rereading one's own existence—however buffoonish and quixotic.

4. I emphasized from the very beginning that the pupils "who have lost the Scripture" do not belong to the hetaeric world, because I rank them as assistants to those creatures for whom, in Kafka's words, there is "an infinite amount of hope."

5. That I do not deny the component of revelation in Kafka's work already follows from my appreciation—by declaring his work to be "distorted"—of its messianic aspect. Kafka's messianic category is the "reversal" or the "studying." You guess correctly that I do not want to shift the path taken by theological interpretation in itself—I practice it myself—but only the arrogant and frivolous form emanating from Prague. I withdrew the argument based on the judges' behavior as untenable (even before your proposals arrived).

6. I consider Kafka's constant insistence on the Law to be the point where his work comes to a standstill, which only means to say that it seems to me that the work cannot be moved in any interpretive direction whatsoever from there. I do not wish to go into explicit detail on this concept.[3]

7. I would like to ask that you elucidate your paraphrase: Kafka "repre-

sents the world of revelation seen from that perspective in which it is returned to its own nothingness."

So much for today. By now you will have in hand the bill I sent you. Best wishes for Escha's recovery, all the best to you.

Yours, Walter

P.S. Still no definitive answer from Weltsch!

Not a line from Spitzer in response to a long letter with my proposals!

1. Notes to this "Kafka letter" to Scholem, drawn from WB's posthumous papers, are printed in *Schriften* 3:1245–46. They correspond only in part with the letter that was actually sent.

2. In his notes, WB adds a sentence not found in the letter: "And everything that Moses accomplished long ago would have be reaccomplished in our world's age."

3. This point is more fully formulated in the notes as well: "In case it [the emphasis Kafka keeps putting on "the Law"] were to have a function in Kafka's work in spite of everything—whether it does is something I want to leave open—an interpretation that takes images as its point of departure, as mine does, is sure to lead to it in the end."

241.* To Gerhard Scholem

September 15, 1934

Dear Gerhard,

I must confess having actually intended to wait to write until I received confirmation that you received my last, numerically arranged observations on Kafka. But my thankful confirmation of the receipt of the check for the Baader forbids postponing these lines any longer. I also owe you thanks for the offprint of the Breuer critique and the copy of the letter to Schoeps. I refer explicitly to these exterior causes, since my inner constitution, which is very exposed at the moment, robs me of all other impetus to write. On the other hand, a lucky coincidence has succceded in creating total solitude around me, since the B[recht]s are gone for a while. I am putting this to use as well as I can for the new piece—I already notified you of it, didn't I?—for the *Zeitschrift für Sozialforschung:* a retrospective recapitulation of the cultural politics of the *Neue Zeit*.[1] The theme has its manageable sides and its drawbacks. That it doesn't belong to my preferred themes is a trait it shares with the epoch of my life in which work on it is embedded. But if I tell you that Weltsch thought to offer me a fee of 60 reichsmarks for the fragmented—abridged by half—printed copy of the Kafka essay, you will understand that for the time being my intense preoccupation with purely literary subjects has clearly reached an end with the "Kafka."

That isn't to say that the "Kafka" itself has reached an end. On the contrary, I intend to nourish it further from a series of considerations I have continued to spin in the meantime—and a remarkable formulation in your letter to Schoeps promises to provide me with a greater insight in the deliberation. It goes: "Nothing ever . . . is, with reference to historical time, more in need of concretization than . . . the . . . "absolute concreteness" of the word of revelation. The absolutely concrete can never be fulfilled at all."[2] That surely states a truth which definitely applies to Kafka, and also thereby broaches a perspective that for the first time makes the historical aspect of his failure obvious. But it will be quite a while before these and other reflections take shape such that I can formulate them definitively. And you will empathize with this all the more because your repeated reading of my work, as well as my commentary in letters, must have made it clear to you that precisely this topic is ideally suited to become the crossroads of the different paths my thought has taken. By the way, in the course of marking that spot more precisely, I won't be able to refrain from making reference to Bialik's essay. Wouldn't it be possible for you to track down the relevant issue of *Der Jude* and lend it to me?

To dwell just a moment longer on external questions—I will hardly make any more headway today on internal ones—I had no other choice than to allow Weltsch—even given such a fee!—to go to press. I asked him, however, in the politest way possible, to revise the fee he had decided on. I hope that at least the collected edition will find its way to me when the time comes. Even as dismal as my library's fate remains—only a fraction of it is here in Svendborg—I still summon up the strength to make appeals now and again; I have, for example, just applied to Samuel Fischer, in order not to leave the attempt undone, to acquire the new "popular edition" of Hofmannsthal's works.—Incidentally, I don't know if Dr. Spitzer is to be relied upon. He hasn't even replied to a detailed letter in which I presented him with detailed proposals—notwithstanding his announcement that they couldn't pay any royalties—for contributions to the Schocken *Almanach!*

Yes, the latest *Fackel* also found its way into my hands. But after such contact even the hands of a Galician would lose their loquacity—not to speak of my lips. A new Timon[3] has truly risen here, who mockingly distributes the yields of a lifetime among false friends!

In closing: How good of you to remember the French translation of the *Berliner Kindheit.* Five sections are done; but I can't consider using them because I had a falling-out with my coworker for reasons that are quite picturesque but unsuited to epistolary portrayal—and which incidentally have nothing to do with the work in question.[4] But perhaps things will once again take a turn for the better, and some restful evening can present you with an account of the splendor and misery of that last summer on Ibiza.[5]

So much for today. In the hope that I will soon be receiving news and with kind regards, not forgetting my wishes for Escha's health: how is she doing?

Yours, Walter

1. If I am not mistaken, Brecht had the whole series of the *Neue Zeit,* the ideological journal of the Social Democratic party. The work itself never got beyond the draft stage, but it receives frequent mention in WB's letters of this period.

2. This sentence had already impressed WB when he first read my "Open Letter."

3. WB is referring to Shakespeare's *Timon of Athens,* one of Karl Kraus's favorite plays: see also WB's letter 243, to Kraft.

4. Jean Selz, whose version of the circumstances under which the relationship was broken off can be read in "Walter Benjamin in Ibiza." Their break took place in March 1934, and the explanation WB hints at here does not agree with Selz's story. But Selz's report about what was probably the only time on Ibiza that WB was intoxicated (or suffering from alcohol poisoning?)—which he witnessed—bears every mark of authenticity (which cannot be said with the same conviction about many other details of his recollections, unless WB had consciously regaled him with lies).

5. This sentence also reflects the background against which the text "Agesilaus Santander" should be interpreted.

242. To Max Horkheimer

Skovbostrand per Svendborg
September 16, 1934

Dear Mr. Horkheimer,

I have no idea of where these lines will reach you, but on the off chance that they will, I briefly want to tell you about my summer.

You are sure to have heard from Mr. [Friedrich] Pollock that—after an atypical project—we agreed on one that will address the cultural-scientific and cultural-political inventory of the *Neue Zeit*. It was of course not only the fortunate circumstance that the journal is available to me on the spot and in its entirety that made me agree to this proposal. Rather, there were two contributing factors.

In the first place, it seems important that, on the basis of a realistic example, I demonstrate for once how collective literary products are particularly suited to materialistic treatment and analysis and, indeed, can only be rationally evaluated when treated in such a way. A journal of the stature of the *Neue Zeit* serves as a model for this. In the second place, however, I intended to serve the goals of the Institute for Social Research in technical terms as well with such a project, whose documentary interest—entirely aside from the author's position—is certifiable.

Although I will conclude my study with the first biennial volume of 1914—during the war, of course, the role of cultural politics in the journal declined significantly—the material I have to examine is distributed over thirty-two volumes (almost all of them double volumes) and is quite extensive. I have therefore not come close to being finished collecting material and will continue to extend my stay here.

This will nonetheless be possible only within limits and I would therefore really like to know whether the journal is available in your library or some other library in Geneva, whether in its entirety or in large part. I consider it a certainty that, through your kind offices, I can get Mehring's *Geschichte der Sozialdemokratie* later, as well as some other works I must consult to complete my preparation.

I truly hope that we will see each other if you get to Europe soon and that we will then be able to discuss the project on the basis of the material I have gathered. It would probably be opportune if we were able to meet in Geneva and this may not be entirely impossible for me since I will be meeting my son in Switzerland, circumstances permitting. If that were to be the case, I would go directly from here to Switzerland. But these plans are still not clear; I would nonetheless be delighted to hear what yours are as soon as possible.

Would you also write me as to whether you might be coming through Paris and when?

I hope that things were to your and the institute's satisfaction in America. For my part, I have reason to be satisfied with my summer. To be sure, this southern tip of Fyn is one of the most remote areas imaginable. The fact that it is so undeveloped not only has its advantages, but contact with the larger world is provided by a variety of visitors and a good radio. This summer in particular it would have been impossible to do without that. A truly memorable experience was living through the Austrian putsch from the very beginning—indeed, it began at the Vienna broadcasting station—as I happened to do.

[. . .]

Sincere regards and best wishes to you and your wife.

Yours, Walter Benjamin

243. To Werner Kraft

Svendborg
September 27, 1934

[. . .] I am still unable to say anything about the details of *Die Fackel*'s[1] long explanation and, indeed, I must leave it open as to whether I will ever be able to do so. The capitulation to Austro-fascism, the glossing over of the white terror instituted against the Viennese workers, the admiration of the rhetoric—equal to Lassalle's—of Starhemberg (whose words I myself happened to hear on the radio)—all of the passages relevant here, which I did read, make any involvement with others something I am not obligated to undertake, regardless of whether I now decide to become more involved. The issue has already been resolved for me in the question, Who is actually left who can still give in? A bitter comfort; but there will be no other casualty on this front even worth mentioning in the same breath as this one. The demon has been stronger than the person or the nonperson: he was unable to remain silent and thus he discovered the downfall of the demon—in self-betrayal.—I would be very grateful if you were to send to this address any comments on my Kafka, as well as the other linguistic glosses you promised me.

1. The political stance assumed by Karl Kraus was at issue.

244.* To Gerhard Scholem

Skovbostrand per Svendborg
October 17, 1934

Dear Gerhard,

The "Kafka" is steadily progressing, and hence I am grateful to you for your recent observations. It remains to be seen whether I will ever be able to arch the bow so that the arrow zings into flight. But whereas my other works tended to find their termination rather quickly, at the point where I took leave of them, I won't be through with this one for a while. The image of the bow suggests why: I am confronted with two ends at once, the political and the mystical. By the way, this is not to say that I have been concerned with the essay these past weeks. The version in your possession will remain valid for a while. I have limited myself to preparing some material for subsequent reflection.

I still haven't had any word from Weltsch; to write him doesn't seem very promising, given the present state of his enterprise.

I am probably correct in assuming that both of our last letters crossed in the mail. In any case, by now you must have long ago received my thanks for the check, interwoven in a lengthy report. But I don't really know how to comply with your request for biographical frescoes and full-length paintings. The overt side of existence has become so precarious for me that I won't touch on it unless necessary; and the pieces I write will help you now and then to visualize the less overt, though no less precarious, side. I won't conceal that at this very moment an exchange of views between us could be especially fruitful. I am readying myself inwardly—my outward circumstances depend on others and not on me—to return to the project of the *Paris Arcades;* you are presumably familiar with its vaguest form. Nonetheless, I am returning to it with significantly changed points of view. One of my next projects will be to work through the quite considerable material generated by my studies to date. Unfortunately, in a letter it is almost impossible to give you an idea either of my intentions or of the difficulties inherent in this project. Incidentally, it probably cannot be written anywhere but in Paris. But for the moment I am not able to afford living there.

The fact that the Institute for Social Research is to emigrate to America doesn't bode well. The upshot could easily be its dissolution, or at least a loosening of my relationship with its members. I don't want to spell out in detail what this means.—If you've read Borkenau's book, then you are better informed about the institute's activities than I am. After your report, it is no longer conceivable that I shall narrow the orbit from which I have circled this fat tome.

I was away from here for a fortnight, in Copenhagen and a small town in the provinces, where I met a woman I know from Germany. Unfortunately, I spent the greater part of my absence confined to bed. At least I discovered the shop of a tattoo artist in Copenhagen and was able to expand my small collection of pictorial broadsides (which I started after being separated from the children's books) by a few marvelous original tattoo patterns from the master craftsman's own hand.[1]

My neighbor is in London. I regret that I wasn't able to get the *Joan*[2] for you—even here copies are extremely scarce. Perhaps you can get it by way of Vienna—the cost is, after all, minimal. I also don't have it here; my collection of the *Versuche,* including the first issue, which contains my handwritten commentary, is still in Berlin. But a new edition of B.'s works is in the making of Malik Verlag. Furthermore, *The Three-Penny Novel* should appear any day now and, if need be, you could have it from me on loan. But you will perhaps be even more interested to learn that a new volume in the Arsène Lupin series—you know the famous gentleman-*cambrioleur*—is to appear shortly in the form of a new book by Ernst Bloch.[3] *Heritage of Our Time* [*Erbschaft dieser Zeit*]—I'm quite keen to see it; first, being curious in general, second, because I would like to learn what I, as a child of my time, am likely to inherit of my work from it. I hope to see Bloch in the near future.

I leave here three days from now. In fact, I will be going to say with Dora, who has taken over an establishment in San Remo. Stefan is still in Germany, but he too is supposed to move down there next spring.

I am writing with clammy fingers in an ice-cold room and can't add much more. Should you see Kraft, please thank him for his letter and tell him that I will write him from Paris.

I return your wishes for the New Year belatedly but most warmly, and my reason for wishing you the best health imaginable is all the more cogent, since you plan—by your own admission—to read Mann's Jacob novel should you fall ill.

Yours, Walter

1. WB's collection of children's books came into Dora Benjamin's possession as part of the financial settlement following the divorce. [What remains of this collection has been acquired by the Institute for the Study of Children's Books of the University of Frankfurt and catalogued in *Die Kinderbuchsammlung Walter Benjamins* (Frankfurt am Main: City and University Library, 1987).—Smith]

2. Brecht's *Saint Joan of the Stockyards* [*Die heilige Johanna der Schlachthöfe*].

3. This bitter remark continues a series of many similar complaints WB made about Bloch in his letters to me before 1933. These reservations placed a major burden on WB's longstanding relationship with Bloch.

245. To Max Horkheimer

San Remo
[1934]

Dear Mr. Horkheimer,

Your letter reaches me at the very moment of my departure from Paris. My sincere thanks for your proposition! I would most gratefully welcome the chance to work in America, regardless of whether it is to do research at your institute or at an institute associated with yours. Indeed, allow me to say that you have my prior consent to any arrangement that seems appropriate to you.

As grateful as I am to your letter for the—albeit uncertain—prospect your proposition opened up for me, it is equally difficult for me to accept that a personal meeting between us must be deferred for a long time. You will have gathered from my last letter that I hoped this meeting would be tangibly near come winter. In the first place, this would have been most welcome for my work. It surely would prove beneficial to it if we were able to work together on the extensive material I have culled from the approximately forty double volumes of the *Neue Zeit*. I put a premium on selecting material that could be dealt with in a variety of ways. I would, in fact, not wish to commit myself to a definitive text without having thoroughly discussed the matter with you. Since, on the other hand, the journal still has my long review article on linguistic sociology in manuscript form,[1] my article on the *Neue Zeit* might perhaps be assigned a deadline that would allow us time for a personal exchange of views.

As important as this project is to me, it of course hardly represents the only or even the most obvious topic of any discussion I would have with you. When you last came through Paris in the spring, we had both counted on seeing each other again sooner than this. At that time, you also turned the conversation to my economic situation and were so kind as to assure me of your readiness to help, even during the time you would not be here. For my part, I promised not to exploit this offer unless absolutely necessary and I have kept my promise. I turned to Mr. Pollock once during that period and, in response to my request, he made available to me the funds for my move to Denmark and for the shipment of part of my library there, which has now taken place. In the meantime, I have succeeded in living on my small annuity all summer and, by selling off some things from my library, I have even managed to afford the long, costly trip on which I am now embarked and of which Paris is but one stage.

That is to say, as much as I regret it, I am unable to remain here. I would basically like nothing better than to do so. Since my last opportunities to work for journals evaporated during the summer—for it is no longer possible for anyone to get money transferred out of Germany—nothing would stand in the way of my tackling the long book that I discussed with you on a number of occasions and that was to be based on studies of Paris I had made over the years. I worked on this material some more during the summer and I now have a clear vision of the book's sturcture. In the opinion of a Parisian friend, it is conceivable that I might well be able to interest local publishers in the thing. However, at the moment I am not in the position of even determining where I will be.

Indeed, as urgently necessary as Paris is to this project, I must be just as happy at the possibility of being put up for one or two months on the Côte d'Azur. This possibility exists since my ex-wife has opened up a small boardinghouse there. It is precisely this circumstance that I have to thank for the fact that I do not have to conclude these lines with a request. But only one to two months of this kind of respite remain ahead of me, and one-quarter of that time will already have elapsed by the time this letter reaches you.

My dear Mr. Horkheimer, I have given you this description in order to make manifest the full significance of my consent to your proposition. Of course, should the opportunity for me to come to America not materialize for a while, I would soon have to consult with you once more about means for my subsistence, cut off as I am from all German sources of aid, even the most modest.

Best wishes to you and your wife, and regards to all.

Yours, Walter Benjamin

1. Appeared in the *Zeitschrift für Sozialforschung* 4 (1935), pp. 248–68.

246. To Werner Kraft

San Remo
November 12, 1934

Dear Mr. Kraft,

As a result of our correspondence, I have become greatly indebted to you in the last few months. Even so, having postponed giving you more detailed information until a quieter moment had arrived, now that I believe that moment to have come, I still cannot go into all the details as much as I would like to. As far as the most important things are concerned, the question is one only of postponement, even though it may well turn out to be a rather long postponement. I kept your most recent letters with those papers I am again turning to, since I will once more begin to work on my Kafka essay.

I do not know whether I wrote you that I had actually already decided to tackle this project again in considerable depth at the time of its "last" completion. A number of circumstances converged to effect such a decision. First of all, my experience that the study brought me to a crossroads in my thoughts and reflections. Devoting additional thought to it promises to do for me precisely what using a compass would do to orient a person on uncharted terrain. Otherwise, should this opinion have required confirmation, for me it would have taken the form of the various and lively reactions that the essay elicited from my friends. You are familiar with Scholem's views on it; I was struck by how accurately you guessed the opposition to the project that was to be expected from Brecht, although you can hardly have a notion of the intensity it occasionally reaches. I have put in writing the most important disagreements on the subject that took place during the summer.[1] Sooner or later you will probably find them reflected in the text itself. Moreover, you have to a certain extent, of course, made these objections your own. It is indeed possible to think of the form of my essay as problematical. But no other form was possible in this instance, for I wanted to have a free hand; I did not want to finish. Historically speaking, it may also still not be the time to finish—least of all at a time when Kafka is viewed as a prophetic author, as he is by Brecht. As you know, I did not use that word but there is much to be said for it and I may still be the one to do it.

Then my essay would become all the more like an instructive lecture, but I do believe that this could only be the case within modest limits, even in the later version. In that version, motifs will become that much more apparent, which you will most likely find much more difficult to accept. I am primarily thinking about the motif of Kafka's having failed. This is very closely related to my decidedly pragmatic interpretation of Kafka. (Or better, this way of looking at things was a primarily instinctive attempt to avoid the false profundity of uncritical commentary; it was the beginning of an interpretation that combines the historical and the nonhistorical aspects of Kafka. The former are still given too short shrift in my version.) I believe in fact that every interpretation that—contrary to Kafka's own feeling, in this case incorruptible and pure—proceeds from the assumption of a body of mystical writing realized by him, instead of just proceeding from the author's own feeling, his rectitude, and the reasons for the inevitable failure, would miss the historical nexus of the entire work. Only at that nexus is a consideration possible that gives the legitimate mystical interpretation its due—an interpretation that is not to be conceived of as the exegesis of his wisdom but of his foolishness. I did not actually do this; not because I did not get close enough to Kafka but because I got too close to him. Nonetheless, Scholem very clearly sensed the limits beyond which even my current version is disinclined to go when he reproached me with passing over Kafka's concept of the "laws." At some later time, I will attempt to demonstrate why the concept of the "laws" in Kafka—as opposed to the concept of "doctrine"—has a predominantly illusory character and is actually a sham.

I hope this will suffice for the time being. I am sorry that I am unable to make a copy of the current version available to you. I regret this all the more since, of course, there is probably not the slightest prospect of seeing the essay published in this or any other form. It therefore occupies an extreme position even in an external sense and is well suited to lead me back to the "essay's" way of looking at things. By the way, I would have liked the essay to have marked an end to this way of looking at things. Thank you for the reference to the essay by Margarete Susman.[2] I would be even more indebted to you if you were to send me your comments on "das alte Blatt."[3]

You are right to propose that we discontinue putting our observations on Kraus in writing. Since I do not know whether you have seen it, however, I would like to make you aware of a small special printing[4] in which friends expressed their gratitude and affection on the occasion of

Kraus's sixtieth birthday. (You may be able to get this private printing through Jaray in Vienna.) It has quite a nice meditation by Viertel; by the way, also a poem by Brecht.

Yes, do write me what you have figured out about Montaigne. I do not know him very well, although I am somewhat more familiar with Lucretius, who is in fact a really wonderful figure. I am indebted to him for some of the most pleasant hours of reading I have been granted since my boyhood. I enjoyed these hours two years ago in the summer when I walked from my room into the sea every morning at 6:30 on the lonely beach of Ibiza in order to bathe. I then went to a remote spot in the forest, to sit on a cushion of moss, protected from the sun, to read Lucretius for an hour before going in to breakfast. And Lucretius affords protection against the various rays of the sun. His chapter on love is surely one of the most remarkable things to be found on the subject in world literature.

I would be happy to receive good news from you soon. I am naturally very interested in everything you can tell me about your perceptions and observations on Palestine. I unfortunately fear that your private circumstances have not been made easier by Germany's new foreign-exchange regulations. Will you be staying there for the time being? You will find my address below. I will probably stay on the *côte* for a few months, whether here or in France.

Before I close I want to recommend to you a little-known book I recently read and which, in terms of its importance to me, I rank ahead of almost all great novels, and right behind *The Charterhouse of Parma*. It is Stevenson's *Master of Ballantrae*. Do get it if you can.

1. The notebook containing the description of these conversations has been preserved among WB's papers. Brecht said that the essay promoted "Jewish fascism."

2. "Das Hiob-Problem bei Franz Kafka," *Der Morgen* 5, no. 1 (1929).

3. In Kafka's "Landarzt."

4. *Stimmen über Karl Kraus zum 60. Geburtstag* (Vienna, 1934). It contained Brecht's "Über die Bedeutung des zehnzeilign Gedichts in der 888. Nummer der *Fackel* (October 1933)."

247. To Alfred Cohn

San Remo
December 19, 1934

Dear Alfred,

I was delighted to find your letter at the place indicated. I took my time reading it, giving it close attention, and gathered from it how, with such a clever touch, you protect the delicate flame of hope from the wind gusts of current historical events. I wish you a well-appointed, domestic hearth in which the flame will one fine day be kindled.

And how are things with me? Such that I am by necessity truly reluctant to tell a shrewd man like you all about it. What should I respond to a person who would tell me that I can thank my lucky stars to be able to pursue my thoughts while strolling or writing without having to worry about my day-to-day existence and while living in the most splendid of areas—and San Remo is truly exceptionally beautiful? And if someone else were to rise up before me in order to tell me to my face that it was pitiful and a disgrace to nest, as it were, in the ruins of my own past,[1] far from all tasks, friends, and means of production—confronted by that man, I would be all the more likely to fall into an embarrassed silence.

I naturally do not lack for daily tasks. But it is once again time to define what I do from a broader perspective and in terms of its totality; I have come to realize the extent to which this is the case after having carefully and systematically begun to go through my material for the *Arcades*. There is unfortunately not the slightest prospect of my soon being able to choose freely where I will be; I will have to be content with being able to leave here. It is also doubtful as to whether this means that I will again be going north. It has been impossible to get any news of Brecht, since he has been in London—and is apparently still there.

In brief, I am not a little envious of your opportunities for bourgeois social intercourse, which I am totally lacking here. I will be compensated for this in the next few days by Stefan's arrival. He is going to spend the Christmas vacation here so that he can transfer to a local school at Easter time, if at all possible.

I learned with rare delight that you are still unable to desist from your old habit of giving me gifts. I would really like to express my gratitude to you once again in person—or to be given the pictorial broadsheet on the spot—but it remains quite doubtful as to whether the coast will lead me all the way to you.[2] Another factor is that the contours of Ibiza, which have engraved themselves so deeply into me, have recently contracted into painful configurations. These words do not only, and not primarily, refer to the death of Jean Jacques Noeggerath[3]—but because the thread of his life happened to intersect a knot of my own life, his death affected me much more than might have been supposed from the nature of our association.

I have nothing very much to tell you today about literature. I know only from hearsay that Bloch's new book was published by Oprecht and Helbling. Bernhard von Brentano reviews manuscripts for them. The book is supposed to include embarrassing and malicious quarrels with me,[4] as I was told by a source who is, to be sure, not infallible. Let's wait and see! Brecht's novel[5] was published by Allert de Lange in Amsterdam. I liked a new book I read by Simenon, *Les suicidés*. You will have probably already noted that for three months I have been tirelessly speaking of Stevenson's novel, *The Master of Ballantrae,* and it will hardly be necessary for me to recommend it to you.—You may be interested in knowing that Hessel has translated Green's *Visionnaire,* which I learned from the *Frankfurter Zeitung.*

So much for today. It would be nice if I did not have to wait all that long for news from you. The most sincere regards to you and Grete.

Yours, Walter

1. WB was living in the Villa Verde Pension, which was run by his ex-wife.
2. Alfred Cohn was in business in Barcelona.
3. Felix Noeggerath's son.
4. *Erbschaft dieser Zeit* (1935). For references to WB, see esp. pp. 275ff.
5. *Der Dreigroschenroman* (1934).

248. To Karl Thieme

San Remo
December 25, 1934

Dear Mr. Thieme,

For a long time now, I have been meaning to express my most sincere gratitude for the bounteous and important evidence of your thoughtfulness. Now the arrival of your most recent parcel and the impending new year, for which you may be assured of my particularly warm wishes, give me a twofold reason to do so.

I could not find a more fitting form to express my gratitude than by responding in detail to your important cultural history of the West.[1] As a written expression of gratitude and one that is subject to the conditions of this kind of expression, it will therefore turn out to be very incomplete indeed. May the few words I now send in advance of a personal discussion with you, something for which I truly hope, be welcome to you in spite of that!

Let me begin with something that seems remote: the more of your letter I read and particularly when I came upon your critique of *devotio moderna,* which illuminates the entire last part, the more often I had to think of my long-deceased friend Florens Christian Rang. In the course of long conversations, which were hardly ever concerned with theology, he introduced me to a world of theological thinking that exhibited profound correspondences with your own. I cannot imagine anything else but that his name is thoroughly familiar to you and that you have known his *Deutsche Bauhütte*[2] for quite a while. Yet it still seems regrettable to me that you were not able to meet the man, for whom all of Western culture continued to be nourished by the content of Judeo-Christian revelation and its history. Your book corroborates this as your position too. In an extensive commentary that is surely one of the most remarkable works of exegesis, he wanted to demonstrate that it was even in force when Renaissance poetry was at its peak—in Shakespeare's sonnets.

After a first reading of your work, it became obvious that I was especially enthralled by the theological analysis of the idea of culture that has held sway since humanism. It seems to me that your concept of the "common truth" presents you with extraordinarily far-reaching insights. Your analysis of neohumanism and of classicism strikes me as eminently perceptive; I read these pages with rapt attention. And in saying this, I hardly need to remind you that my concept of the "common truth"—I do acknowledge such a concept!—is not the same as yours; if I were to add anything to it, it would only be to point out how broad the path is through the breach you have cut through the hieratic wall of humanistic culture.

It is impossible for me to refer to all of the numerous places where you erect small signposts in passing. Clear and well-constructed intellectual landscapes are revealed to anyone who tarries there. Even chasms illuminated by a ray of insight are revealed: your wonderful characterization of Jesuit style as a dispassionately erected prospect of permissible worldly delight; your illumination of Luther's doctrine of sin from the concept of the "damned" bounden duty; your theological characterization of the driving force of the world as an intra-Calvinistic confrontation, e.g. the confrontation of "unbidden" Calvinism with the first Christians who were bidden to answer the question; or your nice proof of the origin of Jünger's "worker-warrior."

Every halfway alert reader can tell from your language that the care and energy you expended on what you had to say were never wasted. Not everyone, however—and only because of this do I allow myself to point it out—will note, as I perchance did, that you delve so deeply into the subject in some places that obsolete phraseology also surfaces. For example, that of pietism, which assumed incomparable form in the figure of Samuel Collenbusch[3] and in which form the man himself can again be heard on your p. 136: "In place of Luther's believer doing good out of gratitude to God for his merciful redemption, there is the believer doing good for the sake of love . . ."

I have said enough to make completely manifest my gratitude to you for having thought of my book in the context of your own; it is not enough—and I am well aware of this—to make any future discussion superfluous or even less urgent. I feel compelled to have such a discussion purely on the strength of this gratitude. With that in mind, I might perhaps—to be sure, only as a matter of expedience—refer you to fragments of a longer essay, "Franz Kafka," which have just appeared in the *Jüdische Rundschau.* I have just been promised offprints, so that I am unfortunately unable to send you one.

The only thing left for me to tell you is with what great interest I read the first four pieces on contemporary lyric poetry[4] which you had sent to me. I found much that was interesting in them, but I must say that I also have some objections. I most vigorously agree with the objection you raise against the doctrine of nature *tel quel*—above all in the section on Elisabeth Langgässer—and which is so forcefully repeated in your essay on St. Francis.[5]

I will most likely remain in San Remo for quite some time yet. Working conditions are certainly unfavorable there, in absolute terms, but they are quite acceptable in relative terms. It is probably not very likely that you will be in the area very soon. I would therefore be all the more delighted to hear from you.

Sincere regards.

Yours, Walter Benjamin

1. *Das alte Wahre: Eine Bildungsgeschichte des Abendlandes* (1934).
2. Appeared in 1924.
3. WB dealt with Collenbusch in the foreword to his letter to Kant in *Deutsche Menschen.*
4. Inclusive reviews in the *Frankfurter Zeitung* (September 21, October 11, November 5, December 5, 1934).
5. "Der Patron der katholischen Aktion," *Franziskanisches Leben* 12 (1936).

249.* To Gerhard Scholem

San Remo
December 26, 1934

Dear Gerhard,

The letter you addressed to me in Denmark has at long last, two weeks ago, found its way to me here. Not so the German essay it announces, which must have gone astray. I hope very much that you can manage to send me another copy soon. Otherwise, I would have to conclude that a higher force is taking great pains to cut me off from the sources of mystical literature—and not merely the pure but the turbid. For example, Bloch's *Heritage of Our Time* has been out for weeks. But do you think I have so much as laid eyes on the book? I know only this much, that restlessness and bickering are about to break loose in the ranks of the faithful, insofar as I am both congratulated on the tribute shown me in the text and defended against the invective it directs at me—allegedly contained in the same passages. Even a letter from the author himself has already arrived. All that I lack is the material itself, which would allow me to make some sense of all this.

But you will permit yourself even less to hesitate in providing me with authentic documents when I confide that I have fallen into the headquarters of the genuine magic Jews. For [Oskar] Goldberg has taken up residence here, and he has delegated his disciple [Adolf] Caspary to the cafés, and the *Wirklichkeit der Hebräer*[1] to the local newspaper stand, while he himself—who knows?—probably spends his time conducting tests of his numerology in the casino. Needless to say, I haven't engaged in conversation with this flank. Less obvious, though unfortunately no less true, is the fact that no opportunities for me to communicate otherwise exist, nor are they foreseeable for me here.

The sheer loneliness in which I spend my days here, and whose effect is most hazardous in the long run, has recently been interrupted by Stefan's presence, if only for a few days. He will be returning to Berlin when school starts—at least those are the plans—in order to be registered at a school here after Easter. After a separation of almost two years, he left me with the best possible impression of his composure and confidence of judgment. He is now sixteen and a serious partner in conversations, which—I regret to say—tend mostly to be serious.

The words with which your last letter touches on my situation cannot be called mistaken. The worst of it is that I am growing weary. And this is an immediate consequence less of my insecure existence than of the isolation in which its vicissitudes tend to place me. This isolation has rarely been more absolute than here, among bathers and tourists from whom I can scarcely expect anything rewarding but from whom—given the circumstances—I am forced day in and day out to reestablish my distance.

Not much would be required to make a trip to Palestine attractive to me; indeed, nothing would be more appropriate than if for once we could together inspect the foundations of our correspondence, which over the years has grown into a skyscraper. I would even be able to raise the fare for the passage, if the cost of the voyage there and back could be spread out over a sufficient period. When you have a chance, please write me in greater detail how you conceive the journey might be organized, whether I might be able to combine it with lectures, etc.

As you have surely seen, the first part of the "Kafka" has recently appeared, and what germinated for so very long has now at least borne reasonable fruit. This publication will induce me, sometime soon, to open my dossier containing suggestions others have made, as well as my own reflections, which—departing from my usual practice—I compiled especially for this essay.[2] My lengthy review essay on the theory of language—which I wrote as a novice, as you will probably notice sooner than I would like—is going to be published in the *Zeitschrift für Sozialforschung* in the foreseeable future. But I have been able to put the learning process resulting from this *coram publico* to good use, and in fact even very recently, through acquaintance with Karl Bühler's *Sprachtheorie.*[3]

To return to the Archives for Social Research, you have perhaps already heard from me or someone else that its administration has moved to America, and in fact just at a moment when *rebus sic stantibus* I set great store in a meeting with its heads. Prior to that, I can't even consider making use of the considerable material I worked through over the summer during my research on the *Neue Zeit.*

Meanwhile, I am busy with intermediate projects: at the moment with a review of Brecht's *Three-Penny Novel,* a book I urge you to read. Enclosed you will find a little filler joke that recently appeared in the *Frankfurter Zeitung.*[4]

A great shame to hear that your effort on Kraft's behalf came to naught! I gather from his letters that life is not easy for him in Palestine. I never met his wife.—I wrote Spitzer not long ago, to notify him of the mailing of my Kafka manuscript, which he had requested. At the same time I was able to confirm receipt of the Schocken *Almanach,* in which—among sundry pieces worth reading—a short passage from the Mishne Torah[5] made an overwhelming impression on me.

Best wishes to you for your semester, a third of its course already run, and to Escha for her recovery.

Yours, Walter

1. Goldberg's magnum opus (1925). Adolf Caspary (born 1898) was one of Goldberg's foremost disciples. (*Die Machinenutopie* [Berlin: David, 1927]).

2. The dossier containing WBs own reflections has been preserved in Frankfurt and printed in the apparatus to *Schriften,* vol. 2. I don't know whether the "observations others have made" (excluding myself) have been preserved in East Berlin among the letters to WB, but I consider this to be probable.

3. See *Schriften* 3:454–55, 468–71.

4. The reference is to the piece "Auf die Minute" [To the minute] (*Schriften* 4:761–63), published in the *Frankfurter Zeitung* (December 6, 1934).

5. Moses Maimomides' magnum opus. It was the passage "Von der Lebensführung des Weisen" (printed in N. Glatzer's translation in the *Almanach des Schocken Verlags für das Jahre 5695* [1934–35], pp. 37–44). (Also published in volume 27 of the Schocken Library, *Rabbi Mosche ben Maimon, ein systematischer Querschnitt durch sein Werk* (1935), pp. 87–92.)

250. To Theodor W. Adorno

San Remo
January 7, 1935

Dear Mr. Wiesengrund,

I presume you are back and I will proceed to answer your long letter of December 17. Not without trepidation—it is so weighty and gets right down to the crux of the matter that there is no prospect of my doing it justice in a letter. It is thus all the more important that, before doing anything else, I once again assure you of the great joy I felt at your vital interest in me. I not only read your letter, but also studied it; it demands to be pondered sentence by sentence. Since you grasped my intentions[1] to a tee, your indications of where I went wrong are of the greatest importance. This applies first of all to your observations on my inadequate mastery of the archaic; it thus perfectly applies to your reservations about the question of the eons and of forgetting. As for the rest, I will yield to your objections to the term "experimental setup" without further ado and will take into consideration your very important observations on the silent film. I have taken the fact that you refer with such particular emphasis to "Investigations of a Dog" ["Aufzeichnungen eines Hundes"] as a hint. It is precisely this piece—probably the only one—that remained alien to me even while I was working on my "Kafka" essay. I also know—and have even said as much to Felizitas—that I still needed to discover what it actually meant. Your comments square with this assumption.

Now that two parts—the first and third—have been published, the way is clear for revision; it is still questionable whether it will finally be published and whether Schocken will publish the expanded version as a book. As far as I can tell at this point, the revision will primarily affect the fourth part which, in spite of the heavy—or perhaps because of the all too heavy—stress placed on it, has not made it possible even for readers like you and Scholem to take a position. Otherwise, Brecht is among those who have been heard from thus far; and therefore, all in all, a sonorous figure has formed around him and there are still some things I can learn by listening to it. I have planned a collection of reflections and I am not yet concerned about how it will be projected onto the urtext. These reflections center on the relationship "allegory = symbol," in which I believe to have captured the antinomy that defines Kafka's works in a way that does greater justice to his way of thinking than the opposition "parable = novel." A more precise definition of the form of Kafka's novels does not as yet exist. I agree with you that it is essential but can be achieved only by indirect means.

I would hope—and this is not at all that unlikely—that some of these questions might remain open until the next time we see each other. That is to say, should there truly be reason to hope in view of a hint from Felizitas, according to which you were considering a trip to San Remo over Easter. I would be delighted if this were the case—indeed, more than you could guess without being able to assess my current isolation. At the moment, however, a brief hiatus in my isolation is imminent; I am expecting Wissing and thus I may yet become the indirect witness to his last months in Berlin, whose coda you experienced directly. And this also makes me want to see you.

I am not looking beyond Easter. Brecht again asked me to come to Denmark and, indeed, right away. Now I will probably not leave San Remo before May in any case. On the other hand, however, I will not allow my stay here to be extended interminably, as valuable a refuge as it is, for in the long run my isolation from friends and the means to work will turn it into a dangerous test of my endurance. Another factor, of course, is that I am completely fettered by the need to do whatever I can to survive, something I constantly feel as crippling. In response to the kind proposition you made in December, for which I sincerely thank you—although, given local circumstances, the institute's 100 Swiss francs will not eliminate my need to struggle to survive, in fact, there is still no reason for me to turn to outsiders with my personal concerns. Even though a minimum degree of freedom of movement and, consequently, a large degree of initiative, could be achieved precisely at this time with the most minimal means. But how?

And on the other hand, you know from experience that a maximum degree of initiative must be summoned to write one's first essays in a foreign tongue. I can feel this in terms of the "Bachofen" essay I am currently writing for the *Nouvelle revue française*. This occasion would provide the opportunity for us to say a lot about the things closest to us. I must put informational material in the foreground for France, where Bachofen is totally unknown—not a single one of his works has been translated. Having just said this, however, I do not want to omit conveying to you my unreserved agreement with your letter of December 5, as far as your comments on Klages and Jung are concerned. In the exact same spirit you indicated, I consider it necessary to learn more about Jung. Do you by chance have available his study of Joyce?

Please tell me where this line is from: "Virtually nothing has done everything well"?[2] And won't you please send me the piece on the tickets for London's transit system to which you allude? In any case, as soon as possible I expect to read your piece about the phonograph record, which addresses such important contexts.

The first copy of Bloch's book that was sent must have missed me; the publisher has promised that a second is on its way. What I really regret is that Bloch, who, no less than the rest of us, surely needs to orient himself on what his friends who are experts have to say, stakes out the spacious compass of his itinerary without recourse to them and is satisfied to let them enjoy the company of his papers.

Have you read *The Three-Penny Novel?* To me it seems to be a consummate success. Write me what you think of it. Also give me detailed information and do not forget to include the state of your own projects.

For today, my most sincere regards.

Yours, Walter Benjamin

1. In WB's Kafka essay.
2. From Adorno's *Tom Sawyer.*

251. To Bertolt Brecht

San Remo
January 9, 1935

Dear Brecht,

What I will do regarding Denmark is still not entirely clear. Horkheimer has written that he intends to find a scholarship for me in America that would enable me to spend a year there. The whole thing is still very much up in the air. But I naturally wrote that I would accept.

It is quite possible that nothing will come of it, in which case I would be happy to come to Denmark. Otherwise things are quite tolerable here as far as external conditions are concerned. On the other hand, my isolation—from people, from news, and from the things I need to work—often goes beyond what is tolerable.

Things were different for you in England. What I would really like to know about in more detail is how? Also what was decided there about your plays and the novel?

I have now read *The* [*Three-Penny*] *Novel* in printed form and indeed with renewed delight in many passages. This time I particularly developed a soft spot for Walley. It seems to me that the book will endure the test of time. I also heard from G. that he considers it a consummate success.

For my review, I had asked Klaus Mann to send me the press notices that have appeared thus far.[1] It can be useful to know what others have made of the book. He wrote me that Landauer sent everything to you. Could you perhaps let me have the cuttings for eight days? I would return them to you by registered mail.

The book on photography is still in manuscript form.[2] I do not know whether a copy is available. It covers everything from the beginnings to the turn of the century. If you want, I could write the author.

I will certainly stay here until Easter; Stefan will then enroll in the local school.

Have you seen Bloch's *Heritage of Our Time?* He talks about you in it.

The next issue of the *Zeitschrift für Sozialforschung* will contain an essay I wrote on linguistics. Otherwise I am in the process of finishing my first lengthy essay written in French, "Bachofen." The only thing to come out of the time I spent in Paris was a discussion with the editor of the *Nouvelle revue française*. The emigrants are depressed; Kracauer especially so. Some, like Heinrich Mann and Kesten, have organized an internal emigration to Nice.

How is the car? If necessary, you can lay a wreath on its cold motor in my name.

Most sincere regards and please convey the same to Heli and the children.

Yours, Walter Benjamin

1. WB wrote a review of Brecht's *Three-Penny Novel* for the journal *Die Sammlung*, published by Klaus Mann; although the essay had been typeset, it did not appear there; see letters 257 and 258, to Scholem and Brecht. It can be found in *Bertolt Brechts Dreigroschenbuch* (Frankfurt, 1960), pp. 187–93.

2. Probably Gisèle Freund's *La photographie française au XIXe siècle* (Paris, 1936). Reviewed by WB in the *Zeitschrift für Sozialforschung* 7 (1938), p. 296.

252. To Werner Kraft

San Remo
January 9, 1935

[. . .] Why aren't you writing me any more about *The Three-Penny Novel?* In my corner of the world, which may well be stylishly central but literarily very remote, I have no idea at all of how the book was received by all and sundry. Since I myself am working on a review at the moment, I asked Brecht to let me have a look at what the newspapers had to say. By the way, as far as his poem in the festschrift for Kraus is concerned, I happen to know that it could not have been withdrawn without obvious rudeness. It is hardly justifiable, however, to draw far-reaching conclusions from the fact that Brecht did not want to exhibit such rudeness, given his uncommon courtesy.[1]

The conjecture you made in your last card, however, that your reservations about my "Kafka" may have hurt my feelings, is even less justified. Without risking my now doing the same thing to you, may I assure you that, in comparison to other objections that have been raised, yours appear like feathered arrows among mortars (by which I by no means want to insinuate that they are poisonous arrows). However, the controversy that has arisen around this work as around no other only confirms that a number of the strategic points in current thinking are present on its terrain and that my efforts to reinforce this thinking are not futile.

You have been promising me your reflections on Palestine for a long time now. I will read them with great interest, and I hope soon.—Seume is one of the most admirable figures of the bourgeousie and some of his letters are truly incomparable.—I have not had fine things like the *Corona* come my way for quite a while now, unless you might be in a position to lend me the issue and include it in the parcel I requested at the beginning. In any case, please be so kind to send me the address of the editorial office.

Have you seen Ernst Bloch's *Heritage of Our Time?* It contains a short chapter about me but of course its viewpoints make no claim to completeness, as the author promptly assured me in a letter.

P.S. A certain Julius Kraft has had a book published with the title *Die Unmöglichkeit der Geisteswissenschaften*. Is he a relative of yours?[2]

1. The disagreements between Brecht and Kraus went back to Kraus's pamphlet "Warum die Fackel nicht erscheint" (*Die Fackel*, 890–905). Brecht reacted with the poem "Über den schnellen Fall des guten Unwissenden."

2. No.

253. To Helene Weigel

San Remo
February 3, 1935

Dear Heli,

I was delighted to receive your letter. I would naturally have liked to have heard how things went for you and Brecht in London. However, I will probably have to continue relying on the scanty information from my correspondents who live there for news about that. Did you see Schoen?

To begin with the most important thing: I have no one with whom to play 66. People here are much too cultured to play cards. This is a lesson for me: people should not aspire to move beyond their own circles! I, of course, have now drifted far away from our regular table and it will certainly be some time before I again show up on its fringes. If the Geneva institute does not send for me to come to America, I will probably visit during the summer. Brecht unfortunately did not send me any clippings about the novel. I would have really liked to know what others made of the book, for the review on which I am currently working. I have not seen a single review because I only read French and Italian papers. Perhaps you could still send me one or two important pieces.

The book you asked about is

Henri Damaye, *Psychiatrie et civilisation* (Paris: Alcan, 1934).

It does not, however, deal with *mass* psychoses, but with bacteria as the cause of individual psychoses. The author's particular thesis is that certain forms of the Koch bacillus do not cause tuberculosis but rather psychosis.

Read Ilf's and Petrov's *Millionaire among the Soviets,* if it is available in German. I am just reading it in the French edition and am discovering some very funny things in it.

Most sincere regards!

Yours, Walter Benjamin

254. To Alfred Cohn

San Remo
February 6, 1935

Dear Alfred,

I am pulling myself together this evening, in spite of a fever and a cold, in order to thank you for your last letter. If the February weather where you are is like the weather here, you will have no end of trouble bringing the children through it safely. The mornings when the sun shines are very warm; once the sun has disappeared in the afternoon, a damp cold immediately sets in and I have been living for a week with its unpleasant consequences.

Your last letter spoke of relatively tolerable conditions and primarily about the prospects of improved conditions. It would be very nice if they had since actually materialized. Meanwhile nothing has changed for me here, except that the spring deadline, beyond which I will probably not extend my stay, is drawing near. In the meantime, I will have to surrender for that long to the hermetic isolation with which I am paying for the relatively pleasant circumstances of my current external existence. This isolation goes far beyond the point at which it could possibly benefit my work, and I am confining myself to hammering out one piece after another without much haste and in a semicraftsmanlike manner. Another consideration is that I must do any relatively concentrated work while in bed, in part due to space factors and in part due to the temperature. This was the only way I was finally able to complete the Bachofen essay, my first long essay in French, and I am planning to do the same thing while working on a review of *The Three-Penny Novel,* which I am just beginning to write for *Die Sammlung*.

Meanwhile, it appears that stabilization in Germany has made tremendous progress; and I would not be surprised if a kind of Brüning regime did not soon come into existence there—unperturbed by Social-Democratic whining and obeisant to the imperial army and navy. The gloomiest and yet probably the most apt image of the future. Under these circumstances, whatever personal ties I still had to Germany are being completely undone. Among the exceptions is my tie to Glück, with whom I am of course not in correspondence but whom I definitely hope to see again this year. On the other hand, not a word from Jula and Fritz. Otherwise it is only occasionally that I hear anything about Ernst from a mutual female friend. Most remarkably, something like a center seems to have materialized for us in England rather than anyplace else. We can, of course, both remember how difficult it is to cultivate French soil. And yet there will be nothing for me but to start over again and again and sometimes I ask myself if I should not have stayed in Paris this winter *à tout prix* and I believe I must reproach myself for missed opportunities. On the other hand—and so as not to overestimate the extent of my own symptoms of inadequacy—I recently entertained myself by putting together a "list of my mistakes and failures of the last two years" and the result was the slight comfort that the former were not at all always prerequisites of the latter.

Yet the more it recedes into the past, the more my first period of emigration on Ibiza appears bathed in a colorful haze. And I say this particularly in order to urge upon you the following questions concerning Ibiza. It may be possible for you to answer some of them based on your own inquiries. Namely, I would really like to know 1) whether the Noeggeraths are still on the island; 2) their whereabouts and 3) whether they still own their lot or have perhaps even built on it; 4) how things are going on Ibiza for the sculptor Jokisch; and 5) whether Guy Selz still has his bar in the harbor?

To come now to your own inquiry,[1] I do not believe that the appropriate way to gather the information you desire is through Scholem. To be sure, I also know of no direct way. But someone I know well—whom you know by name—and whose address I will give you, might be able to find out something for you, perhaps through his relatives or friends there, if you write him in detail and with explicit reference to me. As you know, he himself is not a businessman but a librarian. You must therefore leave no doubt that you are not turning to him for his personal competence (which would be lacking in this regard) but as a conduit to possible experts. Werner Kraft, Jerusalem Rehavia, 37 Ben Maimon Street, c/o Rosenberg. The ink on this had not yet dried when his new address arrived: Rehavia, 31 Alphasi Street.

I get away from here to Nice as often as possible. Not as if there were a lot of people for me there, but there are still one or two. And in addition sensible cafés, bookstores, well-stocked newsstands—in short, everything it is totally impossible to get here. While there, I also lay in a supply of detective fiction. I need quite a lot, since my nights here usually begin at about 8:30. Besides Simenon, Pierre Véry has recently proven to be very good. Otherwise, I have read Ilf's and Petrov's *Millionaire among the Soviets* (translated from the Russian)—the first part is extremely funny, but the later ones are weaker; Drieu La Rochelle's *Comedy of Charlesroi and Other Stories* [*La comédie de Charlesroi*], which contains the novella, "The Deserter" ["Le déserteur"], in which I amazingly discovered an exact description of my own political stance; Montherlant's *Bachelors* [*Les célibataires*], which I probably recommended most highly to you earlier; Guéhenno, *Journal d'un homme de quarante ans,* in which some of the experiences of our generation are well formulated. Of course not as well as Wieland Herzfelde did when he unexpectedly saw me show up in a small suburb of Copenhagen during the summer: "Well, Benjamin. You also probably belong to the generation of '92? We'll surely be seeing each other from time to time. For, you know, the thing about this generation is: that those who were of a more delicate constitution already disappeared before 1914; those who were foolish disappeared between 1914 and 1918; the ones who were left will stick around a while yet."

You will have received Bloch's new book, which I sent you. I would be very grateful if you let me hear what you have to say about it. By resorting to all kinds of tricks, I have repeatedly put off the unthankful and extremely difficult task of writing to him about it, but will be unable to avoid during so for very much longer. The severe reproach I must level against the book (even if I will not level it against the author) is that it in no way corresponds to the circumstances under which it has appeared. Instead, it is as out of place as a fine gentleman who, having arrived to inspect an area demolished by an earthquake, has nothing more urgent to do than immediately spread out the Persian rugs that his servants had brought along and which were, by the way, already somewhat motheaten; set up the gold and silver vessels, which were already somewhat tarnished; have himself wrapped in brocade and damask gowns, which were already somewhat faded. Bloch obviously has excellent intentions and considerable insights. But he does not understand how to thoughtfully put them into practice. His exaggerated claims prevent him from doing this. In such a situation—in a slum—nothing is left for a grand gentleman to do than to give away his Persian rugs as bed covers, to cut his brocade into coats, and to have his splendid vessels melted down.

I am enclosing a list of the issues of the newspaper in which the *Briefe* appear. Because of the upheavals of the past years, I myself have unfortunately been able to get hold of only two complete series, one of which I have to hold in reserve as long as there is the slighest hope that it will be published as a book. Many of the issues are unfortunately out of print. Thus I can be of no further use to you in this regard even though I would be the one most likely to be so.

Another time, perhaps, some commentary on Kafka. But certainly not before I have received a longish report on how things are with you. My view is that I have earned a powerful right to this based on the value of the above.

Most sincere regards.

Yours, Walter

1. About business opportunities in Palestine.

255. To Max Horkheimer

San Remo
February 19, 1935

Dear Mr. Horkheimer,

Let me express my sincere gratitude for your letter of January 28.

I am delighted above all at the prospect of having a personal discussion with you in the near future.

But I would like to tell you now already how important your urgency concerning the essay on Fuchs[1] is to me. After your letter, it is obvious to me that it should take precedence over all other projects. If this has not yet occurred, it is because I have reservations about having Fuchs send any new books—I studied several during the past summer—at a time when my future plans are still unclear. As I already wrote you, it is unfortunately very dubious whether I can manage to stay here past Easter and I dare not even think about what will happen then.

This project would benefit tremendously if I were able to work on it in Paris. Not only to stay in touch with Fuchs while I am working on it—although that too would be of great value—but also to give the piece the broad comparative foundation that you yourself outline in your letter. Staying in Paris would also enable me to pursue Fuchs's sources, which, of course, are what will ultimately give us total insight into his method.

I have been able to complete some important projects here—for example, and most importantly, I wrote a rather long essay on Bachofen in French—but now the isolation in which I find myself is beginning to make itself felt in bibliographical terms as well. Nonetheless, the coming weeks will not be a loss, since I am working on my belletristic essay on French literature.

Every once in a while I even manage to get a commission from Germany—from the *Frankfurter Zeitung*. I mention this not only *à titre de curiosité*, but also to inform you that I am doing everything imaginable to get the situation under control.

[. . .]

The "Kafka" essay you ask about appeared in the *Jüdische Rundschau*, but in such fragmentary form that, should it be of interest to you, I would rather hand you the entire manuscript when we meet than give you an offprint of the article right now.

Will I be able to read the page proofs of the sociolinguistic essay myself?

Please, my dear Mr. Horkheimer, let me know in most intimate detail what form your European projects are taking, since I want to accommodate my own plans to them as much as possible.

In solidarity, I sincerely remain

Yours, Walter Benjamin

1. "Eduard Fuchs, der Sammler und der Historiker" [Eduard Fuchs, collector and historian] *Zeitschrift für Sozialforschung* 6 (1937), pp. 346–80. In *Das Kunstwerk im Zeitalter seiner technischen Reproduzierbarkeit* (Frankfurt, 1963), pp. 95–156. [Also in *One-Way Street and Other Writings,* trans. Edmund Jephcott and Kingsley Shorter (London: New Left Books, 1979.—Trans.]

256. To Max Horkheimer

Nice
April 8, 1935

Dear Mr. Horkheimer,

Many thanks for your kind letter of March 19.

It was delayed in getting to me and the story of this delay at the same time describes the last phase of my own story *in nuce*. I had to leave my place of asylum in San Remo much earlier than I could possibly have predicted. Then I wanted to go to Paris (where I had already had my mail forwarded). If need be, I could have found accommodations in Paris at my sister's. When it became time to go, however, she became severely ill. If I neglected to inform you of all this, it was because I also wanted to avoid the appearance of once again explicitly resorting to your assistance. This was because I am confident that you are doing all you can anyway, and your last letter confirmed that for me. Please accept my sincere gratitude. Nothing is more urgent for me than to link my work to that of the institute as closely and as productively as possible.

It is a pity you are not coming to Europe. On the other hand, I assume that your indispensability is a good indication of the significance the institute has gained in America. I will now, during Easter week, discuss my work schedule in detail with Mr. Pollock and will go to Paris for this at about the same time as he. I hope, in order to stay there! The possibility of this happening will have to be clarified in conversation with Mr. Pollock.

The page proofs of my review article will be sent off to you in the next few days.

I assume your work on authority and family will appear in the institute series.[1] When will it appear? My work on Bachofen is hardly likely to contain much that is new to you. It is meant to introduce Bachofen, who is completely unknown in France and none of whose works have been translated, to the French. With this in mind, I tried to portray him rather than describe his theories.

I hope you and your wife will accept my most sincere regards and wishes!

Yours, Walter Benjamin

1. *Studien über Autorität und Familie: Forschungsberichte aus dem Institut für Sozialforschung* (Paris, 1936).

257.* To Gerhard Scholem

Paris
May 20, 1935

Dear Gerhard,

It has been some time since you last heard from me. You will have guessed the reason. An exceedingly critical period set in after the move to Paris, underscored by external fiascos. Rejection of the "Bachofen" by the *NRF,* which passed it on to the *Mercure de France,* where I can see it languishing now; dissolution of my brief, and still all too long, literary relationship with Klaus Mann, for whom I had reviewed *The Three-Penny Novel* and who returned my review, already typeset, when I refused his unmentionable fee.[1] And a few more things of that ilk, *novissima* in my career, long surpassed in my civil life.

Then, following a short breathing spell, a further circumstance arose that put a halt to my entire correspondence. The institute in Geneva asked for a précis of the *Arcades,* without any commitment on its part. I would even say, out of politeness. Now and then I had hinted here and there about it, never divulging very much. Since this coincided with the annual closing of the Bibliothèque Nationale, I was really alone with my studies on *Arcades* for the first time in many years. And since creative matters have a way of arising all the more unpredictably, the more important they are, so it happened that, with this précis, which I had promised without giving it much thought, the project entered a new phase, in which for the first time it bears more resemblance—even if from afar—to a book.[2]

I don't know how many years my drafts, originally conceived for an essay for *Der Querschnitt* which was never written, date back. I wouldn't be surprised (should this Paris book ever come into being) if it turned out to be the classic nine years, which would exceed the time I spent arching the bow of preparations for the *Trauerspiel* book. But that of course is the real question, since I am not the master of my working conditions. Prospects for really arousing the interest of the institute in Geneva for this book are minimal. It [the book] allows no concessions to be made to any side, and if I know anything about the book at all, then it is that no school will rush to claim it as its own.

Otherwise, I periodically succumb to the temptations of visualizing analogies with the baroque book in the book's inner construction, although its external construction decidedly diverges from that of the former. And I want to give you this much of a hint: Here as well the focus will be on the unfolding of a handed-down concept. Whereas in the former it was the concept of *Trauerspiel,* here it is likely to be the fetish character of commodities.[3] Whereas the baroque book mobilized its own theory of knowledge, this will be the case for *Arcades* at least to the same extent, though I can foresee neither whether it will find a form of representation of its own, nor to what extent I may succeed in such a representation. The title "Paris Arcades" has finally been discarded and the draft is entitled "Paris, Capital of the Nineteenth Century."[4] Privately I call it "Paris, capitale du XIXe siècle," implying a further analogy: just as the baroque book dealt with the seventeenth century from the perspective of Germany, this book will unravel the nineteenth century from France's perspective.

No matter how high an opinion I held of the studies I had made over the course of so many years, I now realize somewhat more clearly what I actually should have been doing, my opinion of them has diminished considerably. Innumerable questions are still unanswered. Admittedly, I am so completely at home in the relevant literature, and all the way down to its *bas fonds,* that I will gain a grasp on its answers sooner or later. In the midst of the incredible difficulties I am faced with, I sometimes enjoy dwelling on the following thought: how much of a dialectical synthesis of misery and exuberance lies in this research, which has been continually interrupted and repeatedly revived over the course of a decade, and which has been driven on into the remotest of regions. Should the book's dialectic prove to be just as sound, then it would find my approval.

The fact that the master plan now lies before me is, by the way, also probably an indirect result of my meeting with one of the institute's directors, which took place immediately after my arrival in Paris. The result was that I could live one (!) month without the customary day-to-day problems. But the month has passed, and I do not at all know what the next one will bring. If I'm supposed to set to work on the Fuchs essay—which, to tell the truth, I have yet to begin—this would be doubly repugnant. On the other hand, it would be a stroke of luck, which I can in no sense rely upon, if the institute really took a material interest in the Paris book.

What I wish for myself now would be to work in the library for a number of months and then be able to travel to Jerusalem after bringing my research to a more or less definitive conclusion in October or November. But even if there are numerous things that leave more of a mark on world events than my desires, we should still both keep the second of these wishes in mind. At the appropriate time I might be able to raise the money here for the trip, by means of a few tricks.

I eagerly await the books you announce: first and foremost, your little Zohar volume. I fear that it comes too late for Bloch, as will be the case with my book as well if it ever gets written—let alone published. Anyway, if Bloch's latest book should ever fall into your hands, you will easily be able to gain an impression of how successful his attempts at burglarizing my property have been. He should be surfacing in Jerusalem before long, accompanied by his new genie, Karola Piotrkowsky, as his wife.[5] Yes, it had almost slipped my mind: he will most likely be coming to Jerusalem with her; she is an architect and wants to build something there.

I am also very interested in Leo Strauss's book. What you tell me about him fits in with the pleasant image of him I have always made for myself.—Even if for the time being I am reading nothing but primary material, I recently happened upon a book whose author you had occasionally pointed out to me, the *Potestas Clavium* by Shestov.[6] I could not examine it very thoroughly but only determined that its polemic against platonic idealism turns out to be more entertaining than in the usual stuff of this genre. I haven't read Berdyaev, whom you mention in your last letter.

Yes, Stefan will soon be attending school in San Remo. My brother, by contrast, is still in Germany, where his wife has a well-paid position with the Soviet trade mission in Berlin. He went abroad once after his release from the concentration camp, but that was just for a holiday.[7] He has a son who is very handsome, judging from pictures I have seen. How very dreadful that your brother's predicament is so desperate. But whose field of vision is not crowded with such images!

Kraft wrote me an almost touching letter in which he offered his services to mobilize an influential Frenchman on my behalf.[8] Naturally I cannot avail myself of this, since setting this very problematic scheme into motion would require an effort that lies far beyond my present concerns. He seems to have traveled deep into the heart of the country and is sending me a nice report about it.

Write me when the occasion arises as to what details you need to make preparations for my coming. Kindest regards to you and Escha,

Yours, Walter

1. Mann had offered him 150 French francs.
2. Compare letters 260 and 261, to Adorno and Horkheimer.
3. According to the famous chapter in the first part of Marx's *Capital*.
4. [*Paris, die Hauptstadt des neunzehnten Jahrhunderts*—Trans.], in *Schriften* 1:406–22 and later in *Reflections*, pp. 146–62.
5. The visit never took place.
6. Shestov's book appeared in German in 1926 [English translation by Bernard Martin (Athens: Ohio University Press, 1968)].
7. Georg Benjamin had visited Switzerland and the northern Italian lakes in the spring of 1934.
8. Probably Charles Du Bos.

258. To Bertolt Brecht

Paris
May 20, 1935

Dear Brecht,

Six weeks ago, by way of Asja, I informed Steffin about the wretched incident with Klaus Mann that deprived me of having my review of your book published. I sent her my manuscript at the same time in the hope that it would reach you while you were in Russia.

As things now stand, I have heard nothing from either you or her, so that I am uncertain whether the contact via Asja worked.

The long and short of it is that I viewed as an insult the proposed honorarium of 150 French francs for a twelve-page manuscript that had been commissioned by the editorial board—without having the slightest inclination to overestimate the market value of my production. In a short letter, I asked for 250 francs and refused to let him have the manuscript for less. Thereupon, even though it was already typeset, it was returned to me.

I would obviously have swallowed Mann's impertinence had I foreseen the result. I showed myself as not clever enough for this world and did so at a point at which cleverness would have meant a lot to me.

You will receive the manuscript of the review at the same time as this letter. One is also being sent to the *Neue deutsche Blätter*. I consider it unlikely, however, that it still might be published there. On the other hand, I asked myself whether—since the book is coming out in Czech—there might not now be a possibility of having my article translated into Czech. Are you in personal contact with your translator?

I still have no idea at all of what will come of Denmark this year. First of all, I would have to know what your plans are. Will you be in Svendborg in the summer?—But something else is also at issue: after my first few weeks in Paris, I concluded that my book—the long one I once told you about—as far from its textual figuration as it may be, is still much closer to it than I had believed. And I have written a detailed précis of it. For this reason, I need to inform myself about a number of things and I can only get this information at the Bibliothèque Nationale. I must therefore try at all costs—and it is devilishly difficult—to stay on in Paris. In any case, please let me know what your plans are from the end of July on, if you have already made any.

"Five Difficulties in Writing the Truth" ["Fünf Schwierigkeiten beim Schreiben der Wahrheit"][1] has the dryness and therefore the unlimited durability of thoroughly classical works. It is written in prose the like of which has heretofore not existed in German. Domke[2] had intended to write you about this.

Greetings to Heli, and my most sincere regards to you.

Yours, Walter Benjamin

1. It was illegally published in *Unsere Zeit* (1934).
2. Martin Domke (born 1892), a lawyer in Berlin; later in Paris and America; a Lichtenberg collector.

259. To Werner Kraft

Paris
May 25, 1935

Dear Mr. Kraft,

I really must thank you for several letters and for more than letters.

I was moved at the fact that my few allusions made my situation so real for you that you gave it some thought in spite of all the difficulties of your own situation.

And it will seem paradoxical to you that a man in my position does not pursue every possibility, whether the most vague or the most remote. But there are the most particular reasons that lead me to disregard the path you suggest in your readiness to help, although I am most sincerely grateful for that readiness. And I will explain these reasons to you because they go to the crux of my current productive situation. I must of course acquiesce in the fact that, in doing so, they will also touch once more on the crux of my material situation.

At the moment, I am unable to judge whether my occasional, and surely most cryptic, allusions informed you that I have for many years quietly indulged in a project that will summarize the views and problems strewn about my writings, within the limits of a defined subject. I may never have mentioned this project. The mass of research that forms its basis is extraordinarily extensive. But this was not the reason that its productive emergence was postponed year after year. And not even economic difficulties constituted the only cause. Rather, they urged upon me a technique of working that allowed me to keep my interest in this project alive for the longest time.

The most profound reason for the Saturnian tempo of the thing was the process of total revolution that a mass of ideas and images had to undergo. They originated in the distant past when I thought in purely metaphysical, even theological, terms and the revolution was necessary so that they could nourish my current disposition with all the force they contained. This process proceeded in silence; I myself was so little aware of its going on that I was terribly surprised when—as a result of an external stimulus—I recently wrote down the outline of the work in just a few days. Let me note here that Scholem knows about the existence of this project, but no one else in Palestine does. Let me ask you not to say anything about what I am planning *to anyone*. You will hear more about it if I go to Palestine in the winter, which is in the realm of possibility. For now, I can only tell you the title. You will be able to gather from that how far-removed this current subject, which dictatorily dominates the economy of my thoughts, is from French classical tragedy.[1] It is called "Paris, the Capital of the Nineteenth Century."

Regardless of how far my research has progressed, or may one day progress, the actual writing of the work will probably be possible only in Paris. Financial difficulty is a factor in this: I do not know how long I will be in a position to finance my stay in Paris. For this reason, I would welcome any intermittent and occasional work. But as far as I am concerned, neither you nor I can approach [Charles] Du Bos for advice. And I would be even less able to make the aforementioned project comprehensible to him. It is—if not heavens, then worlds—removed from his intellectual world. Of course, this does not preclude it from being very important for me to find out where he is at the moment and, indeed, should he be in Paris, it would be very important for you to tell him of my whereabouts. For there are ever fewer contacts with Frenchmen that are somehow useful or even just pleasant.

I was not surprised that the *Nouvelle revue française* did not accept the Bachofen essay. It was an all too easy favor requested by a third party and I began this essay against my own best judgment by yielding to the request. Now the essay is with the *Mercure de France* where not I, but the editor of the *NRF,* submitted it.

Please let me ask you to forgive the unsightly form of the first half of this letter. I began it to the accompaniment of the blare of a radio in a café that was quite unsuited for writing. Now, however, before going on I want to say thank you for your parcel of journals. I have looked through the *Corona,* except for the essay by Jünger. I still have not had the time for that. As always, or almost always, I only enjoyed the essay by Fritz Ernst.[2] What he reports Rahel having said after Goethe's death is beyond compare. It was also very worthwhile for me to become acquainted with the early congratulatory letters Kafka wrote to Brod. You have said everything there is to say about the overall impression made by the commemorative issue[3] and you also found the right words to describe the incident with Klaus Mann, to which I, for my part, will append the following aphorism: "For man is not clever enough for this world."[4]

I think that I will be able to send you a copy of my review of *The Three-Penny Novel* in the very near future, if not at the same time as this letter. Brecht's "Five Difficulties in Writing the Truth" is in the April issue of the Münzenberg journal, the *Neue Zeit,* which is published in Prague and Paris. It is a classical piece and the first completely successful piece of theoretical prose by him of which I am aware.

The question you raise as to where to live during the war is hard to answer because I can hardly count on external circumstances allowing me to do what seems right to me at such a moment, when whatever action taken probably comes too late in any case, but when one must necessarily act within the space of a few hours. From my trip north, I am familiar with a region where life is hard, but where it would be possible with some justification to feel safe, not only from acts of war but also from hunger.[5] I would not feel this way about anyplace in the European or Mediterranean region.

Since we are on the topic of politics, let me at least add that I am just now reading the news about the first major strike in Germany since March 1933. Six thousand workers are on strike in the Chemnitz [. . . ?]-factories.

The poem you included in your last letter seems to sound particularly pure to me and to have its source in a truly fortunate instance of linguistic fulfillment.[6] Thank you for this, as well as for the opportunity to turn my attention once again to *Stiller Herd,*[7] when I get the chance.

1. Kraft had suggested that WB write a book on this topic as the counterpart to his *Trauerspiel* book.
2. "Rahels Traum." Now in *Essais* (Zurich, 1946), 2:211–27.
3. On the occasion of Karl Kraus's sixtieth birthday.
4. From Brecht's *Three-Penny Opera* [*Die Dreigroschenoper*].
5. WB was thinking of the Lofoten Islands. They became a staging area for the war in 1940.
6. "Garten am See," in *Figur der Hoffnung* (Heidelberg, 1955).
7. A manuscript by Kraft.

260. To Theodor W. Adorno

Paris
May 31, 1935

Dear Mr. Wiesengrund,

If these lines have taken their time in reaching you, they will now bring you, in conjunction with what accompanies them, the most complete information about my work and about my internal and external situation.

Before briefly going into the content of the précis, let me touch on the role it plays in my relationship to the institute. This can be disposed of quickly. Because, for the time being, its role is limited to the eventuality that the impetus for its completion came from a conversation I had with Pollock at the end of April. It is obvious that this was an external and disparate impetus. But precisely because of this, it was capable of introducing a disturbance into the large mass that had been carefully protected for so many years from any impact from the outside. Such a disturbance is what makes a crystallization possible. I must stress that the importance of external and heterogeneous factors is exhausted with this eventuality, which is a legitimate and productive factor in the total economy of the project. And it is the concerns expressed in your letter that make me stress that. I see them as understandable concerns and the expression of your most kind interest, even—after such a long interruption in our conversations extending over many years—as unavoidable. They were also faithfully echoed in a letter from Felizitas that arrived this morning. [. . .]

I know that it is the language of purest friendship, of nothing less than that, that led you to assert that you would consider it a true misfortune should Brecht have an influence on this work. Allow me to respond with the following:

If I have ever put my Gracian motto into practice, to wit, "Seek to enlist time on your side in all things," I believe I did so in the way I persevered with this project. It opens with Aragon—the *paysan de Paris*. Evenings, lying in bed, I could never read more than two to three pages by him because my heart started to pound so hard that I had to put the book down. What a warning! What an indication of the years and years that had to be put between me and that kind of reading. And yet the first preliminary sketches for the *Arcades* originated at that time.—Then came the Berlin years, in which the best part of my friendship with Hessel was nourished by many conversations initiated by the *Arcades* project. At the time, the subtitle—no longer in use today—originated: *A Dialectical Fairy Play*. This subtitle points to the rhapsodic character of what I had in mind to present at that time and whose relics—as I recognize today—did not contain any adequate guarantees whatsoever, in formal or linguistic terms. This epoch was also, however, that of a carefree, archaic philosophizing, which was engrossed in nature. What brought about the end of this epoch were the conversations I had with you in Frankfurt, and especially the "historical" conversation in the little Swiss house and, after that, the definitely historical one held around the table with you, Asja, Felizitas, and Horkheimer. It was the end of rhapsodic naïveté. This romantic form had been surpassed in a *raccourci* of development, but I had no concept of another form at that time, and for years afterward. It was also during these years that the external difficulties began that made it seem to me simply a matter of Providence for internal difficulties to have already urged upon me a watchful and dilatory way of working. My decisive meeting with Brecht followed, bringing with it the high point of all aporias relating to the project, from which I was not alienated even now. What might be of significance for the work from this most recent epoch—and it is not slight—however, was not able to assume shape before the boundaries of this significance were unambiguously fixed within me and thus not before "directives" coming from there completely disappeared from consideration.

Everything I am referring to here will, for you in particular, be manifestly reflected in the précis, to which I will now add a few words. The précis, which nowhere repudiates my ideas, is naturally not yet their complete equivalent in all respects. A separate description of the epistemological bases of the baroque book followed only after they had proven their value in the preceding material. This will also be the case here. With that I do not, however, want to guarantee that it will also appear in the form of a separate chapter this time, whether at the end or at the beginning. This question remains open. The précis itself, however, contains crucial references to these bases. You would be the last person to miss them and you will rediscover motifs in them that your last letter raises. Furthermore, the analogies between this book and the baroque book become apparent much more clearly than in any previous stage of the plan (in a way surprising even to me). You must permit me to see in this a particularly significant validation of the melting-pot process that has brought the entire conceptual mass, originally metaphysically mobile, to an aggregate condition in which the world of dialectical images is preserved against all the objections provoked by metaphysics.

At this stage of things (and, to be sure, at this stage for the first time), I can calmly look at what may be brought to bear against the work's method from the side of orthodox Marxism, for example. Conversely, I believe to be on solid footing with it in the Marxist discussion *à la longue,* if only because the crucial question of the historical image is treated here for the first time in its full breadth. Since the philosophy of a work is not only bound to terminology but also to its locus, I do believe that this précis is that of the "large philosophical work" of which Felizitas speaks, even if this designation does not seem to be the most compelling to me. As you know, I am primarily concerned with the "Urhistory of the nineteenth century."

In this work I see the actual, if not the only, reason not to lose courage in the struggle for existence. I can write it only in Paris, from its first to its last word—at first, naturally, only in German—this much is now clear to me, notwithstanding the great mass of preliminary research that laid the groundwork. The minimum I need in Paris is 1,000 francs a month; Pollock put this much at my disposal in May and I am supposed to get the same amount for June. But I need this much money coming in for some length of time in order to be able to continue working. I have enough difficulties to deal with in any case; severe migraine headaches remind me of my precarious existence often enough. Whether and under what title the institute will be able to show an interest in publishing the work and whether it might under certain circumstances be necessary for other projects to provide a basis for its interest—you might be able to clarify this in a conversation with Pollock more readily than I could. I am ready to do any work; but every project of any significance, especially the one on Fuchs, would demand that I put aside the *Arcades* for as long as it takes to write it. (I would prefer not to become more involved with the work on the *Neue Zeit* at the moment. More about that when I get a chance.)

I was so far from assuming that the work, "in the way it is actually conceived," could be published by the institute that I had already verbally assured Pollock of the opposite in April. Nonetheless, an entirely different question is to what extent its new and incisive sociological perspectives, which produce a secure framework for the interpretative buttresses, could establish a basis for the institute's interest in this work. Without this interest, it would not become reality, either in this way or in any other. For at this stage any distance interjected between its design and creation would probably imply radical dangers for any later presentation. The outline, on the other hand, by no means always contains those philosophical explications that form the foundation, but it does have them in the passages that to me are the crucial ones. If you in particular should feel the absence of many a catchword—plush, boredom, the definition of *phantasmagoria*—it is precisely these things that are motifs to which I only had to assign their proper place; their figuration, on which I have in part made considerable progress, did not belong in this précis. This is much less due to reasons of its external appropriation than of its internal appropriation: the old secured certitudes were to be permeated by the new ones I had acquired over the years.

Let me ask you to show the outline you receive to no one, without exception, and to return it to me very soon. It is only there to serve the purposes of my own research. Another one, soon to be produced and, indeed, in multiple copies, will be sent to you later.

San Remo is probably out of the question as a place for us to meet this year. Couldn't you arrange to travel from Oxford to Berlin via Paris? Please give this serious thought!

I would like to see Lotte Lenya, as well as Max Ernst. If you can arrange something, you can be assured of my consent.

It is with great pleasure that I hear that the publication of your book[1] seems to be in the offing. Will I have to wait for our discussion to hear more about it?

[. . .]

Please accept my most sincere regards.

Yours, Walter Benjamin

1. The book was first published in 1956 under the title *Zur Metakritik der Erkenntnistheorie* [*Against Epistemology: A Metacritique*].

261. To Max Horkheimer

Paris
July 10, 1935

Dear Mr. Horkheimer,

I have been eager for quite a while now to send you the précis being mailed at the same time as this letter. Mr. Pollock will of course have alluded to it but I was unable to go through it with him as intended, because of his premature departure.

[. . .]

Let me add that, at Mr. Pollock's urging, I simultaneously had a photocopy made of the studies written for this project. It has been deposited in a safe place and will be made available to you whenever you want.

For the time being, I would rather not add anything substantial about the précis itself. I have been working most assiduously since mid-May to complete my documentation at the Bibliothèque Nationale and the Cabinet des Estampes. Thanks to my situation having been alleviated in these past few months, for which I am indebted to you and Mr. Pollock, I have succeeded in making considerable progress in completing this documentation.

I will of course again put the book on a back burner around the beginning of August in order to write the essay on Fuchs if I do not receive any other instructions from you. On the occasion of my last meeting with him, I heard many interesting things about his beginnings, when the antisocialist law was in force. I want to try to maintain myself in Paris as long as possible in the interests of this essay and of my book.

[. . .]

I was delighted to find your essay on philosophical anthropology[1] in the last issue of the journal. Among its many incisive formulations, the one that made the greatest impression on me was that about the relationship between the structure of the egotistical impulse and the necessity of metaphysical assurance. [. . .]

I hear from Mrs. Favez[2] that you are about to leave New York for a while, if you have not already done so. You have my wishes for a truly lasting recovery.

Sincere regards.
Yours, Walter Benjamin

1. "Bemerkungen zur philosophischen Anthropologie," *Zeitschrift für Sozialforschung* 4 (1935), pp. 1–25.

2. Secretary of the Institute for Social Research in Geneva.

262. To Alfred Cohn

Paris
July 18, 1935

Dear Alfred,

If this response to your letter of the 12th comes to you almost by return mail, it is primarily because I do not want to allow too much time to intervene between my sincerely reciprocating your birthday wishes and the day for which they are meant. Do write me whether I remember correctly that your birthday is on the 21st. If this is incorrect, let me know the day on which you did celebrate it.

There could be no question of celebrating mine. I was all the more content that it came at a time I was enjoying the amenity of an apartment, something I had done without for a long time. My sister recently went abroad—she is in Mallorca—and she let me have her apartment for the weeks she will be gone. Having said this, I have come to the passage in your letter that contains a birthday gift of the most beautiful kind: I refer to your invitation to move into the vacant room. If I am not able to accept this invitation graciously at the moment, on the one hand because I assured my sister that I would not leave her apartment empty and, on the other hand, because I am at the moment unable to interrupt my work at the Bibliothèque Nationale, I still want to reply to you with more than my most sincere gratitude, which is also intended for Grete. I want to reply in the form of a question, namely whether you believe that it might be possible for me to visit you during the second half of September. I am perfectly aware that it will be hardly possible for you to give me a definitive answer now. You should, however, know that I would probably be able to come and see you in Barcelona around that time and I do not have to tell you how much I would like to do that.

I hope by then to have mostly completed the research that binds me to the library. Now that this project is drawing to a close, I have staked out yet another two fields in which to work. The one is the Cabinet des Estampes in which I am attempting to adjust on the basis of pictures the views of objects and relationships that I had formed on the basis of books; the other is the *enfer* of the library[1]—obtaining official permission to use it is one of the few successes I can chalk up for myself in this country. It is extraordinarily difficult to obtain.

I would naturally be delighted to tell you about the project. I will have informed you that I wrote the first synoptic outline for it a few weeks ago. I also had my studies photocopied for safekeeping. Conversely, I am not letting my literary colleagues, even my friends, know anything about the project: nothing of a more detailed nature. It is at a stage in which it would be particularly vulnerable to all conceivable trials and tribulations, not least of all to theft. You will understand that Bloch's "hieroglyphs of the nineteenth century"[2] have made me somewhat skittish.

By the way, I have had my discussion with him. And—subject to unforeseen, belated reactions on his part—I can only hope I have completed the difficult task with which I was confronted, that of leading our relationship out of the critical condition it was in over the last several years without leaving him in the dark about my essentially negative and, indeed, very negative stance toward his last book. This naturally required a high degree of loyalty on his part as well and I am happy to have found that.

It is nice of you to think of my *Briefe* and, above all, of *Berliner Kindheit um 1900*. But it is in a sad state. The various "interested parties," all of whom should go to the devil, achieved nothing but to rob me of all my copies. The only one I have left is my personal copy and I cannot afford to have a copy made of that.

I believe I have not written you since the Congress of Anti-Fascist Writers for the "salvation of culture" was held here. Brecht was here for the occasion and, as you can well imagine, meeting with him was the most pleasant—almost the only pleasant—element of the event for me. Brecht himself came a lot closer to getting his money's worth; this is no wonder, since he has been carrying around a plan for a long satirical novel about intellectuals[3] for years now. The detailed physiognomic acquaintance it was possible to make with individual authors was undeniably interesting for me. More interesting than any of the others was *Gide*, whose habitus at the congress was admired by all observant spectators, not only when he was speaking but just as much when he was silent. But it was also possible to study at leisure figures like [Alfred] Kantorowi[c]z, whom you so accurately identify.

I am extremely fascinated by what you write about Rosenzweig. It is, of course, certain that he was a very remarkable phenomenon. His letters[4] still have not come into my hands, but I will make a note of the book. I want to express one reservation about what you say about Buber in this context. In my relationship to Rosenzweig—in whose *Star of Redemption* [*Der Stern der Erlösung*] I was at one time raptly interested and about which I often heard from Scholem—not the least remarkable thing is that his friendship with Buber was never able to damage my uncommonly deeply rooted aversion to the latter. It might yet occur to us to discuss these things.

Congratulations on having a friend. I have not had a friendship of any importance for me since Ibiza. Among the people I have recently met, it is even rare to make a pleasant acquaintance, like the one I made not long ago of John Heartfield.[5] I had a really good conversation with him about photography. I have even less to report about new reading matter, since all of my reading is devoted exclusively to materials for the *Arcades* project. I made an exception only for Bredel's novel *Die Prüfung,* which Malik Verlag sent me. The book is certainly worth reading. The question as to why the author was not entirely successful in describing a concentration camp gives us much to think about.

The only things left for me to do are to wish you very rapid and, above all, quite lasting success in your endeavors; to wish Grete, whose regards I sincerely reciprocate, the children and you good health; and to wish all of us courage.

Most sincerely yours, Walter

1. The warehouse of the Bibliothèque Nationale in which "risqué" books are stored.
2. *Erbschaft dieser Zeit* (1935), pp. 288ff.
3. The so-called *Tui-Roman*.
4. Franz Rosenzweig, *Briefe* (1935).
5. Wieland Herzfelde's brother.

263. Theodor W. Adorno to Walter Benjamin

Hornberg im Schwarzwald
August 2, 1935

Dear Mr. Benjamin,

Today let me finally attempt to say some things to you about the précis, which I studied most thoroughly and discussed once again with Felizitas, who fully shares my views. It seems in keeping with the importance of the subject—as you know, I rate it extremely high—for me to speak with complete candor and without preamble to get right to the issues that, indeed, I view as being central for both of us in the same sense—but not without prefacing my critical discussion with the statement that the précis seems to be full of the most important concepts even if, due precisely to your way of working, an outline and a "train of thought" can hardly convey a sufficient notion of them. Of these, I should like to point out only the splendid passage about living as leaving behind traces, the incisive sentences about the collector, and the liberation of things from the curse of being useful [. . .]. In the same way, the outline of the Baudelaire chapter as an interpretation of the poet and the introduction of the category of the *nouveauté* (p. 418[1]) seem to me to be consummately realized.

You will deduce from this what you will have expected in any case, namely, that once again the issue for me is the complex defined by these rubrics: Ur-history of the nineteenth century, dialectical image, configuration of myth and modernism. If I thereby refrain from distinguishing between a "material" and an "epistemological" question, this may well be in keeping, if not quite with the external organization of the précis, then in any case with its philosophical core, in whose movement, of course, that antithesis is meant to disappear just as it is meant to do in the two more recent, traditional outlines of dialectics. As a point of departure, let me take the motto on p. 408: *Chaque époque rêve la suivante*. This seems to me to be an important instrument, insofar as all those motifs of the theory of the dialectical image, which basically underlie my criticism, crystallize around that sentence as being *undialectical;* consequently, a clarification of the theory itself could be achieved by its elimination. For the sentence implies three things: the view of the dialectical image as a content of consciousness, albeit a collective one; its linear and, I would almost say, ontogenetic dependence on the future as utopia; the conception of the "epoch" as the pertinent, self-contained subject of the content of consciousness. I think it highly significant that in this version of the dialectical image, which can be called an immanent one, not only is the original theological force of the concept threatened and a simplification introduced that does not attack the subjective nuance but the truth content itself—but, because of this, precisely the social movement within contradiction is forfeited, for the sake of which you sacrifice theology.

If you transpose the dialectical image as "dream" into consciousness, then not only has the concept been demystified and rendered sociable, but precisely through this it has also forfeited that objective liberating power that could legitimize it materialistically. The fetish character of the commodity is not a fact of consciousness but it is dialectical in the preeminent sense of producing consciousness. This means, however, that consciousness or unconsciousness cannot simply replicate it as a dream, but responds to it with an equal measure of desire and fear. But through the *sit venia verbo* replica realism of your present immanent version of the dialectical image, precisely that dialectical power of the fetish character is lost. To return to the language of the glorious first draft of the *Arcades:* if the dialectical image is nothing more than the way its fetish character is apprehended by the collective consciousness, the Saint-Simonian conception of the commodity world may indeed be revealed as utopia, but not as its obverse, namely, as the dialectical image of the nineteenth century as hell. Only this, however, would be able to convey the image of the Golden Age properly and this dual meaning could prove to be extremely crucial precisely for an interpretation of Offenbach: that is, for an interpretation of the underworld and Arcadia—both are explicit categories for Offenbach and could be pursued down to the details of his orchestration. Thus your abandonment of the category of hell in the draft, as well as that of the ingenious passage on the gambler—for which the passage on speculation and the game of chance is no substitute—seems to me to forfeit not only brilliance but also dialectical consistency. I am the last person to fail to see the relevance of the immanence of consciousness for the nineteenth century. But the concept of the dialectical image cannot be derived from the immanence of consciousness. Rather the immanence of consciousness as *intérieur* is itself the dialectical image for the nineteenth century as alienation; there I must also let the second Kierkegaard chapter[2] stand as the stake in the new game. Accordingly, what is required is not to transpose the dialectical image as dream into consciousness, but to dispose of the dream in its dialectical construction and to understand the immanence of consciousness itself as a constellation of the real. More or less like the astronomical phase in which hell wanders through humanity. It seems to me that only an astrological chart of such a journey makes it possible to see history as Ur-history.—Let me attempt to formulate my reservation yet again, exactly the same one, but from a diametrically opposed standpoint. In the spirit of your version of the dialectical image as immanence (with which, to say something positive, I would contrast your earlier concept of it as *model*), you construe the relationship of the oldest to the newest, which of course was already central to the first draft, as one of utopian reference to the "classless society." Thus the archaic becomes a complementary addition instead of itself being the "newest"—and is thus dedialecticized. At the same time, however, the image of classlessness has just as undialectically been backdated as myth instead of becoming truly transparent as a phantasmagoria of hell. Thus the category in which the archaic merges into the modern seems to me much less that of the Golden Age than of catastrophe. I once noted that the recent past always presents itself as if it had been destroyed by catastrophes. I would say *hic et nunc:*

in doing so, however, it presents itself as Ur-history. And it is precisely at this point that I know myself to be in agreement with the boldest section of your book on tragedy.

If eliminating the magical aspect of the dialectical image by representing it as "dream" psychologizes it, by the same token this attempt falls under the spell of bourgeois psychology. For who is the subject of the dream? In the nineteenth century, certainly only the individual; as unmediated replica, however, neither the fetish character nor its monuments can be extrapolated from the individual's dreams. Therefore the collective consciousness is invoked and, indeed, I fear that in the present version it cannot be distinguished from the Jungian one. It is open to criticism from both sides: from the perspective of the social process in that it hypostasizes archaic metaphors where dialectical images are generated by the commodity character, just not in an archaic collective ego, but in alienated bourgeois individuals; from the perspective of psychology in that, as Horkheimer says, the mass ego exists only during earthquakes and mass catastrophes, while otherwise objective surplus value prevails precisely in individual subjects and in opposition to them. The collective consciousness was invented only to divert attention from true objectivity and its correlate, namely, alienated subjectivity. It is up to us to polarize and dissolve this "consciousness" dialectically between society and the single subject, and not to galvanize it as the metaphorical correlate of the commodity character. It should be a clear and adequate warning that no differences remain between classes in the dreaming collective.

The mythic-archaic category of the "Golden Age," however, ultimately also has—and this is exactly what seems socially decisive to me—fateful consequences for the commodity category itself. If the crucial "ambiguity" in the Golden Age (a concept, moreover, that is very much in need of theoretical underpinnings and may by no means simply be allowed to stand as is), namely, that relating to hell, is suppressed, the commodity as the substance of the age consequently simply becomes hell and is negated in a way that would in fact make the immediacy of the primal state appear as truth: thus the demystification of the dialectical image leads directly to purely mythical thinking, and it is here that Klages appears as a danger, just as Jung did earlier. Nowhere, however, does your outline provide more remedies than precisely at this point. Here would be the crucial place for the doctrine of the collector who liberates things from the curse of being useful; if I understand you correctly, this would also be the place for Haussmann, whose class consciousness inaugurates the explosion of the phantasmagoria precisely through the perfection of the commodity character in Hegelian self-consciousness. To understand the commodity as dialectical image simply means to understand it also as the motif of its own destruction and its "sublation" instead of as pure regression to something older. On the one hand, the commodity is the alienated object in which use value withers; on the other hand, it is the surviving object that, having become alien, outlives its immediacy. We have the promise of immortality in commodities and not for people, and—to develop the relationship to the book on the baroque, which you rightly established—the fetish is a treacherously final image for the nineteenth century, comparable only to the death's head. It seems to me that this is where the decisive epistemological character of Kafka lies, especially in Odradek, as the commodity that survives to no purpose: surrealism may come to an end in this fairy tale, just as the *Trauerspiel* does in *Hamlet*. Intrasocietally, however, this means that the mere concept of use value by no means suffices as a critique of the commodity character, but only leads back to a stage prior to the division of labor. This has always been my actual reservation about Berta.[3] Her "collective" and her unmediated concept of function have therefore always been suspect to me, as themselves a "regression." Based on these considerations, whose substance concerns exactly the categories in your précis that may conform to Berta's, you will perhaps understand that my opposition to them is not an insular attempt to rescue autonomous art or anything of the kind, but rather most profoundly addresses those motifs of our philosophical friendship that I regard as basic. If I were permitted to summarize the trajectory of my criticism with a daring stroke, it would have to include the extremes. How could it be otherwise? A restoration of theology, or rather a radicalization of the dialectic down to the glowing core of theology, would concurrently have to mean a most extreme intensification of the sociodialectical, even economic, motif. The motif would also have to be dealt with historically. The commodity character *specific* to the nineteenth century, i.e. industrial commodity production, would have to be worked out materially and much more clearly because, of course, commodity character and alienation have existed ever since the beginning of capitalism, i.e. the age of manufacturing and specifically the age of the baroque—just as, on the other hand, the "unity" of the modern age has lain precisely in its commodity character ever since that time. Only a precise definition of the industrial form of the commodity as one sharply differentiated historically from older forms, however, could produce the complete "Ur-history" and ontology of the nineteenth century: all references to the commodity form "as such" would lend this Ur-history a certain metaphorical character that cannot be tolerated in this crisis. I would like to think that the greatest interpretative results will be achievable if you rely entirely on your way of doing things, processing the material without prejudging it. It certainly poses a difficulty if, by contrast, my criticism moves in a certain theoretical sphere of abstraction, but I know that you will not view it as a problem of Weltanschauung and thus simply dismiss my reservations.

For all that, I hope you will still allow me to make some more concrete and specific observations, which, of course, can be meaningful only against this theoretical background. I would like to suggest the following title: "Paris, Capital of the Nineteenth Century," not "the Capital"—unless the title, *Arcades,* should yet be resurrected along with the section on hell. Dividing the work into chapters based on different men does not strike me as felicitous; it makes for a certain compulsive systematization of the exterior structure with which I am not quite comfortable. Earlier, weren't sections grouped according to materials like "plush," "dust," etc.? The precise relationship Fourier—arcade is not quite clear. I could conceive of the appropriate pattern as a constellation of various urban and commodity materials, a pattern that, in the later section, would be decoded simultaneously as the dialectical image and its theory.—In the motto on p. 406 the word *portique* quite nicely conveys the motif of antiquity; perhaps this would be the place to discuss, in terms of the newest as the oldest, a morphology of the empire in basic terms (as, for example, melancholy is discussed in the baroque book). On p. 407, at any rate, it would be necessary to make completely clear that the conception of the state in the empire as an end in itself is pure ideology. To be sure, based on your subsequent remarks, this seems to be your view of it. The concept of construction is left to stand without any explanation whatsoever. This concept, as alienation from material *and* as mastery of material, is already eminently dialectical and, in my opinion, must also be immediately explained dialectically (there is a sharp distinction between it and the current concept of construction; the very nineteenth-century term *ingénieur* offers a pretext to do so!). The introduction and explication of the concept of the collective unconscious, about which I have already made some basic comments, are, moreover, not completely clear here.—Regarding p. 407, I would like to ask whether cast iron is really the first artificial construction material (bricks!); in general I basically feel uneasy with the word *first.* A correlative formulation might be as follows: Every epoch dreams it is destroyed by catastrophes.—P. 408: The formulation that "the new is permeated by the old" seems highly dubious to me, given my critique of the dialectical image as regression. There is no reversion to the old, but rather the newest, as illusion and phantasmagoria, is itself the old. Without being impertinent, might I remind you of some formulations, including some on ambiguity, in the *intérieur* section of my work on Kierkegaard. Let me add the following: dialectical images as models are not social products but objective constellations in which the social condition represents itself. Consequently, no ideological or social "accomplishment" whatsoever can be attributed to the dialectical image. My objection to your purely negative treatment of reification—your critique of "Klages" in the outline—is based primarily on the passage on the machine on p. 408. The overestimation of machine technology and the machine as such has always been characteristic of bourgeois, retrospective theories: the conditions of production are thus veiled by an abstract reference to the means of production.—The very important Hegelian concept of second nature, since adopted by Georg Lukács and others, belongs on pp. 409ff. The *diable à Paris* could very well lead to hell.—Regarding p. 410: I would very much doubt that the worker would appear "for the last time" as an extra, etc., outside of his class.—The idea of an Ur-history of the feuilleton, to which your "Kraus" contributes so much, is extremely fascinating; this would also be the place for Heine. An old expression taken from journalistic jargon occurs to me here: cliché style. Its origin ought to be investigated. The term "attitude to life" used in cultural or intellectual history is very objectionable.—Your credulous acceptance of the Ur-appearance of technology seems to me to be connected to your overestimation of the archaic as such. I noted this phrase: Myth is not the classless longing of the true society, but rather the objective character of the alienated commodity itself.—P. 411: The conception of the history of nineteenth-century painting as a flight from photography (which, by the way, strictly corresponds to that of music as a flight from the "banal") is quite splendid but also undialectical, i.e. the role of productive forces not incorporated in commodity form in the store of paintings cannot be grasped concretely in this way, but only in the negative of its trace (the precise focal point of this dialectic is probably Manet). This seems to me to be related to the mythologizing or archaicizing tendency of the précis. To a certain extent, the store of paintings becomes, as artifacts of the past, historicist fixed-star images drained of their share of productive force. The subjective role of the dialectic disappears under an undialectical, mythical gaze, that of Medusa.—The Golden Age on p. 412 may well be the true transition to hell.—I am unable to see the relationship of world fairs to the work force and it sounds like pure conjecture; it certainly can be asserted only with the greatest caution.—A grand definition and theory of phantasmagoria naturally belong on pp. 412ff.—P. 413 was a *mene tekel*[4] to me. Along with Felizitas, I remember the overwhelming impression that the Saturn citation once made on us; the citation has not survived my disillusionment. The ring of Saturn would not have to become a wrought-iron balcony, but the balcony would have to become a real ring of Saturn. I am happy not to have to offer you anything abstract here, but rather only your own success: the incomparable moon chapter in *Kindheit,* whose philosophical content would belong here. What you once said about the *Arcades* project occurred to me at this point: that it could be wrested only from the realm of insanity: that it has distanced itself from this realm instead of conquering it, is documented by the interpretation of the Saturn citation, which recoils from it. This is where my actual objections lie. [. . .] This is where I must be brutally frank for the sake of the enormous seriousness of the matter.—The fetish conception of the commodity must be supported by appropriate passages from the person who discovered it. You probably have this in mind.—The concept of the organic that also appears on p. 413 and points to a static anthropology, etc., is probably not tenable either, or only by saying that it merely exists prior to the fetish as such and is thus itself historical, for example, like the "landscape." The dialectical commodity motif of Odradek probably belongs on p. 414.—The workers' movement again seems to function here somewhat like a deus ex machina; to be sure, just as in some analogous forms, the abbreviated style of the précis may be to blame—this is a reservation that applies to many of my reservations. Regarding the passage about fashion: it seems very important to me but in its construction it should be detached from the concept of the organic and related to what is alive—i.e. not, therefore, to a superior "nature"—another thing that occurred to me is the concept of the *changeant,* of the shiny fabric that may well have expressive significance for the nineteenth century, but is also presumably tied to industrial processes. Perhaps you will pursue this. Mrs. Hessel, whose reports in the *FZ* we always read with great interest, is sure to know all about it.—P. 414 is where I have particular reservations about your overly abstract use of the commodity category: as if it had appeared as such "for the first time" in the nineteenth century (let me say parenthetically that the same objection also applies to *intérieur* and the sociology of interiority in my Kierkegaard and precisely at this point everything I object to in your précis also goes for my own earlier study). I believe that the commodity category could be greatly concretized simply by the specifically modern categories of world trade and imperialism. Additionally, perhaps, by the arcade as a bazaar, and maybe also antique stores as world trade markets for the temporal. The significance of compressed distance—perhaps the problems of winning over aimless social strata and imperial conquest. I only mention the things that occur to me; of course, you could unearth incomparably more convincing evidence from your material and define the specific form of the nineteenth-century object world (perhaps from the perspective of its seamy side, that is from its detritus, remains, ruins).—The passage about the office also probably dispenses with historical precision. The office appears to me less as a direct opposite of the *intérieur* than as a relic of older forms of rooms, probably baroque ones (cf. the globes in it, maps, railings, and other material forms).—Regarding the theory of *Jugendstil* on p. 415: if I agree with you that it signifies a decisive shock to the *intérieur,* for me this then excludes the possibility that it "mobilizes all the forces of interiority." Rather it seeks to save and realize them through "externalization" (this is the place for theory, especially that of symbolism, primarily Mallarmé's *intérieurs,* which have exactly the opposite meaning of Kierkegaard's, for example). In *Jugendstil, sexus* takes the place of interiority. It takes recourse to *sexus* because only in sex does the private person confront himself not as intrinsic but as corporeal. This is true of all examples of *Jugendstil* from Ibsen to Maeterlinck and D'Annunzio. After all, it has its origin in Wagner and not in Brahms's chamber music.—It seems to me that concrete is uncharacteristic of *Jugendstil* and is probably part of the remarkable vacuum around 1910. I also consider it probable that authentic *Jugendstil* coincides with the great economic crisis around 1900; concrete belongs to the prewar boom.—P. 415: Let me also draw your attention to the extremely remarkable interpretation of the "master builder" Solness in Wedekind's papers. I am not familiar with pyschoanalytic literature on awakening, but am looking into it. However, is psychoanalysis, which interprets dreams and awakens and which explicitly and polemically disassociates itself from hypnosis (documentation in Freud's lectures), not itself a part of *Jugendstil,* with which it coincides in time? This may be a question of the highest order, which might take us very far. As a corrective to my fundamental criticism, I would like to add the following: if I reject the use of the collective consciousness, it is naturally not in order to leave the "bourgeois individual" intact as the actual substratum. The *intérieur* must be made transparent as social function and its self-containedness must be exposed as illusion. As illusion, however, not vis-à-vis a hypostasized collective consciousness but vis-à-vis the real social process itself. The individual is consequently a dialectical channel, which may not be mythologized away but can only be sublated.—I would again like to emphasize most explicitly the passage about the "liberation of things from the bondage of being useful" as the brilliant turning point for the dialectical salvation of the commodity.—On p. 416, I would be happy if the theory of the collector and of the *intérieur* as an etui were developed as broadly as possible.—On p. 417, I would like to draw your attention to Maupassant's *Nuit,* which appears to me to be the dialectical coda to Poe's *Man of the Crowd* as cornerstone. I find the passage about the crowd as veil wonderful.—P. 418 is the place for a critique of the dialectical image. You undoubtedly know better than I that the theory presented here still does not do justice to the enormous demands of the subject. I would only like to add that it is not ambiguity that is the translation of the dialectic into image, but the "trace" of the image that itself must first be thoroughly dialecticized by the theory. I seem to remember that there is a useful sentence on this in the *intérieur* chapter of my Kierkegaard book. On p. 418, perhaps the concluding stanza of the great *femmes damnées* in the *pièces condamnées*.—The concept of false consciousness, in my opinion, must be used most cautiously and must in any event no longer be used without recourse to its Hegelian [!] origin.—*Snob* was originally not at all an aesthetic but a social concept; it was given currency by Thackery. A sharp distinction must be drawn between *snob* and *dandy;* it would also be well to investigate the history of the snob, for which you of course have the most splendid material, on account of your work on Proust.—The thesis on p. 419 about *l'art pour l'art* and the "total work of art" does not seem to me to be viable in this form. The total work of art and aestheticism in the precise sense of the word are diametrically opposed attempts to escape the commodity character and are not identical: thus Baudelaire's relationship to Wagner is as dialectical as his association with the whore.—On p. 419ff., I simply am not satisfied with the theory of speculation. For one thing, what is missing is the theory of the game of chance, which was so magnificently presented in the preliminary version of the *Arcades;* for another thing, the real economic theory of the speculator is missing. Speculation is the negative expression of the irrationality of capitalistic *ratio*. Perhaps you could also get to the bottom of this passage by "extrapolation to extremes."—On p. 420, an explicit theory of perspective might well be in order; I believe there was something on this in the original version of the *Arcades*. The stereoscope, which was invented between 1810 and 1820, is relevant here.—The nice dialectical conception of the Haussmann chapter could perhaps be brought out more clearly in your presentation than it is in the précis, where the reader must first interpret it.

I must ask you once more to excuse the carping nature of these comments; but I think I at least owe you some specific examples of my basic criticism. [. . .]

In true friendship.

1. The page numbers originally indicated in this letter have been replaced by the page numbers as they appear in *Schriften*, vol. 1.

2. Of Adorno's Kierkegaard book.

3. Pseudonym for Brecht; the letter was sent from National Socialist Germany to the addressee in Paris.

4. [Hebrew for *warning*.—Trans.]

264.* To Gerhard Scholem

Paris
August 9, 1935

Dear Gerhard,

Our latest reports have indeed made their journeys across the Mediterranean very slowly. I hope these lines reestablish the old rhythm of our correspondence.

Your suspicion about my "summer residence" is correct. I am staying in Paris as long as I can somehow hold out. But I have no clear idea where I will go afterward, when this is no longer feasible. The winter months in the remote Danish corner where Brecht lives would probably be all the more difficult to bear, since Brecht himself usually makes his Russian and English trips at that time. On the other hand, how long I can stay here is entirely uncertain. I owe the present, really relatively pleasant weeks—pleasant so long as I utterly refrain from gazing into the future—to the fact that my sister has put her apartment at my disposal during her absence.

I have several weeks of intensive work in the library behind me. They have greatly furthered the documentation for my book. But I now have to interrupt such efforts for a while—without having finished them. No god can save me now from the study of Fuchs. Yes, I have more reason than ever to demonstrate my willingness to comply with the institute's suggestions. The cooperation forthcoming during the negotiations in May did not materialize without my having to disclose the prospect of my disappearing to Palestine for several months and relieving them of having to support me. An attractive perspective for them, as you can imagine, and I am now faced with the delicate task of having to dispel it. I have, as I said, every reason to demonstrate my compliance.

That I have better and more personal reasons to be very sorry to see our meeting postponed won't surprise you. And we dare not expect from a reunion in Europe—which could only be very brief anyway—what several weeks in Palestine would have given us. For my part, insight into your creative work and its circumstances; for you, insight into my work, whose character it is impossible to convey in a letter—even in conversation it would only be feasible if such insight were not limited to occasional isolated ideas. It would thus be all the more rewarding for both of us, since I am getting going on this book with uncommon care, and the greater the isolation in which my work on it proceeds at this stage, the more willing and able I am to put all counsel originating in friendly dialogue to productive use. I believe that its conception, however personal in origin, addresses our generation's most decisive historical interests. No further word should be needed to suggest how very much I would like to familiarize you with it.

Things can essentially be summed up as follows; a précis for the institute—I want to say for superficial, even the most superficial, use—which has been circulating for quite some time, has made me realize the precise point at which constructive work (which simultaneously entails deciding on the literary form and its potential success) will one day have to begin. That day has yet to arrive. Circumstances whose repulsiveness nonetheless implicates me as an accomplice are delaying it. Should I still live to see it, however, I would not grouse about very much anymore.

I don't want to leave the subject without telling you that both of the alternative conjectures you ascribe to it are correct. The work represents both the philosophical application of surrealism—and thereby its sublation [*Aufhebung*]—as well as the attempt to retain the image of history in the most inconspicuous corners of existence—the detritus of history, as it were.

I already informed you, if I remember correctly, of my sister's address, which for the moment is mine. Without knowing whether or not I will still be living here when Mrs. Marx-Steinschneider makes her return visit, I ask that you give it to her.[1] If I have moved, she can get my address from my sister or the concierge. I regret very much having missed seeing her. How can she possibly imagine I would have someone deny that I was here! The climate in Paris is most agreeable at the moment; the social atmosphere less so, stripped as I am of the few acquaintances I have. Even the émigrés gather their few centimes together and take a summer vacation. I am seeing Ernst Bloch—it took a great deal of effort to make my position on his latest book clear to him.[2] I am not discussing my own with him, and you will understand why if you have looked at the section on "Hieroglyphs of the Nineteenth Century" in his. [Siegfried] Kracauer is writing a book on Offenbach, and I have to keep my own reflections under wraps with him as well. All of which is not easy and could be more pleasant.

I am really looking forward to your little Zohar book. Isn't it supposed to appear, if my memory serves me correctly, this September in German?

So let me hear from you as soon as you can. And accept my best wishes for your great Hebrew endeavor. Greetings to you and Escha.

Yours, Walter

1. Marx-Steinschneider and her husband traveled through Paris in October 1935 on their way back from America.

2. No reports or notes concerning this conversation have come to light up to now. Bloch's *Heritage of Our Time* caused WB more than a little agitation, as attested to by a number of letters. Over the years Bloch defended himself frequently against the charges and reservations leveled at his book. But he barely dealt with WB's allegations, which he may well not even have known in this trenchant form.

265. To Gretel Adorno

August 16, 1935

Dear F.,

I believe I am doing the right thing in sending you these few lines. They do not constitute a coming to terms with your long and notable letter of the 2d. I will reserve that for later—and surely not for one letter, but a series of letters in our correspondence—a correspondence that, with its many streams and rivulets, will, we hope, on some not too distant day certainly flow into the channel of our togetherness. No—this letter is not a coming to terms with yours but, if you will, my notice that your letter has been received. But this notice is meant to announce not only that these hands have taken in this letter. And not only that my head took it in, as well as my hands. Instead, before dealing with a single point, I wish to assure you above all how delighted I am to receive your letter because it confirms our friendship and renews our many friendly conversations.

The extraordinary thing about your letter and, given all the precision and urgency of your objections, what is for me so extremely special and seminal is that it always treats the subject in a way that maintains the closest link to its intellectual life as I experienced it; that every one of your reflections—or as good as every one of them—went to the productive heart of the work—not a single one missed the mark. I do not know in which form your reflections will continue to ferment in me, and I know just as little about what their effect will be. In spite of this, two things still seem certain to me: 1) that their effect can only be something beneficial, and 2) only something that will validate and strengthen our friendship.

If it were up to me, this would be all I would say today, because, for the time being, anything more might easily lead us into questionable and unbounded areas. But I will dare to make some very provisional and very few comments, since I would not want these lines, in particular, to seem harsh—and I will not do so without risk. As part of the bargain, you will have to accept that they are more of a confessional than of a purely objective nature.

And so let me say at the outset, although your letter refers with such emphatic phrases to a "first" draft of the *Arcades,* it must be stated that nothing of this "first" draft has been forfeited and not a single word of it has been lost. Please allow me to express it in these terms: what you had in front of you is not draft "number 2," but the *other.* These two drafts are in a polar relationship to each other. They represent the thesis and antithesis of the work. Therefore, "number 2" is for me anything but a conclusion. Its necessity is based on the fact that the insights contained in "number 1" permitted no direct figuration—unless it were an inadmissible "poetic" one. Thus the subtitle, long since abandoned, in the first draft, "A Dialectical Fairy Play."

I now have gotten hold of both ends of the bow—but still do not have the strength to arc it. I can get this strength only through long training, of which my work with source materials represents only one element among others. A concomitant of my unfortunate situation is that, in this second epoch of the project, the other elements must for the time being continue to take a back seat to the elements mentioned above. I know this. And I take this realization into account by proceeding in a dilatory fashion. I do not want to allow an error to have the chance to affect my calculations.

What other elements does this training include? Constructive ones. If W. has reservations about the division of the chapters, he has hit the mark. The organization lacks the constructive moment. I will leave aside the question of whether the direction suggested by both of you is the right one for me to take. This much is certain: the constructive moment means for this book what the philosophers' stone means for alchemy. Otherwise, the only thing I can say for the time being is this: it will have to summarize the opposition in which the book stands in relation to prior and inherited historical research in a way that is new, binding, and very simple. It remains to be seen how.

Having read these lines, your suspicion that something like stubbornness is mixed with my opposition to other reservations will be inevitable. In this instance, I know of no other vice that is at a greater remove from me. And I will overlook the many points on which I am in agreement with you and which I am saving for later examination. (I am rarely so much in agreement with anything as I am with W.'s reflections on the theme of the Golden Age.) No—what I am thinking of at the moment is the passage on Saturn in your letter. I do not at all want to dispute that "the wrought-iron balcony" would have to become "the ring of Saturn." But please let me explain: a single consideration—least of all a consideration of the relevant drawing by Grandville—may by no means be assigned the task of executing this transformation; instead, this task devolves exclusively on *the book as a whole.* It is precisely this book that may not anywhere lay any claim to forms such as those offered to me by my *Berliner Kindheit:* the grounding of this realization within me is an important function of the second draft. The Ur-history of the nineteenth century reflected in the vision of the child playing on its doorstep has a totally different countenance than that in the signs, that they engrave on the map of history.

These thoroughly preliminary observations are limited to some general questions. Without stepping them off to determine their circumference, they leave all details out of consideration. I will touch on many of those later as the opportunity presents itself. In conclusion, however, allow me to refer to a critical issue for me, even at the risk of doing so in the form of a confession. In raising this issue, I suggest two things: how apt W.'s definition of the dialectical image as a "constellation" seems to me, and likewise how undisputed certain elements of this constellation, to which I referred, appear to me: namely, the dream figures. The dialectical image does not draw a copy of the dream—it was never my intention to assert this. But it does seem to me to contain the instances, the moment consciousness dawns as one awakens, and indeed to produce its likeness only from these passages just as an astral image emerges from luminous points. Thus here too yet another bow must be arced, and a dialectic mastered: that between image and awakening. ———

266. To Max Horkheimer

Paris
October 16, 1935

Dear Mr. Horkheimer,

Thank you very much for your letter of September 18. I was naturally delighted to receive it. Since my emigration, the number of people for whom my work validates me has grown very small. On the other hand, the passing of years and my situation in life have caused this work to play an ever greater role in the economy of my life. I was therefore especially delighted by your letter.

Precisely because your opinion of my précis is of such great importance and gives me hope, I would have preferred to avoid any discussion of my situation in this letter. I therefore put off writing it because I was hoping for a "miracle," something excusable in such cases. However, now that I have the proceeds from some very short stories I had written for the *Schweizer Presse,*[1] amounting to some francs that I can count on my fingers, a letter entirely limited to my work has become a luxury I cannot afford. The last time I spoke with Mr. Pollock, I told him that being able to turn to you, should I find myself in a hopeless situation, means more to me than the extent of whatever assistance I might then receive. He understood this and, although the institute's most recent decision provided me with truly meaningful relief for a full three months, I hope and trust that this will not prevent you from considering my case in view of what I said to Mr. Pollock at that time.

My situation is as difficult as any financial position that does not involve debts can possibly be. In saying this, I do not mean to ascribe the slightest credit to myself, but only to say that any help you give me will produce immediate relief. I have reduced my living expenses enormously, compared to what they were in April when I returned to Paris. I am consequently now living as a boarder with some émigrés. Beyond that, I have succeeded in obtaining permission to take my midday meal at a restaurant that has a special arrangement for French intellectuals. In the first place, however, this permission is temporary and, in the second place, I can make use of it only on those days I am not in the library, for the restaurant is very far from there. I will only mention in passing that I ought to renew my *carte d'identité* but do not have the 100 francs this requires. Since it involves a fee of 50 francs, I have also not yet been able to join the Presse Étrangère, which I was urged to do for administrative reasons.

The paradoxical thing about this situation is that my work has probably never been closer to being publicly useful than it is right now. Nothing in your last letter was more encouraging for me than what it had to say in this regard. For me, the value of your acknowledgment is proportional to the perseverance with which I stuck with this project through good times and bad. It is now beginning to take on the features of what I planned for it. And, indeed, recently in an especially decisive form.

When he was here, Mr. Pollock provided the impetus for me to write down the précis. Now your last letter was the occasion for me to set aside the historical image of the work, which I had provisionally fixed, in favor of constructive reflections that will determine the total image of the work. For their part, these constructive reflections may be highly provisional in terms of the form in which I have set them down. I can say nonetheless that they advance the direction of a materialistic theory of art, a beginning that will lead far beyond the draft with which you are familiar. The issue this time is to indicate the precise point in the present to which my historical construction will orient itself, as to its vanishing point. If the pretext for the book is the fate of art in the nineteenth century, this fate has something to say to us only because it is contained in the ticking of a clock whose striking of the hour has just reached *our* ears. What I mean by that is that art's fateful hour has struck for us and I have captured its signature in a series of a preliminary reflections entitled "The Work of Art in the Age of Mechanical Reproduction" ["Das Kunstwerk im Zeitalter seiner technischen Reproduzierbarkeit"].[2] These reflections attempt to give the questions raised by art theory a truly contemporary form: and indeed from the inside, avoiding any *unmediated* reference to politics.

These notes almost nowhere refer to historical material and are not extensive. They are truly basic in nature. I can well imagine that the *Zeitschrift* would be the proper place for them. For my part, it goes without saying that I would rather have you publish this fruit of my labor than anyone else. Under no circumstances would I have it published without having heard your opinion on it.

Considering that the projects I have mentioned take a back seat in my daily work schedule in terms of the amount of time I devote to them and considering that the main part of this schedule is determined by my study of Fuchs and that I work on a lecture for the Institut des études germaniques after that—you will understand that I am fully occupied. Please let me propose that you suggest a deadline for my manuscript on Fuchs so that, given this situation, I have a point of reference.

Your trip to Europe will be another crucial point of reference for me. I am sure that the opportunity will then materialize for us to have a comprehensive discussion. One of the hardships of my existence is that I am unable to discuss the most important concepts of this project with anyone here. Given their current stage of development, I cannot allow myself to treat them frivolously. I have therefore not shown the précis to anyone here. A sentence in your letter about what "may not be omitted" particularly caught my attention. I hope to hear more about this from you, preferably in person.

I am most eager to get your essay on dialectic and hope to learn much from it. The last two issues of the *Nouvelle revue française* have an essay on the same topic. [. . .]

May this letter convey my hopes and my most sincere regards.

Yours, Walter Benjamin

1. "Die Warnung" [The warning], *Basler Nachrichten* (September 26, 1935), and "Rastelli erzählt . . ." [Rastelli narrates], *Neue Zürcher Zeitung* (November 6, 1935).

2. *Zeitschrift für Sozialforschung* 5 (1936), pp. 40–66 (in the translation by Pierre Klossovski). In *Schriften* 1:366–405.

267. To Margarete Steffin

Paris
End of October 1935

Dear Grete,

It has taken me somewhat longer to respond this time, but so much has happened between the day I received your first letter and today. First of all, I moved again—you will find my new address at the end of the letter. There were also some specific difficulties, even if they were of the usual kind, as well as an insurrection of the objects that surround me, fostered by this kind of situation: since I live on the seventh floor, it began with the elevator going on strike, followed by the mass departure of the few belongings I care about, culminating in the disappearance of a very beautiful fountain pen that I consider irreplaceable. This was cause for considerable distress.

Now, while writing you—although nothing in the situation has changed—my distress has decamped, perhaps having been swept away by the fantastic fall storms whistling about my aerie day in and day out. It would have been comforting if your tobacco had arrived during this time. But we can no longer count on my receiving it and should make no further efforts. Otherwise the customs officials will never stop smoking. But thank you so much for your persistence!

I also do not even know whether I already thanked you for the splendid copy of "What Is Epic Theater?" ["Was ist das epische Theater?"] you made for me. I am delighted that you insured the preservation of this important manuscript for me in this way.

Now to matters concerning Brecht. First, I received his "Bemerkungen über die chinesische Schauspielkunst." It is obvious that this is a really excellent essay. It contains some peerless formulations, such as the one about the face as a blank page that is written on by gesture; the one about the neighbor, not the observer, who is depicted—and others. I unfortunately have no personal contact with a single translator here. Conversely, Adrienne Monnier, the publisher of *Mesures,* where I would really like to see the essay appear, does not know a single syllable of German. And the most alarming thing is the suspicion with which her agent views all things German. All of this is simply meant to say that I will be compelled to proceed by circuitous routes and that it is not certain whether I will achieve my goal. The attempt is absolutely worth the effort in any case and I will make that attempt at the next opportunity.

It was very nice to see with my own eyes, in the form of a parable for the theater, just how Brecht uses his experience of the Chinese stage to benefit his own cause. The last piece seems to me, in fact, to be the most perfect example of its kind. There is absolutely no reason for me to hesitate in expressing my opinion on the question you [put] to me regarding the two versions of the scene about [ending missing]

268.* To Gerhard Scholem

Paris
October 24, 1935

Dear Gerhard

Despite the best of intentions, I have been unable to comply with the recommendation at the close of your August letter to let you hear from me soon. Things around me were too bleak and uncertain for me to dare deprive my work of my scarce hours of inner equilibrium. A new move took place during the same period, with everything that precedes and results from moving under such conditions. I finally found some consolation in the opportunity to have a greeting conveyed to you verbally through Kitty Steinschneider.

The immediate cause for writing to you today is to thank you for the Zohar chapter I just received. There can be no question of my reading the book—with the exception of your foreword—from beginning to end. But I did read enough to be able to proffer my highest praise for what you have accomplished. And I can do so without in the least being able to judge the—doubtless immense—technical craftsmanship this translation represents. For the translation is unmistakably informed by the eminent humanity expressed in your ambition to draw such a hermetic text so appropriately and astonishingly close to the unschooled intellect, which is thus able to rely on nothing other than its attentiveness. Translating this text was surely no easier than translating a flawless poem. But translators of poetry are not customarily endowed with the austerity which here both is the precondition of success and imparts the methodological imperative to combine the translation with commentary. In this respect I view your translation as exemplary beyond the pale of the material at hand.

You won't be surprised to learn that this is a matter still close to my heart, even if you probably didn't read the short paper in which it found its expression on Ibiza ("On the Mimetic Faculty" ["Über das mimetische Vermögen"]) in quite that way. Whatever the case, the concept of nonsensuous similarity developed there finds manifold illustration in the way in which the author of the Zohar conceives of the formation of sounds—and written signs to an even greater extent, most likely—as the deposits of cosmic connections. Yet he seems to be thinking of a correspondence that is not ascribed to any mimetic origin. This may well follow from his commitment to the doctrine of emanation, to which my theory of mimesis presents the strongest possible opposition.

I have already taken note of many passages I need to speak with you about. I would like to know more about your thoughts on the origin of the rather strange theory of the moon, pp. 80–81. Furthermore, it would be quite important to examine the doctrine of hell. I suspect I have spotted a misprint on page 90 in the parenthesis containing the exegesis of 1 Samuel 15:29.

In the preface, I found the remarks on Moses de León of particular interest. (Didn't Pflaum write his doctoral dissertation on him??)[1] And then the passage on the primitive and folkloric sides of Zohar demonology.

These sides have a blithe and playful counterpart in your disclosures about the Gutkinds. Yes—I had already given up on them years before leaving Germany. The sole cause was their characteristic folly or numbness in everything regarding simple human relations. They possess extraordinary kindness, and not a slight amount of charm (though I grant this only to Erich, to be sure); nonetheless, they combine this with a far too feeble ability to pick up on things, and their lack of sensitivity turns out to be unbearable in the long run. On the other hand, I approve of the fact that they have found a comfortable and droll existence in America. They always had their minds set on far vistas, and they were always resourceful in developing their contacts.

So as not to spoil you unduly with visitors, fate has decreed that Ernst Bloch's planned trip to Palestine not take place. Hence, the matter rests at the proclamation in your letter to me. What you suggest about Bloch's work doesn't deviate from my own opinion, as you know, and least of all from the one I have of his most recent book. On the other hand, you seem to acknowledge as well—if with a certain reluctance—that my interest in this affair has been satisfied to the extent that I have been spared having to conceal that opinion in its essentials. That has, as I wrote you, meanwhile taken place. And as true as it is that, given these circumstances, the relationship can never evolve to the complete satisfaction of both parties, I will nevertheless most definitely accept responsibility for preserving the association. I, whose weaknesses have surely never included illusions or sentimentality, do so in view of my pure insight into the limitations of this relationship; and, on the other hand, the dispersion of my friends isolates every single one of them, including myself. Weighed against these problems, the way his book treats my writings cannot even become a topic of conversation. I'm only surprised that you discern praise in it, without taking notice of the sometimes drastic reservations.

You didn't send me the printed version of your Kafka poem, and I would like to have it. If nothing of mine [has] arrived for a long time, the causes are, first, that next to nothing has been published and, second, that the papers—e.g., the *Neue Zürcher Zeitung*—tend to provide only a single author's copy, on account of the current crisis.

Despite these circumstances, I have composed a small stack of novellas, just to double and triple my quota of work.[2] One of them should be no trouble to place, if I'm not entirely mistaken, and you will receive it from me then. From time to time I dream about the frustrated book projects—the *Berliner Kindheit um 1900* and the collection of letters—and then I am surprised when I find the strength to embark on a new one. Of course, under such conditions that its fate is even more difficult to predict than the form my own future is likely to take. On the other hand, a book is, as it were, the shelter I step beneath when the weather gets too rough outside. Part of the inclemency is due to Fuchs. But as time passes I am gradually steeling myself against his words, to which I continue to expose myself, having taken a variety of precautions. Moreover, I am considering his books solely to the extent that they treat the nineteenth century. That way, he doesn't lead me too far away from my own work.

This work has recently been decisively advanced by several fundamental observations on aesthetics. Together with the historical outline I drafted approximately four months ago, they will form a kind of grid or systematic point of reference on which all further particulars will have to be inscribed. These reflections anchor the history of nineteenth-century art in the recognition of their situation as experienced by us in the present. I am keeping these reflections very secret, because they are incomparably better suited to theft than most of my ideas. Their provisional formulation is entitled "The Work of Art in the Age of Mechanical Reproduction."

I will be giving a lecture on *Elective Affinities* at the Institut des études germaniques in February.[3] I don't know how long my powers of resistance will last in view of all the circumstances, since I am provided with only the bare necessities for *at most* two weeks a month. The most trifling purchase depends on a miracle taking place. Instead, several days ago I lost my fountain pen—which was an expensive gift, or rather an heirloom. And that was no miracle, rather the most natural consequence of profound ill humor and moreover an instructive confirmation of the saying that he who has nothing will be robbed of what he has.

It seems that today I will not find my way back to more cheerful observations, so this letter ends none too soon. Write soon, and accept my kindest regards for you and Escha,

Yours, Walter

1. Pflaum had written his doctoral dissertation (Tübingen, 1926) on Leone Ebreo (Judah Abrabanel) and his *Dialoghi di Amore*.
2. These novellas are printed as "Kleine Prosa" in *Schriften* 4:721–87.
3. I don't know if this lecture was ever actually delivered.

269. To Kitty Marx Steinschneider

Paris
October 24, 1935

Chère amie,

Your letter arrived yesterday and I want to thank you without letting a moment go by. You know well enough that "success" in such things can in no way be the measure of gratitude. You will therefore be able to understand my gratitude for what it is.

Does this not concurrently provide me with an opportunity to tell you that our long conversation has remained particularly alive in my memory?

I was delighted to hear from you that you conducted this conversation with all the caution appropriate to the issue at hand; I was, of course, entirely sure that this would be the case before I approached you. I will, in fact, be waiting not with decreased but with increased suspense for what you will sooner or later be able to make of things.

There has recently been no change for me in terms of the general aspects of my situation. During the last few weeks, I have been busy writing down some incisive reflections on art theory. Their point of departure was the conversation I had with your husband that morning in the bar. It is as if these reflections, which had always remained concealed during the early part of the waning day, become tangible for me only after having been lured into the light of day. With this in mind, please extend the kindest regards to your husband.

Please write me again as soon as you would like and are able to do so. With news like the kind you sent about Buber, you will always find a very eager listener.

Most sincere regards.
Yours, Walter Benjamin

270. To Werner Kraft

Paris
October 28, 1935

Dear Mr. Kraft,

There are several reasons for my acknowledging your latest news and parcels less quickly than I would have wished. At least the first of these reasons will serve to excuse me. It can be attributed to the particular difficulties of my existence, which have now begun to pile up most threateningly. I will refrain from enumerating the effects in detail; one of them will in any case reach you in the form of my new address.

As you will easily understand, such circumstances demand their own dietary regimen and thus I was not immediately able to answer your last card with the kind of spontaneity that this form of correspondence demands.

Let me first turn to your poem,[1] which made a deep impression on me. The first four stanzas of the poem seem so perfect that it should be able to bear the objection I have to raise about the fifth stanza. The poem ends with the word *end*. The question—as it seems to me—with which you conclude the poem is not able to strike the full resonance of the rich sounding board that the preceding stanzas constructed.

Otherwise, the sorrow contained in these lines interests me no less than their artistic form. And this leads me to the question of whether it might not be possible for you to give me a relatively pragmatic report about your life over there—or about life over there—which, as I freely admit, I have been expecting from you for so long. In this context, you might also tell me in a word what kind of work you have found. [. . .]

Otherwise, I have hardly succumbed to the compulsion to make some kind of sense of the current state of the world. There have already been many cultures on this planet that have perished in blood and horror. It is naturally necessary for us to hope that the planet will some day experience a culture that has gone beyond both of those things—indeed, just like Scheerbart, I am inclined to assume that the planet is waiting for this. But it is terribly doubtful whether *we* will be able to present the planet this gift on its one-hundred- or four-hundred-millionth birthday. And if not, it will ultimately dish out as punishment for us, the planet's heedless well-wishers, the last judgment.

As for me, I am busy pointing my telescope through the bloody mist at a mirage of the nineteenth century that I am attempting to reproduce based on the characteristics it will manifest in a future state of the world, liberated from magic. I must naturally first build this telescope myself and, in making this effort, I am the first to have discovered some fundamental principles of materialistic art theory. I am currently in the process of explicating them in a short programmatic essay.

I am preparing a lecture for the Institute des études germaniques at the Sorbonne for February. I briefly made the rounds of professors and this left me with mixed impressions. [Henri] Lichtenberger is the one who made the most unfavorable impression on me.

Otherwise there is little that is new. And above all, no new books have been read, actually for months now, since the project is taking up all my time. I made one exception for *Horatier und Kuriatier,* a new parable by Brecht, which I recently got to see in manuscript form. It represents an excellent application of certain techniques of Chinese theater, with which he became acquainted during his last stay in Moscow. Many thanks for what you said about my review of *The Three-Penny Novel!* And please write in detail very soon.

1. "Wahnes Frage," in *Figur der Hoffnung*.

271. To Werner Kraft

Paris
December 27, 1935

Dear Mr. Kraft,

Let me express my most sincere gratitude for the informative and valuable letter you wrote on November 9. It was the first letter to have given me a picture of your situation in Palestine, even if only in outline form.

Congratulations on your anthology project for Schocken Books. I can easily imagine that this truly pleases you and that the result will be something delightful. I am not in the least surprised, on the other hand, that you respond to many events and many demands with "secret reluctance." As inadequate as my knowledge of Palestine's material and intellectual situation is, I can still gather from various symptoms that the intellectual breathing space in Palestine is much more constricted than its relatively comfortable political disposition would lead one to assume.

You mention—in connection with your lovely poem—Lev Shestov. It is quite possible that I will meet him sometime very soon. *In Job's Balances* is on the shelf right next to me. I have of course not yet found the right time to start reading it. And in this context, let me ask you not to think me superficial if I do not return to your poem today. I have—I hope without contravening your own wishes—lent it to a friend so that he can make a copy. [. . .]

In conclusion, let me note that I have completed a programmatic essay on art theory. It is called "The Work of Art in the Age of Mechanical Reproduction." In terms of content, it bears no relationship to the long book I mentioned I was planning. Methodologically, however, it is most intimately related to it, since the locus of contemporaneity in the objects whose history is meant to be presented must be precisely fixed before any historical work is undertaken, especially one that claims to be written from the perspective of historical materialism: . . . the fate of art in the nineteenth century.

272. To Theodor W. Adorno

Paris
December 27, 1935

Dear Mr. Wiesengrund,

Before I pass on a message from Max [Horkheimer], which provided me with the first impetus to write these lines, please let me say that I thought of you with profound sympathy when the news of Alban Berg's death reached me yesterday.

You know that when we talked about music, a field that is otherwise quite removed from my sphere of interest, it was only when his work was the subject of conversation that we reached the same intensity as when we discussed subjects in other fields. Specifically, you will no doubt still remember our conversation after the *Wozzeck* performance.

Max asks that you under no circumstances leave the Continent without first having informed him by telegram of where you can be reached before your ocean crossing. It is extremely important for him to speak to you on the Continent, whether in Holland or in Paris. (You can imagine that if it were to be in Paris, I would be extremely delighted and it would also mean a lot to me.)

He specifically wants you to give me the information, since he will keep me up-to-date as to his whereabouts and about the length of his stay in Holland, which begins at the end of the week.

Max, by the way, naturally also knows how much I would like the three of us to get together here in Paris to talk.

Most sincere regards to you and Felizitas.

Yours, WB

273. To Alfred Cohn

Paris
January 26, 1936

Dear Alfred,

I am sincerely grateful for the two brief notes in which you announce the arrival of a letter. They have unfortunately not yet led to results in this new year. And I will now anticipate your letter with a few words of my own.

My thoughts turned to you again just a few days ago—specifically, after I received the news that Noeggerath is giving lectures in Barcelona. To be sure, this news came from an unreliable source, or at least from one lacking in absolute guarantees. I have not been able to find out anything more specific—it cannot be a question of lectures at the university; P. L. Landsberg, Scheler's student, who is a lector at the University of Barcelona and whom I asked about Noeggerath, would surely have known about that.

In any case, I wanted to let you know about Noeggerath's presence in the city; I am sure that he will remember Grete from the early years in Munich and that he would gladly strike up a relationship with the two of you. Of course, I have no way of knowing if this is what you have in mind. It might very well also depend on his condition, which, unfortunately, was not very encouraging when I left Ibiza. Meanwhile, I was also told that he has left the island for good. This is what I might have predicted would happen. The idea was virtually forced upon me by a visit, undertaken in *grande compagnie,* of the building site he had purchased for his island home. If he has now left, my prediction will have been fulfilled after very few years.

For my own part, I still often think back to the island. But I doubt whether my path will lead me to the south when I once again break away from Paris for a while. It is more likely that I will get to Denmark this summer. However, I still do not have a clear notion of things; I only sense that a change of scene would be welcome after spending so much time in one place, which is unusual for me.

For the time being, I will not leave Paris for any length of time—unless political circumstances force me to do so—because the book I am working on keeps me dependent on the Bibliothèque Nationale. Nonetheless, I will soon interrupt my research there for a period of time in order to tackle one or more complete drafts of the book. I have now finished my essay "The Work of Art in the Age of Mechanical Reproduction." It fixes the contemporary locus, whose conditions and problems will set the standard for my retrospective look at the nineteenth century. This programmatic essay should appear in the journal of the institute, and in French. The translation of this essay will be in the hands of an especially talented man; in spite of this, given the subject matter, any translation will probably be difficult to accomplish without harming the text. On the other hand, I feel that the publication of the text in French is something much to be desired in view of my position here.

At approximately the same time as I came to the realization that it would be necessary, at least for the time being, to dispense with an unmediated setting down of my ideas in French, my position seems to be improving somewhat in another way. On the one hand, this is connected with the decision of the institute to unveil a somewhat more intensive action plan in France; on the other, with the growing importance of Adrienne Monnier in the local literary establishment. Over time, I have entered into a relationship with Monnier that is very close to being a friendly relationship in the German sense. You may recall the uncommon sympathy I have always declared for her.

This sympathy has been increased by the political stance she has taken during the past year. *Vendredi* was founded in the second half of that year and you may have come across it. *Vendredi* is a very inexpensive weekly paper that is supposed to have already a circulation of 300,000. It has made the first attempt in a long time to mobilize the literary production of the Left comprehensively. All in all, it has done so very successfully. As far as I know, Gide is very much involved in this experiment, both in terms of his technical advice and financial support. The very important fact that fascism is as good as lacking any literary guidelines is, of course, not limited to France. In France, however, this is being revealed in the right light for the first time—and perhaps even in time. This is the most important achievement of *Vendredi*. The best thing about the paper, besides the elucidation I just mentioned, is to prove that a fear of Communists no longer exists, even among the intellectual vanguard of liberalism. In the same place where authors like Gide or Rolland fix their political position, you come across people like Julien Benda, Alain, and Jules Romains making hardly less energetic, but in any case unambiguous, pronouncements. Furthermore, the rabid polemic that *Vendredi* levels against people like Louis Bertrand, Camille Mauclair, Henri Béraud, and Paul Morand is extraordinarily pleasing for those of us who so completely missed just that kind of political reaction against cryptofascism in German belles lettres. Adrienne Monnier occasionally works for *Vendredi* and plays what can hardly be called a minor role, without actually being a member of the editorial board.

To conclude this literary news with a less important piece of news: should you come across it, read Simenon's *Pitard* immediately. It is a first-rate light novel.

To turn to what is nearest at hand: Do you know whether Ernst [Schoen] went to Moscow or Leningrad? By the way, the aforementioned programmatic essay is with a publisher in Moscow at the moment and I am extremely eager to know whether it will be published in Russia. This is a possibility. Yet a positive decision would surprise me more than a negative one.

Brecht intends to leave America. I heard someone say that the production of *The Mother* was a great success overseas. I still do not know anything more specific about it. I think that the very existence of my letter speaks urgently enough for me to be spared the necessity of asking you in conclusion to respond with news very soon. For today, please simply accept my best wishes and sincere regards.

Yours, Walter

274. To Werner Kraft

Paris
January 30, 1936

Dear Mr. Kraft,

I will write only a few lines today. My reason for writing is to thank you for your last letter, particularly for the beautiful poem, and to tell you briefly about myself.

I was interested in what you wrote about Heine and Brecht. I believe there is much truth in what you say even if I am unable to think of any verses by Heine that might be specifically reminiscent of Brecht. This is understandable, given my limited knowledge of Heine. I am less able to follow you when, with reference to Brecht, you treat the question of whether a poet can create outside tradition. Tradition is surely present in Brecht's work. It is just that we must look for it where we have not often looked before: I am thinking primarily of Bavarian folk poetry, not to mention manifest characteristics that can be traced to the didactic and parabolical sermon of the south German baroque.

It happens that I am now at the point of getting into Heine in my own way. I am reading the prose insofar as it deals with conditions in France. I would be very grateful if you were to refer me to passages in his poetry where his concern with these conditions might also be reflected.

As for your comment on my essay on the theory of language, whose limits were prescribed by its form: it does not anticipate anything about a "metaphysics" of language. And I have structured the essay, albeit not at all manifestly, so that it leads precisely to the place where my own theory of language begins—I put this in writing in a very short programmatic note several years ago on Ibiza. I was very surprised to find significant correlations between this theory and Freud's essay "Telepathie und Psychoanalyse," which you can find in the 1935 *Almanach* of psychoanalysis.

My essay "The Work of Art in the Age of Mechanical Reproduction" will be published in French very soon. The essay is now in the hands of a translator who is considered to be very good; but the difficulties will be extraordinary even for him. The question of where I will be able to publish the German text is still unresolved. I am busy writing some annotations for the essay.

I am currently devoting any time I can find for my book to research in the Cabinet des Estampes. This is where I came across the most splendid portraitist of the city of Paris, Charles Méryon, a contemporary of Baudelaire. His etchings are among the most amazing that a city has ever inspired; it is an immense loss that, as a consequence of Méryon's whims, the plan to have them printed with a commentary by Baudelaire was not carried out.

For today, I hope you will be satisfied with this page.

P.S. It occurred to me just in time to tell you how eagerly I look forward to receiving your notes on language.

And many thanks for the beautiful lines by Mallarmé.[1]

1. Cited by Henri de Régnier in his book of reminiscences, *Donc* (Paris, 1927).

275. To Werner Kraft

Paris
[Spring 1936]

Dear Mr. Kraft,

With sincere gratitude, let me confirm receipt of your particularly fine essay on Else Lasker-Schüler.[1] Reading it, I increasingly came to feel that no one has ever written about this poet with so much love and insight.

At the very beginning of the essay, you have a felicitous (dialectical) grasp of what is inadequate about this phenomenon; but in this case that specifically means that you grasp what is most profound and most vital about her. Your description, therefore, imparts to the women's poetic achievement something like the bliss of the pilot who finds his place by overcoming the force of gravity.

When I have a chance, I want to get the *Konzert*[2] but in the meantime I believe that it will contain very little that will prove to be more beautiful than the quotations within the context of your essay. I am particularly sorry about not being able to do anything about getting it published. The *Zeitschrift für Sozialforschung* is an outlet for specialists that comes out three times a year. Its sphere of interest is precisely demarcated and this essay, on account of its subject matter alone, has nothing in common with that sphere. [. . .]

I am very grateful for your letter of February 15. I will put it among my working papers so that I can make use of its many valuable references to Heine as my research progresses.

In the same letter you mention observations I made about Brecht and tradition. Since, on the one hand, it is likely that we are talking about some very few lines and since, on the other hand, I have completely forgotten what they contained, I will probably not be placing too heavy a burden on you if I ask you to make me a copy of those few words from my letter. At the same time as I make this request, I am particularly sorry to have to leave unanswered your question as to Brecht's attitude toward my Kafka essay. To answer it would, however, mean having to copy a dozen pages of my Danish diary—it contains the most important conversations I had with Brecht in the summer of 1934.[3] I hope to be able to tell you about this sometime in person.

Du Bos is unfortunately very ill again. He has had to cancel his lectures and receptions.—I heard a splendid reading by Paul Valéry at the home of some friends. He read *Le Serpent,* among other things. I would also most prefer to tell you in person about an encounter with Gide at a similar event that took place quite a while ago.

[. . .]

P.S. I have just received your beautiful poem *Die Flöte.*[4] Most sincere thanks.

1. Reprinted in Kraft's *Wort und Gedanke* (Bern, 1959).

2. Published in Berlin, 1932.

3. Published in Walter Benjamin, *Versuche über Brecht* (Frankfurt am Main, 1966), pp. 117–35. [*Understanding Brecht* (London, 1973), pp. 105–21.–Trans.]

4. Unpublished.

276. To Theodor W. Adorno

Paris
February 27, 1936

Dear Mr. Wiesengrund,

I had hoped to be able to send you my essay and this cover letter sooner. But I was unable to free up a single German copy before the French translation was completed. Please forgive me if the one I am now sending shows traces of the translator at work.

Furthermore, if the task of translation were totally finished in all respects, you would be getting the German and French similtaneously. As things now stand, in spite of the fact that it is already in press, I must keep the latter here for a bit so that I can go through it one final time with the translator.

Due to these circumstances, I have also had to put off expressing my gratitude to you for sending me your commemorative essays on the death of Alban Berg.[1] You would have heard something from me about these extraordinary pieces earlier if I had not in fact had to dog my translator's heels for fourteen days, all day long and a good part of the night. You know that the second of these essays is the more accessible to me on account of its more familiar subject matter. I consequently devoted most of my time to it and in fact it seems to me to be extraordinarily beautiful. Many of its passages struck me as being very self-possessed.

For example, at the very beginning in your description of the "stonily delicate" traits, which so wonderfully corresponds to a death mask; and then, the truly astounding sentence, the one that speaks to me directly: "He has undercut the negativity of the world with the hopelessness of his fantasy"—a perspective in which my encounter with the music of *Wozzeck* has again become quite salient. As for some of the other sentences, I will allow myself to go so far as to imagine that you may to some extent have had me in mind while you were writing them; above all, of course, in your reference to the "friendliness of the cannibal." I was also uncommonly delighted with the context in which you cite Berg's sentence about the brass-player accord.

I hope I will not have to wait too long for your letter. No matter how brief the wait may be, I am sure to suffer it with impatience. The two weeks I spent in absolutely intense work with my translator have provided me with some distance from the German text. I usually achieve this only after longer periods of time. I say this not to dissociate myself from it in the least, but rather because I only came to discover at this distance *one* element in the text to which I would particularly like to see you as reader do justice: specifically, its cannibalistic urbanity, a certain circumspection and caution in the act of destruction. I hope this will betray something of the love it reveals for those things closest to you.

I am waiting for the collection of Max [Horkheimer's] essays.[2] I am being entrusted with their translation. Once this work is under way, I definitely assume that we will see each other here. I think and I hope this will soon take place.

Most sincere regards.
Yours, Walter Benjamin

1. "Zur Lulu-Symphonie" and "Erinnerung an den Lebenden." Both essays appeared under the pseudonym Hektor Rottweiler in the Vienna music journal *23,* 24–25 (February 1936).

2. The edition did not materialize.

277. To Kitty Marx-Steinschneider

Paris
April 15, 1936

My dear friend,

I hope that we are on the kind of terms that my silence over such a long time has not awakened the slightest unfounded doubts in you. Or at most occasional doubts about my well-being, which have not necessarily always been unfounded. On the other hand, you will not be surprised if I choose a lull in which to tell you about myself. These lulls do not occur frequently and need not do so.

Spring has arrived in the meantime; the little tree of life, however, pays no heed at all to the season, refuses to sprout even the slightest buds, and at most produces small fruits. Some few friends of nature look up at the last of these that had, of course, already been promised to you. It will arrive at your house in approximately one month packaged as a French text. As for the friends of nature, this is a small group that has been thrown together by chance—consisting of some emigrants, one or two French amateurs, a Russian who shakes his head at the situation, and some individuals of varying origin and sex who display curiosity less for the fruit than for the little tree.

From this short allegory, you will get a fairly accurate idea of my current conditions of production. Strictly speaking, first my supervision of the unusually difficult translation and then clearing up the editorial and technical complications have taken up the major part of my energy in the last two months (if not of my time). I have been compensated for all the annoyance that is almost always connected to such negotiations by the fascination connected to observing the earliest reactions to such a work. Characteristically, they often appear superior to later, as it were official, reactions. I would almost have cause to conclude from these reactions that the place where it appropriately belongs, in Russia, is where it will have the least impact. Here, on the other hand, things are under way to present the work of Gide, Paul Valéry, and others of France's most important writers in a way that is appropriate to it. My essay will be accompanied by a programmatic text I am working on at this very moment.

Otherwise I have been busy working on an essay I am committed to write on the Russian poet Leskov. I agreed to do this as a result of some unpleasant circumstances. He is a little-known but very important contemporary of Dostoyevsky. Are you familiar with him? His works have been translated piecemeal fairly often into German. I am doing it for *Orient und Okzident,*[1] a journal headed by the former Bonn theologian Fritz Lieb. This Lieb is Swiss, a former student of Karl Barth and by far one of the best people I have gotten to know here. He is, moreover, a man of uncommon courage who had played a role in the Swiss uprising of 1918. I am just now reading his work "Das geistige Gesicht des Bolschewismus," which should provide me with the key to his later development, which is just as interesting as it is appealing—and occasionally fascinating.

As for the rest, since I have absolutely no desire to begin making observations on Russian literary history, I will take an old hobbyhorse out of its stall, to discuss Leskov. Using it, I will try to apply to him my oft-repeated observations on the antithesis between *romancier* and storyteller and my old preference for the latter.

Otherwise I am not quite able to decide whether Leskov might be of use to you in terms of your request for literary references. But if one or the other collection of his novellas should ever cross your path, you should take it along in any case. Beyond that, I find myself at a real loss in terms of providing reasonable advice. This is not surprising. On the one hand, I am reading things that are more or less prescribed on account of my work—most of them are in rarely used areas of the stacks of the Bibliothèque Nationale. On the other hand, this has allowed me the freedom to pursue my simple pleasures as a reader, untroubled by all literary considerations. And since personal taste always plays a role in simple pleasures, and not a small role at that, recommending such reading is not a whit more reliable than recommendations of what to eat. Given this reservation, I want to let you know—should I not have done so already?—that I am reading every new novel by Georges Simenon. I think the best of his latest books are *Les Pitard, Le locataire,* and *L'évade*. As you may well imagine, I am at the moment essentially reading no literature at all that is even "relatively highbrow." There are, however, adventure novels that could easily compete with highbrow literature. One of the most splendid adventure novels I recently came across—but it has been known for a long time and was published by Knaur in a German translation—is Philipp Macdonald's *Death in the Desert.* (A film that is not entirely unworthy of the book was based on it.)

Do not assume that I regularly receive the *Jüdische Rundschau.* And you should not in your wildest dreams imagine that what I read there interests me even remotely as much as what you could write me about things having to do with Palestine, on one side of a sheet of stationery. There are, of course, difficulties in formulating questions. For I am always interested in the same thing: what becomes of the hopes that Palestine raises, beyond allowing ten thousand Jews, even one hundred thousand Jews, to eke out a meager existence. A circumstance that, as absolutely essential as it is, may well not run its course without proving to be a new and catastrophic danger among all the dangers threatening Judaism.

(Scholem has also received my discussion of theories of the philosophy of language, which you read, without my having heard one word from him about it. I recently wrote him and also informed him of my new essay on art theory, not without candidly telling hom how wary I am that he will receive it favorably. I can hardly explain the lackluster nature of his rare reports and the long pauses that intervene between them by anything other than the difficulties he himself must be confronting. The prospects of his making a trip to Europe this year, something he seemed to count on last year, will also probably have become uncertain because of this—not to mention the prospects of our getting together.)

I have not been away from Paris for a year and I really need a rest. I intend to visit Brecht in Denmark in a month if possible. But whether it is, is still very uncertain. I would be very happy to be able to spend the summer in Denmark, purely because of the political situation. I have already felt quite uneasy here at times. And I would send you reports from up there that might reveal to you that the possibility of pursuing "peace and fishing" in high latitudes is decidedly more rational than not escaping your "destiny."

Since we are speaking of your destiny, however, we should assume that the next thing you are destined to do is to answer me soon with a long letter.

Most sincere regards, as always.
Yours, Walter Benjamin

1. October 1936, pp. 16–33. In *Schriften* 2:229–58.

278.* To Gerhard Scholem

Paris
May 3, 1936

Dear Gerhard,

With your last letter, our correspondence over this past year has sustained a sorry epilogue. It is an epilogue to which I can proffer nothing more than a mute listener who is able to follow it all too well—even where it moves only in intimations—to intrude with words of no consequence. Of the little that can be expressed, I hope that whatever loneliness you feel vis-à-vis the outside world will be short-lived and will bring about some inner fecundity.

Even if our correspondence these last months hasn't fared much better than you have, at least you can't deny me the testimonial that I have stood by it with patience. Not in vain, if it regains something of its original character as time passes. That's why we must both hope that the elemental spirits of our existence and our work, who are entitled to our dialogue, will not be kept waiting indefinitely on the threshold. On the other hand, one must not disregard the chance that they may be able to converse, set free of the physical zones of our being owing to an imminent purge of geopolitical differences.

For the moment, I can only hope that at least the events in Palestine that come to my attention are exaggerated reports. But that leaves enough to be distressed about in many other respects. Knowing this, I would really like to obtain French citizenship, were it not bound up with costs that could lead to my new nationality being bestowed upon a skeleton.

I read the account of your brother's fate with horror. I don't know him,[1] but the mere fact of having to connect a name to that kind of existence is dreadful. My brother is still in Germany too, but at liberty. He doesn't suffer any direct privation, since my sister-in-law works at the Russian trade mission in Berlin.

As to my own work, it seems to be vastly surpassed by the thoughts you have for it—in every stage of its development. In any case, I take it that you mean the *Paris Arcades* when you refer to the "major project." Nothing has changed there: not a syllable of the actual text exists, even though the end of preparatory studies is now within sight. And for the moment the emphasis is not on the text so much as on the planning of the whole, which needs to be thought through very carefully and will certainly give rise to this or that experiment for some time to come. My last work, whose French version—"L'oeuvre d'art à l'époque de sa reproduction mécanisée"—should be appearing in three weeks' time, has also evolved from this planning. It touches on the major project only superficially, but it indicates the vanishing point for some of its investigations. Of the aforementioned attempts at an overall plan, only one has thus far taken final shape. I will attempt a companion piece to it as soon as I return to this subject.

Unfortunately, I will scarcely be able to sidestep the work on Fuchs this summer; but meanwhile I managed to obtain certain liberties in connection with it.

I hope soon to hear more details of your big Kabbalah project for Schocken; not to speak of the Goldberg critique.

Is Leo Strauss in Palestine?[2] I would not be averse to addressing his works in the journal *Orient und Okzident*—for which I'm writing the Leskov piece. Perhaps you'll be seeing the author; if so, you can prevail upon him to send me the books.

I close for today with most cordial greetings,

Yours, Walter

1. WB had met my brother once, at a Seder in the house of my friend Moses Marx in 1923 but he had forgotten about it.

2. Leo Strauss was in England at that time, from where he traveled to the United States in 1938.

279. To Alfred Cohn

July 4, 1936

Dear Alfred,

I will not let a moment go by without telling you how much your last letter pleased me. Your birthday is another special reason for me to write.

Am I correct in thinking it is on the 1st of July? I assume this is the case and would therefore have written you sooner if your silence had not perplexed me. I was thus doubly pleased to hear from you.

I would have liked to have found something in your lines to indicate a certain change for the better in your external circumstances. The fact that you do not touch on these circumstances gives me reason to believe that nothing has changed yet in this regard; and this is the only shadow to fall on your letter.

Of all the things you have to say about my essay, I was most delighted that you recognized its continuity with my earlier studies in spite of its new, and surely often surprising, tendency—a continuity that is above all surely grounded in the fact that, over the years, I have tried to achieve an increasingly precise and uncompromising idea of what constitutes a work of art.

My attempt to have the essay debated by the local émigré authors was too carefully prepared for it not to produce a rich yield of information. This, however, was almost all it yielded. The most interesting thing was the attempt of those authors who are party members to thwart a debate of my work, if not its actual presentation. They did not succeed and, to the extent that they did not distance themselves completely, they therefore confined themselves to silently following the proceedings. The instinct for self-preservation compensates for deficient perceptivity in such cases: these people feel that their very well-established belletristic industry is threatened by me, but they can spare themselves a confrontation with me for the time being and, in the long run, do not think they are capable of having one. Otherwise, they may well lull themselves into a sense of security with some justification, since Moscow too sees the alpha and omega of literary politics in the fostering of leftist belles lettres. The newly founded *Das Wort*[1] makes me fear that this is so. I will soon hear about this journal in more detail from Brecht, who, with Feuchtwanger and Bredel, is on its editorial board. I think I will go to Denmark in July. For a long time now, I have been playing with the idea of returning to Ibiza for a while. I feel very much in need of rest and a stay in Denmark is more [The rest of the letter is missing.]

1. The first issue of *Das Wort* appeared in Moscow in July 1936.

280. To Max Horkheimer

Skovsbostrand per Svendborg
August 10, 1936

Dear Mr. Horkheimer,

Let me gratefully confirm my receipt of your letters of the 13th and 25th of July, which were forwarded to me here.

I have been at Brecht's for a week. My arrival coincided with a rainy period; the weather has been nice since yesterday, and I am looking forward to country life, something I have had to forgo for a long time.

Even before I received the first of your two letters, I had wanted to write you briefly about the repercussions of my essay that appeared in the last issue of the *Zeitschrift [für Sozialforschung]*. I have not yet seen the actual text of the most interesting of them. It is a statement by Malraux that he made last month at the Writers' Congress in London, where he delivered the plenary address. Since Étiemble was general secretary of the congress, I will get the text from him.

Malraux went into my reflections in front of the congress and confirmed this for me during a meeting in Paris. He went so far as to hold out the prospect of a more detailed consideration of the essay in his next, evidently theoretical, book. I would naturally be pleased if he were to do that. But it should not be forgotten that Malraux is very temperamental; he does not execute each one of his often impulsive plans.

The essay also provided the occasion for a discussion between Jean Wahl and Pierre-Jean Jouve, who is an important poet. I was not present;

I was told about it. Ostertag, the bookdealer from the Pont de l'Europe, told me that this issue of the journal was purchased at his store on several occasions by customers who referred to my essay. Finally, I know that the essay has been repeatedly called to the attention of Jean Paulhan, the editor of the *NRF*. It was suggested that he deal with it in a review in his journal. I am doubtful as to whether he will do this. The circle associated with the *NRF* has the kind of impermeability that has been characteristic of a very specific kind of circle from time immemorial and this holds true threefold when the circles are literary ones.

All in all, this naturally only applies to the journal and not the publishers. Most particularly, not to G.[1] Nonetheless, the unreliability that this grouping imparts to the people involved, and the complications they impose on things, continues to make itself felt in an attenuated fashion in its immediate vicinity. Given these circumstances, you rarely know which agreements are to be viewed as binding and which are not. From my last reports, you have seen how painful it is for me to have to confront all of this now when I am working on your behalf and, on the other hand, how coping with these obstacles steels my will.

It seems to me that it must above all be made impossible for these people to slow down negotiations by appealing to the need to correspond with you. Only a representative officially appointed by you would in fact probably be able to accomplish precisely that. It goes without saying that I am ready to be that person at any time. You may, however, wish to consider whether it may not be more advisable to appoint a Frenchman to this position. He would have a broader view of things and might be able to proceed more efficaciously. In any case, there is no question of Groethuysen doing it, and Étiemble might also feel uneasy filling a dual role. Please let me know what you think.

I am writing Wiesengrund to ask him to arrange things so that we can see each other in Paris at the beginning of October. Étiemble also intends to return around that time and we will then tackle the task of editing the volume.

In my last letter, I enclosed some information that might further clarify the image you have of the September meeting in Pontigny. Information I have obtained since then makes the reserve emanating from your last letter especially understandable. [. . .]

Should the institute consider my reportage worthwhile, you would certainly make my attendance at the meeting possible within the framework of the particulars contained in my last letter. Otherwise I would prolong my stay in Denmark into September in order to be able to return to Paris with the essay on Fuchs completed.

You ask about my cousin, Dr. [Egon] Wissing.

You know from him personally that we have been friends for many years. (Our mutual passion for old books was the first thing that brought us together, in spite of the fact that we are related.) Our friendship became very intimate around the beginning of the thirties so that the death of Wissing's wife, which occurred soon after (1933), also hit me hard.[2]

For Wissing, her death was only the most painful in a whole chain of misfortunes inflicted on him during the last several years. In spite of diagnosed depressive inhibitions, he repeatedly freed himself with great courage and (as his last German intermezzo proves) not less great skill from all entanglements. [. . .] According to the letters he has written from New York that I have received thus far, he seems to be truly succeeding in building a life for himself. [. . .]

In any case, I am tremendously encouraged that you have discovered a relationship to one another and that he has found a mainstay in you and your wife.

Let me extend my sincere regards to you, your wife and your friends.

Yours, Walter Benjamin

1. Probably Bernhard Groethuysen, who was then working for Gallimard.
2. Gert Wissing died in 1934.

281. To Werner Kraft

Svendborg
August 11, 1936

Dear Mr. Kraft,

I am unfortunately indebted to you several times over. To the extent it is possible for me to do so, I would have repaid it long ago if the past month had not denied me the peace that, at such a great distance, is necessary even for some hurried remarks.

In another way, however, the same debt probably borders on the limit of the energy available to me at the time. I refer to the energy needed to expatriate myself spiritually for a short time in a more or less decisive fashion. This is precisely what your *Heine* requires—not your selections, but the materials that underlie them.[1] At the moment I find only the political material to be at all assimilable—not, as I must admit to myself, the poetic material. I found the text valuable and instructive but it would probably be asking the impossible of it to expect it to awaken in me at this time the mood of Heine's poetic voice. Not that this would have kept me from reading your book attentively—but rather, reading it attentively is what made this entirely clear to me. I do not have to tell you that no judgment is implicit in these remarks, but rather an entirely unauthoritative and very conditional reaction.

For the rest, it will not be clearer to anyone than it is to you that it is particularly necessary at the current time to make room for some of the most subjective reactions in order to maintain even the modest disposition to carry on with your work. We can all ask ourselves how long we will be able to consign ourselves to that half of the globe on which we find ourselves, even when summoning up the most extreme recklessness—as we do right now. And whether we will still have time to exchange this half of the globe for the other after a certain amount of time has elapsed.

I do not know whether events in Palestine make it possible for you to give serious attention to those taking place in Spain. In any case, you will agree with me that the conflict over there can become of great importance for us as well. (By the way, I was overcome by a strange feeling yesterday upon hearing the news that Ibiza too has become a theater of the civil war.) I miss not finding any French newspapers here. There is of course not much that is more significant than the effect of Spanish affairs on those of France. I have to depend on translations from Danish papers and on the radio.

I will stay here until the end of the month and even longer if possible. Yet it may turn out that it will be necessary for me to attend a congress in the Bourgogne at the beginning of September. The second issue of *Das Wort* arrived yesterday—this is the new German-language literary journal published in Moscow. As you can imagine, Brecht was very nettled to read some very foolish and disrespectful words about Kraus in the "foreword," which, because it was unsigned, was the responsibility of the editorial board, of which he is also a member. The comments differ all too little from the shameless text that Benkard published in the *Frankfurter Zeitung* on the occasion of Kraus's death. I can well understand that his death has hit you hard. I am grateful to you for the copy of the passage from his girlfriend's letter.

I do not know whether the editorial board of *Das Wort* will retain its present composition for very long, given the circumstances mentioned above. I have an interest in its doing so at least until the attempt has been made, and which can only be undertaken by Brecht, to have the German version of my essay "The Work of Art in the Age of Mechanical Reproduction" published there.

With this I have come to a second situation requiring my apologies. The need to send the French text of the essay to a number of interested parties in Paris has resulted in my having hardly any copies left for my friends. I sent one to Scholem, since he has an almost complete archive of my works. I asked him to make the offprint available to you whenever you wish. It would be very important to me to hear what you think of this essay.

1. *Heine: Gedicht und Gedanke* (Berlin, 1936).

282. To Max Horkheimer

Skovbostrand per Svendborg
August 31, 1936

Dear Mr. Horkheimer,

Thank you for your kind letter of August 17th. You will in the meantime have received my first letter from Denmark.

I was ultimately very pleased that you left everything up to me in regard to the congress in Pontigny and I have reason to be particularly grateful.

I will not attend the congress. Connections by ship to the Continent are such that I would have to leave here a whole week before the congress starts if I wanted to get to it in time. This would be a lost week, both in terms of my recuperation and of my work (which happily coincide here); furthermore, since I sublet my room in Paris until the end of September, I would not quite know where to spend the week. I will therefore remain in Denmark for the time being.

Otherwise, and we will surely feel the same way about this, it is a gloomy summer. I am naturally following events in Russia very closely. And it seems to me that I am not the only one who is at the end of his rope. [. . .]

But who knows what will be on the world's political agenda when we see each other again in, I hope, the not too distant future.

I hope that you will come to enjoy your summer sojourn regardless of the heat. Here, on the other hand, the sun is making itself scarce.

Please accept my most sincere regards, and extend them as well to your wife and Mr. Pollock.

Yours, Walter Benjamin

283. To Max Horkheimer

Paris
October 13, 1936

Dear Mr. Horkheimer,

Before beginning my report, let me express my sincere gratitude to you for having made Wiesengrund's stay here possible. After having been put off for years, our discussion revealed a communality on the most important theoretical goals, which was very satisfying, indeed invigorating. In view of our long separation, this agreement at times had something almost amazing about it.

The material that formed the basis of our discussion: the jazz essay,[1] the reproduction essay, the outline of my book and a number of Wiesengrund's methodological reflections on it—this was enough material for us to tackle the most basic questions. And the time we had together was so short compared to the issues that were pending that, even if the manuscript had been before us, we would hardly have been able to tackle the complex of materialist epistemological criticism as proposed by Weisengrund in his Oxford project.[2] I hope our next conversation will be enriched by this foundation, as well as by certain excerpts from my book, which I intend to tackle after the Fuchs essay has been completed.

The week that has just passed awakened in me the most intense desire that our discussion of the institute's research orientation, as envisioned by you in your letter of September 8th, take place in the near future. Current conditions have made this discussion very necessary and I expect a great deal from it.

Wiesengrund and I have agreed that I for my part will tell you in detail about the status of the translator issue, while he will describe for you the situation at Gallimard's. I do not envy him his task. Nonetheless, I do want to say a few words about things to the extent that I am involved in them.

[. . .] Groethuysen has [. . .] made himself available for an initiative without having thought it through in the least. The one and only thing at issue for him may have been to highlight his presumed influence for you. When he encountered difficulties, he changed his mode of behavior (apparently gradually and without any kind of conscious control).

The extent to which Groethuysen is at the mercy of uncontrolled reflexes became blatantly clear during the last round of negotiations. The subvention issue was one thing that came up for discussion. As you known, this issue was clarified down to the last detail months ago. When I disposed of a related question of his by referring to it, however, Groethuysen assumed the air of a man who finally sees the way ahead clear. That, however, did not prevent him from continuing to avoid giving any definitive information. I am referring to the matter of "slipups." It was impossible to attain any true insight into their mechanics as long as Étiemble kept hold of the translation and Groethuysen by and large continued to set course for the NRF.

[. . .]

In conclusion, let me just say a word to you about how very impressed I was by "Egoismus und Freiheitsbewegung."[3] In so doing, I will ignore all the details that are in part very important to me: the historical aspect of rhetoric, which you pursue from Socrates to the sermon to the contemporary "people's assembly"; your remarks on "the shamanlike weightiness" of our culture industry; your unmasking of its popular appeal to young people. I might perhaps formulate the one thing now of concern to me as follows: in this essay the spirit of those notes that I first heard in the company of Asja Lacis at your place in Cronberg defines the structural context itself. If I understand correctly, a dual set of facts is at issue.

First, there is the transparency with which conventional morality appears as a factotum in the intellectual economy of the neurotic individual. Then there is the critique of the French Revolution in terms of its ideological aspect. And the decisive thing is—the connection between these two moments. The insightfulness with which the anthropological type you characterize emerges like an abortion from the womb of the bourgeois revolution. I believe that the political stamp of your thesis, which represents the reverse of its philosophical truth, can make no greater impression on anyone than on the individual who is at home among the local French intellectuals and has become acquainted with the illusions (and who is yet to become acquainted with who knows what consequences of these illusions!) that are a result of the cult of the great revolution, or rather shape this cult.

Let me close with my most sincere regards to you, your wife, and your friends.

Yours, Walter Benjamin

1. Adorno's "Über Jazz" appeared under the pseudonym Hektor Rottweiler, *Zeitschrift für Sozialforschung* 5 (1936), pp. 235–59.

2. It was first published twenty years later: *Zur Metakritik der Erkenntnistheorie: Studien über Husserl und die phänomenologischen Antinomien* [*Against Epistemology: A Metacritique: Studies in Husserl and the Phenomenological Antinomies*] (Stuttgart, 1956).

3. *Zeitschrift für Sozialforschung* 5 (1936), pp. 161–234.

284. To Max Horkheimer

Paris
December 24, 1936

Dear Mr. Horkheimer,

I would like to thank you doubly and most sincerely. In the first place, for your letter dated December 15th, in which you give me some information that might benefit my son.

[. . .]

I read your essay[1] on Haecker the day before yesterday. I am not familiar with the book you discuss. On the other hand, I dealt with Haecker's *Vergil* several years ago in the *Literarische Welt*.[2] In view of how very moderate it is, your essay breathes—so it seems to me—the unmistakable resolve of a person who is determined for once to call a spade a spade. The Chinese story has a significant place in it.—What you say about the materialist's melancholy touches a specific chord in me: I mean my old love for Gottfried Keller. His splendid sadness was truly the materialist's sadness, shot through with colored threads of joy:

> A shimmering rain slowly fell,
> into which the evening sun shone.

But that's a long story . Of all individuals for whom it was intended as a materialist anthology, for me it is the one whose findings could be most surprising.

Your essay is relevant in another way to the conversation begun yesterday between [Franz] Neumann and myself at our first meeting. Neumann spoke of the catchword currently circulating among the younger generation of American lawyers to the effect that technical terminology should be avoided in jurisprudence as much as possible—not only the traditional terminology of the discipline but every kind of technical terminology—in order to conform completely with everyday language. It is obvious that in this way the law is in danger of being mobilized for any and all demagoguery. In spite of this, it seems to me that what we have here is a tendency that in other areas need not under all circumstances be as double-edged as it is in the area of jurisprudence. I am thinking specifically of the field of philosophy and I ask myself (this was also discussed when Wiesengrund was here) to what extent the "dismantling of philosophical terminology" is a side effect of dialectical-materialistic thinking.

Materialistic dialectics seems to me to deviate from the dogmas of the various schools in that, among other things, it requires the formation of new concepts from case to case; furthermore, in that it requires the kind of concepts that are more deeply embedded in the vocabulary than are the neologisms of jargon. It thereby gives to thinking a certain ready wit and the awareness of this provides thinking with a certain serenity and superiority out of which it can not easily be provoked. What I want to say is that materialistic dialectics might, for a certain period of time, very likely have the advantage of a procedure that for its part may be determined by tactics.

I will stop here in the belief that you will see how much your last texts in particular have helped me arrive at these observations.

Let me in conclusion once more express my gratitude and my most sincere regards.

Yours, Walter Benjamin

1. On Theodor Haecker's *Christ und die Geschichte,* in *Zeitschrift für Sozialforschung* 5 (1936), pp. 372–83.

2. *Schriften* 2:315–23.

285. To Max Horkheimer

Paris
January 31, 1937

Dear Mr. Horkheimer,

Many thanks for your letters of December 30th and January 11th and for the kind wishes you express at the beginning of the second.

[. . .]

As for me, I am devoting my time exclusively to the essay on Fuchs. The text is supposed to be ready in three weeks. I am making the dual nature of the man the basis of my presentation. He exhibited this nature as a popularizer and collector. In this way I hope to set off and emphasize the important characteristics of his nature alongside the limits of his achievement, which cannot be overlooked.

In my last letter I somewhat frivolously touched on a subject that, in the first instance, I should have brought up only in personal conversation. There can naturally be no question of eliminating philosophical terminology. I am in total agreement with you when you say that historical tendencies "that are preserved in certain categories may also not be allowed to be lost in style." I would like to add one further consideration to what you say; and perhaps it will correct what was misleading in my comments. I mean that there is a way of using philosophical terminology to feign a nonexistent richness. This is an uncritical use of technical terms. Concrete dialectical analysis of the particular subject being studied, on the other hand, includes a critique of the categories in which it was apprehended at an earlier level of reality and thought. (What I had in mind the last time was not only the conversation with Neumann but also the dismal example of Mannheim's *Man and Society in an Age of Reconstruction* [*Mensch und Gesellschaft*], to which I was introduced by Wiesengrund.)

Otherwise, general intelligibility surely cannot be a criterion. But it is likely that a certain transparency in details is inherent in concrete dialectical analysis. The general intelligibility of the whole is of course another story altogether. What is pertinent here is to look squarely at the fact you describe: in the long run small groups will play a prominent role in the preservation and transmission of science and art. This is in fact not the time to display in kiosks what we believe to have in our hands, probably not entirely without justification; rather, it seems to be a time to think of storing it where it will be safe from bombs. The dialectics of the thing may consist in this: to give the truth, which is nothing less than smoothly constructed, a place of safekeeping, smoothly constructed like a strongbox.

[. . .]

I was just planning to read Gide's book when I received your reference to it. The passage on religion is excellent, probably the best one in the whole book.—I have no clue about current events in the union.

Let me close for today with sincere regards.

Yours, Walter Benjamin

286.* To Gerhard Scholem

Paris
April 4, 1937

Dear Gerhard,

I was extremely gratified that you so thoroughly understood the character and intention of the volume of letters. Your unfulfilled wish was precisely the same as mine: to expand the book to twice its size. This wish is one I could no longer hope to realize in emigration; at best I might have been able to attempt it with the resources of the Swiss libraries or the British Museum—never in Paris. I also feel sorry for the sake of several commentaries: there is hardly one I would have preferred to write more than that on the incomparable letter written by Rahel on Gentz's death.[1]

I am pleased to hear that your life will soon have a definite shape again, and I congratulate you and your wife on the new apartment. I warmly return your wife's greetings. If this year passes without bringing the outbreak of war, then perhaps we can look into the very immediate future with a little more confidence, and I don't have to tell you that I would be happy to see our reunion bathed in such brighter colors—against either the backdrop of Jerusalem's battlements or that of the grayish blue facades of the boulevards.

Now dress me in your mind's eye in a herald's armor and imagine me at the bow of a four-master cutting through the Mediterranean surf as swiftly as an arrow, because that is the only fitting way to convey the grand news to you: the "Fuchs" is done. The finished text does not entirely have the character of penitence, as my laboring on it quite rightly seemed to you. On the contrary, its first quarter contains a number of important reflections on dialectical materialism, which are provisionally tailored to my book. My subsequent essays will be moving more directly toward that book from now on.

The "Fuchs" has been greeted with great acclaim. I see no reason to hide the fact that the tour de force it achieves is the substantial as well as major cause of this success. I hope you will be getting the printed article before the year is out. It always pleases me to hear of the care you bestow upon the collection of my writings. Troubled premonitions tell me that perhaps only our combined archives could present an exhaustive collection of them. For as conscientious as I am in administering my own, I most likely lost several pieces through the hasty departure from Berlin and the unsettled existence of the early years of emigration. To be sure, only a handful of my own works have been lost—as opposed to almost all of a relatively complete collection of comments published on them. Even you cannot provide replacements for those. With regard to more recent work, I am missing issue number 5 of the first volume of *Das Wort* (Moscow), in which I have an essay on Fascist theories of art. I am not giving up on my efforts to furnish you with one.—A small section of the *Elective Affinities* essay will be appearing in French translation any day now in the *Cahiers du sud.*[2]

I am still waiting for the Hebrew text you promised.

The weather here is marvelous. "I wish someone would come along and take me away"—outside. But it will probably be summer before I get out of doors. The news I have about Stefan sounds better of late.

On that note, I'll close for today. Write very soon.

Most cordially,
Yours, Walter

P.S. I have recently been given *very* precise information about Karl Kraus's last weeks. It is worthy of that illustrious life, and it makes the end of Timon of Athens seem like an invention by Frieda Schanz,[3] compared to the Shakespearean spirit of the age that wrote Kraus's.

1. The reference is to Rahel Varnagen's letter of June 15, 1833, to Leopold Ranke, which was first printed in Varnhagen von Ense's collection *Rahel: Ein Buch des Andenkens für ihre Freunde* (Berlin, 1834), part 3, pp. 576–78.

2. "L'angoisse mythique chez Goethe," *Cahiers du sud* 24, no. 194 (1937): 342–48. The journal's central figures, Jean Ballard (the editor) and Marcel Brion, were among WB's few admirers in France.

3. WB's favorite example of literary vacuity.

287.* To Gerhard Scholem

San Remo
July 2, 1937

Dear Gerhard,

I regret that I haven't satisfied the wish you voiced in your letter of May 7: I have not been prompt in sending you news, let alone been able to provide you with a report on Karl Kraus the day after your letter arrived.

The last few months in Paris have passed rather turbulently. The worsening of the Parisian economic climate, which you were quite right to suspect—and which is more a result of French financial policy than of the world's fair—has forced me to take a series of wearying steps. And, in spite of them, I still haven't managed to secure the continuation of the modest improvement in my living conditions that the spring seemed to promise even on the most minor scale. On the contrary, I am apprehensive when I contemplate the coming months.

You will understand that I mean this quite literally when I tell you that I have yet to set foot on the grounds of the world's fair. I hope that before the year is out you will be seeing the rest of what kept me away from our correspondence. For now, I only want to report that the San Remo weeks are entirely reserved for the study of C. G. Jung. It is my desire to safeguard certain foundations of *Paris Arcades* methodologically by waging an onslaught on the doctrines of Jung, especially those concerning archaic images and the collective unconscious. Apart from its internal methodological importance, this would have a more openly political one as well. Perhaps you have heard that Jung recently leaped to the rescue of the Aryan soul with a therapy reserved for it alone. My study of his essay volumes dating from the beginning of this decade—some of the individual essays date back to the preceding one—teaches me that these auxiliary services to National Socialism have been in the works for some time. I intend to make use of this occasion to analyze the peculiar figure of medical nihilism in literature: Benn, Céline, Jung. It has not yet been settled, though, whether I will be able to land a commission for this work.

By now you will have received "The Storyteller" ["Der Erzähler"]; the next text I can send you will presumably be the "Eduard Fuchs." Since I am understandably very concerned about the comprehensiveness of your archive of my writings, I would like to ask you to order the missing issue of *Das Wort*—volume 1936, no. 5 or 6—directly from the publisher, Jourgaz, 11 Strastnoy Boulevard, Moscow.

We are expecting Stefan from Vienna. I won't be able to form a picture of his development over the last months until I've spoken with him. Unfortunately, the date of his final examinations seems to be postponed further and further into the future.

The prospect of a meeting between us in Palestine, which your letter opens up for me, is—how should I express this?—welcome and full of significance. I must confess that I can fix my gaze upon it only as if through a frosted windowpane. My autonomy vis-à-vis the institute is not what it was two years ago. Even though there is no official tie between us, it would be most unwise on my part to move away from Europe for any substantial amount of time without obtaining New York's permission. If there is a prospect—and this is not out of the question—of having visitors from New York around wintertime, then I would not even attempt to ask for permission.

That is one side of the matter. The other side, though, is that my passport will expire a year from now. It is extremely doubtful that I will receive a new one. That speaks convincingly for postponing my trip to Palestine until this winter, since there may be special difficulties connected with obtaining a visa for Palestine on French temporary papers, which I would be able to get in any case. Meanwhile, I would be glad to hear from you how things look in the large and small world of Palestine. I understand the "large" world as being the English one, the small one *si licet* as that presided over by Buber. I've heard that he has meanwhile embarked on his way there.[1]

I acknowledge, with many thanks, receipt of the work on Sabbatarianism. I would render even more thanks to Schocken if he decided in favor of a German edition of your work.

Are you writing anything on the Kabbalah at the moment?

In closing, I must request your permission to reserve the report on Karl Kraus's last months—for all you may say—for when we see each other. The reason is that I have it secondhand, so you would be getting it thirdhand. Were this to coincide with the switch from the oral to the written, all that remained would be something wholly distorted. It already represents no small risk to attempt to convey verbally some of what vividly caught my attention in the version I heard.

I will most likely be staying in San Remo for another four weeks. A speedy letter from you would have a chance not only of reaching me here but of being answered from here as well.

Most cordial greetings, which I ask you to forward to your wife as well.

Yours, Walter

1. Buber would first move to Jerusalem for good about a year later. He went for a visit in June 1937.

288. To Fritz Lieb

San Remo
July 9, 1937

My dear Fritz Lieb,

This odd stationery may tell you that I am writing from abroad—at least if I designate Paris as home. For at the moment I am "at home" in another sense—in my former wife's home in San Remo. We are expecting Stefan [. . .].

Had we been sitting together—you in the frame of mind you were in when you addressed your letter to me; I in the frame of mind in which I am writing this letter—we would have been able to enjoy the most harmonious sullenness. It remains to be seen, however, whether I will be able to put mine to use as amusingly as you did yours in your wonderful description of Basel. I ask myself whether there might not perhaps be a kind of universal, historical, semiannual period in which demons, instead of those who are simply not free, rejoice at being alive and whether we might not have entered upon such a period. I can imagine that, on account of the conditions of our existence, we will appear distorted to later generations, as if we were dragging around with us a welter of abortions in the form of demonic parasites.

And there is a view onto gloom through whatever window we look. Not to mention through the economic spy hole left to us. A bit of blue fleetingly beckoned to me through it; it has meanwhile clouded over again. Hope of improvement has been postponed; a rise in the cost of living will, however, not be delayed. Do you remember our *quatorze juillet* together? How carefully calculated the displeasure now seems that we dared to utter only in an undertone at that time. If, however, you want to continue to advance your view of the politics of the People's Front, take a look at the French leftist press: all of the leftists cling only to the fetish of the "leftist" majority and it does not bother them that this majority pursues a politics with which the rightists would provoke revolts. In this regard, nothing is more instructive than the evolution of *Vendredi,* which I have been reading every week for two years. The level and intelligence of its contributors (always the same ones!) sink in proportion to the dislocation of the masses standing behind them.

In terms of the technical aspects of work as well, the state of things makes itself felt down to the least detail. Thus my long essay on Eduard Fuchs will not appear for the time being, so as not to influence unfavorably his endless negotiations with the German authorities over the release of his collection; at the same time, I see one of my favorite projects once again lose its almost tangible form. I had intended to write a critique of Jungian psychology, whose Fascist armature I had promised myself to expose. This has also been postponed. I am now turning to a project on Baudelaire.

I have little to say about emigration: even less from here than from Paris. The destructive effect of events in Russia will inevitably continue to spread. And the bad thing about this is not the facile indignation of the staunch fighters for "freedom of thought"; what appears to me to be much sadder and much more inevitable at one and the same time is the silence of thinking individuals who, precisely as thinking individuals, would have difficulty in taking themselves for informed individuals. This is the case with me, and probably also with you.

Gide has published his new book, *Retouches,*[1] which deals with his trip to Russia. I still have not seen it.

Here I will slip in a request: I believe you often have opportunity to acquaint people who might form an opinion of it with my *Deutsche Menschen*. Please do not neglect any opportunity to do so.

It is hardly necessary for me to tell you how delighted I was to receive the Leskov. I am terribly sad that he is giving signs that he may emigrate.

Is it certain that you will be coming to Paris in October? If so, you must now reserve two (in numbers: 2) evenings for us. I hope that you will by then have struck down as if by lightning some of the seven academic Swabians with the morning star of your *Weigel!*[2]

I am enclosing the 35 cts. stamp only because I place value on having Theophrastus[3] view me as a man of honor. It is difficult for me to part with it, because Stefen is sure not to have it. So that he will see, however, that a man of honor is a *gentilhomme,* I am also enclosing a few others.

I will unfortunately have to be in Paris again at the end of the month for the philosophy congress. Write to me soon and still at this address.

Let me express my sincere gratitude for your invitation. Unfortunately, however, I hardly think I will get to Switzerland so soon. And this gratitude is intended just as much for your wife. My most sincere regards and wishes to both you and your wife.

Yours, Walter Benjamin

1. *Retouches à mon retour de l'U.R.S.S.* (Paris, 1937).
2. *Valentin Weigels Kommentar zur Schöpfungsgeschichte und das Schrifttum seines Schülers Benedikt Biedermann: Eine literar-kritische Untersuchung zur mystischen Theologie des 16. Jahrhunderts,* which was first published in Zurich in 1962; Lieb dedicated it to "the memory of my two Paris friends from the House of Israel, Lev Isaakovitsch Schestov and Walter Benjamin."
3. Lieb's son, who, like WB's son Stefan, collected stamps.

289.* To Gerhard Scholem

Paris
August 5, 1937

Dear Gerhard,

These lines, which are to express my gratitude for your letter of July 10, are being written from Paris, at six in the morning. From Paris, because I was summoned away from San Remo to cover the philosophers' congress taking place here; at six in the morning because this congress doesn't leave me with a minute of free time all day.

It would certainly be tempting to write you about the congress in a few words, but the prospect of talking to you about it in person is far more inviting. This brings me to the part of your letter that evokes above all my thanks to you and your wife. I would indeed be happy to come to you, happy to come to Palestine, under the conditions you specify and for the period you have in mind. And I would already be sending you my acceptance today if I were master of my own arrangements. *Rebus sic stantibus,* I will advise the institute of my plans in the next few days. Difficulties—but the kind that would impel me to abandon the plan—should only arise if one of the directors intends to visit Europe this winter.

I hope to be able to accept your invitation in about a month.

Circumstances that would take too long to describe have entailed my following very closely the sessions of the special convention that the Viennese logistical school—Carnap,[1] Neurath, Reichenbach—has been holding. One feels free to say: *Molière n'a rien vu*. The *vis comica* of his debating doctors and philosophers pales in comparison with these "empirical philosophers." I haven't allowed this to deprive me of the chance to listen to the German idealist Arthur Liebert[2] at the main conference. He had hardly uttered his first few words when I found myself carried back twenty-five years into the past, into an atmosphere, to be sure, in which one could have already sensed all the decay of the present. Its products were sitting before me in the flesh in the form of the German delegation. Bäumler is impressive: his posture copies that of Hitler down to the last detail, and his bull neck perfectly complements the barrel of a revolver.—Unfortunately, I missed hearing old Tumarkin (from Bern) speak.[3]

I will be traveling back to San Remo in the middle of next week and will stay there for about a month. If you reply soon, as I very much hope, you can still direct the letter to the Villa Verde. I still don't have a very clear impression of Stefan's present condition; insofar as conclusions may already be drawn, he seems to have partly overcome the crisis in his development.

Under the aforementioned circumstances, I have no choice but to be brief. Allow me to congratulate you most sincerely on your anticipated—or by now received—invitation to New York. (Will you possibly be able to attempt something on your brother's behalf from there, with greater prospects of success?) What pleases me most about the invitation is that it promises us a chance to see each other in case I should not be able to come.

I was pleased to hear that the "Leskov" meant something to you.

A small fragment of my essay on *Elective Affinities* just appeared in French. Publication of the protracted essay on Fuchs seems to be imminent. I am about to embark on another project, which deals with Baudelaire. *En attendant,* in San Remo I have begun to delve into Jung's psychology—the devil's work through and through, which should be attacked with white magic.[4]

So much for today. Please write posthaste. Best of luck with the prolegomena to the Kabbalah book, which I am very pleased to learn will be accessible to me.

Most sincerely,

Yours, Walter

1. In *Briefe* [Frankfurt am Main: Suhrkamp Verlag, 1966—Trans.], p. 735, I read the name as "Bernay," which not only contradicts the way WB wrote his capital *B* but also distorts the name of Paul Bernays. The *C* at the beginning of the word is written in the customary form. Rudolf Carnap (1891–1954), Otto Neurath (1882–1945), and Hans Reichenbach (1891–1953) were the acknowledged central figures of the "Vienna circle" of logistical positivists.

2. Liebert (1878–1946) had long been the editor of the journal *Kant-Studien* until it was "gleichgeschaltet" [forced into line] by the Nazis.

3. In the summer of 1918 we had both attended Anna Tumarkin's lectures in Bern. WB originally planned to write his doctorate under her.

4. WB also expressed his views on C. G. Jung's psychology in letters to Horkheimer and Adorno (as early as 1934!), but as far as I know he did not leave a substantive critique behind in his papers.

290. To Max Horkheimer

Paris
[August 10, 1937]

Dear Mr. Horkheimer,

To my delight, I have heard this very moment that you are coming to Europe sometime in August. I hope this means that I will see you this month or at the beginning of next month.

I will therefore defer the topics about which I recently wanted to write you and limit myself to telling you how much I am looking forward to the imminent publication of my "Fuchs" essay.

I have read your essay, "Traditionelle und kritische Theorie,"[1] as you will assume, in complete agreement. The way you characterize the atmosphere in which our work proceeds and the reasons you give for its isolation are particularly relevant to me. We will certainly also speak about these things.

I will probably leave Paris the same day as Wiesengrund, namely on the 12th. Meanwhile, my son has arrived in San Remo. I will attempt to form my own judgment about the most recent changes in him. [. . .]

May I ask you to write and tell me, immediately after your arrival—if not from New York—where and when I can meet you?

Please proceed on the assumption that I will be able to come without any difficulty from one day to the next, in fact just as easily to Geneva as to Paris.

Sincere regards.
Yours, Walter Benjamin

1. *Zeitschrift für Sozialforschung* 6 (1937), pp. 245–94.

291. To Karl Thieme

Boulogne
October 10, 1937

Dear Mr. Thieme,

Circumstances have confronted me with an unpleasant dilemma that I am resolving by telling you about it. I had the choice of indefinitely putting off writing these lines or else of eliminating from them what might have given them some value in your eyes, if all else fails: observations that I thought to make on your essay "Marxismus und Messianismus."[1]

When I returned home from my summer vacation, I found my room occupied by strangers because of the unforeseeable machinations of my former landlords. I had my hands full transporting my most important papers to safety, i.e. to temporary quarters. I have not yet been able to do the same for my library and thus am for the time being in no position to look at the text of your essay for a second time. I know that, after I read it for the first time, it gave rise to reflections that I planned to communicate to you. We will consequently still have to be patient about this matter. In lieu of that, while I still feel the immediate effect of your criticism of Weidlé, I can at least convey to you my agreement with your most basic reservations about the book: I refer to your objection to the simpleminded attempt to establish a connection with existing efforts of Christian religious art, which have for the most part been influenced by fashion and compromises. But what I might have wished added to this would have been a word about Weidlé's particularly frivolous use of the concept "style." He has no notion of the great extent to which what we call style is also determined by the centuries-long survival of products in which we encounter it. He seems to me to have no insight whatsoever into its historical dimension and it is his flat argumentation from the perspective of a specific "state of affairs" that seems to me to give his representations their journalistic character, which stands in an incongruous relationship to his secular standards.

If I might return for a moment to "The Storyteller," I note that the reference to Origen's concept of apocatastasis was conceived by me simply as an immanent explication of the world of Leskov's imagination. I myself did not want to expound on this subject. I could, however, well imagine that I would have done so at one time; I take it from your letter that Wiesengrund has done so. Where in his works is the concept of fulfillment "without sacrifice" to be found?[2]—I will remain deeply indebted to you for everything you may be able to tell me about the doctrine of the "postponement" of the judgment.

Do you occasionally come across Fritz Lieb in Basel? If so, please give him my regards. Brecht is here at the moment. He spent a little time on a new French production of *The Three-Penny Opera* [*Die Dreigroschenoper*] and is currently rehearsing a small piece with his wife that is set during the time of the Spanish Civil War.[3]

Thank you for inquiring about my *Deutsche Menschen*. It appears that they are making their way in the world. The more tortuously it winds through the German countryside and the less it intersects with its highways, the better!

Everything relegates me, even more than is usually the case, to the limited circle of some few friends and the narrower or broader circle of my own work.

Sincere regards
Yours, Walter Benjamin

1. Presumably "Gemeinsamkeiten und Unterschiede zwischen frühchristlicher und marxistischer Eschatologie," *Religiöse Besinnung* 4 (1931).

2. A phrase Adorno probably used in a letter.

3. *Die Gewehre der Frau Carrar*. Premiere performance on October 16, 1937.

292.* To Gerhard Scholem

Paris
[November 20, 1937]

Dear Gerhard,

This time I'm avoiding letting even the slightest term elapse before replying to your last letter. It contained the announcement of your coming and the critique of the "Fuchs." Both are joined in my mind, just as they are in yours. It is really urgent that we speak with one another soon, indeed it can hardly be delayed. Not that the reservations you have about the "Fuchs" surprise me in the least. But the subject of the work—precisely because it seems so threadbare—offers an opportunity to debate the merits of the method it lets shine through, an opportunity that may not present itself so advantageously soon again. It is well suited to gain us access to the realms in which our debates were originally at home.

Under these circumstances, the dates you have in mind for your stay in Europe are a great disappointment, following the many frustrated schemes for my appearance in Palestine. Does it really surprise you that half a day seems to me less than nothing, after so many years and given the present status of both public events and our private affairs? Half a day is of a dimension that could very easily turn out to be negative, even if the blame for it is not to be sought with one or the other of us. My reservations about this proposal carry all the more weight since no guarantee exists that the summer meeting, if you want to set it for Paris, can take place. I don't yet know where I will be during the summer; I will probably spend a number of weeks with Dora in San Remo. Also under consideration is a trip to Denmark, from where I would like to transfer a part of the fraction of my library back to Paris.

This leads me to the brief remarks I wish to devote to the present state of my private life. I did not recover my former lodgings, and I have struggled along for the last two months with wretched ones that were put at my disposal for free. They are situated at ground level on one of the main thoroughfares outside Paris, where countless trucks roar from morning till night. My ability to work has suffered considerably under these circumstances. I haven't got beyond doing the background reading for the "Charles Baudelaire" I am preparing.

As of January 15th, I will be renting my own place. It has only one room.[1] And yet furnishing it presents me with an unresolved problem. In the interim, I ask that you quickly send what I hope will be more welcome news to me at my sister's address. If you have 65 or 70 francs a day at your disposal, you can make do in Paris rather comfortably.

Sincerely,
Yours, Walter

1. The room was quite spacious, however, as I was able to ascertain during my visit.

293. To Max Horkheimer

San Remo
January 6, 1938

Dear Mr. Horkheimer,

As you know, shortly before the eleventh hour the Wiesengrunds were able to realize our old plan of meeting in my ex-wife's boarding house. My son is also here now. I arrived ten days ago and will stay on a few days longer than the Wiesengrunds, who unfortunately are leaving the day after tomorrow.

A bitter cold front is passing through Italy at the moment. We often have to stay indoors. Still, I hope that their stay here will do Teddie[1] and his wife good; their fear of the ocean crossing occasionally casts a shadow on it.

These have certainly been productive days in terms of our common interests. Teddie read me a number of studies for his *Wagner*.[2] The stunningly new thing about them for me was that, in a totally unfamiliar way, they make socially transparent the state of musical affairs, which could not be any more remote for anyone than it is for me. From another perspective, *one* inclination of this work was of particular interest to me: to lodge the physiognomic directly within the societal space, almost without any psychological mediation. I am eager to have the whole thing in front of me. It is terribly intricate in terms of its motifs.

On a number of occasions, our conversations revolved around my preliminary studies for the "Baudelaire." In recent weeks, I made a rare find that will decisively influence this work: I came upon the last thing Blanqui wrote in his final prison, the Fort du Taureau. It consists of a cosmological speculation. The work is called *L'éternité par les astres*[3] and, as far as I can tell, has been as good as ignored to the present day. (Gustave Geffroy mentions it in his exemplary Blanqui monograph, *L'enfermé,*[4] without knowing what he is dealing with.) It must be admitted that the text appears tasteless and banal when you first leaf through it. Meanwhile, the clumsy reflections of an autodidact, of which most of it consists, prepare the way for speculation about the universe, which is more unexpected coming from this great revolutionary than it would be from anyone else. If hell is a theological subject, this speculation may be defined as theological. While deriving his data from mechanistic natural science, the worldview that Blanqui outlines is in fact an infernal view, and is at the same time, in the form of a natural view, the complement to a social order that Blanqui had to recognize as victorious over him in the last years of his life. The shocking thing is that this outline lacks all irony. It represents unconditional submission, but at the same time the most terrible accusation against a society that has reflected this image of the cosmos as a projection of itself onto the heavens. In its theme of "the eternal return," the piece has the most remarkable relationship to Nietzsche: a more obscure and profound relationship to Baudelaire, whom it almost literally echoes in some splendid passages. I will make the effort to bring this latter relationship to light.

Gide is correct in writing that no poet of the nineteenth century has been talked about more stupidly than Baudelaire. The mark of Baudelaire commentaries is that, in all fundamental aspects, they could have been written the same way had Baudelaire never written *Flowers of Evil*. They are, in fact, challenged in their entirety by his theological writings, by his memorabilia, and above all by the *chronique scandaleuse*. The reason is that the limits of bourgeois thinking and even certain bourgeois ways of reacting would have had to be discarded—not in order to find pleasure in one or another of these poems, but specifically in order to feel at home in the *Flowers of Evil* . . . difficult enough, by the way, even if that were the only condition; but there are others that are obvious and are not any easier to fulfill for anyone whose native language is not French. Once having returned to Paris, I will try to have some French acquaintances read the Baudelaire poems to me.

Together we occasionally tried our hands at the essay for *Maß und Wert*,[5] but did not get beyond some fragments. I assume that you will soon let me know your opinion of the letters from [Ferdinand] Lion.

I am sincerely grateful for your letter of December 5th. I quite understand the disappointment you felt upon receiving *Mesures*. The journal has published issues that are considerably more worth reading. By the way, it is less a mistress than a master of the house who will preside over the planned salon, a patron by the name of Church, who in this way promotes the publication of his own writings. Adrienne Monnier has little influence on the editorial board; I recently heard that she has also turned over its administration to Joseph Corti Books, starting at the end of the year. I very much hope that the next issues will make a better showing. Otherwise, Miss Monnier has not entirely given up on the plan of again starting up her own journal, which is what *Navire d'argent* was years ago.

I was particularly delighted to hear that Monsieur Lyonnet meant something to you. The author writes mostly for children. He has probably never written anything better than this novel.

[. . .]

Might I ask you to allow me to postpone for some weeks my response to your kind inquiry about my personal situation? I will be in a position to calculate my budget precisely only after I get back. An additional factor is that rents under legal rent control will again be in flux after a law passed in the final session of the assembly. I will find out the extent to which I am affected by it only when I am in Paris.

Let me in conclusion express my hope that you have had the time to devote to Montaigne.[6] A social critique of skepticism is new territory and, I believe, well worth knowing.

Please give Mr. Pollock my sincere regards and extend to him my best wishes for the health of his wife. Best wishes to you and your wife for the new year.

Yours, Walter Benjamin

1. Adorno.
2. *Versuch über Wagner* [*In Search of Wagner*] (Berlin and Frankfurt am Main, 1952).
3. Paris, 1872.
4. Paris, 1897.

5. WB wrote this essay on the *Zeitschrift für Sozialforschung* on his own; it appeared in *Maß und Wert* 1 (1937–38), pp. 818–22.

6. "Montaigne und die Funktion der Skepsis," *Zeitschrift für Sozialforschung* 7 (1938), pp. 1–54.

294. To Karl Thieme

Paris
March 9, 1938

Dear Mr. Thieme,

I have had your letter of December and even your well-filled parcel for quite some time now. From the outset, you will have been sure of the eager interest with which I read your review of the Buber-Rosenzweig Bible translation[1] and will have attributed the delay in my response to circumstances having nothing to do with the matter at hand.

It must indeed be attributed to just such circumstances. Among them was a series of very pressing tasks—but the delay was particularly due to the fact that my concentration was repeatedly broken by a move to a small apartment—my first since I emigrated. I am far from having found the most desirable working conditions in my new lodgings; my apartment is besieged by various noises day in and day out. It nonetheless allows me for once to gather together more or less all of my papers, to the extent I was able to salvage them; for another thing, it allows me to have friends over.

I certainly hope that there is a prospect of us spending some quiet hours together at my place the next time you come to Paris.

One of the first people to turn up here was Gerhard Scholem; he stopped in Paris for a few days on his way to New York, where he is to give some guest lectures. Among other things, we talked about Buber. For more than a decade now, we have taken rather different positions on him. Unfortunately being relatively unburdened by expert knowledge, I have an easier time formulating my position unambiguously. The same thing naturally holds for my position on you. In mind of the cursory glance I took at the books of the Bible over the years, I would like to say today that in my heart of hearts I doubted whether the years in which this project was executed truly represented the moment in world history when it might properly have been risked. I agree with you about the fundamental value of such a risk—you will know this to be so from my "Task of the Translator." Specifically in connection with this work, I would like to pose more urgently than you in the question of the temporal index of such an attempt. I am completely convinced by the examples with which you support your objections to the problematical German sentence structure of the Buber translation. I believe I am an even stricter judge of that kind of transgression than you—better yet, I am inclined to look at these transgressions as symptomatic and, at the present moment, to derive from them the most serious reservations about the historical justification of Buber's attempt.

This may also be part of your own reflections; it is, of course, all the more impossible to express such things publicly the more clearly they are illustrated by public conditions. It is obvious that your own project, which is Christian in the best sense of the word, will be something entirely different. The most appealing thing to me about the prospectus was the comments with which you gloss the text in the pneumatological sense. I was hardly less attracted by the basic observations with which you so clearly defend the language against the shoddiness of the commercial artist with which it is saddled by many translators.

If I am not mistaken and if a judgment can be formed on the basis of the one sample, [Richard] Seewald's woodcuts are unfortunately unable to avoid the qualities of commercial art as strictly as you. I would like to hear your opinion of them when you have a chance.

As far as Roeßler[2] is concerned, I was told it was currently a useful habit—or bad habit—of publishers to have the third or fourth hundred copies of a book be counted as a "new edition." In spite of all of this, it is difficult for me to imagine that in one and a quarter years a market has presumably been found for only two hundred copies of the book—as the accounting statement indicates.

I asked around about the book by Grete de Francesco,[3] unfortunately without the desired success. Local publishers are afraid of the production costs incurred by a decently illustrated book.

I really hope to hear good things from you very soon. I may be able to send you some kind of offprint again in the near future. But please do not make me wait for news until then!

Sincere regards.

Yours, Walter Benjamin

P.S. Please let me know whether and when some of your Basel lectures will appear in print. My interest in the figure of the storyteller has not waned.—I am currently trying to search out the book by Jolles[4] to which you referred me.

And, if you would not consider it an annoyance, please try to write me a few words about your latest experiences with Roeßler, to which you allude.

1. "Das ewige Wort in der Sprache unserer Zeit," *Neue Schweizer Rundschau* (February 1938).

2. Attached to the Vita Nova Verlag in Lucerne.

3. *Die Macht des Scharlatans* (1937). Reviewed by WB in the *Zeitschrift für Sozialforschung* 7 (1938), pp. 296ff.

4. Probably André Jolles, *Einfache Formen* (1930).

295. To Karl Thieme

Paris
March 27, 1938

Dear Mr. Thieme,

In the same spirit as your last letter, if not for the same reason, I ask you to forgive me if, by way of exception, the typewriter has imposed itself between us.

I was extremely moved by your letter of the 12th with its passionate reaction to events in Austria; I do not want to put off responding very long. On the other hand, I am so behind in my correspondence that I must seek refuge in extraordinary measures. I cannot prevent a laconic response to your words from giving you an idea of my mood, in addition to an idea of my way of thinking. I fear that your mood will appear almost lighthearted compared to mine.

As for me, to put it bluntly, I hardly know anymore where to get an idea of *sensible* suffering and dying. In the case of Austria, no less than in the case of Spain, the horrible thing seems to me that martyrdom is suffered not in the name of the individual's own cause, but rather in the name of a suggested compromise: whether it is the precious ethnic culture of Austria being compromised by a discredited industry and government-owned business, or revolutionary thought in Spain being compromised by the Machiavellianism of the Russian leadership and the indigenous leadership's worship of Mammon.

In short, no matter how wide I cast my gaze, I find the horizon to be just as doomed as the beings who exist before my eyes. Given all of this, I must still consider myself lucky that my son, who until recently was in Vienna, is now with his mother in Italy.

It hardly bears thinking what is in store for Austrian Jews. In their case, as opposed to what the situation was in Germany, it is impossible for even the well-off to flee. We no longer have even the petty comfort that whispers to us that you and I would have been smarter in the same situation. For I do not believe that.

Did you ever give a thought to the fact that, with the occupation of Vienna, one-fifth or one-sixth of European art treasures is in the hands of the National Socialists?

I am really looking forward to getting your Bible soon.

I still have no plans for the summer. It is nonetheless quite possible that I will be in Paris, should you come in August.

Thank you for the news about Roeßler and sincere regards.

Yours, Walter Benjamin

296.* To Gerhard Scholem

Paris
April 14, 1938

Dear Gerhard,

Your first news from America took a considerable time in coming. It includes much that pleases me.

In the first place, word of the success of your lectures. That must mean that your stay over there is less problematic, at least as far as the language is concerned, than you had initially assumed.

In your ensuing communications, I also hope to profit from this by having you unfurl "cultural and travel images" from the diverse regions and social strata. [*Amerikanische*] *Reisebilder* by Theodor Dielitz was one of my favorite books as a youth, and it was set over there as well.

I further expect that you will initiate me into the secret of Jewish starbirth: courteously return the greetings of the united wizard pair [the Gutkinds].

Mercy really did send me Brod's Kafka biography at my request, and with it the volume beginning with "Description of a Struggle." So it seems that now the six-volume edition lacks only the *Tagebücher und Briefe*. Has it already appeared? If so, where? Please reply without delay.

I speak of Kafka at this point, however, because the biography, in its interweaving of Kafkaesque ignorance and Brodesque sagacity, seems to reveal a district of the spiritual world where white magic and spurious witchcraft interplay in the most edifying manner. I haven't yet been able to read it much, but I at once appropriated for myself the Kafkaesque formulation of the categorical imperative: "Act in such a way that the angels have something to do." I only read it intermittently, my attention and my time are now almost undividedly devoted to the "Baudelaire." Not a word of it has yet been written, but I have been schematizing the whole thing for a week now. The organization is, as goes without saying, decisive. I wasn't to show how Baudelaire is embedded in the nineteenth century, and the vision of this must be seen as fresh as that of a stone that has been lodged in the soil of a forest for decades, and whose imprint—after we have laboriously rolled it away from its place—lies before us with pristine distinctness.

Your portrayal of the conversation with the two Tillichs aroused my profound interest, but caused me much less surprise than you thought it would. The point here is precisely that things whose place is at present in shadow *de parte et d'autre* might be cast in a false light when subjected to artificial lighting. I say "at present" because the current epoch, which makes so many things impossible, most certainly does not preclude this: that the right light should fall on precisely those things in the course of the historical rotation of the sun. I want to take this even further and say that our works can, for their part, be measuring instruments, which, if they function well, measure the tiniest segments of that unimaginably slow rotation.[1]

For these reasons I look forward with some confidence to your encounter with Horkheimer and Wiesengrund, which may have already taken place, if not repeated itself, by the time you receive these lines. My sense of confidence grew through my encounter, just days ago, with the institute's codirector, which turned out to be as genial as it was brief.

I don't yet have a clear view of how my summer will be arranged. As far as I can tell, everything would be very simple if you still have the second half of August free for Paris. I'm not sure if I can be back from Denmark for the first half.—We will certainly return to this point later.

Don't make me wait nearly as long for news this time as last time. Write to me about the "paths and the encounters" that were yours. Convey my kind regards to my New York friends when you get the chance and, whatever happens, don't forget to give them to Moses Marx.

All the best,
Yours, Walter

1. Few passages (if any) in WB's letters to me possess such an unmistakably esoteric, if not almost conspiratorial, tone as this paragraph on his position with regard to the Institute for Social Research. I dare not decide whether the reference to the role of "our works" means the work he did in the orbit of the institute, or instead works by people like him and me. At the time I associated it, given the strange context in which it appears here (and following our conversations in Paris), with both of us, but I am no longer so sure about this.

297. To Max Horkheimer

Paris
April 16, 1938

Dear Mr. Horkheimer,

I am writing this letter three days after my meeting with Mr. Pollock. The meeting went every bit as well as I might have hoped. We spent two very pleasant hours in a small restaurant near Notre Dame. I—an old Parisian!—had to be introduced to this restaurant by Pollock.

As brief as it was, I hope our discussion will result in a useful personal contact for me. I informed Mr. Pollock how desirable I would consider an occasional exchange of ideas with an economist, and he will introduce me to Mr. [Otto] Leichter.

This desire is naturally relasted to my work, which we discussed for a while. I am currently working on my "Baudelaire." It has turned out—and I told Mr. Pollock this—that this is becoming an extensive treatment in which the most important motifs of the *Arcades* project converge. You might just as easily attribute this to the subject as to the fact that the section that had been planned as central to the book is being written first. In my conversations with Teddie, I had anticipated this tendency of my "Baudelaire" to develop into a miniature of the *Arcades*. Ever since San Remo, this has proven to be even truer than I anticipated.

Anyway, Mr. Pollock asked me to inform you of this, because you had originally expected a manuscript of the usual length. I was aware of that but believed it would be all the better if one of my essays were for once to assume the proportions of a longer work. I continue to hope even now that no crucial reservations will stand in its way; I really do not know how I could squeeze the critical aspects of the subject into thirty or forty pages. What I have in mind as its maximum length—I am referring to manuscript pages—is three times that, and perhaps twice that as its minimum length. In the latter case, the length of this work would therefore not be all that different from my "reproduction" essay.

I am currently working on the organization of the essay and have already collected the material I need for it. I found a profusion of material. I give you my word that I will cite as sparingly as possible from the contemporary secondary literature on Baudelaire. Little that has already been said about Baudelaire will have to be repeated and I will not have to go very deeply into his biography. I will cite extensively from the *Flowers of Evil*. I am planning to annotate individual passages of that work; this has not been done thus far for anything other than anecdotal purposes.

The work will be in three parts. Their projected titles are "Idea and Image"; "Antiquity and Modernity"; "The New and the Immutable." The first part will demonstrate the crucial importance of allegory for the *Flowers of Evil*. It shows how the allegorical vision in Baudelaire is constructed. Through this, the fundamental paradox of his theory of art—the contradiction between the theory of natural correspondences and the rejection of nature—should become transparent. An introduction will establish the work's methodological relationship to dialectical materialism in the form of a confrontation of "salvation" with the customary "apologia."

The second part develops the fade-in/fade-out effect as a structural element of the allegorical vision. As a consequence of this effect, antiquity is revealed in modernity, and modernity in antiquity. This process defines the *tableaux parisiens,* those written in verse and those written in prose. The crowd critically affects this transfiguration of Paris. The crowd places itself like a veil in front of the flaneur: it is the latest drug of the isolated individual.—Second, the crowd obliterates all traces of the individual: it is the outcast's latest place of asylum.—Finally, the crowd is the latest and most unfathomable labyrinth in the labyrinth of the city. Through it, previously unknown chthonic features engrave themselves on the cityscape.—What the poet saw as his task was to reveal these aspects of Paris. The concept of this task divides the structure under discussion. In Baudelaire's terms, nothing in his own century comes closer to the task of the hero of antiquity than the task of giving form to modernity.

The third part treats the commodity as the fulfillment of Baudelaire's allegorical vision. It turns out that what is new, which explodes the experience of the immutable under whose spell the poet was placed by spleen, is nothing other than the halo of the commodity. Two excursuses properly belong here. One pursues the extent to which *Jugendstil* appears as preformed in Baudelaire's conception of the new; the other deals with the prostitute as the commodity that most perfectly realizes the allegorical vision. The diffuseness of the allegorical pretext is rooted in this realization. Baudelaire's unique importance consists in having been the first one, and the most unswerving, to have apprehended, in both senses of the word, the productive energy of the individual alienated from himself—agnosticized and heightened through concretization. By this means, the isolated formal analyses that are found in various sections of the work converge in a coherent context.

While the figure of Baudelaire appears in monographic isolation in the first part, his most important virtual and real encounters—those with Poe, with Méryon, with Victor Hugo—come to the foreground in the second part. The third part deals with the historical configuration, where the *Flowers of Evil* joins Blanqui's *Éternité par les astres* and Nietzsche's *Will to Power* [*Der Wille zur Macht*] (the eternal return) by virtue of the idée fixe of the new and the immutable.

If I might use one image to express what I am planning, it is to show Baudelaire as he is embedded in the nineteenth century. The impression he left behind there must emerge as clearly untouched as that of a stone that one day is rolled away from the spot on which it has rested for decades.

I hope that you will consent to my writing the essay based on this plan, which emerges more clearly with each passing day. It seems to me that possible problems concerning its publication will be easier to overcome than new ones that may arise with a change in its internal structure.

I have nothing to report today as far as new publications are concerned. You may have seen Gide's dispute with Céline in the April issue of the NRF. "If one were forced to see in *Bagatelles pour un massacre*[1] anything other than a game, it would be impossible to excuse Céline, in spite of all his genius, for stirring up banal passions with such cynicism and frivolous impertinence" (p. 634). The word *banal* speaks for itself. As you will recall, I was also struck by Céline's lack of seriousness. Gide, being the moralist he is, otherwise pays heed only to the book's intent and not to its consequences. Or, being the Satanist he also is, has he no objections to them?

Since I am now treading on slippery ground, I would like to enclose an especially bizarre and poisonous bloom that has grown in this region. The following sentence can be read in Léon Daudet's *Stupide XIXe siècle:* "Behind Kant is the Jew Hamann, from whom Kant borrows his famous distinction between phenomena and noumena" (p. 185). The book appeared in 1922. When will the alliance between ignorance and baseness that was joined in Germany at precisely that time also become operative here?

By the way, on pp. 96–97 of the same book, you will find a comparison between Montaigne and Renan. I am letting you know about it, although it seemed too uninteresting for me to copy. Should it pique your curiosity, please let me know.

I was really delighted by your telegram, from which I gathered that you liked the review for *Maß und Wert*. Let me thank you for this and at the same time confirm my receipt of your letters of March 7, 15, and 28.—Yesterday I received the issue[2] in which my review appeared in the form of an advertisement for the *Zeitschrift für Sozialforschung*. The review was four printed pages. I am sending it to you at the same time as this letter.—I am glad it is all wrapped up because I considered it possible up to the last moment that Lion might present me with a fait inaccompli. [. . .]

I am looking forward to your "Montaigne." Will it be in the next issue? Please extend my most sincere regards to your wife and friends.

Yours, Walter Benjamin

1. Céline's anti-Semitic book (1937).
2. Of *Maß und Wert*.

298. To Karl Thieme

Paris
May 1, 1938

Dear Mr. Thieme,

No matter how modest the expectations with which you open this letter, I fear you will still be somewhat disappointed in it. In any case, it saddens me to express inadequately my gratitude to you for the gift of your Bible edition.[1]

I do not wish to be so presumptuous as to suggest that the only person who could thank you appropriately is someone with insight into the immense undertaking now behind you. But I would at least have liked, more than anything else, to have interspersed my thanks with evidence of my reading steadily into this work. My own work is the reason this is impossible at this time.

In the last fourteen days, I have nonetheless been able to devote some rather extended breaks from my own work to reading yours. I of course have no right to make a *judgment* that would pretend to even a hint of expert knowledge. In spite of that, I do want to tell you that I had the *impression* of making the acquaintance of something superbly useful. I call the book useful because it seems to me to accomplish something very important and very difficult: holding its own in the face of how our contemporaries read and live. I felt the effects of a lofty seductiveness emanating from the disposition of your text.

What was simply momentous for me was the clarity with which the text's epic and didactic foundations are thrown into relief in your interpretation and in your interpolations. Because of this, the layman feels he is learning something at every turn. And today the alpha and omega of reading the Bible may be to awaken this feeling.

Out of respect for your work, I must leave things at such preliminary comments, at least until a material reason leads me to a more precise examination of one or the other passage. In spite of this, I hope you will recognize the most sincere gratitude in my thanks for the book!

The friend whose visit you announced has not as yet made his appearance. After your letter, he may be certain of a friendly reception even without showing his credentials as a connoisseur of my writings.

Have you seen the journal *Ordo,* published under the auspices of the Comité juif des études politiques, 22 rue Caumartin, Paris IX? It still is not clear to me what these people are after.[2] It seems to me that the journal frequently hits the nail on the head in its critique of the Jews' public conduct and of their public reactions. I wish you would take a look at the thing and tell me what you think of it.

I am reading Benda's *Régulier dans le siécle*. You are sure to have been interested in the man for a long time already and I would welcome hearing what kind of impression he makes on you. Let me ask one question in conclusion. In 1932, I began writing a slender volume, *Berliner Kindheit um 1900*. Perhaps you have seen the parts of it published in the *Frankfurter Zeitung* before Hitler came to power. I have added to this book and revised it extensively in the last few weeks. It will be difficult to find a publisher for it because of its subject matter. If one is found, the book might turn into a noteworthy publishing success. It has something to say to thousands of German refugees. But a publisher might have a harder time recognizing this than the average reader.

Do you have any idea of what the book is like? If not, would it be useful for me to send you its one hundred manuscript pages for fourteen days? Is there anyone within your purview whom you could persuade to take an interest in the thing?

Most sincere regards.

Yours, Walter Benjamin

1. *Herders Laienbibel* (1958).
2. *Ordo* had Jewish-territorial but anti-Zionist tendencies. Alfred Döblin (in the period before his conversion) and Victor Zuckerkandl were among its contributors.

299.* To Gerhard Scholem

Paris
June 12, 1938

Dear Gerhard,

At your request, I'm writing you at length what I think of Brod's *Kafka*. After that, you will find some of my own reflections on Kafka.

You should know from the outset that this letter will be reserved entirely for this subject, which is of profound concern to us both. For news of me, you'll have to be patient for a day or two.

Brod's book is characterized by the fundamental contradiction that obtains between the author's thesis, on the one hand, and the attitude he adopts, on the other. The latter serves rather to discredit the former, not to speak of the other reservations that must be made about it. The thesis states that Kafka found himself on the path to saintliness (p. 49).[1] But the attitude taken by the biographer is one of supreme bonhomie. Its lack of detachment is its most salient feature.

The *very fact* that *this* attitude could avail itself of *this* opinion of the subject robs the book of its authority from the outset. *How* this has been done is illustrated, for instance, by the turn of phrase that introduces "our Franz" to the reader via a photograph (p. 127).[2] Intimacy with the saintly has its own special appellation in the history of religion: pietism. Brod's attitude as a biographer amounts to a pietistic stance of ostentatious intimacy—in other words, the most irreverent attitude imaginable.

This slovenliness in the work's economy is underscored by habits the author may have acquired in the course of his professional activities. At any rate, it is virtually impossible to overlook the traces of his journalistic hackwork, down to the very formulation of his thesis: "The category of saintliness . . . is truly the only correct category in which Kafka's life and work can be considered" (p. 49). Is it necessary to state that saintliness is an order reserved for life, and that artistic creation does not belong to it under any circumstances? And does it need to be pointed out that the epithet of saintliness is nothing more than a novelist's empty phrase when used outside a traditionally established religious framework?

Brod lacks the merest sense of that pragmatic circumspection which should be required of a first biography of Kafka. "We knew nothing of deluxe hotels and were nevertheless happy as larks" (p. 103). On account of the author's striking lack of tact, of a feeling for thresholds and distances, feuilletonistic clichés have seeped into a text that should have been obliged to exhibit a certain dignity, given its very subject. This is not so much the reason for, as evidence of, the extent to which Brod has been denied any authentic vision of Kafka's life. This inability to do justice to his subject becomes especially scandalous where Brod discusses the famous instructions in Kafka's will (p. 198), in which the latter charges Brod with the task of destroying his papers. There if anywhere would have been the ideal place to broach fundamental aspects of Kafka's existence. (He was obviously unwilling to bear responsibility to posterity for a work whose greatness he was well aware of.)

The question has often been considered since Kafka's death; one might have done well to let the matter rest for once. That would have meant some soul-searching on the part of the biographer, of course. Kafka presumably had to entrust his posthumous papers to someone who would be unwilling to carry out his last wishes. And neither the testator nor his biographer would be harmed by looking at things in this way. But that would require the ability to gauge the tensions that permeated Kafka's life.

That Brod lacks this ability is demonstrated by the passages in which he sets out to comment on Kafka's work or style. He doesn't get beyond dilettantish rudiments. The singularity of Kafka's being and his writing is certainly not merely an "apparent one," as Brod would have it, any more than you come near to Kafka's depictions with the insight that they "are nothing but true" (p. 52). Such digressions on Kafka's work are of a kind that render Brod's interpretation of Kafka's Weltanschauung problematic from the very start. When Brod says of Kafka that he more or less followed

Buber's line (p. 198), this amounts to looking for a butterfly in the net over which it casts its fluttering shadow. The "as it were realistic-Jewish interpretation" of *The Castle* suppresses the repulsive and horrible features with which Kafka furnishes the upper world in favor of an edifying interpretation which the Zionist ought to be the first to view with suspicion.

Occasionally, such smugness, so out of keeping with its subject, divulges itself even to a reader who is not all that punctilious. It remained up to Brod to illustrate the intricate difficulties of symbol and allegory, which he considers important for the interpretation of Kafka's work, by the example of the "tin soldier," which constitutes a valid symbol because it not only "expresses much . . . that extends into infinity," but also touches us "through the story of his fate as a tin soldier, in all its detail" (p. 194). One might like to know how the Star of David would look in the light of such a theory of symbols.

Brod's awareness of the deficiency of his own Kafka interpretation sensitizes him to the interpretations of others. It makes one uneasy to see the way he brushes aside the surrealists' by no means foolish interest in Kafka as well as Werner Kraft's in some measure significant interpretations of the short prose pieces. Beyond that, he is clearly making an effort to belittle any future writing on Kafka. "Thus one could go on and on explaining (and some will indeed do so), but necessarily without coming to an end" (p. 53). The emphasis on the words in parentheses is obvious. That "Kafka's many private, accidental failings and sufferings" contribute more to the understanding of his work than do "theological constructions" (p. 174) is unwelcome coming from a man who is resolute enough to base his own presentation of Kafka upon the concept of saintliness. The same dismissive gesture is used against everything that Brod found disturbing in his acquaintanceship with Kafka—psychoanalysis as well as dialectic theology. It allows him to contrast Kafka's style with Balzac's "fraudulent exactness" (p. 52)—and all he has in mind here are those transparent rodomontades that cannot possibly be separated from Balzac's work and its greatness.

None of this originates in Kafka's intentions. Brod all too often misses the assurance, the equanimity so peculiar to Kafka. There is no man alive—as Joseph de Maistre said—who cannot be won over with a moderate opinion. Brod's book does not win one over. It oversteps moderation both in the way in which he pays homage to Kafka and in the familiarity with which he treats him. Both presumably have their prelude in the novel for which his friendship with Kafka served as the subject.[3] The inclusion of passages from that novel by no means represents the least of this biographer's improprieties. By his own admission, the author is surprised that outsiders could believe that the novel contained an affront to the piety due the deceased. "This was misunderstood just as everything else is. . . . People failed to remember that Plato, who in a similar, albeit much more comprehensive way, wrested his friend and teacher Socrates away from Death, all his life seeing him as a companion who continued to live, work, and think by his side, and making him the protagonist of almost every dialogue he wrote after Socrates' death" (p. 64).

There is little chance that Brod's *Kafka* will someday rank among the great standard biographies of men of letters, in a class with Schwab's *Hölderlin* or Bächtold's *Keller*. It is all the more memorable as the document of a friendship that is not among the smallest mysteries of Kafka's life.

You will see from the preceding, dear Gerhard, why an analysis of Brod's biography—even if only in a polemical way—seems to me unsuitable as a vehicle to offer a glimpse of my own image of Kafka. It remains to be seen, of course, whether the following notes will succeed in sketching that image. In any case, they will introduce you to a new aspect, one that is more or less independent of my earlier reflections.

Kafka's work is an ellipse with foci that lie far apart and are determined on the one hand by mystical experience (which is above all the experience of tradition)[4] and on the other by the experience of the modern city dweller. When I speak of the experience of the city dweller, I subsume a variety of things under this notion. On the one hand, I speak of the modern citizen, who knows he is at the mercy of vast bureaucratic machinery, whose functioning is steered by authorities who remain nebulous even to the executive organs themselves, let alone the people they deal with. (It is well known that this encompasses one level of meaning in the novels, especially in *The Trial*). On the other hand, by modern city dwellers I am speaking of the contemporary of today's physicist. If you read the following passage from Eddington's *Nature of the Physical World*, you can virtually hear Kafka speak.

> I am standing on the threshold about to enter a room. It is a complicated business. In the first place I must shove against an atmosphere pressing with a force of fourteen pounds on every square inch of my body. I must make sure of landing on a plank traveling at twenty miles a second around the sun—a fraction of a second too early or too late, the plank would be miles away. I must do this while hanging from a round planet heading outward into space, and with a wind of ether blowing at no one knows how many miles a second through every interstice of my body. The plank has no solidity of substance. To step on it is like stepping on a swarm of flies. Shall I not slip through? No, if I make the venture one of the flies hits me

> and gives a boost up again; I fall again and am knocked upward by another fly; and so on. I may hope that the net result will be that I remain about steady; but if unfortunately I should slip through the floor or be boosted too violently up to the ceiling, the occurrence would be, not a violation of the laws of Nature, but a rare coincidence. . . .
>
> Verily, it is easier for a camel to pass through the eye of a needle than for a scientific man to pass through a door. And whether the door be barn door or church door it might be wiser that he should consent to be an ordinary man and walk in rather than wait till all the difficulties involved in a really scientific ingress are resolved.

In all of literature I know of no printed passage that exhibits the Kafkaesque *gestus* to the same extent. One could effortlessly match almost every passage of this physical aporia with sentences from Kafka's prose, and much speaks in favor of the fact that the "most unintelligible ones" would be among them. If I were to say, as I just did, that there was a tremendous tension between those of Kafka's experiences that correspond to present-day physics and his mystical ones, this would only amount to a half-truth. What is actually and in a very precise sense *folly* in Kafka is that this, the most recent of experiential worlds, was conveyed to him precisely by the mystical tradition. This, of course, could not have happened without devastating occurrences (which I am about to discuss) within this tradition. The long and the short of it is that clearly an appeal had to be made to nothing less than the forces of this tradition if an individual (by the name of Franz Kafka) was to be confronted with *that* reality of ours which is projected theoretically, for example, in modern physics, and practically in the technology of warfare. What I mean to say is that this reality can scarcely still be experienced by an *individual,* and that Kafka's world, frequently so serene and so dense with angels, is the exact complement of his epoch, an epoch that is preparing itself to annihilate the inhabitants of this planet on a massive scale. The experience that corresponds to that of Kafka as a private individual will probably first become accessible to the masses at such time as they are about to be annihilated.

Kafka lives in a *complementary* world. (In this he is precisely on the same level as Klee, whose work in painting is just as essentially *solitary* as Kafka's work is in literature.) Kafka was aware of the complement without being aware of what surrounded him. If one says that he perceived what was to come without perceiving what exists in the present, one should add that he perceived it essentially as an *individual* affected by it. His gestures of terror are given scope by the marvelous *field for play* which the catastrophe will not entail. But his experience was based solely on the tradition to which Kafka surrendered; there was no farsightedness or "prophetic vision." Kafka eavesdropped on tradition, and he who listens hard does not see.

The main reason why this eavesdropping demands such effort is that only the most indistinct sounds reach the listener. There is no doctrine that one could learn and no knowledge that one could preserve. The things one wishes to catch as they rush by are not meant for anyone's ears. This implies a state of affairs that negatively characterizes Kafka's works with great precision. (Here a negative characterization probably is altogether more fruitful than a positive one.) Kafka's work represents tradition falling ill. Wisdom has sometimes been defined as the epic side of truth.[5] Such a definition marks wisdom off as a property of tradition; it is truth in its haggadic consistency.

It is this consistency of truth that has been lost. Kafka was far from being the first to face this situation. Many had accommodated themselves to it, clinging to truth or whatever they happened to regard as such, and, with a more or less heavy heart, had renounced transmissibility. Kafka's real genius was that he tried something entirely new: he sacrificed truth for the sake of clinging to transmissibility, to its haggadic element. Kafka's writings are by their nature parables. But that is their misery and their beauty, that they had to become *more* than parables. They do not modestly lie at the feet of doctrine, as Haggadah lies at the feet of Halakah. When they have crouched down, they unexpectedly raise a mighty paw against it.

This is why, in the case of Kafka, we can no longer speak of wisdom. Only the products of its decay remain. There are two: One is the rumor about the true things (a sort of theology passed on by whispers dealing with matters discredited and obsolete); the other product of this diathesis is folly—which, to be sure, has utterly squandered the substance of wisdom but preserves its attractiveness and assurance, which rumor invariably lacks. Folly lies at the heart of Kafka's favorites—from Don Quixote via the assistants to the animals. (Being an animal presumably meant to him only to have renounced human form and human wisdom owing to a kind of shame—as shame may keep a gentleman who finds himself in a disreputable tavern from wiping his glass clean.) This much Kafka was absolutely sure of: first, that someone must be a fool if he is to help; second, that only a fool's help is real help. The only uncertain thing is: can such help still do a human being any good? It is more likely to help the angels (compare the passage, p. 171, about the angels who get something to do),[6] who could do without help. Thus, as Kafka puts it, there is an infinite amount of hope, but not for us. This statement really contains Kafka's hope; it is the source of his radiant serenity.

I leave you this image, somewhat dangerously foreshortened in perspective, with all the more ease as you may clarify it by means of the views I have developed from different aspects in my Kafka essay in the *Jüdische Rundschau*. What prejudices me most against that study today is its apologetic character. To do justice to the figure of Kafka in its purity and its peculiar beauty, one must never lose sight of one thing: it is the figure of a failure.[7] The circumstances of this failure are manifold. One is tempted to say: once he was certain of eventual failure, everything worked out for him en route as in a dream. There is nothing more memorable than the fervor with which Kafka emphasized his failure. His friendship with Brod is to me above all else a question mark which he chose to ink in the margin of his life.

That seems to bring us back to where we started from, and I place the kindest regards to you at its center.

Yours, Walter

1. [Page references are to Max Brod, *Franz Kafka: A Biography,* trans. G. Humphreys Roberts and Richard Winston, rev. ed. (New York: Schocken, 1963), although this translation has not always been followed.—Smith]

2. [In the original *Franz Kafka: Eine Biographie* (Prague: Heinrich Mercy Sohn, 1937).—Smith]

3. Max Brod's novel *Zauberreich der Liebe* (Berlin: P. Zsolnay, 1928) [*The Kingdom of Love,* trans. Eric Sutton (London: M. Secker, 1930)].

4. WB appropriated this identification from the technical term *Kabbalah,* whose literal meaning is "tradition," as he knew.

5. This definition is to be found in WB's essay "The Storyteller" [*Illuminations,* p. 87].

6. This passage was quoted in letter 296.

7. This aspect emerges as early as WB's letters to me during the summer of 1934.

300.* To Gerhard Scholem

Skovsbostrand per Svendborg
July 8, 1938

Dear Gerhard,

My spring presentiment turned out to be true after all, and it won't prove possible for our fall meeting to take place, much to my dismay, and no doubt to yours as well. The reason, against which all else is powerless, is my work. My stay here is tantamount to monastic confinement; and if it were no more than that, the long trip would be legitimate. But I need this seclusion; I really cannot risk letting a protracted interruption, let alone a change of milieu, to occur before the work has, for all intents and purposes, been finished. Add to this that the local working conditions are superior to those in Paris, and not just because of the seclusion. I have a large garden at my disposal, in peace and quiet, and my desk in front of a window with a clear view of the sound. The small ships that sail past therefore represent my only distraction, apart from the daily chess interlude with Brecht.

Since I am staying at a Svendborg police officer's, in the house next to Brecht's, there presumably won't be any obstacles to an extension of my stay beyond mid-August. If I could at least keep the deadline desired in New York without sacrificing our meeting! But I am afraid that I will have to exceed it after all.

You could do me a good turn in this connection by informing Wiesengrund of this when the occasion presents itself. I will certainly write him myself as well; but first I am waiting for his reply to a detailed letter I sent him from Paris. So you would potentially be doing me a favor if you could slip in a few words to this effect.

Among the reasons that make me sad about the failure of our plans—besides my wish to meet your wife—is my wish to speak with you about the "Baudelaire." I had placed high hopes in such a discussion. It can be summed up as follows: The subject matter necessarily puts into motion the entire mass of thoughts and studies I have launched myself into over the last years. In this sense, I can say that a very precise model of the *Arcades* project would be furnished if the "Baudelaire" were to succeed. Another question is what guarantees there might be for this success. In my opinion, prudence is still best, and that is why I devote a long chain of reflections (which take the *Elective Affinities* essay as their model) to its composition.

Many thanks for your birthday wishes. Your letter did indeed take a remarkably short time—arriving on July 6. I can't say the same about the English offprint you mention. It might still be among my mail in Paris.

I am very pleased to hear that your spoils turned out to be so abundant. Permit me to hope that, once you have the hunting season behind you, you will tell me at some length about the many things that must once again—for who knows how long—be entrusted to our correspondence. I have in mind especially my Kafka letter and your impending visit to the institute.

Hannah Arendt's address is Hôtel des Principautés Étrangères, 6 rue Servandoni.

With kindest regards,

Yours, Walter

301. To Kitty Marx-Steinschneider

Skovbostrand
July 20, 1938

My dear friend,

As you point out, you have now received five letters from me; I do not recall how I dealt with their salutations. With the current salutation, I am weaving a thread of your last letter into mine—and I have no better material than that.

I had been hoping to get a letter from you for a long time. When it finally came, after what was indeed an even longer time, it turned out that my hope had only fallen into a light slumber from which it awakened at the first touch. But if I for my part did not write you much earlier, this was perhaps motivated by the feeling of how few in number our first personal encounters were, not to mention our encounters through correspondence, and by the desire not to deprive them of the abundance of this deficiency. Now the years and the many obstacles that your last letter overcame allow me to hope that it marks the beginning of a somewhat more frequent series of exchanges.

Not all of these obstacles had been overcome when it reached me one morning. For it came right when I had turned my attention to a rather large project after months of living an unsettled existence and of confronting various obstacles. I had gotten into difficulties last fall due to the sudden loss of my lodgings. I was at my ex-wife's place in San Remo for a while; at the end of January, I finally succeeded in getting a small apartment. As a consequence of having had to leave behind in Berlin everything an apartment needs, I was forced to put in several weeks of work. I got behind with my ongoing projects and this always led to more or less disjointed scribbling, which then kept me on the go again for quite some time.

When I received your letter, it had been just a few days since I had gone back to a well-established plan, an essay on Baudelaire, which is part of my project on the last century and which I have had in mind for more than ten years. The essay I am writing, which is more like a book in terms of its organization, should safely round off a part of that project.

I packed up my few things in June and have now been in Denmark for four weeks. I am sitting at a large, massive table in an attic room. On my left are the shore and the quiet, narrow strait that abuts the opposite side of the forest. It is fairly quiet; the motors of the cutters going by make a sound that is all the more pleasing as it allows you to look up and take note of the small boat.

Brecht's house is next door; there are two children there whom I like; the radio; supper; the kindest hospitality and, after a meal, one or two lengthy games of chess. The newspapers arrive so late that you have to pluck up your courage before looking at them.

I saw Scholem in Paris shortly before my departure. Our philosophical debate whose time was long due proceeded in good form. If I am not mistaken, it gave him an image of me as something like a man who has made his home in a crocodile's jaws, which he keeps pried open with iron braces.

We had originally planned to meet once again after his return to Paris from America. But I am unable to interrupt my work and will not return to Paris under any circumstances before the beginning of September.[1] I must therefore ask you to write me at this address.

I would give a lot for you to be able to come into this room just once. I live here as if in a cell. It is not the furnishings that make it that, but the circumstances under which I live in it. They impose a kind of test on me. In spite of my great friendship with Brecht, I must take care to proceed with my project in strict solitude. It contains very specific moments that he is unable to assimiliate. He has been a friend for a long enough time for me to know this and is perceptive enough to respect it. This way everything proceeds very nicely. But it is not always all that easy to avoid talking about what preoccupies you day in and day out. Thus there are moments in which I reread a letter like yours so as to return to my work with resolve. And I think this ought to help bring me another.

I hope that conditions over there are not making your existence all too tumultuous; write me about this as well.

And please allow me to close with my sincere regards.

Yours, Walter Benjamin

1. WB stayed until mid-October, at which time Scholem was already back in Jerusalem.

302. To Gretel Adorno

Skovbostrand per Svendborg
July 20, 1938

Dear Felizitas,

Would you have believed that your birthday wishes would arrive right on the 15th at 12 noon? That is when they did arrive, with the mailman. It is unfortunate that my delight became more acute at the same time as my awareness of my recent failure to send you best wishes. This omission can only be forgiven, not excused. Now I will all the more assiduously keep that date in mind, where it will be well preserved.

I imagine that you will have refreshed your memory on the 15th for the most obvious reason. (With this in mind, I now quite naturally also have a desire to learn whether your sister[1] has gotten married or whether this is still in the offing. You had written me about this in greater detail and I responded. I believe it was in my last letter, to which I still have had no response from the two of you.)

You may have heard how things are going with me from Egon [Wissing], whom I wrote fourteen days ago. I am living in a reasonably quiet room in the closest proximity to Brecht's house. I have a large, sturdy table at which to write—one the likes of which I have not had for years—and a view overlooking a serene strait, past whose shores sailboats and even smaller steamboats glide. Thus, to cite Baudelaire, I live in "contemplation opiniâtre de l'oeuvre de demain." He is the subject of the ouevre in question.

I have devoted eight to nine hours a day to this work for a month now and intend to complete a rough draft of the manuscript before I return to Paris. As much as I regretted it, I therefore had to give up the meeting I had planned to have with Scholem: the interruption would have come during a critical phase of the project. You have meanwhile probably heard all this from him.

In this context, there is some news that I reluctantly pass on to you. You are the first to hear it, and I pass it on not so much into loyal hands as into understanding ones. No matter how hard I try, I will be unable to meet the September 15 deadline.

In a letter I wrote Pollock from here, I told him that it might become necessary for me to extend the deadline a bit. In the meantime, I have had to resolve to reorganize the structure of the project, which I had forcibly imposed upon myself in Paris while suffering from chronic migraines.

After all, we agree that, in a work like this one on Baudelaire, much of what is crucial depends on its conception; it is the conception in which nothing may be forced and in which nothing may be allowed to slide. An additional factor is that some of the fundamental categories of the *Arcades* project are developed here for the first time. Of these categories, that of the new and the immutable occupies first place. I probably told you this in San Remo. Furthermore, motifs that had formerly appeared to me only as spheres of thought, more or less isolated from one another, are brought into conjunction with each other for the first time in this work—and this may give you the best idea of what it is: allegory, *Jugendstil,* and aura.—The denser the conceptual context turns out to be, the more urbanity the linguistic context must of course manifest.

Another factor is the difficulties that are inherent not in the thing itself but in the time (I should say, in the epoch). What I would give to see you—and even for only one week! For the very reason that you would frequently be able to understand what I meant without my uttering more than half a word, you would make it possible for me to gain mastery over its other half! Nothing of the kind exists for me here. On the other hand, I feel that the understanding Brecht shows for the necessity of my isolation is very beneficial. Things would turn out to be much less pleasant without this understanding. But this has made it possible for me to withdraw into my work to such an extent that I have not even read his new, half-finished novel yet.[2] Naturally, I have neither the time nor the opportunity to get involved in something alien to my own work.

The same imperious character that renders my work incompatible with any other involvement also makes it difficult for me to force that work into the confines of an all too restrictive deadline. As certain as I am that the essay will be completed before the end of the year—I would set November 15 as the latest deadline—it would be as foolish of me not to say now that I will not be able to manage without an extension of at least five weeks.

There is naturally nothing left for me to do but to inform Max of this as well. Because, however, my news would reach him even later than this letter will reach you; furthermore, because I only recently wrote Pollock about the situation; because—and this is the decisive factor—I would like to assure myself of your understanding and your help, as well as Teddie's, in this editorial difficulty—for all of these reasons I am writing you, and in such detail.

Even with this, I am not finished. Instead, I immediately want to append a request that may conjure up my entire desk before your eyes. I have found out that the famous R. L. Stevenson wrote about gaslight; there is an essay on gas lamps written by him. All my efforts to get hold of this essay have thus far been in vain. Anything I might say about the importance this essay could have for me would be superfluous. Could you try to get hold of it for me?—Finally: if you can, would you in the next few weeks send me my French books that are still in your possession. I would then be spared problems with customs. The French authorities love to make difficulties for packages containing books. They will go by freight from here to Paris with the rest of my library.

Is what I hear true, that Ernst Bloch is in New York? Let me know if it is, and give him my regards. The last issue of the journal suggests that his student Joachim Schumacher is also there. His contributions to the review section do not seem bad to me (on the other hand, a book he published, *Die Angst vor dem Chaos,* is not a good testimonial to the teaching he enjoyed).

Here I get to see writing that hews to the party line a bit more than what I see in Paris. For example, I recently came upon an issue of *Internationale Literatur*[3] in which I figure as a follower of Heidegger on the basis of a section of my essay on Goethe's *Elective Affinities*. This publication is quite wretched. I think you will have a chance to hear what Bloch makes of it. As for Brecht, he is trying his best to make sense of what is behind Russian cultural politics by speculating on what the politics of nationality in Russia requires. But this obviously does not prevent him from recognizing that the theoretical line being taken is catastrophic for everything we have championed for twenty years. As you know, Tretyakov was his translator and friend. He is most probably no longer alive.

The weather is gloomy and not very conducive to walks: all the better, since there are none to take. My desk is also climatologically privileged: it is located under a weathered roof where the warmth occasionally radiated by infrequent sunbeams is preserved somewhat longer than it is elsewhere. A game or two of chess, which ought to introduce some variety into our lives, take on the color and the monotony of the gray strait, for I seldom win.

My dear Felizitas, I hope you are well; please consider that, under the burden of my work, I need special encouragement to write a letter; give this to me by writing a lot—your letters are *always* short—and please extend my most sincere regards to Teddie, as well as to the others.

Yours, Detlef

I recently saw—for the first time!—Katharine Hepburn. She is magnificent and there is a lot of you in her. Has no one ever told you this?

1. Liselotte Karplus, Egon Wissing's second wife.
2. *Die Geschäfte des Herrn Julius Cäsar* (Berlin, 1957). Published posthumously.
3. A German-language journal published in Moscow from 1930 to 1945; Johannes R. Becher was editor-in-chief.

303. To Max Horkheimer

Copenhagen
September 28, 1938

Dear Mr. Horkheimer,

Let me above all express my sincere gratitude for the lines you wrote on September 6. I often ask myself whether and under what circumstances we will see each other in the foreseeable future. The spirit, wary of the future, looks into the distance.

At the same time as this letter, you will receive the second part of my book on Baudelaire.[1] It includes three sections. Some pages from the beginning of the first are missing; I had to sacrifice them to the completion of the rest of the text and the decision to do so was not all that difficult, since this first section is probably less likely to be considered for publication in the next issue of the journal than the other two. I assume that each of these two sections by itself would have sufficed for the needs of the next issue. If, in spite of that, I am sparing no effort to complete both of them and, beyond that, the most important parts of the first section, it is because it was very important to me to give you a preliminary notion of what the Baudelaire book looks like in its entirety by having you read the second section as a coherent whole.

I might perhaps take this opportunity to summarize briefly how this second section came into being.

In my letter of April 16, I expressed my belief that I would be able to treat all of Baudelaire in 80 to 120 pages. In my letter to Mr. Pollock on July 4, I was still talking about the entire Baudelaire as something I would submit for the next issue of the journal. In the letter I wrote you on August 3, I saw for the first time that it was imperative for the second section to be separated. Not until August 28 could I, or did I have to, inform Mr. Pollock that the second section on its own would exceed the length of a journal article.

As you know, the Baudelaire was originally conceived as a chapter of the *Arcades,* specifically as the penultimate chapter. It was therefore impossible for me to write it before the preceding chapters had been written, and had it been written in this way, it would have been incomprehensible without the preceding chapters. I myself then clung to the notion that the Baudelaire could be written as an extended essay, if not as a chapter of the *Arcades,* with its maximum length being that of an essay the journal could publish. I came to realize as the summer went on that a Baudelaire essay more modest in length that did not repudiate its responsibility to the *Arcades* draft could be produced only as a part of a Baudelaire *book.* To be precise, you will find three essays of this kind enclosed—namely, the three constituent parts, relatively independent of each other, of the completely independent second section of the Baudelaire book.

This book is meant to set down the decisive philosophical elements of the *Arcades* project in what I hope will be definitive form. If, besides the original plan, there was a subject that offered optimal opportunities for the basic conceptions of the *Arcades,* it was Baudelaire. For this reason, the orientation of important material and constructive elements of the *Arcades* to this subject occurred on its own.

To be sure, it is necessary to emphasize that the philosophical bases of the *whole* book cannot be grasped on the basis of the completed second section and are not meant to be grasped on this basis. The synthesis in the third part—its title should be "The Commodity as Poetic Object"—is set up in such a way that it is not possible to catch sight of it from either the first or the second part. This was not only a prerequisite of the final part's independence, but also prescribed by the structure. Within this structure, the first part—Baudelaire as allegorist—poses the question; the third part presents the resolution. The second provides the requisite data for this resolution.

Generally speaking, the function of this second part is that of antithesis. It decisively turns its back on the first part's concern with artistic theory and undertakes a sociocritical interpretation of the poet. This is a prerequisite of Marxist interpretation, but does not on its own fulfill its conception. That is reserved for the third part. There form is meant to come into its own in its material context, just as decisively as it came into its own as a problem in the first part. As antithesis, the second part is the one in which criticism in its narrower sense, namely Baudelaire criticism, has its place. The limits of his achievement had to be clarified in this section; only the third part finally undertakes to interpret his achievement. It will have an independent range of motifs. The basic theme of the old *Arcades* project, the new and the immutable, comes into its own only here; it appears in the concept of the *nouveauté,* which goes to the core of Baudelaire's creativity.

I would anticipate that the evolution that the Baudelaire chapter of the *Arcades* is about to undergo is something the other two chapters of the *Arcades* will also have to undergo at a later time: the chapters on Grandville and on Haussmann.

As soon as I know which part you have chosen to publish in the next issue, I will send an abstract. If I am able to get back to France, a few lacunae in the bibliographical references will also be filled in by that time.

Should you as editor be interested in a montage of brief excerpts, I have indicated the theme of each of them in the margin. If you happen to be interested in this, you might wish to consider the following title, "Sociological Studies of Baudelaire." This title, which otherwise does not have much to recommend it, would have the advantage of being available for you to use if other fragments were published later, whether in the journal or in an annual.

I have translated the French citations; given how many there are, the text would otherwise have become unreadable. I would consider it very desirable if the prose translations of the cited verses appeared as annotations in the part you publish. In many instances, we will probably be dealing with German readers who do not know French. I would if necessary send you these prose versions at the same time as the abstract.

I do not have to tell you under what circumstances I worked on this project the last two weeks. I was in a race against the war. An additional factor was my anxiety about my son in Italy; thanks to the most strenuous efforts, my wife was able to get him to London—this, however, has only momentarily changed the reason to be worried about him.

I have made every effort to keep any trace of these circumstances out of the work, even its external aspects, and have been in Copenhagen for ten days in order to see that a flawless manuscript is produced. I will return to Brecht's tomorrow. Before my departure, he asked me to convey his regards to you, and I am very happy to do so.

I still do not know what my plans are. I have been assured that my Danish residence permit will definitely expire on November 1. Should war break out, I think I must do everything I can to stay in Scandinavia. I would therefore be very grateful if you would give me the names of Danish, but also Swedish and Norwegian, friends—if you have any—to whom I could turn in such a case. If I am able to return to Paris, I will do so as soon as it is feasible.

[. . .]

Let me reciprocate your wife's most sincere regards.

Yours, Walter Benjamin

1. This version of the Baudelaire book has been preserved in manuscript form.

304. To Theodor W. Adorno

Skovbostrand per Svendborg
October 4, 1938

Dear Teddie,

I had just put the finishing touches on the second part of the Baudelaire eight days ago today; two days later the European situation suffered its provisional denouement. Because of the collision of historical events with editorial deadlines, I have had to exert myself to the extreme these past few weeks. This is the reason for my delay in sending these lines.

Yesterday I prepared the several hundred books I have here for shipment to Paris. Now, however, I am increasingly coming to feel that this destination will have to become a transfer point for them as well as for me. I do not know how long it will continue to be physically possible to breathe European air; after the events of the past weeks, it is spiritually impossible even now. This observation is not easy for me to make; but it simply cannot be avoided any longer.

This much may be said to have become indisputably clear: Russia has let its extremity, Europe, be amputated. As far as Hitler's pledge is concerned, to wit, that his European territorial claims have been settled and that the colonial ones could in no way be an occasion for war, I interpret this to mean that any colonial territorial claims will be Mussolini's occasion for war. I expect that Tunisia, inhabited by a large number if not a majority of Italians, will provide the next matter for "negotiation."

You can well imagine how worried I have been in the last few weeks about my wife and above all about Stefan. At the moment it is not necessary to fear the worst. I have known that for only a short time. Stefan is in England; my wife will try to transfer her business to somebody else without suffering too great a loss. In order to save time, she will attempt to relinquish the business only on paper for the time being.

I was in Copenhagen for ten days in order to prepare the Baudelaire manuscript for publication. Copenhagen was enjoying the most magnificent Indian summer imaginable. But this time I saw no more of the city—which I especially love—than what was on the way from my desk to the radio set in the "salon." Fall is now setting in, accompanied by the heaviest rainstorms. I will return a week from this coming Saturday if nothing unexpected comes up. The more natural and relaxed my contract with Brecht has been this past summer, the less equitable I am about leaving him behind this time. For I can see an index of his growing isolation in our communication, which this time was much less problematical than what I had been used to. I do not want to exclude entirely a more banal explanation of the facts—that this isolation diminishes his pleasure in certain provocative tactics that he was inclined to use in conversation; the more authentic explanation, however, is to recognize in his growing isolation the consequences of the loyalty to what we have in common. Given the conditions under which he currently lives, he will be challenged, head-on so to speak, by this isolation during a Svendborg winter.

I still have seen hardly anything at all of his new *Caesar,* because it was impossible for me to read anything at all while I was doing my own work.

I assume you will already have read the second section of the Baudelaire by the time this letter arrives. I was in a race against the war; and in spite of all my choking fear, I felt a feeling of triumph on the day I wrapped up the "flaneur," which had been almost fifteen years in the planning, before the end of the world (the fragility of a manuscript!).

Max will certainly have apprised you of my comments on the relationship of the Baudelaire to the plan of the *Arcades,* something I explained to him in detail in a cover letter. As I formulated it for him, the decisive thing is that a Baudelaire essay that did not repudiate its responsibility to the questions addressed in the *Arcades* could be written only as a section of a Baudelaire *book.* What you know about the book from our conversations in San Remo allows you *per contrarium* to have a fairly precise notion of the function of the completed second section. You will have seen that the critical motifs—the new and the immutable, fashion, the eternal return, stars, *Jugendstil*—are indeed brought up, but not a single one of them was discussed. The task of the third part is to demonstrate the obvious convergence of the basic idea with the plan of the *Arcades.*

I still have not heard very much from you since you moved into the new apartment. I hope to hear from you at length as soon as you have read the Baudelaire. Please also let me know at the same time how your radio project[1] is progressing and primarily what it is actually about. For I am still ignorant of this.

Many thanks for the book on aeronauts: it is currently resting with the rest of your parcel in the boxes waiting to be shipped. I am looking forward to reading it in Paris. Please give Felizitas my sincere thanks for this parcel. I will write her, at the latest from Paris.—You will get the Kierkegaard book, for which I thank you, along with the Löwith[2] by way of Mrs. Favez. I ordered the latter when I needed it for the third part of the Baudelaire. Please let me have it back after you are through with it.

Felizitas was asking about Elisabeth Wiener, but I have heard nothing from her. What is even more important to me is that I have not heard a word from Scholem since he left America. He seems to be hurt at not having found me in Paris. For me, however, everything had to take a back seat to my work. I could never have completed it without the strict seclusion I imposed on myself. Has he given you any sign of himself?

I am eagerly waiting to hear what you might be able to tell me about Ernst Bloch. *En attendant,* every now and then I glance at the city plan of New York that Brecht's son Stefan has mounted on his wall and I walk up and down the long street on the Hudson where your house is.

Most sincere regards.
Yours, Walter

1. Adorno led the music section of the Princeton Radio Research Project.
2. Karl Löwith, *Nietzsches Philosophie der ewigen Wiederkunft des Gleichen* (Berlin, 1935).

305. To Gretel Adorno

Paris
November 1, 1938

My dear Felizitas,

You see the familiar stationery reemerge—and this would mean that, after a fall pregnant with novelties, some things have reverted to the way they were. If you are yearning for a review of my summer, I assume it will be revealed to you as soon as you read the Baudelaire manuscript, if you have not already done so. The manuscript represents the quintessence of the past few months. I am expecting a report on its reception in New York in the next few days and I certainly hope that Teddie will participate in producing it.

You have to let me know soon what you think of New York after taking a second look, especially since this second look must also include some of its freshly baked inhabitants. Thus I primarily expect to hear what you have to say about Ernst Bloch and the relationship both of you have with him. I am no less eager for a description of your everyday life and the way you have organized your existence as a couple and within the circle of your close acquaintances.

I believe that my last letter from Svendborg indicated that—given all the restrictions of my existence in Denmark—I was unenthusiastic about my impending return. I expected drastic changes; nowadays, they are rarely for the best. As it is, I have not yet been able to get around enough to have seen my French acquaintances and find out to what degree my fears were justified. I have spoken only with Adrienne Monnier and my fears never applied to her. On the other hand, I came across changes where I had not expected them. My sister has taken seriously, actually hopelessly, ill. She is now afflicted by a very advanced case of arteriosclerosis in addition to the chronic ailment from which she has been suffering for years. My sister's physical capabilities have been drastically reduced and she is often confined to bed for days on end. Under these circumstances, it is a good thing that I live nearby.—My brother has been transferred to the prison in Wilsnak, where he is kept busy working on the roads. Life is still supposed to be tolerable there. As I often hear from Germany, the nightmare oppressing people in his situation is not so much the upcoming day in prison as the concentration camp that threatens after years of imprisonment.—As far as my wife is concerned, she unexpectedly passed through Paris shortly before my return and is now in London. She seems to want to give running a boardinghouse another try in London. I hope that I will see her here around Christmas and that I will then hear good news about Stefan's prospects in England.

To touch once more on political developments: the rapprochement between Germany and France, which is at the forefront of political efforts, will, I fear, have to distance from one another the few Frenchmen and Germans who are close—directly or indirectly. It is expected that a *statut des étrangers* will be issued by the end of the week. In the meantime I am working on my naturalization, cautiously but without illusions. If my chances of succeeding were doubtful before, the usefulness of succeeding has now also become problematical. The decline of the rule of law in Europe makes any kind of legalization appear deceptive.

I have reason to congratulate myself for every piece of paper I had the foresight to put into your hands in March 1933. As of now, the only thing yielded by my persistent efforts to get some more of my books, but above all my papers, out of Berlin is the virtual certainty that the following things have been destroyed: the complete papers of the two Heinles, my irreplaceable archive on the history of the leftist bourgeois Youth Movement, and finally my youthful writings—among them the 1914 Hölderlin essay.[1]

To close on a more cheerful note, let me add that the Lord who can take so much from those who are awake gives as much to those who are his own in their sleep. [Franz] Hessel, who has sat in Berlin for five and one-half years like a little mouse in the rafters recently arrived in Paris with great testimonials to his legitimacy and with powerful protection. I believe that his story will be a memorable one; I want to have him tell it to me soon.

Did the two of you remember the American primitive paintings I impressed upon you?

Love to you and Teddie.
Yours, Detlef

1. The work was preserved due to a copy in Scholem's possession; it is in *Schriften* 2:375–400.

306. Theodor W. Adorno to Walter Benjamin

[New York]
November 10, 1938

Dear Walter,

The delay in writing this letter threatens to indict me and all of us. But this indictment may already contain the grain of a defense. For it is almost self-evident that a full month's delay in responding to your Baudelaire cannot be attributed to negligence.

The reasons for the delay are all substantive in nature. They have to do with the attitude all of us have to the manuscript but, given my involvement in the *Arcades* project, I might, without being immodest, say that they have to do with my own attitude in particular. I most eagerly looked forward to the arrival of the Baudelaire and literally devoured it. I am full of admiration for the fact that you were able to complete the work by the deadline. And it is this admiration that makes it particularly difficult for me to speak about what has intervened between my passionate expectation and the text itself.

I took your idea of making the Baudelaire a model for the *Arcades* extremely seriously and approached the Satanic arena much as Faust approached the phantasmagoria of the Brocken when he says that it would now solve so many riddles. May I be excused for having had to appropriate Mephistopheles' reply for myself, namely that many riddles pose themselves anew? Can you understand that reading your treatise, one of whose chapters is entitled "The Flaneur," and another is even entitled "Modernism," caused me a certain degree of disappointment?

The basic reason for this disappointment is that, in the parts of it with which I am familiar, the work represents not so much a model for the *Arcades* as a prelude to that project. Motifs are assembled but not developed. In your cover letter to Max, you presented this as your express intention and there is no mistaking the ascetic discipline you allowed to rule, making it possible for you to abstain from conclusive theoretical answers to questions throughout the text and probably even making it possible for you to allow the questions themselves to become apparent only to initiates. But I ask myself whether this kind of asceticism can be sustained in the face of this subject and in a context that places such powerful internal demands on you. As a loyal connoisseur of your writings, I know very well that there is no lack of precedents in the body of your work for this way of going about things. I recall, for example, your essays on Proust and on surrealism in the *Literarische Welt*. Can this method, however, be transferred to the complex of the *Arcades*? Panorama and "trace," flaneur and arcades, modernism and the immutable *without* theoretical interpretation—is this "material" that can patiently wait for interpretation without being consumed by its own aura? Is it not rather the case that when the pragmatic configuration of those subjects is isolated, it conspires almost demonically against the possibility of being interpreted? Once during our unforgettable conversations in Königsstein, you said that each idea in the *Arcades* would actually have to be wrested from a realm in which insanity reigns. I wonder whether it is beneficial for such ideas to be immured behind impenetrable layers of material, as your ascetic discipline demands. In your present text, the arcades are introduced with a reference to the narrowness of the sidewalks, which impedes the progress of the flaneur on the streets. This pragmatic introduction seems to me to prejudice the objectivity of the phantasmagoria, on which I so stubbornly insisted even at the time of our Hornberg correspondence, as much as does, for example, the inclination of the first chapter to reduce the phantasmagoria to the behavior of literary bohemia. You should not worry that I would speak in favor of those who say that the phantasmagoria should survive unmediated in your work or even that the work itself should assume a phantasmagoric character. But the liquidation of the phantasmagoria can be accomplished in its true profundity only if the phantasmagoria is rendered as an objective historicist category and not as a "view" of social characters. It is precisely at this point that your conception diverges from all other approaches to the nineteenth century. However, the redemption of your postulate may not be postponed forever, *ad Kalendas Graecas*, or be "prepared for" by a more harmless description of the state of affairs. This is my objection. To use the old formulation, when, in the third part, Ur-history in the nineteenth century takes the place of the Ur-history of the nineteenth century—most explicitly in the Péguy quote about Victor Hugo—this is merely another way of expressing the same state of affairs.

It seems to me, however, that my objection by no means purely concerns the dubiousness of "abstaining" in relation to a subject that, precisely because of your ascetic attitude toward interpretation, appears to enter a realm to which asceticism is opposed: where history and magic oscillate. Rather, I see the moments in which the text lags behind its own a priori as being closely related to its connection to dialectical materialism—and right here I speak not only for myself but also for Max, with whom I discussed this question in the greatest detail. Let me express myself here in as simple and Hegelian manner as possible. If I am not mistaken, this dialectic lacks one thing: mediation. The primary tendency is always to relate the pragmatic content of Baudelaire's work directly to proximate characteristics of the social history of his time, and preferably economic characteristics when possible. I have in mind, for example, the passage about the wine tax, certain comments about the barricades, or the section I already mentioned about the arcades. The latter seems particularly problematic to me because this is precisely where the transition from a fundamental theoretical consideration of physiologies to the "concrete" representation of the flaneur is particularly flawed.

I have a sense of such artificiality whenever you put things metaphorically rather than categorically. This is particularly the case in the passage about the transformation of the city into an interior for the flaneur. I think that one of the most powerful conceptions in your study is here presented as a mere "as if." There is an extremely close relationship between the appeal to concrete modes of behavior, like that of the flaneur or the later passage about the relationship between seeing and hearing in the city, which, not entirely as a matter of coincidence, enlists a quotation from Simmel, and the kind of materialistic excursuses in which one never completely sheds the anxiety anybody would feel for a swimmer who dives into cold water when covered with the most terrible goose bumps. All of this makes me quite uneasy. Do not fear that I am making use of this opportunity to mount my hobbyhorse. I will content myself with handing it a lump of sugar en passant and for the rest will try to indicate to you the theoretical basis of my aversion to this particular type of concreteness and its behavioristic features. This basis, however, is nothing other than that I consider it methodologically unfortunate to give conspicuous individual characteristics from the realm of the superstructure a "materialistic" twist by relating them to corresponding characteristics of the substructure in an unmediated and even causal manner. The materialistic determination of cultural characteristics is possible only when mediated by the *total process*.

Even if Baudelaire's wine poems are motivated by the tax on wine and by barriers, the recurrence of those motifs in Baudelaire's oeuvre cannot be explained other than by the overall social and economic tendency of the age, i.e. in keeping with the way the issue was raised in your work *sensu strictissimo,* by analysis of the commodity form in Baudelaire's epoch. No one knows the difficulties associated with this better than I do: the phantasmagoria chapter in my Wagner book has undoubtedly revealed its own inadequacy. In its definitive form, the *Arcades* project will not be able to shirk this responsibility. The direct inference from the tax on wine to *L'ame du vin* ascribes to phenomena just that kind of spontaneity, tangibility, and density that they have relinquished in capitalism. There is a profoundly romantic element in this kind of unmediated and, I might almost repeat, anthropological materialism, and I detect it all the more clearly the more blatantly and crudely you confront the Baudelairean world of forms with the necessities of life. The "mediation" I miss and find obscured by materialistic and historiographic invocation is, however, nothing other than precisely the theory from which your work abstains. Bypassing theory affects the empirical evidence. On the one hand, it gives it a deceptively epic character and, on the other hand, deprives phenomena that are experienced only subjectively of their actual historicist importance. This can also be expressed as follows: the theological motif of calling things by their proper name reverts tendentially to a wide-eyed presentation of the bare facts. If you wanted to express it in drastic terms, you might say that your work settled the crossroads of magic and positivism. This location is bewitched. Only theory could break the spell: your own, ruthless, quite speculative theory. It is only its claims I level against you.

Please forgive me if this brings me to a subject that is necessarily of most particular concern for me after my experiences with the Wagner book. I refer to the ragpicker. His destiny as a figure from the lower extreme of poverty simply does not seem to me to capture what the word *ragpicker* suggests as it is used in one of the parts. The part contains nothing of his cringing manner, nothing about the sack thrown over his shoulder, nothing about his voice and the way, in Charpentier's *Louise* for example, it provides as it were the source of black light for an entire opera; nothing of the way jeering children trail behind the old man like the tail of a comet. If I might once more venture into the region of the arcades: the abandonment of sewer and catacomb should have been theoretically deciphered on the basis of the ragpicker. Am I exaggerating, however, in assuming that this failure is related to the fact that the capitalist function of the ragpicker, namely, to make even trash subject to the exchange value, is not articulated. At this point, the asceticism of your work takes on characteristics that would be worthy of Savonarola. For the reprise of the ragpicker in the Baudelaire citation in the third part comes close to grasping this connection. What it must have cost you not to grasp hold of it!

I believe that this brings me to the heart of the matter. The effect emanating from your work as a whole, and by no means only on me and my *Arcades* orthodoxy, is that you have done violence to yourself in it, [. . .] in order to pay a tribute to Marxism that does justice to neither you nor Marxism. It does not do justice to Marxism, because mediation by means of the total social process is missing and you almost superstitiously ascribe to the enumeration of materials a power of illumination, but this power is never reserved for a pragmatic reference but only for theoretical construction. It does not do justice to your most personal substance, since you have denied yourself your boldest and most productive thoughts in a kind of precensorship, even should it be in the form of a postponement, based on materialist categories (which in no way coincide with Marxist categories). [. . .] God knows, there is only one truth and if your intellect takes possession of this one truth in categories that, based on your conception of materialism, you might think are apocryphal, you will have more of this one truth than if you use an intellectual apparatus whose moves your hand unceasingly resists. In the final analysis, there is even more about this one truth in Nietzsche's *Genealogy of Morals* [*Genealogie der Moral*] than in Bukharin's primer. I believe that the thesis I propose is beyond any suspicion of laxity and eclecticism. [. . .] Gretel once joked that you lived in the cavelike depths of your *Arcades* and therefore shrank in horror from completing the work because you feared having to leave what you built. So let us encourage you to allow us into the holy of holies. I believe you have no reason to be concerned for the stability of the shrine, or any reason to fear that it will be profaned.

As regards the fate of your work, quite an unusual situation has arisen in which I have had to act pretty much like the person who is spreading the word: to the sound of a muted drum. Publication in the current issue of the journal was excluded because the weeks of discussions about your work would have intolerably delayed the printing schedule. The plan then was to print the second chapter in extenso and the third in part. Leo Löwenthal was definitely in favor of this. I myself am unambiguously opposed. And indeed, this time not for editorial reasons but for your own sake and that of the Baudelaire study. It does not represent you the way in which this work in particular must represent you. Since, however, I am firmly and totally unalterably convinced that you will be able to produce a Baudelaire manuscript whose impact will be total, I would like to beg you to forgo publishing the current version and to write that other version. It is beyond my ability to surmise whether this would require a new formal structure or whether it could be essentially identical with the concluding section of your Baudelaire *book,* which is yet to come. You are the only one who can decide this. I would like to state explicitly that this request comes from me and does not reflect an editorial decision or a rejection.

[. . .]

Let me close with some epilegomena on the Baudelaire. First, a stanza from Hugo's second Mazepa poem (the man who is supposed to see everything is Mazepa, tied to the back of a horse):

> The six moons of Herschel, old Saturn's ring,
> the pole, curving its nocturnal dawn
> On its northern extremity,
> He sees everything; and for him his unflagging flight
> constantly moves the ideal horizon of this
> Limitless world.

Second, the inclination to "unqualified statements" that you noted, citing Balzac and the description of the employees in *The Man of the Crowd,* surprisingly enough also applies to Sade. He wrote the following about one of Justine's first tormenters, a banker: "Monsier Dubourg, gros, court, et insolent comme tous les financiers."—The motif of the unknown beloved appears in rudimentary form in Hebbel's poem to an "unknown woman," which contains these remarkable lines: "and if I cannot give form and shape to you, then no form will drag you into the grave."—Finally, a few sentences from Jean Paul's *Herbstblumine* that are probably a true find.

> The day received one single sun, but the night a thousand suns and the blue, endless sea of the ether seems to sink down to us in a drizzle of light. How many street lanterns shimmer up and down the whole length of the Milky Way? On top of everything else—these will also be lit, even if it is summer or the moon is shining. Meanwhile, the night adorns itself not only with the cloak full of stars that the ancients described it wearing and that I more tastefully call its *clerical* vestments than its ducal robe, but it takes its beautification much farther and imitates the ladies of Spain. Like them, who when evening falls replace the gems in their headdress with glowworms, the night also embroiders the lower portion of its cloak, on which no stars glitter, with that kind of small creature and the children often take them.

The following sentences from a very different piece in the same collection seem to me to belong in the same context:

> And more of the same; for I noticed not only that Italy is . . . a moonlit Eden for us poor drift-ice people because, by day or night, we find there the living fulfillment of the shared youthful dream of nights spent wandering or singing, but I also asked why people merely walked around and sang in the streets at night like ill-humored night watchmen instead of having entire evening-star and morning-star parties assemble and, in a colorful procession (for every soul was in love), sublimely roam through the most magnificent arbors and the brightest moonlit meadows of flowers, and contribute to this harmonious joy two phrases on the flute, namely the double-ended lengthening of the brief night by sunrise and sunset and the allied two twilights of dawn and dusk.

The idea that the longing that attracts people to Italy is a longing for the country where it is not necessary to sleep is most profoundly related to the later image of the roofed-in city. The light, however, that rests equally on both images is probably none other than that of the gas lantern with which Jean Paul was not familiar.

Yours, *tout entier*

307. To Theodor W. Adorno

Paris
December 9, 1938

Dear Teddie,

You were surely not surprised to see that I did not compose a response to your letter of November 10 from one minute to the next. Your letter gave me a shock, even if the long time it took you to respond made it possible for me to surmise its contents. An additional factor is that I wanted to wait for the galleys you said were coming and I received them only on December 6. The time thus gained made it possible for me to consider your criticism as prudently as possible. I am far from believing it to be unproductive, let alone incomprehensible. I want to try to respond to it in fundamental terms.

A sentence on the first page of your letter will serve as my guide. You write: "Panorama and trace, flaneur and arcades, modernism and the immutable without theoretical interpretation—is this material that can patiently wait for interpretation?" The understandable impatience with which you scrutinized the manuscript for a signpost has, in my estimation, led you astray in some important respects. In particular, you had to arrive at a disillusioning view of the third part once you had missed the fact that modernism is *nowhere* cited in it as the immutable—rather, this important key concept is not used at all in the existing portion of my work.

Since the sentence quoted above in a sense presents a compendium of your objections, I would like to go through it word for word. The panorama is the first thing you mention. It is only remarked on in passing in my text. In fact, the panoramic view is not appropriate in the context of Baudelaire's oeuvre. Since the passage is not intended to have correspondences in either the first or the third part, perhaps it would be best to delete it.—The second item you mention is the trace. In my cover letter, I wrote that the philosophical foundations of the book are not perceptible from the vantage point of the second part. If I wanted to provide a convincing interpretation of a concept like the trace, it had to be introduced with complete impartiality at the empirical level. This could have been done even more convincingly. In fact, my first act after my return was to seek out a most important passage in Poe for my construct of the detective story as deriving from the obliteration or fixation of the traces of the individual in the big-city crowd. But the treatment of the trace in the second part must remain on this level, if it is later to be suddenly illuminated as it appears in critical contexts. This illumination is intended. The concept of the trace will find its philosophical determination in opposition to the concept of aura.

The next item in the sentence being analyzed is the flaneur. As much as I am aware of the profound inner concern, objective as well as personal, that is at the basis of your objections—the ground under my feet is threatening to give way in view of your negative evaluation. Thank God there is an apparently sturdy branch to which I can cling. It is the reference you make elsewhere to the productive tension in which your theory about the consumption of exchange value stands in relationship to my theory about empathy with the commodity soul. I also think that what is at issue here is a theory in the strictest sense of the word and my treatment of the flaneur culminates in it. This is the place, indeed the only one in this section, where theory comes into its own *without obstruction*. Like a single ray of light, it pierces an artificially darkened chamber. This ray, however, broken up by a prism, suffices to give an idea of the nature of the light whose focus is in the third part of the book. Therefore, this theory of the flaneur—later on, I will speak of the ways in which it can be improved at particular points in the text—fundamentally realizes a description of the flaneur I have had in mind for many years.

Moving on, I come to the next term, "arcade." I would much rather not say anything about it, since the fathomless bonhomie of its use will not have escaped you. Why question it? In fact, unless I am thoroughly mistaken, the arcade is not meant to enter the context of the "Baudelaire" in any other way than in this playful form. It appears like the picture of a rocky spring on a drinking goblet. Therefore, the invaluable Jean Paul passage to which you refer me is also not likely to belong in the "Baudelaire."—Finally, as far as modernism is concerned, the text makes clear that this is a term used by Baudelaire himself. The part with this title was not permitted to go beyond the limits prescribed by Baudelaire's own use of the word. Meanwhile, you will remember from San Remo that these limits are in no way definitive. The philosophical reconnaissance of modernism is relegated to the third part, where it is prepared for by the concept of *Jugendstil* and concluded in the dialectic of the new and immutable.

Recalling our conversations in San Remo, I would now like to address the passage in which you yourself brought them up. If, in the name of my own productive interests, I refused in San Remo to adopt as my own an esoteric intellectual development and to disregard the interests of dialectical materialism to that extent [. . .] and get down to the business of the day, in the final analysis this involved not [. . .] mere loyalty to dialectical materialism but also solidarity with the experiences we all have had in the last fifteen years. Thus, even here, my most personal productive interests are at issue; I do not mean to deny that they may occasionally tend to do violence to my original interests. An antagonism exists and I could not dream of wishing to be relieved of it. The problem posed by this work consists in overcoming this antagonism and has to do with the work's construction. What I mean is that speculation will enter upon its necessarily bold flight with some prospect of success only if it seeks its source of strength purely in construction instead of donning the waxen wings of esotericism. Construction determined that the second part of the book would basically be formed out of philological material. Thus the issue is less one of an "ascetic discipline" than a methodological precaution. By the way, this philological part was the only one I was able to anticipate as being independent—a circumstance I had to take into consideration.

When you speak of a "wide-eyed presentation of the bare facts," you are characterizing the genuinely philological stance. This had to be embedded in the construction as such and not only for the sake of results. The nondifferentiation between magic and positivism must in fact be liquidated, as you so aptly formulated it. In other words, the author's philological interpretation must be sublated in Hegelian fashion by dialectical materialists.—Philology is the examination of a text, which, proceeding on the basis of details, magically fixates the reader on the text. What Faust took home black on white is closely related to Grimm's reverence for small things. They share the magical element, which is reserved for philosophy to exorcise, reserved here for the concluding part.

As you write in your Kierkegaard book, astonishment indicates "the most profound insight into the relationship of dialectic, myth, and image." I could be tempted to invoke this passage. Instead I want to propose that it be amended (by the way, just as I plan at another opportunity to amend the subsequent definition of the dialectical image). I believe it should read: astonishment is an excellent *object* of such an insight. The illusion of closed facticity that adheres to any philological examination and that casts its spell on the investigator fades to the degree that the object is construed within a historical perspective. The baselines of this construction converge in our own historical experience. The object thus constitutes itself as a monad. In the monad, everything that was mythically paralyzed as textual evidence comes alive. It therefore seems to me that you misjudge the circumstances if you find a "direct inference from the tax on wine to *L'âme du vin*" in the text. Rather, the juncture was legitimately established in the philological context—not any differently than an ancient author would have established it in his interpretation. It gives the poem the specific gravity it assumes with a genuine reading, something that has not thus far often been given to Baudelaire. Only when this poem has come into its own in this way can the work be affected by the interpretation, or even jolted by it. For the poem in question, an interpretation would not focus on issues of taxation but on the importance of intoxication for Baudelaire.

If you think back to my other works, you will find that the critique of the philologist's stance is an old concern for me—and most profoundly identical with my critique of myth. Each time, the critique provokes the philological work itself. To use the language of my essay on *Elective Affinities,* it pushes for a display of material content in which truth-content is historically revealed. I understand that this side of the issue was of secondary importance for you. Consequently, however, some important interpretations were secondary as well. I am not thinking of interpretations of poems—"A une passante"—or of prose pieces—*The Man of the Crowd*—but primarily of the unlocking of the concept of modernity, which I was especially concerned to keep within philological bounds.

Let me note parenthetically that the Péguy quotation to which you object as an evocation of Ur-history in the nineteenth century belonged where it was because it was necessary at that point to prepare for the realization that the interpretation of Baudelaire may not rely on any chthonic elements. (I had attempted something of the kind in the précis of the *Arcades*.) I therefore believe that the catacomb has no place in this interpretation, no more than the sewer does. On the other hand, Charpentier's opera seems as if it might be very promising; I intend to follow up on your reference when I have a chance. The figure of the ragpicker is of diabolical provenance. In the third part it will reemerge, set off against the chthonic figure of the Hugo-like beggar.

[. . .]

Let me make a candid comment: I believe that it would be rather unfavorably prejudicial to the "Baudelaire" if not a single part of the text—the product of a tension that I could not easily compare with any of my earlier literary efforts—were to be published in the journal. For one thing, the printed form, which distances the author from his text, is of incomparable value. Another factor is that, in this form, the text could be made the subject of a debate, which—as inadequate as the local participants in this debate might be—could compensate me somewhat for the isolation in which I work. I would see the crux of such a publication in the theory of the flaneur, which I regard as an integral part of the "Baudelaire." I am by no means speaking of an unaltered text. As the core of the text, my critique of the concept of the masses, made tangible by the modern metropolis, must be brought out more clearly than it is in the present version. This critique, which I begin in the passages about Hugo, should be orchestrated on the basis of an interpretation of important literary documents. I conceive of the part that deals with the man of the crowd as the model for this. The euphemistic interpretation of the masses—the physiognomic interpretation—could be illustrated by an analysis of the E. T. A. Hoffmann novella that is mentioned in the text. I still need to find a more detailed clarification for Hugo. Theoretical progress is the crucial factor in these views of the masses; its climax is indicated in the text but is not sufficiently emphasized. Hugo and not Baudelaire is at the end of the text. He is the one who has come closest to contemporary experiences with the masses. The demagogue is a constituent part of his genius.

You see that certain points of your criticism appear convincing to me. I of course fear that an *unmediated* correction in the spirit just indicated would be a very delicate matter. The missing theoretical transparency to which you rightly refer is in no way a *necessary* consequence of the philological procedure prevailing in this section. Rather, I see it as the consequence of the fact that this procedure is not made explicit as such. This symptom of a deficiency can in part be attributed to my daring attempt to write the second part of the book before the first. This was also the only way in which the impression could arise that the phantasmagoria was being described instead of being dispersed throughout the construction. The above-mentioned corrections will have an effect on the second part only if it is entirely anchored in the total context. My first task will accordingly be to reexamine the overall construction.

As for the sadness I referred to above, there were sufficient reasons for it, disregarding for now the premonition I mentioned. For one thing, there is the situation of the Jews, in Germany, from which none of us can seal himself off. Another factor is my sister's serious illness. At the age of thirty-seven, she has been found to have hereditary arteriosclerosis. She is almost immobile and consequently almost incapable of working (she probably still has a small amount of capital left at the moment). At her age, the prognosis is almost hopeless. Apart from all this, it is also not always possible to live here free of anxiety. It is understandable that I am making every effort to expedite my naturalization. The necessary steps unfortunately not only take a lot of time but also some money—thus the horizon looks rather ominous to me at the moment from this perspective as well.

The enclosed fragment of a letter to Max dated November 17, 1938, and Brill's enclosed message concern a situation that may destroy my chances of becoming naturalized. You can thus gauge its importance to me. May I ask you to take the matter in hand and ask Max to authorize Brill, promptly and preferably by telegram, to replace my name with the pseudonym *Hans Fellner* for my review in the next issue.

This now brings me to your new essay[1] and consequently to the sunnier part of this letter. In terms of its subject matter, it concerns me in two respects—both of which you have indicated. For one thing, in those parts that relate certain characteristics of the current acoustic apperception of jazz to the optical characteristics of film as I described them. *Ex improviso,* I am unable to decide whether the different distribution of passages of light and shadow in our respective essays derives from theoretical divergences. It is possibly a matter of only apparent differences in point of view, but the fact is that these points of view are brought to bear on different objects and both are equally valid. It may of course not be said that acoustic and optical apperceptions are equally open to revolutionary change. This may be related to why the prospect of a variant hearing that concludes your essay is not made entirely clear, at least to a person for whom Mahler is not a totally luminous experience.

In my essay[2] I tried to articulate the positive moments as clearly as you articulated the negative moments. I consequently see a strength in your essay where there was a weakness in mine. Your analysis of the psychological types engendered by industry and your description of the way in which they are engendered are right on the mark. My essay would have gained in historical plasticity if I myself had paid more attention to this side of things. It becomes more and more obvious to me that the launching of the sound film must be viewed as an industrial action designed to break through the revolutionary primacy of the silent film, which fostered reactions that were hard to control and politically dangerous. An analysis of the sound film would provide a critique of contemporary art that would dialectically mediate between your view and mine.

What particularly appealed to me about your essay's conclusion is the note of reservation you sound at the concept of progress. You at first justify this reserve only in passing and by referring to the history of the term. I would really like to get at its roots and origins. But I cannot conceal the difficulties of this from myself.

Finally, let me address your question concerning the relationship between the view you developed in this essay and the one I presented in the section on the flaneur. Empathy with the commodity presents itself to self-observation or internal experience as empathy with inorganic matter: next to Baudelaire, the star witness to this is Flaubert in his *Temptation of Saint Anthony*. Fundamentally, however, empathy with the commodity may be empathy with the exchange value itself. In fact, under the rubric of "consumption" of exchange value, it is hard to image anything else but empathy with it. You state, "The consumer actually venerates the money he himself spent on the ticket for a Toscanini concert." Empathy with their exchange value turns even cannons into a consumer good that is more gratifying than butter. When it is popularly said of someone that "he is loaded with five million marks," the national community itself then feels it is loaded with a few hundred billion. It empathizes with these billions. Formulating it in this way, I may arrive at the canon that forms the basis of this mode of behavior. I am thinking of the canon underlying the game of chance. The gambler empathizes directly with the sums with which he faces up to the bank or another player. The game of chance in the guise of stock-market speculation paved the way for empathy with exchange value, much as world fairs did. (These were the university at which the masses who were forced away from consumption learned empathy with exchange value.)

I would like to reserve one especially important question for a later letter, if not for a conversation. What does it mean when music and lyric poetry become comical? It is hard for me to imagine that the phenomenon in question has purely negative connotations. Or does the "decline of sacred reconciliation" connote something positive to you? I confess that I cannot quite see my way clear here. Perhaps you will find an opportunity to return to this question.

In any case, let me ask you to write soon. I would appreciate your asking Felizitas to send me Hauff's fairy tales when she gets a chance. I value them because of Sonderland's illustrations. I will write her soon but would also like to hear from her.

As always, most sincerely yours, Walter

1. "Über den Fetischcharakter in der Musik und die Regression des Hörens," in *Dissonanzen: Musik in der verwalteten Welt* (Göttingen, 1963), pp. 9–45.
2. "The Work of Art in the Age of Mechanical Reproduction."

308.* To Gerhard Scholem

Paris
February 4, 1939

Dear Gerhard,

To free my ability to communicate, I had to declare a sort of state of emergency over our correspondence, as you may have inferred from the unusual script.[1] That I have done so is due to your letter of January 25, for which I thank you very much.

If my silence had been transparent to you, your looks would have penetrated in medias res. A period of severe depression accompanied the onset of winter, and all I can say about the depression is *je ne l'ai pas volé.* A number of things coincided. First of all, I was confronted by the fact that my room is practically useless for working in winter. In summer, I have the option of opening the windows and countering the racket the elevator makes with the din of Paris street noises; not so on cold winter days.

This state of affairs coincided most auspiciously with an estrangement from my work's present *sujet:* as I presumably wrote you, in light of editorial demands made by the *Zeitschrift für Sozialforschung,* I finished a part—the second part—of my book on Baudelaire sooner than anticipated. This second part is presented to the reader in three relatively distinct essays. I'd been hoping to see one or the other of them printed in the *Zeitschrift's* latest issue, which just came out. But what came in its stead, at the beginning of November, was an extensively argued letter, from Wiesengrund no less, not necessarily rejecting the work itself but refusing to send it to press.[2]

It is of course impossible for me to introduce you to the details of this problem, which you will surely find of interest, before being able to make the manuscript available to you. I intend to do just that, if you could make do with an uncorrected manuscript, which doesn't always conform to the latest version. In any case, I promise myself to put your point of view, which may well be analogous to Wiesengrund's in essential parts, to good use when I continue the work. And I will *have* to start on that continuation at once.

It isn't easy for me. The isolation in which I live and especially work here creates an abnormal dependence on the reception my work encounters. Dependence doesn't mean sensitivity. The reservations that can be made in the case of the manuscript are reasonable in part and should trouble me all the less, since the key positions of the "Baudelaire" could not and should not emerge in this second part. But this is where I run up against the limits of communication by letter, and now it is my turn to regret that we did not speak with each other in August. Please inform your wife of this regret—modified as befits the subject—as far as my meeting her is concerned.

If I haven't sent you any of my scarce publications in the recent past, the reason is that only seldom do editorial boards these days feel obliged to provide the author with more than a single author's offprint. You have no cause to assume negligence on my part in these matters, since it has been my intention all along to keep your archives of my writings complete. That has become all the more urgent now, since the only fairly substantial collection, apart from yours, is in the hands of a third party and must be considered lost by now. It is among the effects a friend of mine[3] had to leave behind in Barcelona. (As a curiosum, let me tell you that just recently an extremely cursory bibliography of my writings appeared in a small English report by the institute, alongside bibliographies of its other collaborators.) The latest issue of the *Zeitschrift* 7 : 3 contains an essay of mine on Julien Benda in the review section; I am sure you will like it.[4] But what am I to do? I don't have a duplicate copy.

To show you that I do everything within my power, from now on I will on occasion be sending you typewritten manuscripts to be incorporated into the archive. Whereas I must ask you to return quickly the Baudelaire manuscript I promised you, you may consider the accompanying reviews of Hönigswald and Sternberger[5] as dedicated to you. You should get your hands on Sternberger's book *Panorama: Ansichten vom 19. Jahrhundert* at some point, which you surely already know of as an attempt at plagiarism.[6] You will find the Beatrice sonnet enclosed as well.[7]

I take note of the changes in the world of publishing with interest. Rowohlt showed up in my room at about the same time as your news about Schocken being closed down. He had to turn his back on Germany rather hurriedly. He can do no wrong in my book, not because of this, but because he made Hessel's life easier in Berlin for a long time (Hessel himself made it here three months ago)[8] and kept Jewish employees on his payroll as long as he could. I never took him seriously politically. He is going to Brazil, mainly to resettle his family, as I see it, and after that to look around in Europe again. He has his old publishing company halfway intact in Paris at the moment, should the occasion arise.[9] Polgar and Speyer turned up here a short time ago.

Dora passed through Paris six weeks ago. I have the impression that the liquidation of her enterprise in San Remo is going well. Meanwhile, she has opened up a boardinghouse in London, together with an English partner.[10] The chances of Stefan's naturalization appear to be good.[11] It is to be hoped that he will take his final high-school exams in London.

I would like to hear from you about how things are in your part of the world. Aren't the shootings in Jerusalem supposed to have died down somewhat? But above all: is everything all right with your eyes by now?—Hearing that you are still weighing the possibility of having me as a visitor pleased me very much. I'm only afraid that the list of wild and tame peoples whom one has to seek permission from is getting longer by the day.

Your report on America was really marvelous. I was convinced by what you say about country and people (I have taken to relating this part now and then for the edification of a select audience); the passages devoted to the institute hardly introduced thoughts that hadn't been my own for some time. I have all the more reason to thank you for the manner in which you behaved there on the basis of such an accurate assessment of my interests.

There is a doctor living here who treats Shestov's widow. The poor woman sits beneath the volumes of her husband's works, their pages still uncut. What will we leave behind someday, other than our own writings with their uncut pages? To make her interior look a bit more amiable, she hauls away a few of these writings now and then, and in this way I am slowly building up a collection of Shestov's writings. I decided on impulse that I would read *Athens and Jerusalem*[12] someday. If you imagine a good fairy who suddenly gets the urge to transform the filthiest cul-de-sac in the most desolate corner of a large city's outskirts into an inaccessible mountain valley, in which the sides of the mountain flanks plummet as steeply perpendicular as the facades of the block of tenements had before, then you have the image in which Shestov's philosophy appears to me. It is, I believe, rather admirable but useless. One can only take off one's hat to the commentator in him, and I think his style is superb. I hope I'll have occasion to write a review of the book.[13]

The route from Shestov to Kafka is not a long one for anyone who might have decided to disregard the essential. More and more, the essential feature in Kafka seems to me to be humor. He himself was not a humorist, of course. Rather, he was a man whose fate it was to keep stumbling upon people who made humor their profession: clowns. *Amer-*

ika in particular is one large clown act. And concerning the friendship with Brod, I think I am on the track of the truth when I say: Kafka as Laurel felt the onerous obligation to seek out his Hardy—and that was Brod. However that may be, I think the key to Kafka's work is likely to fall into the hands of the person who *is able to extract the comic aspects from Jewish theology*. Has there been such a man? Or would you be man enough to be that man?

Hannah Stern returns your greetings most warmly.

All the best to you and yours,

Yours, Walter

P.S. What is the meaning of your reference to Kafka in connection with the ending of *Three-Penny Novel?*

1. The letter had been typewritten.
2. [See letter 306.—Trans.]
3. Alfred Cohn, to whom WB used to send his writings.
4. *Schriften* 3:550–52.
5. They were first printed in *Schriften* 3:564–69, 572–79.
6. Dolf Sternberger made the following remarks about this review and WB's accusations in the new edition of his book *Panorama oder Ansichten vom 19. Jahrhundert* (Frankfurt am Main: Suhrkamp, 1974) [*Panorama of the Nineteenth Century*, trans. Joachim Neugroschel (New York: Urizen Books, 1977)]: "The judgment W.B. made in Parisian exile at the time, in a manuscript which has only recently come to light, was a painful one for me. I owe him much, not least the sharpening of my eye for the foreign and dead aspects of historical details, as well as a feeling for proceeding configuratively, but I of course did not yet know any of his own relevant works. His essay begins sympathetically, ending in a harsh and angry tone. He too recognized the original critical motivation and characterized it with precision, but he failed to see the 'concept' that would succeed in bringing the remote together, namely, social analysis. He wanted to achieve such an analysis in his own great work on the Paris arcades: my book, related in subject matter, could not possibly satisfy him. I could not then and cannot now confer on class concepts and economic categories the capacity to intercept or illuminate historical conceptions. Benjamin himself believed in it at the time, but could not act accordingly: even in his work, definitions are surpassed by images."
7. See Scholem, *WB*, pp. 208–9.
8. Franz Hessel, one of WB's few close friends, finally left Germany following Kristallnacht, when the atmosphere became imminently dangerous for Jewish writers.
9. Implying that in WB's opinion Rowohlt Verlag's most important authors were Jews (such as Alfred Polgar and Wilhelm Speyer, even though the latter had been baptized).
10. Dora ran a number of such houses in the London neighborhood of Notting Hill until her death in 1964.
11. These prospects were frustrated by the outbreak of the war. Instead, Stefan was deported to Australia in 1941 as an "enemy alien," and the treatment he was subjected to on the ship, where he was under the authority of German Nazis, severely traumatized him. (He later became an antiquarian bookseller in London and died in 1972.)
12. Shestov's last work.
13. This review was never written.

309.* To Gerhard Scholem

Paris
February 20, 1939

Dear Gerhard,

I suggested to Hannah Arendt that she make the manuscript of her book on Rahel Varnhagen available to you.[1] It should be sent off to you in the next few days.

The book made a great impression on me. It swims with powerful strokes against the current of edifying and apologetic Judaic studies. You know best of all that everything one could read about "the Jews in German literature" up to now has allowed itself to be swept along on precisely this current.[2]

I will begin to rework the section "The Flaneur"[3] in the next few days. When that is done, the problem of printing this chapter will be raised once again. For me, among all literary procedures, rewriting is the one I like least. I have greater things in mind, so overcoming that resistance might in this case prove worthwhile.

Entre temps I have returned once again to reflect on Kafka. I am also leafing through older papers and asked myself why you haven't yet sent my criticism of Brod's book to Schocken. Or has this taken place in the meantime?

I hope to hear from you in great detail forthwith.

Most sincerely,
Yours, Walter

1. I kept this manuscript and later was able to send it back to Hannah Arendt when she thought all other copies lost. The book first appeared in 1956 (in English) [*Rahel Varnhagen: The Life of a Jewish Woman,* trans. Richard and Clara Winston, rev. ed. (New York: Harcourt Brace, 1974)], the German original in 1959.

2. WB had bitter memories of the article he had written for volume 5 of the German *Encyclopaedia Judaica* (1930) being completely rewritten by the editors and "purged of everything essential." See the remark he wrote on his copy of the offprint (*Schriften* 2:1521).

3. *Schriften* 1:537–69. [English translation by Harry Zohn in WB, *Charles Baudelaire: A Lyric Poet in the Era of High Capitalism* (London: New Left Books, 1973), pp. 35–66.—Smith.]

310. To Theodor W. Adorno

Paris
February 23, 1939

Dear Teddie,

On est philologue ou on ne l'est pas. After I had studied your last letter, my first inclination was to go back to the significant bundle of papers I have containing your comments on the *Arcades.* Reading these letters, some of which go back quite a ways, was a great tonic: I saw again that the foundations have not been eroded or damaged. Above all, however, these earlier comments enlightened me about your last letter and especially about the kind of reflections appropriate to this type of letter.

"All hunters look alike." This is what you wrote on June 5, 1935, apropos a reference to Maupassant. This leads to a place in the state of affairs to which I will be able to accommodate myself the moment I know the editorial board's final expectations for my treatment of the flaneur. You have given my letter the most felicitous interpretation by making this kind of arrangement. Without relinquishing the place the chapter must occupy in my book on Baudelaire—now that the more evident sociological findings have been secured—I can devote myself to defining the flaneur within the total context of the *Arcades* and in my usual monographic form. Two indications of how this should be conceived follow.

Equality or sameness is a category of cognition; strictly speaking, it is not to be found in sober perception. Perception that is sober in the strictest sense of the word, free of all prejudgment, would always come upon something similar, even in the most extreme case. The kind of prejudice that as a rule accompanies perception without doing any harm can be offensive in exceptional cases. It can mark the person who is perceiving as someone who is *not* sober. This, for example, is the case with Don Quixote. Chivalric romances went to his head. As varied as the things he encounters may be, he always perceives the same thing in them—the adventure awaiting the itinerant knight. Now to Daumier: as you quite correctly suggest, when painting Don Quixote, he paints his own likeness. Daumier also repeatedly comes upon the same thing; he perceives the same thing in all the heads of politicians, ministers, and lawyers—the baseness and mediocrity of the bourgeoisie. In this regard, however, one thing is of primary importance: the hallucination of equality or sameness (which is punctured by the caricature only to reestablish itself as soon as possible; for the further removed a grotesque nose is from the norm, the better it will show as "nose" per se what is typical about the human being with nose) is a comic occasion for Daumier, just as it is for Cervantes. In *Don Quixote,* the reader's laughter rescues the honor of the bourgeois world, in comparison with which the world of the knight is revealed as uniform and simplistic. Daumier's laughter, on the contrary, is directed at the bourgeois; he sees through the equality it flaunts: namely, as the flimsy *égalité* boasted of in Louis Philippe's sobriquet. Through laughter, both Cervantes and Daumier sweep away an equality that they apprehend as historical illusion. Equality has a completely different image in Poe, not to mention in Baudelaire. In *The Man of the Crowd,* you can probably still see flashes of the possibility of an exorcism by means of the comic.

There is no question of this in Baudelaire. Rather, he artificially came to the aid of the historical hallucination of equality, which had taken root along with the commodity economy. And the tropes in which hashish was reflected for him can be deciphered in this context.

The commodity economy arms the phantasmagoria of sameness which, as the attribute of intoxication, as the same time authenticates itself as the central trope of illusion. "With this libation in your body, you will soon come to see Helen in every woman." The price makes the commodity equal to all of those that can be bought for the same price. The commodity does not only and not also establish itself—this is the decisive correction to Sommer's text—in the buyers, but above all in its price. It is precisely in this regard, however, that the flaneur attunes himself to the commodity; he imitates it completely; in the absence of demand for him, namely a market price, he makes himself at home in venality itself. The flaneur outdoes the whore in this; he, as it were, takes her abstract concept for a walk. Only in the flaneur's final incarnation does he fulfill the concept: namely, as the man with a sandwich board.

From the perspective of my Baudelaire study, the revised construct will look like this; I will do justice to the definition of *flanerie* as a state of intoxication; consequently, its connection to the experiences Baudelaire had produced with drugs. I will already introduce the concept of the immutable in the second part as the immutable *phenomenon* while reserving its definitive character as the concept of the immutable *occurrence* for the third part.

You see that I am grateful to you for your suggestions about the type. When I went beyond them, I did so in the most fundamental spirit of the *Arcades* project itself. Balzac consequently distances himself from me, so to speak. He only has anecdotal significance here in that he brings into play neither the comical nor the horrible side of the type. (I believe that Kafka was the first to have redeemed both of them together in the novel; in Kafka, the Balzac types took up solid residence in the illusion: they turned into "the aides," "the bureaucrats," "village residents," "the lawyers" to whom K. is contrasted as the only human being, therefore as an atypical being in all his averageness.)

Second, I will briefly address your desire to introduce the arcades as not just the milieu of someone who acts like a flaneur. I am able to redeem your trust in my archive and will let the remarkable reveries that, around midcentury, built the city of Paris as a series of glass galleries, of winter gardens as it were, have their say. The name of the Berlin cabaret—I will try to find out when it originated—gives you an idea what life in this dream city may have been like.—The flaneur chapter will thus become more like the one that appeared back then in the physiognomic cycle, where it was surrounded by studies on the collector, the forger, and the gambler.

Today I would rather not deal in detail with the comments you make on specific passages. To take one example, your comment on the Foucault citation was clear to me. I cannot agree, among other things, with your questioning Baudelaire's social classification as a petit bourgeois. Baudelaire lived on a small income from some land he owned in Neuilly. He had to share it with a stepbrother. His father was a *petit maître* who had a sinecure as a curator of the Luxembourg gardens during the Restoration. The deciding factor is that Baudelaire was cut off for his entire life from all acquaintance with the world of finance and the upper middle class.

You look askance at Simmel—. Is it not high time to give him his due as one of the forefathers of cultural Bolshevism? (I say this not to support the citation that, in fact, I would not want to do without, but on which too much stress is placed in its current position.) I recently looked at his *Philosophy of Money* [*Philosophie des Geldes*]. There is certainly good reason for it to be dedicated to Reinhold and Sabine Lepsius; there is good reason that it stems from the time in which Simmel was permitted to "approach" the circle around George. It is, however, possible to find much that is very interesting in the book if its basic idea is resolutely ignored. I found the critique of Marx's value theory remarkable.

The observations on the philosophy of absolute concentration in the last issue were a real pleasure.[1] Being homesick for Germany has its problematical sides; homesickness for the Weimar Republic (and what else would this philosophy be?) is simply beastly. The allusions to France in the text take the same tack as my own most personal experiences and reflections. In my last literary report to Max, I could have written a novel about this. The one *fait divers,* that the newspaper of the local branch of the party has recently been made available in the [Hotel] Littré, may give you an idea of the way the wind is blowing. I came upon it when I visited Kolisch.[2] I listened to his quartet give an evening concert and before he left I spent a pleasant hour with him. [. . .] On the same occasion, by the way, I saw Soma Morgenstern,[3] who made it out of Vienna at the last moment.

If you can spare it, I would like to have a look at the book by Hawkins.[4] It would certainly be tempting to investigate a relationship between Poe and Comte. As far as I know, there is none between Baudelaire and him, no more than there is between Baudelaire and Saint-Simon. Comte, on the other hand, was a disciple *attitré* of Saint-Simon for a time when he was about twenty years old. Among other things, he took from the Saint-Simonians the speculations on the mother, but gave them a positivist cachet, coming out with the assertion that nature would succeed in producing in the *vierge-mère* the female being that impregnates itself. You may be interested in the fact that, in the coup d'état of September 2, Comte yielded no less promptly than the Parisian aesthetes. But to make up for that, in his humanistic religion he had previously provided for an anniversary dedicated to the solemn damnation of Napoleon I.

And since we are on the topic of books: Earlier you had referred me to Maupassant's "La nuit, un cauchemar." I have looked through about twelve volumes of his novellas without finding it. Could you let me know what the situation is? A no less urgent request: to send me a copy of your Kierkegaard should you still have one available. I would likewise be very happy to get the *Theory of the Novel* [*Theorie des Romans* by Georg Lukács] on loan.

I am saddened to hear, from Kolisch among others, what your parents have gone through. I hope that in the meantime they have had the good luck to escape.

Let me confirm my receipt of the Hauff with my deepest gratitude. I will write Felizitas next week.

Most sincere regards to both of you.
Yours, Walter

1. Max Horkheimer, "Die Philosophie der absoluten Konzentration," *Zeitschrift für Sozialforschung* 7 (1938), pp. 376–87.

2. Rudolf Kolisch, an important musician; leader and first violinist of the Kolisch Quartet; Arnold Schoenberg's brother-in-law.

3. Born in Poland, Morgenstern [1896–1976] lived in Vienna after the First World War and wrote for the *Frankfurter Zeitung*. He was a friend of Alban Berg and Joseph Roth. He emigrated to New York via Paris.

4. Richmond Laurin Hawkins, *Positivism in the United States (1835–1861)* (Cambridge, Mass., 1938).

311.* To Gerhard Scholem

Paris
April 8, 1939

Dear Gerhard,

Your letter was as sparingly imbued with verdant hope as the streets of Paris are suffused with the green of this cold spring. This made the wintry prospects between the lines of your letter all the more pronounced. Never an enemy of clarity, I am least of all so now, when the years have led me to believe I know exactly what I can or cannot make my peace with. The significance my mentioning a specific sum in my letter of March 14 had—and no other—was that I wanted this second side of the alternative to be represented.

The same conditions that threaten my European situation will in all likelihood make emigration to the U.S.A. impossible. Such a move is only possible on the basis of an invitation, and an invitation could only come about at the instigation of the institute. You are surely aware that the quota is already filled for the next four or five years. I don't think it very likely that the institute, even if it had the power to do so, would want to arrange my invitation at this time. For there is no reason to assume that such an invitation would solve the problem of my livelihood, and the institute, I suspect, would find the immediate linkage of these problems especially irritating.

I haven't heard anything further from the institute since I sent you my last report, but you may find it useful to learn that it brought out a thirty-page informational brochure in English about half a year ago, in which I am rather prominently represented by a cursory bibliography of my writings.

Here in Paris I met with a helpful party in the guise of Hannah Arendt. It remains to be seen whether her efforts will lead to anything. At the moment, I am still getting my stipend—but all guarantees are gone.

The documents I travel on are the French identification papers for *réfugiés provenants d'Allemagne* [refugees of German origin], and these go hand in hand with the French residence permit. They are recognized by England, and that is a sufficient administrative basis for a visa to Palestine. Some time ago—rather a long time, to be sure, and who knows what effect the events in Europe may have had for her—Kitty Marx-Steinschneider showed herself in the course of our conversations in Paris to be willing to facilitate my stay in Palestine. I myself am clearly not in a position to appeal to her, since I did not receive a reply from her to an involved letter, unclouded by personal concerns, which I sent her last summer.

In order to be as thorough as possible on my part: should a stay in Palestine be economically feasible, then I would be able to finance the trip from here.

It was not welcome news to hear that you have reason to complain about your eyes these days. Do you have a doctor there in whom you have complete confidence? I know that this is especially important where eye troubles are concerned.

You can surely understand that I have difficulty applying myself to projects oriented toward the institute at the moment. If you add to this the fact that making revisions is less attractive than new endeavors, anyway, you will understand that reformulating the flaneur chapter is making rather sluggish headway. It will, I hope, prove to be advantageous, if the planned book shows incisive changes. As a consequence, the character of the flaneur in Baudelaire's person may well achieve the plasticity you are probably correct in finding deficient in the present text. To this end, the problem of the "type" will be developed in a philosophically precarious sense. And, at last, the great poem "Les Sept vieillards," which has never been the subject of an interpretation, will be given a surprising yet, as I hope, convincing explanation.

Indeed, your objections do coincide with those of Wiesengrund where you suspected they would. I am not far from admitting that I wanted to provoke them. The overall conception of the "Baudelaire"—which now only exists as a draft, of course—shows the philosophical bow being bent to the greatest extent possible. I was sorely tempted to confront it with a modest, even homegrown method of philological explication, which I give in to now and then in the second part. In this connection, I want to tell you that your suspicion was correct that the passage on allegory has been kept hermetic intentionally.

I could only drop my request that you return the manuscript to me immediately if you were to compensate me with the German or French manuscript of your treatise on Jewish mysticism. You can well imagine how much I desire to study that text. Enclosed is the Brecht sonnet, as a token of appeasement. (The next-to-last word in the second line deviates from the first version I recited to you by heart, as you will remember.)[1]

I would very much like to know what kind of impression *Rahel Varnhagen* made upon you. I am less urgently interested in hearing whether you have ever come across the novel *Der Sohn des verlornen Sohnes,* by Soma Morgenstern, which Erich Reiss published in 1935. If so, let me know what you think about the book. Its author, Heinrich Simon's son-in-law, used to cross my path in Frankfurt some years ago. I have now run into him again here: he left Vienna just in time. The book is the first volume of a trilogy, of which the second volume is already in manuscript form.

Best wishes to you and your wife,

Yours, Walter

On Dante's Poems to Beatrice

Even today, above the dusty vault
In which she lies, whom he could never have
Although he dogged her footsteps like a slave
Her name's enough to bring us to a halt.

For he ensured that we should not forget her.
Writing such splendid verse to her as made
Us listen to the compliments he paid
Convinced that no one ever put it better.

Dear me, what an abuse he started then
By praising in a manner so arresting
What he had only looked at without testing!

Since he made poems out of glimpses, men
Have seen what looks nice in its street attire
And stays bone-dry, as something to desire.[2]

1. The word in question was not *haben* (have), but *vögeln* (screw).
2. Translated by John Willett.

312. To Bernhard von Brentano

Paris
April 22, 1939

Dear Brentano,

Please accept my sincere thanks for your letter. It was also important to me for us to have talked. If the winds of war or of peace do not tear the last threads of the gossamer Indian summer we shared in Germany, we will presumably resume our conversation at some time—both of us the wiser.

Thank you very much for the effort you made on my behalf concerning the Spitteler book. If I get between 150 and 175 francs for it, that would be a fair price. I will send you the book in the next few days, along with the Winkler book.[1]

I agree with you if what you mean to say is that Winkler is among the very few individuals of his generation who do not want everything that was important to my generation to be lost. It is just that Winklerian thinking is substantially unclear to me. But it does seem to me that he provides an entirely clear example of the fact that the experiences of the contemporary individual can no longer be treated idealistically without doing harm to the substance and morality of perception. Winkler proceeds idealistically. And it seems to me that it is basically only the niveau that comes away unharmed.

I do believe that damage could have been done. For, indeed, this thinking does not revolve around just anything at all. (I say this even though I regard authors like Giono or the commercial writer Langgässer with the greatest reservations.) If there is anything in which I recognize an impassioned effort to hold firmly onto finds that are truly worth that effort, it is in the presentation of experience itself that is a factor in Winkler's book. In the essay about Jünger, I like the supposition by virtue of which "experience as a condition of passivity" takes the "place of perception in which the thinking person finds himself from the very beginning in an active relationship to reality." Precisely in what he writes about Jünger, however, this passivity does not seem to me to hold sway and experience does not seem to have had its say. I do not believe that he could have made his peace with Jünger's uncouth metaphysics without doing violence to himself. (By the way, I have nothing against metaphysicians. They are genuine troubadours of brittle reason. But Jünger behaves like a mercenary toward reason.)

The essay on Hölderlin is delightful. Its relationship to [Wilhelm] Michel's study *Hölderlins abendländische Wendung*[2] should be kept in mind. The publisher to some extent disavows the first George essay, but it seems to me by far the most lucid. The well-placed lines about Paul Valéry really seem very auspicious.

What I do miss is that nothing comes out about the circumstances of Winkler's death in the afterword.[3] Political motives may be at the bottom of his suicide, perhaps erotic ones. (The essay about Platen does not suggest that its author was a homosexual; but there is the brief review of Appel's poems.) I would like some information about this in order to get a more precise idea of the author's [image]. This much seems clear to me, namely that he was far from having come to terms with himself.

As of today, there has been no change in my circumstances; that is to say, I live in expectation of being overtaken by bad news. Until it does, I can get by, but I am unable to make provisions for the future. I will count myself lucky if there is enough time between now and such an eventuality for the efforts you are making on my behalf in Basel to yield results. In any case, I want to express my gratitude to you for having set things in motion.

Brecht has decided to give up his house on Fyn, presumably with a heavy heart. This will probably turn out to have been the right thing to do, since the election scheduled for this summer in Denmark may bring about quite a bit of unrest. Brecht is trying to get into Sweden. (In the meantime, I heard yesterday that a mobilization has been ordered in Sweden.)

I am working on a section of my book about Baudelaire that deals with the spectrum of leisure in bourgeois society. It is markedly different from "leisure" in feudal society, where it has the advantage of being flanked by the *vita contemplativa* on one side and by the life-style appropriate to one's class standing on the other. Baudelaire is the most profound practitioner of leisure in the epoch, inasmuch as there were still discoveries left to be made on the basis of this position.

Let me hear from you again.

Sincere regards to you and your wife.
Yours, Walter Benjamin

1. Eugen Gottlob Winkler, *Gestalten und Probleme* (Dessau, 1937), and *Dichter: Arbeiten* (Dessau, 1937).
2. Jena, 1923.
3. Winkler committed suicide in October 1936.

313. To Adrienne Monnier

Paris
April 29, 1939

My dear friend,

Here is the answer I just received from Pontigny. The name of the institution in question is "caisse des recherches scientifiques."

I am entrusting the enclosed copy of my text to you to pass on to Valéry. I was hesitant to inscribe it with a dedication to him, but will do so if you think it appropriate. If you do, please bring the copy to our next meeting, which I hope is imminent.

It might be useful if we could see each other before you visit Valéry. Let me add something you may find useful: from what I heard, the above mentioned *caisse des recherches* received money from the Israélite alliance universelle in order to be able to give some assistance to Jewish scholars. This may be important since Sylvain Lévy, president of the alliance until his death, deemed me worthy of receiving a grant from his organization. That was in 1934; the alliance's money had not yet been merged with that of the *caisse des recherches*.

Do you want to give me a call on Monday morning?

Sincerely yours,
Walter Benjamin

314. To Karl Thieme

Paris
June 8, 1939

Dear Mr. Thieme,

I was very happy to hear the news you gave me concerning your book's uncommon success.[1] I have read it in the meantime, and at least some of the reasons for this success are now clear to me. You demonstrated a skillful touch in how you presented your material. You mastered the most brittle form conceivable, namely, by not concealing this brittleness, unlike the dilettantes who try their hand at conversational form. Am I wrong in assuming that you studied the technique of the *Soirées de Saint-Petersbourg?*

Precisely because you dispensed with all anecdotal details, you were able to achieve a greater urbanity with this form and it really paid off. The popular appeal you often achieve, particularly in the chapter on adolescence, but always without making any concessions, will have contributed to your success. The confrontation between the Dominicans and the Franciscans, but especially your discussion of the matter under dispute between the Jesuits and the Jansenists, seems masterful to me.

In your case urbanity may only be the other side of courage, which is not all that rare. For me, the way your book balances political and theological boldness is an aesthetic spectacle of the highest order. The eschatological speculations of your concluding section are genuine theology, something one rarely encounters anymore nowadays. (Reading your book, I regretted not knowing Barth so that I could do justice to how your way of thinking is related to dialectical theology. My intuition tells me that the opposition must be almost total.) Even though I must be content with an attentive reception of its theological advances, my interest in your book's political intentions is naturally very spontaneous. I sincerely wish your comments on the inadequacy of private sanctification godspeed on their journey to readers. Not all your straightforwardly political statements appear to be unproblematical and it seems to me that your conciseness is too risky, particularly in the passage about the French Revolution. I at least doubt whether the upper middle class can really be described as the original mandator of the movement. I would almost be tempted to suspect sabotage in the censorship office, since distribution of the book has not been suppressed just on the basis of your comment about the people—I am referring to the excellent alternative on p. 41. (The possibilities of sabotage cannot be totally discounted.) The excursus about the "certainty" that is bought with hypocrisy and the condition of "being swept ever farther along" is somewhat more camouflaged but no less impressive.

On the basis of my reading, I once again reminded Lion about your book and would like to think that the matter is well under way. You will find an (anonymous) essay I wrote about Brecht's dramaturgy in the next issue of *Maß und Wert*.[2]

The photographs you requested should be in your hands by now.

Let me close with my most sincere regards.

Yours, Walter Benjamin

P.S. Does the fact that I have not yet heard anything about the book by Münch signify a negative decision?

1. *Am Ziel der Zeiten?* (1939).
2. "What Is Epic Theater?" ["Was ist das epische Theater?"], *Schriften* 2:259–67.

315. To Bernhard von Brentano

Paris
June 16, 1939

Dear Brentano,

Your wonderful sentence, "people don't allow anyone to say anything to them, but you can tell them anything," reminds me to send you a short piece on the storyteller in return for the nice volume of selections you gave me. I published it a few years ago; you are unlikely to have come across it.

I really love Keller's poems and have done so from time immemorial.

Please let me hear from you once again, this time in greater detail?

Kindest regards.
Yours, Walter Benjamin

316. To Margarete Steffin

[June 1939?]

Dear Grete,

I have been back from my Cistercian abbey in Burgundy for fourteen days. As useful as it was to me, thanks to the wonderful library, my stay there was rained out in the literal and every other sense, apart from that one positive aspect. Furthermore, no people were there with whom I could associate. Or if there were any, they were inconspicuous because of the atmosphere. This may have been the case with a Mrs. Stenbock-Fermor. Brecht will perhaps remember the name because of her husband. Shortly before Hitler, he published a Communist commentary on the living conditions of miners.[1]

Two dozen Spanish legionnaires were quartered in the vicinity of the abbey. I had no contact with them; but Mrs. Stenbock-Fermor held courses for them. Since she was very interested in Brecht's works, after my return I sent her *Furcht und Zittern* [*sic*][2] for a few days and she read aloud from it to the Spanish brigadiers (they were mostly Germans and Austrians). She writes that "the chalk cross, the ex-convict, labor service and the hour of the worker made the greatest impression on them and everything was genuinely and simply felt."

By the time you receive these lines, you will probably already know—for Stockholm is of course better provided for in terms of things literary than Svendborg—that portions of the cycle appeared in Pierre Abraham's translation in the June issue of the *Nouvelle revue française;* in all, about six or seven. I have thus far only been able to look at it in the library. The translation seems quite good to me. The *Nouvelle revue française* provided a brief, simple footnote to the effect that Brecht is the author of *The Three-Penny Opera* and *The Seven Deadly Sins* [*Die sieben Todsünden*].

Now for a word on my commentaries on the poems.[3] It is definite that none of them will be published in *Maß und Wert;* instead, I wrote a new essay[4] about Brecht's dramaturgy for that journal as soon as you had given me the news about the disappearance of *Das Wort*. It should appear in a very short time. As far as the commentaries are concerned, it is naturally very important to me for them to be published. I would be very pleased if Brecht would take the initiative and do me the favor of sending them to *Internationale Literatur.* I do not so much have in mind that he should do this as the author of the poems treated in the commentary, but rather in the name of the editorial board of *Das Wort,* since my essay is one of the manuscripts that had been submitted to them. (I am speaking figuratively, for I did not send a manuscript to Erpenbeck but just to you.) Be that as it may, Brecht is in touch with *Internationale Literatur* and I have no contact with it. I think it will be easy for Brecht to inquire whether such commentaries are of interest to these people. But if he does not want to submit them himself, he can surely request that the editorial board ask me to submit them. If the poetry volume appears now,[5] this will make everything easier, whereas it would be very difficult for me to approach *Internationale Literatur* on my own. Please write me about this.

There is unfortunately nothing to report about the Baudelaire at the moment. The New Yorkers have asked me to revise it. If my working conditions were not so unspeakably unfavorable, the revised manuscript would have been completed a long time ago and I believe the revision would include decisive improvements. I am by no means overly sensitive to noise but I am constantly forced to exist under conditions in which a truly noise-sensitive person would not get a single sentence down on paper in years. Now, during the summer, when I would be able to steal some time for myself on my terrace away from the din of the elevator, a good-for-nothing painter who whistles to himself the whole day has established himself on a balcony across the way (and God knows the street is narrow). I often sit there with wagon loads of concrete, paraffin, wax, etc. in my ears, but nothing helps. So much for the Baudelaire, which of course absolutely *must* make progress now.

As usual when a project becomes very urgent, I have taken on some trivial tasks. I put together a small montage—just like my book of letters—for the 150th anniversary celebration of the French Revolution. It is supposed to demonstrate the effect of the French Revolution on contemporary German authors and even on a later generation, up to 1830. While writing it, I again came across some evidence that was willfully obscured by German literary history for a hundred years. Imagine my amazement when, after a careful reading, I determined that, of the two volumes of Klopstock's odes, one-fifth of all the pieces in the second volume of later odes deal with the French Revolution.

I rarely socialize; even though I am not writing, the day still passes with my attempts to do so. I have not even seen Dudow for a long time; but yesterday I heard from Kracauer that he is not well.

Did I write you that I believe I have gotten to the bottom of the mystery surrounding the small parcels of tobacco? They can't be tied. But they will get through customs as samples having no commercial value if you send them in an envelope (with a paper clip). Would you want to try once again? I would like that.

Are you learning Swedish like a good girl? Write soon! Sincere regards to you and Brecht.

Yours, Walter Benjamin

P.S. Karl Kraus died too soon after all. Listen to this: the Vienna gas board has stopped supplying gas to Jews. A consequence of the gas consumption of the Jewish population was that the gas company lost money, since it was precisely the biggest users who did not pay their bills. The Jews preferred to use the gas to commit suicide.

P.P.S. I now have the *Versuche* in their entirety except for 15/16—the only thing missing is the issue with the *Dreigroschenprozeß,* etc. Could you snatch *that* away from Brecht for me? And could you tell me if the *Peakheads* was printed in the *Versuche?*[6] And basically what came out after 15/16?

1. Alexander Graf Stenbock-Fermor, *Meine Erlebnisse als Bergarbeiter* (1929).
2. *Furcht und Elend des Dritten Reiches.* It was then known only in manuscript form.
3. Published posthumously; *Schriften* 2:351–72.
4. "What Is Epic Theater?"
5. *Svendborger Gedichte* (London, 1939).
6. *Versuche,* vol. 8 (essay 17); it was typeset in 1933 but was not printed.

317. To Gretel Adorno

Paris
June 26, 1939

Dear Felizitas,

Today I want to return to my "beloved German." If, however, my letter from Pontigny left you with a true desire for French, you would do me a favor by opening up in good time a copy of the *Flowers of Evil* and looking at it through my eyes. We would then be sure to encounter one another, since my thoughts are now fixed on this text day and night.

Regarding the embodiment of these thoughts, you will not easily rediscover last summer's Baudelaire in it. In its new version, the flaneur chapter—indeed, my time is exclusively devoted to developing it—will try to integrate crucial motifs from my essay on reproduction and from the one on the storyteller in combination with the same kind of motifs in the *Arcades*. I have never been certain in any earlier work to this degree of the vanishing point at which (and, as it now seems, from time immemorial) all of my reflections come together from the most divergent points. I did not have to be told twice that both of you are determined to go forward with the most extreme of my old fund of reflections. One restriction of course remains: for the time being, it is always only the flaneur and not the total complex of the Baudelaire with which you will have to deal. Even without this restriction, the chapter will go far beyond the size of last year's flaneur. Since, however, it will now be divided into three distinct parts—the arcades, the crowd, the type—this will probably make it easier for the editorial staff to cope with. I am still far from completing the final copy. But the era of slow progress is behind me and not a day passes without my putting something down on paper.

To my delight, I recently received the galleys of my review of volume 16 of the *Encyclopédie française*.[1] The complete silence that greeted my review of Sternberger's *Panorama*[2] again went through my mind when I received them. Not even you broke this silence when you recently wrote me about the book itself. (I am familiar with Allan Bott's wonderful collection of photographs.) I would have thought that, completely apart from its critical stance, my essay has something new to say in the observations devoted to the structure of the "genre." Don't you want to write me something about this?

I am chalking up a small literary victory for myself. It has been ten years since I wrote an essay called "What Is Epic Theater?" for the *Frankfurter Zeitung*. At that time, just after the galleys (which I still have) had been printed, it was withdrawn due to Diebold's ultimatum, passed on through Gubler. Now I have found a home for it, with only slight changes, in *Maß und Wert,* initiating a debate on Brecht. You will find it in the next issue.

My summer plans about which you inquired depend on when Schapiro[3] is due to arrive. Or does he plan to spend a long time in Paris? The chances of seeing him would then be a sure thing in any case.—I will not leave France this year, and by no means Paris, before the rough draft of the flaneur is completely finished.

I wonder whether what I asked for as a birthday present will still arrive in good time? I am truthfully not far from viewing the copy of the essay on reproduction as what I wished for. However, so that you will not think there is a deadline for this, I also want my wish for a small book to have been registered. I think I will be delighted if you give me the last book by Robert Dreyfus, who just died. He was an old friend of Proust; he called it *De Monsieur Thiers à Proust* and it contains many stories about Mrs. Straus, which I will happily promise to tell you.

I have not seen the painting by Picasso about which you inquired.

Sincere regards to Teddie. Best wishes,

Yours, Detlef

1. The review never appeared but is preserved in manuscript form.
2. This extant review also remains unpublished.
3. Meyer Schapiro, professor of art history at Columbia University in New York.

318. To Theodor W. Adorno

Paris
August 6, 1939

Dear Teddie,

I believe you are on vacation with Felizitas. These lines will presumably reach you after some delay, giving the Baudelaire manuscript, which was sent to Max a week ago,[1] time to catch up to them.

As for the rest, please do not be angry if these lines look more like an index of headings than a letter. Given the impact of the most horrible weather, I am unusually worn out after my rigorous week-long confinement, which was a prerequisite for the completion of the Baudelaire chapter. But this will not prevent me from telling you and Felizitas how much I am looking forward to the prospect of seeing you again. (I must not completely lose sight of the fact that there will still be difficulties to overcome between this prospect and its realization. I wrote Morgenroth about the sale of my Klee painting; if you see him, don't forget to ask about it.)

No matter how little the new Baudelaire chapter can still be considered a "revision" of one of the chapters you already know, I think that the effect of our correspondence about last summer's Baudelaire will be obvious to you in this version. Above all, I did not have to be told twice how gladly you would trade the panoramic overview of the subject matter for a more precise realization of its theoretical underpinnings. And that you are ready to absolve the climbing expedition required to view the parts of these underpinnings that are at a higher altitude.

Regarding the above-mentioned index of headings, it consists of an index to the many and comprehensive motifs omitted from the new chapter (in comparison with the corresponding flaneur chapter of last summer). These motifs are naturally not to be eliminated from the total complex of the Baudelaire; what I have in mind are in-depth interpretative amplifications where they occur.

The motifs of arcade, noctambulism, the feuilleton, as well as a theoretical introduction of the concept of the phantasmagoria, are reserved for the first section of the second part. The motifs of the trace, the type, and empathy for the commodity soul are earmarked for the third section. The present middle section of the second part will set forth the complete figure of the flaneur but only in conjunction with its first and third sections.

I have taken into account your reservation about the Engels and Simmel quotations that you expressed in your letter of February 1; not, of course, by deleting them. This time I have indicated what is so important to me about the Engels quotation. From the outset, your objection to the Simmel quotation seemed to me to be well-founded. In the present text, it has taken on a less demanding function by virtue of its altered place value.

I am delighted at the prospect of seeing the text in the next issue. I wrote Max how much I have tried to keep anything of a fragmentary nature out of the essay while staying within the prescribed length. I would be happy if no drastic changes (*pour tout dire:* deletions) were destined for it.

I will let my Christian Baudelaire be taken into heaven by nothing but Jewish angels. But arrangements have already been made to let him fall as if by chance in the last third of the ascension, shortly before his entrance into glory.

In conclusion, my dear Teddie, let me thank you for having invited my Jochmann[2] to participate in the impending jubilee issue.

Best wishes to you and Felizitas for a good vacation and a pleasant return home.

Yours, Walter

Dear Felizitas, let me say a special word of thanks for the book by [Robert] Dreyfus[3] and the cover letter announcing its arrival. I often think of both of you.

1. This version of the Baudelaire study was published in the *Zeitschrift für Sozialforschung;* in *Schriften* 1:426–72.

2. Walter Benjamin, "Einleitung zu Carl Gustav Jochmann, *Die Rückschritte der Poesie*" [Introduction to Carl Gustav Jochmann's *Die Rückschritte der Poesie*], 8 (1939), pp. 92–103.

3. *De Monsieur Thiers à Proust.*

319. To Bernhard von Brentano

[Summer 1939]

Dear Brentano,

I recently came into possession of your book[1] again and read it in forty-eight hours. A rare event for me, who usually needs three weeks to read a mystery. But your book is fascinating. I found a subject near and dear to me being treated for the first time: the historical conditions of love, its historical moments and seasons.

A great gamble has paid off for you with the creation of the figure of Countess Orloff: you have summoned on stage a woman for whom years are of no more significance in her love than days are in the short-lived infatuations of our contemporaries. I knew a woman like this really well. She was twenty years older than I and may still be alive. (Based on this knowledge, I believe that the countess is simply predestined for the Goethe cult. Just like the figure I have in mind, she could have said of herself: I have married my Christian Vulpius.) I have always found the most successful formulation of this archaic love, in which the time of waiting is also the time of growth, in Johann Peter Hebel's *Das unverhoffte Wiedersehen*.

With all the sobriety of your presentation and while almost totally abstaining from all description, you have still surrounded your readers with the atmosphere of the capital city. The salon whose windows open up onto the Cornelius Bridge [is] a vignette that reproduces the atmosphere of an entire chapter of Berlin life.

Against the background of historical relationships as they affect the relationship between men and women, the changes in the forms of government appear as wrinkles that have no impact on what is woven into a Gobelin tapestry. (I think that your offhand allusions to the new regime simultaneously contain the sharpest condemnations imaginable of the Weimar Republic.)

Once again—and only now *en pleine connaissance de cause*—let me express my gratitude for the excellent book. I hope that its translation into French—for Grasset?—will soon follow.

You will receive two of my essays in the next few days. The "Baudelaire" is a new publication, which will be followed by others about the poet as circumstances allow.—In [ending missing]

1. *Die ewigen Gefühle* (Amsterdam, 1939; reprint, Darmstadt, 1963).

320. To Adrienne Monnier[1]

Camp des travailleurs volontaires
Clos St. Joseph, Nevers (Nièvre)
September 21, 1939

Dear Miss Monnier,

Your concierge may have told you that I came on Saturday—eight days before war was declared—by your house to say goodbye. Unfortunately, you were not there.

All of us have been greatly affected by the horrible catastrophe. Let us hope that the witnesses to European civilization and the French spirit will survive the murderous rage of Hitler, along with their accounts of it. I would be delighted to hear from you. My address is Camp des travailleurs volontaires, groupement 6 Clos St. Joseph NEVERS (Nièvre).

I am doing as well as can be expected. There is plenty of food. We are impatiently waiting to hear what is in store for us. Able-bodied men are hurrying to enlist. I truly would like to serve our cause to the best of my ability. My physical strength, however, is worthless. I collapsed on the walk from Nevers to our camp. The camp doctors gave me the following order: "at ease—rest."

I have affidavits from Valéry and Romains with me. But I have not yet had the occasion to produce them. A similar affidavit would probably be very helpful, but one that is dated more recently and is more relevant to the situation in which I find myself.

Let me end this letter with sincere wishes for your well-being and the well-being of all the people and values you hold dear.

I remain faithfully yours, my dear Miss Monnier.

Walter Benjamin

1. Written while WB was in the internment camp, in Paris when under threat of occupation, and in flight from the German troops, letters 320–26 were written in French after the outbreak of war.

321. To Gretel Adorno

Camp des travailleurs volontaires
Clos Saint-Joseph Nevers (Nièvre)
October 12, 1939

My dear,

I had such a beautiful dream while lying on my cot last night that I am unable to resist my desire to tell you about it. There are so few beautiful, not to mention pleasant, things about which I can tell you. This is one of those dreams, the likes of which I may have once every five years, that center around the motif of "reading." Teddie will remember the role played by this motif in my reflections on epistemology. The sentence I spoke aloud at the end of the dream happened to be in French. This is another reason to give an account of it in the same language. Doctor Dausse is with me in the dream. He is a friend who took care of me when I had malaria.

I was with Dausse and several others I do not remember. Dausse and I left the group at one point. After leaving the others, we found ourselves at an excavation. I noticed strange kinds of resting places at almost ground level. They were the shape and length of sarcophagi and looked like they were made of stone. As I knelt, however, I realized that I was gently sinking into them like onto a bed. They were covered with moss and ivy. I saw that there were always two of these resting places side by side. Just as I was about to lie down on the one that was next to the one apparently reserved for Dausse, I realized that it was already occupied by other people. So we kept on going. The place resembled a forest but there was something artificial in the way the tree trunks and the branches were arranged, which made this part of the scenery look something like a shipyard. Walking along some beams and climbing some wooden steps, we reached a kind of tiny, planked deck. The women with whom Dausse lived were here. There were three or four of them and they looked very beautiful. The first thing that surprised me was that Dausse did not introduce me. This did not bother me any more than the discovery I made when I put my hat on top of a grand piano. It was an old straw hat, a panama, which I had inherited from my father. (The hat is long gone.) When I took it off, I was shocked to see that a wide slit had been cut into the crown. There were also some traces of red along the edge of the slit.—They brought me a chair. This did not prevent me from taking another one that I placed a short distance away from the table at which everyone was seated. I did not sit down. Meanwhile, one of the women was engaged with graphology. I saw that she was holding something I had written which Dausse had given to her. I was somewhat worried by her graphological analysis because I feared that some of my personal characteristics might be revealed. I went closer. I saw a piece of cloth covered with images. The only graphological element I was able to distinguish was the top part of the letter *d.* Its elongation revealed an extreme aspiration to achieve spirituality. Appended to this part of the letter was a small sail with a blue border, and the sail was billowing as if filled by the wind. That is the only thing I was able to "read"—otherwise, there were only indistinct shapes of waves and clouds. The conversation resolved for a time around this piece of handwriting. I am unable to recall the opinions expressed. But I do know very well that at some point I said precisely this: "It was a matter of turning a poem into a fichu." I had barely uttered these words when something intriguing happened. I noticed that one of the women who was very beautiful was lying on a bed. When she heard my explanation, she made an extremely rapid movement. She pushed aside a bit of the blanket that was covering her as she lay in bed. It took her less than a second to do this. It was not to let me see her body, but to see the pattern of her sheet. The sheet must have had imagery similar to the kind I had probably "written" years ago to give to Dausse. I was quite aware that the woman had made this gesture. But the reason I was aware of it was because of a kind of extrasensory perception. For my bodily eyes were somewhere else. And I was not at all able to distinguish what was on the sheet that had been surreptitiously revealed to me.

After this dream, I could not fall asleep for hours. Out of happiness. And I write you in order to share these hours with you.

There is nothing new. No decision has been made about us thus far. The arrival of a "commission de triage" was announced but we do not know when they will come. My health is not all that good. The rainy weather contributes nothing to its improvement. As for money, there isn't any. We are not allowed more than twenty francs. Your letters would be a great comfort to me. [. . .] A French friend is taking care of my business in Paris with the help of my sister.

Apart from sending me a letter, you can give me no greater pleasure than by sending me the proofs (or the manuscript) of the "Baudelaire."

Please forgive any mistakes you may find in this letter. It is being written in the midst of the perpetual din that has enveloped me for over a month.

Need I add that I am eager to make myself more useful to my friends and the enemies of Hitler than I can be in my present state. I do not cease to hope for a change and I am sure your efforts and your wishes will be joined with mine. Remember me to all our friends.

Love, Detlef

322. To Gisèle Freund

Nevers (Nièvre)
November 2, 1939

My dear friend,

I guessed from some things Sylvia[1] said that you had finally returned. My joy was not diminished at seeing this guess confirmed. The only happy moments I enjoy here come from the few letters I receive that have something special, such as you put into the one you sent. And under these circumstances, happiness equals hope for me.

I hope you will be fully recovered by the time you read these lines. I was very interested in your news from England—I am referring to the news you shared in your last letter, since I had not received any prior to that. I was aware of the treatment of refugees; your description of London, on the other hand, contained some totally unexpected and poignant details. I mainly regret that you were not able to wait for the "sitting" that the government should have granted you for you to take their picture. Let's hope you will have another chance.

By the time I received your letter, I had already heard from Adrienne the good news you mentioned in a postscript. I wrote her two days ago to express my most heartfelt gratitude. In the meantime, I found out that the Pen Club must know all about my situation because Hermann Kesten was released. Kesten was in a camp next to mine. We originally only had a polite relationship, but it has been marked by a sense of loyalty ever since we were at Colombe. We saw each other here two or three times after that. I hear that, when Kesten returned, he was put up at the welcome center of the Pen Club and saw Jules Romains there.

In a letter to Adrienne, I am taking care of the suggestion you made that I request affidavits from my friends attesting to my loyalty. She will show you the relevant passage. I mention in the letter a splendid affidavit written by [Paul] Desjardins. He professes "the greatest admiration" for my work (he even mentions the "Baudelaire"); he also professes a profound esteem for my "invincible attachment to the liberal and democratic ideas" on whose behalf France entered the struggle. [. . .] I do not need to tell you how valuable a few lines from Adrienne herself would be to me. I am however unable to believe that this kind of dossier (which I am trying to assemble) will be enough. It is apparently in Paris where the different cases will be thoroughly reviewed by an interministerial commission. And this is why all my hopes hinge on the process that Adrienne just initiated. This is also why, with her permission, I would like to write a few lines to Benjamin Crémieux.[2] It may be of use to me to inform him that I have not only translated Proust, but that I am the first person to have tried to make [Julien] Green and [Marcel] Jouhandeau familiar names in Germany; and that I am one of those who for years has advocated the work of people like Gide or Valéry there. If both you and Adrienne agree to this, I would appreciate it if you would send me Benjamin Crémieux's address.

I do not need to tell you that I am in complete agreement with you on Montherlant's *Girls* [*Jeunes filles*]. I myself only recently started reading again. I am currently reading Rousseau's *Confessions*. I really like it. You guessed right about the failures.

I deeply regret not having been able to correct the proofs of the "Baudelaire." I had decided to make some changes that would have eliminated what was superfluous. I do not know if the book has already appeared. You will get it in any case. And you must write me what you think of it.

Do not be stingy in sending me news. I think that the number of my joys is very limited, and your handwriting heralds a few of them. Regards to Adrienne and Helen.

Walter Benjamin

1. Sylvia Beach, owner of the bookstore Shakespeare et compagnie and a publisher of Joyce.

2. French literary critic, the translator of Pirandello; WB published an interview with Crémieux in the *Literarische Welt* (December 2, 1927), p. 1.

323. To Max Horkheimer

Paris
November 30, 1939

Dear Mr. Horkheimer,

I must finally give you some sign that I am still alive. I do not know what we may still have to endure; nor do I know if what is yet to come will make the memory of the past few weeks fade in comparison. Right now, however, I am happy to see that these weeks have passed. You can easily imagine that the most painful thing about them was the moral disarray in which everybody was engulfed. If one was not oneself engulfed by it, at least one's neighbors and companions were. If I myself was able in most instances to escape such a moral disarray, I owe this mainly to you. I am speaking not only of your concern for my person, but also of your solidarity with my work. The support you gave me in accepting the "Baudelaire" as you did has been invaluable to me. This must have become clear to you from the letter I sent Mrs. Adorno and also from the telegram I recently sent, which was delayed by formalities.

It was not at all easy to obtain my release. Even though it is not rare to leave the camp for reasons of illness, among others, it is not often that a person may walk out through the front door, namely because of a decision made by the interministerial commission. That is what I was able to do. It is equivalent to an acknowledgment by the French authorities of my absolute loyalty. Even if I would somehow have managed to get out of the camp, I am in Adrienne Monnier's debt for being one of the very first individuals to have their dossiers reviewed by the commission and to be able to leave. She was indefatigable in her efforts on my behalf and absolutely determined. The Pen Club also did something for me at the direction of Jules Romains; Mrs. Favez informed me of steps taken to approach the World Jewish Congress. This was all a great comfort to me. But everything would have taken a very long time to produce results. (The secretary of the Pen Club admitted as much to me when I recently visited him.) I also just learned from Mrs. Favez about your intervention on my behalf with Mr. Scelle and Mr. [Maurice] Halbwachs. Let me belatedly express my most sincere gratitude.

The dossier I had assembled, which contained a small number of selected affidavits testifying on behalf of me and my work, may not have been entirely useless. The letter you sent me while I was in the camp played a prominent role. I hope you will not find me too naïve if I confess that your message deeply touched me, knowing as I did the intent behind the tone of this message. You provided the small branch around which all my hopes crystallized. It was painful to me not to be able to thank you immediately. We were, however, not allowed to send more than two letters a week, and they had to deal with the most basic necessities. For it is a fact that it took me several weeks to gather what I needed to get through the bad weather.

I will not even mention my nervous anxiety. Because you can easily imagine the long-term consequences of the constant din and of the impossibility of getting away from people, if only for one hour. Right now, I feel completely exhausted and I am so tired that I must frequently pause halfway down the street because I am unable to go on. This is certainly due to nervous exhaustion, which will go away provided that the future does not hold anything horrible for us. Quite a few people are now returning to Paris; as for me, it would be impossible for me to get out of Paris because it is extremely difficult to obtain the safe conduct pass a foreign national requires.

The Bibliothèque Nationale has reopened. I hope to get back to my work after I have recuperated a bit, and put some order into my papers. I just received the galley proofs of the "Baudelaire" by way of Geneva; given all the difficulties, the printing errors are minimal. Since I do not know when your essay[1] is scheduled to be published, I allowed myself to ask Mrs. Favez for the proofs of it. I can't wait to see it.

If you have no other task in mind for me, I would like to return to the "Baudelaire" as soon as possible to write the other two parts. They, along with the part with which you are already familiar, will constitute the book as such. (The chapter you are publishing would be the central section of the book. I would cast both the first and third parts as essays that could exist independently of each other.)

One thing I might propose is to do a comparative study of Rousseau's *Confessions* and Gide's *Journal*. I was unfamiliar with the *Confessions* before I read them recently. The book seemed to me to constitute an outline of a social characteristic, of which Gide's *Journal* would represent the decline. (The *Journal* just came out in an unabridged edition.) This comparison should provide a kind of historical critique of "sincerity."

I would really like to hear from you and the Adornos. I intend to write them sometime in any case.

My dear Mr. Horkheimer, please give my best to Mr. Pollock, and please accept assurances of my loyalty and gratitude.

Walter Benjamin

1. "Die Juden und Europa," *Zeitschrift für Sozialforschung* 8 (1939), pp. 115–37.

324. To Gretel Adorno

Paris
December 14, 1939

Dear Felizitas,

You write me in English and I read your letters without any difficulty. I can decipher them more easily than if they were written in German. I am currently looking for an English teacher. I even tried to find one in the camp. But I soon had to give up and, therefore, could not do anything there. I did not delay and have already sent you the only thing I wrote. It was the story of the dream that filled me with happiness. It would be unfortunate if my letter had not reached you. I am almost inclined to think it did not, however, because you make no mention of the dream.

It often happens that, in my thoughts, I am still in the camp. We do not know how things will turn out for those who are still there; even those who were released from the camp cannot be sure of anything. I had hoped to see Bruck[1] again. He is not out yet, however, and I am not sure that he will be any time soon.

Two weeks ago, I received your letter dated November 7. It was really a pleasure to read and I would have responded sooner had I not felt so very weak. During the first few days after my return to Paris, I had to devote all my time (and what little energy I had) to taking care of what was necessary regarding the Baudelaire proofs. The French abstract[2] was actually very inadequate, at least from a linguistic standpoint, and I was happy to have had the chance to redo it. In any case, the next issue seems ready to go to press. It is splendid that the journal of the institute is able to hold its own so brilliantly at a time when the spiritual activity of German émigrés seems to have reached its nadir (because of the contingencies of daily life and of the political situation). In a letter to Max, I put down everything I thought was wonderful about his extraordinary essay.[3] Aside from everything else, the essay manifests magnificent stylistic vigor.

I am curious what Teddie will do about the correspondence between George and Hofmannsthal;[4] it seems as if one thousand years separate us from the time when these letters (which I have not yet seen) were exchanged. On the other hand, it is not recommended that anyone be too up-to-date. I fear that our friend Ernst [Bloch] was too much so; and from what I hear, he appears to be a bit out of touch at the moment, not only with earth but also with world history.

Did you meet Martin Gumpert? He is someone I knew very well a long time ago. Since he just published his autobiography,[5] I wondered whether I might figure in it. This would be the first autobiography in which that would be a possibility.[6]

Max will show you a copy of a letter from the National Refugee Service that raises a serious issue. I doubt that the opportunity this letter offers me would be likely to come up a second time. You will therefore consider it carefully. (I would ask you to do so if I were not certain that you would without being asked.) The issue is extremely complex and it seems impossible to begin without you.

The very first night after I returned home, there was an alert. There has not been one since then, but daily life has undergone drastic changes. The city is plunged into darkness as early as four in the afternoon. No one goes out at night and people fall prey to loneliness. My work would be a real refuge for me right now, and I hope to get back to it one of these days.

Love to you and regards to Teddie. I hope you will forgive me a thousand times over for this stationery; a desire to write you overcame me when nothing else was available.

Detlef

1. Hans Bruck, native of Frankfurt; conductor in Berlin and then in New York.
2. Of the Baudelaire essay; French and English abstracts were appended to German-language contributions in the *Zeitschrift für Sozialforschung*.
3. See note 1 for letter 323.
4. In *Prismen: Kulturkritik und Gesellschaft* (Berlin and Frankfurt am Main, 1955), pp. 232–82 [*Prisms* (Cambridge, Mass., 1990), pp. 187–226—Trans.]; see letter 328, to Theodor W. Adorno.
5. Martin Gumpert, *Hölle im Paradies* (Stockholm, 1939).
6. WB is in fact mentioned in the autobiography.

325. To Max Horkheimer

Paris
December 15, 1939

Dear Mr. Horkheimer,

I just received a letter from the National Refugee Service. A copy is enclosed. I presume that this letter was not sent to me as a result of your efforts, since you said nothing about it. I rather think it is Mrs. Bryher who made the effort to solicit it for me through some of her friends. Mrs. Bryher is editor-in-chief of *Life and Letters Today*. She has been following my work for quite some time and was quite worried about my internment.

I believe that this letter may present me with a real opportunity to improve my situation. It is not at all certain that such an opportunity will come up a second time. My Parisian friends (with, I must say, the notable exception of Miss Adrienne [Monnier]) are unanimous in wanting to see me leave. You, however, know that hasty decisions are not my thing. They are not even close to being my thing. But I am in the habit of following without discussion the advice of tried and true friends (and I will not forget that I would never have had the wisdom to leave Germany as early as March 1933 if Mrs. Adorno had not insisted upon this).

I do not need to tell you how attached I am to France, by virtue both of my relationships and my work. For me, nothing in the world could replace the Bibliothèque Nationale. I can also only rejoice at the welcome France extended to me as early as 1923; and at the goodwill of the authorities and at the devotion of my friends.

This does not exclude the fact that my existence and my research here might be put to the test any day now. Specifically, it may well turn out that, due to the war, strict regulations may have to be imposed that will have to be endured by the best, along with the worst. These reflections are what force me to consider the offer contained in the letter from the Refugee Service.

It goes without saying that your advice will carry the most weight for me in this situation. For I would not like my arrival in America to cause difficulties of a material nature, introducing a discordant element into our friendship. That friendship at the moment constitutes for me not only the sole support of my material existence, but also almost the only moral support I have at my disposal. I am all the more unable to make a hasty decision because I would surely have to take painstaking steps to obtain an exit visa. (It does not even seem certain that I will obtain one before my forty-ninth birthday, which is still a few months away.) I was referring to this in my response to the Refugee Service. I enclose a copy of that response.

Please be as explicit as possible in informing me of your own opinion, namely whether I should stay in France or join you in America. It is really important to me that you consider this request in detail and that you are aware that it does not constitute an attempt on my part to shun my responsibility to what I must unhappily call "my destiny." On the contrary, the only purpose of this request is to allow me to come to a decision in full cognizance of the situation.

I finally saw the proofs of your essay on the Jews and Europe. There has been no political analysis in years that has so impressed me. This is the word we have been awaiting for a long time. And this word could not possibly have made itself heard any earlier. The entire time I was reading this essay, I had the feeling of coming upon truths. I had a presentiment of these truths, rather than really explored them, and they were just expressed with all the necessary strength and dimension. My fierce enmity for the inane, self-satisfied optimism of our left-wing leaders finds more substantial support in your essay. Although you did not mention names, those names are on all our lips.

The nicest thing in your treatment may be the historical construction on the basis of Mandeville and Sade. It is unpredictable and elegant, like a panorama that is revealed to the person who reaches the summit when the light is best.—Your article will be taken very badly by men of affairs and pretentious people. There are many of them everywhere. This is just one more reason for us to take pride in the repercussions the essay will have, and to be extremely curious about what they will be. I envy you the opportunity to watch them happen in complete freedom.

I just received your letter of November 28. Let me express my sincere gratitude for what you had to say about my being released. At the same time you ask about the circumstances surrounding this. My letter of November 30 informed you that I had been told by Mrs. Favez that you had asked for the support of Mr. Scelle and Mr. Halbwachs on my behalf. I do not have the impression that they have done anything. It is true that no absolute assurances are possible in this kind of enterprise. I suspect, however, that they are the kind of people who would not have failed to inform our Paris office if they had done anything at all. All I know is that crucial steps have been taken by a close friend of Miss Adrienne who is one of the most powerful people at the quai d'Orsay. I am therefore hesitant to go see them, while I again must express my gratitude to you for having contacted these professors. I fear I would seem to be reminding them indiscretely of a favor they did not render.

Cordially yours.
Walter Benjamin

326.* To Gerhard Scholem

Paris
January 11, 1940

Dear Gerhard,

I had your letter of December 15 in hand by the end of the month. I hope this one will not require too much time for its trip either.

I was pleased and reassured to hear that you are going about your craft in as unperturbed a manner as the circumstances allow. I particularly hope you won't put off work on your New York lectures any longer. Every line we succeed in publishing today—no matter how uncertain the future to which we entrust it—is a victory wrenched from the powers of darkness. Anyway, it would be all too sad if you were to become negligent of your publications in English precisely when the undersigned is seriously getting down to learning that language. I am negotiating on private lessons at the moment. I intend to take them together with Hannah Stern and her friend.

You want us to "safeguard what we hold in common." As far as I can see, in that respect things are even better taken care of now than they were twenty-five years ago. I am not thinking of us when I say this, but of the arrangements made by the zeitgeist, which has set up markers in the desert landscape of the present that cannot be overlooked by old Bedouins like us. Even though it is a sad thing that we cannot converse with one another, I still have the feeling that the circumstances in no way deprive me of such heated debates as we used to indulge in now and then. There is no longer any need for those today. And it may well be fitting to have a small ocean between us when the moment comes to fall into each other's arms *spiritualiter*.

The isolation that is my natural condition has increased owing to the present circumstances. The Jews seem not even to be holding on to the little intelligence they have left, after all they have been through. The number of those who are able to find their bearings in this world is diminishing more and more. Under these circumstances, I rather enjoyed two short meetings with Dora.[1] She struck me as more quiet and serene than she had been for a long time. The news she gave me about Stefan was not exactly favorable, but not alarming either. By the way, she spoke of signs indicating Italian anti-Semitism will be taken out of circulation in the foreseeable future.

The description you gave me of the lecture at Schocken's soirée is truly gripping. I didn't keep it from Hannah Stern, who returns your greetings most cordially. Your report makes me thirst for revenge, since I am rather slow to see the work of demons in people's shabby behavior. But if I want to slake that thirst, I will have to wait for the first things Schocken himself publishes. Hannah Stern was of the mitigating opinion that Schocken thinks more of Brod alone, in the depths of his soul, than of you and me put together. *Rebus sic stantibus,* I wish you, and—with the requisite distance—your colleague too, every success in his American expedition.

I am very pleased to hear of the influence you have as a teacher, as you can imagine. Tell me as soon as possible what the Scholem school is all about.

The double issue of the institute's journal inaugurating the 1939 volume has just come out. You will find two long essays of mine in it. I'll send you offprints of both, of course, as soon as I can lay my hands on them.[2] Even so, I would dearly advise you to buy the issue or get hold of it some other way. I have a double personal stake in it: first, it will place your propaganda for me on a wider platform, and for another, I want to hear your opinion of the essay "Die Juden und Europa."

Some time ago, you asked about my contributions to *Maß und Wert*. Here's the index (to the extent that you don't own the issues, I am unfortunately unable to get them for you, since the author's copy is all I have in hand. If you are unable to decide in favor of purchasing the ones you are missing—an attitude I certainly could not approve of—then, if worse comes to worst, I could place a typewritten copy at your disposal).

1:5 May–June 1939 ("Über die *Zeitschrift für Sozialforschung*" [On the *Zeitschrift für Sozialforschung*]

1:6 July–August 1938 (*Berliner Kindheit um 1900*)

2:1 September–October 1938 ("Krisenjahre der Frühromantik") [Years of crisis in early romanticism]

2:3 January–February 1939 ("Béguin: *L'ame romantique et le rêve*")
2:6 July–August 1939 ("What Is Epic Theater?")

That should be enough for today. Please accept my most sincere greetings, which are also addressed to your wife.

Yours, Walter

1. During Dora's last stay in Paris, she still tried to prevail on WB to come with her immediately to London, but he refused. It was a fateful decision, which Dora told me about in April 1946, when I first saw her again.

2. Those were the last of his works I was to receive from him: the essay on Jochmann and "On Some Motifs in Baudelaire" ["Über einige Motive bei Baudelaire"] (*Schriften* 2:572–85, 4:605–53). [The latter appears in *Illuminations,* pp. 155–200—Smith.]

327. To Gretel Adorno

Paris
January 17, 1940

My dear Felizitas,

I intend to write you a long letter even though I have received only very brief notes from you. And I have not received any letter at all from Teddie for six months. The last I heard from you was your note dated November 21 (although it was certainly mailed later, because you mention my return to Paris, which was only on the 23d). I heard that you are still not in the best of health. I have nothing very good to say about my health either. It has been extremely difficult for me to walk outside since it has become so cold. I am forced to stop every three or four minutes when walking outside. I naturally went to see a doctor and was diagnosed as having myocarditis, which lately seems to have gotten worse. I am now looking for a doctor who can order a cardiogram; this is rather difficult, for one thing because there are only a few specialists with access to the necessary equipment. Then you must simultaneously try to strike a separate deal with the operator about when he will conduct the test. I have heard that this kind of test is quite expensive.

The weather, my health, and the general state of affairs all conspire to impose on me the most routine, housebound existence. My apartment is heated but not enough to make it possible for me to write if it is very cold. I therefore stay in bed half the time, which is where I am right now. It is true that I have nonetheless had opportunities to go into the city during the last few weeks. This is because I again had to see to all the petty details of civilian life: I had to have my account reopened, I had to reapply for permission to use the Bibliothèque Nationale, etc. Everything required many more steps than you would imagine. It has, however, finally been taken care of. I must tell you that there was a bit of a celebration in the library the first day I went back. Especially in photographic services, where the staff was given quite a few of my personal papers to copy during the last few months, after having photocopied some of my notes years ago.

The most comforting thing recently was a wonderful letter from Max dated December 21. In it, he asked me to resume my reports on French literature. He also asked about what I was planning to work on in the future. My dear Felizitas, I would appreciate it if you would meanwhile take it upon yourself to tell him the importance of his letter for me and, at the same time, to give him this draft of a response. By draft, I mean that I have not yet made up my mind about the bottom line: namely, whether it would be better for me to begin a comparative study of Rousseau and Gide or to begin immediately on the sequel to my "Baudelaire." The fear of having to abandon the Baudelaire once I will have begun writing the sequel is what makes me hesitate. The sequel will be a work of monumental breadth and it would be a delicate matter to have to start and stop again and again. This is, however, the risk I would have to take. I am constantly reminded of it by the gas mask in my small room—the mask looks to me like a disconcerting replica of the skulls with which studious monks decorated their cells. This is why I have not yet really dared to begin the sequel to the Baudelaire. I definitely hold this work more dear to my heart than any other. It would consequently not suffer being neglected even to ensure the survival of its author. (It is true, however, that it is extremely difficult, if not impossible, to come to a practical decision on this matter, even based on pure suppositions. There is no way I can leave Paris without obtaining preliminary authorization. It is extremely hard to get and it would not even be wise to ask for it, since there would be no simultaneous guarantee that I would be able to return.)

Quite aside from my other work, I will be delighted to begin my reports on the latest French books. There is, by the way, a rather funny piece of work that just appeared in Argentina. It is a booklet published by [Roger] Caillois that is an indictment of nazism containing arguments gleaned from the world press, printed without the slightest changes or modifications. It was not necessary to travel to the farthest regions of the intelligible and terrestrial world to write this booklet. On the other hand, Caillois actually published a theory of the pageant in the *Nouvelle revue française,* which I plan to discuss in my first report on French books for Max. I also plan to discuss a curious book written by Michel Leiris, *Manhood: A Journey from Childhood into the Fierce Order of Virility* [*Age d'homme*]. It attracted a lot of attention before the war.

The letter Max wrote on December 21 crossed the letter I sent on December 15. In the meantime, I went to the American consulate, where I was given the usual questionnaire. Question number 14 is as follows:

"Are you the minister of any sect or a professor at a school, seminary, academy or university?" If I am correct, this question will have important consequences for me since, on the one hand, a "yes" would make it possible to get in regardless of the quota (a nonquota visa) and since, on the other hand, the consulate claims that it would take at least five or six years to be admitted under the quota. It would, therefore, be terribly important to list the classes I taught at the Frankfurt Institute. I have not yet filled out the questionnaire because I did not want to mention them without the institute's permission. I will therefore have to put the questionnaire aside until I receive an answer from you. (The consular offices are being transferred to Bordeaux. I will be informed of my number, if I get one, from that office; but only after they get my questionnaire.)

It may not be sheer vanity for me to say that the last issue of the journal seemed to me to be one of the best the institute has published in the past few years. I was very impressed by Max's article and I passed it on to everyone with whom I am in contact. I had quite a few conversations about it, all stressing how solid it is. It occurred to me during these conversations that it might be just as interesting as useful to expand on the question. The question addressed in the article should be expanded by dealing with the way in which the anti-Semitic movement either depends on or stands in opposition to medieval anti-Semitism. This is exactly what Teddie pointed out regarding Wagner ("Der Jude im Dorn").

I took advantage of the publication of parts of the Wagner book to read them again.[1] I then consulted the complete manuscript of the text so that I could compare the passages that made the greatest impression on me when I first read it with the passages I now underlined in the journal. The result of this comparison is that, imbued as I am with the fundamental truth of its global conception, I am currently more than ever attached to certain specific aspects of the question. We will have to return to the topic of reduction (*Verkleinerung*) as an artifice of phantasmagoria. This passage reminded me of one of my oldest projects. You may remember having heard me speak of it: I am referring to the commentary on Goethe's *Neue Melusine*. It might be all the more apropos because Melusine most likely is one of those undinesque creatures you mention toward the end. I was struck by some nice formulations in the summaries: the one concerning the virtual opposition of Freud and Jung in Wagner's work itself; also the one where the homogeneity of Wagnerian "style" is denounced as a symptom of an intimate fall from grace. (One of these days, Teddie will have to compile the passages in his analyses that deal with music as protest and develop the theory of opera contained there.)

To conclude this long letter, let me give you some information about people in whom you are likely to be interested. I recently saw Dora on her way back from London. [. . .]—I do not believe I wrote you that

Glück settled in Buenos Aires almost two years ago. He found a job there that may not be as splendid as his former position, but seems to be very solid. I have not heard anything from him since the war.—Our friend Klossovski, who was declared unfit, left Paris and just got a job in city government in Bordeaux. [Egon Erwin] Kisch, whom you may remember slightly, has just succeeded in being offered a professorship in Chile. And finally, our poor friend [Hans] Bruck is still in a camp. We continue to hope that he will get out soon; but in the meantime he is really suffering. Somebody who will give you news about me in person is Soma Morgenstern. We hear that he is going to leave for New York before spring.

Since postage is really expensive nowadays, Max will forgive me for having entrusted you with some information that is more relevant to him. I trust you will forgive me as well. I hope that you will not make do with sending me one of your small blue notes the next time you write. No matter how pretty they are. I am really counting on you, and on Teddie, to send me a letter that is a few pages long. (I would really like to hear about what he is working on.) Love,

Your old Detlef

P.S. My English lessons are going to start next week.

1. *Versuch über Wagner*. Four chapters of Adorno's Wagner book appeared in the same issue of the *Zeitschrift für Sozialforschung* in which WB's Baudelaire essay appeared.

328. To Theodor W. Adorno

Paris
May 7, 1940

Dear Teddie,

Thank you for your letter of February 29. For the time being, we will unfortunately have to get used to this kind of time span intervening between your writing and the arrival of my response. Another factor is that, as you can easily tell, this letter was not built in a day, any more than Rome was.

I was (and am) naturally delighted at the position you have taken on my "Baudelaire." You may know that the telegram you, Felizitas, and Max had sent reached me in the camp and you can gauge for yourself its importance in my psychic inventory in the months I was there.

I once again read the passages[1] about regressive hearing to which you referred me and can detect the congruence in the orientation of our research. There is no better example of registration that shatters experience than when popular lyrics are set to a melody. (Here it becomes evident that the individual stakes his pride on treating the substance of potential experience in exactly the same way the administration treats the elements of a potential society.) There is no reason to make a secret of the fact that I trace the roots of my "theory of experience" to a childhood memory. My parents naturally took walks with us wherever we spent our summers. There were either two or three of us children. The one I have in mind is my brother. After we had visited one of the obligatory tourist attractions around Freudenstadt, Wengen, or Schreiberhau, my brother used to say, "Now we can say that we've been there." This statement made an unforgettable impression on me. (By the way, I would be surprised if your notion of my view of your essay on the fetish character were correct. Might you not be confusing it with my view of your essay on jazz? I had advised you of my objections to the latter piece. I had followed the former without reservations. It has just recently been on my mind because of some observations you make in it on "musical progress" apropos Mahler.)

There can be no doubt that the concept of forgetting which you inject into your discussion of the aura is of great significance. I will bear in mind the possibility of a differentiation between epic and reflexive forgetting. Please do not think it an evasion if I do not go beyond this today. I clearly remembered the passage in the fifth chapter of the Wagner book to which you allude. But even if, in fact, the issue is a "forgotten human something" in the aura, the issue is not necessarily what is actually present in the work. The tree and the shrub vouchsafed to people are not made by them. Thus there must be something human about objects that is *not* bestowed by the work done. I would, however, like to leave it at that. It seems unavoidable to me that I will again be confronted with the question you raised in the course of my own work. (I do not know whether I will be confronted with it already in the sequel to the "Baudelaire.") The first thing for me to do will be to return to the *locus classicus* of the theory of forgetting, which, as you well know, is represented for me by [Tieck's] *Der blonde Eckbert*.

I believe that it is unnecessary to question the concept of *mémoire involontaire* in order to grant forgetting its due. The childish experience of how a madeleine tasted that one day involuntarily popped into Proust's mind was, in fact, unconscious. It was not the first bite into his first madeleine. (Tasting is a conscious act.) Tasting, however, probably becomes unconscious to the extent that the taste became more familiar. The grown-up's "tasting again" is then naturally conscious.

Since you ask about Maupassant's "Nuit": I read this important piece very carefully. A fragment of my Baudelaire study deals with it and you, of course, will probably see it some day. (*En attendant,* in deep gratitude, I am giving the volume you loaned me to the Parisian office to return to you.)

Regarding the alternative Gide-Baudelaire, Max has been so kind as to leave the choice up to me. I have decided for "Baudelaire"; this is the subject that I now view as the most intransigent; it is most urgent that I satisfy its demands. I will not conceal from you that I have not yet been able to turn to it with the intensity I would have wished. A primary reason for this has been my work on the theses.[2] You will receive some fragments of them during the next few days. To be sure, they in turn represent a certain stage in my reflections on the continuation of the "Baudelaire." I expect that the next few days will be the beginning of a period during which I hope to be able to work uninterruptedly and which I will devote to this continuation.

Now to the George-Hofmannsthal correspondence. Care has been taken that not everything one touches will turn to gold. I am for once in the position of encountering you in an arena in which I feel completely at home, but my modest wish to have firsthand knowledge of the book about which you write remains unfulfilled. Since I am not capable of such firsthand knowledge in the realm of music, you should not take my judgment of your essay too categorically. Be that as it may, as far as I can tell, it is the best thing you have ever written. A series of specific observations follows. I want to preface these with the comment that, for me, the crucial part of the essay resides in its uncommonly assured, striking, and surprising outline of the historical perspective: like the spark that jumps between [Ernst] Mach and Jens Peter Jacobsen, giving the historical landscape a plasticity that basically furnishes the landscape with a bolt of lightning in the evening sky.

What seems to emerge from your presentation is that George's image was more sharply delineated in the correspondence than Hofmannsthal's. The struggle for literary position vis-à-vis the other probably was simply a basic motif of this correspondence, and the aggressor was and remained George. While in a certain sense I find a finished portrait of George in your essay, when it comes to Hofmannsthal much remains in the background. It becomes very clear in some passages that it would be up to you to illuminate specific parts of this background. Your observation about the actor, and even more the one about the child in Hofmannsthal which, for me, culminates in the wonderful quotation from *Ariadne,* which is gripping because of where it appears in your text—this all goes to the heart of the matter. I would have liked to have found your view of the reminiscences from the world of childhood as they occur, lost, in George's "Lied des Zwergen" or "Entführung."

There is one aspect of Hofmannsthal that is very much on my mind but is left untouched. I am not sure whether the allusions with which I want to speak about it to you (perhaps not for the first time?) will really have something new to say. If they do, the question remains as to what extent they will be intelligible to you. I intend to mail these comments regardless of their fragmentary state. There are actually two texts whose rapprochement delineates what I have to say. You yourself refer to one of them, since you cite the *Letter of Lord Chandos*. I am thinking of the following passage: "I do not know how often this Crassus with his moray comes to mind as a mirror image of myself, tossed up over the abyss of the centuries . . . Crassus . . . shedding tears over his moray. And I am forced to think about this figure, whose ridiculousness and contemptibility, in the midst of a senate discussing the most sublime things and ruling the world, catch the eye—I am forced to think about him by something unnameable in a way that seems absolutely foolish to me the very moment I try to express it in words." (The same motif occurs in *Der Turm:* the inside of the slaughtered pig into which the prince had to look when he was a child.) As for the rest, the second of the two passages of which I spoke is also in *Der Turm:* it is the conversation between the doctor and Julian. Julian, the man who, but for a minute suspension of will, a single moment of surrender, lacks nothing to become a part of what is most sublime, is a self-portrait of Hofmannsthal. Julian betrays the prince: Hofmannsthal turned his back on the task that emerges in the Chandos letter. His "speechlessness" was a kind of punishment. The language that Hofmannsthal avoided may be precisely the language that was given to Kafka at about the same time. For Kafka took on the task at which Hofmannsthal failed morally, and therefore also poetically. (The theory of sacrifice to which you refer, which is suspect and built on sand, bears all the traces of this failure.)

I believe that throughout his life Hofmannsthal took the same stance toward his talent as Christ would have taken toward his reign if he had to attribute it to a deal with Satan. It seems to me that Hofmannsthal's uncommon versatility goes hand in hand with his awareness of having betrayed the best within himself. Therefore, no degree of intimacy with the rabble was able to frighten him.

Regardless of this, relegating [Hans] Carossa to a "school" whose head presumably was Hofmannsthal, it is in my opinion still not feasible to speak of the political coordination of German authors *under the sign of this school,* namely of Hofmannsthal himself. Hofmannsthal died in 1929. If it had not been guaranteed him by some other means, he has with his death purchased a non liquet in the criminal case you bring against him. I would think you might want to reconsider this passage; I am almost at the point of requesting you to do so.

You are, of course, right to bring up Proust. I have recently had misgivings about his work; and once again it happens that they coincide with yours. You speak very nicely about the experience of "that's not it"—

precisely the experience that time turns into a lost experience. It now seems to me that there was a deeply hidden (but not for that reason unconscious) model of this basic experience for Proust: namely, the "that's not it" experience of the assimilation of the French Jews. You are familiar with the famous passage in *Sodom and Gomorrha* where complicity among homosexuals is compared with the particular constellation determining the behavior of the Jews among themselves. It was precisely the fact that Proust was only half Jewish that enabled him to have insight into the precarious structure of assimilation, an insight that was brought home to him from the outside by the Dreyfus campaign.

There is not likely to be any book on George that might be even remotely comparable to yours. I have no reservations whatsoever about it; I am not afraid to admit to you that I was most pleasantly surprised. Even if it must appear extremely difficult nowadays to speak of George in any way other than as the poet who in his *Stern des Bundes* has marked out the choreography of the St. Vitus's dance that is passing over Germany's ravaged soil—this was surely not to be expected from you. Yet you have mastered this untimely and thankless task, namely George's "rescue," as decisively as is possible and as unobtrusively as is necessary. In having recognized defiance as the poetic and political foundation of George's work, you have illuminated its most basic characteristics through commentary (significance of translation), as well as critically (monopoly and elimination of the market). Everything is out of the same mold and everything is convincing. There are some passages that would, entirely on their own, prove that the effort you put into this text, no matter how long it has taken, was not wasted. I am thinking of the excellent commentary on the "gentleman," and of portentous quotations such as "the hour is late." Your work has made imaginable what was previously unimaginable and would constitute the beginning of George's afterlife: an anthology of his poems. Some of those are better placed in your text than where you found them.

I would not want to pass over an important point about which we should come to an agreement (and probably could). It concerns what you treat under the rubric of "position." The comparison with smoking hardly does justice to the topic. It could mislead someone into believing that a position is "displayed" or "adopted" in all cases. It is entirely possible, however, to find a position that is unconscious without it therefore being less of a position. And you probably also see things this way since, under the same rubric, you include gracefulness, which is rarely associated with something consciously on display. (Regarding gracefulness, I want to speak only of children and do this without thus wanting to emancipate a natural phenomenon from the society in which it appears, namely to treat it in an inappropriately abstract manner. The gracefulness of children exists, and exists primarily, as a corrective to society; it is one of the pointers toward "undisciplined happiness" that are given us. Holding onto childish innocence, as in a moment of unkindness one could accuse Hofmannsthal of doing (of holding onto the innocence that allowed him to value [Felix] Salten's feuilletons hardly any less highly than my baroque book) does not justify our abandonment of what we can love about him.)

What you had to say about a position in the narrower sense evoked some reservations in me. I want to indicate what they are by a turn of phrase borrowed from your own text. Specifically, the place where you allude to my Baudelaire essay with the felicitous formulation that the lonely person is the dictator of all those who are lonely like him. I do not believe it is too bold to say that we there encounter a position where a human being's essential loneliness comes into view—the loneliness that, far from being the site of the human being's individual fullness, could very well be the site of his historically determined emptiness, of his persona as his misfortune. I understand and share your every reservation when the position displayed is that of fullness (this is, in fact, the way it was understood by George). There is also, however, the inalienable position of emptiness (as is characteristic of Baudelaire's later works). In brief: position as I understand it is distinguished from the kind you denounce just as branding is distinguished from tattooing.

The last two pages of your essay struck me as being like a table for birthday gifts on which the passage about "undisciplined happiness" represents the spark of life. The work is also somewhat like a table covered with gifts in other places as well; the stamp of terminology no more adheres to its ideas than a price tag does to a gift.

In conclusion, I will adopt your good habit of suggesting some things in the form of marginalia. "The last train is just leaving for the mountains" is a sentence that is just as appropriate to the Schwabing atmosphere as [Alfred] Kubin's dream city "Pearl." "Pearl," moreover, is the city in which the "Temple" stands, behind whose walls, which have dry rot, the "Seventh Ring" is preserved.

Relating it to Kraus's critique of George's translation of Shakespeare's sonnets might have given even more weight to your reference to Kraus, especially since you yourself touch on the problem of translation.

George's appreciative judgment of Hofmannsthal replicates Victor Hugo's famous judgment of Baudelaire down to the last detail: "Vous avez créé un frisson nouveau." When George speaks of the granitelike Germanic element in Hofmannsthal, in terms of tone and subject matter he might have had in mind a passage from Hölderlin's letter of December 4, 1801, to Böhlendorf.

The question might be raised in passing as to whether this correspondence may not have been influenced by the correspondence between Goethe and Schiller—the correspondence that, as the documentation of a friendship between two princes among poets, so enormously contributed to the worsening of the air of the upper atmosphere in Germany.

Apropos your "What is noble is so because of what is ignoble"—see Victor Hugo's splendid words: "l'ignorant est le pain que mange le savant."

Your medals for Carossa and Rudolf Borchardt are very nicely cast and, as you can well imagine, the *Devise lucus a non lucendo* you dedicate to symbolism delighted me. The analysis of "Voyelles" [by Arthur Rimbaud], which supports it, also seems thoroughly cogent to me. The intertwining of technique and esotericism, which, as you demonstrate, appeared so early, has become tangible in a regime that establishes political training schools for pilots.

In conclusion, let me say that I am very pleased with the role Jacobsen plays in your essay. Early motifs are no doubt here given their due. In any case, the expanded form of the name of your reflections has an effect similar to that of the appearance of a boy who, rushing from a forest with burning cheeks, approaches us in a cool alley.

You ask about my English lessons. I had already begun lessons with someone else by the time I received the address of a teacher from Felizitas. I fear that my progress, which is not swift, far surpasses my ability to apply my knowledge in conversation. I also thought that Miss Razowski's affidavit was, as you say, a "substantial stimulus." I unfortunately had to change my opinion. Everything I have heard about the current practices of the American consulate (from which I have still heard nothing) agrees that the process of bringing normal cases to a conclusion is very slow. But without my having had anything to do with it, my case has now unfortunately become a "normal" one due to the receipt of the affidavit. Otherwise it would have been possible for me to submit an application for a visitor's visa, like that recently approved for the author Hermann Kesten, for example. [. . .]

To return to the question of a visa, in addition to a letter of appointment, proof of having held an official teaching position has been made a prerequisite for granting a *nonquota* visa (and this is the only thing that would make it possible for me to come very soon). Recently just *that* section in the latter regulation prescribing proof of such employment for *the last two years* before the visa is granted has been interpreted very strictly. This makes me very reluctant to write Schapiro now. I would rather not turn to him before I am assured of being able to put his interest in me to best advantage. This will only be the case when the deadline for my arrival in America has drawn closer; whether it turns out that there is once again some swift progress in the matter of my immigration, or whether the regulations pertaining to granting a *nonquota* visa are again less strictly enforced. The way things are right now, I fear that, even given a letter of appointment, the regulations would be more likely to work against me. I would not hesitate to write Schapiro, however, if you think that he could do something about obtaining an appointment for me.

[. . .]

Do you know Faulkner? If so, I would like to know what you think of his work. I am currently reading *Light in August*.

Your letter arrived without undue delay. I think you can write me in German and that you therefore ought to write me more often. For my part, a letter written in German must of course be the exception.—Send the "Rickert"[3] with your next letter. I, of course, am a student of Rickert (just as you are a student of [Hans] Cornelius) and I am really looking forward to your text.

As always, my most sincere regards. Yours,
Walter Benjamin

1. From Adorno's essay on the fetish character in music, in *Dissonanzen*.
2. *Schriften* 1:494–506.
3. Adorno, review of Heinrich Rickert's *Unmittelbarkeit und Sinndeutung* (Tübingen, 1939), *Studies in Philosophy and Social Science* 9 (1941), pp. 479–82.

329. To Max Horkheimer

Lourdes
June 16, 1940

Dear Mr. Horkheimer,

I promised I would send you news about me as often as possible. Today that news consists primarily of my change of address.

I am sure you will permit me to cut things short today—all the more because I am still extremely tired due to the events of the last two weeks and my trip.

It will surely be unnecessary for me to repeat the request I made in my last letter, namely that you intervene as quickly and as expeditiously as possible with the American authorities. I do not know the present address of the consulate. I am therefore relying on you to mail the consulate my present address from New York. *A letter from the consulate certifying that I could expect my visa with virtually no delay would be of primary importance to me.*

The privileged situation that I currently enjoy would probably allow me to get to New York almost immediately once the visa is delivered. As

I mentioned in my last letter, I presume that the most expeditious way of moving things along would be if I were appointed to a professorship, because this would make it possible for me to obtain a nonquota visa. Chances are that it might be the only way I would get a visa.

Added to the multiple concerns burdening me is my concern about my manuscripts, which I have been forced to leave behind in Paris with all my other belongings.

Give my regards to our friends and please be assured, my dear Mr. Horkheimer, of my deep and sincere attachment.

Benjamin

330. To Adrienne Monnier

Lourdes
[June?] 1940

My dear friend,

I am quickly writing these few lines to you, squeezed into a corner of the table.

I deeply regretted not having seen you again. Unforeseen circumstances forced me to leave for Lourdes where a friend's wife, who left at the same time, was more or less expected.

I have no cause to complain about this event. The place is very inexpensive. I found a bedroom for 200 francs. Given the current state of affairs, the kind welcome I received both from the locals and the authorities is invaluable.

There are lots of people here, mostly Belgian refugees. We hear that things are organized for the best for these people: no trouble, no anxiety. Confidence and a serenity deserving of respect.

I would be delighted if Gisèle [Freund] were to come here if she still has not found an arrangement with which she is truly satisfied. I think Lourdes would really be a good place for her from many perspectives. (I did not know the region, and it is very beautiful.)

I think of you; I will think of you constantly as long as Paris remains in any danger. My mind turns to you not only when I think of Paris, but also when I think of the rue de l'Odéon, which I would commend to the protection of the most powerful and least petitioned of all divinities—but you are also the nexus of many of my thoughts.

Regards. Let me assure you of my deep attachment.

Benjamin

P.S. Please be good enough to send my address to Gisèle, and have her send hers to me. And please give Sylvia [Beach] all the best. Thank you for the beautiful letter from H. and for the book.

331. To Hannah Arendt

Lourdes
July 8, 1940

Dear Hannah,

I hope these lines will find you in Montbahus. Their purpose is to express my gratitude for your card of the 5th, and congratulations for having gotten hold of the man.[1] Please give him my best. (This is in the style of Retz, which is currently shaping mine!)

Mrs. P. found her husband again. It seems he was in rather bad shape.

We received news from Fritz,[2] but it appears that he has not yet been liberated.

I would be in a deeper depression than the one by which I am currently gripped if, as bookless as I am, I had not found in the only book I do have the aphorism that is most splendidly appropriate to my current state: "His laziness supported him in glory for many years in the obscurity of an errant and hidden life" (La Rochefoucauld speaking to Retz). I cite this in the unspoken hope of causing Monsieur sadness.

Your old Benjamin

1. Heinrich Blücher, later Arendt's husband.
2. The psychiatrist Fritz Fraenkel, a friend of WB who lived in the same house in Paris.

332. To Theodor W. Adorno

Lourdes
August 2, 1940

Dear Teddie,

I was delighted to get your letter of July 15 for a number of reasons—for one, that you remembered the day; for another, because of the understanding that emanated from it. No, it truly is not easy for me to write a letter. I spoke to Felizitas about the complete uncertainty in which I find myself concerning my writings. (I have relatively less reason to fear for the papers devoted to the *Arcades* than for the others.[1]) As you know, however, things are such that my personal situation is no better than that of my writings. The measures that came crashing down on me in September could be repeated from one day to the next, but this time with a completely different prognosis. In the last few months I have seen a number of individuals, not so much drift away from their bourgeois existence, as plunge headlong from it, from one day to the next; thus every assurance gives me support, not only the problematical external kind, but also the less problematical internal kind. It was in this sense that I took up the document "à ceux qu'il appartient" with true gratitude. I can well imagine that the letterhead, which was a pleasant surprise, could effectively reinforce the possible impact of this document.

The complete uncertainty about what the next day and even the next hour will bring has dominated my existence for many weeks. I am condemned to read every newspaper (they now come out on a single sheet of paper) like a summons that has been served on me and to detect in every radio broadcast the voice of the messenger of bad tidings. My attempt to reach Marseilles in order to plead my case at the consulate there was in vain. For quite a while now, no permit for a change of residence has been granted to a foreign national. Thus I remain dependent on what all of you are able to do from abroad. I was made particularly hopeful at your holding out the prospect of hearing from the consulate in Marseilles. A letter from this consulate would presumably bring me permission to go to Marseilles. (I am actually unable to make up my mind to establish contact with the consulates in occupied territory. A letter I sent from here to Bordeaux before the occupation received a friendly but insubstantial answer: the documents in question were still in Paris.)

I do hear about your negotiations with Havana and your efforts concerning San Domingo. I am firmly convinced that you are doing what can be done or, as Felizitas says, "more than is humanly possible." My fear is that we have much less time than we assume. And although such a possibility would not have occurred to me fourteen days ago, new information has induced me to ask Mrs. Favez, with the intervention of Carl Burckhardt, to obtain permission for me to go to Switzerland on a temporary basis, if at all possible. I know that there is basically much to be said against this way out; but there is one powerful argument in its favor: time. If only this way out could be realized!—I have written to Burckhardt for help.[2]

I hope that I have thus far given you the impression of maintaining my composure even in difficult moments. Do not think that this has changed. But I cannot close my eyes to the dangerous nature of the situation. I fear that those who have been able to extricate themselves from it will have to be reckoned with one day.

Via Geneva—which is also probably how I will direct these lines—you will receive my curriculum vitae. I have incorporated my bibliography into the biographical information because I lack the resources here to organize it as such in more detail. (All in all, it consists of close to 450 items.) If a bibliography in the narrow sense of the word would still be required, the one in the institute's informational brochure is at your disposal; I could not come up with a better one for you right now.

It is a great comfort to me that you will remain, so to speak, "reachable" in New York and alert, in the actual sense of the word. Mr. Merril Moore lives in Boston at 384 Commonwealth Avenue. Mrs. W. Bryher, the publisher of *Life and Letters Today,* has often called me to his attention. He probably has a good idea of the situation and the will to contribute to changing it. I think it might be worthwhile for you to get in touch with him.

[. . .]

I am sad that Felizitas's condition remains so unstable. [. . .] Please give her my most sincere regards.

Please extend my most sincere gratitude and kindest regards to Mr. Pollock.

All the best,
Yours, Walter Benjamin

P.S. Please excuse the painfully complete signature; it is required.

1. When WB had to flee Paris, his notes and the materials for the *Arcades* project were hidden in the Bibliothèque Nationale with the help of Georges Bataille, who was a librarian there; they have been preserved.

2. Burckhardt's intervention was not successful in persuading the responsible Swiss authorities to come to a positive decision before WB's illegal border crossing into Spain.

Index of Correspondents

Adorno, Gretel (born 1902), née Karplus, Ph.D. Wife of Theodor W. Adorno. Friend of WB since 1928. Letters 210, 217, 223, 226, 229, 231, 265, 302, 305, 317, 321, 324, 327.

Adorno, Theodor W[iesengrund] (1903–69). University professor of philosophy and sociology at the Johann Wolfgang Goethe University in Frankfurt. Director of the Institute for Social Research. 1931: habilitation. 1934: emigrated to Oxford; later went to North America and the Institute for Social Research. 1949: returned to Frankfurt. An intense friendship with WB evolved from their acquaintance in 1923. They spent a lot of time together in Paris and San Remo during the emigration. Letters 213, 250, 260, 272, 276, 304, 307, 310, 318, 328, 332.

Arendt, Hannah (1906–75), author. First marriage to Günter Stern, the son of WB's cousin William Stern. In contact with WB since the beginning of the 1930s, but in particularly close contact during the years of emigration when she directed the Paris office of Youth *Aliyah*. Letter 331.

Belmore, Herbert (born 1983 in Capetown). While still a child, he went to Germany from South Africa with his parents. A schoolmate and close boyhood friend of WB, especially during the time of the Youth Movement. Studied graphics. Went to England in the spring of 1914 and was in Switzerland during the First World War. The friendship ended in 1917. Later a translator in Rome. Letters 1–10, 12, 13, 16–19, 22, 23, 31, 32, 35, 36, 40, 43, 47.

Benjamin, Walter (1892–1940). Letters 195, 202, 204, 237, 263, 306.

Brecht, Bertolt (1898–1956). WB was among the earliest admirers of Brecht's dramatic and lyric work, which WB often praised in public. WB repeatedly traveled from Paris to visit Brecht in Svendborg for lengthy periods and, in long discussions, tried to clarify his own and Brecht's position on political and literary issues. Letters 200, 232, 235, 251, 258.

Brentano, Bernhard von (1901–64). 1925–30: Berlin correspondent for the *Frankfurter Zeitung*. Part of a circle of friends including WB, Benn, Brecht, Bronnen, Rudolf Grossmann, and others. 1932: issued a warning against Hitler in his book *Der Beginn der Barbarei in Deutschland*. 1933: emigrated to Switzerland after the burning of the Reichstag. He wrote his novels, essays, one drama, and a biography, first in Zurich, then in Küsnacht/Zurich. Letters 312, 315, 319.

Buber, Martin (1878–1965). Spent his youth in Lvov. 1916–24: published the journal *Der Jude*. 1926–30: published *Die Kreatur*. Until 1933: honorary professor of the history of religions in Frankfurt. After 1938: professor of social philosophy in Jerusalem. WB published his cityscape of Moscow in *Die Kreatur*. Buber invited him to contribute to *Der Jude* in 1916. Letters 44, 45, 161, 163.

Caro, Hüne (actually Siegfried) (born 1898 in Berlin; died 1979). Close friend of Erwin Löwensohn. Had contact with WB during his years in Switzerland and after that in Berlin. Later lived in Jerusalem. Letter 83.

Cohn, Alfred (1892–1954). Classmate and boyhood friend of WB, with whom he remained in close touch even during the years of emigration. Businessman in Berlin, later in Mannheim, again in Berlin, and finally in Barcelona. 1921: married Grete Radt, who was engaged to WB from 1914 to 1916 when she was a student. After 1936: in Paris. During the Second World War: teacher at the Center for Jewish Pioneers in Moissac. Letters 173, 183, 247, 254, 262, 273, 279.

Freund, Gisèle (born 1908 in Berlin). Journalist and photographer. Met WB when he was in Paris. Both were active in the same literary circles and shared a passion for chess and for photography. WB reviewed Freund's dissertation in the *Zeitschrift für Sozialforschung*. We are indebted to her for some of the best-preserved photos of WB. Letter 322.

Hofmannsthal, Hugo von (1874–1929). In contrast to German university circles, Hofmannsthal recognized WB's overwhelming significance very early and published his essay on the *Wahlverwandtschaften* in *Neue deutsche Beiträge* (1924–25). WB indicated his appreciation of the various versions of Hofmannsthal's *Turm* in several essays. Letters 129, 139, 143, 146, 149, 151, 158, 162, 164, 166, 167, 169, 170, 172, 176, 188.

Horkheimer, Max (born 1895 in Stuttgart; died 1973). Emeritus professor of philosophy and sociology at the Johann Wolfgang Goethe University in Frankfurt. 1925: habilitation from Frankfurt. 1930: professor at Frankfurt and director of the Institute for Social Research. 1933: emigrated. Continuation of the institute under the auspices of Columbia University, New York. 1948: returned from emigration. Knew WB since his stay in Frankfurt. WB became a member of the institute during his emigration. Letters 242, 245, 255, 256, 261, 266, 280, 282–85, 290, 293, 297, 303, 323, 325, 329.

Kraft, Werner (born 1896 in Hannover). Poet and author (until 1933 librarian in Hannover). Studied modern languages in Berlin, where he made WB's acquaintance in 1915. He was in close touch with him until 1921. The contact was resumed in Paris after 1933, first in person and, after Kraft's move to Jerusalem, through correspondence. Letters 239, 243, 246, 252, 259, 270, 271, 274, 275, 281.

Lieb, Fritz (born 1892 in Rothenfluh). 1924: privatdocent for systematic theology in Basel. 1930: to Bonn, where he was made a professor in 1931. 1933: dismissed for political reasons. 1934–36: lived as an emigrant in Paris. 1936: professor at Basel. 1946–47: visiting professor in Berlin. 1958: professor at Basel. 1962: emeritus status. Letter 288.

Marx-Steinschneider, Kitty (born in 1905 in Königsberg). Met WB when she was still Kitty Marx, shortly before she went to Palestine at the beginning of

1933. In the following years she maintained friendly contact with him. Married to Karl Steinschneider in 1933. Lived in Rehovot and later in Jerusalem. Letters 219, 228, 269, 277, 301.

Monnier, Adrienne (1892–1955). Bookdealer and author. Originally a literary secretary, she opened her well-known bookstore at 7 rue de l'Odéon in 1915. In very close contact with French avant-garde literature, especially with Pierre Reverdy, Henri Michaux, and Michel Leiris, and with Valéry. Maurice Saillet published a book with the title *Rue de l'Odéon,* which contains documents relating to Monnier and a number of her works, among them two essays about WB, with whom she was friendly during his years in Paris. Letters 313, 320, 330.

Radt, Jula (born 1894 in Berlin). Sister of Alfred Cohn. Sculptor. Long a close friend of WB, particularly from 1912 to 1915 and 1921 to 1933. 1916–17: in Heidelberg, where she was close to the circle around Stefan George. After that, in Berlin. After 1937: in Holland. 1925: married Fritz Radt, Grete Radt's brother. Letters 152, 154, 155, 159, 224.

Rang, Florens Christian (1864–1924). At first in government service in Prussia. 1895: decided to study theology and returned to the civil service after five years as a pastor. Government minister until 1917. Until 1920: head of the Farmers' Cooperative Union. Thereafter, as a result of a final change of heart, he felt compelled to give up all his offices and became a private citizen. During the last years of his life he was in close contact with WB, whom he met in Berlin circa 1918. Letters 112, 115–24, 126–28, 130, 131.

Rilke, Rainer Maria (1875–1926). WB came into contact with Rilke only shortly before Rilke's death. He valued and quoted Rilke's poems in his youth but never gave his opinion of Rilke in a larger context. He took over the translation of St.-John Perse's *Anabasis,* which Rilke was meant to do. Letters 144, 148.

Rychner, Max (1897–1965). Literary critic. 1921: appointed full professor with a work on G. G. Gervinus. From 1922: editor of the *Neue Schweizer Rundschau,* in which role he became acquainted with WB when trying to get him to contribute to the journal. 1931–37: lived in Cologne as an editor and correspondent. Letters 165, 174, 182, 187, 192, 201, 222.

Sachs, Franz (born 1894 in Berlin). WB's schoolmate and boyhood friend during the Youth Movement until 1914. Studied law and later lived and worked in Johannesburg as a chartered accountant. Letters 14, 21.

Schoen, Ernst (1894–1960). Musician, poet, and translator. WB's schoolmate and later friend. Since his youth, in contact with the family of the composer Busoni. Lived primarily in Berlin; later in Frankfurt as head of broadcasting until 1933. In England from 1933 to 1952, then in Berlin again. WB published "Ein Gespräch mit Ernst Schoen" [A conversation with Ernst Schoen] in the *Literarische Welt* (August 30, 1929). Only the letters WB wrote to him before 1921 are preserved. Letters 25, 33, 34, 37, 38, 48, 52, 54, 59, 62, 68–70, 72, 73, 75, 77, 80, 82, 85, 87.

Scholem, Gershom Gerhard (born 1897 in Berlin; died 1982). Studied mathematics, philosophy, and Semitic studies. 1915: became acquainted with WB. 1918 and 1919: with WB in Bern. Close personal contact up to 1925 when he went to Palestine. 1927 and 1928: another period of personal contact in Paris. After 1925: lecturer and then full professor of the history of Jewish mysticism at the University of Jerusalem. First marriage (until 1936) to Elsa Burchardt; second marriage to Fania Freud. Letters: 41, 42, 46, 49–51, 53, 55–58, 60, 61, 63–67, 71, 74, 76, 78, 79, 81, 84, 86, 88–111, 113, 114, 125, 132–38, 140–42, 145, 147, 150, 153, 156, 157, 160, 168, 171, 175, 177–81, 184–86, 189–91, 193, 194, 196–99, 203, 205–9, 211, 212, 214–16, 218, 220, 221, 225, 227, 230, 233, 236, 238, 240, 241, 244, 249, 257, 264, 268, 278, 286, 287, 289, 292, 296, 299, 300, 308, 309, 311, 326.

Seligson, Carla (1892–1956). Studied medicine and took a lively interest in the Youth Movement. At its height, she was a close friend of WB. 1917: married Herbert Belmore. Her sisters Rika and Traute, who were likewise intensely involved in this circle, committed suicide in the first year of the war (1914–15). Letters 11, 15, 20, 24, 26–30.

Steffin, Margarete (1908–41). Bookkeeper. Born to poor parents. Brecht met her in the winter of 1931/32. She played the servant girl in the first performance of *Die Mutter* (*The Mother*) (January 1932). With brief interruptions, she shared Brecht's exile from 1933 on, and translated Grieg's *Niederlage* and other pieces for Brecht. She died in Moscow on the way to the United States. WB met her in Paris. Letters 267, 316.

Thieme, Karl (1902–63). Born in Leipzig. Studied philosophy, history, and theology. A socialist. Taught at the Deutsche Hochschule für Politik and at the Pädagogische Akademie in Elbing. 1935: emigrated; 1943: became a Swiss citizen. After 1947: taught at the Hochschule für Verwaltungswissenschaften. 1954: professor at the Ausland- und Dolmetscherinstitut of the University of Mainz in Germersheim. Letters 248, 291, 294, 295, 298, 314.

Weltsch, Robert (born 1891 in Prague; died 1985 in Jerusalem). Having emerged from the Prague Zionist circle, he was the editor-in-chief from 1921 to 1939 of the *Jüdische Rundschau,* for which WB wrote his Kafka essay. Later lived in Jerusalem; after 1945 in London. Letter 234.

Wyneken, Gustav (1875–1964). The leader of radical school reform, founder of the Wickersdorf Free School Community. Author of *Schule und Jugendkultur* and publisher of the journal *Der Anfang*. WB's teacher at the Landeserziehungsheim in Haubinda and thereafter in close contact with WB until 1915, particularly between 1912 and 1914. Only WB's letter of repudiation to him, with which WB broke off their relationship, has surfaced. Letter 39.

Weigel, Helene (1900–1971). Diretor of the Berliner Ensemble. Wife of Bertolt Brecht. Letter 253.

General Index

[redacted]
838
Benjamin Benjamin,
Walter,
The correspondence
of Walter Benjamin

9/94

YOU CAN RENEW
BY PHONE!
623-3300

GAYLORD M